HARDPRESS.NET
HOME OF HARD-TO-FIND BOOKS

Journal of the Constitutional Convention of the State of Texas
by Texas. Constitutional Convention

Address:
HardPress
8345 NW 66TH ST #2561
MIAMI FL 33166-2626
USA
Email: info@hardpress.net

JOURNAL

OF THE

CONSTITUTIONAL CONVENTION

OF

THE STATE OF TEXAS,

BEGUN AND HELD AT

THE CITY OF AUSTIN,

SEPTEMBER 6TH, 1875.

PRINTED FOR THE CONVENTION AT THE "NEWS" OFFICE, GALVESTON.
1875.

JOURNAL

OF THE

CONSTITUTIONAL CONVENTION

OF

THE STATE OF TEXAS,-

BEGUN AND HELD AT

THE CITY OF AUSTIN,

SEPTEMBER 6TH, 1875.

———— · · ————

PRINTED FOR THE CONVENTION AT THE "NEWS" OFFICE, GALVESTON.
1875.

JOURNAL

OF

THE CONSTITUTIONAL CONVENTION

OF

THE STATE OF TEXAS, 1875.

HALL OF REPRESENTATIVES, \
AUSTIN, TEXAS, September 6, 1875. ⎰

In pursuance of a proclamation of His Excellency the Governor, of August 23, 1875, the delegates elect to the Constitutional Convention assembled in the Hall of Representatives, in the city of Austin, at 12 M.

Mr. DeMorse called the Convention to order, and moved that Mr. Whitfield be made temporary president.   Carried.

Mr. King offered the following resolution:

Resolved, That the members of this Convention, on the call of the several districts, by their number, present their certificates of election to the secretary, *pro tempore,* and that the secretary enroll the names of the delegates so presenting their certificates of election.

Adopted.

Mr. W. C. Walsh, of Travis, was appointed to act as temporary secretary.

The following delegates came forward and presented their credentials:

B. Abernathy, David Abner, Thomas G. Allison, J. E. Arnim, W. P. Ballinger, J. W. Barnett, Bennett Blake, W. P. Blassingame, John Henry Brown, H. G. Bruce, Ed. Burleson, Ed. Chambers, H. Cline, W. D. S. Cook of Gonzales, G. B. Cooke, of San Saba, W. L. Crawford, E. L. Dohoney, N. H. Darnell, B. H. Davis of Brazos, Bird B. Davis of Wharton, Charles DeMorse, W. W. Dillard, Joe P. Douglass, A. J. C. Dunnam, J.

W. Ferris, Web. Flanagan, J. R. Fleming, George Flournoy, John S. Ford, J. C. Gaither, J. L. German, A. C. Graves, Joseph E. Haynes, J. R. Henry of Limestone, J. L. Henry of Smith, W. C. Holmes, Asa Holt, J. F. Johnson of Franklin, J. H. Johnson of Collin, S. B. Killough, C. B. Kilgore, Henry C. King, Robert Lacy, Thomas Lockett, F. J. Lynch, Mac McCabe, George McCormick, W. P. McLean, B. D. Martin of Hunt, F. M. Martin of Navarro, John S. Mills, John Mitchell, L. W. Moore, J. R. Morris, Lipscomb Norvell, T. L. Nugent, David A. Nunn, G. Pauli, E. B. Pickett, Wm. Neal Ramey, John H. Reagan, R. B. Rentfro, W. Reynolds, E. S. C. Robertson, Joel W. Robinson, L. S. Ross, E. S. Rugely, S. H. Russell of Harrison, Jonathan P. Russell of Wood, Richard Sansom, P. R. Scott, G. A. Sessions, C. R. Smith, Israel Spikes, J. W. Stayton, F. S. Stockdale, Jacob Waelder, H. W. Wade, W. T. G. Weaver, C. S. West, W. W. Whitehead, J. W. Whitfield, and W. B. Wright.

Mr. Ferris offered the following resolution:

Resolved, That the following oath be administered by the proper State officer to the delegates of this Convention: "You do solemnly swear that you will support the constitution of the United States; and that you will faithfully discharge the duties of a delegate to this Convention, to the best of your ability."

Mr. Crawford offered the following substitute:

"I do solemnly swear that I will support the constitution of the United States, and the present constitution of the State of Texas, until the same shall be abrogated and substituted by the constitution now to be made; that I am not disqualified from holding office under sections 30 and 31 of Article 3, nor under section 9 of Article 12, of the constitution of the State of Texas; and that I will faithfully discharge the duties of my office of delegate, to the best of my ability, so help me God."

On motion of Mr. McCormick, the substitute was laid on the table.

The question then recurring on the adoption of the original resolution offered by Mr. Ferris, it was adopted.

On motion of Mr. Brown, a committee of three were appointed to wait on Judge George Moore, of the Supreme Court, for the purpose of having him administer the oath to the delegates.

Mr. Fleming, Mr. Henry, of Smith, and Mr. Martin, of Navarro, were appointed said committee.

The committee appeared with Judge Moore, who, in accordance with the resolution adopted, administered the prescribed oath to the delegates.

Mr. Flournoy moved that it require a majority of all the

votes of the delegates present to the election of officers of the Convention.   Adopted.

On motion of Mr. Allison, the Convention proceeded to the election of a President.

Mr. DeMorse moved that the vote be taken *viva voce*.   Lost.

On motion of Mr. Graves, the President *pro tem.* appointed the following persons as tellers: Mr. Graves, Mr. McCormick and Mr. Weaver.

Nominations being in order, Mr. Burleson nominated Mr. John Henry Brown, of Dallas; Mr. Henry, of Smith, nominated Mr. E. B. Pickett, of Liberty; Mr. Waelder nominated Mr. F. S. Stockdale, of Calhoun county; Mr. McLean nominated Mr. E. L. Dohoney, of Lamar; Mr. Rentfro nominated Mr. Web. Flanagan, who requested that his name be withdrawn, whereupon Mr. Rentfro withdrew the nomination.

The result of the first ballot was as follows: E. B. Pickett, thirty-six; John Henry Brown, six; F. S. Stockdale, fourteen; E. L. Dohoney, twenty-two.

There being no election, the Convention proceeded to a second ballot, with the following result: E. B. Pickett, forty-three; John Henry Brown, two; F. S. Stockdale, twelve; E. L. Dohoney, twenty-three.

Mr. E. B. Pickett having received a majority of all the votes, was declared duly elected President of the Convention.

On motion of Mr. Scott, a committee of three were appointed to wait on the President elect, and conduct him to the chair.

Mr. Scott, Mr. Ballinger and Mr. Ross were appointed as said committee.

The President elect was conducted to the chair and introduced by the chairman of the committee, and addressed the Convention as follows:

Gentlemen of the Convention—I thank you for the high honor you have just conferred upon me in selecting me to preside over your deliberations.   The duties of the position I know and you know are difficult and onerous, but with your assistance I think we can surmount them.   All I can do now is to promise you that I will try to discharge them to the utmost of my humble ability. At the threshold of our labors it might be well that we survey, for a moment, the grounds we are to occupy, and to consider for a few moments some of the duties that lie before us.   We ninety delegates have been selected in our respective districts, out of a population of a million and a half of people, to come here and perform the difficult work of making a new Constitution for this people and for this young and great and growing State.   The people of Texas have confided to us this important trust, and this fact should impress each and every one of us with a serious and solemn sense of the responsibility he is under to himself, to his country, and to posterity; to see to it that the instrument that shall be made here shall be such as shall commend itself, not only to the people of the State to-day, but to the people that may come after us. The people want a new Constitution. They are not satisfied with the present one. They have sent us here to make a new one. We have not come here to make one for ourselves any more than we have for any other ninety men in the State. If we had come here to make one for ourselves, we might then make one as our individual inclinations might wish it to be, but instead of that we have come to make a Constitution for the people. Then how shall we do it? Is it not best that we shall try to make it—not as one, two, three, or a dozen might desire it—but that we should study to find out the wishes of the people and make a Constitution that they will approve. Let us be careful; for if we put anything into the Constitution that the people of the State do not wish there they will take it out by amendment, and they ought to do so. On the other hand, if we leave anything out of the Constitution that the people want in it, they will put it there, and they ought to have it so. If we make a Constitution and the people of this State discover in the near future that it needs amendment, then I say to you that we shall have failed to make such a Constitution as they had a right to expect. Unless we make a Constitution that satisfies them and the times in which we live, and is so adapted that it may continue to serve those who come after us for a very considerable period of time, we will not have fully accomplished our work. These thoughts, it seems to me, can not be too strongly impressed upon us. Gentlemen, there is but one other suggestion I ask the liberty of making. It is almost needless to make it, for you all recognize it and feel its force as strongly as I do. It is this: We should remember, in every part of our work, that we are making an organic law for our own civilization, the most advanced of which the world has any knowledge, and we should keep ourselves on a level with it and look to it that we never at any time sink below it. Hoping that we may be able to make such a Constitution as will satisfy the people and meet the wants and interests of this great and growing State for an indefinite period in the future, that our labors may be harmonious, and that when we have done our work, it may meet the wishes of our constituents, I thank you for the honor you have done me and the attention with which you have listened to my remarks.

The President announced the first business in order the election of a Secretary, and that nominations were now in order.

Mr. West nominated Major Leigh Chalmers, of Travis county; Mr. DeMorse nominated J. F. Beall, of Fort Worth.

The Convention proceed to ballot, with the following result: Chalmers, forty-nine; Beall, thirty-four.

Major Chalmers having received a majority of all the votes, was declared duly elected Secretary of the Convention.

On motion of Mr. Flournoy, Capt. Fred Voight was appointed temporary Sergeant-at-arms.

The election of Sergeant-at-arms being the next business in order, Mr. Allison nominated Capt. Tom Bowers, of Panola county; Mr. Ballinger nominated Mr. Joe Owens, of Galveston; Mr. Moore nominated Capt. M. B. Highsmith, of Bastrop county; Mr. Robertson nominated Mr. Lew Wells, of San Saba; Mr. Martin, of Hunt, nominated B. G. Carter; Mr. Johnson, of Franklin, nominated Noah L. Byars; Mr. Kilgore nominated Mr. Baker; Mr. Haynes nominated J. H. Fitzhugh, of Travis county.

The Convention proceeded to ballot, with the following result: Bowers, fifteen; Wells, eight; Owens, twenty-six; Highsmith, eleven; Carter, nine; Byars, four; Baker, one; Fitzhugh, nine.

No one having received a majority of all the votes, the Convention proceeded to a second ballot.

Mr. McLean offered the following resolution:

Resolved, That the names of all the candidates for Sergeant-at-arms be dropped after the second ballot, excepting the two receiving the highest number of votes.

Adopted.

The Convention then balloted the second time, with the following result: Bowers, seventeen; Owens, thirty-six; Wells, six; Highsmith, seven; Carter, five; Byars, two; Fitzhugh, ten.

There still being no election, the Convention proceeded to a third ballot, with the following result: Bowers, thirty-five; Owens, forty-six.

Mr. Owens having received a majority of all the votes, was declared duly elected Sergeant-at-arms of the Convention.

Mr. Russell, of Wood, offered the following resolution:

Resolved, That the President appoint a committee of three to ascertain and report the officers and employes necessary to complete the permanent organization of this Convention, and that this committee report at the assembling of the Convention to-morrow.

Mr. Reagan offered the following resolution, as a substitute:

Resolved, That the President of this Convention appoint a

committee, consisting of fifteen members, and that said committee report to the Convention, as soon as practicable, what other officers and employes are necessary to facilitate the labors of this Convention.

Resolved further, That said committee, at the same time, report to the Convention the rate of per diem pay and mileage of the members of the Convention, and the rate of compensation of the officers and employes of the Convention.

The substitute was adopted.

Mr. Brown offered the following resolution:

Resolved, That the Sergeant-at-arms be instructed to arrange for drawing for seats by the delegates, on the assembling of the Convention to-morrow.

Mr. Whitfield offered to amend by inserting "that the drawing be by districts."

The amendment was adopted.

The resolution, as amended, was then adopted:

Mr. DeMorse offered the following resolution:

Resolved, That a printing committee, to be composed of five members, be appointed by the President, to provide for the necessary printing for the Convention and the procurement of a daily issue of public journals, containing synoptical reports of the proceedings of the Convention, who shall report as soon as practicable.

Mr. Dohoney offered the following, as a substitute:

Resolved, That the President of the Convention appoint a committee of seven members, to consider and report to the Convention, as soon as practicable, the number and designation of standing committees for the Convention.

The substitute was adopted.

The President appointed the following committee, under the substitute just adopted: Messrs. Reagan, DeMorse, Russell of Wood, Cooke of San Saba, Ross, Whitfield, Ford, Robinson of Fayette, Martin of Navarro, Cook of Gonzales, Ballinger, Barnett, McLean, Whitehead, and Johnson of Collin.

Mr. Stockdale offered the following resolution:

Resolved, That a committee of seven members be appointed by the President on the rules and order of proceeding of the Convention.

Adopted.

The Secretary and Sergeant-at-arms elect came forward and took the oath of office.

Under the resolution just adopted, the President appointed the following members: Messrs. Stockdale, Dohoney, Norvell, West, Ferris, Flournoy and Fleming.

The President appointed the following committee, under Mr. Dohoney's resolution on the subject of standing committees: Messrs. Dohoney, King, Brown, Henry of Smith, Moore and McCormick.

On motion of Mr. Moore, a committee of three was appointed to wait on the Governor, and inform His Excellency that the Convention was now organized and ready to proceed to business.

The President appointed Messrs. Moore, Ferris and Holt.

On motion of Mr. Whitfield, the Convention adjourned until 9 o'clock A. M. to-morrow.

SECOND DAY.

Hall of Representatives, }
Austin, Texas, September 7, 1875. }

Convention met, pursuant to adjournment; roll called; quorum present.   Prayer by the Rev. Mr. John Lovejoy.

The President submitted the following communication to the Convention:

To the President of the Constitutional Convention:

Dear Sir—The "Ministerial Association, of Austin," composed of pastors of various churches, hereby tenders its gratuitous services to the Convention, to open its sessions with prayer daily, and whatever other religious exercises may be needed.

I have the honor to be your obedient servant,

R. H. Willenberg,
President of Association.

On motion of Mr. West, the Convention accepted the services as tendered, and the Secretary was instructed to notify the president of the association of the acceptance of the services tendered, and to return the thanks of the Convention to the association.

Messrs. C. Erhard of Bastrop county, A. O. Cooley of Gillespie county, E. W. Brady of Grimes county, and S. A. McKinney of Denton county, delegates elect, came forward, presented their credentials, and took the oath prescribed by the Convention.

Mr. Reagan, as chairman of a select committee, submitted the following resolution:

Resolved, That the Convention will elect the following named officers, in addition to those heretofore elected, to wit: Two assistant secretaries, who shall, in addition to their other duties, do the engrossing and enrolling for the Convention; one assistant sergeant-at-arms, who shall, in addition to his other duties, be the postmaster of the Convention, and who shall, when necessary, assist the door-keeper; and one door-keeper.

Resolved, That the President of the Convention be authorized to appoint two pages, and not exceeding three porters, for the Convention.

Resolutions adopted.

The Convention then proceeded to the election of a first assistant secretary, Messrs. Ramey, Graves and Chambers acting as tellers.

Nominations being in order, Mr. Robertson, of Bell, nominated H. C. Surghnor, of Bell county; Mr. Cook, of Gonzales, nominated T. J. Pilgrim; Mr. Ramey nominated W. D. R. McConnell; Mr. Nugent nominated A. H. Hutchins; Mr. Abernathy nominated S. M. Hopping; Mr. Cooke, of San Saba, nominated A. H. Latimer; Mr. Kilgore nominated E. W. Terhune; Mr. Holmes nominated Fred. Cockrell; Mr. Chambers nominated J. W. Lane.

The first ballot resulted as follows: Surghnor, ten; Pilgrim, thirteen; McConnell, eleven; Hutchins, ten; Hopping, two; Latimer, twenty; Terhune, three; Cockrell, four; Lane, seven; and Beaumont, one.

Mr. Kilgore withdrew the name of Mr. Terhune.

There being no election, the second ballot was had, with the following result: Surghnor, six; Pilgrim, thirteen; McConnell, seventeen; Hutchins, three; Hopping, two; Latimer, thirty-six; Cockrell, five; Lane, two; and Beaumont, one. No election.

Mr. Rugely offered the following resolution:

Resolved, That in all future elections of officers by this Convention, after the second ballot the names of all shall be dropped except the two receiving the highest number of votes.

Mr. Allison offered the following, as a substitute:

Resolved, That in all elections hereafter for officers of the Convention, where there are more than two candidates, after each ballot the candidate receiving the lowest number of votes shall be dropped.

Adopted.

Third ballot—Pilgrim, twelve; McConnell, eighteen; Hutchins, one; Latimer, fifty-one.

Mr. Latimer having received a majority of all the votes, was declared duly elected first assistant secretary.

Nominations being in order for second assistant secretary, Mr.

George McCormick nominated Mr. J. L. Cunningham; Mr. Martin, of Navarro, nominated G. N. Beaumont; Mr. Bruce nominated W. Shropshire; Mr. Gaither nominated Mr. La-Prelle; Mr. Crawford nominated James M. Speake; Mr. Holmes nominated J. W. Lane; Mr. Sansom nominated T. H. Jones; Mr. Dohoney nominated Nat. Q. Henderson; Mr. Stockdale nominated L. E. Daniels.

The Convention proceeded to ballot, with the following result: Cunningham, twenty-five; Beaumont, sixteen; Shropshire, nine; La Prelle, twelve; Speake, seven; Lane, two; Jones, five; Henderson, five; Daniels, two.

Mr. Gaither withdrew the name of Mr. La Prelle.

Second ballot—Beaumont, twenty; Cunningham, forty-three; Shropshire, nine; Speake, seven; Jones, one; Henderson, one.

Mr. Cunningham having received a majority of all the votes, was declared duly elected second assistant secretary.

The next business in order being the election of an assistant Sergeant-at-arms, Mr. Fleming nominated O. J. Downs; Mr. King nominated R. G. Ellis; Mr. Ford nominated Capt. M. B. Highsmith; Mr. Reagan nominated Sidney Darnell; Mr. Wright nominated A. E. Ivey; Mr. Henry, of Smith, nominated Crockett Williams; Mr. Robertson, of Bell, nominated J. R. Hardeman; Mr. Wade nominated John Hart; Mr. Nunn nominated J. F. Downes.

The result of the first ballot was as follows: Downes, three; O. J. Downs, eight; J. F. Downs, five; Ellis, nine; Highsmith, ten; Darnell, fifteen; Ivey, nineteen; Williams, three; Hardeman, seven; Hart, four; and Plaster, two. No election.

A communication was received from His Excellency, the Governor.

Second ballot—O. J. Downs, three; J. F. Downes, seven; Ellis, three; Highsmith, seven; Darnell, eighteen; Ivey, thirty-nine; Williams, one; and Hardeman, five.

The names of O. J. Downs and M. B. Highsmith were withdrawn, and the Convention proceeded to a third ballot, with the following result: J. F. Downes, four; Darnell, twenty-four; Ivey, fifty-two; Hardeman, three; and Hart, one.

Mr. Ivey having received a majority of all the votes, was declared duly elected assistant Sergeant-at-arms.

Nominations for Door-keeper being next in order, Mr. Ford nominated W. J. Russell; Mr. Robinson, of Fayette, nominated John Ferrell; Mr. Russell, of Wood, nominated W. D. C. Nelson; Mr. Chambers nominated William Fitzhugh; Mr. Ferris nominated Sam Darcy.

The Convention then proceeded to ballot, with the following result: Russell, eighteen; Ferrell, five; Nelson, nineteen; Fitzhugh, eighteen; Darcy, twenty.   No election.

The Convention proceeded to a second ballot, with the following result: Russell, eighteen; Nelson, fifteen; Fitzhugh, twenty-one; Darcy, twenty-seven; Ferrell, four.

There still being no election, the Convention proceeded to a third ballot, and the result was as follows: Russell, seventeen; Nelson, six; Fitzhugh, thirty-one; Darcy, thirty-one.   No election.

Mr. Ford withdrew the name of Mr. Russell.

The fourth ballot was as follows: Fitzhugh, fifty; Darcy, thirty-four.

Mr. Fitzhugh having received a majority of all the votes, was declared duly elected door-keeper.

The following communication of His Excellency the Governor was taken from the President's desk and read:

EXECUTIVE OFFICE, STATE OF TEXAS,
Austin, September 7, 1875.

Hon. E. B. Pickett, President Constitutional Convention:

SIR—Recognizing the honorable body over which you preside as the legitimate representative of the sovereign powers of the people of Texas, assembled in obedience to law and the popular will, for the purpose of altering and reforming the organic law of the State, I have the honor, in behalf of the Executive Department of the State government, to tender the earnest co-operation of all the officers of that department, as far as their aid may be desired in forwarding the labors and advancing the purposes of the Convention.   Having that object in view, reports have been requested of, and made by, the Comptroller of Public Accounts, the Treasurer, Adjutant General, Attorney General, Commissioner of the General Land Office, Chief Justice of the Supreme Court, and Superintendent of Public Instruction, embracing such facts and figures pertaining to their respective departments as were supposed to be desired by the honorable Convention, for use and consideration in its deliberations.   These reports are in the hands of the public printer, and will be laid before the honorable Convention within the next two or three days.   Any information to be found in any of the offices of the Executive Department, not embraced in these reports, will be cheerfully and promptly furnished, upon request from yourself or the honorable Convention.

Feeling fully assured that the labors of the honorable Convention will secure to Texas the blessings of honest, economical, efficient and free government, I tender the Convention, and the individual delegates, my congratulations upon the auspicious circumstances surrounding them, in the general prosperity of the State; my best wishes for an harmonious and pleasant session, and at its conclusion for a happy return to grateful and applauding constituents.   Very respectfully,

RICH'D COKE,
Governor of Texas.

Mr. Flournoy offered the following resolution:

Resolved, That the Convention thanks the Governor for his polite and patriotic communication, and the members will avail themselves of such information as he has offered, as occasion may require.

Adopted.

Mr. Dohoney, chairman select committee, submitted the following report:

To the Hon. E. B. Pickett, President of the Convention:

The undersigned, appointed a committee to consider and report the number and designation of the standing committees for the Convention, herewith submit their report, and respectfully recommend the adoption of the following standing committees, to wit:

1. Committee on Federal Relations, to consist of five members.
2. Committee on State Affairs, to consist of seven members.
3. Committee on Bill of Rights, to consist of nine members.
4. Committee on Legislative Department, to consist of fifteen members.
5. Committee on Judicial Department, to consist of fifteen members.
6. Committee on Executive Department, to consist of fifteen members.
7. Committee on General Provisions, to consist of fifteen members.
8. Committee on Suffrage, to consist of nine members.
9. Committee on Education, to consist of fifteen members.
10. Committee on Agriculture and Stock-raising, to consist of fifteen members.
11. Committee on Public Lands and Land Office, to consist of seven members.
12. Committee on Immigration, to consist of nine members.
13. Committee on Crime and Punishment, to consist of nine members.
14. Committee on Counties and County Lands, to consist of nine members.

15. Committee on Municipal Corporations, to consist of nine members.

16. Committee on Railroad Corporations, to consist of nine members.

17. Committee on Private Corporations, to consist of nine members.

18. Committee on Revenue and Taxation, to consist of nine members.

19. Committee on Printing and Contingent Expenses, to consist of five members.

20. Committee on Engrossed and Enrolled Ordinances, to consist of five members.

21. Committee on Style and Arrangement, to consist of five members.

All of which is respectfully submitted.

> E. L. DOHONEY, Chairman,
> L. W. MOORE,
> GEO. McCORMICK,
> N. H. DARNELL,
> JOHN HENRY BROWN,
> JNO. L. HENRY.

Mr. Lynch moved to strike out from the report "Committee on Federal Relations." Lost.

The report of the committee was adopted.

On motion of Mr. Stockdale, the report just adopted was referred to Committee on Rules.

Mr. Martin, of Navarro, moved a recess of thirty minutes, in order that members might draw for seats. Lost.

Mr. McCormick moved to reconsider the vote of yesterday, adopting the resolution relative to drawing seats. Lost.

On motion of Mr. Martin, of Navarro, the delegates drew their seats, in conformity to the resolution of yesterday.

On motion of Mr. Blassingame, the Convention adjourned until 9 A. M. to-morrow.

THIRD DAY.

HALL OF REPRESENTATIVES,
AUSTIN, TEXAS, September 8, 1875.

Convention met pursuant to adjournment; roll called; quorum present. Prayer by Rev. Dr. Dodge, of Austin. Journal of yesterday read and adopted.

The President announced the following standing committees of the Convention:

Federal Relations—McLean, chairman; Sansom, Lynch, Dunnam, Brady.

State Affairs—Ford, chairman; Barnett, Chambers, Dillard, Johnson of Franklin, Lacey, Goddin.

Bill of Rights—Crawford, chairman; Davis of Brazos, German, Nugent, Nunn, Gaither, Holmes, Haynes, Abner.

Legislative Department—Henry of Smith, chairman; Ferris, Ross, Waelder, Russell of Wood, Weaver, Brown, Fleming, De-Morse, McLean, Murphy, Dohoney, Cardis, Bruce, Russell of Harrison.

Judiciary—Reagan, chairman; Ballinger, West, Henry of Smith, Wright, Ferris, Norvell, Cline, McCormick, Stockdale, DeMorse, Martin of Navarro, Blake, Scott, Douglass, Davis of Brazos.

Executive Department—Ballinger, chairman; King, De-Morse, Russell of Wood, Kilgore, Allison, Burleson, Cooley, Johnson of Collin, Martin of Hunt, Martin of Navarro, Whitehead, Robinson, Spikes, Reynolds.

General Provisions West, chairman; Reagan, Ferris, Dohoney, Crawford, Flournoy, Russell of Wood, Cook of Gonzales, Darnell, McKinney, Rugely, DeMorse, Stockdale, Norvell, Mills.

Suffrage—Dohoney, chairman; Robertson of Bell, Spikes, Scott, Ford, Murphy, Brown, Stayton, Rentfro.

Education—Whitfield, chairman; Moore, Flournoy, Wright, Abernathy, Sansom, Graves, Chambers, Lynch, Ramey, Dunham, Cooke of San Saba, Holt, Rugely, McCabe, Cline.

Agriculture and Stock-raising—Martin of Navarro, chairman; Johnson of Collin, Robertson of Bell, Allison, Sessions, Killough, Barnett, Bruce, Whitehead, Arnim, Flanagan, Henry of Limestone, Scott, Burleson, Robinson.

Public Lands and Land Office—Darnell, chairman; Robertson, Blake, Whitehead, Henry of Limestone, Kilgore, Mitchell.

Immigration—Waelder, chairman; Arnim, Douglass, Erhard, Holmes, Johnson of Franklin, Killough, Martin of Hunt, Davis of Wharton, Russell of Wood.

Crimes and Punishment—Russell of Wood, chairman; Kilgore, Wright, Douglass, Nunn, Crawford, Cardis, McCormick, Abner.

Counties and County Lands—King, chairman; Moore, Nunn, Barnett, Cooke of San Saba, Ballinger, Brown, Henry of Limestone, Morris.

Municipal Corporations—Flournoy, chairman; Crawford, Weaver, Ford, Henry of Smith, King, Davis, Dohoney, Morris.

Railroad Corporations—Ferris, chairman; McLean, Davis of Brazos, Moore, Smith, Holt, Blassingame, Burleson, Flanagan, Stayton.

Revenue and Taxation—DeMorse, chairman; McLean, Ramey, Fleming, Cooke of San Saba, Abernathy, Whitfield, Lacey, Russell of Harrison.

Printing and Contingent Expenses—Cook of Gonzales, chairman; DeMorse, Whitfield, Ford, Allison.

Engrossed and Enrolled Ordinances—Ramey, chairman; Martin of Navarro, Wade, Dillard, Haynes.

Style and Arrangement—Brown, chairman; Stockdale, Ballinger, Ramey, Reagan.

Private Corporations—Stockdale, chairman; Kilgore, Blake, McCormick, Dillard, Nugent, Darnell, Murphy, Lacey, Flournoy.

Mr. Stockdale, as Chairman of Committee on Rules and Order of Proceeding, submitted the following report:

To the Honorable E. B. Pickett, President of the Convention:

The Committee on Rules and Order of Proceeding, beg leave most respectfully to report as follows:

QUORUM.

1. A majority of all the delegates elected to this Convention shall constitute a quorum; but a smaller number may adjourn from day to day and compel the attendance of absent members.

ABSENTEES.

2. In case a less number than a quorum shall convene, the members present may send the Sergeant-at-arms, or any other person or persons, for any or all absentees.

3. No member shall absent himself from the services of the Convention without leave, unless he be sick and unable to attend.

4. A call of the Convention may be demanded by fifteen delegates; and if there be any absent the names of the absentees shall be called again; if they do not answer, the Sergeant-at-arms or a special messenger may be sent for them; and the question pending shall be, without a motion, laid on the table until the absentees appear, or the call be suspended; and until the call be suspended or the Convention full, the Convention shall proceed with the next business in order.

OPEN DOORS.

5. The doors of the Convention shall be kept open, except upon a call of the House.

6. The President shall take the chair at the hour to which the Convention last adjourned.

7. The names of the delegates shall be called, alphabetically; should a quorum not be in attendance, a majority of those present shall be authorized to send the Sergeant-at-arms, or a special messenger, for the absentees. When there is a quorum assembled the journal of the preceding day shall be read, and corrected if necessary.

8. The President shall then call,

    First—For petitions and memorials.
    Second—For reports from standing committees.
    Third—For reports from select committees.
    Fourth—For resolutions and ordinances.
    Fifth—For unfinished business.
    Sixth—For special orders.
    Seventh—For business on the table.

Which shall be disposed of in the order in which they are here presented, unless otherwise directed by the Convention.

DECORUM AND DEBATE.

9. When a delegate is about to speak, in debate, or communicate any matter to the Convention, he shall address the President, standing in his place; and when he has finished he shall sit down.

10. When two or more delegates rise to address the chair, the President shall name the person to speak; but in all cases the delegate who shall first rise and address the chair shall speak first.

11. No member shall speak more than once in any one debate until every member, desiring to do so, shall have spoken; nor shall any member speak more than twice in any one debate, nor longer than fifteen minutes at any one time, without the leave of the Convention.

12. When a member is called to order by the President, or by a delegate, he shall sit down, until the question of order be decided; if the decision be in his favor, he shall be at liberty to proceed; if otherwise, he shall not proceed without leave of the Convention.

13. If a member be called to order for using exceptionable words, they shall be immediately taken down in writing, that the President and Convention may better be enabled to judge of them.

14. Every question of order, shall, in the first instance, be

   2

decided by the President; from whose decision any member may appeal to the Convention.

15. The President may call for the opinion of the Convention upon any question of order.

16. While the President is putting a question, or addressing the Convention, he shall not be interrupted.

17. While a member is speaking, no other member shall interrupt him, except by leave, to explain; nor shall a member speak to any one, or walk across the floor, or otherwise interrupt the business of the Convention. No smoking shall be allowed in the Hall during the session of the Convention.

18. When a question is under debate no motion shall be received, except,

> *First*—To adjourn.
> *Second*—To reconsider.
> *Third*—For the previous question.
> *Fourth*—To amend.
> *Fifth*—To commit.
> *Sixth*—To lay on the table.
> *Seventh*—To postpone for a time certain.
> *Eighth*—To postpone indefinitely.

Which several motions shall have precedence in the order in which they stand arranged.

19. No debate shall be allowed on a motion to adjourn, to lay on the table, or for the previous question.

20. The Convention may punish any delegate for disorderly conduct, and, with the consent of two-thirds, may expel a member.

21. The Convention, during its session, may imprison for forty-eight hours any person not a member, for disrespectful or disorderly conduct in its presence, or for obstructing any of its proceedings.

22. Any member who shall receive a bribe, or shall suffer his vote influenced by promise of preferment or reward, shall be expelled.

23. Every resolution or proposition in any form affecting any provision of the constitution shall be referred to the appropriate committee, without debate. All other resolutions may be acted upon by the Convention upon their introduction.

24. No motion shall be debated until it shall have been seconded.

25. All motions shall be reduced to writing, and be read by the Secretary, if desired by the President or any delegate present.

26. After a motion has been stated by the President, or read by the Secretary, it shall be deemed to be in possession of the Con-

vention, but it may be withdrawn at any time before it is amended or decided.

27. On motion to fill a blank, the largest sum and the longest time shall have precedence.

28. Any member may have the question before the Convention divided, if it be susceptible of a division, into distinct questions.

29. If the question in debate contains several points, any member may have the same divided; but on a motion to strike out and insert it shall not be in order to move for a division of the question. The rejection of a motion to strike out and insert one proposition shall not prevent a motion to strike out and insert a different proposition, nor prevent a motion simply to strike out; nor shall the rejection of a motion simply to strike out prevent a subsequent motion to strike out and insert.

30. No motion to postpone or to commit, having been once decide, shall be again allowed on the same day, at the same stage of the resolution or other question before the Convention.

31. After the morning call, it shall be in order at any time for the Convention to resolve itself into committee of the whole.

PROTESTS.

32. Any member shall have liberty to dissent from or protest against any resolution or ordinance which he may think injurious to the public or an individual, and have the reasons for dissent entered on the journals.

REPORTS.

33. All reports shall be in writing. Every report affecting any provision of the constitution, shall, as of course, lie on the table to be printed, and shall not be acted upon by the Convention until printed and in possession of the delegates for at least one day.

COMMITMENT.

34. When several motions shall be made for the reference of a subject to a committee, they shall have preference in the following order:
> *First*—To a committee of the whole Convention.
> *Second*—To a standing committee.
> *Third*—To a select committee.

RECONSIDERATION.

35. After a question shall have been decided in the affirmative or negative, any member who voted with the majority may, on the day on which the vote was taken, or within the next succeeding day of actual session, move the reconsideration thereof, unless

the resolution, ordinance, message, report, amendment or motion upon which the vote was taken shall have passed out of the possession of the Convention.

36. In all cases a motion to reconsider shall be decided by a majority of the votes.

MODE OF STATING QUESTIONS.

37. All questions shall be distinctly put by the President, and the members shall assent or dissent by answering " yea " or "nay."

38. On a call of three members for the yeas and nays, on any question, they shall be taken; and each member, upon his name being called, unless excused by the Convention, shall, without debate, answer " yea " or " nay."

39. At the desire of any three members present, the yeas and nays shall be entered upon the journal, and the names of the members not voting shall be recorded immediately after those voting in the affirmative and negative.

40. The order of business and the rules of the Convention may be changed or suspended at any time, by a vote of two-thirds.

COMMITTEE OF THE WHOLE.

41. In forming a committee of the whole Convention, the President shall leave the chair, and shall appoint a chairman to preside in committee.

42. The rules of the Convention, as far as applicable, shall be observed in committee of the whole, except as to the limitation of time in debate, and the right to call the previous question and the yeas and nays.

43. Resolutions or ordinances referred to the committee of the whole shall not be defaced or interlined; but all amendments, noting the page and line, shall be duly entered by the Secretary on a separate paper, as the same shall be agreed to by the committee, and so be reported to the Convention; after the report, the matter shall be again subject to debate and amendment, and to be committed.

JOURNAL.

44. The proceedings of the Convention, when not in committee of the whole, shall be entered on the journal as concisely as possible, care being taken to detail a true account of the proceedings. Every report of a committee and vote of the Convention, and a brief statement of the contents of each petition, memorial or other paper presented to the Convention, shall also be inserted in the journal.

ADJOURNMENT.

45. A motion to adjourn shall always be in order, and shall be decided without debate.

STANDING COMMITTEES.

46. Standing committees shall be appointed by the President, to consider and report severally upon the following subjects, and such others as may be referred to them, viz:

1. Committee on Federal Relations, to consist of five members.
2. Committee on State Affairs, to consist of seven members.
3. Committee on Bill of Rights, to consist of nine members.
4. Committee on Legislative Department, to consist of fifteen members.
5. Committee on Judicial Department, to consist of fifteen members.
6. Committee on Executive Department, to consist of fifteen members.
7. Committee on General Provisions, to consist of fifteen members.
8. Committee on Suffrage, to consist of nine members.
9. Committee on Education, to consist of fifteen members.
10. Committee on Agriculture and Stock-raising, to consist of fifteen members.
11. Committee on Public Lands and Land Office, to consist of seven members.
12. Committee on Immigration, to consist of nine members.
13. Committee on Crime and Punishment, to consist of nine members.
14. Committee on Counties and County Lands, to consist of nine members.
15. Committee on Municipal Corporations, to consist of nine members.
16. Committee on Railroad Corporations, to consist of nine members.
17. Committee on Private Corporations, to consist of nine members.
18. Committee on Revenue and Taxation, to consist of nine members.
19. Committee on Printing and Contingent Expenses, to consist of five members.
20. Committee on Engrossed and Enrolled Ordinances, to consist of five members.
21. Committee on Style and Arrangement, to consist of five members.

47. The President of the Convention shall decide all questions not provided for by the standing rules and orders of the Convention, according to parliamentary practice, as laid down by approved modern authors, subject to the right of appeal, as in other cases.

All of which is respectfully submitted.

F. S. STOCKDALE, Chairman Committee.

Report adopted.

On motion of Mr. Stockdale, two hundred copies of the rules and order of proceeding, and also of the standing committees, were ordered printed for the use of the convention.

Mr. Reagan submitted the following report:

COMMITTEE ROOM, September 8, 1875.

Hon. E. B. Pickett, President of the Convention:

Your committee to whom was referred the resolutions, directing them to report to the Convention what other officers and employes were necessary to facilitate its labors, and to report the rate of pay and mileage which should be allowed to the delegates, and the rate of pay of the officers and employes of the Convention, have had the same under consideration; and in addition to the verbal report made by your committee to the Convention this morning, in relation to the election of additional officers for the Convention, recommend further that the President of the Convention appoint two pages, and not exceeding three porters.

It has been the object of your committee to recommend the election and appointment of such officers and employes only as were necessary to facilitate the labors of the Convention, and to avoid recommending the election or appointment of any superfluous officers or employes.

Your committee further recommend that the pay of the delegates to the Convention be five dollars per day, and that their mileage be at the rate of five dollars for every twenty-five miles travel in coming to and returning from the Convention; the distance to be computed by way of the most direct practicable traveled route, not to include deflections from the direct traveled route by railroad or water lines of travel.

This will make the pay and mileage of the delegates to the Convention three-eighths less than the pay and mileage of the members of the Legislature for some years past, with better restrictions against the computation of mileage by circuitous routes.

We also recommend that the President of the Convention appoint a committee of three members, whose duty it shall be to ascertain and report to the Convention the distance to be traveled and the amount payable as mileage to each delegate.

The question of mileage has received the careful consideration of the committee, and while some of the members of the committee were in favor of allowing the traveling expenses of the delegates in lieu of mileage, the rate of mileage fixed upon is believed by the committee not to be in excess of the actual traveling expenses, if any allowance is to be made for the time of delegates while traveling. It is also believed by the committee that on the plan recommended exact equality and fairness may be observed in the payment of mileage; while by allowing traveling expenses we must of necessity leave the amount to be paid, in a considerable degree, to the conscience and discretion of delegates, and thus in some measure embarrass them with this question.

Your committee report to the Convention the accompanying resolutions on these subjects for its consideration.

JNO. H. REAGAN, Chairman,
W. W. WHITEHEAD,
W. P. BALLINGER,
L. S. ROSS,
CHARLES DeMORSE,
MARION MARTIN,
JOEL W. ROBESON,
JNO. W. BARNETT,
J. RUSSEL, of Wood.
JNO. S. FORD,
W. D. S. COOK, of Gonzales.

Resolved, That the pay of the members of the Convention shall be five dollars per day for each day they are in attendance on the Convention, and their mileage in coming to and returning from the Convention, shall be five dollars for every twenty-five miles, the distance to be computed by way of the most direct practicable traveled route, not including deflections by railroads or water lines of travel.

That the pay of the Secretary of the Convention and of his two assistants, of the Sergeant-at-arms and his assistant, and of the Door-Keeper, shall be five dollars each per day; and that the compensation of the pages shall be two dollars and fifty cents each per day, and of the porters two dollars each per day.

Resolved further, That said sums shall be audited and paid out of the appropriation made by the "joint resolution providing for a Convention to frame a Constitution for the State of Texas," approved March 13, 1875, upon the certificate of the President of the Convention, countersigned by the Secretary, which certificate shall be a voucher for the Comptroller.

Resolved further, That the President of the Convention appoint a committee of three delegates, whose duty it shall be to ascertain and report to the Convention the distance to be traveled and the amount of mileage payable to each delegate.

Adopted.

Mr. McLean submitted the following minority report, on the same subject:

Hon. E. B. Pickett, President Constitutional Convention:

The undersigned delegates, members of the committee appointed to consider and report upon the per diem pay and allowance for mileage of members of the Convention, and for other purposes, respectfully report that they can not agree to the report of a majority of the committee, so far as their report relates to the pay and allowance of delegates to the Convention, and offer as a substitute for the committee's resolution touching the pay and allowance of delegates, the accompanying resolution. All the recommendations of the majority meet our approval, excepting what refers to the pay and allowance of delegates.

W. P. McLean,
John Johnson,
J. W. Whitfield.

Resolved, That the pay of delegates to this Convention shall be four dollars per day, and in addition thereto there shall be an allowance of fifteen cents per mile as commutation of traveling expenses to and from the Capital. The amount of mileage is to be computed over the nearest practicable traveled route from the homes of delegates to the Capital of the State, not including the distance in deviations from such nearest route, by traveling on railroads or other public means of transportation. The certificate of the President of the Convention, countersigned by the Secretary, shall be authority for the Comptroller to draw his warrant upon the Treasurer for the payment of claims for pay and allowances under this resolution.

Mr. Reagan moved the adoption of the majority report.

Mr. McLean offered the resolution submitted by the minority as a substitute for the resolution offered by the majority.

Mr. German offered the following amendment to the resolution submitted by the minority: Strike out "five dollars for every twenty-five miles," and insert "two dollars and fifty cents for every twenty-five miles traveled, for those who travel by rail, and five dollars for those who travel otherwise."

Mr. Russell, of Harrison, offered the following, as a substitute for the whole subject matter under consideration:

Resolved, That the delegates to this Convention do serve in this Convention without per diem pay or mileage.

Lost, by the following vote:

YEAS—Abner, Brady, Flanagan, Mitchell, Rentfro, Russell of Harrison, and Wright—7.

NAYS—Messrs. Allison, Abernathy, Arnim, Brown, Blake, Ballinger, Blassingame, Barnett, Burleson, Bruce, Crawford, Chambers, Cook of Gonzales, Cooley, Cline, Douglass, Dillard, DeMorse, Dohoney, Darnell, Dunnam, Erhard, Ford, Flournoy, Fleming, Ferris, German, Gaither, Graves, Holt, Henry of Smith, Henry of Limestone, Holmes, Haynes, Johnson of Franklin, Johnson of Collin, King, Kilgore, Lockett, Lacey, Lynch, McLean, Martin of Navarro, Martin of Hunt, McCabe, Mills, McKinney, McCormick, Moore, Norvell, Nunn, Nugent, Pauli, Reagan, Ramey, Rugely, Robertson of Bell, Robison of Fayette, Ross, Russell of Wood, Spikes, Scott, Sessions, Smith, Stockdale, Stayton, Sansom, Wade, Whitehead, Weaver, Whitfield, West and Waelder—71.

On motion of Mr. Stockdale, the report and resolution of the minority were laid on the table.

On motion of Mr. McLean, the vote just taken was reconsidered.

Mr. German offered to amend the resolution of the minority, by striking out "fifteen cents a mile," and inserting "ten cents per mile."

Mr. Crawford offered the following, as a substitute for the whole subject matter under consideration:

Resolved, That the pay of each member be fixed at five dollars per day, and that there be allowed to each member five cents a mile for the number of miles traveled by the usually traveled route, in going to and returning from the Capital, and in addition thereto the sum of five dollars per day for the number of days necessary to be employed in the travel.

The question recurring on the adoption of the amendment offered by Mr. Gorman, the same was put and lost.

The question then being on the adoption of the substitute offered by Mr. German, the same was put and lost.

The question then recurring on the adoption of the minority resolution, the same was put and lost.

The resolution reported by the majority was then adopted.

Mr. Flanagan moved to reconsider the vote just taken, and to lay the motion to reconsider on the table.   Carried.

On motion of Mr. Cook, of Gonzales, the Secretary was instructed to have printed two hundred copies of the list of standing committees, and of the rules of the Convention.

Mr. Martin, of Navarro, offered the following resolution:

Resolved, That the Sergeant-at-arms provide suitable rooms for the accommodation of the respective committees, and assign the same to said committees.

Adopted.

Mr. Crawford offered the following resolution:

Resolved, That the Secretary of State, provided the same be in his possession or subject to his control, be requested to furnish to the Secretary of this Convention ninety copies of Paschal's Digest of the Laws of Texas, for the use of the members of the Convention during its session.

Adopted.

Mr. McCormick offered the following resolution:

Resolved, That the Sergeant-at-arms be authorized to procure for the use of the members of this Convention a sufficient quantity of stationery and postage stamps; to be paid for out of the fund for contingent expenses.

Adopted.

Mr. DeMorse introduced an ordinance "suspending the operations of the law directing the election of members of the Legislature to meet in January next, and requesting the Governor to intermit his usual proclamation, until after the action of the people on the Constitution to be submitted to them by this Convention."

Read first time.

Mr. Brown introduced an ordinance postponing the general biennial election of December, 1875, as a substitute for the one offered by Mr. DeMorse.

On motion of Mr. Ballinger, the ordinance and substitute were referred to a select committee of seven.

The President announced Messrs. Ballinger, Reagan, West, Henry of Smith, Stockdale, DeMorse, and Brown, as said committee.

Mr. Ramey offered the following resolution:

Resolved, That the constitution, known as the constitution of 1845, and as amended, be made the basis of the action of this Convention in the formation of a new constitution; and that the President of the Convention is hereby required to give the different portions of said constitution to the different committees for their action.

Referred to Committee on State Affairs.

Mr. McLean offered the following resolution:

Resolved, That the Committee on General Provisions be instructed to report a provision, to be incorporated in the constitution, that shall require all lands in the State patented to and otherwise claimed by individuals, in a separate or corporate capacity, in all organized counties, be assessed at a valuation not less than one dollar per acre, and that no lands in other portions of the State, owned or claimed by such parties, shall be assessed at a less amount than fifty cents per acre, and provide for the strict enforcement of this provision.

Referred to Committee on General Provisions.

Mr. Stockdale offered the following resolution:

Resolved, That the rules of the Convention be amended by adding the following:

Rule——. That a motion to lay an amendment to any question on the table shall not, if carried, have the effect to carry with it the original question; but the original question shall, nevertheless, stand as the question before the house.

Rules suspended and the resolution was adopted.

Mr. Russell, of Harrison, offered the following resolution:

Resolved, That this Convention hold one session each day, Sundays excepted, commencing at 9 o'clock A. M., and holding until 1 o'clock P. M.

Mr. Wade proposed to amend by striking out " 1 o'clock P. M.," and inserting " 3 o'clock P. M."

On motion of Mr. Brown, the resolution and amendment were ordered to lie on the table for the present.

Mr. Fleming offered the following resolution:

Resolved, That the Committee on Printing be instructed to contract for twenty copies of such daily papers as the members may select, for the use of each member of this Convention; *provided,* the same shall contain the journals of this body.

Referred to Committee on Printing.

On motion of Mr. Flanagan the Convention adjourned until 9 o'clock A. M. to-morrow.

FOURTH DAY.

HALL OF REPRESENTATIVES,
AUSTIN, TEXAS, September 9, 1875.

Convention met pursuant to adjournment; roll called; quorum present.   Prayer by Rev. E. B. Wright, of Austin.

On motion of Mr. McCormick, Mr. Whitfield was excused, on account of sickness.

Journal of yesterday read and adopted.

The President announced the following members as the Committee on Mileage: Messrs. Martin of Navarro, Abernathy and Stayton.

Mr. West offered the following resolution:

Resolved, That the Committee on Suffrage be instructed to obtain, for the use of the Convention, from the Governor and Secretary of State, a general tabular statement of the number of votes cast in the election for Governor in 1866, 1869 and 1873, together with such other information as the Executive or State Departments may disclose as to the number of legal voters at present in the State; and that they also be instructed to obtain, for the use of the Convention, from any source they may deem best, a general statement of the number of persons now registered and entitled to registration in the State; also to enquire as to the cost and expense of a general election in this State, including the cost of election proclamation, notices, registration, and other expenses to the State, counties and people, and to report to the Convention.

Adopted.

Mr. Darnell offered the following resolution:

Resolved, That all property, both real and personal, of the wife, owned or claimed by her before marriage, and that acquired afterwards, by gift, devise or descent, shall be her separate property, and laws shall be passed more clearly defining the rights of the wife, in relation as well to her separate property as that held in common with her husband. Laws shall also be passed providing for the registration of the wife's separate and communative property in the county in which it is situated.

Read and referred to Committee on General Provisions.

Mr. Darnell offered the following resolution:

Resolved, That the Legislature shall have power to protect, by law, from forced sale a certain portion of the property of all heads of families. The homestead of a family not to exceed two hundred acres of land (not included in a city or town), or any city or town lot or lots in value not to exceed ———— dollars, shall not be subject to forced sale, nor shall the owner, if a married man, be at liberty to alienate the same, unless by the consent of the wife, in such manner as the Legislature may direct; town or city lots may be joining or separate.

Read and referred to Committee on General Provisions.

Mr. Darnell offered the following resolution:

Resolved, That the legal rate of interest shall not exceed eight per cent. per annum, and not more than twelve by contract, with a forfeiture for violation.

Read and referred to the Committee on General Provisions.

Mr. Lynch offered the following resolution:

Resolved, That the Committee on Suffrage be instructed to inquire into the propriety of limiting the right of suffrage to those who pay a poll tax, and report by ordinance or otherwise.

Read and referred to Committee on Suffrage.

Mr. Mills offered the following resolution:

Resolved, That the Sergeant-at-arms be instructed to contract with the Capital Ice Company for a sufficient quantity of ice for the use of the Convention, at a price not to exceed two cents per pound.

Adopted.

Mr. Johnson, of Franklin, offered the following resolution:

Resolved, That the Committee on Legislative Department, be instructed to inquire into the expediency and propriety of incorporating in the constitution the following provision: "The Legislature shall be prohibited from granting, directly or indirectly, public money or anything of value to any individual, company of individuals or corporation, whatever."

Read and referred to Committee on Legislative Department.

Mr. Moore offered the following resolution:

Resolved, That the following shall form a section of the constitution and be a part thereof:

Section —. "The lands granted to the several counties of this State for educational purposes, and known as county school lands, be and are hereby vested in the counties to which they were respectively granted, and said counties are authorized to sell or otherwise dispose of the same, and apply the proceeds thereof to the purposes of said trust."

Read and referred to the Committee on Counties and County Lands.

Mr. Wade offered the following resolution:

Resolved, That venality, malversation, dereliction, and malfeasance are destructive of public spirit and good government, and shall be regarded as high crime; that gifts and rewards, other than as allowed by law, shall not be given to any official, and that the emoluments of any official station shall not be such as to entice the avaricious nor the lovers of leisure; and that the grand juries of the country be required to investigate the conduct, books, and official course of all administrative officers, at least once a year.

Read and referred to Committee on Executive Department.

Mr. Fleming offered the following resolution:

Resolved, That the following section shall be incorporated in the constitution of Texas, under the appropriate caption:

" That the Legislature shall pass laws prohibiting a greater per centum or rate of interest than ten per centum per annum on the amount or value of the contract, and shall, by adequate penalties, provide for the enforcement of this section."

Read and referred to Committee on General Provisions.

Mr. Fleming offered the following resolution:

Resolved, That the following sections shall be incorporated in the constitution of this State, under appropriate captions:

Section ——. " That every railroad corporation, organized or doing business in this State, under the laws or authority thereof, shall have and maintain a public office or place of business, where transfers of stock shall be made, and in which shall be kept, for public inspection, books in which shall be recorded the amount of capital stock subscribed, and by whom, the names of the owners of its stock, and the amount owned by them, respectively; the amount of stock paid in, and by whom; the amount of its assets and liabilities; and the name and place of residence of its officers. The directors of every railroad corporation shall, annually, make a report, under oath, to the Comptroller of Public Accounts, or some officer to be designated by law, of all their acts and doings, which report shall include such matters relating to railroads as may be prescribed by law."

Sec. ——. " The rolling stock, and all other property belonging to any railroad company or corporation in this State, shall be considered personal property, and shall be liable to execution and sale in the same manner as the personal property of individuals; and the Legislature shall pass no law exempting such property from execution and sale."

Sec. ——. " Railroads heretofore constructed, or that may hereafter be constructed in this State, are hereby declared public highways, and shall be free to all persons for the transportation of their persons and property thereon, under such regulations as may be prescribed by law. And the Legislature shall, from time to time, pass laws establishing reasonable maximum rates of charges for the transportation of passengers and freights on the different railroads."

Sec. ——. " The Legislature shall pass laws to correct abuses and prevent unjust discrimination and extortion in the rates of freight and passenger tariffs on the different railroads in this State, and enforce such laws, by adequate penalties, to the extent necessary for that purpose of forfeiture of their property. The Legislature shall pass laws enforcing, by suitable penalties, these provisions."

Read and referred to Committee on Railroad Corporations.

Mr. Nugent offered the following resolution:

Resolved, That the following provision be incorporated in the constitution under its appropriate caption, to wit:

Sec. ——. "In the trial of civil causes and prosecutions for offenses of a less grade than felony, in the several courts of this State, no jury shall be empanelled, unless the parties, or one of them, shall make written application therefor to the court; but this section shall not be so construed as to authorize the State to make such application."

Read and referred to Committee on Legislative Department.

Also—

Resolved, That the following provision shall be incorporated in the constitution, under its appropriate caption, to wit:

Section ——. "No law shall ever be enacted by the Legislature requiring the several counties of the State to provide for the support of petit juries, for the trial of civil causes, and prosecutions for offenses classed as misdemeanors."

Referred to Committee on Legislative Department.

Also—

Resolved, That the following provision be incorporated in the constitution, under appropriate caption, to wit:

Section ——. "The privileges of the writ of *habeas corpus* shall never be suspended in this State."

Referred to Committee on Bill of Rights.

Mr. Haynes offered the following resolution:

Resolved, That the Legislature may pass special laws in regard to farming, fencing and stock-raising.

Referred to Legislative Department.

Mr. Ross offered the following resolution:

Resolved, That all lands in this State shall be rendered for taxation in the counties in which they are situated; and all taxes upon lands shall be assessed and collected in counties where the land lies, and not elsewhere; *provided,* that lands situated in counties not organized may be rendered and the taxes assessed and collected in the counties to which they are severally attached for judicial purposes.

Referred to Committee on Taxation and Revenue.

Mr. Nunn offered the following resolution:

Resolved, That it is the sense of this Convention that the Committee on Legislative Department shall inquire into the expediency, and report in favor of biennial sessions of the Legislature, and for a *special* session only when a public necessity may require.

Referred to Committee on Legislative Department.

Mr. Robertson, of Bell, offered the following resolution:

Resolved, That the Committee on General Provisions shall incorporate in its appropriate place, a provision fixing the rate of interest at 8 per cent., and 10 per cent. by contract.

Referred to Committee on General Provisions.

Mr. McCormick offered the following resolution:

Resolved, That the preamble to the Constitution of the State of Texas shall hereafter read as follows, to wit:

"PREAMBLE:

"We the people of Texas, with reverence for God, and grateful for all his goodness, do, for the better government of the State, make, ordain and establish this Constitution."

Referred to Committee on Bill of Rights.

Mr. Cook, of Gonzales, offered the following resolution:

Resolved, That all representatives of the press be invited to seats within the Hall of the Convention.

Mr. Dohoney offered the following as a substitute:

Resolved, That reporters of newspapers proposing to publish the proceedings of the Convention, or synoptical reports thereof, be and they are hereby invited to occupy seats within the Hall, and near the Secretary's desk, and that the Sergeant-at-arms be instructed to provide suitable seats for their accommodation.

Adopted, and resolution as amended adopted.

Mr. Rugely offered the following resolution:

Resolved, That the Governor shall nominate, and by and with the advice and consent of two-thirds of the Senate, shall appoint the judges of the Supreme and District Courts, and that the Judges of the Supreme Court shall hold their offices for ten years, and the District Judges for six years.

Referred to Judiciary Committee.

Mr. Flournoy offered the following resolution:

Resolved, That the Committee on Private Corporations be instructed to ascertain if there be any person or corporation or combination of persons in the city of Galveston or elsewhere in the State of Texas who have heretofore assumed and are now assuming to exercise the sovereign right of taxing commerce by demanding and receiving tolls or wharfage without authority; and if so to provide just and adequate means for preventing a continuance of the same.

On motion of Mr. McCormick the words " and they be authorized to send for persons and papers," were added, and resolution referred to Committee on Private Corporations.

Mr. Holt offered the following resolution:

Resolved, That Supreme, District and County Judges shall be elected by the people.

Referred to Judiciary Committee.

Mr. Sansom offered the following resolution:

Resolved, That the general provisions of the Constitution of 1845 be the basis of action of the Committee on General Provisions, and that they report the same with such changes as they may deem necessary to the Convention.

Referred to the Committee on General Provisions.

Mr. Nunn offered the following resolution:

Resolved, That in accordance with the theory of republican government, all officers, legislative, executive and judicial, shall be elective by the people, and that the terms of office should be so reduced as to secure an accountability for official conduct to the people.

Referred to the Committee on Legislative Department.

Mr. Allison offered the following resolution:

Resolved, That there be appointed a committee of apportionment, to consist of one member from each Senatorial District, on apportionment of Senatorial and Representative Districts and basis of representation.

Adopted.

Mr. Holmes offered the following resolution:

Resolved, That the following provisions be incorporated in the constitution: That no county in this State, town or municipality, be allowed to give material aid by taxation to any railroad, manufacturing corporation, or educational institution.

Referred to Committee on Legislative Department.

Mr. Haynes offered the following resolution:

Resolved, That the Senate and House of Representatives, when assembled, shall each elect a speaker and its other officers; be judges of the qualifications and election of its members, and sit upon its own adjournments from day to day. Not less than two-thirds of all the members to which each house shall be entitled shall constitute a quorum to do business, but a smaller number may adjourn from day to day, and may be authorized by law to compel the attendance of absent members.

Referred to the Committee on Legislative Department.

Mr. Russell, of Harrison, offered the following resolution:

Resolved, That the following provisions shall be incorporated

3

in the constitution: That taxation shall be equal and uniform, and that no tax on occupation shall be levied.

Referred to the Committee on Tax and Revenue.

Mr. Lynch offered the following resolution:

Resolved, That the Committee on State Affairs inquire into the propriety of abolishing the office of State Geologist.

Referred to Committee on State Affairs.

Mr. Stayton offered the following substitute:

Resolved, That each delegate to this Convention do furnish to the Committee on Mileage, without delay, a statement in writing, showing the residence of such delegate, and further showing the most direct traveled route from the residence of such delegate to the city of Austin.

Mr. Kilgore offered the following substitute:

Resolved, That each member of the Convention furnish the Committee on Mileage the name of the county of his residence, and the county seat of such county.

On motion of Mr. Scott, the original resolution and substitute were laid on the table.

Mr. Wade offered the following resolution:

Resolved, That, for the protection of the civil and religious liberty of the citizen, that the writ of habeas corpus never be suspended; that martial law never be declared; that the liberty of speech and of the press never be abridged; that no citizen, body corporate, city or town be compelled to support any church organization, creed, faith, denomination or association of religion, or to contribute anything to the support or maintainance of any priest, preacher, teacher or director of any such creed, faith, denomination or church organization of religion.

Referred to Committee on Bill of Rights.

The following additions were made to standing committees:

Mr. Stayton, to Committee on Railroad Corporations.

Mr. Cline, to Committee on Education.

Mr. Davis, of Brazos, to Judiciary Committee.

Mr. Russell, of Harrison, to Committee on Taxation and Revenue.

Mr. Flournoy, to Committee on Private Corporations.

Mr. Russell, of Wood, to Committee on Immigration.

On motion of Mr. Stockdale, the Convention adjourned until 9 o'clock A. M. to-morrow.

FIFTH DAY.

HALL OF REPRESENTATIVES, }
AUSTIN, TEXAS, September 10, 1875. }

Convention met pursuant to adjournment; roll called; quorum present. Prayer by Rev. H. V. Philpot, of Austin. Journal of yesterday read and adopted.

On motion of Mr. Wade, a resolution introduced by him on yesterday, and referred to Committee on Executive Department, was taken up and referred to Committee on General Provisions.

Mr. M. H. Goddin, member elect from Walker county, came forward and took the required oath.

The following Committee on Apportionment was appointed by the President:

Second District, Allison, chairman; First District, Whitehead; Third District, Douglas; Fourth District, West; Fifth District, Flanagan; Sixth District, Kilgore; Seventh District, Dillard; Eighth District, Johnson of Franklin; Ninth District, Henry of Limestone; Tenth District, Martin of Hunt; Eleventh District, Wright; Twelfth District, Rugely; Thirteenth District, Reynolds; Fourteenth District, Rentfro; Fifteenth District, Goddin; Sixteenth District, Lockett; Seventeenth District, Robertson of Bell; Eighteenth District, Davis of Brazos; Nineteenth District, Ross; Twentieth District, Brown; Twenty-first District, Chambers; Twenty-second District, Weaver; Twenty-third District, Barnett; Twenty-fourth District, Stayton; Twenty-fifth District, McCormick; Twenty-sixth District, Robeson; Twenty-seventh District, Burleson; Twenty-eighth District, Sansom; Twenty-ninth District, King; Thirtieth District, Ford.

On motion of Mr. Wright, he was excused, and Mr. German, of the same district, was appointed.

Mr. Chambers submitted to the Convention the following telegram:

McKINNEY, September 9, 1875.

To Mr. Chambers, Member of Convention, Austin:

My presence has been indispensable here this week, and I cannot now hold the Denton Court without an ordinance allowing me to open court there at any time during the three weeks allotted to that county. Can't you have an ordinance passed in the morning to that effect? Let me hear at once here.

J. M. LINDSAY.

Mr. Chambers moved that a special committee of three be appointed to consider the telegram, and report to this Convention, by resolution or otherwise.

Carried.

The President appointed as said committee: Messrs. Ballinger, Wright and Flournoy.

On motion of Mr. Brady, Mr. Mills was excused until next Monday.

Mr. Cook, chairman Printing Committee, submitted the following report:

To the Hon. E. B. Pickett, President of the Convention:

SIR—Your Committee on Printing and Contingent Expenses, to whom was referred resolution with regard to subscription for daily papers, to contain proceedings of the Convention, for the use of delegates, have had the same under consideration, and have instructed me to report:

That, in pursuance of what they considered their duties in the premises, they have conferred with the several newspaper publishers of the city of Austin, and have received the following proposals:

The publishers of the *Democratic Statesman* propose to furnish the *Statesman,* with the requisite report, daily, at the following rates:

Nine hundred copies at 4 cents, 1350 copies at 3½ cents, and 1800 copies at 3 cents.

The publishers of the *Evening News* propose to furnish the *Evening News* at two and a half cents, twenty copies for each delegate.

The publisher of the *State Gazette* proposes to furnish daily, the *Gazette,* with full stenographic report of the proceedings of the Convention, at five cents each, twenty copies for each delegate.

The publishers of the Galveston *News* propose to furnish that paper at three cents, any number required.

The publishers of the Houston *Telegraph* propose to furnish that paper daily, with the requisite report, at five cents (500 copies), and cost of composition of journals.

The committee have not felt at liberty to close a contract for the papers, but report the above facts, and ask for further instructions from the Convention.

All of which is respectfully submitted.

W. D. S. COOK, Chairman.

CHARLES DEMORSE,   JOHN S. FORD,
THOS. G. ALLISON,   J. W. WHITFIELD.

Mr. Waelder presented a memorial from a committee of the Texas Medical Association, "asking for a uniform system of sanitary regulations throughout the State."

Read and referred to Committee on State Affairs.

Mr. Russell, of Wood, offered the following resolution:

WHEREAS, In the nature of their government, the government are the great principles necessary to restore confidence and elevate the people to prosperity and happiness; and

WHEREAS, In the nature of their government, the government has no right or power to impose burdens on them for any purpose whatever, except for revenue sufficient to administer the same; therefore be it

Resolved, By the Convention of the people of Texas assembled, that there ought to be a clause placed in the organic law restraining the Legislature, or taxing power of this State, from ever levying taxes upon the people for any purpose whatever, except revenue sufficient to strictly and economically administer the government.

Referred to Committee on General Provisions.

Mr. Martin, of Navarro, offered the following resolution:

Resolved, That the report of the Committee on Printing and Contingent Expenses be received, and the consideration of subscribing for newspapers be indefinitely postponed.

Mr. McLean offered the following as a substitute:

Resolved, That the Committee on Printing is instructed to contract with John D. Elliott, of the *State Gazette,* for 1800 copies daily of the *Gazette,* containing a synoptical report of the daily proceedings of this body, including a statement of the position of each member who may express himself upon each proposition before the body.

Lost.

Mr. McCormick then offered the following as a substitute for the resolution offered by Mr. Martin, of Navarro:

Resolved, That each member of this Convention be allowed to subscribe to twenty copies of any daily paper publishing the proceedings of the Convention, such as the members may select, and at a cost not to exceed three cents per copy.

Lost.

The question then being on the adoption of the original resolution, offered by Martin, of Navarro, it was carried by the following vote:

Yeas—Messrs. Abernathy, Arnim, Blake, Blassingame, Barnes, Burleson, Bruce, Chambers, Cook of San Saba, Cooley, Cardis, Douglas, Dohoney, Davis of Brazos, Erhard, Flournoy, Ferris,

German, Goddin, Holt, Henry of Smith, Henry of Limestone, Holmes, Haynes, Johnson of Franklin, Johnson of Collin, Killough, Lacy, Martin of Navarro, Mitchell, McKinney, Moore, Norval, Pauli, Reagan, Rugely, Robertson, Robeson, Ross, Russell of Wood, Spike, Sessions, Smith, Stayton, Sansom, Wade, Whitehead, Weaver—48.

Nays—Messrs. Allison, Abner, Brown, Brady, Crawford, Cook of Gonzales, Cline, Dillard, DeMorse, Darnell, Dunnam, Davis of Wharton, Ford, Fleming, Flanagan, Gaither, Graves, King, Kilgore, Lockett, Lynch, McLean, Martin of Hunt, McCabe, McCormick, Nunn, Nugent, Reynolds, Rentfro, Russell of Harrison, Scott, Stockdale, Whitfield, West, Waelder—35.

Mr. Stockdale offered the following resolution:

Resolved, " Section 24. That the Legislature may establish new counties for the convenience of the inhabitants of such new county or counties, under the following restrictions:

" 1. No county shall be established of a less area than nine hundred square miles, unless by consent of four-fifths of the Legislature.

" 2. No new county or counties shall be established which shall reduce the old county or counties, or either of them, from which it is taken, to a less area than nine hundred square miles, unless by consent of two-thirds of the Legislature.

" 3. No county shall be established, the boundary line or lines of which shall approach nearer at any point to an established county than twelve miles.

" 4. Every new county, as to the right of suffrage and representation, shall be considered as part of the county or counties from which it was taken, until entitled by numbers to the right of representation.

" 5. No new county shall be laid off containing less than one hundred and fifty qualified jurors, resident at the time therein (nor when the county or counties from which the new county is proposed to be taken, would thereby be reduced below that number of qualified jurors), and in all cases, when from the want of qualified jurors or other causes, the courts can not properly be held in any county, it shall be the duty of the District Judge to certify such fact to the Governor; and the Governor shall, by proclamation, attach such county for judicial purposes to that county the county site of which is nearest the county site of the county so to be attached."

Referred to Committee on Counties and County Lands.

Mr. McCormick introduced the following resolution:

Resolved, That a committee of five be appointed by the President to inquire into the present management of the State Penitentiary, and report what action, if any, is necessary to be taken by this Convention in relation thereto.

Adopted.

Mr. DeMorse introduced the following ordinance:

"PREAMBLE:

"WHEREAS, The first object of natural government is the greatest good to the greatest number; therefore, under the beneficent Providence of a just God, the following provisions of an organic law are ordained for the State of Texas:

"1. All men being equal in political rights, monopolies, perpetuities, or class legislation are unwise and unjust, and will not be allowed.

"2. All legislation must be general in its application and effect, and any having application to classes or persons, or specified localities, except for roads, bridges, mines, harbor improvements, improvement of rivers, stock laws, or laws for the preservation or restoration of peace in disturbed localities, is expressly inhibited and declared void.

"3. The powers of government are comprised in the legislative, executive and judicial, which are equal and co-ordinate, neither having power to revise or control the action of the other.

"4. Money being a creation of government, and its value fixed by legislative sanction, and exorbitant rates of interest, being oppressive to industry and calculated to withdraw this medium of exchange from its legitimate practical uses, and cause its misappropriation to speculative purposes; the conventional rate of interest is fixed at 8 per cent. per annum, which may be increased, by special contract in writing, to 10 per cent. per annum—no more—and any exaction, directly or indirectly, to a greater amount, for the use of money, or by the purchase of the written responsibilities of the party borrowing, shall cause a forfeiture of principal and interest, and release all principals or indorsers to the paper, upon which the money is obtained.

"5. To insure the just representation of minorities, the system of voting in all general, special or municipal elections, shall be by ballot, and shall be the cumulative system; by which, if more than one official is to be elected, the voter may vote for the whole number allowed, and subject to election, or he may concentrate all his votes for any less than the whole number to be elected; that is, if two or three are to be elected, he may vote twice or thrice for one, omitting the remainder, if he so prefers."

Read and referred to Committee on Bill of Rights.

Mr. Brown submitted the following resolution:

Resolved, That every person elected or appointed to any office, agency or trust under this State, or any municipal subdivision thereof, shall, before entering upon the discharge of the duties of such position, take the following oath or affirmation before some officer authorized to administer oaths:

"I do solemnly swear (or affirm) that I will faithfully and impartially discharge and perform all the duties incumbent on me as . . . . . . according to the best of my skill and ability, agreeably to the constitution and laws of the United States and of this State.   I, furthermore, solemnly swear (or affirm) that, since the adoption of the present constitution of the State of Texas, I, being a citizen of this State, have not fought a duel with deadly weapons within this State, nor out of it; nor have I sent or accepted a challenge to fight a duel with deadly weapons; nor have I acted as second in carrying a challenge, nor aided, advised or assisted any person thus offending.   And I, furthermore, solemnly swear (or affirm) that I have not, directly nor indirectly, paid, offered, or promised to pay, contributed, or promised to contribute any money, or other valuable thing, or promised any public office or employment as the reward for the giving or withholding a vote at the election at which I was elected (or appointed) to said office.   So help me God."

Referred to Committee on General Provisions.

Mr. Brown also offered the following resolution:

Resolved, "Art. —, Sec. —, That the following classes of persons, with the exceptions named in this section, shall be entitled to the right of suffrage as electors in this State:

"1. Every male person over twenty-one years of age, who, being a citizen of the United States, shall have resided as a *bona fide* citizen for twelve months in this State, and for six months next preceding any election in the town, city, or county, as the case may be, for municipal, county, or State officers, in which he may offer to vote.

"2. Every male person of foreign birth, who, six months before any such election, shall have declared his intention in accordance with the Federal naturalization laws, to become a citizen of the United States, who shall have, also, for twelve months, resided *bona fide* in this State, and for six months next preceding any election in the town, city, or county, as the case may be, for town, city, county, district, or State officers, or purposes in which he may offer to vote.

"3. That though possessing the foregoing qualification, the following classes of persons shall be denied the right of suffage in any election in this article: Persons insane, or *non compos mentis,* so long as the disease may continue; all persons while confined in county or State prisons; all persons convicted of bribery, forgery, or other high crimes, unless restored to their lost rights in such manner as may be prescribed by law.

"Sec. 2. No registration of voters shall be required in elections for town, city, county, district, or State elections in this State; *provided, however,* that the Legislature shall have the power to enact such provisions as may be deemed necessary, to guard against frauds in elections in cities having over twenty-five thousand population, and in counties bordering on other States or counties.

"Sec. 3. That the Legislature shall enact laws to prevent frauds in elections, imposing penalties appropriate to felonies for such offenses. A person convicted of fraud in elections, whether as a voter, officer of election, candidate for office, or otherwise, shall thereby forfeit his right of suffrage, and neither the Legislature nor any other power shall restore the lost right to such criminal."

Referred to Committee on Suffrage.

Mr. Brown also offered the following resolution:

Resolved, "Sec. ——. That no person shall at the same time hold, exercise, or enjoy the pay, emoluments, or powers of more than one office, appointment, agency, or trust under this State, or any municipal sub-division thereof; nor shall any person, while holding or exercising the functions of any office, appointment, agency, or trust, under the United States, or under any State or Territory of the United States, or under any foreign government, be eligible to any office, appointment, agency, or trust, under this State, or any municipal sub-division thereof; *provided,* that this inhibition shall not extend to the office of postmaster, militia offices without salary, nor to overseers of roads."

Referred to Committee on General Provisions.

Mr. Brown also offered the following resolution:

Resolved, "Sec. ——. That in establishing salaries for teachers, no distinction shall be made in the pay of male and female teachers of the same grade."

Referred to Committee on Education.

Mr. DeMorse offered the following resolution:

Resolved, That in the apportionment of representation, any county which has population sufficient to entitle it to one senator or any given number of representatives, shall elect these by its own vote solely; and for any surplus of population over and above the basis of representation, it may vote in conjunction with other counties, as may be deemed best, for conjoint senators and representatives. The Senate shall not comprise more than thirty members, nor the House of Representatives more than one hundred members, for the next ten years next succeeding the adoption of this constitution.

Referred to Committee on Legislative Department.

Mr. Wade offered the following resolution:

Resolved, That the Committee on Federal Relations inquire into the propriety of laying before the Congress of the United States the proposition to call a Convention of delegates from each State to make a new constitution for the nation, or of requesting that body to submit to the Legislatures of the States such amendments as will abolish the present system of tariff for revenue purposes and adopt a more equal system; also the present system of diplomacy, electoral voting for President, and on abridging the appointing power of the President, or withholding suffrage from all those in the pay and service of government by appointment.

Referred to Committee on Federal Relations.

Mr. Sansom introduced the following resolution:

Resolved, That the property of the wife should be subject to forced sale for the payment of the debts of the husband contracted after marriage.

Referred to Committee on General Provisions.

Also the following resolution:

Resolved, That it is the duty of the State to fix the value of property exempt from taxation.

Referred to Committee on General Provisions.

Also—

That interest on money in this State shall not exceed twelve per cent. per annum, but that the Legislature may fix the legal rate of interest at any sum less than twelve per cent.

Referred to Committee on General Provisions.

Mr. Abernathy introduced the following resolution:

Resolved, That the following be adopted as the preamble to this constitution:

"PREAMBLE:

"Humbly invoking the blessings of Almighty God, the people of the State of Texas do ordain and establish this constitution."

Referred to Committee on Bill of Rights.

Also by Mr. Abernathy the following resolution:

Resolved, That no taxes shall be levied in this State for the purpose of keeping up public roads, but the same shall be kept up by a system of labor by the male citizens of this State between the ages of fifteen and fifty years, as the Legislature may provide by law.

Referred to Committee on State Affairs.

Mr. Robertson, of Bell, introduced the following resolution:

Resolved, That the Committee on General Provisions be requested to inquire into the propriety of incorporating into the constitution the following provision: "That no private corporation be created, except the corporation or individuals composing it pay the cost of the act of incorporation, said cost to be determined by the Legislature and made a part of the act."

Referred to the Committee on General Provisions.

Mr. McLean offered the following resolution:

Resolved, That the Legislature may establish new counties, or change the boundaries of old counties; *provided,* no new county shall be created with less than one thousand persons resident therein subject to a poll tax; nor shall any old county be so reduced that it shall contain within its limits less than said number of persons liable to pay a poll tax, and no old county shall be so reduced in area that the line shall be nearer than ten miles to the courthouse of such old county. When any part of a county is stricken off and attached to another county, the part stricken off shall be obliged to pay its proportion of all the liabilities then existing of the county from which it is taken, and the Legislature shall, in the act detaching such territory, make appropriate provisions for the levy and collection of taxation of the due proportion of indebtedness of such detached territory, in the absence of which legislation, the act detaching such territory shall be null.

Referred to Committee on Counties and County Lands.

Mr. Ramey offered the following resolution:

Resolved, That the special committee appointed under a resolution of this body to determine the mileage of the members of this Convention are hereby required to estimate the distances upon which said mileage is based to the county seat of the county in which each delegate respectively lives.

Mr. Dillard offered a substitute as follows:

Resolved, That the distance shall be computed on an air line from the county seat of each county to the capital, to be ascertained and fixed by the Commissioner of the General Land Office.

On motion of Mr. Martin, of Navarro, both resolution and substitute were laid on the table.

Mr. Johnson, of Franklin, offered the following resolution:

Resolved, That the following provision be incorporated in the constitution, under appropriate caption, viz: "The Legislature shall have no power to grant or authorize any city, town, county, or other political sub-division now existing, or that may hereafter exist, to lend its credit or to grant public money or property of value in aid of, or to any individual, or company of individuals whatever, or to become a stockholder in a company of any kind."

Referred to Committee on Legislative Department.

Mr. Whitehead offered the following resolution:

Resolved, That the Committee on Immigration be, and they are hereby instructed to inquire into the expediency of omitting from the constitution to be framed by this Convention any article or provision establishing a Bureau of Immigration.

Referred to Committee on Immigration.

Mr. Russell, of Harrison, offered the following resolution:

Resolved, That the following provision shall be incorporated in the constitution of the State of Texas, viz: "Every bill which shall have passed the Legislature shall, before it becomes a law, be presented to the Governor. If he approve it, he shall sign it, but if not, he shall return it, with his objections, to the house in which it originated, which shall enter the same upon its journal, and proceed to reconsider it. If, after such reconsideration it again pass both houses by yeas and nays, by a majority of the members of each house, it shall become a law, notwithstanding the Governor's objections. If any bill shall not be returned within three days after it has been presented to the Governor (Sundays excepted), the same shall become a law in like manner as if he had signed it, unless the Legislature, by adjournment, prevent such return. Any bill submitted to the Governor for his approval during the last three days of a session of the Legislature, shall be deposited by him in the office of the Secretary of State within thirty days after the adjournment, with his approval, if approved by him, and with his objections, if he disapproves thereof."

Referred to Committee on Legislative Department.

Also by Mr. Russell, of Harrison, the following resolution:

Resolved, That the following be incorporated in the Bill of Rights of the Constitution, viz: "No person shall ever be imprisoned for debt, except for the non-payment of fines and penalties imposed for violation of law."

Referred to Committee on Bill of Rights.

Mr. Fleming offered the following resolution:

Resolved, That the following section be incorporated in the constitution: "Section —. That no railroad or other transportation company shall grant free passes or tickets, or passes or tickets at a discount, to any officer of this State, legislative, executive, or judicial; and the acceptance of any such pass or ticket by any such officer, shall be a forfeiture of his office."

Referred to Committee on Railroad Corporations.

Mr. Weaver offered the following resolution:

WHEREAS, Free thought, free speech, and free government, are the growth of general education, and constitute the cardinal principles of constitutional liberty and universal intelligence, and is thus the foe to bigotry, despotism and central political power; that neither intelligence, liberty, nor love of country, can be promoted and upheld in any country without *general education;* and

WHEREAS, The State of Texas has a school fund of lands and revenue amply sufficient to educate the children of the State, of all classes and colors *forever,* without the necessity of *direct* taxation from the people for school purposes; and that the lands set apart for school purposes and the revenues comprising the school fund, are the common property of *every citizen of the State;* therefore be it

Resolved, That this constitution take into its own hands the entire public domain of the State of Texas, together with all the lands heretofore appropriated for school purposes, and fix the price of the same, so as to bring it into market as it can be judiciously done, which public revenue shall go to the support of the public free schools of the State, to include all classes of schools, whether universities, academies, or common schools, and whether scientific, agricultural, mechanical, or literary.

Resolved, 2. That this Convention, by proper ordinances, so guard the fund arising from said school revenue as to prevent it from being squandered or appropriated to any other purposes; and thereby securing forever to all the children of this State the greatest wealth of a free country, educated citizens; *and, provided,* that separate free schools shall be established for the education of the negroes.

Referred to Committee on Education.

Mr. Ballinger, chairman select committee, submitted the following report:

Hon. E. B. Pickett, President of the Convention:

Your select committee, to whom was referred the request of the Judge of the Twelfth Judicial District for an ordinance by this Convention to authorize the holding of the District Court of Denton county, which has lapsed by reason of the same not having been opened during the time appointed by law, respectfully report that without having considered the question of the power of the Convention involved in the subject, your committee do not think any exigency apparent which would justify its exercise.

Under existing law, the people and bar understand the court to have lapsed. The relative benefit, or inconvenience, under the circumstances, of now requiring the court to be held, is not sufficiently understood to authorize action by this body, even if the Convention was exercising ordinary legislative functions.

BALLINGER,
WRIGHT,
FLOURNOY.

Report adopted.

Mr. Martin, of Hunt, offered the following resolution:

Resolved, That the Committee on Legislative Department be instructed to inquire into the expediency of inserting in the constitution the following provision: "That after the adoption of this constitution, the first two sessions of the Legislature shall be biennial; the first session limited to ninety days and the second to sixty, and thereafter the Legislature shall meet in regular session once only in every four years, except when the Legislature shall be convened in extra session by the Governor, which extra session shall be limited to thirty days, and when so called, the Legislature shall act upon no measure or measures, except such as may be recommended by the Governor."

Referred to Committee on Legislative Department.

Mr. Ferris offered the following resolution:

Resolved, That the following provision be adopted: "The Legislature shall establish a uniform rate of interest in the State, and such rate of interest shall never exceed eight per cent. per annum when no contract has been made with reference thereto, or twelve per cent. per annum by contract."

Referred to Committee on General Provisions.

Mr. Nugent submitted the following section:

"The Legislature at the conclusion, and before the adjournment of each session, shall cause to be prepared a tabular statement of appropriations of money made at such session. Said statement shall show the amount of each appropriation, the purpose for which it was made, together with the total amount of such appropriations. Said statement shall be published as a part of the general laws of the session, and shall also be published at least once in some newspaper in each Representative or Senatorial District, to be designated by the Governor."

Referred to Committee on Taxation and Revenue.

Mr. Russell, of Harrison, offered the following resolution:

Resolved, That the following provision shall be incorporated in the bill of rights of the constitution:

"That all men have a natural and indefeasible right to worship Almighty God according to the dictates of their own conscience; that no person shall, on account of his opinion on the subject of religion, be rendered ineligible to any office of profit or trust under this State; nor be disqualified from testifying, or from serving as a juror; that no human authority can control or interfere with the rights of conscience; that no person ought, by any law, be molested in his person or estate, on account of his religious persuasion or profession, or want of the same; but the liberty of conscience hereby secured shall not be so construed as to excuse acts of licentiousness, nor to justify practices inconsistent with the good order, peace, or safety of this State, or with the rights of others."

Referred to Committee on Bill of Rights.

Mr. Ross offered the following resolution:

Resolved, That the Legislature shall provide by law for the appointment of special judges of the District Court in all cases where the presiding judge shall for any cause be disqualified from sitting, and whenever by reason of the absence, sickness, or other inability of the presiding judge, any term of his court for any county of his district would otherwise not be held. The venue of cases may be changed under such regulations as may be prescribed by law.

Referred to Committee on Legislative Department.

Mr. Holmes offered the following resolution:

Resolved, That each county in the State be divided into five divisions, equal according to population, and that the qualified voters of each division elect one magistrate, who, together with the other magistrates, shall compose the county court.

2. That the qualified voters of each of said divisions elect one constable, who, in addition to the regular duties of the office, shall be *ex-officio* deputy sheriff of the county.

Referred to Committee on Judiciary.

Mr. McCormick offered the following resolution:

Resolved, That the following section shall be incorporated under the appropriate article:

"Sec. ——. No judge of any court in this State during his term of service shall hold any other office, appointment, or public trust, and the acceptance thereof shall vacate his judicial office; nor shall he during such term, or within one year thereafter, be eligible to any political office."

Referred to Judiciary Committee.

Mr. Pauli offered the following resolution:

Resolved, That all State and county taxes shall be collected in lawful money of the United States only, and that no bonds or scrip of any kind are receivable therefor.

Referred to Committee on Revenue and Taxation.

Mr. Dohoney offered the following resolution:

Resolved by the Constitutional Convention of the State of Texas, That the following be adopted as an article in the proposed new constitution, to wit:

" ARTICLE —.

" OFFICIAL QUALIFICATIONS.

"Section 1. No person who is a disbeliever in the existence of a God shall hold any office in this State.

"Sec. 2. No person holding an office of profit under the United States shall, during the continuance in such office, hold any office of profit under this State, nor shall any person, at the same time hold two offices under this State.

"Sec. 3. No person having heretofore held office under the United States, or under any State, and who shall have been impeached, or convicted of malfeasance or misfeasance in office, or who shall have been guilty of any defalcation or default in the discharge of the duties of such office, shall hold office in this State, and no officer who shall hereafter be guilty of any such defalcation or default in office, shall thereafter hold any office in this State.

"Sec. 4. No person who has heretofore been convicted of felony in any State shall hold office in this State; and no person who shall hereafter be convicted of felony shall thereafter hold any office in this State.

"Sec. 5. No person who shall hereafter fight a duel, or assist in the same as a second, or send, accept, or knowingly carry a challenge therefor, or agree to go out of this State to fight a duel, shall hold any office in this State.

"Sec. 7. No drunkard or other person who is in the habit of risking money on games of chance, or contingent results, shall hold any office in this State.

"Sec. 7. No drunkard or other person who is in the habit of getting under the influence of intoxicating liquor, shall hold any office in this State.

"Sec. 8. All officers, both civil and military, under the authority of this State, shall, before entering on the duties of their respective offices, take and subscribe an oath, or affirmation, to support the Constitution of the United States and of this

State, and that they are subject to none of the disqualifications
enumerated in this article, and that they will faithfully demean
themselves in office."

Referred to Committee on General Provisions.

The chair announced the following committee to inquire into
the management of the State Penitentiary: Messrs. McCormick, Brown, Dunnam, Arnim and Mills.

Mr. Stockdale asked to be relieved from acting as chairman of
the Committee on Private Corporations.

On motion of Mr. Flanegan he was excused.

On motion of Mr. Flournoy, Mr. Wright was made chairman
of said committee.

Mr. German offered the following resolution:

Resolved, That the following provisions shall be adopted:

"That members of the House of Representatives shall be
chosen by the qualified electors, and their term of office shall be
two years from the date of general election; and the regular sessions of the Legislature shall be once only in every two years,
and of not more than sixty days' duration.

Referred to Committee on Legislative Department.

On motion of Mr. Bruce, Mr. Graves was added to the Committee on Railroad Corporations.

On motion of Mr. Henry, of Smith, Mr. Kilgore was added
to the Committee on Judiciary.

On motion of Mr. Dohoney, Mr. German was added to the
Committee on Railroad Corporations.

On motion of Mr. Robertson, of Bell, Mr. Smith was added
to the Committee on Revenue and Taxation.

On motion of Mr. Russell, of Wood, Mr. Weaver was added
to the Committee on Judiciary.

On motion of Mr. Davis, of Brazos, Mr. Johnson, of Franklin, was added to the Committee on Bill of Rights.

On motion of Mr. Cook, of Gonzales, Mr. Burleson was added
to the Committee on Revenue and Taxation.

Mr. West offered the following resolution, which was referred
to the Committee on General Provisions:

Resolved, That the following shall constitute article —, section
—, of the constitution:

"All claims, locations, surveys, grants and titles to land of any
kind, which are declared null and void by the Constitution of the
Republic, or State of Texas, are and the same shall remain
forever null and void.

"Sec. —.   There shall be one General Land Office in the

4

State, which shall be at the seat of government, where all titles which have heretofore emanated or may hereafter emanate from the government, shall be registered; *provided,* that hereafter no title issued prior to the 13th of November, 1835, by the Mexican authorities, shall be received or registered in said Land Office."

Mr. Robertson, of Bell, offered the following resolution:

Resolved, That the Committee on Public Lands and Land Office be requested to incorporate the following provision in the constitution:

"That all genuine outstanding land certificates granted to early settlers, soldiers and colonists, for services rendered, may at any time, at the option of the holder, be located on any portion of the public domain of the State, but any and all of said certificates that shall be outstanding when all of the land of the State shall be absorbed and appropriated, shall become void. Homesteads shall be granted to actual settlers out of the public domain."

Referred to Committee on Public Lands.

Mr. Cook, of Gonzales, submitted a communication of Mr. Kidd, representative reporter for the Houston *Telegraph,* addressed to the Printing Committee, and asked that it be spread upon the journals of the Convention.

On motion of Mr. Brown, the communication was laid on the table.

On motion of Mr. Allison, the Convention adjourned until 9 o'clock A. M. to-morrow.

SIXTH DAY.

HALL OF REPRESENTATIVES, ⎱
AUSTIN, TEXAS, September 11, 1875. ⎰

Convention met pursuant to adjournment; roll called; quorum present. Prayer by Rev. T. B. Lee, of Austin. Journal of yesterday read and adopted.

Mr. Stayton presented the memorial of Pryor Lee on the subject of old land certificates that have not been satisfied.

Referred to Committee on Public Lands and Land Office.

Mr. Robertson, of Bell, offered the following resolution:

Resolved, That a committee of three be appointed to ascertain and report to this Convention on Monday next, or as soon as practicable, whether a stenographer can be secured to report the full proceedings of this Convention, and if one can be found, at what cost per day.

Adopted.

The President announced Messrs. Robertson, DeMorse and Stockdale as said committee.

Mr. Cook, of Gonzales, offered the following resolution:

Resolved, That for all accounts made for contingent expenses of this Convention against the contingent fund thereof, the approval of the Committee on Contingent Expenses, signed by the Secretary and countersigned by the President of the Convention, shall be sufficient authority for the Comptroller to draw his warrant on the Treasurer for the payment of the same; which shall be paid out of the funds appropriated by joint resolution of the second session of the Fourteenth Legislature, to defray the expense of this Convention.

Adopted.

Mr. West offered the following resolution.

Resolved, That the Sergeant-at-arms be required to make the necessary arrangements to furnish water for the use of this Convention until the cisterns shall be replenished by rain.

Adopted.

Mr. Abernathy offered the following resolution:

Resolved, That none of the waters of this State shall be poisoned or otherwise polluted so as to destroy fish; the Legislature shall enact laws to protect the fish from wasteful destruction in the waters of this State.

Referred to Committee on General Provisions.

Mr. Burleson offered the following resolution:

Resolved, That no debt shall be contracted by any county or municipal corporation except with the consent of two-thirds of both branches of the Legislature, nor under any circumstances shall an indebtedness be contracted in excess of — per cent. of the assessed value of the taxable property of such county or corporation.

Referred to Committee on Municipal Corporations.

Mr. Burleson also offered the following resolution:

Resolved, That the failure of an officer made by law a collector of taxes, to pay over the revenue collected, should be made a felony and punished as such.

Referred to Committee on Taxation and Revenue.

Mr. Graves offered the following resolution:

Resolved, That the following section shall be incorporated in the constitution under the appropriate caption:

"No lottery shall be authorized by this State; and the buying and selling of lottery tickets within this State is prohibited."

Referred to Committee on General Provisions.

Mr. Fleming offered the following resolution:

Resolved, That a committee of one from each Senatorial District be appointed by the President to apportion the State into Judicial Districts.

Adopted.

Mr. Nunn offered the following resolution:

Resolved, That the Judiciary Committee be instructed to inquire into the expediency of reporting in favor of defining by law the powers of the judicial tribunals, to punish for contempt of court, and to secure the citizen against the exercise of capricious, arbitrary or absolute power, by defining and limiting the causes that can be held as contempt of court, so that no such power can be exercised, except so far as may be necessary, to preserve the dignity and independence of the judiciary and to secure the enforcement of proper discipline in the court for the transaction of public business, and to provide a mode of proceeding, that while consistent with the dignity of the court, shall protect the citizen against capricious and absolute power.

Referred to Committee on Judiciary.

Mr. King offered the following resolution:

Resolved, That the following provision be incorporated in the constitution of the State of Texas:

"No act of the Legislature except for appropriations, shall take effect or be in force, until ninety days after the adjournment of the session of which it was enacted, unless in case of emergency, (which must be expressed in the preamble, or in the body of the act,) the Legislature shall by a vote of two-thirds of all the members elected to each house otherwise direct; said vote to be taken by yeas and nays and entered upon the journal."

Referred to Committee on Legislative Department.

Mr. Holmes offered the following resolution:

Whereas, The necessity for the secret and inquisitorial service of the grand jury does not now exist and is contrary to the principles of free government, and is the source of civil discord and dissensions between citizens of communities, and the cause of unnecessary expense to the State, and unreasonable delay in the execution of justice; therefore be it

Resolved, That the following provisions be incorporated in the constitution:

"That every presentment for indictment on going before the grand jury, shall be certified to by the magistrate in whose jurisdiction the offense originated, accompanied with the evidence relating thereto."

Referred to Committee on Judiciary.

Mr. Chambers offered the following resolution: ·

Resolved, That the following provisions shall be adopted:

"1. All the public lands heretofore appropriated by law to common school purposes, shall be forever held sacred for that purpose, and no Legislature shall ever pass any law to divert it from that purpose.

"2. That the Legislature shall provide by law from time to time for the sale of said lands and for the safe-keeping and disbursement of the proceeds of the sales of the same."

Referred to Committee on Education.

Mr. Sansom offered the following resolution:

Resolved, That all the male inhabitants of this State, of twenty-one years of age and over, shall be qualified electors; *provided,* that, if a tax be levied for public schools, any voter failing or refusing to pay said tax shall not vote until the tax has been paid. *And provided further,* that in municipal corporations all appropriations, for other than police purposes, shall be submitted to a vote of the property-holders and tax-payers of said corporations, and that no poll-tax shall be levied by said corporations.

Referred to Committee on Suffrage.

Mr. Robertson, of Bell, offered the following resolution:

Resolved, That the Committee on Judiciary be requested to incorporate the following provisions in the constitution under the appropriate heads:

"That six Supreme and twenty-five District Judges be elected.

"That Supreme Judges receive a salary of three thousand five hundred dollars each.

"That District Judges receive a salary of two thousand five hundred dollars each.

"That Judges of the Supreme Court hold their offices six years."

Referred to the Committee on Judiciary.

Mr. Robertson also offered the following resolution:

Resolved, That the Committee on General Provisions be requested to incorporate in the constitution, under its appropriate head, the following provisions:

"That all officers be elected by the people, both State and County, except Secretary of State and the Superintendents of the Asylums.

" That no power of suspending same be exercised except by a vote of two-thirds of both Houses of the Legislature.

" That the Legislature meet biennially, to be convened in extra session by the Governor only in case of emergency, and then only to transact such business as the Governor may designate in his proclamation.

" That the per diem pay of members of the Legislature shall not exceed five dollars.

" That the Legislature shall have no power to make any grant or to authorize the making of any grant of public money or thing of value, to any individuals, municipal or other corporations whatsoever; *provided,* that this shall not be so construed as to prevent the grant of aid in a case of public calamity.

" That the Legislature shall have no power to authorize any county, city, town, or other political corporation or sub-division of the State now existing, or that may hereafter be created or established, to lend its credit or to grant public money or thing of value in aid of or to any individual association or corporation of value in aid or to any individual, association or corporation association or company.

" That no municipal government in this State shall incur a debt for internal improvement or otherwise, except by a vote of a majority of those owning real estate in such municipalities.

" That all lands heretofore granted to counties for school purposes shall forever remain the property of the counties, to be managed and disposed of by the county commissioners of the counties, as the Legislature may prescribe, the revenues arising therefrom to be used only for school purposes.

" That the lands heretofore set aside for school purposes shall remain a perpetual school fund, and shall be leased or otherwise disposed of as may be provided by law, but the fee to said lands shall never pass out of the State."

Referred to Committee on General Provisions.

Mr. Barnett offered the following resolution:

Resolved, That the following section shall be incorporated in the constitution:

" Sec. ——.   The Legislature shall, at the first session after the ratification of this constitution, provide by law for the filing of an abstract of titles and the payment of taxes on all patented land in the several counties of this State."

Referred to Committee on Revenue and Taxation.

Mr. Flournoy offered the following resolution:

Resolved, That the following section shall be embraced in the constitution.

"Sec. ——.   The Legislature shall have power, and it shall be their duty, to protect by law from forced sale a certain portion of the property of all heads of families, and of unmarried adults, male and female.   The homestead of a family not to exceed 200 acres of land (not included in a city, or town or village), or any city, town or village lot or lots, not to exceed in value $5000 at the time of their designation as a homestead, and without reference to the value of any improvements thereon, shall not be subject to forced sale for debts, except they be for the purchase thereof, for the taxes due thereon, or for labor and material expended thereon; nor shall the owner, if a married man, be at liberty to alienate the same, unless by the consent of the wife, and in such manner as may be prescribed by law, nor shall any mortgage or trust deed, or other lien thereon be valid except to secure the purchase money therefor or the payment for the improvements thereon, although the same may have been executed by the husband alone, or jointly with his wife.   But the Legislature shall provide for the separate registration of the homestead (designated as such) in the county clerk's office of the county wherein the same may be situated, and the claim of homestead shall not thereafter be entertained, except as to the property so registered as such.   If the homestead shall not have been acquired and registered prior to the death of the husband or wife, or other head of a family, no homestead or other property in lieu thereof shall be set apart out of the estate of such deceased person until all claims against the same shall have been fully paid; *provided,* that any property claimed and registered as a homestead shall be liable to forced sale to satisfy any lien or mortgage that may have been created thereon prior to such registration."

Referred to Committee on General Provisions.

Mr. McCormick offered the following resolution:

Resolved, That the following section shall be incorporated in the constitution:

"Ministers of the Gospel being by their profession dedicated to the service of God, ought not, therefore, to be diverted from their functions; therefore no minister of the Gospel, priest or preacher, of any denomination whatever, shall ever be eligible to the Legislature."

Referred to Committee on Legislative Department.

Mr. Erhard submitted the following propositions, to make our schools useful, practicable and economical:

Resolved, "1. That the control of schools shall be left to the management and control of each county and its sub-divided school districts.

" 2. That the school patrons in each school district, or separate school, shall choose their own teacher or teachers.

" 3. That the scholastic year shall consist of two sessions of twenty weeks each.

" 4. That no county shall pay for the building of school houses or benches, much less the State; each community must provide such for itself.

" 5. That the patrons of any school shall determine the salary of the teacher or teachers.

" 6. That unless otherwise provided for hereafter, each patron, able to pay, shall pay two dollars for each child per month, and that the paying patrons shall select three of their number to determine who are unable to pay.

" 7. That the deficiency of the teachers' salary per session shall be paid out of the county treasury, provided a certificate be presented by the teacher, signed by the appointed committee of three of the school in which he was employed.

" 8. That the county treasurer shall report such moneys paid out by the County Court, and after a due estimate, the citizens of such school district shall be taxed sufficient to cover said deficiency.

" 9. Should there be any public school fund, then the Comptroller of the State shall turn the same over to the several counties *pro rata,* according to the number of scholars in each county, and the county shall put said *pro rata* to the credit on tax rolls to such persons who have paid tuition for their children.

" 10. That teachers of freedmen's schools shall be examined by competent persons appointed by the County Court of the county wherein they teach, and if incapable, shall be discharged.

" 11. Each county wherein schools exist for colored youths, they shall select three citizens, who shall, as often as they deem best, go and examine that the teachers perform their duties diligently, or to hear the complaints of parents or guardians, and for want, or neglect, or cruel punishment, or immorality, shall discharge said teachers.

" 12. There shall be no compulsory education.

" 13. All persons between six and twenty-one years of age can avail themselves of school education; *provided,* those who have to be maintained by public taxation shall, after having acquired a knowledge of reading, writing and arithmetic, then be discharged, so that the public may not be farther taxed for them.

" 14. That whenever there shall be a sufficient public school fund to pay the tuition of all youths in the State, then no one shall be required to pay or be taxed for tuition, but all other regulations shall continue in force.

"15. There shall be separate schools for the white and colored children.

"16. That the next Legislature select teachers from Austin and other prominent institutions of learning in Texas, and request them to make a report in writing, which they consider the best books for schools, and after considering said reports, the Legislature shall adopt a uniform system of school books for the State of Texas, to be used in all schools, except high colleges or universities; those institutions being independent, may select their own course.

" 17. That at a suitable time the Legislature may establish a normal school for the proper training and education of male and female teachers for elementary schools."

Referred to Committee on Education.

Mr. Brown submitted the following sections:

"Sec. ——. All genuine claims for land against the State of Texas, whether certificate or headright, scrip or bounty warrant, which were in existence before the 1st of January, 1875, are declared to be valid and entitled to be located, surveyed and patented on the vacant and unappropriated public domain of the State."

Referred to Committee on General Provisions.

"Sec. ——. Every office created by this constitution, or by the Legislature under its authority, shall have a fixed period of tenure, and whenever vacated by death, resignation or other cause, the vacancy, whether filled by appointment or election, shall be filled for the unexpired term only."

Referred to Committee on General Provisions.

"COUNTY COURTS.

" Sec. ——. Every organized county, now or hereafter in existence in this State, shall be divided into a convenient number of civil districts, not to be less than two nor more than ten, as population or territory or both combined may render necessary for the convenience of the people. The number of such districts may be increased from two to ten by the County Court; or the public interest may render necessary and the boundaries of the same may be changed from time to time by the County Court when deemed necessary.

"The first sub-division of the present organized counties shall be made by the County Courts now in existence prior to the first election for county officers, provided for by this constitution.

"Sec. ——. The County Courts of each organized county in this

State, now or hereafter in existence, shall consist of a county chief justice, who shall be elected by the general vote of the county, and shall be the presiding justice of said court; and also one county commissioner, to be elected by the voters of each civil district separately. Said chief justice and county commissioners shall serve for two years from the day of their election and until their successors shall be elected and qualified. They shall take the constitutional oath of office before entering upon the discharge of their duties, and shall execute such bonds as may be provided by law.

" Sec. ——. The County Court shall hold regular sessions at least four times in each year, at such times as may be provided by law. Said court may also hold special or adjourned sessions, under such regulations as may be prescribed by law, and shall receive such per diem compensation as may in like manner be prescribed, but the members thereof shall not be allowed pay for more than three days at any one session, whether regular, special or adjourned.

" Sec. ——. The County Court shall have general supervision, jurisdiction and control over the public business of the county relating to county taxes, public buildings, poor houses, alms-houses, work-houses, houses of correction, roads, bridges and ferries, paupers and insane persons, in accordance with the laws on those subjects; and also all such other powers and jurisdictions as may be prescribed by law.

" JUSTICES COURTS.

" Sec. ——. In each civil district of every organized county, nor or hereafter existing in this State, there shall be elected two justices of the peace and one constable, who shall hold their respective offices for two years from the day of their election and until their successors shall be elected and qualified."

Referred to Committee on Judiciary.

Also, offered the following resolution in favor of amending the constitution of the United States:

WHEREAS, In view of evils in the legislation of the Congress of the United States, admitted to exist by all parties and sections; therefore

Resolved by the people of Texas in Convention assembled, That the senators and representatives in Congress from this State are hereby instructed to propose to Congress the two amendments following to the constitution of the United States, to be passed by that body and submitted to the several States for ratification:

" Sixteenth Amendment—Congress shall pass no bill, excepting appropriation bills, embracing more than one general subject matter, which shall be expressed in its title.

"Seventeenth Amendment—When an appropriation bill covering separate objects or items, may be passed by Congress, and submitted to the President for his consideration, he may approve a portion of the objects or items, and withhold his approval of other objects or items. If Congress be in session at the time his objections to such objects or items shall be communicated to the house in which the bill originated, as is provided in other cases, whereupon the question shall be separately upon each object or item objected to—'shall the proposition pass, the objections of the President to the contrary, notwithstanding?' and such objects or items as may thus pass each house of Congress by a vote of two-thirds of the members present, shall be and become a part of the law. Those objects or items not so receiving a vote of two-thirds of each house, shall be and remain of no force and effect. But should Congress not be in session, the President in approving portions of the bill and objecting to other portions, shall endorse on the same the portions to which he objects, and such portions shall have no force or effect in the law so approved."

Resolved, That the President of this Convention is instructed to transmit a copy of this resolution to each of our senators and representatives in Congress.

Referred to Committee on Federal Relations.

Mr. West offered the following resolution:

Resolved, That section ——, of article ——, of the constitution, shall be and read as follows:

"No senator or representative shall, during the term for which he may be elected, whether he resign, or shall have resigned his said office or not, be eligible to the Senate of the United States, or to any civil office of profit under this State, which shall have been created, or the emoluments of which may have been increased during such term; and no member of either house of the Legislature shall, during the term for which he is elected, whether he resign or shall have resigned his said office or not, be eligible to any office or place, the appointment of which may be made in whole or in part by either house of the Legislature; nor shall the members thereof be capable of voting for a member of their own body, whether such member resign, or shall have resigned his said office, for any office whatever, except it be in such cases as are herein provided for. The President for the time being of the Senate and Speaker of the House of Representatives shall be elected from their respective bodies."

Referred to Committee on Legislative Department.

Mr. West offered the following resolution:

Resolved, That section —, of article —, of the constitution shall be and read as follows:

"No bill of attainder, *ex post facto* law, retroactive law, or any law impairing the obligations of contracts shall be made, and no person's property shall be taken, or damaged, or applied to public use, without just compensation being made, unless by the consent of such person; nor shall any law be passed depriving a party of any remedy for the enforcement of a contract which existed when the contract was made."

Referred to Committee on Bill of Rights.

Mr. Weaver offered the following resolution:

Resolved, That there shall be established an inferior court in each county in this State, to be styled the County Court, which shall have civil jurisdiction over all actions of debt and damages where the amount in controversy shall not exceed $500, but they shall not have jurisdiction to enforce liens on real estate, or to try actions settling titles to real estate. Said court shall have general probate powers of the estates of deceased persons, guardians, minors, lunatics, etc. It shall also have jurisdiction over all misdemeanors and felonies where imprisonment in the penitentiary shall not exceed five years. Said court shall hold its sessions monthly, at the county seat of each county, and shall be open at all times to try crimes and misdemeanors.

"2. There shall be elected by the qualified voters of each county a judge and clerk of said court. Said judge shall be a licensed lawyer, resident of the county and a practicing attorney of at least five years standing. The salary, powers, term and duties of said county judge to be further prescribed by law."

Referred to Committee on Judiciary.

Mr. Crawford offered the following resolution:

Resolved, That the Committee on Revenue and Taxation be required to report on the propriety of establishing a perpetual public school fund on the following basis:

1. Apply exclusively the suffrage poll tax of two dollars.

2. Apply from the State revenue an amount not to exceed one-tenth of the same.

3. Apply the interest arising from the present school fund, and such interest as may arise from any fund hereafter created by the sale of school lands, as well as the rent money entire which may arise from the lease of said lands.

4. Authorize any school district which may be created by law to levy a special tax, not to exceed twenty-five cents on the $100, for school purposes, provided that said special tax shall not be

levied except by the consent of a majority of the voters of said district, who shall represent or own a majority of the taxable property in said district, to be ascertained at a public election held for that purpose.

Referred to Committee on Revenue and Taxation.

Mr. Holt offered the following resolution to deprive juries of the right of commuting capital punishment to imprisonment for life.

Resolved, That in all cases where by law it may be provided that capital punishment may be inflicted, the jury shall not have the right in their discretion to substitute imprisonment or hard labor for life.

Referred to Committee on Crimes and Punishments.

Mr. Kilgore introduced the following resolution:

Resolved, That the preamble of the proposed new constitution shall read as follows:

" PREAMBLE.

"We, the people of Texas, grateful to Almighty God for the privilege of choosing our own form of government, do establish this constitution."

Referred to Committee on Bill of Rights.

Also by Mr. Kilgore the following resolution:

Resolved, That section —— of the proposed new constitution shall read as follows:

"Sec. ——. Every free male person twenty-one years of age, a citizen of the United States who shall have resided in this State twelve months next preceding an election and the last six months in the district, county, city or town in which he offers to vote, and shall have paid all poll tax to which he is subject by law, shall be deemed a qualified elector in this State (Indians not taxed excepted), and should such qualified elector be absent from his own county on the day of an election, he shall be permitted to vote in any county in the district of his residence for district officers, and in any county in the State for State officers. No soldier, seaman or marine in the army or navy of the United States shall be entitled to vote at any election in this State."

Referred to Committee on Suffrage.

Mr. McCormick offered the following resolution:

Resolved, That the following section be incorporated in the constitution:

"No Governor, Lieutenant Governor or member of the Legislature of this State shall be eligible to a seat in the Congress of the United States for five years after the termination of the term of office for which they may have been elected."

Referred to Committee on General Provisions.

Mr. Rugely introduced the following resolution:

Resolved, That the right of trial by jury shall be inviolate; the Legislature shall pass such laws as may be needed to maintain its purity and efficiency. No person is qualified to serve upon any jury who is not a citizen of the State and resident of the county; who has been convicted of felony; who is deaf, dumb, blind, or who can not understand and read and write the English language.

Referred to Committee on Judiciary.

Mr. Brady offered the following resolutions:

Resolved, That the following be incorporated in the constitution:

Sec. —. In all civil cases the right of trial by jury shall remain inviolate."

Also—" Sec.—. That no money shall be drawn from the treasury for the use and benefit of any religious or theological institution whatever."

Also—" Sec. —. No law shall ever be passed restraining the free expression of thought, opinions and ideas, or restricting the right to speak, write or print freely on any subject whatever; but, for the libelous abuse of that right, every person shall be responsible.

" Sec. —. In all prosecutions for libel the truth of the matters alleged to be libelous may be given in justification."

Also—" Sec. —. Excessive bail shall not be required; excessive fines shall not be imposed; cruel and unusual punishments, such as burning, branding, thumb-screws, the rack, torture, poisoning, breaking upon the wheel, the stocks, pillory, whipping and the like, shall not be inflicted. All penalties shall be proportioned to the nature of the offense."

All of which were referred to Committee on Bill of Rights.

Also by Mr. Brady, the following resolution:

WHEREAS, The people of Texas, through their Legislatures, have granted and reaffirmed, through many consecutive years, charters to railway companies giving them the right to charge and collect fares and freights as is stipulated in said charters; and,

WHEREAS, The people of Texas have acquiesced in said charters, through their Legislatures exceeded their constitutional powers in granting said charters; now,

Therefore, It is the sense of the people that it would be dishonorable and dishonest to assume at this time to gainsay such grants and to attempt to modify or divert the same by retroactive provisions and without the consent of the companies invested with said charters.

Referred to Committee on Railroad Corporations.

Mr. Ferris offered the following resolution:

Resolved, That the Committee on Public Lands and Land Office take into consideration the propriety of making the Land Office Department self-sustaining from fees.

Referred to Committee on Public Lands and Land Office.

Mr. Flanagan offered the following resolution:

Resolved, That no person elected or appointed to any office in the federal government by the Legislature or any portion of the people of Texas, shall be eligible to any other office under the constitution, or which is elected by the Legislature or any part of the people of Texas, during the full term for which such person was so elected or appointed, except in the cases provided in this constitution, or in which offices are declared not incompatible.

Referred to the Committee on General Provisions.

By Mr. Rentfro:

Resolved, That the following shall be incorporated in the constitution, under its appropriate caption:

"Sec. ——. The right of trial by jury, as heretofore enjoyed, shall remain inviolate; but a jury for the trial of civil or criminal cases in courts not of record, may consist of less than twelve men, as may be prescribed by law. Hereafter a grand jury shall consist of twelve men, any nine of whom concurring, may find an indictment or a true bill.

Referred to Committee on Bill of Rights.

Mr. DeMorse offered the following concerning education:

"Public education being the most reliable safeguard of republican government, it is provided that all grants of land heretofore made for that purpose by the Congress of the Republic and the Legislature of the State shall be preserved for their predestined uses, and that one-tenth of the annual revenue of the State shall be divided between the several counties of the State in proportion to population, to be subdivided among the several school districts according to the number of scholars reported within the ages of eight and fourteen years, and that provision shall be made by law for the division of the several counties into school districts, which through trustees may tax themselves for educational purposes to such an extent as two-thirds of the freeholders of each school district may authorize by annual vote not exceeding one-half of one per cent.; and it is enjoined upon the several Legislatures of the State to carefully consider all practicable schemes for providing a permanent and extended system of public education for as great a portion of each year as may be practicable with reference to population and property, and as a part thereof a special annual poll tax of not less than two dollars *per capita* for educational purposes shall be levied by act of the State Legislature to be added to the annual reservation of one-tenth of the general revenue assigned to school purposes.

Referred to Committee on Education.

Mr. Robinson offered the following resolution:

Resolved, That each county in the State be divided into as many justices' precincts as the conveniences of the population may require.

Referred to Judiciary Committee.

Mr. Crawford introduced the following resolution:

Resolved, That the Committee on Printing be required to report a resolution authorizing the President to receive sealed proposals at his desk for three days after the report of said resolution for the printing of this body, and at the expiration of said time to open said proposals and thereupon by the consent of this Convention to award said printing to the lowest responsible bidder.

Mr. Stockdale offered an amendment, which was afterwards withdrawn.

Mr. Crawford offered a substitute for resolution and amendment, as follows:

Resolved, That the President of this Convention be authorized to receive sealed proposals at his desk for the printing of this body until Monday, the 13th inst., at 12 o'clock, at which time he shall open the same and award the said printing by the consent of this Convention to the lowest responsible bidder.

Mr. Henry, of Smith, offered the following resolution:

Resolved, That the Committee on Printing be directed to receive sealed proposals to do the printing of this body, and to contract with the lowest responsible bidder for the same.

On motion of Mr. Stockdale, the original resolution, together with amendments and substitutes were referred to Committee on Printing.

Mr. Waelder offered the following resolution:

Resolved, That the Committee on Judiciary inquire into the expediency of dividing the State into convenient districts for the meeting of judges of the district courts *in banc,* who shall compose courts of appellate jurisdiction to decide cases on appeal from the district courts of the State, and from whose decisions there shall be an appeal only to the court of last resort, under certain limitations and restrictions.

Referred to Committee on Judiciary.

Mr. Ballinger offered the following resolution:

Resolved, That trial by jury in civil causes arising on contracts should not be so restricted as not to be open to modification by the Legislature, so that in classes of cases which require it, a less expensive and more practical system may be adopted.

2. That whenever a jury is empanneled for the trial of any case, civil or criminal, the discharge of a juror from death, sickness or other cause, shall not produce a mistrial, but the remainder of the jury may render a verdict.

Referred to Committee on Bill of Rights.

Mr. Haynes offered the following resolution:

Resolved, That the Legislature shall have no power to grant divorces, but may authorize the courts to grant them for such causes as may be specified by law, but such laws shall be general and uniform throughout the State.

2. The Legislature shall have no power to authorize lotteries for any purpose, and shall pass laws prohibiting the sale of lottery tickets in this State.

3. The Legislature shall have no power to change the names of persons or pass acts adopting or legitimatizing persons, but shall, by general laws, confer this power on the courts.

Referred to Committee on General Provisions.

Mr. Dohoney introduced the following resolution:

Resolved, That the President of the Convention be, and he is hereby authorized, to appoint an additional standing committee, to consist of seven members, on " Ordinances of the Convention."

The resolution was adopted.

Mr. Arnim offered the following resolution:

Resolved, That in order to establish a uniform system of public free schools throughout the State, the Committee on Education be instructed to inquire into the expediency of the State reassuming the control of all lands granted to counties for educational purposes; but if such re-assumption of control be deemed injudicious and impracticable, then the amount derived from such counties, from the utilization of their school funds as a yearly revenue, subject to be used for educational purposes, shall be deducted out of the sum apportioned to such counties in the distribution of the revenues derived from the perpetual State school fund.

5

Resolved further, That no taxes shall be levied or collected in this State for educational purposes, except as a poll-tax.

Referred to Committee on Education.

Mr. Martin, of Navarro, from the Committee on Mileage, made the following report:

To the Hon. E. B. Pickett, President of the Convention:

The special committee to whom was referred the resolution to estimate the mileage of the members of the Convention by the nearest traveled route, have carefully considered the distance for each member, and have herein estimated the same according to the resolution of the Convention, making the total amount of number of miles 34,932, and total amount paid as mileage $6,986 40.   Respectfully submitted,

MARION MARTIN, Chairman.

B. ABERNATHY,

JOHN W. STAYTON.

STATEMENT OF MILEAGE OF THE MEMBERS OF THE CONVENTION OF 1875:

NAME.	COUNTY.	MILES.	AMOUNT.
Allison, Thos G.	Panola	608	$121 60
Abner, David	Harrison	628	125 60
Abernathy, B.	Camp	652	130 40
Arnim, J. E.	Lavaca	175	35 00
Ballinger, W. P.	Galveston	430	86 00
Barnett, J. W.	Parker	428	85 60
Brady, E. W.	Grimes	300	60 00
Blake, B.	Nacogdoches	480	96 00
Blassingame, W.	Grayson	532	106 40
Brown, John W.	Dallas	402	80 40
Bruce, H. G.	Johnson	324	64 80
Burleson, Ed.	Hays	60	12 00
Cardis, Louis	El Paso	1,462	292 40
Chambers, Ed.	Collin	466	93 20
Cline, H.	Harris	330	66 00
Cook, W. D. S.	Gonzales	124	24 80
Cooke, G. B.	San Saba	212	42 40
Cooley, A. O.	Gillespie	170	34 00
Crawford, W. L.	Marion	660	132 00
Davis, B. H.	Brazos	192	38 40
Davis, Bird	Wharton	282	56 40
Darnell, N. H.	Tarrant	432	86 40
Dohoney, E. L.	Lamar	620	124 00
DeMorse, Charles	Red River	676	135 20

NAME.	COUNTY.	MILES.	AMOUNT.
Dillard, W. W.	Bowie	700	$140 00
Dunnam, A. J. C.	Trinity	462	92 40
Douglass, J. P.	Cherokee	480	96 00
Erhard, C.	Bastrop	68	13 60
Ferris, J. W.	Ellis	340	68 00
Flanagan, Webster	Rusk	530	106 00
Fleming, J. R.	Comanche	300	60 00
Flournoy, George	Galveston	430	86 00
Ford, J. S.	Cameron	780	156 00
Gaither, J. C.	Falls	194	38 80
German, J. L.	Fannin	544	108 80
Goddin, M. H.	Walker	350	70 00
Graves, A. C.	Coryelle	200	40 00
Henry, J. L.	Smith	500	100 00
Henry, J. R.	Limestone	275	55 00
Haynes, J. E.	Caldwell	60	12 00
Holmes, W. C.	Grayson	532	106 40
Holt, Asa	Van Zandt	472	94 40
Johnson, J. F.	Franklin	600	120 00
Johnson, John	Collin	466	93 20
Killough, S. B.	Robertson	250	50 00
Kilgore, C. B.	Gregg	538	107 60
King, H. C.	Kendall	214	42 80
Lacy, Robert	Leon	314	62 80
Lockett, Thomas	Washington	206	41 20
Lynch, F. J.	DeWitt	196	39 20
McLean, W. P.	Titus	600	120 00
McCormick, G.	Colorado	196	39 20
McCabe, L. H.	Fort Bend	296	59 20
McKinney, S. A.	Denton	482	96 40
Martin, Marion	Navarro	388	77 60
Martin, B. D.	Hunt	508	101 60
Mills, John S.	Grimes	300	60 00
Mitchell, John	Burleson	132	26 40
Moore, L. W.	Fayette	136	27 20
Morris, J. R.	Harris	330	66 00
Murphy, J. B.	Nueces	420	84 00
Norvell, L.	Jasper	616	123 20
Nugent, T. L.	Erath	320	64 00
Nunn, D. A.	Houston	476	95 20
Pauli, G.	Lee	100	20 00
Pickett, E. B.	Liberty	438	87 60
Ross, L. S.	McLennan	200	40 00

NAME.	COUNTY.	MILES.	AMOUNT.
Ramey, W. M.	Shelby	540	$108 00
Reagan, John H.	Anderson	400	80 00
Rentfro, R. B.	Montgomery	300	60 00
Reynolds, W.	Waller	230	46 00
Robertson, E. S. C.	Bell	100	20 00
Rugely, E. S.	Matagorda	432	86 40
Russell, H. H.	Harrison	628	125 60
Robeson, Joel W.	Fayette	136	27 20
Russell, J.	Wood	612	122 40
Spikes, I.	Kaufman	452	90 40
Scott, P. R.	Cass	660	132 00
Sessions, G. A.	Freestone	354	70 80
Smith, C. R.	Milam	150	30 00
Stockdale, F. S.	Calhoun	332	66 40
Stayton, J. W.	Victoria	256	51 20
Sansom, R.	Williamson	50	10 00
Wade, H. W.	Hunt	508	101 60
Whitehead, W. W.	Tyler	552	110 40
Wright, W. B.	Lamar	620	124 00
Weaver, W. T. G.	Cooke	542	108 40
Whitfield, J. W.	Lavaca	200	40 00
West, C. S.	Travis	00	00 00
Waelder, J.	Bexar	150	30 00

Total number of miles.......... 34,775
Total amount, at 20 cents per mile. $6,955 00

Mr. Fleming moved to reduce the number of miles reported by the committee from three hundred and twenty-four miles to three hundred miles, as the mileage properly due him going to and returning from Comanche to Austin.

Carried.

Mr. Johnson, of Franklin, moved that his mileage be reduced from the report of the committee of six hundred and fifty-two miles to six hundred miles.

Carried.

Mr. Flournoy moved to add forty miles to Mr. Rugely's mileage, the distance reported by the committee being less than the actual distance traveled.

Carried.

Mr. McLean moved to reduce his mileage from six hundred and seventy-two miles, as reported by the committee, to six hundred miles.

Carried.

Mr. Robertson, of Bell, moved to reduce his mileage from one hundred and twenty miles, as reported by the committee, to one hundred miles.

Carried.

Mr. Brady moved to reduce his mileage from three hundred and sixteen miles to three hundred miles, that being the distance actually traveled.

Carried.

Mr. Kilgore moved to deduct from his own mileage, as reported by the committee, thirty-eight miles, and add to Mr. Flanagan's mileage thirty miles, these being the actual and correct statements of the distances.

Mr. Ramey moved the adoption of the report of committee, which was carried.

Mr. Goddin, of Walker, submitted the following communication:

AUSTIN, TEXAS, September 11, 1875.

Hon. E. B. Pickett, President of the Convention:

SIR—I respectfully tender my resignation as a member of the Convention from the Fifteenth Senatorial District, to take effect from date. Very respectfully,

M. H. GODDIN, of Walker,

Member of the Convention.

On motion of Mr. Flanagan the resignation was accepted, and Mr. Goddin withdrew from the floor of the House.

On motion of Mr. Ramey, Mr. Gaither was added to the Committee on Revenue and Taxation.

On motion the Convention adjourned until 9 o'clock A. M. Monday.

SEVENTH DAY.

HALL OF REPRESENTATIVES, ⎫
AUSTIN, TEXAS, September 13, 1875. ⎰

Convention met pursuant to adjournment; roll called; quorum present. Prayer by the Rev. Mr. Grasty.

J. B. Murphy, delegate elect from the Thirtieth District, on motion of Mr. Ford, came forward, presented his credentials, took the prescribed oath and his seat.

Journal of Saturday read and adopted.

The President announced the following Committee on Judicial Districts:

Twenty-fifth District, McCormick, Chairman.· First District, Norvell; Second District, Blake; Third District, Nunn; Fourth District, Reagan; Fifth District, Russell, of Harrison; Sixth District, Henry, of Smith; Seventh District, Crawford; Eighth District, DeMorse; Ninth District, Martin, of Navarro; Tenth District, Martin, of Hunt; Eleventh District, Wright; Twelfth District, Flournoy; Thirteenth District, Davis, of Wharton; Fourteenth District, Cline; Fifteenth District, Brady; Sixteenth District, Lockett; Seventeenth District, Smith; Eighteenth District, Lacy; Nineteenth District, Fleming; Twentieth District, Ferris; Twenty-first District, Johnson, of Collin; Twenty-second District, Holmes; Twenty-third District, Nugent; Twenty-fourth District, Stockdale; Twenty-Sixth District, Moore; Twenty-seventh District, Cook, of Gonzales; Twenty-eighth District, West; Twenty-ninth District, King; Thirtieth District, Murphy.

Mr. Waelder introduced a memorial on the subject of suffrage. Referred to Committee on Suffrage.

Mr. Ballinger introduced a memorial on the subject of usury. Referred to the Committee on General Provisions.

Mr. Darnell offered the following resolution:

Resolved, That all land which may have been granted to railroads or other incorporated companies, by way of subsidies, which have been or may hereafter be forfeited, shall be set apart, together with all the public domain for common school purposes, the redemption of genuine land certificates, and to actual settlers, in such manner as the Legislature shall direct; *provided,* that all certificates for land, which were rejected by the traveling or local boards of Land Commissioners, to detect fraudulent land certificates which have not been established by law, shall be forever barred from location.

Referred to Committee on Education.

Mr. Dohoney reported as follows:

To the Hon. E. B. Pickett, President of the Constitutional Convention:

Your Committee on Suffrage, having had under consideration the resolution of this body instructing them to call on the Executive and State Departments for the number of votes cast at the several elections held in this State, in the years 1866, 1869 and 1873, also to obtain and report the present registered vote of the State, and to ascertain the probable cost of a general election in the State, instruct me to report to your honorable body that they have performed that duty, and herewith submit the following report, to-wit:

The total vote of the State cast for the office of Governor at the election in 1866, as shown by the returns in the office of the Secretary of State, is sixty thousand six hundred and eighty-two (60,682).

The total vote cast for the office of Governor in 1873, amounts to one hundred and thirty-nine thousand six hundred and forty-nine (139,649).

The returns of the election of 1869 can not be found, and are reported to have been taken out of the State by General Reynolds, United States army.

The total registered vote of the State, as far as the same has been ascertained up to August 1, 1875, is one hundred and ninety-one thousand two hundred and sixty-three votes, (191,263).

This does not embrace the vote in a number of unorganized counties, nor the vote of the counties of Harrison and Camp yet to hear from.

Your committee are satisfied from the information they have obtained that the total registered vote of the State must exceed two hundred thousand (200,000); and that a full and complete registration in the State would give a vote of not less than two hundred and twenty-five thousand, (225,000).

They submit herewith a tabular statement from the office of the Secretary of State, showing the vote by counties for Throckmorton and Pease in 1866, and the aggregate thereof; also the vote for Coke and Davis in 1873, by counties, and the aggregate thereof; and the registered vote of the several counties, as reported to the office of the Secretary of State, up to August 1, 1875—which statement is marked "Exhibit A," and made a part of this report:

TABULAR STATEMENT OF ELECTION RETURNS FOR GOVERNOR FOR THE YEARS 1866 AND 1873 AND OF THE REGISTERED VOTE IN 1875.

COUNTIES.	1866.			1873.			Registered Vote, 1875.
	Throckmorton.	Pease.....	Total.....	Coke.....	Davis.....	Total.....	
Anderson ..	910	23	933	1,135	916	2,051	2,848
Angelina...	273	124	397	462	116	578	741
Aransas....	.....	.....	......	172	29	201	239
Archer	.....	.....	......	.....	.....	......	......
Atascosa ...	140	71	211	389	31	420	684
Austin.....	690	534	1,224	913	902	1,815	2,490
Bandera ...	42	3	45	156	27	183	299
Bastrop....	671	376	1,047	1,090	1,144	2,234	2,861
Baylor.....	.....	.....	......	.....	.....	......	......
Bee	75	11	86	114	7	121	176
Bell.......	495	112	608	1,862	198	2,060	3,408
Bexar	966	1,030	1,996	1,832	1,234	3,066	4,338
Blanco.....	92	50	143	202	64	266	......
Bosque	236	40	276	755	89	844	......
Bowie	322	6	328	530	268	798	1,260
Brazoria ...	336	34	370	336	1,092	1,428	1,836
Brazos.....	413	11	424	1,197	816	2,013	2,500
Brown.....	.....	.....	......	167	5	172	317
Burleson ...	494	113	607	1,085	581	1,666	1,510
Burnet	107	136	243	474	108	582	928
Caldwell...	413	101	514	740	480	1,220	1,434
Calhoun ...	192	106	298	218	227	445	635
Callahan ...	.....	.....	......	.....	.....	......	8
Cameron...	157	280	437	433	221	654	1,255
Camp	.....	.....	......	.....	.....	......	......
Cass.......	.....	.....	......	863	396	1,259	2,000
Chambers ..	59	.....	59	208	49	257	......
Cherokee ..	1,046	93	1,139	1,486	527	2,013	......
Clay.......	.....	.....	......	76	.....	76	370
Collin	1,044	121	1,165	1,690	288	1,978	......
Colorado...	582	329	911	.....	.....	......	2,923
Coleman ...	.....	.....	......	.....	.....	......	......
Comal	190	363	553	363	345	708	882

TABULAR STATEMENT OF ELECTION RETURNS — *Continued.*

COUNTIES.	1866.			1873.			Registered Vote, 1875.
	Throckmorton.	Pease....	Total....	Coke....	Davis....	Total....	
Comanche..	121	24	145	500	14	514	874
Concho	....	....	....	....	....	....	....
Cooke	512	28	540	1,128	57	1,183	2,492
Coryell.....	274	18	292	1,121	45	1,166	1,833
Crockett ...	....	....	....	....	....	....	....
Dallas......	921	267	1,188	2,028	336	2,364	5,779
Dawson	....	....	....	....	....	....	....
Delta......	....	....	....	....	....	....	796
Denton	654	142	796	1,249	118	1,367	2,476
DeWitt	408	95	503	545	553	1,098	1,458
Dimmit....	....	....	....	....	....	....	....
Duval	....	....	....	....	....	....	....
Eastland ...	....	....	....	....	....	....	264
Edwards ...	....	....	....	....	....	....	....
Ellis	525	89	614	1,528	122	1,650	2,384
El Paso....	....	....	....	447	46	493	797
Encinal	....	....	....	....	....	....	....
Erath......	224	131	355	376	58	434	917
Falls	373	88	411	834	738	1,572	2,109
Fannin ...	921	384	1,255	1,531	559	2,090	3,102
Fayette	696	606	1,302	1,677	1,551	3,228	4,300
Fort Bend..	373	15	388	261	1,159	1,428	1,848
Franklin ...	....	....	....	....	....	....	985
Freestone ..	495	7	502	1,070	602	1,672	2,154
Frio.......	....	....	....	69	13	82	....
Galveston ..	596	177	773	2,492	1,023	3,515	5,538
Gillespie ...	52	261	313	104	344	448	650
Goliad.....	195	181	376	292	224	516	....
Gonzales...	....	....	....	1,054	415	1,469	2,020
Grayson ...	875	153	1,028	2,265	495	2,760	6,082
Gregg	....	....	....	308	154	462	1,514
Grimes.....	764	17	781	1,329	1,600	2,929	4,013
Guadalupe..	458	206	664	....	....	....	2,200
Hamilton ..	129	2	131	187	6	193	333
Hardeman..	....	....	....	....	....	....	....

TABULAR STATEMENT OF ELECTION RETURNS — *Continued.*

COUNTIES.	1866.			1873.			Registered Vote, 1875.
	Throckmorton.	Pease....	Total....	Coke....	Davis....	Total....	
Hardin.....	73	34	107	136	20	156	280
Harris.....	1,398	132	1,530	2,966	2,169	5,135	7,204
Harrison...	796	6	802	....	.....	......	......
Haskell	.....	....	......	....	.....	......	......
Hays	184	11	195	525	152	677	1,197
Henderson .	463	84	547	763	249	1,012	1,509
Hidalgo ...	64	324	388	60	72	132	203
Hill.......	375	29	404	1,302	148	1,450	1,961
Hood......	.....	....	......	773	32	805	822
Hopkins ...	1,058	134	1,192	1,871	193	2,064	2,616
Houston ...	582	181	763	1,014	1,058	2,072	2,565
Hunt......	712	54	766	1,469	139	1,605	2,178
Jack......	31	20	51	.....	....	......	200
Jackson....	134	36	170	164	244	408	449
Jasper	312	14	326	345	121	466	932
Jefferson...	143	3	146	277	71	348	468
Johnson ...	555	25	580	1,407	35	1,442	.....
Jones......	.....	.. ..	......	.....	.....	......	......
Karnes	192	3	195	185	88	273	372
Kaufman ..	698	44	742	1,070	142	1,212	1,761
Kendall....	17	135	152	70	200	270	384
Kerr	65	41	106	143	77	220	272
Kimball ...	.....		......	....	.....	......	......
Kinney	.....	....	......	94	114	208	355
Knox.....	.....		......	....	.....	......	......
Lamar	1,181	165	1,346	1,792	598	2,390	3,731
Lampasas .	89	80	169	375	13	388	594
La Salle....	.....	....	......	....	....	......	......
Lavaca	729	37	766	.....	...	......	2,002
Lee........	.....	....	......	.....	.....	......	1,225
Leon	362	73	435	1,103	462	1,565	2,123
Liberty ...	333	8	341	.....	.....	......	800
Limestone..	393	61	454	1,231	337	1,568	1,938
Live Oak...	91	7	98	115	13	128	67
Llano......	98	21	119	108	7	115	......

TABULAR STATEMENT OF ELECTION RETURNS — *Continued.*

COUNTIES.	1866.			1873.			Registered Vote, 1875.
	Throckmorton.	Pease....	Total....	Coke....	Davis....	Total....	
McCulloch..	36	8	44	.....	.....	......	52
McLennan..	639	85	724	1,631	878	2,509	3,317
McMullen..	.....	.....					
Madison....	226	4	230	449	177	626	.....
Marion.....	404	4	408	1,018	1,195	2,213	.....
Mason. ...	8	61	69	82	41	123	225
Matagorda..	192	39	231	186	388	574	789
Maverick...	.....	.....	.....	71	65	136	201
Medina	19	217	236	76	326	402	.....
Menard	.....	.....	......	74	54	128	178
Milam	520	14	534	997	138	1,135	2,300
Montague ..	110	30	140	426	51	477	1,002
Montgom'ry	538	41	579	689	708	1,397	2,384
Morris. ...	.....	.....	......	.....	.....	......	896
Nacogdoch's	666	22	688	987	395	1,382	1,947
Navarro....	554	19	573	1,212	462	1,674	2,577
Newton	.....	.....	......	265	96	361	491
Nueces.....	146	134	280	199	313	51	1,035
Orange.....	104	1	105	.....	.....	......	327
Palo Pinto.	72	1	73	262	3	265	436
Panola.....	567	26	593	1,114	284	1,398	1,858
Parker.....	529	145	674	955	184	1,139	2,000
Pecos......	.....	.....	......	.....	.....	......	292
Polk.... ...	461	49	510	447	159	606	.....
Presidio....	.....	.....	......	.....	.....	......	.....
Rains......	.....	.....	......	251	40	291	495
Red River.	1,057	48	1,105	1,321	439	2,260	.....
Refugio....	121	33	154	139	19	158	.....
Robertson..	493	8	501	1,162	1,000	2,162	5,392
Rockwall...	.....	.....	... .	229	33	262	861
Runnels....	.....	.....					
Rusk	971	126	1,097	1,796	1,302	3,098	.....
Sabine.....	186	27	213	.....	.....	......	729
Somerville..	.....	.....	......	.....	.....	.....	......
S.Augustine	286	8	294	.....	.....	......	......

TABULAR STATEMENT OF ELECTION RETURNS — *Continued.*

COUNTIES.	1866. Throck-morton.	Pease....	Total....	1873. Coke....	Davis....	Total....	Registered Vote, 1875.
San Jacinto	.....	.....	......	.....	.....	.....	954
San Patricio	.....	....	......	91	12	103	158
San Saba...	130	11	141	291	2	293	494
Shackelford.	.....	.....	......	.....	.....	......	190
Shelby.....	435	120	555	676	402	1,078	1,332
Smith	1,168	110	1,278	1,589	1,339	2,928	2,740
Starr	287	29	316	100	97	197	335
Stephens...	.....	.....	......	.....	.....	......	.....
Tarrant....	628	121	749	1,820	138	1,958	2,543
Taylor.....	.....	.....	......	.....	.....	.....	.....
Throck'ton.	.....	.....	......	.....	.....	......	.....
Titus	878	67	945	1,702	250	1,952	1,250
Tom Green.	.....	.....	......	.....	.....	......	241
Travis	601	368	969	2,167	1,416	3,583	4,488
Trinity.....	347	27	374	450	70	520	.....
Tyler......	328	44	372	556	13	569	.....
Upshur	888	7	895	1,166	605	1,771	1,625
Uvalde.....	46	27	73	148	22	170	.....
Van Zandt .	401	176	577	651	244	895	.....
Victoria....	275	125	400	450	517	967	1,166
Walker.....	601	3	604	774	877	1,651	2,126
Waller.....	.....	.....	......	.....	.....	.....	1,800
Washington.	982	252	1,234	1,697	2,324	4,021	3,837
Webb......	.....	.....	......	91	512	603	1,028
Wharton...	186	21	207	.....	.....	.....	816
Wichita....	.....	.....	......	.....	.....	.....	.....
Wegefarth .	.....	.....	......	.....	.....	.....	.....
Wilbarger..	.....	.....	......	.....	.....	.....	.....
Williamson .	433	268	701	1,127	208	1,335	.....
Wilson.....	.....	.....	......	330	93	423	932
Wise	218	119	337	584	66	650	1,295
Wood......	254	265	519	681	169	850	1,366
Young.....	.....	.....	......	.....	.....	...	195
Zapata.....	.....	120	120	.....	.....	......	.....
Zavalla.....	.....	.....	......	.....	.....	......	.....
Total....	48,631	12,051	60,682	70,155	35,157	105,312	144,343

As to the cost and expense of a general election, they respectfully report that the act of the Legislature of 1874, (General Laws, pages 23 and 24) provides that the proclamation for a general election may be published for a period not to exceed three months, in two newspapers in each Congressional District. The estimate of Secretary of State is that such a proclamation published in weekly newspapers, at regular rates, would cost $2,205, and that the same, published in daily papers, would cost about $12,442 50.   The cost of printing and furnishing election blanks would probably be $125.   The cost of registration is ten cents for each person registered, which is paid by the respective counties, and will probably amount to $25,000.

All of which is respectfully submitted for the information and use of the Convention.

E. L. DOHONEY, Chairman.

Laid over under the rules.

Mr. Ford, from Committee on State Affairs, reported as follows:

COMMITTEE ROOM, }
AUSTIN, September 11, 1875. }

To the Honorable E. B. Pickett, President of the Convention:

The Committee on State Affairs, to which was referred a resolution suggesting that "the constitution of 1845 be made the basis of the new constitution, and that the President of the Convention be required to give out the different portions of said constitution to the different committees for their action," have had the same under consideration, and have directed that it be recommended to the favorable notice of the Convention.

JOHN S. FORD, Chairman.
Committee on State Affairs.

Laid over under the rules.

Also by Mr. Ford, from Committee on State Affairs:

COMMITTEE ROOM, }
AUSTIN, September 11, 1875. }

To the Honorable E. B. Pickett, President of the Convention:

The Committee on State Affairs, to which was referred a resolution concerning the abolition of the taxes levied "for the purpose of keeping up public roads," and recommending that a system of labor be formed for said purpose, have had the same under consideration, and have instructed me to report the following as a substitute for said resolution, and to recommend its adoption:

Resolved, That no taxes shall be levied in this State for the opening, repairing, and keeping up public roads, but that the same shall be done by a system of labor by the male citizens of this State between the ages of eighteen years and forty-five years; and the Legislature of this State shall, at its first session after the adoption of this constitution, pass a law to carry this provision into effect.

JOHN S. FORD, Chairman.
Committee on State Affairs.

Laid over under the rules.

Mr. Cook, of Gonzales, from the Committee on Printing, submitted the following report:

To the Honorable E. B. Pickett, President of the Convention:

Your Committee on Printing and Contingent Expenses, having conferred with all the representatives of the press now in the city, and invited from them proposals for doing the printing probably to be required by the Convention, beg leave to report:

That they have carefully considered all the proposals received by them for such printing, and that they deem that made by the *Galveston News*, to print the journals of the Convention, five hundred (500) copies, usual type and style, at one-sixth of a cent (1-6c.) per page, the lowest and best bid.

The publishers of the *Galveston News* also propose to print the constitution we may form, usual style, pamphlet form, twenty 'thousand (20,000) copies, at three and seven-twentieths (3 7-20c.) cents per copy, regardless of number of pages. This we also deem the lowest and best bid.

The publisher of the *Evening News,* printed in this city, proposes to print such matter as may be required for the use of delegates, in bill form, at two cents (2c.) per page, and this the committee consider the lowest and best bid for that class of work.

The publisher of the *Evening News* further proposes that in the event the Convention employ a stenographic reporter of the proceedings of the Convention, to print such proceedings at one cent (1c.) per page, which we deem the lowest and best bid for that class of work.

The committee, therefore, recommend that the propositions of the publishers of the *Galveston News* for printing the journals and constitution be accepted, and that such work be awarded to them. And that the propositions of the publisher of the *Evening News* for printing bills, resolutions, ordinances, etc., be accepted, and that such work be awarded to him, and that the printing of the daily proceedings of the Convention be awarded to him, if such work should be desired.

All of which is respectfully submitted.

W. D. S. COOK, Chairman.

Mr. Crawford offered the following amendment:

Add after the words "be accepted," on their entering into bond, with good and sufficient sureties, in the sum of five thousand dollars, payable to the Governor of the State, conditioned for the faithful performance of the work.

The amendment was adopted.

Mr. Reagan offered the following resolution:

Resolved, That all fines, penalties, forfeitures, and escheats, which have accrued to the Republic and State of Texas, under their constitutions and laws, shall accrue to the State of Texas; and the Legislature shall, by law, provide a method for determining what lands have been forfeited or escheated; and

WHEREAS, It is the duty of the State government to give repose and security to the titles to lands in this State; and

WHEREAS, After the lapse of about forty years, persons, including non-residents of the State and aliens, are still depositing in the General Land Office, and causing to be recorded in the several counties of this State, grants and titles, or pretended grants and titles to lands, which had their origin prior to the declaration of independence of the Republic of Texas;

Resolved, That the Committee on the General Provisions of the Constitution inquire into the expediency of incorporating in the general provisions of the constitution, a declaration that no grant, title, bond, contract, agreement or power of attorney, or other evidence of right to or interest in land, having its origin or being dated before the 2d day of March, A. D. 1836, which has not heretofore been deposited in the General Land Office or recorded in the proper county, shall after the adoption of this constitution, be deposited in the General Land Office, or recorded in any county in this State, or used as evidence in any of the courts of this State.

Mr. Wade offered the following resolution:

Resolved, That a system of free public schools is essential to the prosperity of a State, and that the lands heretofore set apart for school purposes be utilized under a proper system of lease which will raise a distributive fund for the support of free public schools, and that the title to said land never be permitted to pass from the State.

Referred to Committee on Education.

Mr. Johnson, of Collin, offered the following resolution:

Resolved, That all property, real and personal, belonging to any railroad or other corporation in the State, shall be assessed and paid in the county in which the same is situated. And that this body be instructed to provide proper constitutional provisions to enforce and carry out the objects herein named. And that this resolution be referred to the Committee on Railroad Corporations.

Referred to Committee on Railroad Corporations.

Mr. Johnson, of Collin, offered the following resolution:

Resolved, That all lands situated in the State of Texas shall be assessed, and the taxes upon the same shall be paid, in the county in which the same is located; and that the tax collector shall be authorized to advertise and sell lands not rendered, without a decree of any court, and in the same year that taxes may be due and not paid.

Referred to Committee on Revenue and Taxation.

Mr. DeMorse offered the following resolution:

It shall be a part of the oath of office of every person elected or appointed to official position in the State, that—

"I have not, since my election (or appointment) received, and will not, during the continuance of my term of office, receive any gift, courtesy, accommodation, free ticket, or compensation, from any railroad or other corporate company, or any private individual, other than may be extended to citizens of the State generally."

Referred to Committee on General Provisions.

Mr. Johnson, of Franklin, offered the following resolution:

Resolved, That the Committee on General Provisions be instructed to inquire into the necessity of reporting a constitutional provision requiring the Legislature, at its first session, to enact a local option act, in reference to the sale of intoxicating liquors as a beverage, whereby the County Court of each county in the State shall be required upon the written application of ...... voters, to order an election of the qualified voters of any town, city, school district, or justice's precinct within said county, or an election within the county itself, as to whether the sale of intoxicating liquors as a beverage, shall be licensed within the proposed limits; and if a majority of those voting vote against such license, then such sale of intoxicating liquors as a beverage shall be prohibited within the specified bounds.

Referred to Committee on General Provisions.

Mr. Morris offered the following resolution:

Resolved, That railroads be taxed upon their gross receipts as base of value.

Referred to the Committee on Revenue and Taxation.

Mr. Lynch offered the following resolution:

Resolved, That the Comptroller of Public Accounts be authorized and instructed to invest all funds belonging to common schools, now in United States bonds, together with amount of cash on hand, in Texas bonds, said amount to be held sacred as part of permanent school fund of this State.

Referred to Committee on Education.

Mr. Abernathy offered the following preamble and resolution :

PREAMBLE—For the high esteem we have for the ministry of the gospel, we think they should be faithful to the one high vocation.

Resolved, That no minister of the gospel shall be entitled to a seat in the Legislature of this State, except he first be elected to the same.

Referred to Committee on General Provisions.

Mr. Martin, of Navarro, offered the following resolution :

Resolved, That any person who shall directly or indirectly offer, give or promise any money or thing of value, testimonial, privilege or personal advantage to any executive or judicial officer or member of the Legislature, to influence him in the performance of any of his public or official duties, shall be guilty of bribery, and be punished in such manner as shall be provided by law.

And any member of the Legislature or executive or judicial officer who shall solicit, demand, or receive, or consent to receive, directly or indirectly, for himself, or for another, from any company, corporation, or person, any money, office, appointment, employment, testimonial, reward, thing of value, or enjoyment, or of personal advantage, or promise thereof, for his vote or official influence, or for withholding the same, or with an understanding, expressed or implied, that his vote or official action shall be in any way influenced thereby, or who shall solicit or demand any such money or other advantage, matter or thing aforesaid, for another, as the consideration of his vote, or official influence, or for withholding the same, or shall give or withhold his vote or influence in consideration of the payment or promise of such money, advantage, matter, or thing, to another, shall be held guilty of bribery within the meaning of this constitution, and shall incur the disabilities provided for said offenses with a forfeiture of the office or position he may hold, and such other additional punishment as is or shall be provided by law.

Referred to Committee on General Provisions.

Mr. Weaver offered the following resolution :

Resolved, That in all civil cases a majority verdict shall decide the issue.

Referred to Committee on Judiciary.

6

Mr. Henry, of Smith, offered the following resolution:

Resolved, That it shall be the duty of the Legislature to protect from forced sale a certain portion of the property of all heads of families, citizens of this State. The homestead of a family not to exceed in area two hundred acres, or in value two thousand dollars, (not included in a town, city, or village) or any city, town, or village lot or lots, not to exceed in value the sum of two thousand dollars, shall not be subject to forced sale for debt, except it be for the purchase thereof, for the taxes assessed thereon, for labor and materials expended thereon, or for the enforcement of voluntary liens thereon, nor shall the owner, if a married man, be at liberty to alienate or encumber the same, unless by the consent of the wife, and in such manner as may be prescribed by law.

Referred to Committee on General Provisions.

Mr. Rentfro offered the following resolution:

Resolved, That the following be incorporated in the State constitution, under the caption of general provisions:

"WHEREAS, It is best for the interests of the State at large that no individual should himself be the first incumbent of an office in the creation of which he has aided; therefore no member of this Convention shall be eligible for election to any office, whether of honor, trust, or profit, by this constitution created, at the first general election held under this constitution, or for the space of twelve months after its adoption by the people."

Referred to Committee on General Provisions.

Mr. Graves offered the following resolution:

WHEREAS, The Sergeant-at-arms and the Assistant Sergeant-at-arms have no time to assist the Door-keeper; and

WHEREAS, The Door-keeper is not able to attend to all the duties devolving upon him; therefore

Resolved, That this body proceed at once to the election of an Assistant Door-keeper, who shall have the same pay as the Door-keeper.

Laid over under the rules.

Mr. Fleming offered the following resolution:

Resolved, That the following sections shall be incorporated in the constitution, under the appropriate captions:

"All land, whether owned by persons or corporations, shall be assessed for taxation, and the taxes paid, in the county where situated when organized, and shall pay tax according to its value. Lands not rendered for assessemnt shall be assessed by the proper assessing officer, and in no case shall be valued at less than one dollar per acre. All proceedings to enforce the collection of taxes shall be *in rem*, without reference to the owner or claimant, and taxes on land are declared to be a special lien thereon.

" 2.   The Legislature shall provide by law a summary proceeding in the District Courts by which collection of taxes on land shall be enforced through judgments and judicial sales as fast as the tax is due and unpaid. As many tracts or parcels of land as can be conveniently embraced in one suit may be proceeded against in one action, rendering separate judgments against each tract. But one writ shall issue in each suit or action, which shall be published at least four weeks prior to the day on which the court commences, and shall describe each tract of the land as near as may be by reference to the county map or the name of the original grantee or patentee, or the number and volume of the patent, or in any other way that is descriptive; *provided,* that it shall not be necessary to describe it by metes and bounds. No judgment or sale under these proceedings shall be held invalid by reason of any irregularity in the proceedings, and the deed of conveyance made in pursuance thereof shall be held to vest a good and perfect title in the purchase, subject to be impeached only for actual fraud or want of jurisdiction in the court rendering the judgment; *provided,* the former owner shall within two years from the date of the purchaser's deed have the right to redeem the land upon payment to the purchaser of eight times the amount of money paid for the land.

" 3. The owner or *bona fide* claimant of land thus proceeded against shall at any time before final judgment is rendered, have the right to make himself a party to the suit and make defense, and when in that mode issues are formed, the court may allow severance and separate trial as to the tracts of land about which contests are made.

" 4. Lands in unorganized counties shall be proceeded against in counties to which such unorganized counties are attached for judicial purposes.

" 5. The Legislature shall by appropriate enactment give effect to this article."

Referred to Committee on Revenue and Taxation.

Mr. McCormick introduced the following resolution:

Resolved, That the following section shall be incorporated in the constitution:

" Sec. ——.   No railroad corporation in existence at the time of the adoption of this constitution shall have the benefit of any future legislation, except on condition of complete acceptance of all the provisions of this constitution applicable to railroads.   And in case any railroad corporation in this State shall refuse to accede to the provisions of this constitution applicable to railroads within thirty days after the adoption hereof by the people, the Governor of this State shall proceed at once to collect from such corporation all moneys loaned by this State to such corporation out of the school fund or other funds of this State."

Referred to Committee on Railroad Corporations.

Mr. McKinney offered the following resolution:

Resolved, That the title to all lands heretofore donated to the several counties in this State for school purposes shall remain inviolate in the respective counties as a vested right and may be disposed of by the County Court of each county under such rules and regulations as may be prescribed by law, and the proceeds arising from the sale of the same shall belong to the respective counties to which said lands were originally granted, and shall form a permanent school fund belonging to each respective county, which shall be under the control and supervision of the County Court of each county, and shall be loaned only on unincumbered real estate security of double the value of the loan, with personal security in addition thereto; the interest arising from the same shall be an available school fund belonging to the respective county to which said land was originally donated, and may be annually expended for the benefit and support of public free schools in said county, under such rules and regulations as may be prescribed by law.

Referred to Committee on Counties and County Lands.

Mr. Robeson of Fayette, offered the following resolution:

Resolved, That this Convention suspend the collection of the tax of $\frac{1}{4}$ of one per cent. levied for the year 1875 to keep up roads and bridges, until the constitution now being framed shall be voted on by the people.

Referred to Committee on Taxation and Revenue.

Mr. Martin offered the following resolution:

Resolved, That a member who has a personal or private interest in any measure or bill proposed or pending before the Legislature shall disclose the fact to the House of which he is a member, and shall not vote thereon.

Referred to Committee on Legislative Department.

Also the following:

Resolved, That no money raised for the support of the public schools of this State shall be appropriated to or used for the support of any sectarian school.

Referred to Committee on Education.

Mr. Gaither offered the following resolution:

Resolved, That the Judiciary Committee be instructed to inquire into the propriety of restricting the number of jurors in all cases to six.

Referred to Committee on Judicial Department.

Mr. Kilgore offered the following resolution:

Resolved, That section —— Bill of Rights shall read as follows:

SECTION ——. The privilege of the writ of habeas corpus shall never be suspended in this State, except when, in case of rebellion or invasion, the legislature shall declare the public safety requires it.

Referred to Committee on Bill of Rights.

Mr. Allison moved to change his mileage to five hundred and eighty miles.

The President ruled the motion out of order, as the mileage of the delegates had been fixed by the committee and the question disposed of by the Convention.

Mr. McLean offered the following resolution:

Resolved, That the following provision be incorporated in the constitution, to wit:

" That no person who shall have been a member of this Constitutional Convention shall be eligible to any office of honor, profit, or trust in this State, or as a representative or senator in the Congress of the United States, within one year next succeeding the adoption of this constitution by the people of the State. That this resolution shall not affect any member who now holds any of the offices referred to."

Referred to Committee on Federal Relations.

Mr. Holmes offered the following resolution:

Resolved, That the Legislature shall have no power to extend time for the completion of the contract to any railroad corporation or manufacturing establishment contrary to the terms of the charter granted to the same.

Referred to Committee on Legislative Department.

Mr. Whitfield offered the following resolution:

Resolved, That the Superintendent of Public Instruction be requested to furnish to this Convention the scholastic population of the State, the amount of money distributed *per capita* for the year 1875, and the amount of money required to maintain public free schools in this State for four months each year, and the amount due teachers for services already performed.

The resolution was adopted.

Mr. German offered the following resolutions:

Resolved, That the following shall be a provision of the constitution:

"That the Legislature shall pass no law extending the time for the construction of any of the works of internal improvement in this State."

Referred to Committee on Legislative Department.

Mr. Russell, of Harrison, offered the following resolution:

Resolved, That the following provision be incorporated in the constitution, viz:

"There shall be a State board of equalization, consisting of the Governor, Comptroller and State Treasurer. The duty of said board shall be to adjust and equalize the valuation of real and personal property among the several counties in the State, and it shall perform such other duties as may be prescribed by law."

Referred to Committee on Revenue and Taxation.

Mr. Cook, of Gonzales, offered the following resolution:

Resolved, That provision be made in the constitution that no one shall be eligible as a juror to sit in a case of felony who is under indictment, or has been tried for a similar offense.

Referred to Committee on Judiciary.

Mr. Pauli offered the following resolution, with the request that the substance thereof be made a part of the constitution:

"Sunday being considered and established in and throughout the State as a day of rest and recreation, be it and it is hereby

"*Resolved,* That no law or any portion of law shall be passed by any Legislature enforcing the observance of that day to such an extent as to make the same burdensome and oppressive to the mental and social liberty of any one or any class of moral, peaceable and law-abiding citizens."

Referred to Committee on Bill of Rights.

Mr. Brown offered the following, to be incorporated in the constitution:

"ARTICLE —.

"CORPORATIONS.

"Section 1. All existing charters, or grants of special or exclusive privileges, under which a *bona fide* organization shall not have taken place, and business been commenced in good faith, at the adoption of this constitution, shall hereafter have no validity in this State.

"Sec. 2. No corporation, after the adoption of this constitution, shall be created by special laws; nor shall any existing charter be extended, changed or amended by special laws, except those for charitable, penal or reformatory purposes, which are under the patronage and control of the State.

"Sec. 3. The Legislature shall not remit the forfeiture of the charter of any corporation now existing, or alter or amend such forfeited charter, or pass any other general or special laws for the benefit of such corporations.

"Sec. 4.   The exercise of the power and right of eminent domain, shall never be so construed or abridged as to prevent the taking, by the general assembly, of the property and franchises of incorporated companies already organized, or that may be hereafter organized, and subjecting them to the public use, the same as that of individuals.   The right of trial by jury shall be held inviolate in all trials of claims for compensation, when in the exercise of said right of eminent domain, any incorporated company shall be interested either for or against the exercise of said right.

"Sec. 5.   The exercise of the police power of the State shall never be abridged, or so construed as to permit corporations to conduct their business in such manner as to infringe the equal rights of individuals, or the general well being of the State.

"Sec. 6.   In all elections for directors or managers of any incorporated company, each shareholder shall have the right to cast as many votes in the aggregate as shall equal the number of shares so held by him or her in said company, multiplied by the number of directors or managers to be elected at such election; and each shareholder may cast the whole number of votes, either in person or by proxy, for one candidate, or distribute such votes among two or more candidates, and such directors or managers shall not be elected in any other manner.

"Sec. 7.   No corporation shall engage in business, other than that expressly authorized in its charter, or the law under which it may have been or hereafter may be organized, nor shall it hold any real estate for any period longer than six years, except such as may be necessary and proper for carrying on its legitimate business.

"Sec. 8.   No corporation shall issue stock or bonds, except for money paid, labor done, or property actually received, and all fictitious increase of stock or indebtedness shall be void.   The stock and bonded indebtedness of corporations shall not be increased, except in pursuance of general law, nor without the consent of the persons holding the larger amount in value of the stock first obtained at a meeting called for the purpose, first giving sixty days public notice, as may be provided by law.

"Sec. 9.   Dues from private corporations shall be secured by such means as may be prescribed by law, but in no case shall any stockholder be individually liable in any amount over or above the amount of stock owned by him or her.

"Sec. 10. No corporation shall issue preferred stock without the consent of all the stockholders.

"Sec. 11. The term "corporation," as used in this article, shall be construed to include all joint stock companies or associations having any powers or privileges not possessed by individuals or partnerships.

"Sec. 12. The power to tax corporations and corporate property shall not be suspended or surrendered by act of the Legislature."

Referred to Committee on General Provisions.

Also by Mr. Brown:

"RAILROADS.

"Sec. ——. It shall not be lawful in this State for any railway company to charge for freight or passengers a greater amount for the transportation of the same for a less distance than the amount charged for any greater distance, and suitable laws shall be passed by the Legislature to enforce this provision, but excursion and commutation tickets may be issued at special rates.

"Sec. ——. Any railroad corporation or association, organized for the purpose, shall have the right to construct and operate a railroad between any points within this State, and to connect at the State line with railroads of other States. Every railroad company shall have the right, with its road, to intersect, connect with or cross any other railroad, and shall receive and transport each the other's passengers, tonnage and cars, loaded or empty, without delay or discrimination.

"Sec. ——. Railways heretofore constructed, or that may hereafter be constructed in this State, are hereby declared public highways, and railroad companies common carriers. The Legislature shall pass laws to correct abuses and prevent unjust discrimination and extortion in the rates of freight and passenger tariffs on the different railroads in this State; and shall, from time to time, pass laws establishing reasonable maximum rates of charges for the transportation of passengers and freight on said railroads, and enforce all such laws by adequate penalties.

"Sec. ——. Every railroad or other corporation, organized or doing business in this State under the laws or authority thereof, shall have and maintain a public office or place in this State for the transaction of its business, where transfers of stock shall be made, and where shall be kept, for public inspection, books in which shall be recorded the amount of capital stock subscribed, the names of the owners of the stock, the amounts owned by them respectively, the amount of stock paid and by whom, the transfer of said stock, with the date of transfer, the amount of

its assets and liabilities, and the names and places of residence
of its officers.   The directors of every railroad company shall
hold one meeting annually in this State, public notice of which
shall be given thirty days previously, and shall report annually,
under oath, to the State Comptroller, or some officer designated
by law, all of their acts and doings, which report shall include
such matters relating to railroads as may be prescribed by law.
The Legislature shall pass laws enforcing, by suitable penalties,
the provisions of this section.

" Sec. —.   The rolling stock and all other movable property
belonging to any railroad company or corporation in this State,
shall be considered personal property, and shall be liable to execution and sale, in the same manner as the personal property of
individuals; and the Legislature shall pass no law exempting
any such property from execution and sale.

" Sec. —.   No railroad or any corporation, or the lessees, purchasers or managers of any railroad corporation, shall consolidate the stock, property or franchises of such corporation, with,
or lease, or purchase the works or franchise of, or in any way
control any railroad corporation owning or having under its
control a parallel or competing line; nor shall any officer of such
railroad corporation act as an officer of any other railroad corporation owning or having the control of a parallel or competing line.   The question whether railroads are parallel or competing lines, when demanded, shall be decided by a jury, as in
other civil issues.

" Sec. —.   If any railroad company organized under the laws
of this State, shall consolidate by sale or otherwise, with any
railroad company organized under the laws of any other State,
or of the United States, the same shall not thereby become a
foreign corporation, but the courts of this State shall retain
jurisdiction in all matters which may arise as if said consolidation had not taken place.   In no case shall any consolidation
take place, except upon public notice of at least sixty days to
all stockholders, in such manner as may be provided by law.

" Sec. —.   The Legislature shall pass no law for the benefit of
railroad or other corporations, or any individual or association
of individuals, whether retrospective, curative or confirmatory
in its operation, which imposes on the people of any county or
municipal sub-division of the State, a new liability in respect to
transactions or considerations already past.

" Sec. —.   No law shall be passed by the Legislature granting
the right to construct and operate a street railroad within any
city, town, village, or on any public highway, without first ac-

quiring the consent of the local authorities having control of the street or highway proposed to be occupied by such street railroad; and the franchises so granted shall not be transferred without similar assent first obtained.

"Sec. —. No railroad corporation in existence at the time of the adoption of this constitution, shall have the benefit of any future legislation, except on condition of complete acceptance of all the provisions of this constitution applicable to railroads.

"Sec. —. No president, director, officer, agent, or employe of any railroad company, shall be interested, directly or indirectly, in furnishing material or supplies to such company, or in the business of transportation as a common carrier of freight or passengers over the works owned, leased, controlled or worked by such company.

"Sec. —. No discrimination in charges or facilities in transportation, shall be made between transportation companies and individuals, or in favor of either, by abatement, drawback or otherwise; and no railroad company, or any lessee, manager or employe thereof, shall make any preference in furnishing cars or motive power.

"Sec. —. No railroad or other transportation company shall grant free passes or tickets, or passes or tickets at a discount, to members of the general assembly, judges of courts, or any State, or county, or municipal officer; and the acceptance of any such pass or ticket, by a member of the Legislature, or any such officer, shall be a forfeiture of his office."

Referred to Committee on Railroad Corporations.

Mr. Robertson, of Bell, offered the following resolution:

Resolved, That the Committee on General Provisions be requested to incorporate in the constitution, under the appropriate caption, the following:

"That the salary of the Governor shall be four thousand dollars per annum.

"Commissioner of the General Land Office, Comptroller of Public Accounts and Secretary of State, shall each receive a salary of three thousand dollars per annum.

"The Attorney General shall receive a salary of two thousand dollars per annum, with such fees as may be allowed by law.

"The District Attorneys shall each receive a salary of five hundred dollars per annum, with such fees as may be allowed by law.

"That the Superintendents of the Lunatic, Deaf and Dumb, and Blind Asylums, shall each receive the sum of twenty-five hundred dollars per annum."

Referred to Committee on General Provisions.

Mr. Russell, of Harrison, offered the following resolution:

Resolved, That the following provisions shall be incorporated in the constitution:

"That it shall be the duty of the Legislature to provide by law for the publication of all forced sales decreed by any court in this State, or under execution, in some newspaper which will give the greatest publicity to the same in the county where the property is to be sold.

Referred to Committee on General Provisions.

Mr. Wade offered the following resolution:

Resolved, That a clause be placed in the constitution requiring the Legislature, at its first session, after its adoption, to repeal all superfluous laws, revise, condense, and provide for the speedy digesting of the laws of the State, and that such session shall be held every tenth year thereafter.

2. That a copy of the laws thus revised and digested shall be furnished one voter in every ten throughout the State, to be selected or appointed by the County Court of each county.

Referred to Committee on General Provisions.

Mr. Douglass offered the following resolution:

Resolved, Any member of either house shall have liberty to dissent from, or protest against any act or resolution which he may think injurious to the public or an individual, and have the reason for dissent entered on the journals.

Referred to Committee on Legislative Department.

Mr. Allison offered the following resolution:

Resolved, That the Judiciary Committee inquire into the expediency of declaring theft felony only when the amount stolen exceeds —— dollars.

Resolved, That owing to the great and increasing costs and expense of District Courts, the Judiciary Committee inquire into the expediency of enlarging the jurisdiction of Justices of the Peace in civil cases, and also in criminal cases not amounting to felony.

Referred to Committee on Judiciary.

Mr. Moore introduced the following, to become a clause in the Bill of Rights:

"The sovereign power of this State is inherent in, resides, and remains with the people thereof. The government which they create is but an agent, under the limitations thereof, for the expression of this sovereignty. And it follows from this fundamental and inalienable principle, that there is no power in the government, by grant or contract, to confer upon any individual or association of individuals immunities, emoluments or franchises which shall not be subject to the control of the sovereignty of the people for their safety and happiness."

Referred to Committee on Bill of Rights.

Mr. Ferris offered the following resolution:

Resolved, That the following provisions be inserted in the constitution:

"Sec. —.   The Legislature shall provide such revenue as may be needful, by levying a tax, by valuation, so that every person and corporation shall pay a tax in proportion to the value of his, her, or its property.   Such value to be ascertained by some person or persons, to be elected or appointed in such manner as the Legislature shall direct, and not otherwise; but the Legislature shall have power to tax peddlers, auctioneers, brokers, hawkers, bankers, merchants, commission merchants, showmen, jugglers, inn-keepers, grocery-keepers, liquor dealers, toll bridges, ferries, insurance, telegraph and express interests or business, vendors of patents, circuses, keepers of billiard tables and games, and persons or corporations owning or using franchises and privileges, in such manner as it shall from time to time direct by general law, uniform as to the class upon which it operates.

"Sec. —.   The specification of the objects and subjects of taxation shall not deprive the Legislature of the power to require other subjects or objects to be taxed, in such manner as may be consistent with the principles of taxation fixed in this constitution."

Referred to Committee on Revenue and Taxation.

Mr. Brady offered the following resolution:

Resolved, That the following be incorporated in the constitution:

"Sec. —.   Every citizen of the United States, and every person of foreign birth, who may have declared his or her intention to become a citizen of the United States, according to law, not less than one, nor more than five years before he or she offers to vote, who is twenty-one years old, or older, at the time of the election, and possessing the following qualifications, shall be entitled to vote at all elections by the people:

"First—He or she shall have resided in the State at least one year immediately preceding the election at which he or she offers to vote.   .

"Second—He or she shall have resided in the county, city or town where he or she offers to vote, at least sixty days immediately preceding the election."

Referred to Committee on Suffrage.

Mr. Rentfro introduced the following resolution:

Resolved, That the following provision be incorporated in the State constitution under its appropriate caption:

"Sec. ——.   Every male citizen of this State who shall have attained the age of twenty-one years, shall, under the exceptions contained in this constitution, be eligible to any office of any character whatsoever provided for by this constitution."

Referred to Committee on Bill of Rights.

Mr. Flournoy offered the following resolution:

Resolved, That the following be adopted as a part of the constitution:

" Article ——.

Section ——.   The maximum charges for freight and passage on all railroads now in operation or hereafter to be operated in the State of Texas, shall be at the rate of five dollars per ton per one hundred miles for freight, and three cents per mile for passage.   The Legislature shall never increase, but may at any time reduce the above named maximum rates, in whole or in part, and it shall be their duty to do so whenever consistent with justice to the companies owning such railroads, always allowing them reasonable compensation.

" All railroad companies now in operation in the State of Texas are required, within ninety days after the adoption of this constitution by the people, to file in the office of the Secretary of State, an acceptance of the provisions of the first section of this article; and if any such company or companies shall fail to file such acceptance within the time above prescribed, then the Legislature shall never thereafter grant any relief, aid or assistance in any form whatever to any company so failing.

" Nevertheless such company, as all other railroad companies in Texas, shall be subject to civil remedies, and the officers, agents and employes thereof to the criminal prosecutions hereinafter contemplated.

" Besides the civil remedy of the State and of any person aggrieved by a violation of the provisions of section 1 of this article, the Legislature shall, at its first session after the adoption of this constitution by the people, and at subsequent sessions as needed, pass such laws as may be applicable, providing for the punishment criminally of any officer, agent or employee of any railroad company, who shall demand or receive, in any manner whatsoever, a larger sum or compensation for freight or passage, than that fixed in the first section of this article, or than that that may hereafter be fixed by the Legislature.

" In addition to the general oath prescribed for members of the

Legislature, each member thereof shall, before entering upon his duties as such, be also required to swear that he will, while a member of the Legislature, faithfully endeavor to provide for the strict enforcement of the first, second, and third sections of this article."   ·

Referred to the Committee on Railroad Corporations.

The President announced the following standing Committee on Ordinances:

Messrs. Stockdale, Stayton, Wade, Brown, Cook of San Saba, Smith, Davis of Brazos.

Mr. Henry, of Smith, moved to add Mr. Nunn to Committee on Judiciary.

Carried.

Mr. King moved to add Mr. Cooley to Committee on Counties and County Lands.

Carried.

Mr. Dohoney moved to add Johnson, of Franklin, to Committee on General Provisions.

Carried.

Mr. Flanagan moved to add Mr. Brady to Committee on Apportionment.

Carried.

Mr. Ford moved to add Mr. Murphy to Committee on Judiciary.

Carried.

Mr. Brown moved to adjourn to 9 o'clock A. M. to-morrow.

Carried.

EIGHTH DAY.

HALL OF REPRESENTATIVES, }
AUSTIN, TEXAS, September 14, 1875. }

Convention met pursuant to adjournment; roll called; quorum present.   Prayer by Rev. Mr. Talliaferro.   Journals read and adopted.

The President announced the following Committee on Old Land Titles and Mexican Grants.

Messrs. Reagan, Wright, Robertson of Bell, Ballinger, Henry of Smith, West and Ferris.

Mr. Ford offered the following resolution:

Resolved, That the following be incorporated as a provision of the constitution:

"Judges of the Supreme Court and of the District and Criminal Courts, and the judges of any court of record which may be created or established by law in pursuance of this constitution, are prohibited from taking an active part in the discussion of political questions, and from becoming active partisans in the election of Federal, State, district and county officers, during their respective terms of office. Any judge of any court of record who shall during his term of office violate the provisions of this clause, shall, upon conviction, be removed from office. The Legislature, during their first session after the adoption of this constitution, shall pass a law providing for the speedy trial of any judge so offending."

Referred to Committee on Judiciary.

Mr. Norvell offered the following resolution:

Resolved, That the following shall be Article — of the constitution:

"ARTICLE —.
"JUDICIAL DEPARTMENT.

"Section 1.   The judicial power of this State shall be vested in one Supreme Court, in District Courts, and in such inferior courts as the Legislature may from time to time establish; and such jurisdiction may be vested in corporation courts as may be deemed necessary, and be directed by law; *provided,* that no judge of any court, except those of the Supreme and District Courts, shall receive a salary from the State.

"Sec. 2.   The Supreme Court shall consist of a Chief Justice and two Associated Justices, any two of whom shall form a quorum.

"Sec. 3.   The Supreme Court shall have appellate jurisdiction only, which shall be co-extensive with the limits of the State; but shall not extend to or embrace cases of misdemeanor or interlocutory judgments; nor shall it extend to or embrace cases commenced in any other court except the District Court, and such cases relating to the estates of decedents and wards commenced in the Probate Court and brought into the District Court by appeal or *certiorari,* as may be designated by law. And the Supreme Court and the judges thereof shall have power to issue the writ of *habeas corpus,* and under such regulations as may be prescribed by law may issue writs of *mandamus,* and such other writs as shall be necessary to enforce its own jurisdiction, and also to compel a judge to proceed to trial and judgment in a cause. And the Supreme Court shall hold its sessions once every year at not more than three places in the State.

"Sec. 4.   The Supreme Court shall appoint its own clerk,

who shall hold his office for four years, and be subject to removal by the said court for neglect of duty, misdemeanor in office, and such other causes as may be prescribed by law.

" Sec. 5.   The Judges of the Supreme and District Courts shall be elected by the qualified electors of the State, in the manner prescribed by law.   The Judges of the Supreme Court shall hold their offices for six years, and the Judges of the District Court shall hold theirs for four years; *provided,* the election for District Judges shall be confined to their respective Districts.

" Sec. 6.   The State shall be divided into twenty-four Judicial Districts, which number shall not be increased previous to the expiration of four years from the first general election under this Constitution, but may thereafter be increased not exceeding two Districts within each succeeding period of four years; *provided,* the Legislature shall have power to change the Judicial Districts whenever they may deem it expedient.   For each District there shall be elected a Judge, who shall have resided in the State for three years next preceding his election, and in the District for one year next preceding his election, and who shall continue to reside in the District during his term of office, and hold the Courts at one place in each county not less than twice in each year, in such manner as may be prescribed by law.

" Sec. 7.   The Judges of the Supreme Court shall have resided in the State for five years next preceding their election, and shall receive a salary not less than three thousand five hundred dollars annually, and the Judges of the District Court a salary not less than two thousand five hundred dollars annually, and the salaries of the Judges shall not be increased or diminished during their continuance in office.

" Sec. 8.   The Judges of the Supreme and District Courts shall be removed by the Governor on the address of a majority of each House of the Legislature, for willful neglect of duty, misconduct, habits of drunkenness, oppression in office, incompetency, or other reasonable cause which shall not be sufficient ground for impeachment; *provided, however,* that the cause or causes for which such removal shall be required, shall be stated at length in such address, and entered on the journals of each house; *and provided further,* that the cause or causes shall be notified to the Judge so intended to be removed; and he shall be admitted to a hearing in his own defense before any vote for such address shall pass; and in all such cases the vote shall be taken by yeas and nays, and entered on the journals of each house respectively.

" Sec. 9.   All Judges of the Supreme and District Courts

shall, by virtue of their offices, be conservators of the peace throughout the State. The style of all writs and process shall be 'The State of Texas.' All prosecutions shall be carried on in the name and by the authority of the 'State of Texas,' and conclude, 'against the peace and dignity of the State.'

"Sec. 10. The District Court shall have original jurisdiction of all criminal cases, of all suits in behalf of the State to recover penalties, forfeitures, and escheats, and of all cases of divorce, and of all suits, complaints, and pleas whatever, without regard to any distinction between law and equity, when the matter in controversy shall be valued at or amount to two hundred and fifty dollars, exclusive of interest; and the said courts or the judges thereof, shall have power to issue all writs necessary to enforce their own jurisdiction and give them a general superintendence and control over inferior jurisdictions. And in the trial of crimial cases the jury trying the same shall find and assess the amount of punishment to be inflicted, or fine to be imposed; except in cases where the punishment inflicted or fine imposed shall be specifically fixed by law. The District Court shall also have appellate jurisdiction in criminal cases originating in inferior courts, with such exceptions, and under such regulations as the Legislature may prescribe.

"Sec. 11. There shall be a Clerk of the District Court for each county, who shall be elected by the qualified voters, and who shall hold his office for two years, subject to removal by information, or by presentment of a grand jury and conviction by a petit jury. In case of vacancy, the Judge of the District shall have the power to appoint a clerk for the unexpired term. The Clerk of the District Court shall be Recorder for the county, and *ex-officio* Clerk of the Probate and County Court.

"Sec. 12. There shall be elected by the qualified electors of the State, an Attorney General for the State, and a District Attorney for each judicial district, who shall hold their offices for two years: *provided,* That the election for District Attorneys shall be confined to their respective districts. The Attorney General shall receive an annual salary not less than two thousand dollars, and the District Attorneys, each, an annual salary not less than five hundred dollars, which shall not be increased or diminished during their continuance in office.

"Sec. 13. . There shall be elected in each county, by the qualified voters, one Sheriff, who shall hold his office for two years, and be commissioned by the Governor. Vacancies in the office of Sheriff shall be filled by election for the unexpired term.

7

" Sec. 14. Each county shall be divided into five justice's precincts.   There shall be elected in each county, by the qualified voters, five Justices of the Peace, one of whom shall reside, after his election, at the county seat, and shall be the Chief Justice; and no two of said justices shall reside in the same justice's precinct.   They shall hold their offices for two years, be commissioned by the Governor, and should a vacancy occur, an election shall be held for the unexpired term.

" Sec. 15.   There shall be elected in each county, by the qualified voters, as may be directed by law, one constable for each justice's precinct, who shall hold his office for two years; and the constable shall perform the duties required by law.   Vacancies in the office of constable shall be filled by election for the unexpired term.

" Sec. 16.   There shall be in each county of the State a Probate Court, one term of which shall be held by the Chief Justice, at the county seat, in each month.   The Probate Court shall have jurisdiction for appointing guardians, for the probate of wills, for granting letters testamentary, and of administration, for settling the accounts of executors, administrators, and guardians, and for the transaction of business appertaining to estates; and the District Courts shall have original and appellate jurisdiction, and general control over said Probate Court, and original jurisdiction and control over executors, administrators, guardians, and minors, under such regulations as may be prescribed by law.

" Sec. 17. Justices of the Peace shall have concurrent jurisdiction with the District Court of all misdemeanors, and such civil jurisdiction as shall be provided by law. The Justices of the Peace in each county, or any three of them, shall constitute the County Court, with such jurisdiction over the local affairs, interests, and police matters in the county, as the Legislature shall prescribe.   Justices of the Peace shall be, *ex-officio,* Notaries Public.   They shall also perform the duties of Coroner, except such as may, by law, be devolved upon Constables.

" Sec. 18.   No judge shall sit in any case wherein he may be interested, or where either of the parties may be connected with him by affinity or consanguinity, within such degree as may be prescribed by law, or where he shall have been of counsel in the cause.   When the Supreme Court, or any two of its members shall be thus disqualified to hear and determine any cause or causes in said court, or when no judgment can be rendered in any case or cases in said court, by reason of the equal division of opinion of said judges, the same shall be certified to the Governor of the State, who shall immediately commission the requisite number of persons learned in the law for the trial and determination of said case or cases. When the Judges of the District Court are thus disqualified, the parties may, by consent, appoint a proper person to try the said case; and the judges of the said courts, may exchange districts, or hold courts for each other, when they may deem it expedient, and shall do so when directed by law. The disqualification of judges of inferior tribunals, shall be remedied as may be prescribed by law.

"Sec. 19. Should a vacancy occur in the office of Supreme or District Judge, Attorney General or District Attorney, the same shall be filled by election for the unexpired term.

"Sec. 20 Sheriffs, Clerks of the District Court, and Justices of the Peace shall receive such fees or other compensation as may be provided by law.

"Sec. 21. Each qualified voter in a county shall also be a qualified juror in the county, provided he be a freeholder in the State.

"Sec. 22. In the trial of all causes in equity in the District Court, the plaintiff or defendant shall, upon application in open court, have the right of trial by jury, to be governed by the rules and regulations prescribed in trials at law.

"Sec. 23. In all causes arising out of a contract, before any inferior judicial tribunal, when the amount in controversy shall exceed ten dollars, the plaintiff or defendant shall, upon application to the presiding officer, have the right of trial by jury.

"Sec. 24. In all cases where Justices of the Peace or other judicial officers of inferior tribunals, shall have jurisdiction in the trial of causes, where the penalty for the violation of a law is fine or imprisonment (except in cases of contempt), the accused shall have the right of trial by jury."

Referred to Committee on Judiciary.

Mr. Brady offered the following resolution:

WHEREAS, The Hon. M. H. Goddin, a delegate to this Convention from the Fifteenth Senatorial District, has tendered his resignation as such delegate, thus causing a vacancy in the representation in said district; therefore

Resolved, That the President of this Convention be and he is hereby instructed to order an election to be held in said district, to fill said vacancy caused by the resignation of the Hon. M. H. Goddin, in ten days from the passage of this resolution.

Referred to a select committee of three.

Mr. Brown offered the following resolution:

Resolved, That the Committee on Railroad Corporations be

instructed to consider the propriety of requiring that no railroad or part of railroad hereafter constructed in this State, shall pass within three miles of a county seat without passing through and maintaining a depot in such town, unless prevented from so doing by natural obstacles, such as hills, mountains, or streams, the truth of which shall be a judicial question.

Referred to Committee on Railroad Corporations.

Mr. Brown also offered the following resolution:

Resolved, That the Committee on Revenue and Taxation be instructed to take into consideration the propriety of providing that all taxes on lands in this State, not situated in an organized county, shall be assessed and collected, under uniform provisions of law, by the Comptroller, at the seat of government.

Referred to Committee on Revenue and Taxation.

Mr. Haynes offered the following resolution:

Resolved, That the Legislature shall pass no law requiring the citizens of this State to pay a tax or license to sell their productions in any market in the State, nor grant to any corporation the power to pass such laws or ordinances.

Referred to Committee on Revenue and Taxation.

Mr. Gaither offered the following resolution:

Resolved, That the following clause shall be inserted in the next State constitution:

" That no separate Criminal Court shall be created in any county in the State of Texas unless said county contains at least twenty-five thousand inhabitants."

Referred to Committee on Judiciary.

Mr. Nunn offered the following resolution:

Resolved, That the Attorney General be and he is hereby requested to furnish to this Convention such information as to the amount and character of the business in the courts of this State as may be in his possession, and that the same be referred to the committee for dividing the State into judicial districts.

Adopted.

The following is the report of special committee:

Convention Hall,
Austin, September 14, 1875.

To the Hon. E. B. Pickett, President of the Convention:

The special committee to which was referred a resolution " to ascertain and report to this Convention on Monday next, or as soon as practicable, whether a stenographer can be secured to report the full proceedings of this Convention, and if one can be obtained, at what cost per day," beg leave to report that they have performed that duty, with the following result:

That the services of Mr. George Gibbons can be obtained at ten dollars per day, confining his services to the report of the debates.

Your committee would suggest that in connection with this report of debates, it would be essential to have a condensed report of the journals, which would have to be made by the journal clerk, as it would be impracticable for the stenographic reporter to do more than take notes and write out debates.

The committee recommend the passage of the accompanying resolution.

All of which is respectfully submitted.

E. S. C. ROBERTSON, Chairman.

Resolved, That the services of Mr. Geo. Gibbons be engaged at ten dollars per day, to report the debates of the Convention, and that the Committee on Printing be authorized to contract for the publication of the same.

Lost.

Mr. Fleming offered the following resolution:

Resolved, That the following section be incorporated in the constitution, under its appropriate caption:

" That no officer of this State nor of any county, city or town, shall receive directly or indirectly, for salary, fees and perquisites more than five thousand dollars net profit per annum, and any and all sums in excess of this amount shall be paid into the State, county, city, or town treasury, as shall hereafter be directed by appropriate legislation."

Referred to the Committee on Legislative Department.

Mr. West offered the following resolution:

Resolved, That the Committee on Federal Relations be, and are hereby, instructed to inquire into, and as far as practicable to ascertain, the condition of our Mexican and Indian frontiers; the character and extent of depredations on the persons and property of the people of this State; by whom done and whether with the sanction or acquiescence of any foreign government; whether the depredators, by the character of their arms or clothing, have the appearance of having any official position, and if so, under what government; and where and in what manner they seek refuge; as well as the disposition made of property, if any, taken by such parties.

Also as to our Indian frontier, whether and what character of depredations have been committed on the settlers; by what Indians; and whether attributable to mismanagement or infidelity of officers in charge of that service; and, also, as to the amount in value and character of the property lost by our citizens, whether by depredations on the Mexican or Indian border; as also the expenses incurred by the State of Texas in giving protection to her citizens against such depredations; and, also, to obtain from the Executive and Adjutant General's office all the information on these matters that they can.

Referred to Committee on Federal Relations.

Mr. Johnson, of Collin, offered the following resolution:

Resolved, That every person who has or shall have right of entry into any real estate, consisting of lands, tenements or hereditaments, shall make entry therein within two years next after this right shall have accrued; and, on failure so to do, shall be forever barred thereafter; *provided,* that married women, infants, insane persons, and all others laboring under a disability to sue, shall have two years in which to make entry next after their disabilities shall have been removed.

Referred to Committee on General Provisions.

Mr. Russell, of Harrison, offered the following resolution:

Resolved, That the following provision be incorporated in the constitution, viz:

"That there shall be elected by the qualified voters of each Judicial District in this State one District Judge, who shall, in addition to other qualifications, be a man of good moral character and a resident citizen of the district two years next preceding his election; shall have attained the age of thirty-five years, and shall have been a licensed practicing lawyer in this State for the ten years next preceding his said election; that the tenure of said office shall be for the term of (8)) eight years, and the annual salary of the same shall be the sum of —— dollars, and shall not be increased or diminished during said term."

Referred to Committee on Judiciary.

Mr. DeMorse offered the following resolution:

Resolved, That the following be referred to the Committee on the Judicial Department:

Adjudication of civil causes by the courts shall be based upon the principle that while it is the duty of the State to provide tribunals for the settlement of difficulties, it is not just that the State, as a political body, or that individuals not personally interested, should bear the cost of adjudication.

Referred to Committee on Judiciary.

Mr. Waelder offered the following resolution:

Resolved, That the Committee on Judiciary inquire into the expediency of providing not less than two terms of the District Court in each county, but authorizing and requiring the Legislature to fix more than two terms for such counties as may, by reason of their populations, or for other causes, require it — thus leaving the number of terms to be held in each county to be so regulated by the Legislature as to meet the wants of the several counties.

Referred to Committee on Judiciary.

Mr. Dohoney offered the following resolution :

Resolved, That the Committee on the Legislative Department be instructed to inquire into the expediency of inserting a provision in the Constitution, inhibiting the Legislature from passing any law to license the sale of intoxicating liquors as a beverage.

Referred to Committee on Legislative Department.

Mr. Flournoy offered the following resolution :

Resolved, That the Courts of this State shall not, hereafter, entertain any claim' to real estate which originated from the States of Coahuila and Texas, or from the Republic of Texas, unless the evidences of title to such real estate shall have been of record in the county where the same is situated, or in one of the counties from which the county in which the same is situated has been organized for more than ten years preceding the 1st day of January, 1875.

Referred to select committee of seven on Old Lands, Land Titles, etc.

Mr. Kilgore offered the following resolution :

Resolved, That section —, Bill of Rights of the proposed new Constitution, shall read as follows:

" Section —. Private property shall not be taken for public purposes without just compensation first made or secured to the owner thereof, as soon as the actual damage and the value of the property taken can be ascertained by arbitrators selected according to law, who shall not take into consideration any advantage that may result to said owner on account of the improvement for which it is taken."

Referred to Committee on Bill of Rights.

Mr. Ballinger offered the following resolution :

Resolved, That the Committee on the Judicial Department insert the following sections in the articles of the constitution on the Judicial Department:

" Section —. When any Judge of a District Court shall fail to attend to hold court at the beginning, or at any time during the term appointed by law, a failure to hold or continue the session of said court shall not be caused thereby; but the practising lawyers in attendance on said court shall thereupon proceed to elect one of their number who shall be the Judge of said court, take oath as such, and have and perform all the duties of judge for the term of said court, while the regular Judge continues absent.

"Sec. —. When any District Judge or any special judge of a District Court, as provided in the preceding section, shall be disqualified from trying any cause on the docket of said court, no change of venue, on account of such disqualification shall be necessary, but on the call of such cause the parties shall agree to a special judge to try and make all orders in the same, or on failure so to agree, the practising lawyers in attendance on the court shall elect one of their number who shall take the oath and be the lawful judge in said cause."

Referred to Committee on Judiciary.

Mr. Smith offered the following resolution :

Resolved, That the Committee on Education be instructed to inquire into the propriety and utility of incorporating in the constitution the following provisions:

"Section —. The Legislature shall establish and maintain a State University as soon as the university fund will permit; also, establish and maintain one school of a high grade of learning, and such primary schools in each county in this State as will insure the gratuitous instruction of all persons in this State within the scholastic age prescribed by law.

"Sec. —. The President of the University shall be the President of the 'Board of Education,' and shall have the supervision and control of public instruction throughout the State, in such manner and under such restrictions as the Legislature may prescribe.

"Sec. —. The moneys and lands heretofore granted, or which may hereafter be granted, for the endowment and support of a university, shall constitute a special fund for the endowment and maintenance of said university; and the Legislature shall not have power to appropriate the university fund, nor the interest thereon, for any other purpose than the endowment and support of said university.

"Sec. —. The proceeds arising from the sale or rent of county public school lands shall be expended for the use of public schools in the county to which the lands belong, in such manner as the Legislature may direct.

"Sec. —. All the lands heretofore, or which may hereafter be, set apart by the Legislature for public schools, and all moneys, bonds and other property now belonging to the public school fund, all lands escheated to the State, the net proceeds from sales of estrays, unclaimed dividends or distributive shares of the estates of deceased persons, or from fines, penalties and forfeitures, all gifts, grants or devises that may hereafter be made to this State, and not otherwise appropriated by the terms of the grant, shall be sacredly preserved as a public school fund and faithfully appropriated in the manner prescribed by law to establish and maintain free public schools in this State, and for no other purpose; *provided,* That the proceeds arising from sales of estrays or from fines, penalties and for forfeitures shall be appropriated in the counties where the sales are made, and the fines and for-forfeitures are collected.

"Sec. —. The Legislature shall, as soon as the public funds are sufficient, carry into effect the provisions of this constitution by appropriate legislation."

Referred to Committee on Education.

Mr. King offered the following resolution:

Resolved, That the committee on the Executive Department be instructed to inquire into the expediency of incorporating into the constitution the following provision:

"Every bill which shall have passed both houses of the Legislature shall be presented to the Governor; if he approve, he shall sign it, but if not, he shall return it with his objections to the house in which it shall have originated, who shall enter the objections at large upon the journals and proceed to reconsider it; if, after such reconsideration, two-thirds of the members present shall agree to pass the bill, it shall be sent, with the objections, to the other house, by which it shall likewise be reconsidered; if it shall be approved by two-thirds of the members present of that house, it shall become a law; but in such cases the votes of both houses shall be determined by yeas and nays, and the names of the members voting for or against the bill shall be entered on the journals of each house respectively. If any bill shall not be returned by the Governor within ten days (Sundays excepted) after it shall have been presented to him, the same shall be a law in like manner as if he had signed it, unless the Legislature shall, by their adjournment, prevent its return, in which case it shall not become a law without the approval of the Governor. No bill shall become a law after the final adjournment of the Legislature, unless approved by the Governor within thirty days after such adjournment. If any bill presented to the Governor contain several items of appropriation of money, he may object to one or more of such items, while approving of the other portion of the bill. In such case he shall append to the bill, at the time of signing it, a statement of the items to which he objects; and the appropriation so

objected to shall not take effect. If the Legislature be in session
he shall transmit to the house in which the bill originated a
copy of such statement, and the items objected to shall be separately reconsidered. If on reconsideration one or more of such
items be approved by two-thirds of the members of each house
present, the same shall be a part of the law notwithstanding the
objections of the Governor.

"All the provisions of this section in relation to bills not approved by the Governor shall apply in cases in which he shall
withhold his approval from any item or items contained in a
bill appropriating money."

Referred to Committee on Executive Department.

Mr. Wade offered the following resolution:

Resolved, That for judicial purposes the State be divided into
three supreme districts, and that each supreme district be divided
into seven sub-districts; each supreme district shall elect one
Supreme Judge and seven District Judges, who shall be residents of the supreme districts and take their districts by lot and
hold their office six years.

Referred to Committee on Judiciary.

Mr. Holmes offered the following resolution:

Resolved, That there be added to the eleemosynary institutions
of the State an inebriates' asylum, for the cure of drunkenness
and the reform of inebriates; the revenue necessary for the support of the same to be collected from the liquor dealers of the
State, under the name of the Inebriates' Asylum tax, which tax
shall be known as occupation tax.

Referred to Committee on General Provisions.

Mr. Cooley offered the following resolution:

Resolved, That the following shall constitute a part of the
proposed constitution, to-wit:

"Sec. ——.   It shall be the duty of the Legislature, whenever
necessary, to provide adequate protection for the persons and
property of all citizens of this State against incursions, attacks
and depredations by Indians and the inhabitants of any foreign
State; and, for this purpose, the Legislature may incur indebtedness, borrow money and make appropriation thereof in such sum
or sums as may be required."

Referred to Committee on Legislative Department.

The President announced the following committee on Mr.
Brady's resolution to fill vacancy occasioned by resignation of
Mr. Goddin.

Messrs. Brady, Davis and Flournoy.

Mr. German offered the following resolution:

Resolved, That the Committee on Education be required to inquire into the propriety of including the lands set apart for the purpose of building two universities and the proceeds of the sale thereof as a part of the permanent school fund for the purpose of keeping up public schools.

Referred to Committee on Education.

Mr. Martin, of Hunt, offered the following resolution:

Resolved, That the Committee on Federal Relations be instructed to ascertain the amount of money expended for the defense and protection of the frontier by this State since its admission into the Union under the present constitution, and to report to this Convention such proceeding as it may deem necessary and proper, to have the same reimbursed by the Government of the United States.

Referred to Committee on Federal Relations.

Also by Mr. Martin, of Hunt, the following resolution:

Resolved, That the Committee on Legislative Department be instructed to inquire into the expediency of incorporating a provision in the constitution requiring the Legislature to establish by law a Board of Equalization in the several counties of this State, whose duty it shall be to equalize and make uniform the taxes on real estate.

Referred to Committee on Legislative Department.

Mr. Weaver offered the following resolution:

WHEREAS, A number of resolutions have been introduced partially disfranchising all the members of this Convention, therefore, in order to be impartial and make a clean sweep of all (chaplains excepted) connected with this body, be it

Resolved, That neither one of the secretaries, sergeant-at-arms, door-keepers, or any officer or appointee of this Convention, nor any newspaper reporter of the same, shall hold any office until five years after the adoption of this constitution; and not then unless he is elected by the sovereign people.

Referred to Committee on General Provisions.

BUSINESS ON THE PRESIDENT'S DESK.

WHEREAS, The sergeants-at-arms have no time to assist the door-keeper; and, whereas, the door-keeper is not able to attend to all the duties devolving upon him, therefore, be it

Resolved, That this body proceed at once to the election of an assistant door-keeper, who shall have the same pay as door-keeper.

September 13th, taken up and referred to a special committee of three, consisting of Messrs. Kilgore, Brown and West.

Mr. Flournoy moved to reconsider the vote refusing to adopt

the resolution by Mr. Robertson, of Bell, concerning the employment of a phonographic reporter.

Mr. Mills offered the following amendment:

That said phonographer shall report said debates in a round, legible hand, ready for the printer, without additional charge.

Mr. Allison moved to postpone action on the question until to-morrow.

Lost.

The amendment of Mr. Mills was then adopted.

The resolution was then adopted.

On motion of Mr. Henry, Mr. Ramey was added to the Committee on Legislative Department.

Carried.

Mr. Robertson, of Bell, moved to add Mr. Henry, of Limestone, to the Committee on Taxation and Revenue.

Mr. Dohoney moved to add Mr. Rugely to the Committee on Legislative Department.

Carried.

Mr. Russell, of Harrison, moved to add Mr. Holmes to the Committee on General Provisions.

Carried.

Mr. King moved to adjourn to 9 o'clock A. M. to-morrow.

Carried.

NINTH DAY.

HALL OF REPRESENTATIVES,
AUSTIN, TEXAS, September 15, 1875.

Convention met pursuant to adjournment; roll called; quorum present. Prayer by Rev. Dr. Dodge.

On motion of Mr. Ferris, Mr. Smith was excused from attendance on account of sickness.

Journals read and adopted.

The following is the report from Committee on Printing and Contingent Expenses:

To the Hon. E. B. Pickett, President of the Convention:

Your Committee on Printing and Contingent Expenses having received a proposal from Messrs. C. Von Boeckmann & Son to print the constitution, about to be framed, in the German language, in pamphlet form, small pica type, including translation, at the rate of one third of one cent ($\frac{1}{3}$c.) per page, have had the same under consideration and have instructed me to report:

"That they consider the proposal a reasonable one, and in as much as many German citizens of the State are unable to read the English language, they recommend that three thousand copies of the constitution be printed in the German language, and that the contract for doing such printing be awarded to said C. Von Boeckmann & Son.

"W. D. S. Cook, Chairman."

Report was adopted.

Mr. Cook, of Gonzales, from Committee on Printing, asked leave for his committee to retire.

Permission granted.

Mr. Weaver moved to reconsider the vote adopting report from Committee on Printing, just taken, to print three thousand copies of the constitution in the German language.

Mr. Rentfro moved to lay the motion on the table.

Carried.

The following is the report from the Special Committee:

To Hon. E. B. Pickett, President of the Convention:

The select committee to whom was referred the resolution to elect an Assistant Door-keeper for the Convention beg leave to report that they have had before them the Sergeant-at-arms and other officers under him, and having inquired fully into the matter, are satisfied there is no necessity for an Assistant Door-keeper. The officers now are Sergeant-at-arms, Assistant Sergeant-at-arms, Door-keeper and three porters, which the Sergeant-at-arms informs the committee are ample to do the work without further addition. Indeed, he has already made the arrangements necessary to have the duties incumbent on the officers on the floor of the Convention performed promptly and efficiently, and so distributed as not to be specially burdensome on any one of them. We therefore recommend that the resolution do not pass.

Kilgore,
Brown, of Dallas,
West.

Adopted.

The following is the report from Select Committee on Resolutions providing for an election in the Fifteenth Senatorial District:

Committee Room, }
Austin, September 15, 1875.}

To the Hon. E. B. Pickett, President of the Convention:

Sir—Your select committee to whom was referred the resolution providing for an election in the Fifteenth Senatorial District, to fill the vacancy caused by the resignation of the Hon.

M. H. Goddin, of Walker county, have had the same under advisement, and respectfully ask leave to report the following resolution and recommend its adoption :

Resolved, That a vacancy having occurred in the representation of the Fifteenth Senatorial District in this Convention by the resignation of the Hon. M. H. Goddin, of Walker county, His Excellency the Governor be and is hereby authorized and requested to order an election to be held in said district to fill said vacancy on Saturday, the 25th day of September, 1875.

Respectfully,

E. W. BRADY, Chairman, for Committee.

Mr. McCormick offered the following substitute :

WHEREAS, It appearing to the satisfaction of the Convention that at the election held for delegates thereto in the Fifteenth District, one M. H. Goddin, of Walker county, received the certificate of election, and it appearing to the satisfaction of the members hereof that said M. H. Goddin is and was at the time he received the certificate of election *non compos mentis* and therefore ineligible to a seat in this Convention ;

And it further appearing that at the election for delegates in said district D. C. Dickson received the next highest number of votes, and that said Dickson is a pure, good man and the true representative of the good people of the said district ;

And further, that the said Goddin having in a fit of drunkenness and passion, resigned his seat in this Convention ; therefore be it

Resolved, That in the opinion of this Convention the said D. C. Dickson is the true representative of the good people of the Fifteenth Senatorial District.

Resolved further, That D. C. Dickson, upon taking the oath prescribed by the Convention, is admitted to a seat in the same.

Mr. McCormick moved to refer report and substitute to a select committee of five.

Lost.

Mr. Flournoy moved to lay the substitute on the table.

Carried.

The question recurring on the adoption of the report of the committee, Mr. Crawford moved to postpone action on the matter and make the subject special order for to-morrow after the morning call.

Mr. Martin, of Navarro, offered the following amendment:

Said election to be ordered by the President of this Convention.

The amendment was lost.

Mr. Dohoney offered the following amendment:

Strike out of the resolution the word "request" and insert "authorize."

Mr. Johnson, of Franklin, offered the following amendment:

Strike out the word "requested" and insert the word "instructed."

Mr. Sansom moved to lay amendments on the table, whereupon the yeas and nays were called, and the Convention refused to lay the amendments on the table by the following vote:

Yeas—Messrs. Abner, Brady, Cooke of San Saba, Cline, Davis of Brazos, Davis of Wharton, Flournoy, Fleming, Ferris, Henry of Tyler, Henry of Limestone, Killough, McCabe, Mitchell, McCormick, Norvell, Pauli, Reagan, Reynolds, Rentfro, Ross, Russell of Harrison, Russell of Wood, Sansom, Wade, West—26.

Nays—Messrs. Allison, Abernathy, Arnim, Brown, Blake, Ballinger, Blassingame, Barnett, Burleson, Bruce, Crawford, Chambers, Cooley, Douglass, Dillard, Dohoney, Darnell, Dunnam, Erhard, Ford, German, Graves, Holmes, Haynes, Johnson of Franklin, Johnson of Collin, King, Kilgore, Lockett, Lacy, Lynch, Martin of Navarro, Martin of Hunt, McKinney, Moore, Murphy, Nunn, Nugent, Raimey, Rugely, Robertson of Bell, Spikes, Scott, Stockdale, Stayton, Whitehead, Wright, Weaver, Whitfield, Waelder—50.

Mr. Johnson, of Franklin, withdrew his amendment.

Mr. Dohoney's amendment was accepted and the resolution of the committee adopted.

Mr. Flournoy moved to reconsider the vote just taken and lay that motion on the table.

Carried.

Mr. West, by leave, submitted the following reports from Committee on General Provisions:

COMMITTEE ROOM,
AUSTIN, September 14th, 1875.

To the Hon. E. B. Pickett, President of the Convention:

The Committee on General Provisions, to whom was referred a resolution to fix the tax valuation of lands in this State, beg leave to report that they have examined the same and recommend that it be referred to the Committee on Revenue and Taxation.

Respectfully submitted,
C. S. WEST, Chairman.

COMMITTEE ROOM, ⎱
AUSTIN, September 14, 1875. ⎰

To the Hon. E. B. Pickett, President of the Convention:

The Committee on General Provisions to whom were referred two resolutions as to Spanish and Mexican land titles, beg leave to report that they have examined the same and recommend that they be referred to the Select Committee on Spanish and Mexican titles.

Respectfully submitted,
C. S. WEST, Chairman.

COMMITTEE ROOM, ⎱
AUSTIN, September 14, 1875. ⎰

To the Hon. E. B. Pickett, President of the Convention:

The Committee on General Provisions to whom was referred a resolution as to the payment of the costs of charter by all private corporations, beg leave to report that they have examined the same and recommend that it be referred to the Committee on Private Corporations.

Respectfully submitted,
C. S. WEST, Chairman.

COMMITTEE ROOM, ⎱
AUSTIN, September 14, 1875. ⎰

To the Hon. E. B. Pickett, President of the Convention:

The Committee on General Provisions to whom was referred a resolution as to validating certain land certificates, have examined the same, and beg leave to recommend that the same be referred to the Committee on Public Lands and Land Office.

Respectfully submitted,
C. S. WEST, Chairman.

COMMITTEE ROOM, ⎱
AUSTIN, September 14, 1875. ⎰

To the Hon. E. B. Pickett, President of the Convention:

The Committee on General Provisions to whom was referred a resolution restraining the Legislature from levying any tax except for revenue purposes, beg leave to report that they have examined the same and recommend that the resolution be referred to the Committee on Legislative Department.

Respectfully submitted,
C. S. WEST, Chairman.

COMMITTEE ROOM, }
AUSTIN, September 14, 1875. }

To the Hon. E. B. Pickett, President of the Convention:

The Committee on General Provisions, to whom were referred a series of resolutions as to the salary of the Governor and other State officers, beg leave to report that they have examined the same and recommend that the resolutions as to the salary of the Governor, Secretary of State, Comptroller, and Superintendents of the different Asylums, be referred to the Committee on Legislative Department, and that the resolutions as to the salaries of the Attorney General and District Attorney be referred to the Committee on Judiciary Department.

Respectfully submitted,

C. S. WEST, Chairman.

The following is the report of the Superintendent of Education, complying with a resolution of the Convention passed on the 13th instant.

DEPARTMENT OF EDUCATION, STATE OF TEXAS, }
AUSTIN, September 14, 1875. }

To the Hon. E. B. Pickett, President of the Convention:

SIR—I have the honor to acknowledge the receipt of a resolution passed by the Honorable Convention on the 13th inst., requesting certain information relative to the school affairs of the State, as follows, to-wit:

"*Resolved,* That the Superintendent of Public Instruction be requested to furnish this Convention (1) the scholastic population of the State; (2) the amount of money distributed *per capita* for the year 1875; and (3) the amount of money required to maintain public free schools in this State for four months each year; and (4) the amount due teachers for services already performed."

Responding to said resolution, I have the honor to reply as follows, viz:

1. The census of the scholastic population of the State was taken between the dates July 4, 1874, and November 20, 1874, in almost every county. The total scholastic population of counties from which reports were received, and estimates from the best data in this Department for counties from which reports were not received, give in the aggregate three hundred and thirteen thousand and sixty-one children (313,061).

The law requires the census of scholastic population be taken annually, on the first Saturday in July. The census returns, due for 1875, have not all been received at this Department. The number is largely increased over the reports of 1874; and we estimate the present scholastic population at three hundred and fifty thousand (350,000).

2. The amount appropriated from the State School Fund for the year ending August 31, 1875, was five hundred thousand dollars, ($500,000), but for convenience in distributing, the sum of $499,959 05 only was apportioned, which gave, *per capita,* one dollar and fifty-nine cents ($1 59), to the scholastic population.

3. In response to the third inquiry of the honorable Convention, I beg to suggest that we find some difficulty in answering. Under the law as it now stands the salaries of teachers vary to an extent that renders it impossible to determine what might be the actual expenses of public schools for four months.

The returns in this department for the year ending August 31, 1874, show the cost per pupil in the public free schools, as averaged throughout the State, was $1 56 per month, or $6 24 for four months. The returns in the aggregate for the scholastic year ending August 31, 1875, show a great variation in the price of tuition *per capita* in the several counties of the State. In counties where there has been proper administration by the local officers, the rate per month for each pupil has not exceeded seventy-eight cents; while in other counties where there was a neglect of public interests and a total disregard to economy, the cost *per capita* has been reported as high as two dollars per month. We are satisfied, however, that throughout the State the cost per pupil for each month in the public free schools, during the scholastic year ending August 31, 1875, has not exceeded one dollar and fifty cents, ($1 50), or six dollars for four months, *per capita.*

The annual report from the county officers were not due to this department until the close of the scholastic year, August 31, 1875; I am, therefore, unable to give the total cost of that year from actual reports. We may, however, safely estimate that under a proper administration, which can be secured by a wise law, the rate of tuition per month, *per capita,* need not, nor should it exceed in the aggregate $1 50, giving as the total expense for four months tuition of 350,000 children the sum of two million and sixty thousand dollars, ($2,060,000).

4. I regret my inability to answer, at present, the amount due teachers for services already performed. As heretofore stated, the annual reports from county officers, which contain the data from which that amount will be ascertained, were not due until after the 31st ultimo; I trust, however, that said

reports will reach the department in time to furnish the information requested at an early day.

Very respectfully,

O. N. HOLLINGSWORTH,

State Supt. Pub. Inst.

On motion of Mr. Russell, of Wood, two hundred copies of the report were ordered printed.

Mr. McCormick offered the following resolution:

Resolved, That the substance of the following sections be incorporated in the proposed constitution:

"All male citizens of this State, between the ages of sixteen and forty-five years, shall be required to work upon the public roads of this State, under such regulations and exceptions as the Legislature may prescribe.

"The Legislature shall enact such laws as may be necessary to keep open and in good repair the public roads of this State, and may authorize the levy of a tax of not more than one-tenth of one per cent. upon all the property in the State, to be used in building bridges and keeping the same in repair, provided that the tax collected shall be expended in the county paying the same."

Referred to Committee on General Provisions.

Mr. Russell, of Harrison, offered the following resolution:

WHEREAS, Under the present constitution "all unsatisfied genuine land certificates shall be surveyed and returned to the General Land Office by the first day of January, 1875, or be forever barred;" and

WHEREAS, There is now in existence and outstanding unsatisfied genuine land certificates that were not surveyed and returned to the General Land Office, as prescribed by the constitution, and are now barred; and

WHEREAS, A number of the holders and owners of said certificates were debarred from locating, surveying and returning said certificates, as prescribed by the present constitution, by reason of the same having been lost and no time existed for application for duplicates, and for other good and valid causes beyond and without their control; and

WHEREAS, A number of the holders and owners of said certificates had, previous to January 1, 1875, located the same in good faith, in accordance with the requirements of the constitution of 1869, and it has since transpired that without any fault or neglect of the said parties their certificates were located on lands previously located, and there remained no sufficient time to have the same relocated prior to January 1st, 1875; therefore

Be it resolved and ordained by the people of Texas, in Convention assembled, That the rights and interests of the holders and owners of all unsatisfied genuine land certificates in existence, but not located, returned and surveyed as prescribed by the constitution of 1869, on the first day of January, 1875, shall not be affected by reason of the non-location, survey and return of the same, nor shall the validity of said certificates be affected; but that said certificates shall be revived and in full force and effect, and shall be subject to location, return and survey on any of the unlocated lands of the State for five years next after the adoption of this constitution.

Referred to Committee on Public Lands and Land Office.

Mr. Erhard offered the following resolution:

Resolved, That those delegates from counties adjacent to the frontier, or such counties wherein no newspapers are published, be allowed thirty copies each of some paper in the city of Austin which publishes the proceedings of this Convention, in order that said people may be informed of the proceedings of this body, and that said members make a report according to the provisions of the foregoing.

Referred to Committee on Printing and Contingent Expenses.

Mr. Pauli offered the following resolution:

Resolved, That any Justice of the Peace in his own precinct of jurisdiction act as administrator *pro tempore* in all cases where impartial and immediate action in regard to the estate of a deceased person is necessary.

In all cases where the Justice of the Peace is notified of the death of a person in his precinct, he shall at once summon three, or as many citizens of good standing as may be prescribed by law, to investigate—

First, how the person so deceased came to his or her death, namely: Whether from natural cause, by accident, or through violence committed by some other person or persons. If from the latter cause, the Justice of the Peace is to issue at once the necessary warrant or warrants for the immediate apprehension and arrest of such offender or offenders, and the same be brought to justice.

Second. If the estate of the deceased, either by the last will and testament or by virtue of relationship, is assigned to an administrator, then to report this fact to the County Court.

Third. If the estate is left without protection, and no person attainable who has a legal right to administer on said estate, or if under the circumstances the same needs immediate attention to keep it from being squandered—under the latter probabilities the Justice of the Peace shall, with the assistance of the three already summoned citizens, or as the probate law of the county may direct, take an inventory of all the property of the deceased, real and personal, and make returns thereof without unnecessary delay to the County Court in open session. The property so returned shall then remain under the protection and management of said court, for such length of time and under such regulations as may hereafter be provided for by law in this State.

Referred to the Committee on Judiciary.

Mr. Ballinger offered the following resolution:

Resolved, That the Committee on the Judiciary Department shall provide in the article on that department:

"Sec. ——. That the Supreme and District Judges of this State shall be appointed on the nomination of the Governor, by and with the advice and consent of the Senate."

The form of each nomination shall be in substance as follows:

"I herewith nominate . . . . to be Judge of . . . . . . , and I declare that he is, in my judgment, the best appointment to be made to that office, without regard on my part, to personal or partisan considerations."

"That such nomination shall not be acted on by the Senate for at least ten days, during which time the Governor shall, when requested by the Senate, appear before the Senate and give them information and hear their advice respecting such nomination; and the Governor shall also, at their request, lay before the Senate all recommendations of said nominee and of all other persons for such office."

Referred to Committee on Judiciary.

Mr. Rentfro offered the following resolution:

Resolved, That the following be and constitute the preamble to the State constitution, to-wit:

" PREAMBLE.

"We, the people of the State of Texas, acknowledging with grateful hearts the goodness of the Great Legislator of the Universe, in affording us, in the course of His providence, an opportunity, deliberately and peaceably, without fraud, violence or surprise, of entering into an original, explicit and solemn compact with each other, and of forming a new constitution of civil government for ourselves and posterity, do agree upon, ordain and establish the following declaration of rights, and frame of government, as the constitution of the State of Texas."

Referred to Committee on Bill of Rights.

Also, by Mr. Rentfro, the following resolution:

Resolved, That the following provision shall be incorporated in the State constitution under its appropriate caption, to wit:

" Sec. ——. It is the right of every man to worship or *not* to worship a Supreme Being, as his reason may direct; and no citizen shall be hurt, molested, or restrained in his person, liberty, or estate, for his religious profession or sentiments, or for the absence on his part of any religious profession or sentiment; *provided,* he does not disturb the public peace, infringe upon public mortality, or obstruct others in their religious worship."

Referred to Committee on Bill of Rights.

Also, by Mr. Rentfro, the following resolution:

Resolved, That the following be and constitute a part of the State constitution:

" Sec. ——. The people of this State have the sole and exclusive right of governing themselves as a sovereign State; and do and forever hereafter shall exercise and enjoy every power, jurisdiction, and right, which is not, or may not hereafter, be, by them, expressly delegated to the United States of America."

Referred to Committee on Bill of Rights.

Mr. Robertson, of Bell, offered the following resolution:

Resolved, That the Committee on General Provisions be requested to insert in the constitution, under its appropriate caption the following provisions:

" That the retailing of spirituous, vinous, or other intoxicating liquors may be prohibited in the vicinity of any school, or in any town in this State, by a vote of a majority of the people thereof, and the Legislature shall pass the necessary law to carry into effect this provision.

" That the right of appeal in both criminal and civil cases be provided for, from the lowest, through all the courts, to the highest.

" That the Legislature may tax incomes, and the occupations of retailing spirituous liquors, insurance, peddling, chiromancy and all other exhibitions commonly designated as shows and none other."

Referred to Committee on General Provisions.

Mr. Robertson, of Bell, also offered the following resolution:

Resolved, That the Committee on General Provisions be requested to insert in the constitution, under its appropriate caption, the following provisions:

" That all freemen, when they form a social compact, have equal rights; and no man or set of men is entitled to exclusive separate public emoluments or privileges, but in consideration of public services.

"No religious test shall ever be required as a qualification to any office or public trust in the State.

"All men have a natural and indefeasible right to worship God according to the dictates of their own conscience; no man shall be compelled to attend, erect or support any place of worship, or to maintain any ministry against his consent; no human authority ought in any case whatever to control or interfere with the rights of conscience in matters of religion, and no preference shall be given to any religious societies or modes of worship. But it shall be the duty of the Legislature to pass such laws as may be necessary to protect every religious denomination in the peaceable enjoyment of their own mode of worship.

"Every person shall be at liberty to speak, write or publish his opinions on any subject, being responsible for the abuse of that privilege; and no law shall ever be passed curtailing the liberty of speech or of the press.

"No person shall be denied the right to hold office in the State on account of his profession, trade, business or calling; but all men shall be equal before the law."

Mr. Erhard offered the following resolution:

Resolved, That there shall be a General Superintendent of Schools, and the Governor and Secretary of State shall be *ex officio* members of said board.

1. That whenever the State establishes a State University, he shall, with the consent and advice of the Senate, appoint seven Curators.

2. The Legislature shall carefully guard over the University lands, inquire into it whether any are sold; if for cash, how the funds were deposited: if sold on credit, to enforce the payment forthwith, whenever payment is due.

3. Until we have an University the Superintendent shall guard the interest of the University lands; and if any is sold the whole proceeds thereof shall be applied for the use and benefit of the University.

4. If at any time there should be a surplus fund not needed by the University, then said money shall be invested either in United States bonds or bonds of the State of Texas.

5. The foregoing section shall also apply to funds pertaining and belonging to the public school fund, or the public school fund may be loaned on real estate, to be first appraised by three disinterested persons where the property mortgaged lies, and shall be double the value of the amount loaned out.

6. No public school fund or university fund or funds belonging to either shall in anywise be used for any sectarian institution.

7. That the scholastic year shall begin on the first Monday in October of each year.

8. That each teacher of a public school shall teach at least six hours a day, but the hours to begin or end shall be determined by the patrons of each school district.

Referred to Committee on General Provisions.

Mr. Flournoy offered the following resolution:

Resolved, That whenever the wages or pay of a married man, for his labor, shall not amount to more than two dollars per day, and of a single man to more than one dollar per day, the same shall never be the subject of garnishment. And whenever garnishments shall, in any case, apply to wages or salary, the same shall relate only to the overplus of the above-named amounts.

Referred to Committee on General Provisions.

Mr. Reynolds offered the following resolution:

Resolved, That the following be ingrafted, under its proper caption, in the State constitution:

"Sec. ——. That all elections in this State shall be free and open; and no power, civil or military, shall at any time interfere to prevent the free exercise of the right of suffrage."

Referred to Committee on Bill of Rights.

Mr. Reynolds also offered the following resolution:

Resolved, That the courts of justice shall be open to every person, and a certain remedy afforded for every injury to person, property or character, and that right and justice shall be administered without sale, denial or delay.

Referred to Committee on Bill of Rights.

On motion of Mr. Stockdale Mr. Stayton was added to the select committee on old Mexican Grants and Land Titles.

Mr. Ross moved to reconsider the vote taken yesterday by which the employment of a stenographic reporter was authorized.

Mr. Rentfro moved to lay the motion to reconsider on the table, whereupon the yeas and nays were called and resulted as follows:

YEAS—Messrs. Abernathy, Brown, Brady, Crawford, Cline, Dillard, DeMorse, Dohoney, Dunnam, Davis of Brazos, Erhard, Ford, Flournoy, Ferris, Henry of Tyler, Johnson of Franklin, King, Kilgore, Killough, Lockett, McCabe, Morris, Mitchell, Moore, Murphy, Norvell, Nunn, Pauli, Reagan, Rugely, Reynolds,

Rentfro, Robertson of Bell, Stockdale, Whitehead, Wright, Whitfield, and West—38.

NAYS—Messrs. Allison, Arnim, Abner, Blake, Ballinger, Blassingame, Barnett, Burleson, Bruce, Chambers, Cook of Gonzales, Cooke of San Saba, Cooley, Douglass, Fleming, German, Gaither, Graves, Holt, Henry of Limestone, Holmes, Haynes, Johnson of Collin, Lacy, Lynch, Martin of Navarro, Martin of Hunt, Mills, McKinney, McCormick, Nugent, Ramey, Robeson of Fayette, Ross, Russell of Harrison, Russell of Wood, Spikes, Scott, Sessions, Stayton, Wade, and Waelder—42.

The question recurring upon Mr. Ross' motion to reconsider, Mr. West moved a call of the house.

Absentees—Messrs. Darnell, McLean, Weaver and Flanagan.

On motion of Mr. Russell, of Harrison, Mr. Flanagan was excused on account of sickness.

On motion of Mr. Brown, the call was suspended.

Mr. Stockdale moved to adjourn until 9 o'clock to-morrow.

The yeas and nays were called and stood—

YEAS—Blake, Ballinger, Brady, Crawford, Cook of Gonzales, Cooke of San Saba, Cline, Cooley, Douglass, Dillard, DeMorse, Dohoney, Davis of Brazos, Davis of Wharton, Erhard, Ford, Flournoy, Ferris, Henry of Tyler, Johnson of Franklin, King, Killough, Lockett, McCabe, Morris, Mitchell, Moore, Murphy, Norvell, Nunn, Pauli, Reagan, Reynolds, Rentfro, Robertson of Bell, Robeson of Fayette, Stockdale, Sansom, Wright, West, Waelder—41.

NAYS—Allison, Abernathy, Arnim, Abner, Brown, Blassingame, Barnett, Burleson, Bruce, Chambers, Dunnam, Fleming, German, Gaither, Graves, Holt, Henry of Limestone, Holmes, Haynes, Johnson of Collin, Kilgore, Lacy, Lynch, Martin of Navarro, Martin of Hunt, Mills, McKinney, McCormick, Nugent, Raimey, Rugely, Ross, Russell of Harrison, Russell of Wood, Spikes, Scott, Sessions, Stayton, Wade, Whitehead, Whitfield—41.

So the Convention adjourned to 9 o'clock A. M. to-morrow, pending Mr. Ross' motion to reconsider.

TENTH DAY.

HALL OF REPRESENTATIVES, ⎫
AUSTIN, TEXAS, September 16, 1875. ⎰

Convention met pursuant to adjournment; roll call; quorum present. Prayer by Rev. E. B. Wright, of Austin. Journals read, corrected and adopted.

Mr. West presented the petition of J. H. Hutchins and Alfred Grooms, relative to services rendered in the Land Office during the war.

Referred to Committee on Ordinances.

Mr. Nugent presented the memorial of T. R. Orenbaun, relative to doing away with fences in prairie counties, and school lands.

Referred to Committee on Counties and County Lands.

The following reports of committees were then read:

To the Hon. E. B. Pickett, President of the Convention:

The Committee on Legislative Department, having considered the resolution referred to it in relation to empanneling juries, ask to be allowed to report the same back, and recommend that it be referred to the Committee on Judicial Department.

JNO. L. HENRY, Chairman.

To the Hon. E. B. Pickett, President of the Convention:

The Committee on Legislative Department, to whom was referred resolution in regard to giving aid by municipal corporations, beg leave to report the same back, and recommend that the same be referred to the Committee on Municipal Corporations.

JNO. L. HENRY, Chairman.

To the Hon. E. B. Pickett, President of the Convention:

Your Committee on the Legislative Department, to whom was referred resolution relating to the appointment of special judges, having considered the same, instruct me to report it back and ask that it be referred to the Committee on Judicial Department.

JNO. L. HENRY, Chairman.

To the Hon. E. B. Pickett, President of the Convention:

The Committee on the Legislative Department, to whom was referred resolution in relation to support of petit juries, have had the same under consideration, and ask leave to report it back and recommend that it be referred to the Committee on the Judiciary Department.

Jno. L. Henry, Chairman.

Committee Rooms, }
Austin, September 16, 1875. }

To the Hon. E. B. Pickett, President of the Convention:

The Committee on General Provisions, to whom were referred a series of resolutions concerning municipal corporations, county school lands and public school lands, beg leave to report that they have carefully considered the same and herewith return the same, and recommend that the resolution as to municipal corporations be referred to the Committee on Municipal Corporations; that the resolution as to county school lands be referred to the Committee on Counties and County Lands; that the resolution as to public school lands be referred to the Committee on Education.

All of which is respectfully submitted.

C. S. West, Chairman.

Mr. Lockett offered the following resolution:

Resolved, That the public free schools of this State shall be taught at least four months during the scholastic year, and that the Legislature shall pass laws to enforce and carry out this provision. *Provided, further,* that the school officers of towns, cities and districts may continue them for a longer period; and that the Directors may levy a tax for the continuance of the same.

Referred to Committee on Public Schools.

Also, by Mr. Lockett, the following resolution:

Resolved, That article 3, section 2, of the constitution of 1866 be and constitute a part of the constitution now being made, under its proper caption, with the words "Africans and the descendants of Africans" stricken out, and which shall read as follows:

"Every free male person who shall have attained the age of twenty-one years and who shall be a citizen of the United States, and shall have resided in this State one year next preceding an election, and the last six months within the district, county, city or town in which he offers to vote (Indians not taxed excepted), shall be deemed a qualified elector; and should such qualified elector happen to be in any other county situated in the district in which he resides at the time of an election, he shall be permitted to vote for any district officer; *provided,* that the qualified electors shall be permitted to vote anywhere in the State for

State officers; *and provided, further,* that no soldier, seaman or marine in the army or navy of the United States shall be entitled to vote at any election created by this constitution."

Referred to Committee on Suffrage.

Mr. Robertson, of Bell, offered the following resolution:

Resolved, That all claims, locations, surveys, grants, and titles to land, which are declared null and void by the constitution of the Republic of Texas, are and the same shall forever remain null and void; that all certificates for headlight claims issued to fictitious persons, or which were forged, and all locations and surveys thereon, are and the same were null and void from the beginning.

Referred to Committee on General Provisions.

Mr. Dillard offered the following resolution:

WHEREAS, All original power and sovereignty resides with the people, and they alone can delegate power or authority to govern either in the executive, legislative or judicial departments of the government; therefore,

Resolved, That all officers, either of the legislative, executive or judicial departments of the government, be elected by the people.

Referred to Committee on Legislative Department.

Mr. Whitfield offered the following resolution:

Resolved, That an additional porter be employed by the President whose duty it shall be, in addition to other duties, to attend the State Library and see that books are not taken therefrom without leave or by irresponsible parties; he shall keep the Library open from 7 o'clock A. M. to 6 o'clock P. M. during the session of this Convention.

Adopted.

Mr. West offered the following resolution:

Resolved, That section —— of article —— of the constitution shall read as follows:

"No man or set of men shall ever be exempted, relieved or discharged from the performance of any duty or service imposed by general law, by special legislation. Exemptions from the performance of public duty or service shall only be made by general laws passed by the votes of two-thirds of the members of both houses of the Legislature."

Referred to Committee on General Provisions.

Mr. Ballinger offered the following resolution:

Resolved, That the property of counties, cities and towns, owned and held only for public purposes, and essential to the performance of their public duties, such as public buildings and the sites therefor, fire engines and all other property used for extinguishment of fires, etc., should be exempt from execution and forced sale; and that the Committee on Municipal Corporations be directed to report an appropriate provision in the constitution to cover proper exemptions of property of counties, cities and towns in this State.

Referred to Committee on Municipal Corporations.

The Convention then proceeded to the consideration of unfinished business on the President's desk, which being the motion of Mr. Ross to reconsider the resolution to employ a phonographic reporter, Mr. Wright made this point of order, viz.: that the motion to reconsider was out of order, for the reason that the question had been once reconsidered, and that by the employment of the stenographer, the question under rule 35 had passed out of the control of the house.

The chair ruled against the point of order.

Mr. Waelder offered the following resolution:

Resolved, That the matter of the employment of a stenographer be referred to the Committee on Printing and Contingent Expenses, with instructions to report upon the matters to be reported by the stenographer, and what disposition shall be made of the reports when made, the probable expense, etc.; and that until the committee report and the action of the Convention thereupon, the stenographer shall be regarded as unemployed, and that the motion to reconsider be postponed until the coming in of the report.

The chair ruled the resolution out of order.

Mr. West moved to postpone the question of reconsideration until to-morrow, and that it be made the special order after the morning call was through. The yeas and nays were called and the motion lost by the following vote:

YEAS.—Crawford, Erhard, Ford, Henry of Tyler, King, Kilgore, McLean, Moore, Murphy, Norvell, Rentfro, Stockdale, Wright, West—14.

NAYS—Allison, Abernathy, Arnim, Abner, Brown, Blake, Ballinger, Blassingame, Barnett, Burleson, Brady, Bruce, Chambers, Cook of Gonzales, Cline, Cooley, Douglass, Dillard, DeMorse, Dohoney, Darnell, Dunnam, Davis of Brazos, Davis of Wharton, Flournoy, Fleming, Ferris, German, Gaither, Graves, Holt, Henry of Limestone, Holmes, Haynes, Johnson of Franklin, Johnson of Collin, Killough, Lockett, Lacy, Lynch, Martin of Navarro, Martin of Hunt, McCabe, Mills, Mitchell, McKinney, McCormick, Nunn, Nugent, Pauli, Reagan, Ramey, Rugely, Reynolds, Robertson of Bell, Robeson of Fayette, Ross, Russell of Harrison, Russell of Wood, Spikes, Scott, Sessions, Stayton, Sansom, Wade, Whitehead, Whitfield, Waelder—68.

The question then recurring upon Mr. Ross' motion to reconsider the same was put, and the yeas and nays being demanded the vote was reconsidered by the following vote:

YEAS.—Allison, Abernathy, Arnim, Abner, Brown, Blake, Ballinger, Blassingame, Barnett, Burleson, Brady, Bruce, Crawford, Chambers, Cook of Gonzales, Cooke of San Saba, Cooley, Dillard, Darnell, Davis of Brazos, Davis of Wharton, Erhard, Fleming, Ferris, German, Gaither, Graves, Holt, Henry of Limestone, Holmes, Haynes, Johnson of Franklin, Johnson of Collin, Kilgore, Killough, Lacy, Lynch, Martin of Navarro, Martin of Hunt, McCabe, Mills, Mitchell, McKinney, McCormick, Moore, Nugent, Pauli, Ramey, Reynolds, Robeson of Fayette, Ross, Russell of Harrison, Russell of Wood, Spikes, Scott, Sessions, Stayton, Wade, Whitfield, Waelder—60.

NAYS.—Cline, Douglass, DeMorse, Dohoney, Dunnam, Ford, Flournoy, Henry of Tyler, King, Lockett, McLean, Murphy, Norvell, Nunn, Reagan, Rugely, Rentfro, Robertson of Bell, Stockdale, Sansom, Whitehead, Wright, West—23.

Mr. Flournoy offered the following as a substitute for the resolution:

Resolved, That the stenographic reporter be employed to report only the debates on the proposed constitution, or some part thereof; and that the Committee on Printing be instructed to contract with him, at reasonable rates, and also to contract for the publication of the same in some daily newspaper, and for the furnishing of fifteen copies of such newspaper to each of the members of this Convention.

Mr. Russell, of Wood, moved to indefinitely postpone the whole subject matter.

Mr. Nunn proposed to amend the substitute, as follows:

The stenographer shall continue in the employment of the Convention under the contract made heretofore, until the further action of this Convention.

Withdrawn.

Mr. Crawford offered the following amendment, which was accepted:

That the detail of said contract be reduced to writing by the committee, with estimate of cost of session of forty-five days, and referred to this body for its approval or rejection.

On motion of Mr. Scott, the main question was ordered, which being the adoption or rejection of Mr. Flournoy's resolution, the yeas and nays were called, and stood:

YEAS—Allison, Abner, Brown, Blake, Ballinger, Brady, Crawford, Cline, Douglass, Dillard, DeMorse, Dohoney, Darnell, Dunnam, Davis of Brazos, Davis of Wharton, Erhard, Ford, Flournoy, Ferris, King, Kilgore, Lockett. McCabe, Morris, Mills, Mitchell, Moore, Murphy, Norvell, Nunn, Reagan, Rugely, Reynolds, Rentfro, Stockdale, Sansom, Whitehead, Wright, Whitfield, West, Waelder—42.

NAYS—Mr. President, Abernathy, Arnim, Blassingame, Barnett, Burleson, Bruce, Chambers, Cook of Gonzales, Cooke of San Saba, Cooley, Fleming, German, Gaither, Graves, Holt, Henry of Tyler, Henry of Limestone, Holmes, Haynes, Johnson of Franklin, Johnson of Collin, Killough, Lacy, Lynch, McLean, Martin of Navarro, Martin of Hunt, McKinney, McCormick, Nugent, Pauli, Ramey, Robertson of Bell, Robeson of Fayette, Ross, Russell of Harrison, Russell of Wood, Spikes, Scott, Sessions, Stayton, Wade—43.

So the substitute was lost.

The question then recurring on the motion of Mr. Russell, of Wood, to indefinitely postpone the whole subject matter, the same was put, and the yeas and nays being demanded, stood:

YEAS—Allison, Abernathy, Arnim, Abner, Brown, Blake, Blassingame, Barnett, Burleson, Bruce, Chambers, Cook of Gonzales, Cooke of San Saba, Cooley, Fleming, German, Gaither, Graves, Holt, Henry of Limestone, Holmes, Haynes, Johnson of Franklin, Johnson of Collin, Killough, Lacy, Lynch, Martin of Navarro, Mills, McKinney, McCormick, Nugent, Ramey, Ross, Russell of Harrison, Russell of Wood, Spikes, Scott, Sessions, Wade and Whitfield—41.

NAYS—Ballinger, Brady, Crawford, Cline, Douglass, Dillard, DeMorse, Dohoney, Darnell, Dunnam, Davis of Brazos, Davis of Wharton, Erhard, Ford, Flournoy, Ferris, Henry of Tyler, King, Kilgore, Lockett, McLean, Martin of Hunt, McCabe, Morris, Mitchell, Moore, Murphy, Norvell, Nunn, Pauli, Reagan, Rugely, Reynolds, Rentfro, Robertson of Bell, Robeson of Fayette, Stockdale, Stayton, Sansom, Whitehead, Wright, West, Waelder—43.

So the motion was lost.

The question being the adoption of the original resolution, Mr. Crawford moved to adjourn until 9 o'clock to-morrow.

The yeas and nays were called, and the Convention refused to adjourn by the following vote:

YEAS—Abernathy, Brady, Crawford, Cooke of San Saba, Dillard, DeMorse, Dohoney, Davis of Brazos, Davis of Wharton,

Flournoy, Ferris, Kilgore, Lockett, McLean, Mills, Mitchell, Moore, Murphy, Norvell, Pauli, Rugely, Scott, Sansom—23.

NAYS—Allison, Arnim, Abner, Brown, Blake, Ballinger, Blassingame, Barnett, Burleson, Bruce, Chambers, Cook of Gonzales, Cline, Cooley, Douglass, Darnell, Dunnam, Erhard, Ford, Fleming, German, Gaither, Graves, Holt, Henry of Tyler, Henry of Limestone, Holmes, Haynes, Johnson of Franklin, Johnson of Collin, King, Killough, Lacy, Lynch, Martin of Navarro, Martin of Hunt, Morris, McKinney, McCormick, Nunn, Nugent, Reagan, Ramey, Reynolds, Rentfro, Robertson of Bell, Robeson of Fayette, Ross, Russell of Harrison, Russell of Wood, Spikes, Sessions, Stockdale, Stayton, Wade, Whitehead, Wright, Whitfield, Waelder—59.

The yeas and nays were then called upon the adoption or rejection of the original resolution, and stood—

YEAS—Abernathy, Brady, Cline, Douglass, DeMorse, Dohoney, Darnell, Dunnam, Davis of Brazos, Erhard, Ford, Flournoy, Ferris, Henry of Tyler, King, Kilgore, Lockett, McLean, Morris, Murphy, Norvell, Nunn, Reagan, Rugely, Robertson of Bell, Stockdale, Stayton, Sansom, Whitehead, Wright, West—31.

NAYS—Allison, Arnim, Abner, Brown, Blake, Ballinger, Blassingame, Barnett, Burleson, Bruce, Crawford, Chambers, Cook, of Gonzales, Cooke of San Saba, Cooley, Dillard, Davis of Wharton, Fleming, German, Gaither, Graves, Holt, Henry of Limestone, Holmes, Haynes, Johnson of Franklin, Johnson of Collin, Killough, Lacy, Lynch, Martin of Navarro, Martin of Hunt, McCabe, Mills, Mitchell, McKinney, McCormick, Moore, Nugent, Pauli, Ramey, Reynolds, Rentfro, Robeson of Fayette, Ross, Russell of Harrison, Russell of Wood, Spikes, Scott, Sessions, Wade, Whitfield, Waelder—53.

So the resolution was lost.

Mr. Brown in the chair.

Mr. McCormick moved to reconsider the vote just taken, and to lay the motion on the table.

The chair ruled the motion out of order.

Mr. McCormick appealed, and the Convention sustained the chair.

Mr. Martin, of Navarro, offered the following resolution:

Resolved, That the stenographic reporter shall receive the amount of compensation agreed upon with the committee to the present date.

Adopted.

Mr. Dillard offered the following resolution:

WHEREAS, The convention has now been in session ten days,

and many resolutions, petitions and memorials have been presented, read and referred; and,

WHEREAS, It greatly retards the action of this body, by holding daily sessions, as all of the work must first be shaped in the committee rooms; and,

WHEREAS, The great and important duty devolves upon each and every member to adopt that course which will best promote the true interest of the people; therefore,

Resolved, That the Convention do now adjourn until Monday, the 25th day of September, 1875, at 9 o'clock A. M., that the committees may have sufficient time to mature and prepare their report.

Laid over under the rules.

On motion of Mr. Kilgore, Mr. Martin, of Navarro, was added to Committee on General Provisions.

On motion of Mr. Stockdale, the Convention then adjourned to 9 o'clock A. M. to-morrow.

ELEVENTH DAY.

HALL OF REPRESENTATIVES, }
AUSTIN, TEXAS, September 17, 1875. }

Convention met pursuant to adjournment; roll called; quorum present.

On motion of Mr. Mills, Mr. Rentfro was excused from attendance on account of sickness.

Journals of yesterday were read and adopted.

The following communication from the Attorney General, with accompanying report, was then read, and, on motion of Mr. Nunn, two hundred copies of the report were ordered printed:

ATTORNEY GENERAL'S OFFICE, }
AUSTIN, September 15, 1875. }

To the Hon. E. B. Pickett, President of the Convention:

SIR—In compliance with a resolution of the Convention, I have the honor to transmit herewith a table showing the number of criminal and civil cases upon the dockets of the various District Courts of the State, at their last regular terms, together with the number of each disposed of, which has been compiled from reliable data furnished me by District Clerks.

I am, sir, with great respect, your obedient servant,

GEO. CLARK, Attorney General.

A TABLE

Showing the Business of the District Courts in the several Counties of the State.

COUNTIES.	No. of Criminal Cases last term of District Court.	No. Disposed of.	No. of Civil Cases last term of Court.	No. Disposed of
Anderson	241	58	264	45
Angelina	84	39	45	25
Aransas	31	10	29	14
Atascosa	71	22	22	15
Austin	187	21	102	25
Bastrop	268	22	109	40
Bee	68	22	11	1
Bell	263	45	137	14
Bexar	381	153	303	120
Blanco	32	3	37	11
Bowie	100	23	120	16
Brazoria	72	17	140	36
Brazos	333	99	267	202
Brown	48	18	48	30
Burnet	106	33	48	26
Caldwell	254	48	134	55
Calhoun	54	11	44	15
Cameron	64	24	40	23
Cass	40	13	100	14
Clay	51	5	17	3
Colorado	183	29	185	89
Comal	22	3	20	5
Cook	103	31	122	50
Dallas	696	222	832	180
Delta	43	15	51	9
Denton	254	64	152	38
DeWitt	205	38	70	27
Ellis	153	45	179	64
Falls	251	57	234	34
Fannin	192	92	237	70
Fort Bend	181	40	203	81
Freestone	149	36	97	31
Galveston	138	54	1151	219
Gillespie	38	10	35	16
Gonzales	350	78	169	67
Grayson	260	108	527	125
Gregg	109	25	59	11
Grimes	158	25	97	50

A Table showing the Business of District Courts—Continued.

COUNTIES.	No. of Criminal Cases last term of District Court.	No. Disposed of.	No. of Civil Cases last term of Court.	No. Disposed of.
Gaudalupe	239	35	104	86
Hamilton	96	15	33	9
Hardin	26	9	20	4
Harris	214	14	528	210
Hayes	89	35	40	23
Hidalgo	26	1	8	4
Hill	220	89	112	84
Hood	64	1	109	12
Hopkins	102	45	254	9
Houston	424	121	417	84
Hunt	212	49	182	88
Jack	106	14	36	15
Jackson	25	11	17	9
Jasper	45	12	38	11
Jefferson	42	12	28	4
Johnson	258	44	218	55
Karnes	74	24	38	20
Kaufman	225	32	188	46
Kendall	20	9	16	7
Kerr	28	4	9	5
Kinney	81	23	37	12
Lamar	332	125	418	111
Lampasas	60	34	49	14
Lavaca	252	70	76	41
Leon	108	9	58	1
Liberty	81	19	136	87
Limestone	282	52	194	53
Live Oak	73	19	19	6
Llano	86	18	26	12
McLennan	455	62	428	164
Mason	55	10	25	6
Matagorda	44	11	87	15
Medina	84	—	23	12
Menard	42	5	14	5
Milam	220	31	146	4
Montague	77	18	66	35
Montgomery	153	35	135	54
Nacogdoches	97	—	86	27
Navarro	110	30	185	63
Newton	46	—	35	—

A Table showing the Business of District Courts—Continued.

COUNTIES.	No. of Criminal Cases last term of District Court.	No. Disposed of.	No. of Civil Cases last term of Court.	No. Disposed of.
Orange	36	10	23	8
Palo Pinto	66	—	45	12
Panola	171	28	105	31
Parker	146	25	108	30
Rains	85	34	33	10
Red River	160	37	241	65
Robertson	221	31	371	160
Rockwall	21	4	32	13
Rusk	635	202	127	49
Sabine	306	5	40	7
San Jacinto	40	15	53	23
San Patricio	38	32	36	13
San Saba	46	25	23	12
Shelby	210	55	36	19
Smith	421	30	185	50
Starr	41	11	15	4
Tarrant	184	55	323	164
Titus	149	60	132	24
Travis	643	168	428	99
Upshur	203	36	80	14
Victoria	208	37	75	14
Walker	106	32	56	28
Waller	131	1	88	34
Washington	344	41	410	150
Webb	25	8	30	25
Wharton	93	21	64	10
Wilson	102	53	36	20
Wise	105	26	74	30
Wood	224	53	153	37
Young	—	—	3	—
Total	16,666	3,940	14,451	4,258

No Reports from the following Counties.

Bandera,	Erath,	Nueces,
Bosque,	Fayette,	Polk,
Burleson,	Goliad,	Refugio,
Chambers,	Harrison,	San Augustine,
Cherokee,	Henderson,	Trinity,
Collin,	Lee,	Tyler,

A Table showing the Business of District Courts—Continued.

Comanche,	Madison,	Uvalde,
Coryell,	Marion,	Van Zandt,
El Paso,	Maverick,	Williamson.

GEO. CLARK, Attorney General.

The following reports from the Committee on Judiciary Department were read:

COMMITTEE ROOM, }
AUSTIN, September 17, 1875. }

To the Hon. E. B. Pickett, President of the Convention:

The Judiciary Committee instruct me to say that it has under consideration the subject of the latter portion of the accompanying resolutions, and the remainder and principal part of them relate to the business of the Committee on the Legislative Department of the Constitution; and they instruct me to report them back to the Convention, and ask their reference to the Committee on the Legislative Department.

JOHN H. REAGAN, Chairman.

COMMITTEE ROOM, }
AUSTIN, September 16, 1875. }

To the Hon. E. B. Pickett, President of the Convention:

The Committee on the Judiciary direct me to report the accompanying resolutions back to the Convention, and to ask that they be referred to the Committee on the Executive Department.

JOHN H. REAGAN, Chairman.

Mr. Davis, of Brazos, offered the following resolution:

Resolved, That the following proviso shall constitute the closing clause of section — in article — of the constitution:

"*Provided,* that on the death of the husband or wife, or both, the homestead shall descend and vest in like manner with the other real property of the deceased, and shall be governed by the same laws of descent and distribution; but it shall not be partitioned among the heirs of the deceased during the lifetime of the surviving husband or wife, or so long as the survivor may elect to use or occupy the same as a homestead, or so long as the guardian of the minor children of the deceased may elect so to use and occupy the same."

Referred to Committee on General Provisions.

Also, by Mr. Davis, of Brazos, the following resolution:

Resolved, That section — of article — of the constitution shall read as follows:

"The salaries of State, county and municipal officers shall not be increased during their term of office; nor shall the term of any officer be extended for a longer period than that for which such officer was elected or appointed. But the Legislature may reduce the salaries of officers who shall neglect the performance of any legal duty."

Referred to the Committee on General Provisions.

Also, by Mr. Davis, of Brazos, the following resolution:

Resolved, That section — of article — of the constitution shall read as follows:

" No corporation, after the adoption of this constitution, shall be created except upon the condition that the charter of such corporation shall at all times be subject to amendment and repeal by the Legislature. Nor shall any existing charter be extended, changed or amended, nor shall any benefit be conferred by future legislation upon such corporation, except upon the same condition."

Referred to Committee on General Provisions.

Also, by Mr. Davis, of Brazos, the following resolution:

Resolved, That section — of article — of the constitution shall read as follows:

" The Legislature shall, as soon as practicable, provide for the establishment of a State University, for the promotion of literature and the arts and sciences, including an agricultural and mechanical department; and the "Agricultural and Mechanical College of Texas," established by an act of the Legislature, passed April 17th, 1871, located in the county of Brazos, shall be and is hereby constituted a branch of the State University, for instruction in agriculture, the mechanic arts and the natural sciences connected therewith.

" The University lands and the proceeds thereof, and all moneys belonging to the University fund, and all grants, donations and appropriations heretofore made under former laws of this State, for the maintenance and support of a State University, and all other lands and appropriations that may hereafter be granted by the State, shall be and remain a permanent fund for the use of the State University. The interest arising from the same shall be annually appropriated for the support and benefit of said University.

"And it shall be the duty of the Legislature to take measures for the protection, improvement, or other disposition of said lands, and, as soon as may be done, to provide effectual means for the permanent security and investment of the funds of said State University."

Referred to Committee on Education.

Mr. Russell, of Wood, offered the following resolution:

WHEREAS, It is well known that several incorporated cities in the State have been exacting *enormous direct tax, license tax* and *privilege tax* from venders of *fresh meats* and *vegetables;* and,

WHEREAS, Such direct tax, license tax, and sale of privilege for the vending of fresh meats and vegetables in certain wards of these incorporated cities, have exceeded, in some instances, the *enormous sum of eleven hundred dollars per annum;* and,

WHEREAS, Such enormous taxes are the cause of *suffering* and *want* among the *poorer class,* who are unable to secure the *absolute necessaries of life* on account of the *high prices* necessarily charged for such articles; and,

WHEREAS, The sale of fresh meats and vegetables are *prohibited* in *these cities* unless the *municipal laws* are complied with; therefore, be it

Resolved, That the Legislature shall not pass any special or general law whereby any incorporated town or city shall be allowed to levy and collect a special, direct, license or privilege tax exceeding fifty dollars per annum from any person or firm who are venders of fresh meats, or a special, direct, license or privilege tax exceeding ten dollars per annum from any person or firm who are, or may be, venders of vegetables, fruit, poultry, eggs, milk or butter.

Referred to Committee on Towns and City Corporations.

Mr. Ramey offered the following resolution:

Resolved, That in each county in this State there shall be established a County Court, to consist of one chief justice and four commissioners, to be elected by the people of the whole county; and no two of said court, at the time of their election, shall reside in the same district.

The members of said court shall receive such per diem, perform such duties, and hold courts at such times as may be prescribed by law.

In the decision of such questions as may come before said court upon county matters, the yeas and nays of the individual members shall be entered upon the minutes of the said court.

Referred to Committee on Judiciary.

Mr. Mills offered the following resolution:

Resolved, That the following shall be a section of the constitution:

"Sec. ——.   All qualified electors shall be qualified jurors."

Referred to Committee on General Provisions.

Mr. Wade offered the following resolution:

WHEREAS, A resolution having passed this Convention allowing the delegates hereof envelopes and postage stamps, to be charged as current expenses of this body; therefor be it

Resolved, That the amount thus furnished any one delegate shall not exceed fifteen dollars, account to be kept by the Sergeant-at-arms.

Mr. Nunn proposed to amend by inserting " five " instead of " fifteen."

Accepted.

Mr. Kilgore proposed to strike out " five " and insert " one."

Lost.

On motion of Mr. Allison the resolution was referred to the Committee on Printing and Contingent Expenses.

Mr. Morris offered the following article:

" ARTICLE —.

" Sec. —. It shall be the duty of the Legislature of this State to make suitable provisions for the support and maintenance of a system of public free schools for the gratuitous instruction of all the inhabitants of this State between the ages of eight and sixteen years.

" Sec. —. There shall be a Superintendent of Public Instruction, who shall be elected by the people. The Superintendent shall hold his office for the term of four years. He shall receive an annual salary of three thousand dollars. In case of vacancy in the office of Superintendent, it shall be filled by appointment of the Governor, until the next general election.

" Sec. —. The Superintendent shall have supervision and control of the public free schools of the State, and shall perform such other duties concerning public instruction as the Legislature may direct. The Legislature shall lay off the State into convenient school districts, and shall provide for the formation of a board of school directors in each district. It may give the district boards such legislative powers, in regard to the schools, school-houses and school fund of the district, as may be deemed necessary and proper. It shall be the duty of the Superintendent of Public Instruction to recommend to the Legislature such provisions of law as may be found necessary, in the progress of time, to the establishment and perfection of a complete system of education, adapted to the circumstances and wants of the people of this State. He shall at each session of the Legislature furnish that body with a complete report of all the free schools in the State, giving an account of the condition of the same, and the progress of education within the State. Whenever required by either house of the Legislature, it shall be his duty to furnish all information called for in relation to public schools.

"Sec. —. The Legislature shall establish a uniform system of public free schools throughout the State.

"Sec. —. As a basis for the establishment and endowment of said free schools, all the funds, lands and other property heretofore set apart and appropriated, or that may hereafter be set apart and appropriated, for the support and maintenance of public schools shall constitute the public school fund; and all sums of money that may come to this State hereafter from the sale of any portion of the public domain of the State of Texas, shall also constitute a part of the public school fund; and the Legislature shall appropriate all the proceeds resulting from sales of public lands of said State to such public school fund; and the Legislature shall set apart for the benefit of public schools one-fourth of the annual revenue derivable from general taxation, and shall also cause to be levied and collected an annual poll tax of one dollar on all male persons in the State between the ages of twenty-one and sixty years; also, a tax of two per cent. on the gross earnings of all railroads, steamship lines and insurance companies of this State; also, all the fines collected for carrying concealed weapons and disturbances of the peace; also, all moneys collected for license for selling malt and spirituous liquors, for the benefit of public schools; and said fund and the income derived therefrom and the taxes and other moneys herein provided for school purposes shall be a perpetual fund, to be applied as needed, exclusively for the education of all the scholastic inhabitants of this State, and no law shall ever be made borrowing or appropriating such fund for any other purpose or use whatever.

"Sec. —. The Legislature shall, if necessary, in addition to the income derived from the public school fund and from taxes for school purposes provided for in the foregoing section, provide for the raising of such amount by taxation in the several school districts in the State as will be necessary to provide the necessary school houses in each district and insure the education of all the scholastic inhabitants of the several districts.

"Sec. —. The public lands heretofore given to counties shall be under the control of the board of school directors of their respective counties, and shall never be sold except by act of Legislature, four-fifths of the members elected to such Legislature voting in favor of granting such authority; in such case, the proceeds shall become a permanent school fund of the county to which said lands belonged, and to be invested in the bonds of the State of Texas, and the interest shall be used each year toward maintaining the free schools of such county. The board of school directors shall have authority to rent or lease the school lands of their counties, under such regulations as the Legislature may prescribe, and the proceeds to be used as directed in this section; *provided,* that no lease shall run for a longer period than ten years.

"Sec. ——. The Governor, Attorney General, and Superintendent of Public Instruction shall constitute a board, to be styled the Board of Education, and shall have the general management and control of the perpetual school fund; they shall define the course of studies in the public schools, and direct the class and kind of apparatus and books to be used therein; to prescribe the duties of the boards of school directors, having authority to remove them and appoint others to fill vacancies, and generally do all things to establish and maintain a system of public free schools for at least four months in each and every year, not inconsistent with the provisions of this constitution, under such regulations as the Legislature may hereafter prescribe.

"Sec. ——. The Superintendent of Public Instruction, the Comptroller of Public Accounts, and the Commissioner of the General Land Office, shall constitute a board to be styled the Board of Commissioners, they shall have control of all the public land known as the alternate sections, and such other lands, (except the four leagues belonging to each county in the State,) heretofore set apart, or that may hereafter be set apart for the use and benefit of the common schools; they shall be authorized to sell these lands at not less than fifty cents per acre, under such regulations as the Legislature may prescribe, and the title to such lands shall be made in the name of the State of Texas.   The Commissioner of the General Land Office shall keep a correct and separate record of all such sales.   The Board of Commissioners will on the accumulation of every ten thousand dollars invest the same in the bonds of the State of Texas, and deposit the same with the State Treasurer.

"Sec. ——. The Legislature shall at its first session, and from time to time thereafter as may be necessary, provide all needful rules and regulations for the purpose of carrying into effect the provisions of this article.   It is made the imperative duty of the Legislature to see to it that all the children in the State, within the scholastic age are, without delay, provided with ample means of education.   The Legislature shall annually appropriate for school purposes, and to be equally distributed among all the scholastic inhabitants of the State, the interest accruing on the school fund and the income derived from taxation for school purposes; and shall from time to time, as may be necessary, invest the principal of the school fund in the bonds of the State of Texas, and the bonds already belonging to the school fund, and those to be hereafter purchased as provided for in this article, are declared not to be of doubtful obligation."

Referred to Committee on Education.

Mr. Robertson, of Bell, offered the following resolution:

Resolved, That the Committee on the Legislative Department be requested to insert in the constitution, under the appropriate caption, the following provision:

"That the Legislature shall provide for a thorough and equal assessment of all the property in the State, and for the condemnation and sale under judgment of court of all lands in arrears for taxes.

"The Legislature shall pass no special law when a general law can be made applicable.

"All county officers shall hold their offices for two years.

"That all officers, both State and county, elective under this constitution, shall be elected within sixty days after the adjournment of this Convention, and shall assume the duties of their offices as soon as practicable after the election."

Referred to Committee on Legislative Department.

Mr. Norvell offered the following resolution:

Resolved, That the following section shall be embraced in the constitution in its appropriate place:

"Sec. ——. In all civil suits the time between the 28th day of January, A. D. 1861, and the 30th day of March, A. D. 1870, shall not be computed in the application of any statute of limitations."

Referred to Committee on General Provisions.

Mr. DeMorse offered the following resolution:

Resolved, That no lottery or gift enterprise shall be authorized or permitted within this State, nor shall the sale of tickets in lotteries, gift enterprises or other evasions involving the lottery principle, established or existing in other States, be sold in this State, and it shall be the duty of the Legislature to pass stringent laws to prevent the sale of such tickets.

Referred to Committee on Legislative Department.

Mr. Erhard offered the following resolution:

Resolved, That in incorporated towns no one shall vote for any municipal officer or any other election pertaining to said corporation unless he has $500 worth of taxable property.

In incorporated towns or cities three assessors, appointed or elected, shall annually assess all the property of the citizens residing within the limits of said corporation.

Corporations keeping their roads in their limits in order shall be exempt from all road laws.

Referred to the Committee on Municipal Corporations.

Mr. Reagan offered the following resolution:

Resolved, That the Committee on Judiciary be instructed to inquire into the propriety of making such provision in the constitution as will prevent the members of the County Courts from passing on questions in relation to their own fees of office or compensation.

Referred to Committee on Judiciary.

Mr. Moore offered the following:

WHEREAS, The appointment of relatives and other personal favorites to places of public trust by those vested with power of appointment, is detrimental to the public service; therefore be it

Resolved, That the Committee on General Provisions be requested to incorporate in the constitution, provisions of the following import:

" 1. That no officer in this State vested with power of making appointments to office shall appoint thereto any one related to him by affinity or consanguinity, and all such appointments heretofore made shall become vacant upon the acceptance of this constitution; *provided,* that the incumbent thereof shall hold his office on appointment till his successor shall qualify.

" 2. That when appointment to office shall be made by any officer, he shall take and subscribe the following oath:

" ' That the appointment of .... to the office of .... has not been made with reference to personal friendship; and that said .... is not related to me by affinity or consanguinity, and that said appointment is the best I could make,' which oath shall be deposited as may be provided by law; and the Legislature shall pass suitable laws for the violation of these provisions."

Referred to Committee on General Provisions.

Mr. Ferris offered the following resolution:

Resolved, That the Judiciary Committee take into consideration the propriety of making the following provisions:

" Sec. —. The Supreme Court shall consist of one Chief Justice and six Associate Justices. It shall have the power at any session to separate and divide itself into two courts, each to consist of the Chief Justice and three Associate Justices. Each court so separated shall have the power to hear and decide all appellate causes, civil or criminal: of such court three members shall constitute a quorum, and the concurrence of three shall be necessary to every decision. In all cases of difficult adjudication, or when there may be a conflict of opinion, of which the court shall be the judge, or when the separate court can not make a decision, the court shall hear and decide upon the same as one united court, of which four members shall constitute a quorum, and the concurrence of four shall be necessary to a decision.

"Sec. —. After the year of our Lord one thousand eight hundred and eighty, should it appear necessary for the disposition of appellate causes, inferior appellate courts of uniform organization and jurisdiction may be created in districts formed for that purpose, to which such appeals and writs of error as the Legislature may provide may be prosecuted from district and other courts, and from which appeals and writs of error shall lie to the Supreme Court in all criminal cases of a grade not less than felony, and cases in which a franchise or title to real estate, or the validity of a statute is involved, and in such other cases as may be provided by law. Such appellate courts shall be organized, and held at such times and places, and in such manner, as may be provided by law. Such appellate courts may be created for a part of, or the whole State, as may appear necessary. And the Legislature, on forming such appellate courts, shall have the power to limit appeals to the Supreme Court and modify its operation."

Referred to Committee on Judiciary.

Mr. Pauli offered the following resolution:

Resolved, That the Committee on Revenue and Taxation be instructed to see into the propriety of establishing in this State a standing Board or Committee of Assessment of Taxes, in order that a just and equal assessment of the real value of all the property taxable may be obtained and rigidly enforced.

Referred to Committee on Revenue and Taxation.

Mr. Russell, of Harrison, offered the following resolution:

Resolved, That the indebtedness of the State of Texas shall never exceed the sum of two and one-half per cent. of its taxable property.

Referred to Committee on General Provisions.

Mr. Sansom introduced the following resolution:

Resolved, That no civil office not provided for in the constitution shall be created by the Legislature.

Referred to Committee on General Provisions.

Mr. Kilgore offered the following resolution:

Resolved, That Frederick Voight be and is hereby authorized and directed to contract with a competent workman for certain repairs needed in and about the Capitol building, to-wit:

The plastering on the wall, near the ceiling, on the north side of the hall; repairing the sash and putting in the glass needed in the hall and in the window over the stairway and for putting in the glass needed in the windows of the Capitol Library and the roof on north side of building.

And that the bill for such repairs shall be paid out of any moneys subject to appropriation by this Convention.

Referred to Committee on State Affairs.

Mr. Waelder offered the following resolution:

Resolved, That the Committee on Suffrage inquire into the propriety of embodying the following provision in the constitution:

" Sec. —. Every male person, (Indians not taxed excepted) who shall have attained the age of twenty-one years, and who shall be (or who shall have declared his intention to become) a citizen of the United States, and shall have resided in the State one year next preceding an election, and the last six months within the district or county in which he offers to vote, and is duly registered as may be. provided by law, and has paid his State and county taxes thirty days previous to an election, shall be deemed a qualified elector. And should such qualified elector happen to be in any other county, situated in the district in which he resides, at the time of an election, he shall be permitted to vote for a district officer, and any qualified voter shall be permitted to vote anywhere in the State for State officers ; *provided,* that no soldier, seaman or marine in the army or navy of the United States, shall be entitled to vote at any election to be held under the laws of this State.

" Sec. —. Every qualified elector who has lived sixty days in any incorporated city or town in which he offers to vote, and shall have paid his corporation taxes thirty days before an election, (and none other) shall be entitled to vote in elections held in such incorporated city or town."

Referred to Committee on Suffrage.

Mr. Cline offered the following resolutions:

1. A general diffusion of knowledge being essential to the preservation of the liberties of the people, the Legislature shall establish a system of public instruction, and maintain public schools during not less than six months in each year, for the free education of all minor children in this State between the ages of six and eighteen years.

2. The supervision of public instruction shall be vested in a board, composed of the Superintendent of Public Instruction as President, with the Governor, Secretary of State and Attorney

General *ex-officio*—whose powers and duties shall be defined by law.

3. Every county shall constitute a district, and shall have a district superintendent and board of directors, whose selection, qualifications,. powers and duties shall be prescribed by law ; *provided,* that a city may become a district, and that several districts may have the same district superintendent.

4. The Board of Public Instruction may remove any district superintendent or director for cause, and fill a vacancy by appointment for the unexpired term.

5. The State free school fund shall consist of all escheats, lands and land certificates and bonds heretofore set apart for public schools, and the income from said fund, together with not less than one-fourth of the revenue of the State, shall be annually appropriated and distributed among the districts and expended for schools.

6. The county school fund shall consist of four leagues of land —granted and to be granted in trust for public schools—and any other vested property in the several counties, and the income from such fund, together with the proceeds from sale of estrays, fines and forfeitures, all tax on dogs, polls and occupations, and not less than one-fourth of the ad valorem taxes on property, shall be annually expended for its schools.

7. The State and county permanent school fund shall be invested in bonds of the United States and bonds of the State of Texas; the county fund may also be invested in first mortgages on unincumbered real estate in the county—paying taxes on double the value of the loan—together with personal security.

8. No grant shall be made from any public fund to any institution, church or school controlled by any ecclesiastical body, nor in aid of any particular opinions of conscience, creed or church.

Referred to Committee on Education.

Mr. Erhard offered the following resolution:

Resolved, That the Legislature inquire into the expediency to stipulate and fix an annual salary for district and county clerks and for sheriffs, proportioned to the amount of labor each has to perform, which certainly depends on the number of inhabitants of each county, and in that case the law pass, then the usual fees of said officers to be paid over into the county treasury.

Referred to Committee on Legislative Department.

Mr. Stayton offered the following resolutions:

Resolved, That the Committee upon Crimes and Punishments be instructed to report a provision to be incorporated into the constitution, making it the imperative duty of the Legislature to cause to be erected and maintained a house of correction, to which all persons under eighteen years of age, who may be convicted of any crime which under the law may be a felony, shall be sent for punishment.

Referred to Committee on Crimes and Punishments.

Resolved, That the following be incorporated in the constitution:

" Sec. ——. The Legislature, at its first session after the ratification of this constitution by the people, shall by law establish in each organized county of the State a poor farm, of not less than one hundred acres of land, upon which shall be erected a poor house, a workshop, a hospital and a house of correction, and all necessary outbuildings for taking care of, managing and employing and supplying the wants of its indigent and poor inhabitants; and under such regulations as the Legislature may direct, all persons committing petty offenses in the county may be committed to the house of correction for correction and employment; and the Legislature shall, at its first session after the ratification of this constitution, set apart one league of land for the use and benefit of each organized county, in order to enable the county to carry out this provision, and the said league of land, or the proceeds derived from the sale of the same, shall be used only in establishing said poor farm and building said poor house of correction, as provided for by this section.

Referred to Committee on General Provisions.

Mr. German offered the following resolution:

Resolved, That the Committee on Legislative Department be required to report a clause to prohibit the Legislature from granting any more subsidies of land or money to railroads or other corporations.

Referred to Committee on Legislative Department.

Mr. Stockdale offered the following resolution:

1. No law or laws of this State shall be suspended, except by the Legislature, which may only suspend in the same manner as laws are made or repealed. Whenever a law is suspended, it shall be for a time certain.

2. The writ of *habeas corpus* is a writ of right. The right to have this writ from the proper court or judge shall never be suspended, except by act of the Legislature. The Legislature shall never suspend this right, except there be such hostile invasion of the State, by organized or armed force, as shall put in peril the safety of the State; or such rebellion, within the State, as shall make it necessary in order to preserve the authority of the State government, and only in these cases in reference to arrest upon

charges, made upon oath, of treason, conspiracy to commit treason, or some other offense, defined by law, against the authority of the government.   Nor shall any person be held in arrest upon a charge of offense against the authority of the government, except under a judicial warrant.   When the right is suspended, in accordance with the foregoing conditions, then a person in arrest, under judicial warrant, may be held in a place of safety and removed, as circumstances may require, by the Executive or under his authority, and shall be so safely held without the benefit of trial, bail or mainprize until the act suspending the right shall be repealed, or shall expire by its own limitation.

3. Every suspension of the right of the writ of *habeas corpus* by act of the Legislature shall be for a time certain not to exceed ..... months.

Referred to Committee on Bill of Rights.

Mr. Waelder offered the following resolution:

Resolved, That the following be made a part of the constitution:

"MODE OF CALLING A CONVENTION AND AMENDING THE CONSTITUTION OF THIS STATE.

"Sec. 37. The Legislature, by a vote of three-fourths of all the members of each house, with the approval of the Governor, shall have power to call a convention of the people, for the purpose of altering, amending or re-forming the constitution of this State; the manner of electing delegates to the Convention, the time and place of assembling them, to be regulated by law.

"Sec. 38. The Legislature, at any biennial session, by a vote of two-thirds of all the members of each house, may propose amendments to the constitution, to be voted upon by persons legally qualified to vote for members of the House of Representatives of the State; which proposed amendments shall be duly published in the public prints of this State, at least three months before the next general election for representatives to the Legislature, for the consideration of the people; and it shall be the duty of the several returning officers, at said general election, to open a poll for, and make returns to the Secretary of State, of the number of legal votes cast at said election, for and against said amendment, and if more than one be proposed, then the number of legal votes cast for and against each of them; and if it shall appear, from said return, that a majority of the votes cast upon said proposed amendment, or amendments, have been cast in favor of the same, and two-thirds of each house of

10

the Legislature, at the next regular session thereafter, shall ratify said proposed amendment, or amendments, so voted upon by the people, the same shall be valid to all intents and purposes, as parts of the constitution of the State of Texas; *provided,* that the said proposed amendments shall, at each of said sessions, have been read on three several days in each house of the Legislature, and the vote thereon shall have been taken by yeas and nays; and, *provided further,* that the rule in the above proviso shall never be suspended by either of said houses."

Referred to Committee on Legislative Department.

Mr. Cline offered the following resolution:

1. The judicial power shall be vested in one Supreme Court, in District Courts, County Courts, Municipal Courts, Magistrates and Criminal Courts.

2. The Supreme Court shall have original jurisdiction of impeachment of State executive officers and District Judges, and appellate jurisdiction of all cases in which the construction of the constitution, or the constitutionality of a statute or charter, is drawn in question; of all cases of debt wherein the sum claimed (exclusive of interest) shall exceed $2,000; of all other cases wherein the sum claimed (exclusive of interest) shall exceed $500; of all criminal cases where the penalty is death or imprisonment for five years.

3. The District Court shall have original jurisdiction of such impeachment of inferior officers and magistrates, as may be prescribed by law; and appellate jurisdiction and supervision over inferior courts as may be prescribed by law; and general original jurisdiction of suits for debt and damages wherein the amount claimed (exclusive of interest) shall exceed $500; of divorce, status, lands, liens, writs in equity, and such criminal and other causes as may be prescribed by law.

4. The County Court shall have original jurisdiction in all cases of misdemeanor or petit larceny at common law. In all cases of wills, succession, guardianship, and administration of estates of decedents, minors, lunatics, and drunkards. In suits at law for debt or damages where the sum claimed (exclusive of interest) shall be not less than $100, nor more than $1,000. The municipal magistrate and Criminal Courts shall have such jurisdiction as may be prescribed by law.

5. The Judges of the Supreme, District and Criminal Courts shall be learned in the law, experienced at the bar during .... years; nominated by the Governor and confirmed by the Senate, and shall hold office during good behavior, and be paid by the State.

6. The Judges of the County Courts shall be learned in the law, experienced at the bar during .... years; elected by their county, and shall hold office four years, and be paid a salary fixed by the County Commissioners out of the county treasury. The judge shall preside over the Commissioner's Court.

7. The Supreme Court shall appoint their clerk. The County Clerk shall be elected for four years, and shall have the custody of all county records; attend the District, County, Criminal and Commissioners' courts of his county, and perform such other duties as may be prescribed by law.

8. The magistrates, sheriffs, constables and county commissioners shall be elected by the county, shall hold office four years, and shall have such powers and duties and compensation as may be prescribed by law.

9. The Governor, by and with the advice and consent of the Senate, shall commission special judges having the same qualifications required for the Supreme Court, who shall hear and determine causes on the dockets of the Supreme Court at the date of the ratification of this constitution, to hold such commission until the dockets of the Supreme Court shall be cleared of all causes ready to be tried when called.

Such special judges may be assigned as follows: One special judge, with two Judges of the Supreme Court to sit at Tyler; one special judge, with two Judges of the Supreme Court, to sit at Galveston; and two special judges, with the Chief Justice of the Supreme Court, to sit at Austin, or *vice versa.*

Referred to Committee on Judiciary.

Mr. Murphy offered the following resolution:

The Legislature shall, at its first session, provide for a change of venue in civil and criminal cases.

Referred to the Committee on Legislative Department.

Mr. Cline offered the following resolution:

Resolved, That the Committee on Agriculture and Stock-raising inquire what provision may be proper to adjust and protect the interests of farmers and stock raisers; to secure inspection of hides and stock in counties where stockraising is one of the principal interests of the people.

Referred to Committee on Agriculture and Stock-raising.

On motion of Mr. Moore Mr. Robeson, of Fayette, was excused for four days, beginning to-morrow.

Mr. McCormick offered the following resolution:

Resolved, That the Committee on Revenue and Taxation be required to report upon the propriety of incorporating in the constitution a provision that all collectors of State, county, municipal and school taxes specify in the receipt given by them for such taxes, the several items of real and personal property upon which such tax is demanded.

And also the propriety of releasing each tax-payer from the payment of taxes until such itemized bill for the same is presented him. And that said itemized bill shall show for what purposes said taxes are levied, whether for school, general revenue, or other purposes.

Referred to the Committee on Revenue and Taxation.

On motion of Mr. Waelder Mr. King was excused temporarily on account of sickness.

Mr. Johnson, of Franklin, offered the following resolution:

Resolved, That the Judiciary Committee be required to inquire into the propriety of incorporating a provision in the constitution that will effectually prohibit gambling of every character in this State.

Referred to Committee on Judiciary.

The Convention then proceeded to consider business on the President's desk.

Report of Committee on State Affairs, on resolution making the constitution of 1845 the basis of the constitution about to be framed, was taken up.

Mr. Dohoney in the chair:

Mr. DeMorse moved to indefinitely postpone action on the subject.

Carried.

Mr. Dillard's resolution to adjourn until Monday, September 20th, was then taken up.

Mr. Reagan offered the following amendment:

Resolved, That when the Convention adjourns to-morrow, it adjourn over until Monday, the 27th inst., to enable the committees to prepare their reports for the action of the Convention.

Accepted.

On motion of Mr. Whitfield the substitute as amended was laid on the table.

Mr. Mills moved to adjourn until Tuesday morning, 21st inst., at 9 o'clock.

By leave, Mr. Flournoy offered the following resolution:

Resolved, That the Convention do adjourn after each meeting for the next ensuing ten days as soon as the minutes shall have been read. And the members of the various committees shall devote themselves energetically to the preparation of the business of the Convention.

Laid over under the rule.

On motion of Mr. Flournoy the Convention adjourned until 9 o'clock A. M. to-morrow.

TWELFTH DAY.

HALL OF REPRESENTATIVES, }
AUSTIN, TEXAS, September 18, 1875. }

Convention met pursuant to adjournment; roll called; quorum present.   Prayer by Rev. Mr. Abernethy.

Journals of yesterday read and adopted.

Mr. Ford presented a memorial from L. G. Lincicum on the subject of embodying in the new constitution a law guaranteeing equality of rights to the practitioners of all the various schools of medicine.

Referred to Committee on General Provisions.

Mr. Russell, of Wood, presented a petition from the heirs of Verner, memorializing the Convention to reopen the courts of the State for the adjudication of old Mexican land grants.

Referred to Committee on Mexican Land Titles.

The following reports of committees were then read:

COMMITTEE ROOM, }
AUSTIN, September 18th, 1875. }

To the Hon. E. B. Pickett, President of the Convention:

The Committee on General Provisions, to whom was referred a series of resolutions concerning the Superintendent of Public Instruction and a State University, instruct me to return the same, and recommend that they be referred to the Committee on Education.   Respectfully submitted,

C. S. WEST, Chairman.

COMMITTEE ROOM, }
AUSTIN, September 17, 1875. }

To the Hon. E. B. Pickett, President of the Convention:

The Committee on State Affairs, to which was referred the resolution requiring them to "inquire into the propriety of abolishing the office of State Geologist," have had the same under consideration, and have instructed me to report as follows:

Up to the present time the labors of the State Geologist have not been productive of any visible good results, yet as Texas is a growing State, and the great natural resources she possesses are almost unknown and undeveloped, it would not be prudent to restrict the Legislature from continuing said office, if the exigencies of the public good should require it.

JOHN S. FORD, Chairman.

COMMITTEE ROOM,
AUSTIN, September 17, 1875. }

To the Hon. E. B. Pickett, President of the Convention:

The Committee on State Affairs, to which was referred the resolution relating to the repairing of the capitol building, under the superintendence of F. Voigt, have had the same under consideration, and have instructed me to report the said resolution back, and recommend its adoption by the Convention.

JOHN S. FORD, Chairman.

Mr. Mills offered the following amendment:

"Provided that the cost of the same shall not exceed seventy-five dollars."

Adopted.

Mr. Martin, of Navarro, moved to lay the resolution on the table.

The ayes and nays were demanded, which resulted as follows:

YEAS—Arnim, Brown, Blassingame, Barnett, Brady, Bruce, Dohoney, Darnell, Erhard, Flournoy, Fleming, German, Gaither, Graves, Holt, Henry of Smith, Henry of Limestone, Haynes, Johnson of Collin, Lynch, Martin of Navarro, Martin of Hunt, Mills, Mitchell, McKinney, Moore, Norvell, Pauli, Reagan, Rugely, Robertson of Bell, Ross, Scott, Sessions, Smith, Sansom, Wade, Whitehead, Wright—39.

NAYS—Mr. President, Allison, Abner, Blake, Ballinger, Cook of Gonzales, Cooke of San Saba, Cline, Cooley, Douglass, Dillard, DeMorse, Dunnam, Davis of Brazos, Davis of Wharton, Ford, Ferris, Flanagan, Holmes, Johnson of Franklin, King, Kilgore, Killough, Lockett, Lacy, McCabe, Morris, McCormick, Murphy, Nunn, Nugent, Ramey, Reynolds, Russell of Harrison, Spikes, Stockdale, Stayton, Waelder, West, Whitfield—40.

The question being on the adoption of the resolution, as amended, the yeas and nays were called for with the following result:

YEAS—Allison, Abner, Blake, Ballinger, Burleson, Crawford, Cook of Gonzales, Cooke of San Saba, Cline, Cooley, Douglass, Dillard, DeMorse, Dunnam, Davis of Brazos, Davis of Wharton, Ford, Ferris, Flanagan, Holmes, Johnson of Franklin, King, Kilgore, Killough, Lockett, Lacy, Martin of Hunt, McCabe, Morris, McCormick, Murphy, Nunn, Nugent, Pauli, Ramey, Reynolds, Russell of Harrison, Stockdale, Stayton, Sansom, Waelder, West, Whitfield—43.

NAYS—Abernathy, Arnim, Brown, Blassingame, Barnett, Brady, Bruce, Chambers, Dohoney, Darnell, Erhard, Flournoy, Fleming, German, Gaither, Graves, Holt, Henry of Smith, Henry of Limestone, Haynes, Johnson of Collin, Lynch, Martin of Navarro, Mills, Mitchell, McKinney, Moore, Norvell, Reagan, Rugely, Robertson of Bell, Ross, Russell of Wood, Spikes, Scott, Sessions, Smith, Wade, Whitehead, Wright—40.

By which the resolution was adopted.

To the Hon. E. B. Pickett, President of the Convention:

Your Committee on Printing and Contingent Expenses, to whom was referred resolution, "that those delegates from counties adjacent to the frontier, or such counties wherein no newspapers are published, be allowed thirty copies each of some paper in the city of Austin which publishes the proceedings of this Convention," have had the same under consideration, and have instructed me to report it back to the Convention, and recommend that it be not adopted.

W. D. S. Cook, Chairman.

The report was adopted.

Also reported as follows:

To the Hon. E. B. Pickett, President of the Convention:

Your Committee on Printing and Contingent Expenses, to whom was referred preamble and resolution, in regard to furnishing members with envelopes and postage stamps, have had the same under consideration, and have, unanimously, instructed me to report the same back with the following resolution, and recommend its adoption, viz.:

Resolved, That the Sergeant-at-arms be and he is hereby directed to furnish each delegate and officer with postage stamps, stamped envelopes and stamped wrappers, to the amount of ten dollars each, and no more, for and during the session of this Convention."

W. D. S. Cook, Chairman.

Mr. Nunn moved to strike out ten dollars and insert five dollars.

Mr. Dillard moved to strike out ten dollars and insert nothing. Lost.

Mr. McCormick moved to indefinitely postpone the whole matter. Lost.

Mr. Ballinger offered the following as a substitute for the resolution and amendment:

Resolved, That the Sergeant-at-arms furnish the stationery, postage stamps, wrappers, etc., required by members, making a report of the amount received by each member, to be published in the proceedings of the Convention.

The substitute was then adopted by the following vote:

YEAS—Allison, Arnim, Abner, Brown, Blake, Ballinger, Blassingame, Burleson, Brady, Bruce, Crawford, Chambers, Cook of Gonzales, Cooke of San Saba, Cline, Cooley, Dillard, DeMorse, Dohoney, Darnell, Dunnam, Davis of Brazos, Davis of Wharton, Erhard, Ford, Fleming, Ferris, Flanagan, German, Gaither, Graves, Henry of Limestone, Haynes, Johnson of Franklin, Johnson of Collin, Kilgore, Killough, Lacy, Lynch, Martin of Navarro, Martin of Hunt, McCabe, Morris, McKinney, McCormick, Moore, Murphy, Nugent, Pauli, Reagan, Ramey, Rugely, Reynolds, Robertson of Bell, Ross, Russell of Harrison, Russell of Wood, Scott, Sessions, Smith, Stockdale, Stayton, Sanson, Whitehead, Wright, Waelder, Whitfield—67.

NAYS—Abernathy, Barnett, Douglass, Flournoy, Holt, Henry of Smith, Holmes, King, Lockett, Mills, Mitchell, Norvell, Nunn, Spikes, Wade, West—16.

Mr. Whitfield offered the following resolution:

Resolved, That the Committee on Printing and Contingent Expenses be instructed to contract with some newspaper published in the city of Austin for the publication of the daily journal; and deliver to each delegate five copies of the same.

Mr. Martin, of Navarro, proposed to amend by striking out " five " and inserting " one."

Mr. McCormick moved to amend the amendment by inserting "one to every three delegates."

Lost.

Mr. Martin's (of Navarro) amendment lost and the resolution adopted.

Mr. McCormick moved to reconsider the vote just taken and to lay the motion on the table.

Carried.

Mr. Burleson offered the following resolution:

Resolved, That the Legislature, at the first session after the adoption of the present constitution, shall provide for the assessment and collection of all back taxes due the State and counties.

Referred to Committee on Revenue and Taxation.

Mr. Scott offered the following resolution:

Resolved, That the following shall be a part of the constitution:

"It shall be the duty of the Legislature to provide for the settlement of differences by arbitration where parties shall elect that mode of trial."

Referred to Committee on Legislative Department.

Mr. Brown offered the following resolution:

" GENERAL PROVISIONS.

"Sec. —. No person shall be prosecuted in any civil action or criminal proceeding for or on account of any act by him done, performed or executed between the first day of January, one thousand eight hundred and sixty-one, and the twentieth day of August, one thousand eight hundred and sixty-six, by virtue of military authority vested in him, or in pursuance of orders from any person vested with such authority by the government of the United States, or of this State, or of the late Confederate States, or any of them, to do such act. And if any action or proceeding shall have been, or shall hereafter be instituted, against any person for the doing of any such act, the defendant may plead this section in bar thereof."

Referred to Committee on General Provisions.

Mr. Ramey offered the following resolution:

Resolved, That in every county in this State there shall be elected by the qualified voters thereof a County Clerk, who shall be the Clerk of the District, County and Probate Courts of said counties respectively. Shall also be Recorder for the same, and perform such other duties as may be required by law. But in counties containing 10,000 inhabitants, or more, the Legislature may make provisions to divide the duties of said office and provide for the electing of two clerks in each county, one to be denominated District and the other County Clerk, each to perform such duties as may be prescribed by law.

Referred to the Executive Committee.

On motion of Mr. Waelder, the Convention adjourned to 9 o'clock A. M. Monday.

THIRTEENTH DAY.

HALL OF REPRESENTATIVES, }
AUSTIN, TEXAS, September 20, 1875.

Roll called; quorum present; prayer by Rev. Mr. Lee.

On motion of Mr. Mills, Messrs. Cline and Morris were excused one day.

On motion of Mr. Chambers, Mr. McKinney was excused temporarily on account of sickness.

Journals read and adopted.

Report from Committee on Legislative Department:

COMMITTEE ROOM, ⎫
AUSTIN, September 20, 1875. ⎭

To the Hon. E. B. Pickett, President of the Convention:

The Committee on the Legislative Department, to whom were referred sundry resolutions, have had the same under careful consideration, and instruct me to report the accompanying articles as a substitute for the whole subject matter and recommend their adoption.

JOHN L. HENRY, Chairman.

"ARTICLE —.

"LEGISLATIVE DEPARTMENT.

" Section 1. The Legislative power of this State shall be vested in a Senate and House of Representatives, which together shall be styled "the Legislature of the State of Texas."

" Sec. 2. The Senate shall consist of thirty members, and the House of Representatives of ninety members, until the first apportionment after the adoption of this constitution; when, or at any apportionment thereafter, both houses may be increased by the Legislature, the Senate not to exceed thirty-three members and the House of Representatives not to exceed one hundred members.

" Sec. 3. The Senators shall be chosen by the qualified electors for the term of four years, and shall, after the first election under each apportionment, be divided by lot into two classes. The seats of the senators of the first class shall be vacated at the expiration of the first two years, and those of the second class at the expiration of four years, so that one-half of the senators shall be chosen biennially thereafter.

" Sec. 4. The members of the House of Representatives shall be chosen by the qualified electors, and their term of office shall be two years from the day of their election.

" Sec. 5. The Legislature shall meet every two years at such time as may be prescribed by law, and at other times when convened by the Governor. The first session under this constitution shall convene on the .... day of .... 1876.

" Sec. 6. No person shall be a senator, unless he is a citizen of the United States, and at the time of his election a qualified elector of this State, and shall have been a resident of this State five years next preceding his election, and the last year thereof a resident of the district for which he shall be chosen, and shall have attained the age of thirty years.

"Sec. 7.   No person shall be a representative unless he be a citizen of the United States, and at the time of his election a qualified elector of this State, and shall have been a resident of this State two years next preceding his election, the last year thereof a resident of the district for which he shall be chosen, and shall have attained the age of twenty-one years.

"Sec. 8.   Each house shall be the judge of the qualifications and election of its own members, but contested elections shall be determined in such manner as shall be provided by law.

"Sec. 9.   The Senate shall, at the beginning and close of each session, and at such other times as may be necessary, elect one of its members President *pro tempore,* who shall perform the duties of the Lieutenant Governor in any case of absence or disability of that officer, and whenever the said office of Lieutenant Governor shall be vacant. The House of Representatives shall, when it first assembles, organize temporarily, and thereupon proceed to the election of a Speaker from its own members. And each house shall choose its other officers.

"Sec. 10.   Two-thirds of each house shall constitute a quorum to do business, but a smaller number may adjourn from day to day, and compel the attendance of absent members, in such manner and under such penalties as each house may provide.

"Sec. 11.   Each house may determine the rules of its own proceedings, punish members for disorderly conduct, and, with the consent of two-thirds, expel a member, but not a second time for the same offense.

"Sec. 12.   Each house shall keep a journal of its proceedings, and publish the same; and the yeas and nays of the members of either house on any question shall, at the desire of any three members present, be entered on the journal.

"Sec. 13. When vacancies occur in either house, the Governor, or the person exercising the power of the Governor, shall issue writs of election to fill said vacancies; and should the Governor fail to issue a writ of election to fill any such vacancy, within twenty days after it occurs, the returning officer of the district, in which such vacancy may have happened, shall be authorized to order an election for that purpose.

"Sec. 14.   Senators and representatives shall, except in cases of treason, felony, or breach of the peace, be privileged from arrest during the session of the Legislature, and in going to and returning from the same, allowing one day for every twenty miles, such member may reside from the place at which the Legislature is convened.

"Sec. 15. Each house may punish, by imprisonment, during its sessions, any person not a member for disrespectful or disorderly conduct in its presence, or for obstructing any of its proceedings; *provided,* such imprisonment shall not, at any one time, exceed forty-eight hours.

"Sec. 16. The sessions of each house shall be open, except when the Senate is in executive session.

"Sec. 17. Neither house shall, without the consent of the other, adjourn for more than three days, nor to any other place than that where the Legislature may be sitting.

"Sec. 18. No senator or representative shall, during the term for which he may be elected, be eligible to any civil office of profit under this State, which shall have been created, or the emoluments of which may have been increased during such term; no member of either house shall, during the term for which he is elected, be eligible to any office or place, the appointment to which may be made, in whole or in part, by either branch of the Legislature, and no member of either house shall vote for any other member for any office whatever, which may be filled by a vote of the Legislature, except in such cases as are in this constitution provided. Nor shall any member of the Legislature be interested, either directly or indirectly, in any contract with the State, or any county thereof, authorized by any law passed during the term for which he shall have been elected.

"Sec. 19. No judge of any court, Secretary of State, Attorney General, clerk of any court of record, or any person holding a lucrative office under the United States or this State, or any foreign government, shall be eligible to the Legislature.

"Sec. 20. No person who at any time may have been a collector of taxes, or who may have been otherwise entrusted with public money, shall be eligible to the Legislature, or to any office of profit or trust under the State government, until he shall have obtained a discharge for the amount of such collections, or for all public moneys with which he may have been entrusted.

"Sec. 21. No member shall be questioned in any other place for words spoken in debate in either house.

"Sec. 22. A member who has a personal or private interest in any measure or bill, proposed, or pending, before the Legislature, shall disclose the fact to the house of which he is a member, and shall not vote thereon.

"Sec. 23. If any senator or representative remove his residence from the district or county for which he was elected, his office shall thereby become vacant, and the vacancy shall be filled as prescribed in section 13 of this article.

"Sec. 24. The members of the Legislature shall receive from the public treasury such compensation for their services as may, from time to time, be provided by law, not exceeding five dollars per day for the first sixty days of each session, and after that not exceeding two dollars per day for the remainder of the session; except the first session held under this constitution, when they may receive not exceeding five dollars per day for the first ninety days. In addition to per diem the members of each house shall be entitled to mileage in going to and returning from the seat of government; which mileage shall not exceed five dollars for every twenty-five miles, the distance to be computed by the nearest and most direct route of travel by land, regardless of railways or water routes; and the Comptroller of the State shall prepare and preserve the table of distances to each county seat now or hereafter to be established, and by such table the mileage of each member shall be paid; but no member shall be entitled to mileage for any extra session that may be called within one day after the adjournment of a regular session.

"Sec. 25. The State shall be divided into Senatorial Districts of compact and contiguous territory, according to the number of qualified electors, as nearly as may be, and each district shall be entitled to elect one senator; and no single county shall be entitled to more than one senator.

"Sec. 26. The members of the House of Representatives shall be apportioned among the several counties, according to the number of population in each, as nearly as may be, on a ratio obtained by dividing the population of the State, as ascertained by the most recent United States census, by the number of members of which the house is composed; *provided*, that whenever a single county has sufficient population to be entitled to a representative, such county shall be formed into a separate representative district, and when two or more counties are required to make up the ratio of representation, such counties shall be contiguous to each other, and where any one county has more than sufficient population to be entitled to one or more representatives, such representative or representatives shall be apportioned to such county, and for any surplus of population it may be joined in a representative district with any other contiguous county or counties.

"Sec. 27. Elections for senators and representatives shall be general throughout the State, and shall be regulated by law.

"Sec. 28. The Legislature shall, at its first session after the publication of each United States decennial census, apportion the State into Senatorial and Representative districts, agreeably to the provisions of sections 25 and 26 of this article; and until after the next decennial census, when the first apportionment shall be made by the Legislature, the State shall be, and it is hereby, divided into Senatorial and Representative districts as follows:

SENATORIAL DISTRICTS.

First District—Liberty, San Jacinto, Tyler, Jefferson, Jasper, Orange, Hardin, Newton and Polk.

Second District—Houston, Angelina, San Augustine, Nacogdoches and Sabine.

Third District—Rusk, Panola and Shelby.

Fourth District—Harrison.

Fifth District—Marion, Bowie, Cass and Morris.

Sixth District—Red River, Titus, Franklin and Hopkins.

Seventh District—Camp, Upshur, Gregg and Smith.

Eighth District—Cherokee, Anderson and Henderson.

Ninth District—Lamar, Fannin and Delta.

Tenth District—Wood, Van Zandt, Kaufman, Rains, Rockwall and Hunt.

Eleventh District—Grayson and Cook.

Twelfth District—Collin and Denton.

Thirteenth District—Dallas and Ellis.

Fourteenth District—Navarro, Limestone and Freestone.

Fifteenth District—Leon, Brazos and Robinson.

Sixteenth District—Grimes, Trinity, Madison and Walker.

Seventeenth District—Montgomery, Waller, Fort Bend and Wharton.

Eighteenth District—Harris and Chambers.

Nineteenth District—Galveston, Brazoria and Matagorda.

Twentieth District—Austin, Washington and Burleson.

Twenty-first District—Falls, Milam and Bell.

Twenty-second District—Johnson, Hill and McLennan.

Twenty-third District—Tarrant, Parker, Wise, Montague, Clay, Jack, Young and unorganized counties, first of them.

Twenty-fourth District—Coryell, Bosque, Hamilton, Brown, Coleman, Moore, Erath, Hood, Summerville, Palo Pinto, Eastland, Shackleford, and unorganized counties of Runnels, Baylor, Comanche, Callahan, Jones and Stephens.

Twenty-fifth District—Travis, Williamson, Burnett and Lampasas.

Twenty-sixth District—Fayette, Bastrop and Lee.

Twenty-seventh District—Colorado, Lavaca and Gonzales.

Twenty-eighth District—Calhoun, Victoria, DeWitt, Aransas, Refugio, Bee, Goliad, Karnes, Wilson, Jackson and Atascosa.

Twenty-ninth District—Cameron, Hidalgo, Starr, Webb, Maverick, Kinney, Uvalde, Medina, Nueces, San Patricio, Live Oak, Frio, and the unorganized counties of Duval, Encinal, McMillen, La Salle, Dimitt and Zavalla.

Thirtieth District—Bexar, Comal, Bandera, Kendall, Kerr, Gillespie, Mason, Menard, Tom Green, Pecos, Presidio, El Paso, and the unorganized counties of Concho and Crockett.

Thirty-first District—Guadalupe, Caldwell, Hays, Blanco, Llano, San Saba, and unorganized county of McCulloch.

REPRESENTATIVE DISTRICTS.

First District—One representative—Liberty, Hardin and Jefferson.

Second District—San Jacinto, Polk and Tyler, one.

Third District—Jasper, Newton and Orange, one.

Fourth District—San Augustine and Sabine, one.

Fifth District—Houston, one.

Sixth District—Nacogdoches and Angelina, one.

Seventh District—Rusk, one.

Eighth District—Panola and Shelby, one.

Ninth District—Rusk, Panola and Shelby, one.

Tenth District—Harrison, one.

Eleventh District—Marion, Morris, Cass and Bowie, three.

Twelfth District—Red River, one.

Thirteenth District—Titus and Franklin, one.

Fourteenth District—Hopkins, one.

Fifteenth District—Smith, Gregg, Upshur and Camp, three.

Sixteenth District—Lamar, one.

Seventeenth District—Fannin, one.

Eighteenth District—Lamar, Fannin and Delta, one.

Nineteenth District—Hunt and Rockwall, one.

Twentieth District—Kaufman, Rains, Wood and Van Zandt, two.

Twenty-first District—Henderson, one.

Twenty-second District—Anderson, one.

Twenty-third District—Cherokee, one.

Twenty-fourth District—Leon, one.

Twenty-fifth District—Robertson, one.

Twenty-sixth District—Brazos, one.

Twenty-seventh District—Grimes, one.

Twenty-eighth District—Grimes and Madison, one.

Twenty-ninth District—Walker and Trinity, one.

Thirtieth District—Montgomery, one.

Thirty-first District—Harris, two.
Thirty-second District—Harris and Chambers, one.
Thirty-third District—Galveston, two.
Thirty-fourth District—Galveston, Brazoria, Matagorda, one.
Thirty-fifth District—Wharton, Fort Bend and Waller, two.
Thirty-sixth District—Austin, one.
Thirty-seventh District—Washington, one.
Thirty-eighth District—Washington and Burleson, one.
Thirty-ninth District—Falls, Milam and Bell, three.
Fortieth District—Limestone, one.
Forty-first District—Freestone, one.
Forty-second District—Navarro, one.
Forty-third District—Ellis, one.
Forty-fourth District—Dallas, two.
Forty-fifth District—Collin, one.
Forty-sixth District—Grayson, two.
Forty-seventh District—Grayson and Collin, one.
Forty-eighth District—Cook, one.
Forty-ninth District—Denton, one.
Fiftieth District—Clay, Montague and Wise, and unorganized counties west of Clay, one.
Fifty-first District—Tarrant, one.
Fifty-second District—Parker, Jack and Young, and unorganized counties west of them, one.
Fifty-third District—Johnson, one.
Fifty-fourth District—Hill, one.
Fifty-fifth District—McLennan, one.
Fifty-sixth District—Jackson, Calhoun, Victoria, DeWitt, Aransas, Refugio, Bee and Goliad, two.
Fifty-seventh District—Colorado and Lavaca, two.
Fifty-eighth District—Gonzales, one.
Fifty-ninth District—Fayette, one.
Sixtieth District—Bastrop, one.
Sixty-first District—Fayette and Lee, one.
Sixty-second District—Caldwell, Guadalupe and Hays, two.
Sixty-third District—Travis, one.
Sixty-fourth District—Travis and Blanco, one.
Sixty-fifth District—Williamson and Lampasas, one.
Sixty-sixth District—Coryell, Hamilton, Brown, Coleman, and unorganized county of Runnels, one.
Sixty-seventh District—Bosque, Summerville and Hood, one.
Sixty-eighth District—Erath, Comanche, Palo Pinto, Eastland, Shackleford, and unorganized counties of Stephens, Jones, Callahan and Taylor, one.

Sixty-ninth District—Bexar, one.

Seventieth District—Bexar and Comal, one.

Seventy-first District—Uvalde, Medina, Bandera, Kendall, Kerr, Gillespie, Menard, and unorganized counties of Edwards and Kimball, one.

Seventy-second District—Llano, Mason, San Saba, Burnet, McCulloch and Concho, one.

Seventy-third District—El Paso, Presidio, Pecos, Tom Green and Crockett, one.

Seventy-fourth District—Cameron, Hidalgo, Starr, Zapata and Webb, one.

Seventy-fifth District—Nueces, Frio, Maverick and Kinney, and the unorganized counties of Duval, Encinal, McMullen, La Salle, Dimitt and Zavalla, one.

Seventy-sixth District—San Patricio, Live Oak, Karnes, Wilson and Atascosa, one.

Seventy-seventh District—Cherokee, Rusk, Panola, Shelby and Harrison, one.

" PROCEEDINGS.

"Sec. 29. The enacting clause of all laws shall be: 'Be it enacted by the Legislature of the State of Texas.'

"Sec. 30. No law shall be passed except by bill, and no bill shall be so amended, in its passage through either house, as to change its original purpose.

"Sec. 31. Bills may originate in either house, and, when passed by such house, may be amended, altered or rejected by the other.

"Sec. 32. No bill shall have the force of a law until it has been read on three several days in each house and free discussion allowed thereon; but in cases of imperative necessity (which necessity shall be stated in a preamble), four-fifths of the house in which the bill may be pending may suspend this rule, the yeas and nays being taken on the question of suspension and entered upon the journals.

"Sec. 33. All bills for raising revenue shall originate in the House of Representatives, but the Senate may amend or reject them as other bills.

"Sec. 34. After a bill has been considered and defeated by either house of the Legislature, no bill or resolution, containing the same substance, shall be passed into a law during the same session.

"Sec. 35. No bill (except general appropriation bills, which may embrace the various subjects and accounts, for and on ac-

11

count of which moneys are appropriated,) shall contain more than one subject, which shall be expressed in its title. But if any subject shall be embraced in an act, which shall not be expressed in the title, such act shall be void only as to so much thereof, as shall not be so expressed.

" Sec. 36. No law shall be revived or amended by reference to its title; but in such case the act revived, or the section or sections amended, shall be re-enacted and published at length.

" Sec. 37. No bill shall be considered unless it has been first referred to a committee, returned therefrom, and printed for the use of the members.

" Sec. 38. The presiding officer of each house shall, in the presence of the house over which he presides, sign all bills and joint resolutions passed by the Legislature, after their titles have been publicly read before signing, and the fact of signing shall be entered on the journal.

" Sec. 39. No law passed by the Legislature, except the general appropriation act, shall take effect or go into force until ninety days after the adjournment of the session at which it was enacted, unless in the case of an emergency (which emergency must be expressed in the preamble or in the body of the act), the Legislature shall, by a vote of two-thirds of all the members elected to each house, otherwise direct; said vote to be taken by yeas and nays and entered upon the journals.

" Sec. 40. When the Legislature shall be convened in special session, there shall be no legislation upon subjects other than those designated in the proclamation of the Governor calling such session; and no such session shall be of longer duration than thirty days.

" Sec. 41. Every bill which shall have passed both houses of the Legislature, shall be presented to the Governor, who, if he approve, shall sign it; but if not, he shall return it, with his objections, to the house in which it originated; such house shall enter the objections at large upon its journals and proceed to re-consider such bill. If, after such reconsideration, two-thirds of the members present shall agree to pass the bill, it shall be sent, with the objections, to the other house, by whom it shall likewise be re-considered. If approved by two-thirds of the members present of that house, it shall become a law; but in such cases the votes of both houses shall be taken by yeas and nays, and the names of the members voting for or against the bill, shall be entered on the journals of each house respectively. If any bill shall not be returned by the Governor within ten days, Sundays excepted, after it shall have been presented to him, the same shall become a law in like manner as if he had signed it, unless the Legislature, by their adjournment, prevent its return, in which case it shall be a law, unless he shall file the same with his objections in the office of the Secretary of State, and give notice thereof by public proclamation within thirty days after such adjournment. The Governor may approve any appropriation, and disapprove any other appropriation in the same bill. In such case he shall, in signing the bill, designate the appropriations disapproved, and return a copy of such appropriations, with his objections, to the house in which the bill shall have originated; and the same proceedings shall then be had as in the case of other bills disapproved by the Governor; but if the Legislature has adjourned before the bill is returned to the house, he shall return the same to the Secretary of State, with his objections.

"REQUIREMENTS AND LIMITATIONS.

"Sec. 42. The Legislature shall pass such laws as may be necessary to carry into effect the provisions of this constitution.

"Sec. 43. The first session of the Legislature under this constitution shall provide for revising, digesting or codifying and publishing the laws, civil and criminal; and a like revision, digest or codification and publication may be made every ten years thereafter.

"Sec. 44. The Legislature shall provide by law for the compensation of all officers, servants, agents and public contractors not provided for by this constitution, but shall not grant extra compensation to any officer, agent, servant or public contractor after such public service shall have been performed, or contract entered into for the performance of the same; nor grant, by appropriation or otherwise, any amount of money out of the Treasury of the State, to any individual, on a claim, real or pretended, when the same shall not have been provided for by pre-existing law.

"Sec. 45. The power to change the venue in civil and criminal cases shall be vested in the courts, to be exercised in such manner as shall be provided by law; and the Legislature shall pass laws for that purpose.

"Sec. 46. The Legislature shall, at its first session after the adoption of this constitution, enact effective vagrant laws.

"Sec. 47. The Legislature shall pass laws prohibiting the establishment of lotteries or gift-enterprises in this State, as well as the sale of tickets in lotteries, gift-enterprises or other evasions involving the lottery principle, established or existing in other States.

"Sec. 48. The Legislature shall not have the right to levy

taxes or impose burdens upon the people, except to raise revenue sufficient for the economical administration of the government, in which shall be included the following purposes:

" The payment of all interest upon the bonded debt of the State, that may become due during the term for which each Legislature is elected; the benefit of the sinking fund, which shall not be more than two per centum of the public debt; the support of public schools; the payment of the cost of assessing and collecting the revenue; the payment of all officers, agents and employes of the State government, and all incidental expenses connected therewith; the support of the eleemosynary institutions of the State; the enforcement of quarantine regulations on the coast of Texas; the protection of the frontier.

" Sec. 49. The Legislature shall have no power to contract or authorize the contracting of any debt or liability on behalf of the State, (except in cases of insurrection or invasion, and then only to the amount of five hundred thousand dollars) or to issue bonds or other evidences of indebtedness therefor, except in the renewal of existing bonds, when they can not be paid at maturity out of the sinking fund or other resources.

" Sec. 50. The Legislature shall have no power to give or to lend, or to authorize the giving or lending, of the credit of the State in aid of, or to any person, association or corporation, whether municipal or other, or to pledge the credit of the State in any manner whatsoever for the payment of the liabilities, present or prospective, of any individual, association of individuals, municipal or other corporation whatsoever.

" Sec. 51. The Legislature shall have no power to make any grant, or to authorize the making of any grant, of public money to any individual, association of individuals, municipal or other corporation whatsoever; *provided,* that this shall not be so construed as to prevent the grant of aid in a case of public calamity.

" Sec. 52. The Legislature shall have no power to authorize any county, city, town or other political corporation, or subdivision of the State, to lend its credit or to grant public money or thing of value in aid of, or to any individual, association or corporation whatsoever, or to become a stockholder in such corporation, association or company.

" Sec. 53. The Legislature shall have no power to grant, or to authorize any county or municipal authority to grant any extra compensation, fee or allowance to a public officer, agent, servant or contractor, after service has been rendered, or a contract has been entered into and performed in whole or in part; nor pay, nor authorize the payment of any claim hereafter created against any county or municipality of the State, under any agreement or contract made without express authority of law.

"Sec. 54. The Legislature shall have no power to release or alienate any lien held by the State upon any railroad, or in anywise change the tenor or meaning, or pass an act explanatory thereof; but the same shall be enforced in accordance with the original terms upon which it was acquired.

"Sec. 55. The Legislature shall have no power to release or extinguish, or authorize the releasing or extinguishing, in whole or in part, the indebtedness, liability or obligation of any corporation or individual to this State, or to any county or other municipal corporation therein.

"Sec. 56. The Legislature shall not pass any local or special law authorizing the creation, extension or impairing of liens; regulating the affairs of counties, cities, wards or school districts; changing the names of persons or places; changing the venue in civil or criminal cases; authorizing the laying out, opening, altering or maintaining roads, highways, streets or alleys; relating to ferries or bridges, or incorporating ferry or bridge companies, except for the erection of bridges crossing streams which form boundaries between this and any other State; vacating roads, town plats, streets or alleys; relating to cemeteries, grave-yards or public grounds not of the State; authorizing the adoption or legitimation of children; locating or changing county seats; incorporating cities, towns or villages, or changing their charters; for the opening and conducting of elections, or fixing or changing the places of voting; granting divorces; creating offices or prescribing the powers and duties of officers in counties, cities, towns, election or school districts; changing the law of descent or succession; regulating the practice or jurisdiction of, or changing the rules of evidence in any judicial proceeding or inquiry before courts, Justices of Peace, Sheriffs, Commissioners, arbitrators or other tribunals, or providing or changing methods for the collection of debts, or the enforcing of judgments, or prescribing the effect of judicial sales of real estate; regulating the fees or extending the powers and duties of Aldermen, Justices of the Peace, Magistrates or Constables; regulating the management of public schools, the building or repairing of school houses and the raising of money for such purposes; fixing the rate of interest; affecting the estates of minors or persons under disability; remitting fines, penalties and forfeitures, or refunding moneys legally paid into the treasury; exempting property from taxation; regulating labor, trade, mining and manufacturing; declaring any named person of age;

extending the time for the assessment or collection of taxes, or otherwise relieving any assessor or collector of taxes from the due performance of his official duties, or his securities from liability; giving effect to informal or invalid wills or deeds; summoning or empanneling grand or petit juries; for limitation of civil actions; and in all other cases, when a general law can be made applicable, no local or special law shall be enacted.

"Sec. 57. No local or special law shall be passed, unless notice of the intention to apply therefor shall have been published in the locality, where the matter or thing to be affected may be situated, which notice shall state the substance of the contemplated law, and shall be published at least thirty days prior to the introduction into the Legislature of such bill and in the manner to be provided by law; the evidence of such notice having been published shall be exhibited in the Legislature, before such act shall be passed.

Article 1, section 16, of the constitution of Georgia, declares that "no person shall be abused in being arrested, while under arrest, or in prison."

The constitution of Delaware, article 1, section 11, declares that in the construction of jails "proper regard shall be had to the health of the prisoners," and the constitution of Tennessee, in addition to the requirement that prisons shall be "*safe and comfortable,*" requires the Legislature to provide for the "*humane treatment of prisoners.*"

Other reference might be given, but these will suffice to show that the insertion of the section prepared by us on this subject would not be the introduction of a novelty in organic law.

We think in view of our recent history it would be eminently proper to declare in this solemn form the enlightened and humane views we hold upon this subject, and in so doing lay down an unchangeable rule for the guidance of our law-makers and courts in affording protection to this unfortunate class of our people. We can not, if we would, shut our eyes to the fact that a convict is still a living being; that he has a body that can be starved and tortured, and feelings that can be wantonly lacerated. When he enters the walls of a prison to serve out his sentence for a giving time he is in the custody of the State. To the State only can he appeal for food and for protection against brutal outrage. He has offended against the law and must pay the penalty. Beyond requiring him to pay this penalty, and while so doing, as far as possible to be self-sustaining, the State has no demands upon him. To the penalty should not be added needless misery and degradation.

To impose harsh conditions not necessarily embraced in the due execution of the sentence, is to inflict an injury which naturally awakens in the breast of the sentenced a feeling of hatred towards society itself, and produces a demoralization which leads to crimes of a worse character after the appointed term is served out.   Take a man who had always borne the character of a good citizen, who, in the transport of passion, commits an offense which consigns him to the penitentiary—starve him, apply the lash, ride him on " the horse," in other words, treat him as a brute—and not as a human being during his confinement, and you produce a feeling of despair and desperation which makes him ripe for any crime when his prison doors are opened.   In such cases does not society itself offend?

We have also prepared a section upon the subject of a house of correction for juvenile offenders.   We think it should be made the duty of the Legislature at its first session after the adoption of this constitution, to provide for the immediate establishment of such an institution, in which all juvenile offenders under the age of eighteen years, not punishable under the direction of the county authorities, shall be confined, and preventing any such offenders, except in case of sentence for life, from being sent to the penitentiary.   The constitutions of several of the States contain provisions upon this subject.   A list of some twenty States, with the character of the reformatory institutions established by them, will be found on page 128 of the report of the Commissioners.

Twenty years ago our State committed itself to the policy of adopting such an institution by making full provision therefor in the Penal Code, art. 187 *et seq.*   Our legislators then declared that the principal design of a house of correction was to reform and improve the moral condition and character of juvenile offenders, and that all officers charged with the duty of the management and discipline thereof should use kind and presuasive measures to produce the reformation of the persons under their care.   The necessity for action in this direction is now urgent. From the best information we can obtain, the number of convicts now confined in the Penitentiary, under twenty-one years of age, is not less than one thousand, some of them are mere children, and in a statement of the Inspector, furnished the Commission, two of them are reported as being under *ten years of age.*

The mingling of young persons with hardened and depraved convicts can but prove pernicious.   No better school to educate them in crime could be devised.   In the end society must lose by so manifest a disregard of a wise philanthropy and indiffer-

ence to its best interests.   To take a mere child for driving stock
from its accustomed range, or even for stealing a yearling, worth
perhaps two dollars (things that some of his neighbors may have
grown rich by doing, and whose wealth enables them to successfully defy the law) and send him to the Penitentiary, not only
disgracing him for life but placing him beyond the reach of
moral instruction and in daily association with the vile, the des-
perate and the hardened criminal, is, it seems to us, a great wrong,
a wrong to the youthful offender and an injury to society.   The
percentage of juvenile convicts sent to houses of correction and
who are afterwards returned, is very small compared to the number of those of the older offenders confined in the penitentiaries.
With the former the statistics show that reformatory efforts have
been crowned with success.   We sincerely trust that the Convention will agree with us as to the importance of requiring the establishment of such an institution as is contemplated in the section prepared by us.   We have now about two thousand penitentiary convicts in this State, and the number is rapidly increasing—perhaps in no State in the Union is the number so
large.   Their management and the utilization of their labor present questions for consideration that may well arrest the attention of this body.   The Fourteenth Legislature at its last session
passed a law for the building of two additional penitentiaries,
and we understand they have already been located.   If we are
to judge of the probable cost of these additional penitentiaries,
machinery, etc., by the cost of the one at Huntsville, the State
will soon be called upon to make an outlay of something like a
million of dollars, to say nothing of the money required to pay a
retinue of officers and guards for their management.   If it is the
policy to keep all convicts confined in prison walls and matters
go on as they are now, several more penitentiaries will soon
be required.

"ARTICLE —.

"MODE OF CALLING A CONVENTION AND AMENDING THE CONSTI-
TUTION OF THIS STATE.

"Section 1. The Legislature, by a vote of three-fourths of all
the members of each house, with the approval of the Governor,
shall have the power to call a convention of the people, for the
purpose of altering, amending, or reforming the constitution of
this State; the manner of electing delegates to the convention,
the time and place of assembling them, to be regulated by the
law calling such convention.

"Sec. 2. The Legislature, at any biennial session, by a vote
of two-thirds of all the members of each house, may propose

amendments to the constitution, to be•voted upon by the qualified electors for members of the House of Representatives, which proposed amendments shall be duly published once a week for four weeks, commencing at least three months before the next election for representatives to the Legislature, in one weekly newspaper of each county, in which such a newspaper may be published; and it shall be the duty of the several returning officers at said election, to open a poll for, and make returns to the Secretary of State, of the number of legal votes cast, at said election, for and against said amendment; and if more than one be proposed, then the number of votes cast for and against each of them; and if it shall appear from said return that a majority of the votes cast upon said amendment or amendments, have been cast in favor of the same, and two-thirds of each house of the Legislature, at the next regular session thereafter, shall ratify said proposed amendment or amendments, so voted upon by the people, the same shall be valid, to all intents and purposes, as part of the constitution of the State of Texas; *provided,* that the said proposed amendments shall, at each of said sessions, have been read on three several days in each house of the Legislature, and the vote thereupon shall have been taken by yeas and nays; *and provided further,* that the rule in the above proviso shall never be suspended by either house.

Mr. Russell, of Harrison, gave notice of a minority report from the Committee on Legislative Department.

Mr. Brown moved that 400 copies of the report and proceedings just read be printed for the use of the Convention.

Mr. Wade moved to amend by substituting 200 copies.

Mr. Brown's motion carried, and 400 copies ordered.

Mr. West presented a memorial from the Texas State Medical Association and physicians of Travis county.

Referred to Committee on State Affairs.

Mr. Cook, of Gonzales, submitted the following report:

Committee Room, }
Austin, September 17, 1875. }

To the Hon. E. B. Pickett, President of the Convention:

Your Committee on Printing and Contingent Expenses, in pursuance of resolution of this date adopted by the Convention, have contracted with John D. Logan & Co., publishers of the *Evening News,* for publishing the daily journals of the Convention in the *Evening News,* and to deliver to each delegate daily five copies of the same, for the sum of eleven dollars and twenty-five cents ($11 25) per day, and have instructed me to report accordingly.   W. D. S. Cook, Chairman.

On motion of Mr. Mills the report was adopted.

Mr. McCormick submitted the following report:

COMMITTEE ROOM, ⎫
AUSTIN, September 18, 1875. ⎭

To the Hon. E. B. Pickett, President of the Convention:

Your committee, to whom was referred the resolution to inquire into the present management of the State Penitentiary, and report what action, if any, is necessary to be taken by this Convention in relation thereto, beg leave to submit the following report and recommendations:

During the past summer the public mind was greatly excited over the alleged mismanagement of the Penitentiary by the present lessees. Charges, apparently well founded, of cruelty to and abuse of convicts were in general circulation. His Excellency, Governor Coke, in obedience to a public demand, and acting upon information in his possession, which fully justified, if it did not impel the course pursued by him, promptly appointed a special commission, composed of Hon. A. J. Peeler, Assistant Attorney General, and the Hons. D. H. Triplett and Tillman Smith, to make a thorough investigation into the matter and report thereon. This commission visited in person the Penitentiary at Huntsville and various points at which convicts were employed outside of the walls. Their report, copies of which can be obtained by the members of this Convention from the Secretary of State, is full and exhaustive, and embraces among other things, the history of the present lease, with copies thereof, the laws of the State concerning the Penitentiary, the condition of the Penitentiary when it went into the hands of the lessees, a schedule of the property, its value, etc., turned over to them, the expenditures made by the lessees in the way of improvements, and their estimated value, the manner in which the various officials have discharged their duties, and the manner in which the convicts have been fed, clothed, lodged, punished, etc. We have examined this report with care, and have no reason to doubt the statements made or the correctness of the conclusions reached by the commissioners, who seem to have discharged their duty with great ability, faithfulness and strict impartiality. The evidence taken by them is on file in the Governor's office, and was placed by His Excellency at our disposal, but owing to its voluminousness, the length of time required to examine it in detail, the fact that the report of the commission gives in brief its purport and effect, we have thought it neither desireable nor necessary to encumber our report with extracts therefrom.

That the convicts have not been properly fed, clothed and lodged; that they have been, in many instances, subjected to cruel and shocking punishments, is established beyond doubt.

Since the report of the Commissioners, matters seem to have improved somewhat, except as to food—this at times has been wholly insufficient. The Governor, as we learn, has been in constant apprehension that he would, on this and other accounts, be compelled to resume possession for the State. Stringent rules and by-laws for the government of the Penitentiary, framed to secure, as far as possible, humane treatment of the convicts, have been put in operation by the Governor and Directors. Excessive and harsh punishments, at the hands of irresponsible guards, are now seldom, if at all, inflicted. For the sake of humanity and for the credit of the State, it can but be gratifying that reforms, which were so much needed, were so promptly inaugurated.

But we do not believe it possible, under the present leasing system, with the convicts scattered about over the State, on railroads and plantations, as they must necessarily be, owing to the want of capacity of the buildings at Huntsville, to secure the convicts proper treatment. Not only is it out of the question to properly care for and protect them from abuse while this is the case, but reformatory measures are wholly impracticable.

The latter we regard (and it has been so declared by our laws from the beginning) as one of the chief objects of punishment, and should not be lost sight of. While there is a considerable difference of opinion as to the positive and general beneficial effects of moral and secular instruction upon convicts, all agree that what is known as a "good-time law," accomplishes much in the way of stimulating them to obedience to prison rules and regulations, and to good conduct. By this law the convict who is industrious and observant of the rules and regulations of the prison, is allowed certain time by which his sentence is shortened. A copy of such a law, with some comments thereon, will be found on page 119 of the report of the Commissioners.

We think this reformatory measure, which is now adopted by nearly all the States, is of sufficient importance to direct, by constitutional provision, its adoption in this State, and have prepared a section, to be incorporated in its appropriate place, not only requiring the passage of such a law, but authorizing the Legislature in their discretion to extend its benefits to persons now undergoing sentence. Another section has also been prepared by us, which we think ought to be incorporated in the constitution, which declares in substance that all convicts and persons undergoing sentence of imprisonment in any penitentiary, house of correction, house of refuge, jail, or other place in this State, shall be fed, clothed, lodged and treated with care and humanity; that no greater amount of labor shall be required of them than their health and strength may render proper; that they shall not be subjected to cruel, unusual and degrading punishment, and requiring the Legislature to pass appropriate laws to secure all such persons humane treatment and to punish all violators of such provision or the laws which may be passed for the enforcement thereof. In the opinion of some the insertion of such a provision in the fundamental law may seem too much like legislation. We find, however, in the constitution of New Hampshire, part 1, article 18, this provision: "All penalties ought to be proportionate to the nature of the offense. No wise Legislature will affix the same punishment to the crimes of theft, forgery and the like which they do to those of murder and treason. Where the same undistinguishing severity is exerted against all offenses, the people are led to forget the real distinction in the crimes themselves, and to commit the most flagrant with as little compunction as they do the lightest offenses. For the same reason, a multitude of sanguinary laws is both impolitic and unjust, *the true design of all punishment being to reform,* not to *exterminate mankind.*"

We think it is time to pause before going further in this direction. We believe that the expense of erecting more than one additional penitentiary can be avoided. To begin at the beginning the fault lies, to a great extent, in our criminal laws. For many offenses for which persons should be punished in their county, by being compelled to work in chain gangs, if necessary, on the public roads or in county work houses, they are now sent to the penitentiary.

We have heard of instances where persons, some of them children, have been sent to the penitentiary for the theft from a house of a box of matches, a plug of tobacco, or some other article of insignificant value. With proper changes in our criminal law, and applying, if need be, through authorized legislation or executive pardon the benefits of such changes to those already convicted, and who have served a sufficient length of time to pay the penalty of their offenses, according to the more just standard to be adopted, and further by extending the benefit of the "good-time law" to those already convicted, and by removing from the penitentiary to a house of correction all the juvenile convicts. We believe that the present penitentiary will hold all the convicts that ought to be thus confined. We think before any additional penitentiaries are built that these measures should be adopted, and especially. a house of correction established for the younger offenders.   Then if the present Penitentiary be found insufficient, a new one could be built, if the excess was not large, some of the convicts under proper regulations to prevent their escape and to insure their proper treatment, might be employed on public works.   The labor of a considerable number could no doubt be utilized in the building of the house of correction referred to.

Before concluding our report we desire to again advert to the fact that the Penitentiary may suddenly be thrown back upon the State.   If the lessees should be unable to feed and clothe the convicts, no other alternative would be left.   We have reason to believe that the Governor has been in constant apprehension of such a contingency.   With two thousand convicts suddenly thrown upon his hands, without a dollar with which to buy food and clothing or employ guards, his position would be most embarrassing.   He has sought and will we believe continue to avert such an issue, but still it may come, and, it seems to us, the Convention should take such action as may be in its power to enable him, if the State is forced to resume possession, to do so.   We should, in justice to ourselves, have taken more time in the preparation of this report, but for the fact that we thought it important to bring the matters herein contained to the attention of the Convention at an early day, that they might receive mature consideration.

We respectfully ask to be discharged from the further consideration of this subject.

SECTIONS PROPOSED TO BE INCORPORATED IN THE NEW CONSTITUTION AND RECOMMENDED BY THE COMMITTEE.

" Section ——. All convicts and persons undergoing sentence of imprisonment in any penitentiary, house of correction, house of refuge, jail, or other place in this State. shall be fed, clothed, lodged and treated with care and humanity. and no greater amount of labor shall be required of them than their health and strength may render proper, nor shall they be subjected to any cruel, unusual or degrading punishment : and the Legislature shall pass appropriate laws to secure to all such persons humane treatment and to punish all violators of this section and of the laws passed for the enforcement hereof.

" Sec. ——. The Legislature shall pass such 'good-time' and other laws as will encourage all convicts and others sentenced to imprisonment to industry, obedience and good conduct during their confinement, and may extend the benefits of such laws to all now undergoing sentence.

"Sec. ——. The Legislature shall, at its first session after the adoption of this constitution, provide for the establishment of a house of correction, in which all juvenile offenders under the age of eighteen years, not punishable under the direction of county authorities, shall be confined, and such juvenile offenders shall not be sent to a penitentiary unless sentenced to imprisonment for life."

GEO. McCORMICK, for Committee.

Mr. Mills offered the following resolution:

WHEREAS, The present Constitutional Convention having reduced their salaries three-eighths of the original amount, or that which was paid members of the Legislature, and have promised their constituents and the people generally to practice rigid retrenchment; therefore be it

Resolved, That it is the sense of this Convention that all State officers created by the new constitution shall be subject to a like reduction. That the salary of the Governor shall be $3,125; that of Supreme Judges $2,812 50 each, and of District Judges $2,187 50 each, and all other State officers in like proportion.

Mr. Mills moved to adopt the resolution.

Mr. Flournoy moved its reference to Committee on Stock and Stock-raising.

On motion of Mr. Martin, of Navarro, the resolution was referred to Committee on Executive Department.

Mr. Ford offered the following resolution:

Resolved, That the Committee on Printing and Contingent Expenses be instructed to inquire into the expediency of printing the new constitution in the Spanish language, and report by resolution or otherwise.

Adopted.

Mr. Robertson, of Bell, offered the following resolution:

Resolved, That the Commissioner of the General Land Office be requested to furnish the President of this Convention with a tabular statement of the number of acres of land, the titles to which are on file in said office, issued by the King of Spain, the Viceroys of Mexico, the Republic of Mexico, the State of Tamaulipas, and the State of Coahuila and Texas, previous to the second day of March, 1836.

Also, the number of acres of land granted by the Republic of Texas, either as head-rights, bounty, donation, scrip or otherwise.

Also, the number of acres patented by the Republic of Texas.

Also, the number of acres granted by the authorities of the State of Texas, either as head-rights, bounty, donation or otherwise, railroads excepted.

Also, the number of acres patented by the State of Texas on all classes of claims, railroads excepted.

Also, the number of acres of land of all classes of claims, (railroads excepted), the field notes of which are on file in the General Land Office, but on which no patents have issued.

Also, the number of acres of land granted to railroads, canals, ditches, and the clearing out of rivers and bayous, respectively, since the second day of March, 1836, up to the present time.

Also, the number of acres, the certificates to which have been issued to railroad, canal, ditch, river and bayou companies, respectively.

Also, the number of acres that have been patented to said companies.

Also, the number of acres, the field notes of which have been returned to the General Land Office by virtue of said certificates, the patents to which have not been issued.

Also, a statement of the annual expenses of said office; and

Also, a statement of the annual revenues of said office.

Also, the number of acres in the entire area of Texas, according to the Land Office computation.

Adopted.

On motion of Mr. Fleming the Convention adjourned till 9 o'clock, A. M., to-morrow.

FOURTEENTH DAY.

Hall of Representatives. }
Austin, Texas, September 21, 1875. }

Convention met pursuant to adjournment; roll called; quorum present. Prayer by Rev. W. H. D. Carrington.

Journals of yesterday read and adopted.

On motion of Mr. McCabe, Mr. Reynolds was temporarily excused on account of sickness.

Mr. Flournoy, Chairman of the Committee on Municipal Corporations, made the following report:

COMMITTEE ROOM, }
AUSTIN, September 21, 1875. }

To the Hon. E. B. Pickett, President of the Convention:

SIR—Your Committee on Municipal Corporations, to whom was referred the following resolution—

"*Resolved,* That in incorporated towns no one shall vote for any municipal officer or any other election pertaining to said corporation, unless he has $500 worth of taxable property; in incorporated towns or cities three assessors, appointed or elected, shall annually assess all the property of the citizens residing within the limits of said corporation; corporations keeping their roads in their limits in order shall be exempt from all road laws,"

Have instructed me to report back the same, with the suggestion that it be referred to the Committee on Suffrage.

All of which is respectfully submitted,

GEORGE FLOURNOY, Chairman.

Also—

COMMITTEE ROOM, }
AUSTIN, September 21, 1875. }

To the Hon. E. B. Pickett, President of the Convention:

SIR—Your Committee on Municipal Corporations, to whom was referred the enclosed resolutions, have instructed me to report that they have under consideration the first section of said resolutions, and suggest that the second and third sections thereof be referred to the Committee on Counties and County Lands.

All of which is respectfully submitted.

GEORGE FLOURNOY, Chairman.

The Select Committee, to whom was referred the resolution and proposed ordinance providing for the postponement of the election for members of the Legislature, presented the following report:

COMMITTEE ROOM, }
AUSTIN, September 20, 1875. }

To the Hon. E. B. Pickett, President of the Convention:

The undersigned, constituting a majority of the select committee, to whom was referred a resolution and also a proposed ordinance providing for the postponement of the election for members of the Legislature and other officers, to be held according to the existing laws of the State, on the first Tuesday of December, 1875, beg leave to make the following report:

They have carefully considered the subject, and have availed themselves of all sources of information that were accessible to them. It is not their purpose, nor do they deem it necessary, that they should enter in this connection at length into the consideration of the question as to the extent of the powers of this Convention, and under what circumstances or conditions it can exercise such powers as it may possess. In the matter under consideration, they have arrived at the conclusion that this Convention has the power, and that it is its duty to the people of the State to postpone said election, and the assembling of the Legislature in January next.

One of the main abuses that this body has been assembled by the people to inquire into and correct, is the almost unlimited power now vested in the Legislative Department of this State by the present constitution.

The Convention has directed one of its standing committees to examine into and report upon the existing abuses in that department, and to suggest the remedy for them.

This duty that committee has performed, and their report is now before this body. They recommend very important and necessary changes in the organization of that department of the State government, restricting its powers, altering its sessions, the number of its members, and making many other important alterations.

That most of the changes recommended will be adopted by this body and accepted by the people of the State, there is no doubt.

While then this body, in the plain discharge of its duties, is in the act of thoroughly reforming and reorganizing this branch of the government, it seems to the majority of the committee, not only to be proper but to constitute an important part of the duty enjoined on them by their election to postpone for the present the meeting of the Legislature, when its assembling in January next could have no other effect than to create confusion, conflict, embarrassment, and add greatly to the expenses of the people of the State, without any corresponding benefit to be derived from their assembling together.

It is to be presumed that the Legislature, that passed the joint resolution providing for taking the popular vote as to the assembling of the present Convention, would have provided a mode of obviating the difficulties and embarrassments attending an election in December, to the convening of the Legislature in January next.

But it was a subject practically beyond legislative control, for

12

it was impossible for that body to foresee and in advance determine at what period this body would end its labors, or on what day it would submit its work to the people. No action could then be taken by them, because it was a matter for which they could not provide. It was a subject intimately connected with that of the submission of the work of the present Convention to the people, a duty which specially devolves upon the Convention. If they believe the election in December next presents an obstruction or greatly embarrasses the people, and will in some measure tend to prevent them from passing fairly and fully upon the merits of the instrument submitted to them, it is within the scope of their authority, and clearly within the line of their duty, to take all the steps necessary and proper to enable the will of the people to be freely and fairly ascertained.

The direct expense to the State arising from ordering the election, issuing proper notices, preparing, printing and distributing instructions and forms to the different officers of the State charged with the due execution of the election laws, together with the expense of an entirely new registration, will not fall short of $30,000, and may greatly exceed that amount. The mileage and per diem of the members of the Legislature alone may, and probably will, reach the sum of $100,000; that of the three last Legislatures exceeded that sum. The other contingent expenses will probably reach the sum of $30,000.

The expense and loss of time to the voters in the State, would not fall short of $150,000. In addition to this, it must be borne in mind that there is practically no limitation on the power of the Legislature to create a public debt, and but little limitation on their power to appropriate public money. We may safely assume that other expenses incurred by them will increase the estimate of expenses above made, and that the total expense to the people and the State, of this unnecessary and useless election and assembling of the Legislature will exceed $300,000. Furthermore, under the act of Congress, of 25th July, 1866, providing that the Legislature of each State, which is chosen next preceding the expiration of the term for which any United States senator from such State is chosen, was elected, shall, on the second Monday after they meet, elect a United States senator; it becomes the duty of the Legislature which meets on the second Monday in January next, to elect a United States senator. If, prior to the fourth of March, 1877, a new Legislature should assemble, organized under the provisions of the constitution that may be framed by this Convention, it would also be beyond all doubt a Legislature chosen next preceding the expiration of the time for which one of the United States senators from Texas was elected, and it would also be their duty, under this act of Congress, to elect a United States senator. If they did not exercise this power, a very serious question would arise as to whether the Legislature that met in January, 1875, was the proper body to elect a United States senator. If the Legislature, organized under the provisions of the constitution framed by this body, should elect a United States senator, then it would result that there would be two persons, both elected and both claiming at the same time to be duly elected, to the Senate of the United States.

By refusing to postpone the election in December next, we become directly responsible to the people for all the expenses incurred and other evil consequences resulting from this state of affairs.

Again, if the Convention should work harmoniously together, there is no reason why they may not complete their work and have a constitution ready for submission to the people by the first of November next. The Convention of 1845, whose duties were very arduous, involving as it did a change from an independent Republic to a State of the Union, only sat fifty-three days. If, then, we can in sixty days complete our work, there is no good reason why it should not be submitted to the people on the first Monday in January. This would give them sixty days to consider it. The Convention of 1845 did not give as much as sixty days' notice. That constitution was framed on the 27th of August, 1845, and ratified by the people on the second Monday in October, 1845. The Convention of 1866 submitted their work to the people with notice of only sixty days. Since then the means of communication throughout the State have greatly increased, and now within sixty days information can be conveyed throughout the State as fully as it could be done in ninety days in 1845 or 1866. If, then, in accordance with approved precedents in this State, this body should complete its work in sixty days and submit it for the acceptance or rejection of the people in January next, as we believe can be done, and probably will be done, we would have the spectacle of a Legislature assembled at a cost of thousands of dollars, to our already tax-burthened people to accomplish nothing, and whose official existence, if the constitution was submitted to the people on the second Monday in January, and on that day accepted by them, would end on the day that it commenced. By virtue of the power which this Convention has to regulate the time, manner and conditions on which its work shall be submitted to the people, we believe it can prevent the occurrence of such a state of things; it is a power incidental to and growing out of the express and unqualified grant of power to them from the people to frame and provide for putting in operation the constitution. Its exercise is necessary in order that the people may be able at the least possible expense and without embarrassment from other matters growing out of the assembling of the Legislature, to vote fully and fairly on the merits of the instrument submitted to them.

The undersigned have examined the subject in its various aspects, and the ordinance which they herewith submit makes provision so that in case the proposed constitution is rejected, elections for members of the Fifteenth Legislature and other State, district and county officers may be ordered by the Governor. It also provides for the continuance in office of the present incumbents until their successors are elected and qualified.

Should there arise any great unforeseen public emergency before the constitution is voted upon, the Governor, under the provisions of the ordinance reported, would have the power by his proclamation to convene the Fourteenth Legislature in extraordinary session.

The majority of the committee can not see how or in what manner any conflict of authority or serious inconvenience or injury to the public interest can result from the passage of the ordinance contemplated, nor have they any reason to apprehend any conflict from any quarter. On the contrary, they believe it will be the duty of every officer of the State, from the highest to the lowest, to co-operate earnestly and cheerfully with the Convention in saving this heavy and worse than useless expense to the State, and in preventing all the inconvenience, conflict, embarrassment and confusion that will be certain to flow from the election in December next.

It is to be regretted that the committee are not all of one mind on this important matter. But the power of the Convention to pass the ordinance in question appears so well founded and so clear, and the duty of exercising that power so imperative, that they do not hesitate to recommend the adoption of the accompanying ordinance, which they have prepared as a substitute for the resolutions and ordinance that were referred to them.

Respectfully submitted.

CHARLES DeMORSE,
F. S. STOCKDALE,
C. S. WEST,
JOHN HENRY BROWN.

While I did not participate in the preparation of the ordinance and report on this subject, I concur with the majority of the committee in their conclusions.

JOHN II. REAGAN.

ORDINANCE.

"AN ORDINANCE POSTPONING THE GENERAL ELECTION OF DECEMBER, A. D. 1875, AND FOR OTHER PURPOSES.

"WHEREAS, It is provided by law under the existing Constitution that a general election for members of the Legislature, Assessors and Collectors, and some other officers, shall be held on the first Tuesday in December, A. D. 1875; and

"WHEREAS, By authority of law and the sanction of the people, delegates, legally elected, are now assembled in Convention to frame a new constitution for the State of Texas; and

"WHEREAS, The election of a Legislature and other officers, and the coming together of the Legislature to hold its session under the existing laws and constitution, are, for the time being, unnecessary, and will cause great public expense, and are likely to produce confusion in putting a new constitution in operation, if one shall be established; together with doubts as to the validity of the election of a United States Senator if two Legislatures shall assemble during the next year; and can only aggravate the evils, to remedy which this Convention was assembled by the people; and

"WHEREAS, It is the duty of the Convention to save to the State the unnecessary expense, and to prevent the occurrence of the other evils aforesaid; now, therefore,

"*Be it ordained by the people of the State of Texas, in Convention assembled,* That the holding of the election as provided by the laws under the existing constitution, to be held on the first Tuesday in December, A. D. 1875, be, and the same is hereby suspended and postponed; and all officers of this State are hereby prohibited from holding, and from, in any manner, aiding in the holding of said election; and any election held on that day is hereby declared to be void and of no effect.

"Sec. 2. The terms of office of the members of the present Legislature, and of all other officers, whether State, district or county officers, whose terms of office by existing laws or constitution will expire on said first Tuesday in December, A. D. 1875, or at any time thereafter, before a general election is held, be, and the same are hereby extended; and said members of the Legislature and other officers shall remain in office and continue to exercise the powers and perform the duties of their places and offices, under existing laws and pursuant to the existing constitution until their successors are duly elected and qualified in accordance with the further provisions of this ordinance, or until they are superceded by the establishment of a new constitution.

"Sec. 3. In case the new constitution, when submitted to the people, be rejected by them, then the Governor of the State of Texas shall, within ten days after the official promulgation of such rejection, issue his official proclamation, fixing a day for a general election, to be held in accordance with existing laws, giving sixty days notice of such election, at which election there shall be elected all the members of the Legislature and other officers, which, but for this ordinance, would have been chosen on the first Tuesday in December, A. D. 1875; and the election so held shall be deemed and taken to be, and it is hereby declared shall be, a general election under the existing laws and constitution of the State of Texas. And the Governor shall also name in said proclamation the day on which the Legislature shall assemble. When the Legislature shall be assembled pursuant to the proclamation of the Governor, its session shall be taken and deemed to be, and it is hereby declared that it shall be, the first session of the Fifteenth Legislature under the existing constitution and laws of this State. And the terms of office of the members of the Legislature and other officers elected according to the provisions of this ordinance shall expire and determine at the same time and in the same manner as if they had been elected on said first Tuesday in December, A. D. 1875."

Mr. Ballinger submitted the following report:

To the Hon. E. B. Pickett, President of the Convention:

The undersigned members of the Select Committee, to which was referred ordinances for the postponement of the election in December, are unable to concur in the conclusions of the majority of the committee recommending an ordinance by the Convention for that purpose. The subject is of such importance that we deem it our duty to make known our dissent from the majority, and to state very briefly the heads of our own conclusions, after most careful deliberation:

We are unable to recognize, on the part of this Convention, any rightful authority to put in force the ordinance recommended by the committee.

This Convention was elected by the people of the State under a law of the last Legislature, which provided as follows:

"That a Convention to frame a new constitution for the State of Texas, shall assemble at the city of Austin, on the first Monday in September, 1875, for the purpose of framing a constitution."

We think that the only power possessed by the Convention, under their election by the people, held in pursuance of this law, is, to "*frame*"—that is, to plan, to devise, to form—a constitution; and to submit the same to the people of the State for their adoption or rejection.

We think that this submission of the constitution to the people is not merely a political duty of the Convention, but that it is legally, indispensably *necessary,* under the construction of its powers derived from its election under the above law; and that, without the ratification of the people, the Convention, by and of itself, has no power to ordain and establish a constitution, or any part thereof.

We think that, outside of its duty to frame and submit a constitution to the people, the Convention has no powers of sovereignty; no powers, legislative, executive or judicial.

Whilst we recognize fully that the Convention does possess the power to put in force the measures necessary to the submission of the constitution to the people, so as to secure their free and full action for its adoption or rejection, we are wholly unable to appreciate that the election in December can, in any manner whatever, obstruct the submission to the people of the constitution to be framed by the Convention, or their action upon the same.

The considerations involved as to the elections in December are alone those of economy, convenience, etc., and are not within the cognizance of this Convention. The Legislature, in full view of the situation, declined to postpone the election in December. This recurrence may operate as something of a grievance to the people. Or, it may be, on the other hand, that interference by the Convention, depriving the State of its regular legislative body, depriving districts and counties of their legal officers, and keeping in place those whose terms will have expired, dislocating a regular State election, and putting the official authority to be exercised in this State by many officers for two years (should the constitution not be ratified,) on the hazards of the doubtful power now being exercised; it may be, we say, that this will be productive of a degree of inconvenience and confusion of far greater magnitude than the slight benefits which are possible to result from this ordinance.

Whatever may be the contrast of results of this character, however, it is our thorough conviction that cognizance of them is wholly beyond the authority of this Convention. It will be a usurpation of the most dangerous principle. If the Convention can suspend a general election, and prolong the tenure of legislators, and district and county officials expiring under the existing constitution and laws, we do not perceive what the Convention could not do. It could suspend or prolong, at pleasure, the executive officers of the government, and the judicial officers of the government. All individual rights would be subject to it. Its will would demark the extent of its power.

The undersigned do full justice to the motive alone of public good which actuates the committee. Our forbearance may afford protection against further dangers beyond the present ordinance. But we establish a principle, we set an example, which only needs evil times, or may only need a day of high excitement or passion, to be a principle and example of most dangerous augury.

If the regulation of the elections in December can be brought within the range of the powers of this Convention to provide a new organic law for the State,—if it should have any place in the government we are to frame—the ordinance to effect it should be submitted to the ratification of the people and receive the same sanction on which all and every part of the constitution will depend.

W. P. BALLINGER,
JNO. L. HENRY.

On motion of Mr. Dohoney, the consideration of the two reports was postponed until Thursday next, after morning call, and 400 copies were ordered printed.

Mr. Flournoy offered the following resolution:

Resolved, That the following be referred to Committee on Railroads:

"Section 1. The charges for freight or passage on each railway in this State, which is now being or may hereafter be operated therein, shall, as to such railway, and for the same class of freight or passage, be at all times equal and uniform for each mile that such railway may transport freight or passengers within this State; *provided,* that charges for greater distances may be proportionally smaller than for less distances on the same class of freight or passengers; but shall always, for the same distance on any part or all of their line or lines be equal and uniform; *and provided further,* that no distinction or discrimination whatever shall be made between freight or passengers transported for the same distance on the main line of any railway and any branch or branches connected therewith, and under the same general or special ownership, management or control.

"Sec. 2. The Legislature shall, at its first session after the adoption of this constitution, and from time to time thereafter, pass all needful laws and provide such civil and penal remedies as will secure a just and prompt execution of the letter and purpose of the two preceding sections; and the district and inferior courts of all and each of the counties through which, or any part of which any railway shall be operated, shall be invested with civil and criminal jurisdiction of all claims for damages and criminal prosecutions growing out of a violation of this constitution or of such laws as may be passed in pursuance thereof."

Referred to Committee on Railroad Corporations.

Mr. Johnson, of Collin, offered the following resolution:

Resolved, That the Committee on Judicial Department be instructed to so frame appropriate clauses in the constitution as to give to Justices of the Peace jurisdiction in ordinary civil suits to the amount of five hundred dollars, and in criminal cases, under such limitations as may be deemed necessary, over all petty offenses and misdemeanors under the grade of felony.

Referred to Committee on Judiciary.

Also the following:

Resolved, That the Committee on Education be instructed to embody the substance of the following propositions in the educational part of the constitution, to wit:

That the school law should be revised so that fewer officers and commissions will have to be paid out of the school fund; that the district trustees should have power to appoint and remove teachers in their districts; that the Board of School Directors be abolished and their duties performed by a county superintendent. That the office of State Superintendent be abolished, and his duties be transferred to the State Treasurer, and that all grants of land heretofore or hereafter to be made by the State Legislature for public school purposes be so guarded by constitutional provision that they can not, under any circumstances, be diverted from their intended objects and purposes.

Referred to Committee on Education.

Mr. Whitfield offered the following resolution:

Resolved, That the following be incorporated in the constitution in the provisions regulating the Judiciary Department:

"The Judges of the Supreme and District Courts shall be elected by the people, as follows:

"The State shall be divided into five Supreme Court Districts, and each Supreme Court District into five Judicial Districts in compact and convenient form, and by the qualified voters of each Supreme Court District there shall be elected by the qualified voters thereof one Supreme Court Judge and five District Judges, one for each Judicial District.

"The District Judges shall be residents of their respective districts, but the Legislature may provide that the District Judges shall alternate so that no District Judge shall hold the courts in the same district more than twice successively.

"The Supreme Judges shall hold office for a term of eight years, and the District Judges for a term of four years."

Referred to Committee on Judiciary.

Mr. Holmes offered the following resolution:

WHEREAS, At common law, murder, manslaughter and other felonies are regarded as offenses against the State and does not recognize the offense and injury to persons; therefore, be it

Resolved, That any person may have civil redress for damages resulting from any felony committed to his injury, and that no property shall be exempt from forced sale to satisfy the damages assessed by a jury trying the same.

Referred to Committee on General Provisions.

Mr. Ramey offered the following resolution:

Resolved, That each county in this State shall be divided into not less than *five* nor more than *twelve* districts, and in each district there shall be elected one Justice of the Peace, who shall have such jurisdiction in both civil and criminal causes, hold courts at such times and places, and receive such fees as may be determined by law.

Such Justices shall act as Notaries Public, and perform such other duties as may be prescribed by law.

Each district as aforesaid shall elect its own Justice, for two years, at such time as may be required by law: and shall at the same time elect one Constable for the same period of time, to perform such duties as may be prescribed by law.

Referred to Committee on Judiciary.

Mr. Waelder offered the following resolution:

Resolved, That the Committee on General Provisions inquire into the expediency of incorporating a clause in the constitution by which statutes of limitation may be made available to actual occupants of unappropriated public lands, as against the State.

Referred to Committee on General Provisions.

Mr. Brown offered the following:

"GENERAL PROVISIONS.

"Sec. ——. No Supreme, District, County, or other Judge, Justice of the Peace, Mayor or Recorder of a town or city, shall sit in the trial of any cause or issue while in a state of intoxication. The Legislature shall provide by law appropriate penalties for such offense.

"Sec. ——. It shall be an offense for the Attorney General, any

District, County or City Attorney, any County, District or Supreme Court Clerk, or the deputy of such clerk, any Sheriff or Deputy Sheriff, or any Constable, or City Marshal, or the deputy of either, to officiate in the court to which he may belong, during its sitting, while in a state of intoxication. The Legislature shall provide by law appropriate penalties for such offense.

"Sec. ——. Any grand or petit juror in this State, whether in State, County or Municipal Courts, who, after being sworn and empanneled, shall appear before the court in a state of intoxication, prior to his discharge as such juror, shall be liable to such penalty as may be prescribed by law. The Legislature shall provide by law appropriate penalties for such offense.

"Sec. ——. On the day or days of all elections in this State, whether State, district, county or municipal, general or special, all dram or drinking houses, by whatever name called, in the town or vicinity of any such election, shall be closed throughout such day or days; nor shall any intoxicating drink be sold or given away therein; nor, on such day or days shall any merchant, or other dealer sell at retail or give away, in such town or vicinity, any intoxicating drink. The Legislature shall provide by law appropriate penalties for such offense.

"Sec. ——. Habitual drunkenness shall be adequate cause for suspending or removing any public officer in this State, whether State, district, county or municipal; the fact of such drunkenness to be a matter of judicial inquiry, to be determined by court and jury. The Legislature shall enact adequate laws to enforce this provision."

Referred to Committee on General Provisions.

Mr. Murphy offered the following resolution:

Resolved, That the following be embraced in the constitution:

"ARTICLE ——.

"MILITIA.

"Section 1. The Legislature shall provide by law for organizing, arming, and disciplining the militia of this State, in such manner as they shall deem expedient, not incompatible with the constitution and laws of the United States.

"Sec. 2. No licensed minister of the gospel shall be required to perform military duty.

"Sec. 3. The Governor shall have the power to call forth the militia to execute the laws of the State, to suppress insurrections, repel invasions and raiders."

Referred to the Committee on Judiciary.

Mr. McLean offered the following resolution:

Resolved, That the Committee on Revenue and Taxation be

instructed to report an ordinance to prohibit the creation of any debt by the Legislature against the State, and also to extend the same provision to all municipal corporations in the State.

Referred to Committee on Revenue and Taxation.

Mr. West offered the following resolution:

Resolved, That the Committee on Private Corporations be instructed to inquire into and report to this Convention the propriety of incorporating into the constitution the following provision:

"The Legislature shall provide by law, that in all elections for directors, managers or trustees of incorporated companies created by or under the laws of this State, every stockholder shall be entitled, for each share of stock owned by him, to as many votes as there are directors, managers or trustees to be elected, and may, in person or by proxy, cast them all for one candidate or distribute them among as many candidates as he shall think fit; and such directors, managers or trustees shall not be elected in any other manner."

Referred to Committee on Private Corporations.

Mr. West also offered the following resolution:

Resolved, That the Committee on Suffrage be instructed to inquire into and report to this Convention the propriety of incorporating into the constitution the following provision, viz:

"The House of Representatives shall consist of three times the number of the members of the Senate, and the term of office shall be two years. Three representatives shall be elected in each legislative district, at the first general election after the adoption of this constitution, and every two years thereafter. In all elections of representatives aforesaid each qualified voter may cast as many votes for any one candidate as there are representatives to be elected from his district, or may distribute the same, or equal parts thereof, among the different candidates as he shall see fit, and the candidates receiving the highest number of votes shall be declared elected."

Referred to Committee on Suffrage.

Mr. McCormick offered the following resolution:

Resolved, That the following be incorporated in the constitution:

"That all patents issued from the Land Office to assignees upon forged assignments are and shall be void."

Referred to Committee on General Provisions.

Mr. McCormick also offered the following resolution:

Resolved, That the following shall be incorporated in the constitution:

"The Legislature shall prohibit by law the intermarriage of persons of the white and black races."

Referred to Committee on General Provisions.

Mr. Dohoney offered the following resolution:

Resolved, That the Committee on General Provisions be instructed to inquire into the expediency of inserting a provision in the constitution authorizing the Legislature to enact local or special laws for the different sections of the State in reference to fences, for agriculture and stock-raising.

Referred to Committee on Agriculture and Stock-raising.

Mr. Sansom offered the following resolution:

Resolved, That the Legislature have power to enact such laws as will enable the Governor to appoint for each land district of the State a board of three scientific and practical land surveyors, whose duty it shall be, when called upon by parties having conflicting or badly defined division land lines, after taking the required oath, to go upon the ground and correct and adjust any discrepancies that may exist, making and defining *well* the corners and lines, subject to appeal or not, as the Legislature may direct.

Referred to Committee on General Provisions.

Mr. Stockdale offered the following resolutions:

Resolved, That the Commissioner of the General Land Office be, and he is hereby, requested to furnish the Convention, for its information, with an engraved map of the State of Texas, marked with colored lines, showing:

1. Each municipality, and the date of the creation and organization thereof, with each county and the date of its organization, and every successive change of the boundary thereof, with the date at which it was made.

2. That he furnish another map showing every Surveyor's District that has existed in this State, with the modifications thereof, if any, and the dates thereof, with the boundaries of the old colonies, and the date of the colonial contracts.

Referred to Committee on Public Lands and Land Office.

On motion of Mr. McLean, Mr. Johnson, of Collin, was added to Committee on Revenue and Taxation.

On motion of Mr. Russell, of Wood, Mr. Murphy was added to Committee on Crimes and Punishments.

On motion of Mr. DeMorse, Mr. Ross was added to Committee on Revenue and Taxation.

On motion of Mr. Holmes, Mr. West was added to Committee on Lands and Land Office.

On motion of Mr. West, Mr. Davis, of Brazos, was added to Committee on Education.

On motion of Mr. Ross, Mr. Flournoy was added to Committee on Railroad Corporations.

On motion of Mr. McCormick, the Convention adjourned until 9 o'clock A. M. to-morrow.

FIFTEENTH DAY.

HALL OF REPRESENTATIVES,
AUSTIN, TEXAS, September 22, 1875.

Convention met pursuant to adjournment; roll called; quorum present. Prayer by Rev. J. F. Johnson.

Journal read and adopted.

Mr. Louis Cardis, delegate elect from El Paso, came forward, presented his credentials, took the oath prescribed, and his seat as a delegate.

Mr. Stockdale presented the memorial of Pryor Lea, asking that a clause be inserted in the new constitution authorizing the Legislature to make equitable arrangements with corporations in relation to chartered rights.

Mr. Wade offered the following resolution:

WHEREAS, Vigilant and faithful representation is required by the people of Texas; therefore be it

Resolved, That if any member of this Convention shall hereafter be absent from the calls of this house for more than four days in succession, without excuse, adjudged good by the house, the seat of such member may be declared vacant, on motion, under the two-thirds rule, and the Governor authorized to fill all such vacancies, by appointment, from the district in which the member thus relieved was elected.

Laid on the table, to come up in its order.

Mr. Nunn offered the following resolution:

Resolved, That the Committee on Public Education be instructed to inquire into the expediency of establishing by law a system of public instruction or of aid to general education, and of fixing the same on a basis of all the present available school fund and resources of the State, with an addition of an ad valorem tax of not less than one-tenth or more than one-eighth of one per cent. on the taxable property of the State, and of a poll tax of not less than two dollars or more than five dollars, and the requirement of the payment by each voter of said poll tax at least four months next before the election as a condition of the exercise of the elective franchise; and to make provision for the sale of the school lands belonging to counties, to be used for the benefit of the counties respectively, and also to dedicate all the unappropriated public lands of this State to the school fund, to be sold as early as possible and proceeds applied to the benefit of the general school fund of the State.

Mr. Erhard offered the following resolutions:

Resolved, That defaulters of any county, State or other public funds, shall be considered felons, and imprisoned in the State Penitentiary, and that the Legislature define the crime and the punishment.

Resolved, That in any court the verdict of nine jurors shall be sufficient to decide in any civil or criminal case.

Referred to Committee on Judiciary.

Mr. Wright offered the following resolution:

Resolved, That the Legislature nor any county shall ever levy and collect for county purposes a tax which shall exceed in the aggregate in any one year one-fourth of the amount of the tax levied by the State, save and except to build courthouses and jails and to keep the same in repair; and all taxes so raised shall be levied alone on such subjects of taxation as may be levied by the State.

Referred to Committee on General Provisions.

Mr. Dillard offered the following resolution:

Resolved, That the Committee on Revenue and Taxation be instructed to create two separate officers in each county in the State, that of tax assessor and tax collector, and that there shall be elected in each county in the State one tax assessor and one tax collector, who shall hold their offices for two years.

Referred to Committee on Taxation and Revenue.

Mr. Weaver offered the following resolution:

Resolved, That woman, being by the ordinances of nature, the mother of all living human beings, that, if we accept Hebrew traditions, the word "Eve" typically means the mother of all living, and that, as mother, wife, sister and daughter, she has the first care of our lives, is our nurse in childhood, our mentor in youth, our companion, helper and consoler in manhood, our comforting, ministering and sustaining angel in death, even at the birth, trial, death and resurrection of Jesus, in the beautiful faith of Christianity, constant to him in the midst of mobocracy and despotism; and that in history, wherever she has had the power to speak and act for herself, in the great majority of cases, she has risen above the masses, like the full moon out of night's bosom, to shine with the light of beauty, virtue, charity and truth, over the moral darkness around her; and that, in this land of republican faith and representative, democratic government, by every recognition of modern, enlightened Christian civilization, she is morally and mentally man's equal; that the same "inalienable rights" that Jefferson has made household words in every land, where human liberty has found a home or an advocate, are as much woman's as man's; that she is a citizen as much of these United States, by the same natural rights of citizenship, as man; that the elective franchise, being founded on these natural rights of the people, and inasmuch as woman is of the people, and must be governed by the laws made by the people, and is often a taxpayer, there is no reason, political, human or divine, (Paul to the contrary notwithstanding,) why she should not have the same rights at the ballot-box that man has.

Resolved further, That the writer hereof believes that the presence of woman at the ballot-box, as an American sovereign, connected with the feminal influence of a virtuous woman, as a legal voter, would do more to protect that shrine of the people's rights than all the laws to guard the elective franchise that have heretofore been passed.

Referred to Committee on Suffrage.

On motion of Mr. Brown, of Dallas, the Convention adjourned to 9 o'clock A. M. to-morrow.

SIXTEENTH DAY.

HALL OF REPRESENTATIVES, }
AUSTIN, TEXAS, September 23, 1875. }

Convention met pursuant to adjournment; roll called; quorum present; prayer by the Rev. R. H. Talliafero.

Journal of yesterday read and adopted.

Mr. Burleson offered the following resolution:

Resolved, That the Committee on Revenue and Taxation be and is hereby instructed to investigate and report whether it be practicable, under the constitution of the United States, to compel the owners of continuous inter-State lines of communication, who reside in the United States but not in Texas, to pay the same taxes upon the one-half of their packet vessels, and upon so much of their railway property as is used in Texas, as if they were resident citizens of Texas.

Referred to Committee on Revenue and Taxation.

On motion of Mr. Brown, Mr. Cardis was added to the Committee on Printing and Contingent Expenses.

On motion of Mr. Cocke, of San Saba, Mr. Russell. of Wood, was added to the Committee on Revenue and Taxation.

Mr. Robertson, of Bell, offered the following resolution:

WHEREAS, The encouragement of agriculture and the mechanical arts and the general diffusion of knowledge being of the first importance to the settlement and proper development of all the resources and interests of Texas; therefore,

Resolved, That the Committee on Revenue and Taxation be requested to insert in the constitution, under the appropriate caption, the following provisions:

"That all agricultural and mechanical implements in actual use on farms and in workshops shall be exempt from taxation.

"That all printing presses, types and material actually used in the publication of newspapers, not to exceed $2000, shall be exempt from taxation."

Referred to Committee on Revenue and Taxation.

Mr. Allison offered the following resolution:

Resolved, That the following be incorporated as a part of the constitution:

"In case of the inability of any judge of a court of record to discharge the duties of his office with efficiency, by reason of continued sickness, drunkenness, or physical or mental infirmity, the Legislature, two-thirds of the members of each house concurring, shall remove such judge from office. But each house shall state on its respective journal, the cause for which it shall wish his removal, and give him notice thereof, and he shall have the right to be heard in his defense, in such manner as shall be prescribed by law; and should any judge of a court of record neglect or fail to hold a term of his court as prescribed by law, except in case of sickness himself, or serious sickness of his family, or providential hindrance, he shall forfeit, as may be provided by law, not less than one-twelfth of his annual salary.

Referred to Committee on Judiciary.

Mr. Sansom presented the petition of sundry citizens of Georgetown in Williamson county, on the subject of the sale of liquor in said town.

Referred to Committee on State Affairs.

13

On motion of Mr. King, Mr. Stockdale was added to the Committee on Counties and County Lands.

On motion of Mr. Floudnoy, Mr. McCormick was added to the Committee on Railroad Corporations.

BUSINESS ON THE PRESIDENT'S TABLE.

The resolution of Mr. Wade relative to declaring vacant seats of members who absent themselves from this Convention for four days in succession, was taken up and on motion of Mr. Brown laid on the table.

The report of the Committee on Legislative Department taken up.

Mr. McLean moved to postpone the consideration of the subject until 10 o'clock to-morrow morning, and make it the special order for that hour.

The yeas and nays were called on the question, and it was carried by the following vote:

YEAS — Abernathy, Arnim, Abner, Brown, Blake, Barnett, Crawford, Chambers, Cook of Gonzales, Cooke of San Saba, Cline, Cooley, Cardis, Douglass, DeMorse, Dohoney, Darnell, Dunnam, Davis of Brazos, Erhard, Ford, Fleming, Gaither, Graves, Henry of Smith, Holmes, Johnson of Franklin, Johnson of Collin, King, Kilgore, Killough, Lockett, Lacy, McLean, Martin of Navarro, Martin of Hunt, McCabe, Morris, Mitchell, McKinney, McCormick, Norvell, Nunn, Pauli, Reagan, Ramey, Rugely, Robertson of Bell, Robeson of Fayette, Ross, Spikes, Smith, Stockdale, Sansom, Whitehead, Wright, Whitfield, West, —58.

NAYS—Allison, Ballinger, Blassingame, Burleson, Bruce, Dillard, Ferris, Flanagan, German, Holt, Henry of Limestone, Haynes, Lynch, Murphy, Nugent, Russell of Harrison, Russell of Wood, Scott, Sessions, Stayton, Wade, Weaver, Waelder—23.

On motion of Mr. Stockdale, the Convention proceeded to the consideration of the special order, viz: The reports to the majority and minority of the select committee on the subject of postponing the election in December next for members of the Legislature, the majority of the committee reporting an ordinance to that effect.

On motion of Mr. Stockdale, the Convention adjourned until 2½ o'clock P. M.

EVENING SESSION — 2½ O'CLOCK.

Convention met; roll called; quorum present.

Discussion of pending question resumed and continued until

5½ o'clock, when, on motion of Mr. McCormick, the Convention adjourned until 7½ o'clock, P. M.

NIGHT SESSION—7½ o'clock.

Convention met; roll called; quorum present.

Discussion on the pending question again resumed and continued until 10½ o'clock, and upon motion of Mr. Martin, of Navarro, the Convention adjourned by the following vote:

YEAS—Abernathy, Abner, Ballinger, Bruce, Crawford, Cooke of San Saba, Cline, Cooley, Douglass, DeMorse, Dohoney, Davis of Brazos, Erhard, Flournoy, Ferris, Henry of Smith, Holmes, Johnson of Franklin, Kilgore, Lockett, McLean, Martin of Navarro, Martin of Hunt, McCabe, Morris, Mills, Mitchell, Moore, Norvell, Nunn, Pauli, Rugely, Robeson of Fayette, Scott, Sessions, Smith, Sansom, West, Waelder—39.

NAYS—Allison, Brown, Blake, Barnett, Burleson, Chambers, Cook of Gonzales, Cardis, Dillard, Darnell, Dunnam, Ford, Fleming, Flanagan, Gaither, Holt, Henry of Limestone, Haynes, Johnson of Collin, Killough, Lacy, Lynch, McKinney, McCormick, Murphy, Nugent, Ramey, Robertson of Bell, Ross, Russell of Harrison, Spikes, Stayton, Wade, Whitehead, Whitfield—35.

SEVENTEENTH DAY.

HALL OF REPRESENTATIVES, ⎫
AUSTIN, TEXAS, September 24, 1875. ⎭

Convention met pursuant to adjournment; roll called; quorum present. Prayer by Rev. Dr. Dodge, of Austin.

Journals of yesterday were read and adopted.

On motion of Mr. Ballinger, Mr. Rugely was excused for ten days.

Mr. West presented a memorial from the widows and heirs of Wm. A. Smith.

Referred to Committee on State Affairs.

Mr. Scott presented a petition from members of the bar of Cass county relative to the election of our judiciary.

Referred to Committee on Judiciary.

Mr. King presented a memorial from Charles Montague, of Bandera.

Referred to Committee on Lands and Land Office.

Mr. Blassingame presented a memorial from the Aldermen of the city of Sherman.

Referred to Committee on Education.

Mr. Russell, of Wood, offered the following resolution:

Resolved, by the People of Texas in Convention assembled, That the resolution introduced in this body, on the 22d inst., by the honorable gentleman from Cook county, recommending the incorporation of woman suffrage in the organic law of this State, be, and the same is hereby, expunged from the journals of this Convention, by drawing a black line or mark around said resolution.

Referred to Committee on Suffrage.

Mr. Cooley offered the following resolution:

Resolved, That the Committee on Public Lands and Land Office inquire into the expediency of adopting a provision of the constitution requiring the Legislature to provide for donating public lands to all settlers thereon who have attained the age of sixteen years.

Referred to Committee on Public Lands and Land Office.

Mr. Martin, of Hunt, offered the following resolution:

Resolved, That the Adjutant General be requested to furnish this Convention with a list of the officers and men employed in the defense and protection of the frontier from the commencement of the administration of Gov. Davis to the present time; the amount of appropriations for that purpose, and when made; the rank and pay of officers and men; the cost of quartermasters and commissary's stores, *itemized;* cost of transportation from place of purchase to point of destination, with kind of transportation; where forces have been stationed; number of Indians killed or captured; amount of stock recovered, and when, kind and value thereof; cost per head of keeping soldiers in said service; and what troops, if any, are kept by the general government on the frontier; where stationed; and whether State troops when mustered into service are under command of State or Federal officers.

The resolution was adopted.

UNFINISHED BUSINESS TAKEN UP, VIZ.:

The report of the majority and minority of the Select Committee on the question of postponing the general election of December, 1875, for members of the Legislature.

Pending discussion of the question (Mr. Johnson of Franklin, having the floor) the hour for the special order arrived.

On motion of Mr. Flournoy, the consideration of the special

order was postponed until the pending business could be disposed of.

On motion of Mr. Whitfield, the main question was ordered, which being the passage of the ordinance reported by the majority of the committee postponing the general election of December, 1875, and for other purposes, the same was put, and the yeas and nays being called, the ordinance passed by the following vote:

YEAS—Allison, Abernathy, Arnim, Brown, Blake, Blassingame, Barnett, Burleson, Crawford, Chambers, Cook of Gonzales, Cooke of San Saba, Cardis, Dillard, DeMorse, Darnell, Dunnam, Davis of Brazos, Erhard, Ford, Flournoy, Fleming, Ferris, Gaither, Graves, Holt, Henry of Limestone, Holmes, Haynes, Johnson of Franklin, Johnson of Collin, Kilgore, Killough, Lacy, Lynch, Martin of Navarro, Martin of Hunt, McKinney, McCormick, Moore, Murphy, Nunn, Reagan, Ramey, Robertson of Bell, Robeson of Fayette, Ross, Russell of Wood, Spikes, Scott, Sessions, Stockdale, Whitehead, Wright, Whitfield, West—56.

NAYS—Abner, Ballinger, Bruce, Cline, Cooley, Douglass, Dohoney, Davis of Wharton, Flanagan, Henry of Smith, King, Lockett, McCabe, Morris, Mills, Mitchell, Norvell, Nugent, Pauli, Reynolds, Russell of Harrison, Smith, Stayton, Wade, Waelder—25.

Pending call of the roll, Messrs. German and Sansom asked to be excused from voting, being interested in the question.

Excused.

Mr. Flournoy moved to reconsider the vote just taken and to lay the motion on the table.

Carried.

The Convention then resumed the consideration of the special order, viz: The Legislative Department, as reported by the committee.

Mr. Waelder moved that the Convention go into Committee of the Whole on the pending question, and that he be excused from acting as chairman of the Committee.

Carried.

The Convention went into Committee of the Whole, Mr. Stockdale, chairman.

The committee arose, reported progress, and asked leave to sit again.

Report adopted.

Mr. Brown offered the following resolution:

Resolved, That the ordinance this day passed by this Convention, entitled "An ordinance postponing the general election of December, A. D. 1875, and for other purposes," shall be duly enrolled, signed by the President of the Convention, countersigned by the secretary, and deposited in the office of the Secretary of State; and that the President of the Convention is hereby instructed to inform the Governor of such action, and report the fact back to the Convention to be entered of record on its journals.

Adopted.

On motion of Mr. McCormick, the use of the hall was granted to Mr. Mood, of Georgetown, to deliver a lecture.

On motion of Mr. Russell, of Harris, the Convention adjourned until 9 o'clock to-morrow.

EIGHTEENTH DAY.

HALL OF REPRESENTATIVES, }
AUSTIN, TEXAS, September 25, 1875.}

Convention met pursuant to adjournment; roll called; quorum present. Prayer by the Rev. R. H. Wilenburg, of Austin.

Journals of yesterday were read and adopted.

On motion of Mr. Killgore, Mr. Flanagan was excused from attendance on the Convention until October 4th, proximo.

Mr. Stockdale presented the memorial of sundry citizens of Wilson county in regard to legislative apportionment.

Referred to Committee on Legislative Apportionment.

On motion of Mr. Whitfield, Mr. Brown was added to Committee on General Provisions.

Mr. Martin, of Navarro, reported as follows:

COMMITTEE ROOM, }
AUSTIN, September 24, 1875.}

To the Hon. E. B. Pickett, President of the Convention:

Your committee, to whom was referred the resolution to inquire into the expediency of inserting a provision in the constitution, authorizing the Legislature to enact local or special laws for the different sections of the State, in reference to fences for agriculture and stock-raising, have had the same under careful consideration, and instruct me to report the accompanying resolution, and recommend its adoption.

MARION MARTIN, Chairman.

Resolved, That the following section be incorporated in the constitution, in the article relating to the legislative department:

"Sec. —.The Legislature shall pass general laws authorizing any county in the State, by a vote of two-thirds of the qualified voters, voting at any general election, to adopt a fence system in such county for the protection of farmers and stock-raisers."

Laid over to come up under the rule.

Mr. Whitfield made the following report:

COMMITTEE ROOM, }
AUSTIN, September 25, 1875. }

To the Hon. E. B. Pickett, President of the Convention:

Your committee, to whom was referred a memorial of certain citizens of Grayson county, beg leave to return said memorial to your honorable body, and request that it be referred to the Committee on Suffrage, as it is more appropriate matter for that committee.   Yours respectfully,

J. W. WHITFIELD, Chairman.

Report adopted.

Mr. Ford submitted the following report:

COMMITTEE ROOM, }
AUSTIN, September 24, 1875. }

To the Hon. E. B. Pickett, President of the Convention:

The Committee on State Affairs, to which was referred the petition of the people of Georgetown, Williamson county, asking for the privilege of voting upon the question of prohibiting the sale of spirituous liquors, etc., have had the same under consideration, and have instructed me to report the following resolution and to ask for its adoption by the Convention:

"*Resolved,* That the Committee on General Provisions be instructed to inquire into the expediency of requiring the Legislature of this State to pass a law to enable different localities by a majority vote of their legal voters, to prohibit the sale of intoxicating liquors within certain prescribed and clearly defined limits, and providing for punishing violations of said law."

JOHN S. FORD, Chairman.

Laid over under the rules.

Mr. Pauli offered the following resolution:

Resolved, That the printed report of any standing committee after remaining on the desk of each member the stipulated time, be considered and acted upon in the following manner:

That a certain number of sections of the report be referred to a certain number of members of the Convention (not members of the respective standing committees) for their particular consideration.

That, for this object the President shall assign as many sections of the report to as many select committees as may be expedient, to learn the different opinions on the changes or amendments to the original report, and to make these as compact as possible.

That these respective select committees shall then, at their earliest convenience, lay their amendments and charges, in writing, together with the original report, before the Convention in such form as to, inasmuch as possible, stop all unnecessary embarrassment of the Secretary, and expedite the work of the Committee of the Whole.

Laid over under the rule.

On motion of Mr. Dohoney the Convention resolved itself into Committee of the Whole (Mr. Dohoney, Chairman,) on Art. . . "Legislative Department," as reported by the committee on that subject.

Committee arose, and through their chairman reported progress and asked leave to sit again.

Report adopted.

On motion of Mr. Mills, the Convention adjourned until Monday morning, 9 o'clock.

NINETEENTH DAY.

HALL OF REPRESENTAIIVES, }
AUSTIN, TEXAS, September 27, 1875. }

Convention met pursuant to adjournment; roll called; quorum present; prayer by the Rev. Mr. Philpot, of Austin.

On motion of Mr. Ramey, Mr. Allison was excused from attendance on the Convention on account of sickness.

On motion of Mr. Cooley, Mr. Waelder was excused from attendance on the Convention on account of sickness.

Mr. Stayton presented the memorial of sundry citizens of Wilson county in regard to judicial apportionment.

Referred to Committee on Judiciary.

Mr. Ramey, chairman of the Committee on Engrossed and Enrolled Ordinances, made the following report:

COMMITTEE ROOM, }
AUSTIN, September 27, 1875. }

To the Hon. E. B. Pickett, President of the Convention:

SIR—Your committee on "Engrossed and Enrolled Ordinances" beg leave to report that they have carefully examined and compared "An ordinance postponing the general election of

December, A. D. 1875, and for other purposes," and find the same correctly engrossed and enrolled.

Respectfully,
WM. NEAL RAMEY, Chairman.

Report accepted.

Mr. Flournoy offered the following resolution:

Resolved, That the Convention hereafter hold two sessions each day, the first to begin at 9 o'clock A. M., and the second at 2¼ o'clock P. M.

Adopted.

Mr. Mills offered the following resolution:

Resolved, That the Secretary of State be requested to furnish this Convention with a statement of the registered vote of the State, by counties, as it now stands, and a hundred copies be printed for the use of this body.

Laid on the table.

Mr. Martin, of Navarro, offered the following resolution:

Resolved, That the President appoint a select committee of five to report an ordinance or provision in the constitution that will secure the most effective and speedy collection of all back taxes, as well as all future taxes.

Adopted.

Mr. Ballinger offered the following resolution:

Resolved, That the Committee on Municipal Corporations shall report a proper exception or provision in the constitution which shall secure to the city of Galveston, and other cities on the Gulf coast, the right to create the debt and issue valid bonds therefor, which may be necessary to build such breakwater, seawall or other improvement as will protect said city or cities against all injury or danger from the waters of the Gulf coast.

Referred to Committee on Municipal Corporations.

Mr. Brady offered the following resolution:

WHEREAS, The chairmen and members of the various committees of this Convention have no time, apart from their respective duties as representatives, to act as committee clerks; be it

Resolved, That the Convention at once go into an election for one general committee clerk.

Laid over under the rules.

Mr. Barnett offered the following resolution:

Resolved, That the five dollars per day allowed the delegates of this Convention be limited to sixty days, and one dollar per day allowed for the remainder of the session.

Referred to Committee on Printing and Contingent Expenses.

BUSINESS ON THE TABLE.

The following report was taken up and adopted:

COMMITTEE ROOM, }
AUSTIN, September 24, 1875. }

To the Hon. E. B. Pickett, President of the Convention:

The Committee on State Affairs to which was referred the petition of the people of Georgetown, Williamson county, asking for the privilege of voting upon the question of prohibiting the sale of spirituous liquors, etc., have had the same under consideration, and have instructed me to report the following resolution, and to ask for its adoption by the Convention:

Resolved, That the Committee on General Provisions be instructed to inquire into the expediency of requiring the Legislature of this State to pass a law to enable different localities by a majority vote of their legal voters, to prohibit the sale of intoxicating liquors within certain prescribed and clearly defined limits; and providing for punishing violations of said law.

JOHN S. FORD, Chairman.

The following report was taken up and referred to the Committee on General Provisions:

COMMITTEE ROOM, }
AUSTIN, September 24, 1875. }

To the Hon. E. B. Pickett, President of the Convention:

Your Committee to whom was referred the resolution to inquire into the expediency of inserting a provision in the constitution, authorizing the Legislature to enact local or special laws, for the different sections of the State in reference to fences for agriculture and stock-raising, have had the same under consideration and instruct me to report the accompanying resolution and recommend its adoption:

MARION MARTIN, Chairman.

Resolved, That the following section be incorporated in the constitution, in the article relating to the Legislative Department:

" Section ——. The Legislature shall pass general laws authorizing any county in the State, by a vote of two-thirds of the qualified voters, voting at any general election, to adopt a fence system in such county, for the protection of farmers and stock-raisers."

The following resolution was taken up and referred to Committee on State Affairs:

"' *Resolved,* That the printed report of any standing committee, after remaining on the desk of each member the stipulated time, be considered and acted upon in the following manner:

" That a certain number of sections of the report be referred to a certain number of members of the Convention (not members of the respective standing committees) for their particular consideration.

" That, for this object, the President shall assign so many sections of the report to as many select committees as may be expedient, to learn the different opinions on the changes or amendments to the original report, and to make these as compact as possible.

" That these respective select committees shall then, at their earliest convenience, lay their amendments and changes, in writing, together with the original report, before the Convention in such form as to, inasmuch as possible, stop all unnecessary embarrassment of the Secretary, and expedite the work of the Committee of the Whole."

Mr. Russell, of Wood, moved that the Committee of the Whole be requested to report back the " Legislative Department" article, and report progress, and ask to be discharged from a further consideration of the subject in Committee of the Whole.

Carried.

Mr. Dohoney, as said chairman, reported that the Committee of the Whole had considered said article, and had adopted sections 1, 2, 3 and 4, with an amendment to section 2, as follows:

" Sec. 2, line 1, between the words ' chosen ' and ' by,' insert ' after every apportionment.' "

On motion of Mr. West, the amendment was lost.

The Convention proceeded to consider the article by sections.

Section 1 adopted.

Sec. 2.   Mr. Brown offered the following amendment:

Add, "And after the census of 1890 the Senate may be increased to the number of forty and the House to the number of one hundred and twenty representatives."

Mr. Wade offered the following as a substitute for Mr. Brown's amendment:

In the sixth line, after the word "thereafter," strike out the remainder of the section and add: " The Senate may be increased to forty members and the House of Representatives so as not to exceed one member to every twenty thousand inhabitants."

Lost.

Mr. Brown's amendment was also lost.

Mr. DeMorse offered the following amendment:

At the end of Sec. 2 add: " At the period of each apportionment, the terms of the Legislature previously elected shall expire."

Mr. West offered the following as a substitute for the amendment:

Add to Sec. 2: "And after each apportionment there shall be a general election for senators and representatives."

Adopted.

Mr. Kilgore offered the following as a substitute for Sec. 2:

" The Senate shall consist of thirty members and the House of Representatives of ninety members, until the first apportionment after the adoption of this constitution, when, or at any apportionment thereafter, the House of Representatives may be increased by the Legislature.

Lost.

Mr. Crawford offered the following as a substitute for the section:

" The Senate shall consist of thirty members, until the first apportionment after the year A. D. 1880, when, or at any apportionment thereafter, it may be increased by the Legislature, but the Senate shall never consist of more than fifty members.

" The House of Representatives shall consist of ninety members, until the first apportionment after the year A. D. 1880, when, or at any apportionment thereafter, the number of representatives may be increased by the Legislature, but there shall never be more than one representative for every 20,000 inhabitants.

"At the first election after each apportionment there shall be an election for all of the senators and representatives."

Laid on the table.

On motion of Mr. McCormick the section was adopted.

Mr. Whitfield offered the following amendment to Sec. 3: In Sec. 3, line 11, strike out "four" and insert "two," and strike out the remainder of section.

On motion of Mr. Mills the amendment was laid on the table by the following vote:

YEAS—Abner, Ballinger, Blassingame, Brady, Bruce, Crawford, Cook of Gonzales, Cooke of San Saba, Cline, Cooley, Douglass, Dillard, DeMorse, Dohoney, Dunnam, Davis of Brazos, Davis of Wharton, Erhard, Fleming, Ferris, German, Gaither, Henry of Smith, Holmes, King, Killough, Lockett, Lacy, Lynch, McCabe, Morris, Mills, Mitchell, Moore, Nunn, Nugent, Pauli, Reagan, Ramey, Reynolds, Robeson of Fayette, Ross, Russell of Harrison, Russell of Wood, Scott, Smith, Stayton, Sansom, Wade, Wright, Weaver, West—52.

NAYS—Abernathy, Arnim, Brown, Barnett, Burleson, Chambers, Cardis, Darnell, Ford, Flournoy, Graves, Holt, Henry of Limestone, Haynes, Johnson of Franklin, Johnson of Collin,

Kilgore, McLean, Martin of Navarro, Martin of Hunt, McKinney, McCormick, Murphy, Norvell, Robertson of Bell, Spikes, Sessions, Whitehead, Whitfield—29.

On motion of Mr. German Sec. 3 was adopted.

Mr. Martin, of Navarro, moved that the Convention proceed to consider the article by sections, perfect the same, and pass on without acting finally upon the section.

Carried.

Mr. McCormick offered the following amendment to section 5:

In ninth line strike out "two" and insert "four." In line twenty, after the word "Governor" insert the words "upon extraordinary occasions when the public safety requires."

On the question of the adoption of striking out "two" and inserting "four," the yeas and nays were called for, and the amendment lost by the following vote:

YEAS—Arnim, Chambers, Holmes, Johnson of Collin, Kilgore, McCormick, Smith, Stayton, Whitfield—9.

NAYS—Abernathy, Abner, Brown, Blake, Ballinger, Blassingame, Barnett, Burleson, Brady, Bruce, Crawford, Cook of Gonzales, Cooke of San Saba, Cline, Cooley, Cardis, Douglass, Dillard, DeMorse, Dohoney, Darnell, Dunnam, Davis of Brazos, Davis of Wharton, Erhard, Ford, Flournoy, Fleming, Ferris, German, Graves, Holt, Henry of Smith, Henry of Limestone, Haynes, Johnson of Franklin, King, Killough, Lockett, Lacy, Lynch, McLean, Martin of Navarro, McCabe, Morris, Mills, Mitchell, McKinney, Moore, Murphy, Norvell, Nunn, Nugent, Pauli, Reagan, Ramey, Reynolds, Robertson of Bell, Robeson of Fayette, Ross, Russell of Harrison, Russell of Wood, Spikes, Scott, Sessions, Sansom, Wade, Whitehead, Wright, Weaver, West—71.

Mr. McCormick withdrew his second amendment.

Mr. DeMorse offered the following as an additional section to come in between section 5 and section 6:

Insert after section 5 as an additional section: Every member of the Legislature, before entering upon the duties of his position, shall have the following oath administered to him:

"I will faithfully represent the interests of my constituency and the general interests of the State. I will observe and sustain the constitution of the State and the constitution of the United States; and I have not since my election received, and will not during the continuance of my term of office receive, any gift, accommodation, free ticket or compensation, from any railroad or other corporate company, other than shall be extended to citizens of the State generally, nor any unusual accommodation or compensation from any private individual."

Mr. Crawford made this point of order, viz: That under rule twenty-three, the section being new matter, not before considered by the Convention, should be referred without debate to some standing committee.

The chair ruled against the point of order.

Mr. Crawford appealed, and the Convention sustained the chair.

Mr. Mills offered the following amendment to Mr. DeMorse's additional section: Add " or used a free pass or tried to borrow the same."

Mr. McCormick moved to lay the amendment on the table. Lost.

Mr. Moore offered the following amendment: "And that to procure my election I have not paid nor promised to pay, nor will I pay any sum of money or any other thing of value, or any expense incurred therefor to any person whatever."

The question upon the adoption of Mr. Mills's amendment was put, and the amendment adopted by the following vote:

YEAS—Abernathy, Abner, Blassingame, Burleson, Brady, Crawford, Cook of Gonzales, Cooke of San Saba, Cooley, Cardis, Dillard, Dohoney, Davis of Brazos, Ford, Flournoy, Holt, Henry of Smith, Holmes, Johnson of Franklin, Johnson of Collin, Kilgore, Killough, Lockett, Lynch, Martin of Navarro, Martin of Hunt, McCabe, Mills, Mitchell, Moore, Murphy, Nugent, Pauli, Reagan, Ramey, Reynolds, Ross, Russell of Harrison, Russell of Wood, Scott, Smith, Wade, Weaver—43.

NAYS—Arnim, Brown, Blake, Ballinger, Barnett, Bruce, Chambers, Cline, Douglass, DeMorse, Darnell, Dunnam, Davis of Wharton, Erhard, Fleming, Ferris, German, Graves, Henry of Limestone, King, Lacy, McLean, McKinney, McCormick, Norvell, Nunn, Robertson of Bell, Robeson of Fayette, Spikes, Sessions, Stayton, Sansom, Whitehead, Wright, Whitfield, West —36.

Mr Moore's amendment was then adopted.

The question then recurring upon the adoption of Mr. DeMorse's amendment as amended, the same was put and the yeas and nays being called, the amendment was lost by the following vote:

YEAS—Abernathy, Arnim, Blassingame, Burleson, Chambers, Cooley, Cardis, DeMorse, Dohoney, Dunnam, Graves, Henry of Limestone, Holmes, Johnson of Franklin, Johnson of Collin, Kilgore, McLean, Martin of Navarro, Martin of Hunt, Mills,

Mitchell, McKinney, McCormick, Moore, Nunn, Nugent, Reynolds, Robertson of Bell, Robeson of Fayette, Ross, Russell of Harrison, Russell of Wood, Sessions, Smith, Weaver, Whitfield—36.

Nays—Abner, Brown, Blake, Ballinger, Barnett, Brady, Bruce, Crawford, Cook of Gonzales, Cooke of San Saba, Cline, Douglass, Dillard, Darnell, Davis of Brazos, Davis of Wharton, Erhard, Ford, Flournoy, Fleming, Ferris, German, Holt, Henry of Smith, Haynes, King, Killough, Lockett, Lacy, Lynch, McCabe, Murphy, Novell, Pauli, Reagan, Ramey, Spikes, Scott, Stayton, Sansom, Wade, Whitehead, Wright, West—44.

Mr. McLean moved to reconsider the vote just taken and to postpone the consideration of the same for the present.

Mr. Mills offered the following amendment:

In Sec. 6, line 25, strike out " five " and insert " three" years; in same section, line 27, strike out " thirty " and insert " twenty-five " years.

Lost.

Mr. Martin, of Navarro, offered the following substitute for sections 6 and 7:

" No person shall be a senator or representative,unless he be a citizen of the United States and a qualified elector of this State and shall have resided in their respective counties or districts one year next preceding their election, and shall continue therein during their term of service."

Lost.

Mr. Dillard offered the following substitute for sections 6 and 7:

" No person shall be a senator or representative unless he be a citizen of the United States, and, at the time of his election, a qualified elector of this State, and shall have been a resident of this State five years next preceding his election, and the last year thereof a resident of the district for which he shall be chosen."

The yeas and nays being called on the question, the substitute was lost by the following vote:

Yeas—Arnim, Brady, Bruce, Crawford, Dillard, Ford, Fleming, Graves, Henry of Limestone, Haynes, Johnson of Collin, Martin of Navarro, Martin of Hunt, Mitchell, McCormick, Moore, Norvell, Reagan, Scott, Wright, Whitfield—21.

Nays—Abernathy, Abner, Brown, Blake, Ballinger, Blassingame, Barnett, Burleson, Chambers, Cook of Gonzales, Cooke of San Saba, Cline, Cooley, Douglass, DeMorse, Dohoney, Darnell, Dunnam, Davis of Brazos, Davis of Wharton, Erhard, Flournoy, Ferris, Gaither, Holt, Henry of Smith, Holmes, Johnson of Franklin, King, Kilgore, Killough, Lockett, Lacy, Lynch, McLean, McCabe, Morris, Mills, McKinney, Murphy, Nunn, Nugent, Pauli, Ramey, Reynolds, Robertson of Bell, Robeson of Fayette, Ross, Russell of Harrison, Russell of Wood, Spikes, Sessions, Smith, Stayton, Sansom, Wade, Whitehead, Weaver, West—59.

Mr. Whitfield offered the following amendment:

Section 6, line 27, strike out "thirty" and insert "twenty-four."

The yeas and nays being called, the amendment was lost by the following vote:

YEAS—Abernathy, Arnim, Brown, Barnett, Brady, Bruce, Crawford, Chambers, Dillard, Darnell, Ford, Fleming, Graves, Henry of Limestone, Haynes, Johnson of Collin, Kilgore, Lockett, Martin of Navarro, Martin of Hunt, Mills, Mitchell, McCornick, Moore, Norvell, Pauli, Reagan, Ross, Scott, Sessions, Wade, Whitehead, Wright, Whitfield—34.

NAYS—Abner, Blake, Ballinger, Blassingame, Burleson, Cook of Gonzales, Cooke of San Saba, Cline, Cooley, Douglass, De Morse, Dohoney, Dunnam, Davis of Brazos, Davis of Wharton, Erhard, Flournoy, Ferris, German, Gaither, Holt, Henry of Smith, Holmes, Johnson of Franklin, King, Killough, Lacy, Lynch, McLean, McCabe, Morris, McKinney, Murphy, Nunn, Nugent, Ramey, Reynolds, Robertson of Bell, Robeson of Fayette, Russell of Harrison, Russell of Wood, Spikes, Smith, Stayton, Sansom, Weaver, West—47.

Mr. Kilgore proposed to amend section 6, line 27, by striking out "thirty" and inserting "twenty-six."

Mr. Brady proposed to amend the amendment by striking out "thirty" and inserting "seventy."

Lost.

And Mr. Kilgore's amendment adopted.

Mr. Martin, of Navarro, proposed to amend section 6, line 25, by striking out "five years," and inserting "three years."

Mr. Cook of Gonzales, proposed to amend section 9, line 36, by striking out "and close;" also strike out the remainder of the sentence after the word "President," in line 37.

The yeas and nays being called upon the adoption of the amendment, stood as follows:

YEAS—Arnim, Blassingame, Barnett, Burleson, Bruce, Chambers, Cook of Gonzales, Cardis, Flournoy, Fleming, Gaither, Graves, Holt, Holmes, Haynes, Johnson of Franklin, Johnson of Collin, Lacy, Lynch, Martin of Navarro, Martin of Hunt Mills, McKinney, McCormick, Murphy, Nugent, Robertson of Bell,

Robeson of Fayette, Ross, Russell of Wood, Spikes, Scott, Sessions, Wade, Weaver, Whitfield—36.

NAYS—Abernathy, Abner, Brown, Ballinger, Brady, Crawford, Cooke of San Saba, Cline, Cooley, Douglass, Dillard, DeMorse, Dohoney, Darnell, Dunnam, Davis of Brazos, Davis of Wharton, Erhard, Ford, Ferris, German, Henry of Smith, Henry of Limestone, King, Kilgore, Killough, Lockett, McLean, McCabe, Morris, Mitchell, Moore, Norvell, Nunn, Pauli, Reagan, Ramey, Russell of Harrison, Smith, Stayton, Sansom, Whitehead, West—43.

On motion of Mr. Sansom, the Convention adjourned until 2½ o'clock P. M.

EVENING SESSION—2½ o'CLOCK.

Convention met; roll called; quorum present.

The Convention resumed the consideration of Article —, "Legislative Department."

Mr. Russell, of Harrison, proposed to amend section 10, line 1, by striking out the words "two-thirds" and inserting "a majority."

Lost.

Mr. Ballinger proposed to amend section 18, line 83, by striking out all from the word "eligible" in 83d line down to the word "Legislature" in 84th line, and insert the words "or to any other office in this State or the government of the United States elected by any part of the people of this State or by the Legislature."

Mr. Wright proposed to amend the amendment by striking out of it all that related to the government of the United States.

Adopted, and amendment as amended lost.

Mr. Kilgore offered the following amendment to section 81:

After the word "provided" in line 87 insert "and members of the Legislature shall, in addition to the oath of office prescribed by this constitution, swear that they will not as such vote for any member thereof, during the term for which he was elected, for any office of profit or trust under the government of the United States."

On motion of Mr. Martin, of Navarro, the amendment was laid on the table by the following vote:

YEAS—Abernathy, Arnim, Blassingame, Barnett, Burleson, Brady, Bruce, Crawford, Chambers, Cook of Gonzales, Cooke of San Saba, Dillard, DeMorse, Dohoney, Darnell, Dunnam, Davis of Brazos, Davis of Wharton, Ford, Flournoy, Fleming, Ger-

14

man, Gaither, Graves, Holt, Henry of Smith, Henry of Limestone, Holmes, Haynes, Johnson of Franklin, Johnson of Collin, King, Killough, Lockett, Lacy, Lynch, McLean, Martin of Navarro, Martin of Hunt, McCabe, Morris, McKinney, Moore, Murphy, Norvell, Nunn, Pauli, Reagan, Reynolds, Robertson of Bell, Robeson of Fayette, Ross, Russell of Harrison, Russell of Wood, Spikes, Scott, Sessions, Smith, Stayton, Sansom, Wade, Whitehead, Weaver, Whitfield—64.

Nays—Ballinger, Cline, Cooley, Douglass, Erhard, Ferris, Kilgore, Mills, Mitchell, McCormick, Nugent, Wright, West—13.

Mr. West gave notice that he would move a reconsideration of the vote adopting the resolution providing for two sessions a day for the Convention.

Mr. Murphy propsed to amend section 19, line 93, by inserting after the word "shall," "during the term for which he is elected or appointed."

Adopted.

Mr. Reagan offered the following as a substitute for all of section 24, down to the word "days," in line 113:

"Sec. 24. The members of the Legislature shall receive from the public treasury such compensation as may have been provided by law, not exceeding six dollars per day, for the first sixty days of each session, and after that not exceeding two dollars per day for the remainder of the session. The members of the first Legislature to be elected under this constitution, shall receive five dollars per day for their services; and during its first session may receive that sum for ninety days; *provided,* that the pay of members of the Legislature shall not be increased during the term for which they are elected.

Mr. Fleming moved to lay the amendment on the table.

Carried by the following vote:

Yeas—Abernathy, Arnim, Abner, Brown, Blake, Ballinger, Blassingame, Barnett, Burleson, Brady, Bruce, Chambers, Cook of Gonzales, Cooke of San Saba, Cardis, Douglass, DeMorse, Dohoney, Darnell, Dunnam, Davis of Brazos, Davis of Wharton, Erhard, Ford, Flournoy, Fleming, Ferris, German, Gaither, Graves, Holt, Henry of Smith, Henry of Limestone, Holmes, Haynes, Johnson of Franklin, Johnson of Collin, King, Kilgore, Killough, Lockett, Lacy, Lynch, McLean, Martin of Navarro, Martin of Hunt, McCabe, Morris, Mitchell, McKinney, McCormick, Moore, Murphy, Nugent, Pauli, Reynolds, Robertson of Bell, Robeson of Fayette, Ross, Russell of Harrison, Russell of Wood, Spikes, Scott, Sessions, Smith, Stayton, Sansom, Wade, Whitehead, Wright, Weaver, Whitfield, West—73.

Nays—Crawford, Cline, Cooley, Dillard, Mills, Norvell, Nunn, Reagan, Ramey—9.

Mr. Reagan offered the same substitute, after striking out "six dollars," and inserting "five dollars."

Mr. Henry, of Smith, moved to lay it on the table.

The yeas and nays were called, and the substitute laid on the table by the following vote:

Yeas—Abernathy, Arnim, Abner, Ballinger, Blassingame, Barnett, Burleson, Brady, Bruce, Chambers, Cook of Gonzales, Cooke of San Saba, Douglass, DeMorse, Dohoney, Davis of Brazos, Davis of Wharton, Flournoy, Fleming, Ferris, German, Gaither, Graves, Henry of Smith, Henry of Limestone, Holmes, Johnson of Franklin, Johnson of Collin, Killough, Lacy, Lynch, McLean, Martin of Navarro, Martin of Hunt, Morris, Mitchell, McKinney, McCormick, Murphy, Nugent, Reynolds, Robertson of Bell, Robeson of Fayette, Ross, Russell of Harrison, Russell of Wood, Sessions, Smith, Stayton, Wade, Wright, Weaver—52.

Nays—Blake, Crawford, Cline, Cooley, Cardis, Dillard, Darnell, Dunnam, Erhard, Ford, Holt, Haynes, King, Kilgore, Lockett, McCabe, Mills, Moore, Norvell, Nunn, Pauli, Reagan, Ramey, Spikes, Scott, Sansom, Whitehead, Whitfield, West—29.

Mr. Fleming moved to strike out line 111 of section 24.

Mr. DeMorse offered the following as a substitute for the amendment:

Strike out line 111, and the word "session" in line 112, and amend so as to read: "Not exceeding five dollars per day for sixty days, and no pay thereafter."

Mr. Russell, of Wood, moved to lay the amendment on the table.

Carried by the following vote:

Yeas—Abernathy, Arnim, Abner, Blake, Ballinger, Blassingame, Burleson, Brady, Bruce, Cook of Gonzales, Cooke of San Saba, Cline, Cooley, Cardis, Douglass, Dohoney, Darnell, Dunnam, Davis of Brazos, Davis of Wharton, Erhard, Flournoy, Ferris, Graves, Holt, Henry of Smith, Henry of Limestone, Holmes, Haynes, Johnson of Franklin, King, Kilgore, Killough, Lockett, Lacy, Martin of Navarro, Martin of Hunt, McCabe, Mills, McKinney, Moore, Murphy, Norvell, Nunn, Pauli, Reagan, Ramey, Reynolds, Robeson of Fayette, Russell of Wood, Spikes, Scott, Sessions, Smith, Stayton, Sansom, Wade, Whitehead, Weaver—59.

Nays—Barnett, Crawford, Chambers, Dillard, DeMorse, Ford, Fleming, German, Gaither, Johnson of Collin, Lynch,

McLean, Morris, Mitchell, McCormick, Nugent, Robertson of Bell, Ross, Wright, Whitfield—20.

Mr. Ferris offered the following amendments:

On page 5, line 110, strike out "sixty days" and insert "ninety days;" same page, line 113, strike out "for the first ninety days" and insert "for the entire session."

Mr. German moved to lay the amendment on the table.

Carried by the following vote:

YEAS—Abernathy, Arnim, Abner, Blake, Blassingame, Barnett, Burleson, Bruce, Cook of Gonzales, Cooke of San Saba, Douglass, Dillard, DeMorse, Dohoney, Darnell, Dunnam, Davis of Brazos, Flournoy, Fleming, German, Gaither, Graves, Holt, Henry of Limestone, Holmes, Haynes, Johnson of Franklin, Johnson of Collin, Kilgore, Killough, Lacy, Lynch, McLean, Martin of Navarro, Martin of Hunt, McKinney, McCormick, Moore, Murphy, Nugent, Pauli, Ramey, Robertson of Bell, Robeson of Fayette, Ross, Russell of Wood, Spikes, Scott, Sessions, Smith, Stayton, Sansom, Wade, Whitehead, Wright, Whitfield—57.

NAYS—Ballinger, Brady, Crawford, Chambers, Cline, Cooley, Cardis, Davis of Wharton, Erhard, Ford, Ferris, Henry of Smith, King, Lockett, McCabe, Morris, Mills, Mitchell, Nunn, Reagan, Reynolds—21.

Mr. Nugent offered the following amendment:

Amend by adding to the section: "The members of the Legislature shall also receive in lieu of all allowances for stationery and postage such sum as may be provided by law, not to exceed the sum of thirty dollars for each member."

On motion of Mr. Martin, of Navarro, the amendment was laid on the table.

Mr. McCormick moved to amend sec. 24, line 111, by striking out "two" and inserting "one."

Laid on the table.

Mr. Brady offered the following amendment:

"Sec. 24.   The members of the Legislature shall receive from the public treasury, as compensation, a salary of $300 for the term for which they are elected. And in the event of an extra session being called, they shall receive five dollars per day. They shall receive mileage at the rate of five dollars for each twenty-five miles necessarily traveled in going to and returning from the capital; but no member shall be entitled to mileage for any extra session that may be called within one day after the adjournment of a regular session."

On motion of Mr. Martin, of Navarro, the amendment was laid on the table.

Mr. Ballinger proposed to amend section 24 by inserting after the word "days" in line 113, the words "and after that not exceeding two dollars per day for the remainder of the session."

Adopted.

Mr. McCormick offered the following amendment:

Strike out sections 25 and 26, and substitute for section 25 the following:

"Sec. 25. The State shall be divided into Senatorial Districts of contiguous compact territory, according to the number of inhabitants as near as may be; and each district shall be entitled to elect one senator and three representatives."

On motion of Mr. Martin, of Navarro, the Convention adjourned until 9 o'clock to-morrow morning.

TWENTIETH DAY.

Hall of Representatives, \
Austin, Texas, September 28, 1875.

Convention met pursuant to adjournment; roll called; quorum present. Prayer by Rev. Mr. Wright, of Austin.

Journal of yesterday read and adopted.

Mr. Brown submitted the following additional rules for the guidance of the Convention:

"Every resolution or ordinance, before it becomes a part of the constitution, shall be read on three several days.

"The first reading shall be for information, and upon being read a first time, if not reported by a committee, it shall be referred to the appropriate committee without debate.

"Upon a second reading of a resolution or ordinance, it shall be subject to commitment or amendment.

"The final question upon the second reading shall be, 'Whether it shall be engrossed and read a third time.'

"No amendment shall be received at the third reading of a resolution or ordinance without the consent of two-thirds of the members present.

"It shall be in order, at the third reading of a resolution or ordinance, to move its commitment; and should such commitment take place and any amendment be reported by the committee, the said resolution or ordinance shall be considered as on its second reading.

"Business on the table shall be taken up in the following order:

"First — Simple resolutions.

"Second—Resolutions and ordinances on the second reading.

"Third—Resolutions and ordinances on the third reading."

Referred to Committee on Rules.

Mr. Mills offered the following amendment to the rules:

"Rule —.   After the yeas and nays have been ordered and vote has actually begun, no member shall have the right to speak or have the subject matter explained."

Laid over under the rule.

Mr. Mills submitted the following memorial, which was read and referred to Committee on Lands and Land Office.

To the Honorable the members of the Constitutional Convention of the State of Texas:

*   *   *   *   *   *   *   *   *

Your memorialists are Mary J. Thompson, the widow, and Maggie J. Weldy (who is intermarried with S. Weldy) and Jennie C. Thompson, the children of the identical Henry N. Thompson, who was first lieutenant in the company of volunteers commanded by George W. Burroughs in the war for Texan independence.   Said company originally belonged to the first regiment of permanent volunteers, commanded by Colonel Joseph Rogers, but your memorialist, Mary J. Thompson, believes that, upon the organization of the Army of Texas, in 1837, said company was placed in the second regiment of permanent volunteers. And your memorialists respectfully represent that said company was organized and equipped in the town of Zanesville, Ohio, where they now reside; that said Lieutenant Thompson remained in the service of Texas until his company and regiment were honorably discharged; that he is now dead, and your memorialists are very poor; therefore they pray that your honorable body may grant to the said Mary J. Thompson the land to which her said husband was entitled under the laws of Texas, but for which he never made application.

> M. J. THOMPSON,
> S. WELDY,
> MAGGIE J. WELDY,
> JENNIE C. THOMPSON.

The following communication was taken from the President's desk, read, and referred to the Committee on Public Lands and Land Office:

GENERAL LAND OFFICE, }
AUSTIN, September 27, 1875. }

To the Hon. E. B. Pickett, President of the Convention:

SIR — I have the honor to acknowledge the receipt of a communication from the Secretary of the Convention, inclosing copy of a resolution adopted by the Convention on the 20th day of September, instant.

I desire to inform the honorable body over which you preside that I can not possibly furnish the information sought within a less time than six months.   If, under the circumstances, it is desired that I should begin the work, you will please advise me, and I will place all the available force of the office upon it.

Very respectfully,

Your obedient servant,

J. GROOS,

Commissioner General Land Office.

Mr. Russell, of Harrison, presented the petition of sundry citizens of Longview, asking that occupation tax on selling goods by sample be abolished.

Referred to Committee on Revenue and Taxation.

Mr. Cook, of Gonzales, submitted the following report:

COMMITTEE ROOM, }
AUSTIN, September 27, 1875. }

To the Hon. E. B. Pickett, President of the Convention:

Your Committee on Printing and Contingent Expenses, to whom was referred resolution directing said committee to inquire into the expediency of having the new constitution printed in the Spanish language, have had the same under consideration, and have instructed me to report the following resolution and recommend its adoption, viz:

"*Resolved*, That the Committee on Printing and Contingent Expenses be and they are hereby authorized to contract, on the best terms they can obtain, for the translation of the new constitution in the Spanish language, and the printing of three thousand copies of the same for distribution among the Spanish-speaking citizens of the State."

W. D. S. COOK, Chairman.

Adopted.

Mr. Haynes offered the following resolution:

Resolved, That the Commissioner of the General Land Office be requested to furnish this Convention with a statement showing the yearly expense of running said office, and the amount of fees collected in said office for work done and turned over to the State; the number of employes required to do the work; the amounts drawn by them as salaries from the State. The said statement to show the cost of carrying on the said Land Office, over and above the amounts received as fees.

Adopted.

Mr. Russell, of Wood, offered the following resolution:

Resolved, That it is the sense of this Convention that there ought to be a clause in the present constitution inhibiting the Attorney General or any other officer of the State from employing attorneys or clerical force, unless the same is authorized by pre-existing statute.

Referred to Judiciary Committee.

Mr. Moore offered the following resolution:

Resolved, That the Committee on Printing be authorized and directed to make a contract for the printing of one thousand copies of the constitution in the Bohemian language.

Mr. Mills moved to lay the resolution on the table.

Lost by the following vote:

YEAS — Brown, Blake, Blassingame, Barnett, Brady, Bruce, Chambers, Douglass, Dohoney, Dunnam, Davis of Wharton, Graves, Holt, Holmes, Johnson of Franklin, Lacy, Martin of Navarro, Martin of Hunt, Morris, Mills, Ramey, Russell of Wood, Spikes, Sansom, Wade, Weaver — 26.

NAYS—Allison, Abernathy, Arnim, Abner, Ballinger, Burleson, Crawford, Cook of Gonzales, Cooke of San Saba, Cline, Cooley, Cardis, Dillard, DeMorse, Darnell, Davis of Brazos, Erhard, Ford, Flournoy, Fleming, Ferris, German, Gaither, Henry of Smith, Henry of Limestone, Haynes, Johnson of Collin, Kilgore, Killough, Lockett, Lynch, McCabe, Mitchell, McKinney, McCormick, Moore, Murphy, Norvell, Nunn, Nugent, Pauli, Reagan, Rentfro, Robertson of Bell, Robeson of Fayette, Ross, Russell of Harrison, Scott, Sessions, Smith, Stockdale, Stayton, Whitehead, Wright, Whitfield, West — 56.

The President announced the following Select Committee, authorized by a resolution of Mr. Martin, of Navarro, to provide for an effective and speedy collection of all taxes due, or to become due, the State: Messrs. Martin, of Navarro, chairman, Waelder, Norvell, Henry of Smith, and West.

Mr. Brown offered the following, to come in after the preamble to the Bill of Rights, under the head of

" BOUNDARIES.

" In accordance with the following treaties, acts and joint resolutions, to-wit:

" The treaty concluded between Spain and the United States

of America, on the 22d of February, 1819, and ratified on the 22d of February, 1821;

"The treaty concluded between the United States of America and the United Mexican States, January 12, 1828, and ratified April 5, 1832;

"An act of the Congress of the Republic of Texas, approved December 19, 1836;

"A joint resolution of the Legislature of the State of Texas, approved April 29, 1846;

"An act of the Congress of the United States of the 5th of July, 1848, accepted and assented to by the State of Texas by the act of November 2, 1849;

"And an act of the Congress of the United States, (commonly called the compromise act), approved September 9, 1850; accepted and assented to by an act of the Legislature of the State of Texas, approved on the 25th day of November, 1850 —

"The boundaries of the State of Texas are hereby declared to be and shall forever remain as hereinafter set forth, to-wit:

"Beginning in the middle of the mouth of Sabine Bay or Pass, on the Gulf of Mexico; thence up the middle of Sabine Bay or Lake to the mouth of the Sabine river; thence up the central channel of said river to latitude 32 degrees north; thence due north, on the line established in the year 1840, to Red river; thence up the Rio Roxo, or Red river, to the one hundredth degree of longitude west from London and twenty-three west from Washington; thence due north to the parallel of thirty-six degrees and thirty minutes north latitude; thence due west to the meridian of one hundred and three degrees of longitude west from Greenwich; thence due south to the thirty-second degree of north latitude; thence due west, on the line of thirty-two degrees north latitude, to the channel of the Rio Bravo del Norte, otherwise called the Rio Grande; thence with the channel of said river to its mouth in the Gulf of Mexico; thence, on a line drawn three marine leagues from the shore of the Gulf of Mexico, to the beginning, at the mouth or pass of Sabine Bay."

Referred to Committee on Bill of Rights.

The Convention then proceeded to the consideration of unfinished business, the pending question being Mr. McCormick's substitute for sections 25 and 26. Taken up and consideration of the sections and substitute passed over for the present.

Mr. Nunn proposed to amend line 156, section 32, by striking out "a" and inserting the words "which necessity shall be stated in."

Lost.

Mr. Brown proposed to insert after preamble the words " or in the bill itself."

Lost.

Mr. Stockdale offered the following amendment:

Section 34, line 163, strike out the words " or resolution."

Adopted.

Mr. Cook, of Gonzales, offered the following amendment:

Add to the beginning of the 164th line the words " shall originate in the same house in which the original bill originated, and ".

Lost.

Mr. Cook moved to strike out sec. 37.

On motion of Mr. Mills the amendment was laid on the table.

Mr. West offered to amend the section by striking out the words " and printed for use of the members."

Adopted.

Mr. Martin, of Navarro, offered the following amendment:

Sec. 37, line 175, between " committee " and " returned " insert " and ".

Adopted.

Mr. Ballinger proposed to amend section 37, line 175, by striking out " returned therefrom " and inserting " reported thereon."

Adopted.

Mr. Nunn proposed to strike out " a " and insert " the " in line 183, in section 37.

Lost.

Mr. Nugent proposed to amend section 38, line 177, by striking out the words " and joint resolution."

Lost.

Mr. Wade proposed to strike out of section 38, line 178, the words " their title " and insert the word " they."

Lost.

Mr. Dohoney, by leave, offered the following amendment to section 34:

Add to the section the words, " After a resolution has been acted on and defeated, no resolution containing the same subject shall be considered at the same session."

Adopted.

Mr. Stockdale, by leave, offered to amend section 37 by adding " and no bill shall be passed which has not been presented and referred to and reported from a committee at least three days before the adjournment of the Legislature."

Adopted.

Mr. Flournoy proposed to amend section 40 by striking out all after the word "session" in line 187 down to the word "no" in the 189th line.

Mr. Ballinger offered to amend by inserting after the first word "session" in line 189 the words "or presented to them by the Governor."

Mr. Johnson, of Collin, moved to lay Mr. Flournoy's amendment on the table.

Carried by the following vote:

YEAS—Allison, Abernathy, Brown, Blake, Ballinger, Blassingame, Barnett, Burleson, Brady, Bruce, Chambers, Cook of Gonzales, Cooke of San Saba, Douglass, Dillard, DeMorse, Darnell, Dunnam, Davis of Brazos, Fleming, Ferris, German, Gaither, Graves, Holt, Henry of Smith, Henry of Limestone, Holmes, Haynes, Johnson of Franklin, Johnson of Collin, King, Kilgore, Killough, Lacy, Lynch, McLean, Martin of Navarro, Martin of Hunt, McCabe, Morris, Mills, Mitchell, McKinney, Moore, Murphy, Nugent, Pauli, Reagan, Ramey, Reynolds, Robertson of Bell, Robeson of Fayette, Ross, Russell of Harrison, Russell of Wood, Spikes, Scott, Sessions, Smith, Stockdale, Stayton, Sansom, Wade, Whitehead, Weaver—66.

NAYS—Arnim, Abner, Crawford, Cline, Cooley, Dohoney, Davis of Wharton, Erhard, Ford, Flournoy, Lockett, McCormick, Norvell, Nunn, Rentfro, Wright, Whitfield, West—18.

The question recurring on Mr. Ballinger's amendment, Mr. DeMorse offered the following as a substitute for the amendment:

"Strike out the words "designated in the proclamation of the Governor calling such session" and insert the words "may be presented to them by the Governor."

Mr. Dillard moved to lay Mr. Ballinger's amendment on the table.

Lost.

Mr. German moved to reconsider the vote just taken.

Lost by the following vote:

YEAS—Allison, Abernathy, Arnim, Blassingame, Barnett, Burleson, Brady, Bruce, Dillard, Dunnam, Fleming, German, Graves, Holt, Henry of Limestone, Haynes, Johnson of Collin, Lynch, Martin of Navarro, Miils, Robertson of Bell, Robeson of Fayette, Ross, Russell of Wood, Spikes, Scott, Sessions, Sansom, Wade, Whitfield—30.

NAYS—Abner, Blake, Ballinger, Crawford, Chambers, Cooke of San Saba, Cline, Cooley, Douglass, DeMorse, Dohoney, Darnell, Davis of Brazos, Davis of Wharton, Erhard, Ford, Flournoy, Ferris, Gaither, Henry of Smith, Holmes, Johnson of

Franklin, King, Kilgore, Killough, Lockett, Lacy, McLean, Martin of Hunt, McCabe, Morris, Mitchell, McKinney, McCormick, Moore, Murphy, Norvell, Nunn, Nugent, Pauli, Reagan, Ramey, Reynolds, Rentfro, Russell of Harrison, Smith, Stockdale, Stayton, Whitehead, Wright, Weaver, West—52.

The question recurring upon Mr. DeMorse's substitute for Mr. Ballinger's amendment, it was put and substitute lost.

The question on Mr. Ballinger's amendment was put and the amendment adopted by the following vote:

YEAS—Arnim, Abner, Brown, Blake, Ballinger, Brady, Crawford, Chambers, Cook of Gonzales, Cooke of San Saba, Cline, Cooley, Cardis, Douglass, DeMorse, Dohoney, Darnell, Dunnam, Davis of Brazos, Davis of Wharton, Erhard, Ford, Ferris, Gaither, Henry of Smith, Holmes, King, Kilgore, Lockett, Lacy, Lynch, McCabe, Mills, Mitchell, McCormick, Moore, Murphy, Nugent, Pauli, Ramey, Reynolds, Rentfro, Russell of Harrison, Smith, Stockdale, Stayton, Whitehead, Wright, Weaver, West—50.

NAYS—Allison, Abernathy, Blassingame, Barnett, Burleson, Bruce, Dillard, Flournoy, Fleming, German, Graves, Holt, Henry of Limestone, Haynes, Johnson of Franklin, Johnson of Collin, Killough, McLean, Martin of Navarro, Martin of Hunt, Morris, McKinney, Norvell, Nunn, Reagan, Robertson of Bell, Robeson of Fayette, Ross, Russell of Wood, Spikes, Scott, Sessions, Sansom, Wade, Whitfield—35.

Mr. Martin, of Navarro, offered the following amendment:

Add to section 24 the words "or called session."

Adopted.

Mr. Chambers moved to strike out section 41, as it more properly belonged to the Executive Department.

Lost.

Mr. Martin, of Navarro, offered the following amendment:

Add to section 41 the words "within twenty days after adjournment of the Legislature."

Mr. Stockdale offered the following as a substitute for the amendment:

Section 41, line 206, strike out the word "thirty," and insert "ten."

Lost.

Mr. Russell, of Harris, offered the following amendment:

Section 41, line 195, strike out the words "two-thirds," and insert the words "a majority;" also strike out in lines 197 and 198 the words "two-thirds," and insert in lieu thereof "a majority."

On motion of Mr. Henry, of Smith, the amendment was laid on the table by the following vote:

YEAS—Arnim, Brown, Blake, Ballinger, Blassingame, Barnett, Burleson, Bruce, Chambers, Cook of Gonzales, Cooke of San Saba, Cardis, Douglass, Dillard, DeMorse, Darnell, Dunnam, Davis of Brazos, Erhard, Ford, Flournoy, Fleming, Ferris, German, Gaither, Graves, Holt, Henry of Smith, Henry of Limestone, Holmes, Haynes, Johnson of Franklin, Johnson of Collin, King, Kilgore, Killough, Lacy, Lynch, McLean, Martin of Navarro, Morris, Mitchell, McKinney, McCormick, Moore, Murphy, Norvell, Nunn, Nugent, Pauli, Reagan, Ramey, Rentfro, Robertson of Bell, Robeson of Fayette, Ross, Russell of Wood, Spikes, Scott, Sessions, Smith, Stockdale, Stayton, Sansom, Wade, Whitehead, Wright, Weaver, Whitfield—69.

NAYS—Abernathy, Abner, Brady, Cline, Cooley, Dohoney, Davis of Wharton, Lockett, Martin of Hunt, McCabe, Mills, Reynolds, Russell of Harrison—13.

On motion of Mr. McCormick, a further consideration of the pending subject was postponed until 9 o'clock to-morrow.

Mr. Flournoy offered the following amendment to the standing rules.

Resolved, That rule 38 be amended by striking out "three" and inserting "nine," in the first line of said rule; and amend rule 39 by substituting "nine" for "three," in the first line of said rule.

Mr. Flournoy moved to suspend the rules in order to consider the amendments.

Mr. Rentfro moved to adjourn till 9¼ o'clock to-morrow morning.

Lost.

Question on suspension of rules was put, and lost by the following vote:

YEAS—Abernathy, Arnim, Brown, Blake, Ballinger, Blassingame, Burleson, Chambers, Cook of Gonzales, Cooke of San Saba, Cardis, Douglass, Dillard, Darnell, Dunnam, Davis of Brazos, Erhard, Ford, Flournoy, Gaither, Graves, Holt, Henry of Smith, Henry of Limestone, Holmes, Kilgore, Killough, Lacy, Lynch, McLean, Martin of Navarro, Morris, McCormick, Murphy, Nunn, Nugent, Russell of Wood, Sessions, Smith, Stockdale, Stayton, Wade, Whitehead, Wright, Weaver, Whitfield—46.

NAYS—Abner, Barnett, Brady, Bruce, Crawford, Cline, DeMorse, Dohoney, Davis of Wharton, Fleming, Ferris, German, Haynes, Johnson of Franklin, Johnson of Collin, King, Lockett, Martin of Hunt, McCabe, Mills, Mitchell, McKinney, Moore, Norvell, Pauli, Reagan, Ramey, Reynolds, Rentfro, Robertson of Bell, Robeson of Fayette, Ross, Russell of Harrison, Spikes, Scott, Sansom, West—37.

Mr. Whitfield moved to suspend the rule requiring two sessions per day, until Monday next.

Carried.

Mr. German moved to reconsider the vote refusing to adopt the additional section offered by Mr. DeMorse, to come in between sections 5 and 6, and to postpone the same for the present.

Carried.

Mr. Brady moved to reconsider the vote taken yesterday on section 9, abolishing the office of Lieutenant Governor, and to postpone its consideration for the present.

Carried.

On motion of Mr. Dillard, the Convention adjourned until 9 o'clock A. M. to-morrow.

TWENTY-FIRST DAY.

HALL OF REPRESENTATIVES, ⎫
AUSTIN, TEXAS, September 29, 1875. ⎭

Convention met pursuant to adjournment; roll called; quorum present; prayer by the Rev. Mr. Dodge. of Austin.

Journal of yesterday were read and adopted.

The Chair submitted the following communication:

AUSTIN, TEXAS, September 29, 1875.

.*To the Constitutional Convention:*

I have the honor to report to the Convention, that, on the 27th day of September, 1875, the ordinance entitled, "An ordinance postponing the general election of December, A. D. 1875, and for other purposes," passed by the Convention on the 24th day of September, A. D. 1875, was duly enrolled, signed by the President of the Convention, countersigned by the Secretary, and deposited in the office of the Secretary of State, and the Governor informed of the action had in relation to said ordinance.

E. B. PICKETT,
President of the Convention.

Mr. Dohoney offered the following resolution:

WHEREAS, The people of the frontier of Texas, for years past, have been, and now are, suffering from depredations committed by lawless bands, organized beyond the border to invade our territory; and,

WHEREAS, These bands do invade Texas at its most exposed points, murder our citizens, carry their women and children into captivity, burn and pillage their homes, and steal and carry away their property; and,

WHEREAS, The United States forces, placed at the disposal of the general commanding the military district including our frontier, are wholly inadequate to the protection thereof, by reason of which the State of Texas, for years past, has been compelled, at great expense, to furnish troops for the protection of her own frontier; therefore,

Be it resolved by the Constitutional Convention of the State of Texas, That the President appoint a select committee of seven members of this body, with instructions to inquire into the extent of the aforesaid depredations and the causes thereof; to correspond wit hthe commander of the United States forces on said frontier and the citizens of the State who are exposed to the aforesaid depredations; and to prepare and present to the Congress and people of the United States a memorial, setting forth the condition of said frontier, and urging prompt measures for its adequate protection.

2. *Be it further resolved,* That our senators and representatives in Congress be, and they are hereby requested to lay before the President of the United States and the Secretary of War the exposed condition of our frontier; to secure, if possible, an adequate force for its protection, placed at the disposal of the commanding general; to lay the whole matter of frontier protection before Congress, and demand both adequate protection for the future, and reimbursement for all sums of money heretofore expended by the State for the protection of its own frontier.

3. That copies of this preamble and resolutions be furnished to our senators and representatives in Congress, and also to Major General E. O. C. Ord, United States Army, commanding the military district embracing our frontier.

Adopted.

Mr. Mills offered the following resolution:

Resolved, That section —— shall be a portion of the constitution, and shall read as follows:

"Section ——. No greater rate of interest shall be allowed on other amounts and contracts, when no interest is specified, than eight per centum per annum; but twelve per centum shall be allowed by special contract on maturity, and no greater. And all contracts, notes, and bills of exchange, providing for no payment or higher rate of interest, shall be null and void, and the creditor contracting for a higher rate of interest than twelve per centum per annum, shall forfeit the whole debt.

" Nor shall any note, bill, or contract in which a greater rate of interest than twelve per centum, as provided for, either directly or indirectly, be collectable, in the hands of any persons whatsoever.

"And it shall be a felony for any person to transfer any note, bill or other contract on which such usurious interest is charged, either directly or indirectly, and the Legislature shall pass all laws necessary to enforce this provision."

Referred to Committee on General Provisions.

Mr. Brown offered the following resolution, to be referred to the Committee on Public Lands and Land Office.

" Sec. ——. The Legislature shall have power to reserve from sale, location, or appropriation otherwise, except as herein provided, townships or districts of the public domain, not to exceed thirty-six sections of six hundred and forty acres each in any one townships or districts, for a term of five years after their settlenies of actual settlers. Such reservations, commencing in what is commonly known as the Pan Handle of Texas, may be extended westerly to the western limits of the State and south and southwesterly through the vacant and unappropriated public domain of the State to the Rio Grande. But between such townships or districts there shall always be a space of at least twenty-five miles. Such townships or districts shall be designated, surveyed and marked in such manner as may be provided by law.

" Sec. ——. The Legislature shall have power to grant to each head of a family who may settle in any such township or district three hundred and twenty acres of land, on condition that he or she shall reside thereon for the period of three years, and to single men, on the same condition, one hundred and sixty acres of land.

" Sec. ——. The Legislature may exempt all settlers in such townships or districts, for a term of five years after their settlement, from the payment of all State taxes on property owned by them within such township or district.

" Sec. ——. The Legislature may enact special laws, providing in each such district, until the same may become part of an organized county, for the election of a Justice of the Peace and a Constable, to be clothed with such powers as may be prescribed by law."

Referred as indicated.

Mr. Brady offered the following resolution:

Resolved, That the following be incorporated in the constitution:

" Sec. ——. The Legislature shall pass laws providing for taking the census of the State in the year 1885, and every ten years thereafter."

Referred to Committee on General Provisions.

The Convention then proceeded to the consideration of unfinished business, viz: Article ——, Legislative Department:

Mr. Flournoy offered the following amendment to section 41:

Strike out in line 206 the words " and give notice thereof by public proclamation."

Adopted.

Mr. Sanderson proposed to amend section 48 by striking out line 246.

Laid on the table.

Mr. Henry, of Smith, proposed to amend section 48, line 240, by striking out " shall " and inserting " may."

Adopted.

Mr. Wright offered the following amendment:

Amend section 48 by striking out line 248 and inserting " the support of the Blind Asylum, the Deaf and Dumb Asylum, and the Insane Asylum."

Adopted.

Mr. McCormick moved to reconsider the vote just taken.

Mr. Wade offered the following amendment:

In section 48, line 245, after the word " debt " insert " and for the payment of the present floating debt."

Withdrawn.

Mr. Davis, of Brazos, offered to amend, as follows:

Amend section 48 by adding after the word " schools," in line 246, the following: "And colleges and universities under the control of the State."

Lost.

Mr. Ferris offered the following substitute for section 49:

" Sec. 49. The aggregate amount of debts hereafter contracted by the Legislature shall never exceed the sum of one hundred thousand dollars, except in case of war, to repel invasion, or suppress insurrection; and in no case shall a debt be created, or bonds issued, except by a vote of two-thirds of both houses of the Legislature."

Mr. Stockdale proposed to amend the amendment by adding: "Except in the renewal of existing bonds, when they can not be paid at maturity out of the sinking fund or other resources."

15

Accepted by Mr. Ferris.

The question being on the adoption of the amendment, the yeas and nays were called and the substitute adopted by the following vote:

YEAS—Allison, Abernathy, Abner, Brown, Blake, Ballinger, Blassingame, Burleson, Brady, Bruce, Crawford, Cook of Gonzales, Cooke of San Saba, Cline, Cardis, Douglass, Dillard, Dohoney, Davis of Brazos, Davis of Wharton, Erhard, Flournoy, Ferris, Gaither, Henry of Limestone, Holmes, Haynes, Johnson of Franklin, Johnson of Collin, King, Killough, Lockett, Lynch, Martin of Navarro, Martin of Hunt, McCabe, Morris, Mills, Mitchell, McKinney, Moore, Nunn, Pauli, Ramey, Reynolds, Rentfro, Ross, Russell of Harrison, Spikes, Scott, Sessions, Smith, Stockdale, Stayton, Weaver—55.

NAYS—Arnim, Barnett, Chambers, Cooley, DeMorse, Darnell, Dunnam, Fleming, German, Graves, Holt, Henry of Smith, Kilgore, Lacy, McLean, McCormick, Norvell, Nugent, Reagan, Robertson of Bell, Robeson of Fayette, Russell of Wood, Wade, Whitehead, Wright, West—26.

Mr. Reagan offered the following substitute for section 49:

"Sec. 49. No debt shall be created by or on behalf of the State except to supply casual deficiencies of revenue, repel invasions, suppress insurrection, defend the State in war or pay existing debt; and the debt created to supply deficiencies in the revenue shall never exceed in the aggregate, at any one time, two hundred thousand dollars."

Mr. Mills proposed to amend the substitute by adding the words "and for school purposes."

Mr. McCormick moved to lay the amendment to the substitute on the table.

Carried by the following vote:

YEAS — Allison, Abernathy, Arnim, Brown, Blake, Blassingame, Burleson, Bruce, Chambers, Cook of Gonzales, Cooke of San Saba, Cardis, Douglass, DeMorse Darnell, Dunnam, Davis of Brazos, Flournoy, Fleming, Ferris, Gaither, Graves, Holt, Henry of Smith, Henry of Limestone, Holmes, Johnson of Franklin, Johnson of Collin, King, Kilgore, Killough, Lacy, Lynch, McLean, Martin of Navarro, McKinney, McCormick, Norvell, Nunn, Nugent, Reagan, Ramey, Robertson of Bell, Robeson of Fayette, Ross, Russell of Wood, Spikes, Scott, Sessions, Smith, Stockdale, Stayton, Wade, Whitehead, Wright, Weaver—56.

NAYS—Abner, Ballinger, Barnett, Brady, Crawford, Cline, Cooley, Dillard, Dohoney, Davis of Wharton, Erhard, Lockett,

Martin of Hunt, McCabe, Morris, Mills, Mitchell, Pauli, Reynolds, Rentfro, Russell of Harrison—21.

The question on the adoption of Mr. Reagan's substitute was then put and substitute adopted by the following vote:

YEAS—Allison, Arnim, Abner, Brown, Blake, Ballinger, Barnett, Burleson, Crawford, Cook of Gonzales, Cooke of San Saba, Cooley, Cardis, Darnell, Davis of Brazos, Davis of Wharton, Erhard, Ford, Ferris, Graves, Holt, Henry of Limestone, Haynes, Johnson of Collin, King, Kilgore, Killough, Lacy, Lynch, Martin of Navarro, Mills, McKinney, McCormick, Moore, Murphy, Norvell, Nunn, Reagan, Ramey, Robertson of Bell, Russell of Harrison, Spikes, Scott, Sessions, Smith, Stockdale, Whitehead, West—48.

NAYS—Abernathy, Blassingame, Brady, Bruce, Chambers, Cline, Douglass, Dillard, DeMorse, Dohoney, Dunnam, Flournoy, Fleming, German, Gaither, Henry of Smith, Holmes, Johnson of Franklin, Lockett, McLean, Martin of Hunt, McCabe, Morris, Mitchell, Nugent, Pauli, Reynolds, Rentfro, Robeson of Fayette, Ross, Russell of Wood, Wade, Wright, Weaver—34.

Mr. Arnim offered the following amendment:

Section 51, line 264, after the word "money" insert "public land, or anything of value."

Mr. Arnim withdrew his amendment.

On motion of Mr. Russell, of Wood, Mr. Ramey was added to Committee on Crimes and Punishments.

Mr. German offered the following amendment:

Section 51, line 264, after the word "money" insert "public lands, or other thing of value."

On motion of Mr. Ross, the Convention adjourned until 9 o'clock to-morrow morning, pending Mr. German's amendment.

TWENTY-SECOND DAY.

HALL OF REPRESENTATIVES, }
AUSTIN, TEXAS, September 30, 1875. }

Convention met pursuant to adjournment; roll called; quorum present. Prayer by Rev. Dr. Talliafero, of Austin.

Journals of yesterday read and adopted.

On motion of Mr. Flournoy the select committee authorized by Mr. Dohoney's resolution on affairs on our frontier, was increased from seven to eleven.

Mr. Wright asked and obtained leave of absence for a few days from attendance on the Convention.

Mr. Mills was also excused for a few days.

Mr. Kilgore presented the memorial of the bar of Longview on the subject of Judicial Districts.

Referred to Committee on Judicial Districts.

The chair announced the following Select Committee on Frontier Affairs: Messrs. Flournoy, Dohoney, Ford, Fleming, King, West, Barnett, Weaver, Ross, Cardis and Mills.

Mr. Robertson, of Bell, submitted a communication from L. K. Tarver and others, of Belton, on the subject of Judicial Districts.

Referred to the Committee on Judicial Districts.

Mr. Erhard presented the petition of sundry citizens of Bastrop county on the subject of payment of certain claims for ranging service before the war.

Referred to the Committee on Revenue and Taxation.

Mr. Ballinger, chairman of the standing Committee on Executive Department, submitted the following report and article, "Executive Department."

To the Hon. E. B. Pickett, President of the Convention:

The committee, to which was referred the preparation of an article on the Executive Department in a new constitution for the State, together with various resolutions relating thereto, having had the same under consideration, instruct me to report the accompanying article, styled the "Executive Department," and the committee recommend its adoption by the Convention.

W. P. BALLINGER, Chairman.

"Article ——.
"EXECUTIVE DEPARTMENT.

"Section 1. The Executive Department of the State shall consist of a Governor, who shall be the chief executive officer of the State, a Lieutenant Governor, Secretary of State, Comptroller of Public Accounts, Treasurer, Commissioner of the General Land Office, Attorney General, and Superintendent of Public Instruction.

"Sec. 2. All the above officers of the Executive Department (except Secretary of State,) shall be elected by the qualified electors of the State, at the time and places of election for members of the Legislature.

"Sec. 3. The returns of every election for said executive officers, until otherwise provided by law, shall be made out, sealed up, and transmitted by the returning officers prescribed by law, to the seat of government, directed to the Secretary of State, who shall deliver the same to the Speaker of the House of Representatives, as soon as the Speaker shall be chosen, and the said Speaker shall, during the first week of the session of the Legislature, open and publish them in the presence of both houses of the Legislature; the person having the highest number of votes for said officers respectively voted for at said election, and being constitutionally eligible, shall be declared by the Speaker, under the Legislature, to be elected to said office; but if two or more persons shall have the highest and equal number of votes for any of said officers, one of them shall be immediately chosen to such office by joint vote of both houses of the Legislature. Contested elections for any of said offices shall be determined by both houses of the Legislature.

" Sec. 4. The Governor shall be installed on the first Thursday after the organization of the Legislature, or as soon thereafter as practicable, and shall hold his office for the term of two years, or until his successor shall be duly installed. He shall not be eligible to election more than four years out of six successive years. He shall be at least thirty years of age, a citizen of the United States, and have resided in this State at least five years immediately preceding his election.

" Sec. 5. He shall, at stated times, receive as compensation for his services, an annual salary of five thousand dollars, and no more, and shall also have the use and occupation of the Governor's mansion, fixtures and furniture.

" Sec. 6. During the time he holds the office of Governor he shall not hold any other office, civil, military or corporate; nor shall he practice any profession and receive compensation, reward, fee, or the promise thereof for the same; nor receive any salary, reward or compensation, or the promise thereof, from any person or corporation for any service rendered or act performed during the time he is Governor, or to be thereafter rendered or performed.

" Sec. 7. He shall be commander-in-chief of the military forces of the State, except when they are called into the actual service of the United States. He shall have power to call for the militia to execute the laws of the State, to suppress insurrections and repel invasions.

" Sec. 8. The Governor may, on extraordinary occasions, convene the Legislature at the seat of government, or at a different place in case that should be in possession of the public enemy, or of the prevalence of disease thereat. His proclamation therefor shall state specifically the purpose for which they are convened, and the Legislature shall enter upon no business except that for which they were convened, or which may be presented to them by the Governor.

" Sec. 9.   The Governor shall, at the commencement of each session of the Legislature, and at the close of his term of office, give to the Legislature information by message of the condition of the State; and he shall recommend to the Legislature such measures as he may deem expedient.   He shall account to the Legislature, and accompany his message with a statement of all public moneys received and paid out by him from any funds subject to his order, with vouchers; and at the commencement of each regular session he shall present estimates of the amount of money required to be raised by taxation for all purposes.

" Sec. 10.   He shall cause the laws to be faithfully executed; and shall conduct in person, or in such manner as shall be prescribed by law, all intercourse and business of the State with other States and with the United States.

" Sec. 11.   In all criminal cases, except treason and impeachment, he shall have power, after conviction, to grant reprieves, commutations and pardons, and under such rules as the Legislature may prescribe, he shall have power to remit fines and forfeitures.   With the advice and consent of the Senate, he may grant pardons in cases of treason; and to this end he may respite a sentence therefor until the close of the succeeding session of the Legislature; *provided,* that in all cases of remissions of fines or forfeitures, or grants of reprieve, commutation or pardon, he shall file in the office of the Secretary of State his reasons therefor.

" Sec. 12.   All vacancies in State or district offices, except members of the Legislature, shall be filled, unless otherwise provided by law, by appointment of the Governor, which appointment, if made during its session, shall be with the advice and consent of two-thirds of the Senate present.   If made during the recess of the Senate, the said appointee, or some other person to fill said vacancy, shall be nominated to the Senate during the first ten days of its session; if rejected, said office shall immediately become vacant; and the Governor shall, without delay, make further nominations, until a confirmation take place; but should there be no confirmation during the session of the Senate, the Governor shall not thereafter appoint any person to fill such vacancy who has been rejected by the Senate, but may appoint some other person to fill the vacancy until the next session of the Senate, or until the regular election to said office, should it sooner occur.   Appointments to vacancies in offices elective by the people shall only continue until the first general election thereafter.

"Sec. 13 During the sessions of the Legislature the Governor shall reside where its sessions are held, and at all other times at the seat of government ; except when by act of the Legislature he may be required or authorized to reside elsewhere.

"Sec. 14. Every bill which shall have passed both houses of the Legislature shall be presented to the Governor for his approval. If he approve he shall sign it, but if he disapprove it he shall return it with its objections to the house in which it originated, which house shall enter the objections at large upon their journal and proceed to reconsider it.   If, after such reconsideration, two-thirds of the members present agree to pass the bill, it shall be sent with the objections to the other house, by which likewise it shall be reconsidered, and if approved by two-thirds of the members present of that house, it shall become a law; but in such cases the votes of both houses shall be determined by yeas and nays, and the names of the members voting for and against the bill shall be entered on the journal of each house respectively.   If any bill shall not be returned by the Governor with his objections within ten days (Sundays excepted) after it shall have been presented to him, the same shall be a law in like manner as if he had signed it, unless the Legislature by their adjournment prevent its return, in which case it shall be a law, unless he shall file the same with his objections in the office of the Secretary of State and give notice thereof by public proclamation within twenty days after such adjournment. If any bill presented to the Governor contains several items of appropriation, he may object to one or more of such items while approving the other portion of the bill. In such case he shall append to the bill at the time of signing it a statement of the items to which he objects, and no item so objected to shall take effect. If the Legislature be in session, he shall transmit to the house in which the bill originated a copy of such statement, and the items objected to shall be separately considered. If, on reconsideration, one or more of such items be approved by two-thirds of the members present of each house, the same shall be part of the law notwithstanding the objections of the Governor. If any such bill, containing several items of appropriation, not having been presented to the Governor ten days (Sundays excepted) prior to adjournment, be in the hands of the Governor at the time of adjournment, he shall have twenty days from such adjournment within which to file objection to any item or items thereof and make proclamation of the same, and such item or items shall not take effect.

" Sec. 15. Every order, resolution or vote to which the concurrence of both houses of the Legislature may be necessary, except on questions of adjournment, shall be presented to the Governor, and before it shall take effect shall be approved by him, or, being disapproved, shall be repassed by both houses, and all the rules, provisions and limitations shall apply thereto prescribed in the last preceding section in the case of a bill.

" Sec. 16. There shall also be a Lieutenant Governor, who shall be chosen at every election for Governor by the same electors, and in the same manner, continue in office for the same time, and possess the same qualifications. The electors shall distinguish for whom they vote as Governor and for whom as Lieutenant Governor. The Lieutenant Governor shall, by virtue of his office, be President of the Senate, and have, when in committee of the whole, a right to debate and vote on all questions, and when the Senate is equally divided to give the casting vote. In case of the death, resignation, removal from office, inability or refusal of the Governor to serve, or his impeachment, or absence from the State, the Lieutenant Governor shall exercise the powers and authority appertaining to the office of Governor until another be chosen at the periodical election, and be duly qualified, or until the Governor impeached, absent or disabled, shall be acquitted, return, or his disability be removed.

" Sec. 17. Whenever the government shall be administered by the Lieutenant Governor, or he shall be unable to attend as President of the Senate, the Senate shall elect one of their own members as President for the time being; and if, during the vacancy of the office of Governor the Lieutenant Governor should die, resign, refuse to serve, or be removed from office, or be unable to serve, or if he shall be impeached, or absent from the State, the President of the Senate for the time being shall in like manner administer the government until he shall be superseded by a Governor or Lieutenant Governor. The Lieutenant Governor shall, whilst he acts as President of the Senate, receive for his services the same compensation which shall be allowed the Speaker of the House of Representatives, and no more; and during the time he administers the government as Governor shall receive the same compensation which the Governor would have received had he been employed in the duties of his office, and no more. The President, for the time being, of the Senate, shall, during the time he administers the government, receive in like manner the same compensation which the

Governor would have received had be been employed in the duties of his office.   If the Lieutenant Governor shall be required to administer the government, and shall, whilst in such administration, die, resign, or be absent from the State during the recess of the Legislature, it shall be the duty of the Secretary of State to convene the Senate for the purpose of choosing a President for the time being.

"Sec. 18.   The Lieutenant Governor and President of the Senate, succeeding to the office of Governor, shall, during the entire term to which they succeed, be under all the restrictions and inhibitions imposed in this constitution on the Governor.

"Sec. 19.   There shall be a seal of the State, which shall be kept by the Secretary of State, and used by him officially, under the direction of the Governor.   The seal of the State shall be a star of five points, encircled by olive and live-oak branches, and the words 'The State of Texas.'

"Sec. 20.   All commissions shall be in the name and by the authority of the State of Texas, be sealed with the State seal, signed by the Governor, and attested by the Secretary of State.

"Sec. 21.   There shall be a Secretary of State, who shall be appointed by the Governor, by and with the advice and consent of the Senate, and shall continue in office during the term of service of the Governor elect.   He shall authenticate the publication of the laws, and keep a fair register of all official acts and proceedings of the Governor, and shall, when required, lay the same, and all papers, minutes, and vouchers relative thereto, before the Legislature, or either house thereof, and shall perform such other duties as may be required of him by law.   He shall receive for his services an annual salary of two thousand dollars, and no more.

"Sec. 22.   The Attorney General shall hold his office for two years, and until his successor is duly qualified.   He shall represent the State in all suits and pleas in the Supreme Court of the State in which the State may be a party, and give legal advice, in writing, to the Governor and other executive officers when requested by them, and perform such other duties as may be required by law.   He shall reside at the seat of government during his continuance in office.   He shall receive for his services an annual salary of two thousand dollars, and no more, besides such fees as may be prescribed by law.

"Sec. 23. The Comptroller of Public Accounts, the Treasurer, and the Commissioner of the General Land Office, shall each hold office for the term of four years, and until his successor is qualified; receive an annual salary of two thousand five hundred dollars, and no more; reside at the capital of the State during his continuance in office, and perform such duties as are, or may be, required of him by law. They, and the Secretary of State, shall not receive to their own use any fees, costs, or perquisites of office, or other compensation. All fees that may be payable by law for any service performed by any officer specified in this article, or in his office, shall be paid, when received, into the State treasury.

"Sec. 24. An account shall be kept by the officers of the Executive Department, and by all officers and managers of State institutions, of all moneys and choses in action received and disbursed or otherwise disposed of by them severally, from all sources, and for every service performed; and a semi-annual report thereof shall be made to the Governor under oath. The Governor may at any time require information in writing from any and all of said officers or managers upon any subject relating to the duties, condition, management and expenses of their respective offices and institutions, which information may be required by the Governor under oath, and the Governor may also inspect their books, accounts, vouchers and public funds, and any officer or manager who at any time shall make a false report or give false information, shall be guilty of perjury, and punished accordingly.

"Sec. 25. The Legislature shall pass efficient laws facilitating the investigation of breaches of trust and duty by all custodians of public funds, and providing for their suspension from office on reasonable cause shown, and for the appointment of temporary incumbents of their offices during such suspension.

"Sec. 26. The Governor, by and with the advice and consent of two-thirds of the Senate, shall appoint a convenient number of Notaries Public for each county, who shall perform such duties as now are or may be prescribed by law."

Report received, to come up in its order.

Mr. Fleming moved to have two hundred copies of the report and article printed.

Mr. Haynes moved to amend by inserting "ninety copies."

Mr. Stayton moved to amend by inserting "four hundred copies."

Mr. Fleming's motion carried, and two hundred copies ordered printed.

The following communication from the Commissioner of the General Land Office was taken from the President's desk, read and referred to the Committee on Public Lands and Land Office.

GENERAL LAND OFFICE, }
AUSTIN, September 29, 1875. }

To the Hon. E. B. Pickett, President of the Convention:

SIR—I have the honor to acknowledge the receipt of a copy of a resolution, adpoted by the Convention on the 28th inst., requesting statement showing the annual expenditure necessary to carry on the business of the General Land Office, the amount of fees collected by said office and paid into the State treasury, the number of employes and the salaries paid them.

In compliance with said request I hand you the following statements:

Exhibit "A" shows the amount of office and patent fees received by the office during each of the past four fiscal years, beginning August 31st, 1871, and ending September 1st, 1875.

The term " office fees " embraces all sums received for the examinations, statements, copies and certificates to railroad and other companies for internal improvements.

Exhibit " B " shows the appropriations made by the Legislature for the support of the Land Office for each of six fiscal years, beginning September 1st, 1870, and ending August 31st, 1876. None of these appropriations include the amount paid annually for printing the blanks required by the office. The orders for the necessary blanks are sent to the " Printing Board " and paid for out of the appropriation for public printing.

A comparison of the appropriation for the year ending August 31st, 1875, with the amount of fees received by the office during the same period, shows the receipts to have exceeded the appropriation by eight thousand three hundred and forty dollars ($8340). But this instance can not be taken as a criterion; the large excess of office fees received during the year just closed over any preceding year is attributable to the large number of certificates issued to railroad companies and companies for improving the navigation of the rivers of this State. It is not likely the revenue of the office from the same source will ever be as large. As it is impossible to say in advance what will be the receipts of the office for the next year, I can not state (to use the language of the resolution) what " the cost of carrying on the said Land Office, over and above the amounts received as fees," will be.

The revenue of the office could be very materially increased by charging a fee of 25c. upon each certificate, transfer, field note, or other document required by law, or permitted to be filed. If the present fee, $4, charged for certificates, authorizing the location of land issued by this office was increased, the amount received by reason of such increase would add largely to the revenue of the office.

Exhibit " C " shows the number of employes in said office, and the amount paid them per month.

The annual appropriation necessary for wood, stationery and postage, is $3000.

I am, very respectfully,

Your obedient servant,

J. J. GROOS, Commissioner.

EXHIBIT " A."

Showing amount of office and patent fees paid into the General Land Office for the fiscal years 1871, 1872, 1873 and 1874, the fiscal year beginning September 1, and ending August 31.

September 1, 1871, to August 31, 1872:

Office Fees...	$12,779 00
Patent Fees..	4,734 00
Total	**$17,513 00**

September 1, 1872, to August 31, 1873:

Office Fees...	$20,242 00
Patent Fees	9,457 00
Total	**$29,699 00**

September 1, 1873, to August 31, 1874:

Office Fees...	$20,620 00
Patent Fees..	17,425 00
Total	**$38,045 00**

September 1, 1874, to August 31, 1875:

Office Fees...	$27,854 00
Patent Fees..	24,886 00
Total	**$52,740 00**

EXHIBIT " B."

Showing appropriations made for the General Land Office for the fiscal years 1871, 1872, 1873, 1874, 1875 and 1876, beginning on September 1, and ending August 31:

September 1, 1870, to August 31, 1871.............	$42,700 00
September 1, 1871, to August 31, 1872.............	42,900 00
September 1, 1872, to August 31, 1873.............	62,683 00
September 1, 1873, to August 31, 1874.............	76,100 00

September 1, 1874, to August 31, 1875.......... $44,400 00
September 1, 1875, to August 31, 1876.......... 46,550 00

EXHIBIT "C."

Statement showing the number of employes of the General Land Office, and their salaries, for the month of September, 1875:

Commissioner	$250	00
Chief Clerk	166	66
Chief Draftsman	166	66
Spanish Translator	166	66
Receiving Clerk.............................	150	00
Six Clerks, at $116 66......................	699	96
Two Clerks, at $108 33......................	216	66
Fourteen Clerks, at $13,000 per annum........	1,083	33
Four Draftsmen, at $125 per month...........	500	00
Ten Draftsmen, at $100 per month............	1,000	00
One Night Watchman.........................	41	66
One Porter	33	33

Total number, exclusive of Commissioner... 42 } Total............. $4,474 92

Mr. Dohoney submitted the following report:

COMMITTEE ROOM,
AUSTIN, September 30, 1875.

To the Hon. E. B. Pickett, President of the Convention:

The Committee on Suffrage, to whom was referred various memorials and resolutions in reference to the right of suffrage, and proposed extensions thereof, as well as limitations thereon, have had the same under careful consideration, and the majority of said committee instruct me to report the accompanying article on suffrage as a substitute for the whole, and respectfully recommend its adoption by the Convention, as a part of the constitution.

E. L. DOHONEY, Chairman.

"ARTICLE —.
"SUFFRAGE.

Section 1. The following classes of persons shall not be allowed to vote in this State, to-wit: First, persons under twenty-one years of age; second, idiots and lunatics; third, all inmates of State asylums, and all paupers supported by any county; fourth, all persons convicted of bribery in receiving money, intoxicating drinks, or other thing of value, for their votes, also all persons convicted of any felony; fifth, all soldiers and marines employed in the service of the army or navy of the United States.

"Sec. 2. The following classes of persons shall be entitled to vote at all elections of the people held in this State: First, every male person over twenty-one years of age, and subject to none of the foregoing disqualifications, who, being a citizen of the United States, shall have resided for twelve months in this State, and for six months in the county, next preceding any election at which he may offer to vote, and who, in addition thereto, shall have paid all poll taxes due by him to the State and county before said election; second, every male person of foreign birth subject to none of the foregoing disqualifications, who, six months before any such election shall have declared his intention to become a citizen of the United States, in accordance with the Federal naturalization laws; who shall have resided in this State twelve months, and in the county in which he offers to vote six months, next preceding any election; and who, in addition thereto, shall have paid all poll taxes due by him to the State and county before said election.

"Sec. 3. Every qualified elector in this State who shall have resided for six months next preceding any election at which he may offer to vote, in any incorporated town or city, and who, in addition thereto, shall have paid all taxes due said town or city that have accrued against him since the adoption of this constitution, shall be entitled to vote at elections held in such incorporated town or city; *provided,* that in elections for the creation of debt for the improvement of such town or city, or for other purpose, freeholders only shall vote.

"Sec. 4. All elections of the people in this State shall be by ballot, and under such regulations as the Legislature may prescribe.

"Sec. 5. Voters shall in all cases, except treason, felony or breach of the peace, be privileged from arrest during their attendance at elections, and in going to and returning therefrom.

Mr. Rentfro, from the same committee, made the following minority report:

COMMITTEE ROOM, }
AUSTIN, September 29, 1875. }

To the Hon. E. B. Pickett, President of the Convention:

The undersigned, a member of the Committee on Suffrage, to which committee were referred certain resolutions, etc., relating to the qualification of electors, would respectfully submit that he can not entirely concur in the majority report and attached sections. In the main he most heartily indorses the sections so submitted by the majority of said committee, and concurs in the qualifications therein stated, yet he feels it to be his duty, as a representative in part of the people of this State, most earnestly to protest against the requirements as set forth in the latter portions of 1st and 2d clauses of section 2 of said majority report. Said clause, after stating certain qualifications as to sex, age, etc., reads as follows: "And who, in addition thereto, shall have paid all State and county poll taxes for at least .... days before said election."

In part second of said article 2d the same language occurs with reference to naturalized citizens. The undersigned would submit, that although it is a principle of a republican form of government that taxation and representation should go hand in hand, yet he feels that a requirement of the payment by the electors of this State of poll taxes, as a prerequisite to the exercise on their part of the "elective franchise," would be a perversion of that principle; that said provision, if incorporated in the State constitution, would, although presumably general in its operation, militate most severely against the interests of the working classes of the State. He submits, that if the doctrine that an elector should exhibit his tax receipt before being allowed a voice in the selection of his rulers obtains in any degree, that payment of all taxes of every character whatsoever should be required as a prerequisite to the right of voting from any and all persons. He insists that if said provision is asked to be incorporated in the State constitution for the purpose of raising revenue, that the amounts derived therefrom will be wholly insufficient to carry out the end desired. On the other hand, if said provision has for its object a partial restriction of the right of suffrage, he believes the sentiment of the people of the State to be unqualifiedly opposed to any provision having for its object the attainment of such an end. He maintains that said provision would practically deprive of the right of voting many good citizens of this State, and believing, as he does, that the exercise of the "elective franchise" in a republican government is a *right* and not, as it has erroneously been termed, a *privilege,* he feels that he would be false to the duty which, as a delegate, he owes to the working classes of this State, if he did not most earnestly protest against an incorporation in the organic law of any provision tending to hinder the electors in the free exercise of that *right*. Maintaining that the right of voting should be free; that no provisions should be placed in the organic law, which while it cannot affect the rights of those whom fortune has blessed with an abundance, yet may operate most disastrously against the rights of the poor; and believing that the portion of said section as above will so do, the undersigned, with all respect to the majority of said committee, must ask leave to differ with said majority, and assigning the above as some few of his objections to the said sections, while concurring in the remainder, respectfully submits the above as his protest and report in the premises.   R. B. Rentfro.

Mr. Cook, of Gonzales, moved to have 100 copies of reports and article printed.

Mr. Dohoney moved to have 100 copies of the reports and 200 copies of the article printed.

On motion of Mr. Chambers the question was divided and 100 copies of the reports and 200 copies of the article ordered printed.

Mr. Russell, of Harrison, submitted the following ordinance and resolution:

ORDINANCE.

Whereas, The late disastrous storm on the coast of the State of Texas ruined and placed in a condition of want and distress the people residing in the counties hereinafter named; and

Whereas, In their said condition they are totally unable at present to pay the State taxes due by them for the year 1875; and to exact of them said tax would be to further embarrass and distress them and impose upon them additional ills and burdens; therefore

Be it ordained by the people of Texas in Convention assembled, That the collection of the State tax levied for the year 1875 upon the property of the people residing in the counties of Chambers, Brazoria, Matagorda and Calhoun, be and the same is hereby restrained and enjoined; and that the sheriffs and tax collectors of said counties are hereby forbidden and enjoined from the collection of said tax; and that the tax-payers in said counties are hereby relieved and exempted from the payment of said tax due for the year 1875.

Resolved, further, That a committee of seven be appointed by the President to inquire into and report upon the ordinance, and that they be authorized to report for the relief of any other counties on said coast not named in this ordinance.

On motion of Mr. Russell, of Wood, the ordinance was referred to the Committee on Revenue and Taxation.

Mr. Erhard offered the following resolution:

Resolved, That the State of Texas sustain and uphold a Bureau of Immigration; that we may find a market for our school lands, and obtain labor, also to encourage trade and commerce and to develop our State generally.

Immigrants, particularly those who do not understand the English language, need good and disinterested advice, the necessity of which all those will appreciate who ever were in any foreign country.

In the preamble of the Declaration of Independence, the fathers of the Republic of the United States stated as one of their grievances that the British King had refused to pass laws to encourage immigration hither. The grandure of wealth of the United States is due to immigration. The unparalleled success of the great West and California is due to a well regulated immigration bureau.

The Republic of Texas induced immigration by giving heads of families, and even young men of seventeen years of age, liberal land grants, being well aware their newly-acquired Republic would be valueless without immigration.

Referred to Immigration Committee.

Mr. Kilgore offered the following resolution:

WHEREAS, There are now but two pages for the Convention to perform the duties heretofore performed by four; and

WHEREAS, The labor of two pages are very burdensome and require their constant attention; therefore

Be it resolved, That the per diem of said pages, from and after the passage of this resolution, shall be three dollars ($3) per day.

Laid over under the rules.

Mr. Erhard offered the following:

Every married woman shall have her title to property received at marriage or inherited hereafter recorded, and she shall have sole control over it; she may exchange, buy or sell in her own right, but her property shall be liable for all contracts she makes. No property to be sold under forced sale unless it bring two-thirds of its value; but it shall be offered for sale each continuous six months till it bring said value. Proper notices being posted each time as in first instance.

Referred to Committee on General Provisions.

Mr. Stockdale submitted the following report:

To the Hon. E. B. Pickett, President of the Convention:

The Committee on Rules, to which was referred resolutions making additional rules for the government of the Convention,

16

beg leave to report that they have duly considered the same, and now return them and recommend that they be adopted. The committe also present, in addition to the rules referred to them, the accompanying rule, and recommend that it be also adopted.

All of which is respectfully submitted.

F. S. STOCKDALE, Chairman.

Rule 1. Every resolution or ordinance, before it becomes a part of the constitution, shall be read on three several days.

The first reading shall be for information, and upon being read a first time, if not reported by a committee, it shall be referred to the appropriate committee, without debate.

Upon a second reading of a resolution or ordinance, it shall be subject to commitment or amendment.

The final question upon the second reading shall be "Whether it shall be engrossed and read a third time."

Rule 2. No amendment shall be received at the third reading of a resolution or ordinance without the consent of two-thirds of the members present.

It shall be in order, at the third reading of a resolution or ordinance, to move its commitment; and should such commitment take place, and any amendment be reported by the committee, the said resolution or ordinance shall be considered as on its second reading.

Rule 3. Business on the table shall be taken up in the following order:

First—Single resolutions.

Second—Resolutions and ordinances on the second reading.

Third—Resolutions and ordinances on the third reading.

Rule. 4. Whenever any article of the constitution shall be passed, upon its third reading, under the foregoing rules, it shall be, as of course, referred to the Committee on Style and Arrangement. When the whole constitution is reported back to the Convention by said committee, it shall then be considered by the Convention as on its second reading, and acted upon according to the same rules and order as provided for resolutions and ordinances in the foregoing rules.

Adopted.

Mr. Nunn moved to reconsider the vote refusing to adopt the amendment of Mr. Davis, of Brazos, to section 48, article —, Legislative Department, viz: by adding after the word "schools" in line 246 the words "and colleges and universities under the control of the State."

Motion passed over for the present.

Mr. Whitfield, chairman of the Committee on Education, made the following report:

COMMITTEE ROOM, }
AUSTIN, September 30, 1875. }

To the Hon. E. B. Pickett, President of the Convention:

Your Committee on Education, to whom was referred various resolutions, have carefully considered the same, and a majority of the committee instruct me to report the following and recommend its passage.

J. W. WHITFIELD, Chairman.
L. W. MOORE,
WM. NEAL RAMEY,
W. B. WRIGHT,
A. C. GRAVES,
FRAN's J. LYNCH,
B. ABERNATHY,
GEORGE FLOURNOY,
EDWARD CHAMBERS.

"ARTICLE —.

"EDUCATION.

"Section 1. A general diffusion of knowledge being essential to the preservation of liberties of the people, it shall be the duty of the Legislature of this State to make suitable provisions for the support and maintenance of public schools.

"Sec. 2. All funds, lands and other property heretofore set apart and appropriated, or that may hereafter be set apart and appropriated for the support of public schools, all the alternate sections of land reserved by the State out of grants heretofore made or that may hereafter be made to railroads or other corporations of any nature whatever, one-half of the public domain of the State, and all sums of money that may come to the State from the sale of any portion of the same, shall constitute a perpetual public school fund.

"Sec. 3. And there shall be set apart annually not more than one-tenth of the annual revenue derivable from taxation for general purposes, and such poll tax as may by law be levied under the provisions of this constitution, which shall also constitute a part of the public school fund.

"Sec. 4. The lands herein set apart to the perpetual school fund shall be sold under such regulations, at such time, and upon such terms as may be prescribed by law, and the Legislature shall not have power to grant any relief to the purchasers thereof. The Comptroller shall invest the proceeds of such sale, and of those heretofore made, in the bonds of this State, if the same can be obtained, otherwise in United States bonds, and the United States bonds now belonging to said fund shall likewise be invested in State bonds, if the same can be obtained.

"Sec. 5. The principal of all bonds, or other funds, and the principal arising from the sales of lands hereinbefore set apart to said school fund, shall be the permanent school fund, and all the interest derivable therefrom, and the taxes herein provided, shall be the available school fund, which shall be applied annually to the support of public schools, and no law shall ever be made appropriating any part of the permanent or available school fund to any other purpose whatever, except as hereinafter provided.

"Sec. 6. All public lands which have been heretofore, or may be hereafter, granted to the various counties of this State for public schools, are of right the property of said counties respectively, to which they are granted, and entitled thereto, and is hereby vested in said counties, subject to the trust created in the grant.

"Sec. 7. So soon as the available school fund may be sufficient, the Legislature shall establish and maintain free public schools throughout the State for a period of not less than four months in each year, and may authorize any county to establish public schools in such county whenever the available fund apportioned to such county as herein provided, together with the fund realized from the sale of the lands of the county, shall be sufficient to maintain public schools in such county for not less than four months in each year. But until such time the available school fund hereinbefore provided shall be distributed to the several counties of the State according to the scholastic population. The distribution to be made by the Governor, the Comptroller and the Treasurer, who for this duty shall constitute a school board. The fund shall be distributed to the counties and applied in aid of private schools in such mode as the Legislature may provide.

"Sec. 8. All lands heretofore granted for the benefit of the Lunatic Asylum, the Blind Asylum, the Deaf and Dumb Asylum and the Orphan Asylum, together with such donations as may have been or may hereafter be made to either of them, are hereby set apart to provide a permanent school fund for the support and maintenance and improvement of said asylums; but the Legislature shall have the power, whenever deemed advisable, to provide for the sale in part or in whole of said lands. The proceds of said lands when realized, together with all moneys severally donated to such asylums or either of them, shall be invested in bonds of the State of Texas, if obtainable; if not, in bonds of the United States, in such manner as the Legislature shall provide. And the proceeds of the interest thereon shall be a several available fund for each of said asylums, and for no other purpose.

"Sec. 9. Separate schools shall be provided for the white and colored children, and impartial provision shall be made for both."

Mr. Stansom, from the same committee, submitted the following minority report:

> COMMITTEE ROOM, }
> AUSTIN, September 30, 1875. }

To the Hon. E. B. Pickett, President of the Convention:

The undersigned, members of your Committee on Public Education, beg leave to state that they are unable to concur in the report submitted by the majority of said committee, for the following reasons, viz:

They believe the education of children to be a private duty— devolved upon the parent by God, as is manifest both from the laws of nature and revelation — and to the end that the parent may be enabled to discharge this great duty, the same laws confer on him the right to control his children; and they do not believe that a democratic government can, without violating the great principles of personal freedom and individual right upon which it is founded, either relieve the parent of this duty by laying it upon the shoulders of another, or deprive him of this right by assuming it.

They are unable to see how a government established for the protection of private property can, without subverting the purposes of its creation, take by taxation the private property of a portion of its citizens and apply it to the use of another portion of its citizens, unless it be given in compensation for services rendered the State or for the preservation of life.

They are satisfied that no system of public free schools, which does not enforce the regular attendance at the schools of all the children within the scholastic age, will or can secure the object sought to be attained. And they find it very difficult to discover the right of a free government to impose *public* duties upon those of its citizens who have not attained their majority which it does not even claim the right to impose on older citizens.

They believe that a system of public education, by passing the control of the children into the hands of the State, and empowering the State to prescribe the qualifications of teachers and the course of instruction, endangers religious liberty — as, in their view, religious liberty implies not only the right of the parent to worship God according to the dictates of his own conscience, but as well his right to direct the religious instruction of his children.

They believe that a system of public education designed to embrace the entire scholastic population of the State, and to be supported by taxation, is not adapted to the condition of the people of this State, and that they do not desire such a system.

They believe that the benefits to be derived from any system of public education, even the most perfect, if not altogether valueless, are certainly a very poor compensation for the sacrifice of principle necessary to its adoption by a free people.

They are so far, however, from undervaluing the importance of education, that they deem it the duty of the Convention to make out of the public means at the disposal of the State, the most ample provision for the free tuition of all the indigent orphan children in the State, and prospectively for, at least, the partial instruction of all the children of the State; and this they believe may be accomplished without the violation of any valuable principle by the adoption of the articles herewith respectfully submitted.

R. Sansom,
Asa Holt,
A. J. C. Dunnam,
G. B. Cooke.

"Article ——.

" Section 1.   To promote the general diffusion of knowledge, the lands heretofore set apart by the Republic or State of Texas, and the moneys, bonds and other property now owned by the State, which have been devoted to the use or support of public free schools, and in addition thereto one-half of the public domain now subject to disposal by the State, shall constitute the basis of a permanent fund, to be called the general educational fund; *provided,* that the title to lands given to the State for the use and benefit of public free schools, shall be surrendered to the donors at their option; but the right of the State to improvements put upon said lands by the State shall not be thereby affected.

" Sec. 2.   The Legislature shall provide for the sale of all the lands set apart in section one of this article, which have been located, or which may hereafter be located, by railroad or other corporations, and for the sale of all other property therein set apart.   And all moneys derived from the sale of the same shall be invested in bonds of the State or of the United States.

" Sec. 3.   The interest accruing on the general educational fund shall be distributed annually by the Comptroller of Public Accounts between the respective counties of the State, according to their scholastic population, and shall be distributed as follows: First, to the payment of tuition for four months in each year of all the indigent orphan children of the State, between the ages of eight and sixteen years. The remainder to be applied, *pro-rata*, to the payment of tuition of all the children of the State within said ages. But the State shall not levy a tax to support a system of public free schools."

Mr. Cline gave notice that he would submit a separate minority report at a future time.

Mr. Whitfield moved to have two hundred copies of the articles, reported by the majority and minority, printed, and that they be made the special order for Tuesday next at 10 o'clock A. M.

Carried.

The following communication from the Adjutant General was taken from the President's desk and read:

ADJUTANT GENERAL'S OFFICE,
STATE OF TEXAS,
AUSTIN, September 30, 1875.

To the Hon. E. B. Pickett, President of the Convention:

SIR — I have the honor to submit statements of the strength and cost of all troops that have been called out for frontier protection since the inauguration of Governor Davis, and to the present time.

To make a list of all officers and men, and to separate and itemize accounts of quartermasters, commissary and transportation, would require the examination of vouchers filed in the Comptroller's office for the last six years, and it is doubtful if it could be completed in time to lay it before your honorable body.

I have no information in regard to the number and disposition of United States troops in Texas.

The State forces are under the command of their own officers.

Very respectfully, your obedient servant,
WM. STEELE, Adjutant General.

Frontier Forces Organized under Law approved June 13, 1870.

Letter of Co.	Station— Counties	Captains	Lieut.	Surgeon	Sergeant	Corp'l	Buglers	Farriers	Privates	Total	Mustered In	Mustered Out
A	Mason	Franklin Jones	1	1	3	4	1	1	50	62	August 25, 1870	November 12, 1870.
B	Erath	A. H. Cox	1	1	3	4	1	1	50	62	September 8, 1870	May 15, 1871.
C	Kerr	J. W. Sansom	1	1	3	4	1	1	50	62	August 25, 1870	May 31, 1871.
D	Uvalde	J. R. Kelso	1	1	4	4	...	1	50	62	September 10, 1870	January 20, 1871.
E	Fort Inge	H. J. Richarz	1	1	3	4	1	1	50	61	September 9, 1870	June 15, 1871.
F	Wise	D. P. Baker	1	1	3	4	1	1	39	50	November 5, 1870	June 15, 1871.
G	Starr	C. G. Falcon	1	1	3	4	1	1	43	55	October 8, 1870	April 30, 1871.
H	Zapata	B. Chamberlain	1	1	3	4	1	1	39	50	November 15, 1870	February 28, 1871.
I	Mason	J. M. Hunter	1	1	3	4	...	1	43	55	September 12, 1870	January 24, 1871.
K	Lampasas	J. M. Harrell	1	1	3	4	1	1	50	62	September 16, 1870	February 16, 1871.
L	Gillespie	H. R. V. Biberstein	1	1	3	4	...	1	50	61	October 10, 1870	May 31, 1871.
N	El Paso	G. Garcia	1	...	3	4	1	1	39	50	August 21, 1870	June 15, 1871.
O	Kimble	P. Kleid	1	...	3	4	1	1	49	60	August 29, 1870	May 31, 1871.
P	Coleman	J. P. Swisher	1	1	3	8	1	1	50	62	September 6, 1870	February 6, 1871.
14		14	14	12	48	55	11	18	652	814		

Capt. Falcon, Company G, reports that on April 21, 1871, his company recovered 130 head of cattle from thieves at Las Curvas, on the Rio Grande, wounding one of the thieves.

Captain Chamberlain, Co. H, February 25, 1871, reports the arrest by his company of several cattle thieves.

Capt. Cox, Co. B, reports that on May 4, 1871, Sergeant R. V. Parker and 11 men of his company attacked and defeated a band of 40 Indians, on Rocky Creek, Palo Pinto county, killing 10 warriors and recapturing 40 horses; four men of company wounded.

Capt. Sansom, Co. C, reports that on October 27, 1870, a pursuit of Indians and recapture of 6 horses and 2 mules.

Capt. Richarz, Co. E, December 4, 1870, reports an Indian raid in numbers from Mexico, and the pursuit and recapture of 5 horses.   December 9, 1870, reports an engagement with Indians; 8 killed and 15 wounded; 3 Rangers killed, amongst whom the captain's son.

Capt. Baker, Co. F, reports, February 7, 1871, an engagement between 10 men of his company and 40 Indians; 2 Indians killed (one a chief) and several wounded; captured 2 horses and 1 mule.

Capt. Swisher, Co. P, January 23, 1871, reports a skirmish with Indians; 1 killed and several wounded; recaptured 38 horses; 1 Ranger wounded.

RECAPITULATION.— Recovered 130 cattle, 94 horses and mules; Indians killed, 21 ; Rangers killed, 3 ; Rangers wounded, 5.

The cost of this force (which was paid from the proceeds of the sale of bonds authorized to be issued and sold by act approved August 5, 1879,) was as follows:

To Quartermaster Stores	$12,922 65
Transportation	13,943 70
Forage and Rations	119,054 88
Interest	527 49
Ordnance and Stores	76,640 05
Medical Supplies	4,426 70
Services	225,655 01
	$453,170 48
Amount lost through James Davidson and G. W. Honey	5,826 03
	$458,996 51

Making average cost per man, $2 90 per day.

The members of this force were allowed by law: Captains and Surgeons, $100 per month; Lieutenants, $80 per month; Sergeants, $54 per month; Corporals and Farriers, $52 per month; Buglers and privates, $50 per month, with subsistence for officers and men and forage for horses. Horses, clothing, and camp and garrison equipage were furnished by the men at their own expense.

The ordnance (Winchester carbines, ammunition, accoutrements and equipments, $76,640 05) was purchased by the State and issued to this force, and the value of such arms, etc., stopped from pay due the men for services.

Minute Companies Organized under Laws approved November 25, 1871, for one Year from Date of Organization.

COMPANY.	STATION—COUNTY.	COMMANDED BY.	NO. MEN.	ORGANIZED.
A	Blanco	James Ingram	19	Jan. 4, 1872.
B	Wise	G. W. Stevens	19	March 2, 1872.
C	Kendall	C. A. Patton	19	Feb. 4, 1872.
D	Comanche	J. A. Wright	19	May 25, 1872.
E	Kerr	C. Schwethelm	19	April 6, 1872.
F	Gillespie	B. F. Casey	19	April 18, 1872.
G	Brown	G. H. Adams	19	June 5. 1872.
I	Cooke	J. M. Waide	19	April 24, 1872.
K	Bandera	R. Ballantyne	19	July 2, 1872.
L	Coleman	J. M. Elkins	19	Volunteer without pay.
M	Lampasas	G. E. Haynie	19	Aug. 10, 1872.
N	San Saba	W. H. Ledbetter	19	Aug. 13, 1872.
O	Burnet	John Alexander	19	Aug. 19, 1872.
P	Parker	J. C. Gilleland	19	Aug. 19, 1872.
Q	Llano	F. C. Stewart	19	Aug. 21, 1872.
R	Mason	Daniel Herster	19	Aug. 26, 1872.
S	Jack	N. Atkinson	19	Aug. 23, 1872.
T	Palo Pinto	D. H. McClure	19	Aug. 22, 1872.
U	Montague	J. J. Willingham	19	April 20, 1872.
V	Medina	Geo. Habey	19	Sept. 6, 1872.
W	Webb	J. D. Martinez	19	Oct. 2, 1872.
X	Maverick	Man. Ban	19	Oct. 8, 1872.
Y	Uvalde	D. A. Bates	19	Oct. 12, 1872.
Z	Erath	C. M. O'Neal	19	Oct. 12, 1872.

Total number of men, 480.

Lieut. Ingram, Company A, February, 1872, reports heavy bodies of Indians in his district; capture of one white woman by them.   Unsuccessful pursuit.

August 16, 1872, reports Indians in county.   Scout pursued, but compelled to withdraw; two Indians killed, several wounded; three Rangers wounded.

Lieut. Stevens, Company B, April 13, 1872, reports his company captured 13 horses from Indians.

July 30, 1872, reports — horses captured from Indians by his company.

August 11, 1872, reports fight of himself and eight men of his company with one hundred Indians on August 3, 1872.   All his horses lost; one Ranger killed; the chief and twenty Indians killed.

Lieut. Hudson, Company F, August 26, 1872, reports a citizen killed by Indians.   Scout pursued and captured two horses from them.

Lieut. Waide, Company I, reports 50 horses recaptured from Indians.

RECAPITULATION.— Recovered, 65 horses; Indians killed, 23; Rangers killed, 1; Rangers wounded, 3.

The cost of this force was paid from the proceeds of the sale of bonds issued for frontier defense, by act approved August 5th, 1870.   For particulars, see next exhibit of minute companies.

The officers and men of this force were allowed $2 per day, for ten days in each month, when Indians were in their respective counties.

Besides their pay, the State furnished them with arms, ammunition and accoutrements only, which remained the property of the State.   They were armed with the balance of Winchester carbines, etc., purchased by the State for the forces of 1870-'71.

Minute Companies Reorganized under Law approved November 25, 1871, after their first year of Service had expired.

COMPANY.	STATION—COUNTY.	COMMANDED BY	NO. MEN.	RE-ORGANIZED.
A	Blanco.........	S. B. Gray	19	April 1, 1873.
B	Wise	G. W. Stevens..	19	Aug. 7, 1873.
C	Kendall.......	J. C. Nowlin ...	19	March 1, and Jan. 3, 1874.
D	Comanche	W. C. Watkins..	19	Sept. 18, 1873.
E	Kerr	H. Schwethelm..	19	April 7, 1873.
F	Gillespie.....	B. F. Casey	19	Nov. 21, 1873.
G	Brown	G. H. Adams...	19	Aug. 12, 1873.
I	Cooke	J. M. Waide ...	19	April 24, 1873.
L	Coleman	J. M. Elkins....	19	Nov. 7, 1873.
M	Lampasas......	E. W. Greenwood	19	Sept. 12, 1873.
N	San Saba	W. H. Ledbetter.	19	Sept. 19, 1873.
P	Parker	J. C. Gilleland..	19	Oct. 29, 1873.
Q	Llano.........	J. M. Smith....	19	Sept. 29, 1873.
R	Mason	C. C. Smith	19	Dec. 9, 1873.
T	Palo Pinto....	J. H. Caruthers.	19	Oct. 1, 1873.
U	Montague	J. J. Willingham	19	May 31, 1873.
Z	Erath.........	N. Keith.	19	Mar. 29, 1873.
No. 1.	Kerr	S. R. Merritt....	.....	Sept. 7, '73.
No. 2.	Gillespie......	Geo. Laremore..	.....	Nov. 21, '73.
No. 3.	Kinney.......	J. H. Kennedy..	.....	Jan. 6, '73.
No. 4.	Callahan	J. W. Jones....	.....	Oct. 6, '73.
No. 5.	Menard.......	P. H. Mires....	.....	Aug. 25, '73.
No. 6.	....	....	.....	....

(No. 1–5 marked: Without Pay.)

Sergeant Carter, Company G, in March 27, 1874, engaged a party of Indians and recaptured three horses and some Indian trophies in San Saba county.

Lieut. Elkins, Company L, June 9, 1873, recaptured eighty horses in a fight with Indians. June 11, 1873, had a running fight of fifteen miles with Indians. Killed one and wounded two. November, 1873, engaged a party of Indians. Killed three, and recaptured seventeen horses.

Lieut. Ledbetter, Company N, October 30, 1873, engaged seven Indians.

Lieut. Schwethelm, Company E, June 29, 1873, had a running fight with fifteen Indians. Captured seven horses and mules. February 22, 1874, had a running fight with Indians.

Lieut. Stevens, Company B, September 9, 1873, had a fight with Indians. Captured ten horses. February 5, 1874, followed Indians and recaptured all their loose stock.

RECAPITULATION — Recovered 117 horses; Indians killed, 4.

The cost of this force, and that of the Minute Companies organized in 1872, as per previous exhibit, (which was *in part* paid from the balance, so far as it would admit, of proceeds of bonds issued for frontier defense, by act approved August 5, 1870,) was as follows:

Mileage ....$	692	50
Services	55,032	85
Ordnance and stores	4,519	600
Transportation	735	82
Courier service	274	00
Rent of arsenal	500	00
Horses lost in action..................	1,220	00
Telegraphing	3	60
Medical supplies	90	00
Postage	121	01
Advertising	96	00
Printing	50	00
Total	$63,335	38

The amount due to these companies for their services, and for which there was not sufficient proceeds of sale of bonds in the Treasury, was made good by a deficiency appropriation by the first session of the Fourteenth Legislature. The amount paid on account of this force from said appropriation can not be given, as the rolls and accounts were submitted to the Auditorial Board, who, after acting upon them, referred them directly to the Comptroller, without filing them in the Adjutant General's office.

This force, like the minute companies of 1872, was allowed $2 per day for each officer and man, for ten days in each month, when Indians were in their respective counties.

ed out by Gover
ir cost subject to
for four months

NDED BY	Lieuts.	Sergts.	Corp'ls.
Stevens . .	2	4	8
astin . . .	2	4	8
cAdams	2	4	8
lunter . .	2	4	8
reen . . .	2	4	4
ampbell	2	4	8
ackett . .	. .	2	4
onnell . .	2	4	8
	14	30	56

s having recaptur
or the above forc
73, (previous ex
roved May 4, 18
paid on the au
the law of the F
ation.
expenditure hav
Board, and from
to make specific

Frontier Battalion and Minute Companies Organized under Law Approved April 10, 1874.

Companies.	Station. County.	Field and Staff.	Commanded by.	Lieutenants.	Sergeants.	Corporals.	Privates	Total.	Mustered In.	Mustered Out.
		J. B. Jones, Major.						1	May 2, '74.	{ Resigned
		M. M. Kenney, Q. M.						1	" 16, "	{ Mar. 16, '75.
		S. G. Nicholson, Surg.						1	June 9, "	"
A	Stephens	Capt.	J. R. Waller	2	6	6	63	78	May 25, "	April 30, '75.
B	Young	"	G. W. Stevens	2	6	6	63	78	" 16, "	May 31, "
C	Archer	"	E. F. Ikard	2	6	6	63	78	" 20, "	Mar. 31, "
D	Menard	"	C. R. Perry	2	6	6	63	78	" 25, "	May 31, "
E	Coleman	"	W. J. Maltby	2	6	6	63	78	" 30, "	" 31, "
F	Kerr	"	Neal Coldwell	2	6	6	63	78	June 4, "	June 4, "
	El Paso	Lieut.	Til. Montes		2	2	20	25	May 27, "	Nov. 27, "
	Webb	"	Ref. Benavides		2	2	20	25	June 13, "	Nov. 13, "
	Nueces & Rio Grande	Capt.	War'n Wallace	2	4	4	39	50	" 29, "	Sept. 29, "
9		3	7 Capts., 2 Lts.	14	14	44	457	571		

El Paso County Minute Men served six months.
Webb   "   "   "   five   "
Nueces   "   "   "   three   "

In December, 1874, five companies of the Frontier Battalion were reduced to one Lieutenant and thirty non-commissioned officers and privates, and Company "F," (which was ordered to the Rio Grande,) was reduced to one Captain, two Lieutenants and forty-three non-commissioned officers and privates.

May 7, 1874, Captain Ikard, Company C, with six men attacked ten Indians. Drove them (fighting) fifteen miles; hit an Indian, who fell from his horse.

July 11, 1874, Lieut. G. W. Campbell, Company C, and twenty men, attacked a camp of seventy-five to eighty Indians. Captured 43 horses and mules, and some camp equipage.

July 12, 1874, Lieut. B. F. Best, Company E, recovered 2 horses taken by Indians.

July 12, 1874, Major J. B. Jones, with Capt. G. W. Stevens, Company B, and Lieut. J. T. Wilson, Company A, and thirty-four men, engaged over one hundred and twenty-five Indians at Lost Valley; three Indians killed and three wounded; two Rangers killed, two wounded, and 12 Rangers' horses killed and disabled.

July 25, 1874, Sergt. M. T. Israel, Company E, and twenty-one men struck a party of six Indians near the head of Clear-Fork, of Brazos; three Indians killed, one Ranger wounded.

August 22, 1875, Capt. N. Coldwell, Company F, gave unsuccessful pursuit to nine Indians; captured 1 horse.

May 28, to June 12, 1874, Capt. Waller's Company A, arrested over twenty-two cattle thieves and desperadoes; killed two murderers who resisted arrest, and captured 800 head of cattle — returned them to owners.

July 29 and 30, 1874, Capt. Perry's Company D, arrested several criminals.

May 10, 1874, Capt. Maltby and Lieut. Connell captured 2 horses, etc., from horse thieves.

Sept. 15, 1874, Lieut. T. Montes, El Paso, Company M. M., with twelve men, attacked seven Indians, killing two, recaptured 5 horses, saddles, etc. Recovered a boy stolen by these Indians eight months previous.

November 18, 1874, Lieut B. F. Best, Company E, and sixteen men, overtook a party of Indians in Brown county, killed three and wounded one. One Indian's horse killed and two captured; two Rangers wounded; one Ranger's horse killed.

November 17, 1874, Lieut. J. W. Millican, Company A, overtook a party of Indians in Shackelford county, and recaptured two horses and two mules.

November 21, 1874, Lieut. D. W. Roberts, Company D, engaged eleven Indians in Menard county, killed five and captured one; captured 3 horses, arms, etc. Lieut. L. P. Beaver kept up the pursuit, when the Indians took refuge in a cave, where one was killed and one wounded.

December 18, 1874, a detachment of three men of Company

D fought nine Indians, killed two and wounded two, recaptured 16 horses and all their camp equipage.

May 8, 1875, Major J. B. Jones, with his escort, engaged seven Indians and killed five; one Ranger wounded; one Ranger's horse killed and two wounded.

RECAPITULATION.—Engagements, 16; trails followed, 30; desperadoes and cattle thieves arrested, 28; desperadoes and cattle thieves killed, 8; Indians killed, 24; Indians wounded, 10; Indians captured, 1; Rangers killed, 2; Rangers wounded, 6; Rangers' horses killed, 14; recovered from Indians (boy), 1; recaptured horses and mules, 78; recaptured cattle, 1,000.

Probably the greatest benefit derived to the State from this force was the driving back (after a severe engagement on July 12, 1874,) of a large Indian war-party commanded by Lone Wolf, that invaded Texas for the purpose of revenge. The loss of life and property which was thus prevented can not be estimated.

The cost of this force was $300,000, appropriated May 4, 1874. The average cost per man per day, $2 30.

The supplies, with rare exceptions, were delivered at the company's stations by the contractors.

The transportation furnished the companies were pack mules for scouting and one two-horse wagon for camp equipage.

17

Frontier Battalion Reorganized for three months, from June 1, 1875, under Law Approved April 10, 1874.

Companies.	Station. County.	Field and Staff.	Commanded by.	Sergeants.	Corporals.	Privates.	Total.	Mustered in.	Mustered out.
		J. B. Jones, Major....		....	....	....	1		
		S. G. Nicholson, Surg.		....	....	....	1		
B	Young.	Lieut.	G. W. Stevens.	3	2	35	41	June 1, 1875.	Aug. 31, 1875.
D	Menard	"	D. W. Roberts	3	3	34	41	" 1, "	" 31, "
E	Coleman	"	B. S. Foster....	3	3	34	41	" 1, "	" 31, "
F	Kerr....	Capt.	N. Coldwell	3	3	34	41	" 28, "	" 31, "
		2	1 Capt. 3 Lieuts.	12	11	137	166		

Frontier Battalion Reorganized for twelve months, from September 1, 1875, under Law Approved April 10, 1875.

Companies.	Station. County.	Field and Staff.	Commanded by.	Sergeants.	Corporals.	Privates.	Total.	Mustered in.
		J. B. Jones, Major					1	
		S. G. Nicholson, Surg.					1	
A	Young	Lieut.	Ira Long	3	3	34	41	Sept. 1, 1875.
B	Mason	"	G. W. Stevens	3	3	37	41	" 1, "
D	Mason	"	D. W. Roberts	3	3	34	41	" 1, "
E	Coleman	"	B. S. Foster	3	3	34	41	" 1, "
F	Kerr	"	N. Coldwell	3	3	34	41	" 1, "
		2	5 Lieutenants.	15	12	173	207	

August 7, 1875, Lieut. Roberts, Company D, after following Indians four hundred miles attacked them on Staked Plains; killed one, wounded one.   Recovered a Mexican captive and recaptured 23 horses.

RECAPITULATION.— Indians killed, 1; Indians wounded, 1; captive recovered, 1; horses recaptured, 23.

The cost of these forces to September 1, 1875, is included in the amount ($300,000,) mentioned in previous exhibit.

The present force since September 1, 1875, will be paid out of the appropriation of $150,000 made by the last Legislature; and this appropriation will have to apply to such other companies as it may be necessary to call out under the law authorizing the organization of the Frontier Battalion.

The Washington County Volunteer Militia Company, Capt. L. H. McNelly commanding, with one lieutenant, four sergeants, three corporals and twenty-five privates, was organized July 25, 1874, for duty in DeWitt county, to assist the civil authorities, and was mustered out March 31, 1875.

The sum of $17,403 00 was appropriated by the last Legislature to pay this company and two Galveston companies: the Washington Guards and Lone Star Rifles.

Capt. McNelly's company was reorganized April 1, 1875, for duty on the Rio Grande. On June 12, 1875, this company overtook a party of sixteen Mexican thieves, killed fifteen, wounded one, and recaptured two hundred and sixty-three head of cattle. One ranger killed.

In July, 1875, recaptured three hundred head of cattle from a party of Mexican thieves, who, hearing of the company's approach in pursuit, deserted the herd and succeeded in escaping.

In June, July and August, 1875, the company recovered from the other side of the Rio Grande forty-three horses belonging to parties in Texas.

	KILLED					WOUNDED					CAPT'D				RECOVER'D				COST
	Indians	Mexicans	Outlaws	Rangers	Rangers' Horses	Indians	Mexicans	Outlaws	Rangers	Rangers' Horses	Indians	Mexicans	Outlaws	Indian Captives	Horses and Mules	Cattle	Engagem'ts fought	Trails followed	
Forces of 1870-71, 14 companies	21					15			5						94	130			$458,996 51
Minute Companies of 1872-73, 24 companies	23			1					3	8					65				63,335 88
Minute Companies of 1873-74, 24 companies	4														117				} 121,476 56
Ranger Companies called out Nov. 1, 1873, 7 co's																			
Total, under Gov. E. J. Davis's administr'n, 4 y'rs	48			4	8	15			8				28		276	130			$643,808 45
Frontier Bat. from May '74, to May 31, '75, 9 co's	24		8	3	14		1		6	10		1	28	1	78	1000	15	39	} $300,000 00
Frontier Bat. from June 1, '75, to Aug. 31, '75, 4 cos.	1						1		1						33		1	1	
L. H. McNelly's Company, on Rio Grande, 1 company	15		1	1				1						2	43	568			
Total, under present administration, 1 y'r 7½ mo's	25	15	3	3	14	1	1	1	6	11		1	28	2	144	1568	16	30	$800,000 00
General total	23	15	3	7		1	1	1	14	11		1	28	2	420	1698	16	30	$643,808 45

On motion of Mr. King, the communication was referred to the Committee on Frontier Affairs.

Mr. King moved that one hundred copies of the communication be printed.

Lost.

On motion of Mr. Martin, of Navarro, Mr. Martin, of Hunt, was added to the Committee on Frontier Affairs.

On motion of Mr. Russell, of Harrison, Mr. Pauli was added to the Committee on Immigration.

The Convention then proceeded to the consideration of the unfinished business, viz: Mr. German's amendment to section 51, article —— Legislative Department, viz: After the word "money" in line 264 insert the words "public land or other thing of value."

Mr. West moved to pass over the consideration of the pending question until the reports from the Committees on Education and Public Lands and Land Office shall be made to the Convention and printed, in order that the subject of the disposition of the public lands should be considered as an entirety.

Mr. Kilgore moved to adjourn until 9 o'clock to-morrow.

By leave, the following amendments were read for information:

By Mr. Russell, of Wood: Add to the amendment: "provided this clause shall not be so construed as to prevent actual settlers from pre-emption privileges, nor the State from making valid titles to her lands when sold."

By Mr. Flournoy—Substitute for the amendment: in line 264 insert the words "or land" after the word "money," and add to the section the following words: "Or of portions of the public domain for internal improvements, or to actual settlers, by general law alone."

The Convention then adjourned, under Mr. Kilgore's motion, to 9 o'clock A. M. to-morrow.

TWENTY-THIRD DAY.

HALL OF REPRESENTATIVES, }
AUSTIN, TEXAS, October 1, 1875. }

Convention met pursuant to adjournment; roll called; quorum present; prayer by Rev. Mr. Lee, Rector of St. David's Church, at Austin.

Journal of yesterday read and adopted.

Mr. Russell, of Harrison, asked and obtained leave of absence for a few days from the Convention.

On motion of Mr. Rentfro, Mr. McCabe was excused from attendance on the Convention for a few days.

On motion of Mr. Moore, Mr. Lockett was excused from attendance on the Convention for a few days after to-day.

Mr. Darnell, chairman of Committee on Public Lands and Land Office, submitted the following report and article:

COMMITTEE ROOM,
AUSTIN, September 29, 1875.

To the Hon. E. B. Pickett, President of the Convention:

The Committee on Public Lands and Land Office have considered the memorials, ordinances and resolutions referred to them, together with such other matters proper for them to consider, and beg leave to submit the following sections as a substitute for the same and recommend that they be incorporated in the constitution.

N. H. DARNELL, Chairman.

" ARTICLE —.
" PUBLIC LANDS AND LAND OFFICE.

" Section 1. There shall be one General Land Office in the State, which shall be at the seat of government, where all land titles which have emanated, or may hereafter emanate, from the State shall be registered, except those titles the registration of which may be prohibited by this constitution, and the Legislature may, from time to time, establish such subordinate offices as may be deemed necessary.

" Sec. 2. All unsatisfied genuine land certificates barred by section 4, article 10, constitution of 1869, by reason of the holders or owners thereof failing to have them surveyed and returned to the Land Office by the first day of January, 1875, are hereby revived, and may be located on any of the vacant lands in the State.

" Sec. 3. The Legislature shall not hereafter grant public lands to any person, persons, or corporation; nor shall any certificate for land be sold at the Land Office except to actual settlers upon the same, and in lots not to exceed one hundred and sixty acres, except as may be otherwise specially provided in this constitution.

" Sec. 4.   All lands granted to railway companies which have not been alienated in conformity with the terms of their charters and the laws of the State under which the grants were made are hereby declared forfeited to the State and subject to location and survey as other vacant land.

"Sec. 5. To every head of a family without a homestead there shall be donated one hundred and sixty acres of public land, upon the condition that he will select and locate said land and occupy the same three years, and pay the office fees due thereon. To all single men, eighteen years of age, shall be donated eighty acres of public land upon the terms and conditions prescribed for heads of families.

"Sec. 6. The State of Texas hereby releases to the owner or owners of the soil all mines and minerals that may be on the same, subject to taxation as other property."

On motion of Mr. Darnell, one hundred copies of the report and article were ordered printed for the use of the Convention.

Mr. Stayton offered the following resolution:

Resolved, That a select committee of seven be appointed to inquire and report as to the expediency of inserting into the constitution a provision providing for the reservation of a certain quantity of the public lands of the State, and for donating the same for the purpose of aiding in the construction of railways in the western and southeastern portions of this State, as the increase in population will render it practicable so to do, in such manner as will equalize the different portions of the State in benefits heretofore and hereafter to be received by such donations.

Mr. Nugent proposed to amend by inserting "northwestern."

Adopted.

Mr. Flournoy proposed to amend by striking out "western, northwestern and southeastern portion" and inserting the "State of Texas."

Lost.

The question on the adoption of the resolution as amended was then put, and the resolution adopted by the following vote:

YEAS—Allison, Abner, Brown, Blake, Ballinger, Barnett, Burleson, Crawford, Chambers, Cook of Gonzales, Cooke of San Saba, Cline, Cooley, Cardis, Douglass, DeMorse, Darnell, Dunnam, Davis of Brazos, Erhard, Ford, Flournoy, Fleming, Ferris, Gaither, Henry of Smith, Holmes, Haynes, King, Kilgore, Killough, Lockett, Lynch, Martin of Hunt, McCabe, Morris, Moore, Murphy, Norvell, Pauli, Reagan, Ramey, Reynolds, Robeson of Fayette, Spikes, Sessions, Smith, Stayton, Sansom, Whitehead, Weaver, Whitfield, West, Waelder—54.

NAYS—Abernathy, Arnim, Blassingame, Brady, Bruce, Dillard, Dohoney, German, Graves, Holt, Henry of Limestone,

Johnson of Franklin, Johnson of Collin, Lacy, McLean, Martin of Navarro, Mitchell, McKinney, McCormick, Nunn, Nugent, Rentfro, Robertson of Bell, Ross, Russell of Wood, Scott, Stockdale, Wade—28.

Mr. Wade offered the following sections, which were referred to the Committee on Judiciary:

"Section 1. Every civil suit that may be commenced in any court of record having original jurisdiction shall be submitted and decided, or shall be ordered to be arbitrated, at the option of the parties, within one year from and after the end of the appearance term of such suit and not thereafter; or shall be dismissed at the cost of the party failing to submit or to consent to an award of arbitration.

"Sec. 2. Every such suit, when appealed or taken up by a writ of error, shall be submitted and decided within one year from and after the same shall have been docketed in the court to which appeal is taken, or shall, at the option of the parties, within one year from and after its appearance term in the appellate court, and not thereafter, be ordered to be arbitrated, or on the expiration of the year shall be dismissed at the cost of the party failing to submit or to consent to an award of arbitration.

"Sec. 3. Judges of courts who neglect or fail to decide such suits when submitted within the year, or to order an arbitration when the parties consent thereto, shall forfeit one-fourth of their salaries, and may be otherwise punished as may be prescribed by law; and attorneys who neglect or fail to submit such suits, or to consent to an order of arbitration within the time prescribed shall forfeit to their clients all fees they may have been paid touching such suits, and shall be forever barred from directly or indirectly collecting any fees for work done in or concerning such suits.

"Sec. 4. In cases of arbitration as herein prescribed, the arbitrator or arbitrators shall render an award within one year from and after the end of the term at which the order of arbitration was made and not thereafter.

"Sec. 5. The Legislature shall enforce the foregoing four sections, as from time to time may be found necessary, by appropriate legislation, and shall not have the power to extend the time limited or to relieve any judge or attorney for neglecting or failing to comply with the requirements thereof, save by means of a public law and when prevented from compliance by the act of God or of the public enemy.

Mr. Nunn offered the following resolution:

WHEREAS, A report from the Adjutant General was presented

to this Convention on the 30th of September, in obedience to the previous order, and the same was referred, without reading, to a special committee; and

WHEREAS, It is believed that members of this Convention voted for said motion to refer with the understanding that the said report would not thereby be withdrawn from publication, but would be published in the official journal, as part of the daily proceedings of this body; and

WHEREAS, The said report has not been published, and, it being desirable that the information therein contained should be placed before every delegate of this Convention; therefore, be it

Resolved, That two hundred copies of the said report be printed for the use of the Convention.

Adopted.

Mr. Rentfro offered the following resolution:

Resolved, That the Secretary of the Convention be instructed to purchase or procure, for the use of the Committee on Senatorial Apportionment, three large maps of the State of Texas, provided, that the same contain all the existing counties of this State.

Lost.

The Convention then proceeded to the consideration of unfinished business and business on the table.

Mr. Brady moved to take up the resolution in relation to electing a Committee Clerk.

On motion of Mr. McCormick, the resolution was laid on the table.

Mr. Kilgore called up his resolution relative to additional pay for Pages.

Mr. West proposed to amend by adding: "Also, the pay of the Porters, Door-keepers, Sergeant-at-arms, Clerks and Secretary be increased in the same proportion."

Laid on the table.

Mr. Dillard moved to lay the resolution on the table.

Lost by the following vote:

YEAS—Allison, Brown, Blake, Blassingame, Barnett, Burleson, Bruce, Chambers, Dillard, DeMorse, Dohoney, Darnell, Dunnam, Davis of Brazos, Erhard, Ford, German, Graves, Holt, Henry of Smith, Haynes, Johnson of Collin, Killough, Martin of Hunt, McCabe, McKinney, Moore, Norvell, Nunn, Nugent, Pauli, Reagan, Ramey, Robertson of Bell, Russell of Wood, Spikes, Wade, West—38.

NAYS—Abernathy, Arnim, Abner, Ballinger, Brady, Crawford, Cook of Gonzales, Cline, Cooley, Cardis, Douglass, Davis of Wharton, Fleming, Ferris, Henry of Limestone, Holmes, Johnson of Franklin, King, Kilgore, Lacy, Lynch, McLean, Martin of Navarro, Morris, Mitchell, McCormick, Murphy, Reynolds, Rentfro, Robeson of Fayette, Scott, Sessions, Smith, Stockdale, Stayton, Sansom, Whitehead, Weaver, Whitfield, Waelder — 40.

The question then recurring on the adoption of the resolution, the yeas and nays were called, and the resolution lost by the following vote:

YEAS — Arnim, Abner, Ballinger, Brady, Crawford, Cook of Gonzales, Cooke of San Saba, Cline, Cardis, Fleming, Ferris, Henry of Limestone, Holmes, Johnson of Franklin, King, Kilgore, Lacy, Lynch, McLean, Martin of Navarro, McCabe, Morris, McCormick, Murphy, Reynolds, Rentfro, Robeson of Fayette, Scott, Sessions, Smith, Stockdale, Stayton, Sansom, **Whitehead,** Weaver, Whitfield, Waelder — 37.

NAYS—Allison, Abernathy, Brown, Blake, Blassingame, Barnett, Burleson, Bruce, Chambers, Douglass, Dillard, DeMorse, Dohoney, Darnell, Dunnam, Davis of Brazos, Erhard, Ford, German, Graves, Holt, Henry of Smith, Haynes, Johnson of Collin, Killough, Martin of Hunt, Mitchell, McKinney, Moore, Norvell, Nunn, Nugent, Pauli, Reagan, Ramey, Robertson of Bell, Russell of Wood, Spikes, Wade, West—40. . . . .

The consideration of the article on Legislative Department again resumed.

Mr. Flournoy corrected his amendment by striking out " internal improvements " and inserting " railroads."

On motion of Mr. McCormick, the further consideration of the subject was passed for the present.

Mr. German proposed to amend section 56 by adding after line 329 the words " for incorporating railroads or other works of internal improvements."

Adopted by the following vote:

YEAS—Allison, Abernathy, Arnim, Ballinger, Blassingame, Barnett, Burleson, Bruce, Chambers, Dillard, DeMorse, Dohoney, Dunnam, Davis of Brazos, Erhard, Ford, Flournoy, Fleming, Ferris, German, Gaither, Graves, Holt, Henry of Limestone, Holmes, Haynes, Johnson of Franklin, Johnson of Collin, Kilgore, Killough, Lacy, Lynch, McLean, Martin of Navarro, McCabe, Morris, Mitchell, McKinney, McCormick, Moore, Murphy, Norvell, Nunn, Nugent, Ramey, Rentfro, Robertson of Bell, Robeson of Fayette, Ross, Russell of Wood, Spikes, Scott, Sessions, Smith, Stockdale, Stayton, Sansom, Wade, Whitehead, Weaver, Whitfield—61.

NAYS—Abner, Blake, Crawford, Cook of Gonzales, Cooke of San Saba, Cline, Douglass, Davis of Wharton, Henry of Smith, King, Pauli, Reynolds, West, Waelder—14.

Mr. Dohoney offered the following amendment:

Amend section 56, line 331, by adding at the end thereof the words " but local or special laws may be enacted for the different sections of the State in reference to fences for the benefit of agriculture or stock-raising."

Mr. Stockdale proposed to substitute the amendment by the following:

" Except as otherwise provided in this constitution."

Adopted.

Mr. West offered the following amendment:

Provided, Nothing herein contained shall be so construed as to prohibit the Legislature from passing special laws for the preservation of the game and fish of this State in certain localities.

Adopted.

Mr. Crawford offered the following amendment:

Amend section 53, lines 276 and 277, by striking out the word " hereafter."

Adopted.

Mr. Stayton proposed to add " towns " after the word " cities," in line 289.

Adopted.

Mr. Ramey proposed to amend section 16, by striking out the word " when," in line 74, after the word " except " and the word " is," in same line, and insert " when " instead.

Adopted.

Mr. Russell, of Wood, offered the following amendment to section 44:

Add: " Nor employ any one in the name of the State unless authorized by pre-existing law."

Adopted.

Mr. Martin, of Navarro, offered the following independent section:

" All stationery, printing, paper and fuel, used in the Legislature and other departments of government, shall be furnished, and the printing, binding and distributing of the laws, journals, department reports and all other printing and binding, shall be performed under contract, to be given to the lowest, responsible bidder, under such regulations as shall be provided by law. And no member or officer of any department of the government shall be in any way interested in such contract, and all such contracts shall be subject to the approval of the Governor, Comptroller and State Treasurer."

Mr. McCormick offered the following amendment to the amendment.

Add the words, " paper, ink, pens, pencils, blotters, etc., and general supplies."

Laid on the table.

Mr. Martin, of Navarro, withdrew his amendment.

Mr. Johnson proposed to amend section 47 by adding in line 237 the words·" and shall pass laws prohibiting gambling of every character in all places."

Lost.

Mr. Waelder offered to amend section 43 by adding " and when so revised, digested or codified and published, shall be the statutory laws, civil and criminal, of this State, and all laws not therein contained, or in conflict therewith, shall be regarded as repealed."

Lost.

Mr. Stayton offered the following amendment to section 53:

In line 278 strike out the word " express."

Adopted.

Mr. Wade proposed to amend by inserting in section 48, line 245, the words " and for the present floating debt of the State."

Adopted.

Mr. Henry, of Smith, offered the following additional section:

" Sec. —. The Legislature shall hold its sessions at the city of Austin, which is hereby declared to be the seat of government."

Adopted.

On motion of Mr. Dillard the Convention adjourned until 9 o'clock A. M. to-morrow.

TWENTY-FOURTH DAY.

HALL OF REPRESENTATIVES, }
AUSTIN, TEXAS, October 2, 1875. }

Convention met pursuant to adjournment; roll called; quorum present; prayer by Rev. Mr. Groety, of Austin.

Journal of yesterday read and adopted.

On motion of Mr. Cook, of Gonzales, Mr. Burleson was excused from attendance on the Convention until Tuesday.

Messrs. Morris and Gaither were excused until Tuesday next, and Messrs. Graves and Johnson of Franklin, for to-day.

The President announced the following select committee, in pursuance of Mr. Stayton's resolution in relation to setting apart a portion of the public domain, to encourage railroads, in south-eastern, western and north-western Texas, viz: Mr. Stayton, Chairman; Messrs. Nugent, Whitehead, Blassingame, DeMorse, Martin of Hunt, and Johnson of Collin.

Mr. Murphy presented a memorial from S. T. Foster, asking the exemption of all uniformed military companies from jury service, which, together with the following section, was referred to the Committee on State Affairs:

"Sec. ——. That the active members of all uniformed and armed volunteer companies in this State, consisting of at least thirty-two non-commissioned officers and privates, shall be ex-empt from jury service."

Mr. Martin, of Hunt, submitted a communication from D. R. Coulter, of Hunt county, on the subject of taxation, which was referred to the Committee on Revenue and Taxation.

Mr. Crawford, Chairman of Committee on Bill of Rights, submitted the following report:

> COMMITTEE ROOM,
> AUSTIN, October 2, 1875.

To the Hon. E. B. Pickett, President of the Convention:

Sir—The Committee on Bill of Rights, to whom was referred the consideration of a preamble—"Boundaries of the State and Bill of Rights"—having considered these subjects, as well as the various resolutions referred to them, direct me to return the following articles as the result of their labor, and to recommend to the Convention the adoption of the same.

Respectfully submitted.

W. L. CRAWFORD, Chairman.

"PREAMBLE.

"Humbly invoking the blessings of Almighty God, the people of the State of Texas do ordain and establish this constitution.

"ARTICLE 1.

"BOUNDARIES.

"In accordance with the following treaties, acts, and joint resolutions, to wit:

"The treaty concluded between Spain and the United States of America on the 22d of February, 1819, and ratified on the 22d of February, 1821;

"The treaty concluded between the United States of America

and the United Mexican States, January 12, 1828, and ratified April 5, 1832;

"An act of the Congress of the Republic of Texas, approved December 19, 1836;

"A joint resolution of the Legislature of the State of Texas, approved April 29, 1846;

"An act of the Congress of the United States of the 5th of July, 1848, excepted to by the State of Texas, by the act of November 2, 1849; and

"An act of the Congress of the United States (commonly called the compromise act, approved September 9, 1850, accepted and assented to by an act of the Legislature of the State of Texas, approved on the 25th day of November, 1850—

"The boundaries of the State of Texas are hereby declared to be, and shall forever remain, as hereinafter set forth, to-wit:

"Beginning in the middle of the mouth of Sabine Bay or Pass, on the Gulf of Mexico; thence up the middle of Sabine Bay or Lake to the mouth of the Sabine river; thence up the central channel of said river to latitude 32 degrees north; thence due north, on the line established in the year 1840, to Red river; thence up the Rio Roxo or Red river to the one hundredth degree of longitude west from Greenwich and twenty-three west from Washington; thence due north to the parallel of thirty-six degrees and thirty minutes north latitude; thence due west to the meridian of one hundred and three degrees of longitude west from Greenwich; thence due south to the thirty-second degree of north latitude; thence due west, on the line of thirty-two degrees north latitude, to the channel of the Rio Bravo del Norte—otherwise called the Rio Grande; thence with the channel of said river to the Gulf of Mexico; thence, on a line drawn three marine leagues from the shore of the Gulf of Mexico, to the beginning at the mouth or pass of Sabine Bay.

"ARTICLE 2.

"That the general, great and essential principles of liberty and free government may be recognized and established, we declare that—

"Section 1. Texas is one of the free and independent States of the United States of America, and that the maintenance of our free institutions and the perpetuity of the Union depend upon the preservation of the right of local self-government, unimpaired, to all the States.

"Sec. 2. All political power is inherent in the people, and all free governments are founded on their authority, and instituted for their benefit. The faith of the people of Texas stands pledged to the preservation of a republican form of government, and, subject to this limitation only, they have at all times the inalienable right to alter, reform, or abolish their government, in such manner as they may think expedient.

"Sec. 3. All freemen, when they form a social compact, have equal rights, and no man, or set of men, is entitled to exclusive separate public emoluments or privileges but in consideration of public services.

"Sec. 4. No religious test shall ever be required as a qualification to any office or public trust in this State; nor shall any one be excluded from holding office on account of his religious sentiments, provided he acknowledge the existence of a Supreme Being.

"Sec. 5. No person shall be disqualified to give evidence in any of the courts of this State on account of his religious opinions, or for the want of any religious belief, but all oaths, or affirmations, shall be administered in the mode most binding upon the conscience, and shall be taken subject to the pains and penalties of perjury.

"Sec. 6. All men have a natural and indefeasible right to worship God according to the dictates of their own consciences. No man shall be compelled to attend, erect, or support, any place of worship, or to maintain any ministry, against his consent. No human authority ought, in any case whatever, to control or interfere with the rights of conscience in matters of religion; and no preference shall ever be given by law to any religious societies, or mode of worship. But it shall be the duty of the Legislature to pass such laws as may be necessary to protect every religious denomination in the peaceable enjoyment of their own mode of public worship.

"Sec. 7. No money shall be appropriated or drawn from the treasury for the benefit of any sect or religious society, theological or religious seminary; nor shall property belonging to the State be appropriated for any such purposes.

"Sec. 8. Every citizen shall be at liberty to speak, write or publish his opinion on any subject, being responsible for the abuse of that privilege. And no law shall ever be passed curtailing the liberty of speech, or of the press. And in all civil or criminal actions for libel, the truth thereof may be given in evidence to the jury, and if it shall appear that the alleged libelous matter was published with good motives, and for justifiable ends, it shall be a sufficient defense.

"Sec. 9. The people shall be secure in their persons, houses, papers and possessions, from all unreasonable seizures or searches, and no warrant to search any place, or to seize any person or thing, shall issue without describing them as near as may be, nor without probable cause, supported by oath or affirmation.

"Sec. 10. In all criminal prosecutions, the accused shall have a speedy public trial by an impartial jury. He shall have the right to demand the nature and cause of the accusation against him, and to have a copy thereof. He shall not be compelled to give evidence against himself. He shall have the right of being heard by himself or his counsel, or both; shall be confronted with the witnesses against him, and shall have compulsory process for obtaining witnesses in his favor. And no person shall be held to answer for a criminal offense unless on indictment of a grand jury, except in cases in which the punishment is by fine or imprisonment otherwise than in the penitentiary, in cases of impeachment, and in cases arising in the army, or navy, or in the militia, when in actual service, in time of war or public danger.

"Sec. 11. All prisoners shall be bailable by sufficient sureties, unless for capital offenses, when the proof is evident; but this provision shall not be so construed as to prevent bail after indictment found, upon an examination of the evidence by a judge of the supreme or other court of record, upon the return of a writ of *habeas corpus,* returnable in the county where the offense is committed.

"Sec. 12. The writ of *habeas corpus* is a writ of right, and shall never be suspended. The Legislature shall enact laws to render the remedy speedy and effectual in all proper cases.

"Sec. 13. Excessive bail shall not be required, nor excessive fines imposed, nor cruel or unusual punishment inflicted. All courts shall be open, and every person, for an injury done him in his lands, goods, person or reputation, shall have remedy by due course of law.

"Sec. 14. No person, for the same offense, shall be twice put in jeopardy of life or liberty, nor shall a person be again put upon trial for the same offense after a verdict of not guilty.

"Sec. 15. The right of trial by jury shall remain inviolate. The Legislature shall pass such laws as may be needed to regulate the same, and to maintain its purity and efficiency.

"Sec. 16. No bill of attainder, *ex post facto* law, retroactive law, or any law impairing the obligation of contracts, shall be made.

"Sec. 17. No person's property shall be taken, damaged, destroyed or applied to public use, without adequate compensation being made, unless by the consent of such person; and, when

18

taken, except for the use of the State, such compensation shall be first made, or secured by a deposit in money, and no irrevocable or uncontrollable grant of special privileges or immunities shall be made; but all privileges and franchises granted by the Legislature shall be subject to the control thereof.

"Sec. 18. No person shall ever be imprisoned for debt.

"Sec. 19. No citizen of this State shall be deprived of life, liberty, property or privileges, or in any manner disfranchised, except by the judgment of his peers, or the law of the land.

"Sec. 20. No citizen shall be outlawed, nor shall any person be transported out of the State for any offense committed within the same.

"Sec. 21. No conviction shall work corruption of blood or forfeiture of estate, and the estates of those who destroy their own lives shall descend or rest as in case of natural death.

"Sec. 22. Treason against the State shall consist only in levying war against it, or adhering to its enemies, giving them aid and comfort; and no person shall be convicted of treason, except on the testimony of two witnesses to the same over act, or on confession in open court.

"Sec. 23. Every citizen shall have the right to keep and bear arms in the lawful defense of himself or the State, but the Legislature shall have power by law to regulate the wearing of arms with a view to prevent crime.

"Sec. 24. The military shall at all times be subordinate to the civil authority.

"Sec. 25. No soldier shall in time of peace be quartered in the house or within the enclosure of any citizen without the consent of the owner, nor in time of war but in a manner prescribed by law.

"Sec. 26. Perpetuities and monopolies are contrary to the genius of a free government, and shall never be allowed, nor shall the law of primogeniture and entailments ever be in force in this State.

"Sec. 27. The citizens shall have the right in a peaceable manner to assemble together for their common good, and to apply to those invested with the power of government for redress of grievances or other purposes, by petition, address or remonstrance.

"Sec. 28. No power of suspending laws in this State shall be exercised except by the Legislature.

"Sec. 29. Emigration from the State shall not be prohibited, and no appropriation of money shall be made to aid immigrants to the State.

"Sec. 30. To guard against transgressions of the high powers herein delegated, we declare that every thing in this 'Bill of Rights' is excepted out of the general powers of government, and shall forever remain inviolate, and all laws contrary thereto, or to the following provisions, shall be void."

On motion of Mr. Davis, of Brazos, two hundred copies of the report and article were ordered printed for use of the Convention.

Mr. Russell, of Wood, submitted the following report:

COMMITTEE ROOM, }
AUSTIN, October 2, 1875. }

To the Hon. E. B. Pickett, President of the Convention:

SIR—Your Committee on Immigration, to whom was referred sundry resolutions relative to establishing and maintaining a Bureau of Immigration, have carefully considered the same; and I am instructed by a majority of the committee to report that, in their opinion, the people ought not to *be taxed for any such purposes,* and therefore respectfully recommend that a clause be put in the organic law restraining the Legislature from ever appropriating money for such purposes.

Respectfully submitted,

J. RUSSELL, Charman.
SAM. B. KILLOUGH,
JULIUS E. ARNIM,
WM. C. HOLMES,
JOE. P. DOUGLAS.

Report received and passed to the orders of the day.

Messrs. Waelder and Erhard gave notice of minority reports.

UNFINISHED BUSINESS.

The Convention then proceeded to consider article —, Legislative Department.

Mr. Reagan proposed the following amendment to article —, mode of calling a cenvention and amending the constitution:

Section 1, line 1, strike out the words " three-fourths " and insert " two-thirds."

Adopted.

Mr. Brown offered the following amendment:

Section 1, line 2, after the word " house " insert the words " taken by yeas and nays and entered on the journal."

Adopted.

Mr. Stayton offered the following amendment:

Amend by striking out all after the word " favor " in section 2, line 19, and insert " thereof, the same shall be valid to all intents and purposes as a part of the constitution of the State of

Texas, and the same shall be so declared by a joint resolution of the Legislature at the first session thereof after such election."

Mr. Allison offered the following as a substitute for the amendment:

Section 2, line 19, strike out "two-thirds" and insert "a majority."

Lost.

Mr. Moore offered the following as a substitute for the amendment:

Strike out in line 19, after the word "of," all down to the word "so," in line 21, and insert "either of them," and strike out all after the word "Texas" in line 23, and insert "and the Governor shall by his proclamation so declare."

(Mr. Stockdale in the chair.)

Mr. Ballinger offered the following as a substitute for the section and amendments:

"Sec. 2. The Legislature, at any biennial session, by a vote of two-thirds of all the members elected to each house, to be entered by yeas and nays on the journal, may propose amendments to the constitution, to be voted upon by the qualified electors for members of the House of Representatives, which proposed amendments shall be duly published once a week for four weeks, commencing at least three months before an election, the time of which shall be specified by the Legislature, in one weekly newspaper of each county in which such newspaper may be published; and it shall be the duty of the several returning officers of said election to open a poll for and make returns to the Secretary of State of the number of legal votes cast at said election for and against said amendments; and if more than one be proposed, then the number of votes cast for and against each of them; and if it shall appear from said election that a majority of the votes cast have been cast in favor of any amendment, the said amendment so receiving a majority of the votes cast shall become a part of the constitution, and proclamation thereof shall be made by the Governor."

Adopted by the following vote:

Yeas—Abner, Ballinger, Blassingame, Barnett, Brady, Cook of Gonzales, Cooke of San Saba, Cline, Douglas, Dohoney, Dunnam, Davis of Wharton, Erhard, Ferris, German, Holt, Henry of Limestone, Holmes, Haynes, King, Lynch, Martin of Navarro, Martin of Hunt, Moore, Murphy, Norvell, Nunn, Nugent, Pauli, Reagan, Robertson of Bell, Robeson of Fayette, Spikes, Sessions, Smith, Stockdale, Stayton, Whitehead, Weaver —39.

Nays—Allison, Abernathy, Arnim, Brown, Blake, Bruce, Crawford, Chambers, Cooley, Cardis, Dillard, DeMorse, Darnell, Davis of Brazos, Ford, Flournoy, Fleming, Henry of Smith, Johnson of Collin, Kilgore, Killough, Lacy, McLean, Mitchell, McKinney, McCormick, Rentfro, Ross, Russell of Wood, Scott, Wade, Whitfield, West, Waelder—34.

Mr. Pickett moved to strike out section 1 of the article under discussion.

Mr. McCormick offered a substitute for the section as follows:

"Section 1. The people of the State may call a Constitutional Convention at any time and in any manner that a majority of them may, by their voice expressed at the ballot box, desire; and no laws shall be passed curtailing or preventing the exercise of this great inalienable right."

Accepted by Mr. Pickett as a substitute for his motion.

Mr. Flournoy offered the following as a substitute for the entire article:

"ARTICLE —.

"Section 1. The Legislature shall, at the expiration of ten years, after the adoption of this constitution, submit for the action of the people the question of convention or no convention, to reform, amend or alter the constitution; and unless a majority of the votes cast at an election on such question be in favor of a convention, no such convention shall be held; but the same question shall be submitted at the expiration of each ten years thereafter until the majority of the votes cast shall have been in favor of such convention. The mode of ascertaining the will of the people as above provided shall be prescribed by law; but this shall not be construed to interfere with the right of the people to assemble in convention at any time whenever they so will it."

Mr. Martin, of Navarro, proposed to amend the substitute by striking out "ten years" and inserting "twenty years."

On motion of Mr. Holt, the main question was ordered.

Question on Mr. Martin's (of Navarro) amendment put and amendment lost.

Question on Mr. Flournoy's substitute for the article was put and lost.

Mr. McCormick, by leave, withdrew his substitute, and the question on Mr. Pickett's motion to strike out the first section was put and carried by the following vote:

Yeas—Allison, Abernathy, Arnim, Abner, Blake, Blassingame, Barnett, Brady, Crawford, Chambers, Cook of Gonzales, Cooke of San Saba, Douglas, Dillard, DeMorse, Darnell,

Dunnam, Flournoy, Ferris, German, Holt, Henry of Limestone, Holmes, Haynes, Johnson of Collin, King, Kilgore, Lynch, McLean, Martin of Navarro, Martin of Hunt, McKinney, McCormick, Norvell, Nugent, Pauli, Reagan, Ramey, Robeson of Fayette, Ross, Russell of Wood, Spikes, Scott, Sessions, Stockdale, Stayton, Whitehead, Weaver, Whitfield—49.

NAYS—Brown, Ballinger, Bruce, Cline, Cooley, Cardis, Dohoney, Davis of Brazos, Erhard, Ford, Fleming, Henry of Smith, Killough, Lacy, Mitchell, Moore, Murphy, Nunn, Reynolds, Robertson of Bell, Smith, Wade, West, Waelder—24.

Mr. Dohoney offered the following as section 1 of the article:

"Section 1. The Legislature may, at any regular session, by a vote of two-thirds of all the members of each house, pass a joint resolution, to take the sense of the qualified electors of the State, at the next succeeding general election, upon the proposition to call a Constitutional Convention; and if at such election a majority of those voting vote in favor of calling a Constitutional Convention, the Legislature, at the next succeeding session, shall pass a joint resolution calling a Constitutional Convention, which convention, when it shall assemble, shall frame a constitution, and submit the same to a vote of the qualified electors of the State for ratification or rejection; and if a majority of those voting at such election shall vote in favor of the ratification of said constitution, it shall, by proclamation of the Governor, be declared the constitution of the State."

Mr. DeMorse offered the following as a substitute for Mr. Dohoney's substitute for section 1:

"The Legislature, by a majority of all the members, shall have the power to suggest, and provide by appropriation, for a convention of the people, for the purpose of creating a new organic law, and shall submit the proposition to a popular vote, and, a majority of the people approving, the succeeding Legislature shall, by a majority, recognize their will, and provide that no general election shall be held until the convention shall have assembled, and provided therefor to suit the exigency; but this section shall not be considered as in any degree questioning the sovereign right of the people to assemble and create organic law, without authorization from any legislative body, and by such means as they may prefer."

Mr. Reagan moved to lay both substitutes on the table.

Mr. Murphy moved to adjourn until 9 o'clock A. M. Monday. Lost.

The question on laying the substitute on the table was put, and the substitute laid on the table by the following vote:

YEAS—Allison, Arnim, Abner, Blake, Blassingame, Barnett, Brady, Crawford, Chambers, Cook of Gonzales, Cooke of San Saba, Douglas, Dillard, Darnell, Dunnam, Davis of Brazos, Flournoy, Fleming, German, Holt, Henry of Limestone, Holmes, Haynes, Johnson of Collin, King, Kilgore, Killough, Lacy, Lynch, Martin of Navarro, Martin of Hunt, McKinney, McCormick, Murphy, Norvell, Nugent, Pauli, Reagan, Robeson of Fayette, Ross, Russell of Wood, Spikes, Scott, Sessions, Stayton, Whitehead, Weaver, Whitefield—48.

NAYS—Abernathy, Brown, Ballinger, Bruce, Cline, Cooley, Cardis, DeMorse, Dohoney, Erhard, Ford, Ferris, Henry of Smith, McLean, Mitchell, Moore, Nunn, Ramey, Reynolds, Robertson of Bell, Smith, Stockdale, Wade, Waelder—24.

Mr. Cardis moved to reconsider the vote refusing to adopt the resolution augmenting the pay of pages.

Passed over for the present.

Mr. Robertson, of Bell, proposed to amend section 2, line —, after the word "votes," by inserting the words "of the State has been."

Mr. Scott moved to adjourn until 9 o'clock Monday morning. Lost.

Mr. Dohoney offered the following resolution:

Resolved, That Nat. Q. Henderson, who has rendered efficient service in the inception of the labors of this Convention, in assisting to make up the journals of this body for the first five days of its session, be allowed twenty-five dollars for his services; and the certificate of the Secretary of the Senate, approved by the President, shall be sufficient for the Comptroller to draw his warrant for said amount.

An amendment was offered that the same shall be paid out of the salaries of those whom he assisted.

On motion of Mr. Scott, the Convention adjourned until 9 o'clock A. M. Monday.

TWENTY-FIFTH DAY.

HALL OF REPRESENTATIVES, }
AUSTIN, TEXAS, October 4, 1875. }

Convention met pursuant to adjournment; roll called; quorum present; prayer by the Rev. Mr. Wright, of Austin.

Journal of Saturday read and adopted.

On motion of Mr. Whitehead, Mr. Dunnam was excused from attendance on the Convention for a few days.

Mr. Reagan submitted a letter from J. Langston on the subject of crimes and punishments.

Referred to the Committee on Crimes and Punishments.

Also, a letter from John M. McDonald on the subject of school lands in Henderson county.

Referred to the Committee on Counties and County Lands.

Mr. Dohoney presented the memorial of S. G. W. Hiatt on the subject of woman suffrage.

Mr. Martin, of Navarro, moved to reject the memorial.

Mr. Martin, of Navarro, withdrew his motion, and Mr. Blassingame renewed it.

On motion of Mr. Dillard the main question was ordered, which being the rejection of the memorial, the same was put, and the Convention refused to reject by the following vote:

YEAS—Allison, Abernathy, Arnim, Abner, Brown, Blake, Blassingame, Barnett, Bruce, Chambers, Dillard, Dunnam, Davis of Wharton, Graves, Holt, Henry of Limestone, Johnson of Collin, Killough, Lacy, Lynch, Martin of Navarro, McKinney, Moore, Murphy, Norvell, Ramey, Ross, Russell of Wood, Scott, Sessions, Smith, Whithead—32.

NAYS—Ballinger, Brady, Crawford, Cook of Gonzales, Cooke of San Saba, Cooley, Cardis, Douglas, DeMorse, Dohoney, Darnell, Davis of Brazos, Erhard, Ford, Flournoy, Fleming, Ferris, German, Henry of Smith, Holmes, Haynes, King, Kilgore, McLean, Martin of Hunt, Mitchell, McCormick, Nunn, Nugent, Pauli, Reagan, Robertson of Bell, Robeson of Fayette, Spikes, Stockdale, Stayton, Wade, Weaver, Whitfield, West Wadder—41.

The memorial was referred to the Committee on Suffrage.

Mr. DeMorse, chairman of the Committee on Revenue and Taxation, submitted the following reports:

To the Hon. E. B. Pickett, President of the Convention:

The Committee on Taxation, to whose consideration was referred a proposed ordinance to relieve certain counties from taxation, on account of damages resulting from flood and storm, direct me to report said ordinance back to the Convention, and express their opinion that the committee has no authority in the premises, and doubts the propriety of any action by the Convention in this direction.

To the Hon. E. B. Pickett, President of the Convention:

The Committee on Revenue and Taxation, to which was referred a memorial from Bastrop county relative to pay of

Rangers, long due, direct me to report the memorial back to the Convention, and suggest that the subject be referred to the first session of the Legislature under this constitution.

Respectfully,

CHARLES DeMORSE,
Chairman of Committee on Revenue and Taxation.

Reports received.

Mr. Cook, of Gonzales, reported as follows:

COMMITTEE ROOM, }
AUSTIN, October 4, 1875. }

To the Hon. E. B. Pickett, President of the Convention:

Your Committee on Printing and Contingent Expenses, to whom was referred resolution authorizing and directing them to make a contract for printing one thousand copies of the constitution in the Bohemian language, have had the same under consideration, and have instructed me to report the same back to the Convention and recommend its adoption.

W. D. S. COOK, Chairman.

Report adopted.

Mr. Cardis offered the following resolution:

WHEREAS, The frontier of this State is constantly depredated upon by armed bands of Indians and others; and

WHEREAS, The Democratic party of this State is solemnly pledged to the protection of this suffering people; therefore, be it

Resolved, That the Committee on Revenue and Taxation be instructed to report a provision to be embodied in the constitution of this State, removing taxation from this people for a certain period of time, allowing the said amount to go to the protection of the frontier, the people thereof to be allowed the privilege of protecting themselves, with no other assistance from the State than the removal of said tax for the time specified

Referred to Committee on Revenue and Taxation.

Mr. Ballinger offered the following resolution:

Resolved, That to aid in giving security to life and property on the coast of Texas, whenever any county, city or town shall expend, in good faith, for the construction of a permanent seawall or breakwater on said coast the sum of ten thousand dollars, for every ten thousand dollars so expended the State of Texas will grant to said county, city or town certificates for—— sections of the vacant and unappropriated public domain of the State, to be held or disposed of only as a trust for the further construction of said works.

Referred to Committee on Municipal Corporations.

Mr. Erhard offered the following resolution:

Resolved, That the Legislature regulate the pardoning power, to-wit: All petitions for pardons shall be signed before the District Clerk, who shall certify that the signatures are genuine; that the pardon shall be signed, or granted, after investigating the merits of the case, by the Governor and Attorney General, and attested by the Secretary of State.

Referred to Committee on General Provisions.

UNFINISHED BUSINESS AND BUSINESS ON THE TABLE.

Resolution to pay Nat. Q. Henderson, $25 for services rendered at the commencement of the session, taken up.

Mr. Martin, of Navarro, withdrew his amendment, and the resolution was lost.

The Legislative Department again taken up.

Mr. Robertson, of Bell, offered the following amendment:

Insert in line —, after the word "votes," the words "of the State has been".

Adopted.

Mr. Fleming proposed to amend section 25, line 123, by striking out after the word "of" the words "compact and".

Adopted.

Mr. Murphy offered the following additional sections:

"ARTICLE —.
"MILITIA.

"Section 1. The legislature shall provide by law for organizing, disciplining and arming the militia of this State, not incompatible with the constitution and laws of the United States.

"Sec. 2. No licensed minister of the Gospel shall be required to perform military duty.

"Sec. 3. The Governor shall have the power to call forth the militia to repel raiders."

Mr. Reagan moved to strike out section 3 of the amendment.

Mr. Murphy, by leave, withdrew his amendment.

Mr. Nunn called up his motion to reconsider the vote refusing to adopt an amendment by Mr. Davis, of Brazos, to section 48, line 246, viz:

After "schools" add "and colleges and universities under the control of the State."

Vote reconsidered.

Mr. Flournoy offered the following as a substitute for the amendment:

Section 48, line 246½, "To raise no more than forty thousand dollars (in the aggregate) to be applied to the completion of the State Agricultural and Mechanical College."

Mr. DeMorse offered the following substitute for the amendment and substitute:

"Section 48, line 246, after "schools" add "and the maintenance and support of the Agricultural and Mechanical College of Texas."

Mr. Flournoy accepted the same as a substitute for his amendment.

Mr. Ballinger moved to substitute the amendment as follows:

Add to line 248 the words "and maintenance and support of the Agricultural and Mechanical College of the State."

Accepted by Mr. DeMorse.

Mr. Dohoney proposed to amend the amendment by adding "and such other colleges, universities and normal schools as may be established by law."

Lost.

Mr. Norvell proposed to amend the amendment by striking out the words "maintenance and support," and insert "completion and repair."

Lost.

Mr. Stayton offered to amend as follows:

Add after the word "schools," in line 246, the following words: "in which shall be included colleges and universities established by the State."

Adopted.

And Mr. DeMorse's amendment adopted.

Mr. Weaver moved to reconsider the vote refusing to adopt Mr. Dohoney's substitute to section 1, article —, mode of amending the constitution.

Mr. German moved to reconsider the vote adopting Mr. DeMorse's amendment to section 48, line 246.

On motion of Mr. Flournoy the pending question was postponed until to-day week.

Mr. Flournoy's resolution to amend the rules relating to the yeas and nays was taken up and lost.

Mr. Mills's resolution on the same subject was taken up and lost.

Mr. Martin's (of Navarro) report as chairman of Committee on Agricultural and Stock-raising, reporting a resolution and section — on the subject of a fence law, was taken up and referred to the Committee on General Provisions.

The report of the Committee on Executive Department, with article —, taken up.

Mr. Fleming offered the following amendment:

Amend section 1 by striking out in line 4 the words "and Superintendent of Public Instruction."

Adopted.

Mr. Russell, of Wood, proposed to amend by striking out in lines 2 and 3 the words "Lieutenant Governor."

Lost.

Mr. West proposed to amend by striking out of lines 6 and 7, section 2, the words "except Secretary of State."

Lost.

Mr. Norvell proposed to amend as follows:

Add to section 3 the words "in joint session."

Adopted.

Mr. Whitfield proposed to amend section 4, line 26, by striking out "two" and inserting "four."

The yeas and nays were called upon the amendment, and the Convention adopted the amendment by the following vote:

YEAS—Abernathy, Arnim, Abner, Brown, Blake, Ballinger, Blassingame, Cook of Gonzales, Cardis, DeMorse, Dohoney, Dunnam, Davis of Brazos, Davis of Wharton, Erhard, Ford, Fleming, Ferris, Henry of Smith, Johnson of Collin, Kilgore, Killough, Lacy, Lynch, Martin of Hunt, Mitchell, McCormick, Moore, Murphy, Pauli, Reagan, Ramey, Reynolds, Robertson of Bell, Robeson of Fayette, Ross, Spikes, Scott, Smith, Stockdale, Stayton, Whitfield, Waelder—43.

NAYS—Allison, Barnett, Brady, Bruce, Crawford, Chambers, Cooke of San Saba, Cooley, Douglas, Dillard, Darnell, Graves, Holt, Henry of Limestone, Holmes, Haynes, King, Martin of Navarro, McKinney, Norvell, Nugent, Russell of Wood, Sessions, Wade, Whitehead, Weaver, West—27.

Mr. Kilgore offered the following amendment:

Section 4, line 28, strike out "six" and insert "eight."

Adopted.

Mr. Waelder proposed to amend as follows:

Insert "he shall not be eligible for more than two terms in succession, in lieu of the words commencing "he," in line 27, to "years," in line 28.

Mr. Martin, of Navarro, moved to reconsider the vote adopting Mr. Kilgore's amendment.

Lost.

The Convention adjourned, pending Mr. Waelder's amendment.

EVENING SESSION—2½ o'clock.

Convention met pursuant to adjournment; roll called; quorum present.

Question pending when the Convention adjourned, viz: Mr. Waelder's amendment again taken up and lost.

Mr. Brown moved to amend by striking out " Thursday," in section 4, line 24, and insert " Monday."

Lost.

Also amend by inserting " shall" between " and " and " have," in line 29, section 4.

Adopted.

Mr. Johnson, of Collin, moved to amend by striking out " $5000 " and insert "$4000" in section 5, line 32, as salary of the Governor.

Mr. Wade moved to insert " $3000 " in gold.

Lost.

Mr. German moved to amend by striking out " $5000 " and inserting " $3000."

Lost.

Mr. Kilgore proposed to amend by inserting " $4500."

The yeas and nays were called upon the question of the adoption of the amendment, and the Convention refused to adopt the amendment by the following vote:

YEAS—Abner, Brown, Ballinger, Cooke of San Saba, Douglas, Dillard, Erhard, Henry of Smith, Kilgore, Moore, Reagan, Whitfield—12.

NAYS—Allison, Abernathy, Arnim, Blake, Blassingame, Barnett, Brady, Bruce, Crawford, Chambers, Cook of Gonzales, Cooley, Cardis, DeMorse, Dohoney, Darnell, Davis of Brazos, Davis of Wharton, Ford, Flournoy, Fleming, Ferris, German, Graves, Holt, Henry of Limestone, Holmes, Haynes, Johnson of Collin, King, Killough, Lacy, Lynch, McLean, Martin of Navarro, Martin of Hunt, Mitchell, McKinney, McCormick, Murphy, Norvell, Nugent, Pauli, Ramey, Reynolds, Robertson of Bell, Robeson of Fayette, Ross, Russell of Wood, Spikes, Scott, Sessions, Smith, Stockdale, Stayton, Wade, Whitehead, Weaver, West, Waelder—60.

The question recurring on Mr. Johnson's (of Collin) amendment, the yeas and nays were called, and the amendment was lost by the following vote:

YEAS—Allison, Abernathy, Arnim, Abner, Barnett, Brady, Bruce, Chambers, Cook of Gonzales, Darnell, Flournoy, Fleming, Graves, Holt, Henry of Limestone, Holmes, Haynes, Johnson of Collin, Killough, Lacy, Lynch, McLean, Martin of Navarro, Martin of Hunt, Mitchell, McKinney, Nugent, Pauli, Ramey, Robertson of Bell, Russell of Wood, Spikes, Scott, Wade, Weaver—35.

NAYS—Brown, Blake, Ballinger, Blassingame, Crawford, Cooke of San Saba, Cooley, Cardis, Douglas, Dillard, DeMorse, Dohoney, Davis of Brazos, Davis of Wharton, Erhard, Ford, Ferris, German, Henry of Smith, King, Kilgore, McCormick, Moore, Murphy, Norvell, Reagan, Reynolds, Robeson of Fayette, Ross, Sessions, Smith, Stockdale, Stayton, Whitehead, Whitfield, West, Waelder—37.

Mr. Nugent proposed to amend the salary of Governor by striking out $5000 and inserting $3500.

Mr. McCormick moved to lay the amendment on the table.

The yeas and nays were called and the amendment laid on the table by the following vote:

YEAS—Abernathy, Abner, Brown, Blake, Ballinger, Cook of Gonzales, Cooke of San Saba, Cooley, Cardis, Douglas, Dillard, DeMorse, Dohoney, Darnell, Davis of Brazos, Davis of Wharton, Erhard, Ford, Flournoy, Ferris, Henry of Smith, Henry of Limestone, King, Kilgore, Killough, Lynch, Martin of Navarro, McCormick, Moore, Murphy, Norvell, Reagan, Robeson of Fayette, Ross, Sessions, Smith, Stockdale, Stayton, Whitehead, Weaver, Whitfield, West, Waelder—43.

NAYS—Allison, Arnim, Blassingame, Barnett, Brady, Bruce, Crawford, Chambers, Fleming, German, Graves, Holt, Holmes, Haynes, Johnson of Collin, Lacy, McLean, Martin of Hunt, Mitchell, McKinney, Nugent, Pauli, Ramey, Reynolds, Robertson of Bell, Russell of Wood, Spikes, Scott, Wade—26.

Mr. German moved to reconsider the vote refusing to adopt Mr. Johnson's (of Collin) amendment to strike out $5000 and insert $4000.

On motion of Mr. Scott the main question was ordered and the vote was reconsidered.

The question recurring on the adoption of the amendment, the yeas and nays were called, and the amendment adopted by the following vote:

YEAS—Allison, Abernathy, Arnim, Abner, Brown, Blassingame, Barnett, Burleson, Brady, Bruce, Chambers, Cook of Gonzales, Darnell, Davis of Wharton, Flournoy, Fleming, German, Graves, Holt, Henry of Limestone, Holmes, Haynes, Johnson of Collin, Killough, Lacy, Lynch, McLean, Martin of Navarro, Martin of Hunt, Mitchell, McKinney, Nugent, Pauli, Ramey.

Reynolds, Rentfro, Robertson of Bell, Robeson of Fayette, Russell of Wood, Spikes, Scott, Sessions, Wade, Weaver—44.

NAYS—Blake, Ballinger, Crawford, Cooke of San Saba, Cooley, Cardis, Douglas, Dillard, DeMorse, Dohoney, Davis of Brazos, Erhard, Ford, Ferris, Henry of Smith, King, Kilgore, McCormick, Moore, Murphy, Norvell, Nunn, Reagan, Ross, Smith, Stockdale, Stayton, Sansom, Whitehead, Whitfield, West, Waelder—32.

Mr. Martin, of Navarro, offered the following amendment:

Section 4, strike out all between the words "installed," in line 27, and "he," in line 28.

Adopted.

Mr. Crawford proposed to amend section 5, as follows:

"He shall receive no fees or perquisites or extra compensation for the performance of any duties connected with his office."

Lost.

Mr. Henry, of Smith, offered the following amendment:

Add after the word "move," in line 32, the words "until otherwise provided by law."

Lost.

Mr. Murphy offered the following amendment:

Section 7, line 44, amend by adding after the word "invasion," the words "and raiders from the Mexican Republic."

Lost.

Mr. Stayton offered the following amendment:

Add to section 7, after the word "invasion," in line 44, the following, "by troops under the direction or control of other States or governments, or by predatory bands therefrom."

On motion of Mr. Robertson, of Bell, the Convention adjourned until 9 o'clock A. M., to-morrow, pending Mr. Stayton's amendment.

TWENTY-SIXTH DAY.

HALL OF REPRESENTATIVES,
AUSTIN, TEXAS, October 5, 1875.

Convention met pursuant to adjournment; roll called; quorum present; prayer by Rev. William Brush, D. D.

Journal of yesterday read and adopted.

On motion of Mr. Davis, of Brazos, A. T. McKinney, delegate elect from the Fifteenth District, to fill the vacancy occasioned by the resignation of Mr. Goddin, came forward, presented his credentials, took the prescribed oath and his seat in the Convention.

Mr. Reagan, Chairman of the Committee on Judiciary, reported back a resolution declaring defaulters felons, and asked that it be referred to the Committee on Crimes and Punishments.

Referred as asked.

Also reported back a memorial of the citizens of Wilson county, and asked that it be referred to the Select Committee on Apportionment.

Referred as asked.

Mr. Scott submitted a memorial from the bar and citizens of the counties of Harrison, Gregg, Cass, Bowie and Wood, relative to the necessity of taking action in reference to certain railroads in this State.

Referred to Committee on Railroad Corporations.

Mr. Waelder, from the Committee on Immigration, submitted the following minority report and article:

To the Hon. E. B. Pickett, President of the Convention:

The undersigned, dissenting from the report of the majority of the Committee on Immigration, begs leave to submit the accompanying article for the consideration of the Convention:

While I am free to concede that the Immigration Bureau has not accomplished, to the extent anticipated, the purpose of its establishment, I am yet of the opinion that the effort to induce immigration to our young State should not be given up.

It will scarcely be disputed that many, if not all parts of Texas need population—men with strong arms and ready hands to till her soil and engage in the various industrial pursuits which will reward the laborer for his work, to whatever branch of business he may turn his attention. Neither can it be denied that our State offers facilities to the classes indicated, equal to any that are offered by any other section of the country.

It is as true, that in relation to the soil, climate and productions, the agricultural, mineral and other resources of the different sections of the State, but little is known abroad; at least there is not that general knowledge which the emigrant from other States and countries would desire to have before selecting this as a new home.

If, then, we desire immigration, should we not furnish information of the advantages which the State offers to the settler within its limits? Is it not right that the State should publish this information in some authentic form?

With this view and for this purpose I recommend the establishment and maintenance of a Bureau of Agriculture, Statistics and Immigration, by which the desired information can be gathered, compiled and disseminated, and through the means of which immigration may be drawn to our borders.

Not only would the information thus furnished be important to the seekers of new homes from other States and countries, but it would also be of great service to the present citizens and inhabitants of this State, giving them more complete and more accurate knowledge than they now have of the populations, productions, capacities, and resources of the different sections.

It is true that private enterprise has done much to impart knowledge of the subjects mentioned; but who can doubt that the same and more extended information, coming from a public officer, by authority of the State, would be regarded as more reliable, and therefore more acceptable?

The expense of this bureau would be trifling, as compared with what other States, or even individuals and associations of individuals, have done and are doing in the same direction. A bureau of the character recommended would simply require, in addition to a chief, and probably not more than one clerk, an appropriation for stationery, printing and postage, and the occasional employment of an agent for a limited time to attend to specific duties pertaining to the efficient workings of the system.

With the greatest desire to administer the affairs of the State in the most economical manner, the comparatively trifling sum required would be more than repaid by the knowledge which the system would impart to the citizens of the State, to say nothing of the advantages which would flow from the increase of population, adding to our material wealth, importing and creating property for taxation.

If all sections of the State do not need, or desire, increase of population, there are other sections whose prosperity would be enhanced thereby.

In justice to them, and for the general advantage of th   '
State, I ask that some plan may be inaugurated which will produce the results indicated.

Without entering into further detail, I submit this minority report, and respectfully ask its favorable '
Convention.   JACOB WAELDER,
                    Of the Committee on Immigration.
        "ARTICLE —.
    "AGRICULTURE, STATISTICS AND IMMIGRATION.
"Section 1. The Legislature shall provide for the establish-
19

ment, maintenance and support of a Bureau of Agriculture, Statistics and Immigration, which bureau shall be charged with the gathering, publishing and dissemination of correct statistical information as to the population, productions, industrial and agricultural capacity, mineral and other resources of the different sections of, and by that and such other means as may be provided by law, encourage immigration to this State; *provided,* that the average of appropriations per year for the above purposes shall not exceed the sum of . . . . . thousand dollars."

On motion of Mr. Moore, one hundred copies of the report and article were ordered printed.

Mr. Ford, chairman of Committee on State Affairs, reported as follows:

COMMITTEE ROOM,
AUSTIN, October 4, 1875.

To the Hon. E. B. Pickett, President of the Convention:

The Committee on State Affairs, to which was referred the memorial of the widow and heirs of the late W. A. Smith, have had the same under consideration, and instruct me to report the accompanying section, and recommend that it be adopted by the Convention as a part of the new constitution.

JOHN S. FORD, Chairman.

"Sec. ——. The Legislature shall make provision by law to have all claims and demands justly and lawfully due by the existing State government, or by any of its predecessors, and which shall be presented within one year from a date specified by law, and not thereafter, either adjudicated or audited; *provided,* that such claims and demands have not heretofore been either adjudicated or audited; *and, provided also,* that said claims and demands originated prior to the 28th day of January, 1861, or subsequent to the 5th day of August, 1865; and that they are not in contravention of the constitution and laws of the United States; and all claims and demands not so presented shall be and remain forever barred."

Mr. Moore offered the following resolution:

Resolved, That when, in considering any of the articles of the constitution as reported, amendments are offered, which affect such articles as may not yet be reported by the suitable committee, said amendments shall be referred without debate to said committee.

Laid over under the rules.

The Convention then proceeded to consider the unfinished business, viz: Mr. Stayton's amendment to Executive Article.

Mr. Kilgore proposed to substitute the amendment by the following:

Section 7, add after the word "invasion," line 44, the words "whether by armies or by bands of lawless men."

Pending discussion on the amendment, the hour arrived for the special order, viz: The article on education.

On motion of Mr. Whitfield, the special order was postponed until Friday next at 10 o'clock A. M.

The Convention proceeded with the consideration of the pending subject, Mr. Kilgore's substitute:

Lost.

Mr. Ballinger offered the following as a substitute for the amendment:

"It shall be the duty of the Legislature to provide by law for the protection of the frontier from armed incursions and bands of robbers, and for calling forth the militia for that purpose."

Lost.

Mr. King offered the following as a substitute for Mr. Stayton's amendment:

"Sec. 1. In line 44 strike out the word "and" and add the following words, "and protect the frontier from hostile incursions by Indians or other predatory bands."

Accepted by Mr. Stayton.

On the question of the amendment the yeas and nays were called, and the amendment adopted by the following vote:

YEAS—Abner, Brown, Ballinger, Blassingame, Barnett, Burleson, Brady, Bruce, Crawford, Chambers, Cook of Gonzales, Cooke of San Saba, Cooley, Cardis, Dillard, DeMorse, Dohoney, Darnell, Davis of Brazos, Erhard, Ford, Flournoy, Fleming, Ferris, Gaither, Graves, Henry of Limestone, Holmes, Haynes, Johnson of Collin King, Kilgore, Killough, Lockett, Lynch, Mitchell, McKinney of Walker, McCormick, Moore, Murphy, Nugent, Pauli, Reynolds, Rentfro, Ross, Spikes, Smith, Stockdale, Stayton, Whitfield, West, Waelder—52.

NAYS—Allison, Abernathy, Arnim, Blake, Douglas, German, Holt, Henry of Smith, Johnson of Franklin, Lacy, Martin of Navarro, Martin of Hunt, Mills, McKinney of Denton, Norvell, Nunn, Reagan, Ramey, Robertson of Bell, Robeson of Fayette, Russell of Wood, Scott, Sessions, Sansom, Wade, Whitehead, Weaver—27.

Mr. Scott moved to reconsider the vote taken on yesterday refusing to strike out of section 1 the words "Lieutenant Governor."

Lost by the following vote:

YEAS—Abner, Blassingame, Barnett, Brady, Bruce, Chambers, Cook of Gonzales, Davis of Wharton, Flournoy, Fleming, German, Gaither, Graves, Holt, Haynes, Johnson of Franklin, Johnson of Collin, Lockett, Lynch, Martin of Navarro, Martin of Hunt, Mills, Mitchell, McKinney of Denton, McCormick, Murphy, Pauli, Reynolds, Rentfro, Robertson of Bell, Robeson of Fayette, Ross, Russell of Wood, Spikes, Scott, Wade, Weaver, Whitfield—38.

NAYS—Allison, Abernathy, Arnim, Brown, Blake, Ballinger, Crawford, Cooke of San Saba, Cooley, Cardis, Douglas, Dillard, DeMorse, Dohoney, Darnell, Davis of Brazos, Erhard, Ford, Ferris, Henry of Smith, Henry of Limestone, Holmes, King, Kilgore, Killough, Lacy, McKinney of Walker, Moore, Norvell, Nunn, Nugent, Reagan, Ramey, Sessions, Smith, Stockdale, Stayton, Sansom, Whitehead, West—40.

Mr. Kilgore proposed to strike out of section 8, line 47, the word "disease" and insert "epidemic."

Mr. Davis, of Brazos, proposed to amend as follows:

Section 8, strike out the balance of the section after the word "place" in line 46, and insert: "Should the casualties of war, or the prevalence of contagious diseases, render it unsafe to meet at the seat of government."

Lost.

Mr. Kilgore's amendment lost.

Mr. Ballinger offered the following amendment:

Add to section 8, "and shall not continue in session longer than thirty days."

Mr. Waelder offered the following amendment:

Strike out all after the word "convened," in line 49, to the end of the section.

Adopted.

Mr. Crawford offered the following amendment:

Strike out all after "convened," in line 50, and insert: "Until they have taken final action thereon. Nor shall they afterward enter upon any legislation, except it be to meet the exigencies which necessitated the convening of the Legislature in extra session. The Governor shall convene no extraordinary session for a longer period than thirty days."

Lost.

Mr. Dohoney moved to amend by striking out section 14, as the same was provided for, and properly belonged to article —, "Legislative Department."

Lost.

Mr. Stockdale offered the following amendment:

Strike out of section 14 all after the word " adjournment," in line 110, and insert the following: " If any bill, except the general appropriation bill, containing appropriations for more than one object be presented to the Governor, he shall return it, for that reason, to the house in which it originated without his approval, if the Legislature be in session; if not, then to the State Department, as heretofore provided."

Lost.

Mr. Nugent proposed to strike out "will," in line 99, and insert " shall."

Adopted.

Mr. Flournoy proposed to amend section 14 as follows:

Strike out of lines 109 and 110 the words: " and give notice thereof by proclamation;" and the words: " and make proclamation of the same," in line 124.

Lost.

Mr. Mills moved to amend section 17, after the word "more," in line 157, " except mileage."

Withdrawn.

Mr. Brown offered the following amendment:

Section 17, lines 156 and 157, strike out the words " Speaker of the House of Representatives," and insert " members of the Senate."

Adopted.

Mr. Waelder proposed to strike out all of section 17 after the word " office," in line 163.

Adopted.

Mr. Pauli offered the following amendment:

Strike out, in line 160, all after the words " no more," down to and including the words " his office," in line 163.

Lost.

Mr. Waelder offered the following amendment:

Strike out the three first lines to and including the word " and " in line 4 of section 17.

Adopted.

Mr. Murphy proposed to amend by striking out of line 169 the word " and " and inserting the word " or," and strike out " they " and insert " he."

Adopted.

Mr. Scott offered the following amendment:

Section 19, strike out down to the word " the " in line 175, and insert the following:

" There shall be a seal of the State, which shall be kept by the Governor and used by him officially."

Lost.

Mr. Martin, of Hunt, offered the following amendment:

Amend section 18 by inserting the word "may" before the word "succeed" in line 170.

Adopted.

Mr. McCormick proposed to add after the word "Texas," in line 176, the words and figures "1836."

Adopted.

Mr. Brady proposed to amend section 21 by striking out all after the word "State," in line 180, down to and including the word "elect," in line 182, and insert "who shall be elected by the qualified voters of the State for a term of four years."

Lost.

Mr. Mills proposed to amend by striking out "$2000" and inserting "$1800" as the salary of Secretary of State.

Lost.

Mr. Allison proposed to amend as follows:

Section 21, line 188, add after the words "$2000" the words "$500," so as to read "$2500 and no more."

On motion of Mr. Russell, of Wood, laid on the table by the following vote:

YEAS—Abernathy, Arnim, Abner, Brown, Blassingame, Barnett, Burleson, Brady, Bruce, Chambers, Cook of Gonzales, Cooke of San Saba, Douglas, Dillard, DeMorse, Dohoney, Darnell, Davis of Brazos, Erhard, Ford, Flournoy, Fleming, Ferris, German, Gaither, Graves, Holt, Henry of Limestone, Holmes, Haynes Johnson of Franklin, Johnson of Collin, Lockett, Lacy, Lynch, Martin of Navarro, Martin of Hunt, Mills, Mitchell, McKinney of Denton, McKinney of Walker, McCormick, Moore, Murphy, Nugent, Pauli, Ramey, Reynolds, Rentfro, Robertson of Bell, Robeson of Fayette, Ross, Russell of Wood, Spikes, Scott, Sessions, Smith, Sansom, Wade, Weaver, Whitfield—61.

NAYS—Allison, Blake, Ballinger, Crawford, Cooley, Henry of Smith, King, Kilgore, Norvell, Nunn, Reagan, Stockdale, Stayton, Whitehead, West, Waelder—16.

Mr. Whitfield proposed to amend section 22, line 189, by striking out "two" and inserting "four."

Lost.

Mr. Scott moved to reconsider the vote taken on yesterday extending the tenure of office of the Governor to four years.

Mr. Davis, of Brazos, moved to adjourn.

Lost.

On motion of Mr. Stockdale a call of the Convention was ordered.

Mr. German moved to suspend the call.

Lost.

Roll called.

Absentees—Messrs. Cline, Cardis, Ford, Flanagan, Henry of Limestone, Killough, Lynch, Mills.

Mr. Murphy moved to excuse Mr. Cardis.

Carried.

Messrs. Lynch, Mills and Killough appeared and answered.

On motion of Mr. Rentfro the call was suspended.

On motion of Mr. Whitfield the Convention adjourned to 2½ o'clock, pending Mr. Scott's motion.

EVENING SESSION—2½ o'clock.

Convention met; roll called; quorum present.

Mr. McKinney, of Walker, was added to the Committees on General Provisions and Crimes and Punishments, on motion of Mr. Mills and Mr. Russell, of Wood, respectively.

Question pending when the Convention adjourned—viz., Mr. Scott's motion to reconsider—taken up.

On motion of Mr. Scott, the consideration of the motion was passed for the present.

Mr. Martin, of Navarro, moved to reconsider the vote amending the article in regard to the seal of the State.

Carried, and amendment lost.

Mr. Ramey moved to reconsider the vote refusing to adopt the amendment increasing the salary of the Secretary of State.

Mr. Flournoy proposed to amend section 22 by inserting after the word " party," in lines 191 and 192, the following:

" And shall especially inquire into the charter rights of all private corporations, and from time to time, in the name of the State, take such action in the courts as may be proper and necessary to prevent any private corporation from exercising any power, or demanding or collecting any species of tax, toll, freight or wharfage, not authorized by law; and shall, whenever sufficient cause exists, seek a judicial forfeiture of such charters, unless otherwise expressly directed by law."

Adopted.

Mr. Moore proposed to amend by adding to the section: "*Provided,* That the fees which he may receive shall not amount to more than $2,000 annually."

Adopted.

Mr. Darnell proposed to amend section 23, line 200, by striking out the word " four," and inserting " two."

Adopted by the following vote:

YEAS—Allison, Abernathy, Abner, Brown, Blake, Blassingame, Burleson, Brady, Bruce, Crawford, Chambers, Cook of Gonzales, Cooke of San Saba, Cooley, Douglas, Dillard, Dohoney, Darnell, Davis of Wharton, Flournoy, Ferris, German, Graves, Holt, Holmes, Haynes, Johnson of Franklin, Johnson of Collin, Lacy, Martin of Navarro, Martin of Hunt, Mills, Mitchell, McKinney of Denton, McKinney of Walker, Murphy, Norvell, Nugent, Pauli, Reagan, Reynolds, Rentfro, Robeson of Fayette, Russell of Wood, Scott, Sessions, Sansom, Wade, Whitehead, Weaver, West—51.

NAYS—Arnim, Ballinger, DeMorse, Davis of Brazos, Erhard, Ford, Fleming, Gaither, Henry of Smith, Henry of Limestone, King, Kilgore, Killough, Lockett, Lynch, Moore, Ramey, Robertson of Bell, Ross, Spikes, Smith, Stayton, Whitfield, Waelder —24.

Mr. German proposed to amend section 23, line 201, (salaries of Treasurer, Comptroller, and Commissioner of Land Office), by striking out "$2,500," and inserting "$2,000."

Mr. Reagan moved to strike out "$2,500," and insert "$3,000." Lost by the following vote:

YEAS—Blake, Ballinger, Cooley, DeMorse, Erhard, Gaither, Henry of Smith, Holmes, King, Lynch, McKinney of Walker, McCormick, Reagan, Robertson of Bell, Smith, Stockdale, Stayton, Sansom, Weaver, West, Waelder—21.

NAYS—Allison, Abernathy, Arnim, Abner, Brown, Blassingame, Barnett, Burleson, Bruce, Crawford, Chambers, Cook of Gonzales, Cooke of San Saba, Douglas, Dillard, Dohoney, Darnell, Davis of Brazos, Davis of Wharton, Flournoy, Fleming, Ferris, German, Graves, Holt, Henry of Limestone, Haynes, Johnson of Franklin, Johnson of Collin, Kilgore, Killough, Lockett, Lacy, Martin of Navarro, Martin of Hunt, Mills, Mitchell, McKinney of Denton, Moore, Murphy, Norvell, Nugent, Pauli, Ramey, Reynolds, Rentfro, Robeson of Fayette, Ross, Russell of Wood, Spikes, Scott, Sessions, Wade, Whitehead, Whitfield—55.

Mr. Cooley offered the following as a substitute for the amendment:

Strike out the word "receive," in line 200, and insert the following therefor:

"The Comptroller of Public Accounts shall receive an annual salary of four thousand dollars, and the Treasurer and Commissioner of the General Land Office each."

On motion of Mr. Holt, the substitute was laid on the table.

Mr. Martin, of Navarro, moved to lay the amendment offered by Mr. German on the table.

Carried by the following vote:

YEAS—Allison, Abernathy, Arnim, Abner, Brown, Blake, Ballinger, Burleson, Cook of Gonzales, Cooke of San Saba, Cardis, Douglas, Dillard, DeMorse, Dohoney, Darnell, Davis of Brazos, Erhard, Ford, Flournoy, Ferris, Gaither, Holt, Henry of Smith, Henry of Limestone, Holmes, Haynes, King, Kilgore, Lacy, Lynch, Martin of Navarro, Martin of Hunt, McKinney of Walker, McCormick, Moore, Murphy, Norvell, Reagan, Ramey, Robertson of Bell, Robeson of Fayette, Ross, Spikes, Sessions, Smith, Stockdale, Stayton, Sansom, Whitehead, Weaver, Whitfield, West, Waelder—54.

NAYS—Blassingame, Barnett, Brady, Bruce, Crawford, Chambers, Cooley, Fleming, German, Graves, Johnson of Franklin, Johnson of Collin, Killough, Lockett, McLean, Mills, Mitchell, McKinney of Denton, Nugent, Pauli, Reynolds, Rentfro, Russell of Wood, Scott, Wade—25.

Mr. Stayton offered to amend by striking out the words " and no more," in section 23, line 201, and insert "until otherwise provided by law."

On motion of Mr. Graves the amendment was laid on the table.

Mr. Scott called up his motion to reconsider the vote taken yesterday fixing the tenure of office of the Governor at four years, and the vote was reconsidered.

The question on the adoption of the amendment to strike out "two" and insert "four" was then put, and the amendment lost by the following vote:

YEAS—Arnim, Ballinger, Cardis, DeMorse, Davis of Brazos, Erhard, Ford, Fleming, Ferris, Gaither, Henry of Smith, Henry of Limestone, Kilgore, Killough, Lynch, McCormick, Moore, Murphy, Ramey, Robertson of Bell, Robeson of Fayette, Ross, Spikes, Smith, Stayton, Whitfield, Waelder—27.

NAYS—Allison, Abernathy, Abner, Brown, Blake, Blassingame, Barnett, Burleson, Brady, Bruce, Crawford, Chambers, Cook of Gonzales, Cooke of San Saba, Cooley, Douglas, Dillard, Dohoney, Darnell, Flournoy, German, Graves, Holt, Holmes, Haynes, Johnson of Franklin, Johnson of Collin, King, Lockett, Lacy, McLean, Martin of Navarro, Martin of Hunt, Mills, Mitchell, McKinney of Denton, McKinney of Walker, Norvell, Nugent, Pauli, Reagan, Reynolds, Rentfro, Russell of Wood, Scott, Sessions, Stockdale, Sansom, Wade, Whitehead, Weaver, West—52.

Mr. Dohoney moved to reconsider the vote adopting the amendment striking out a portion of lines 27 and 28, section 4.

Carried, and the Convention refused to strike out the lines.

Mr. Whitfield proposed to amend section 4, line 28, by striking out the words "at least thirty years of age" and insert "a qualified elector."

Lost by the following vote:

YEAS—Brown, Brady, Crawford, Dillard, Davis of Wharton, Ford, Fleming, Kilgore, Martin of Navarro, Martin of Hunt, McCormick, Norvell, Pauli, Rentfro, Whitfield—15.

NAYS—Allison, Abernathy, Arnim, Abner, Blake, Ballinger, Blassingame, Barnett, Burleson, Bruce, Chambers, Cook of Gonzales, Cooke of San Saba, Cooley, Douglas, DeMorse, Dohoney, Darnell, Davis of Brazos, Erhard, Flournoy, Ferris, German, Gaither, Graves, Holt, Henry of Smith, Henry of Limestone, Holmes, Haynes, Johnson of Franklin, Johnson of Collin, King, Killough, Lockett, Lacy, Lynch. McLean, Mills, Mitchell, McKinney of Denton, McKinney of Walker, Moore, Murphy, Nugent, Reagan, Ramey, Reynolds, Robertson of Bell, Robeson of Fayette, Ross, Russell of Wood, Spikes, Scott, Sessions, Smith, Stockdale, Stayton, Sansom, Wade, Whitehead, Weaver, West, Waelder—64.

Mr. Murphy offered the following amendment:

Section 24, line 219, insert between the words "be" and "guilty" the words "removed from office and adjudged."

Adopted.

Mr. Stockdale proposed to amend the amendment just adopted as follows:

Strike out in lines 219 and 220 all after "perjury," and insert "and so adjudged and punished accordingly and removed from office."

Adopted.

Mr. Scott proposed to amend section 24, line 218, by inserting between the words "shall" and "make," the word "wilfully."

Adopted.

Mr. Murphy offered the following amendment:

Section 26, line 228, insert between the words "county" and "who," the words "not to exceed six."

Mr. Brady proposed to substitute the amendment as follows:

Amend section 26, by adding: "Provided not more than two shall be appointed in each justice's precinct."

Lost, and amendment lost.

Mr. Brady moved to reconsider the vote by which "Superintendent of Public Instruction" was stricken out of section 1, lines 4 and 5.

Lost by the following vote:

YEAS—Brown, Ballinger, Barnett, Brady, Crawford, Cooley, Cardis, Dillard, DeMorse, Dohoney, Davis of Brazos, Davis of Wharton, Erhard, Ford, Ferris, Henry of Smith, King, Kilgore, Lockett, Martin of Hunt, Mills, Mitchell, McKinney of Walker, McCormick, Moore, Pauli, Reynolds, Rentfro, Smith, Whitfield, West, Waelder—32.

NAYS—Allison, Abernathy, Arnim, Abner, Blake, Blassingame, Burleson, Bruce, Chambers, Cook of Gonzales, Cooke of San Saba, Douglas, Darnell, Flournoy, Fleming, German, Gaither, Graves, Holt, Henry of Limestone, Holmes, Haynes, Johnson of Franklin, Johnson of Collin, Killough, Lacy, Lynch, McLean, Martin of Navarro, McKinney of Denton, Norvell, Nugent, Reagan, Ramey, Robertson of Bell, Robeson of Fayette, Russell of Wood, Spikes, Scott, Sessions, Stockdale, Stayton, Sansom, Wade, Whitehead, Weaver—46.

Mr. Brown moved to adjourn until 9 o'clock A. M. to-morrow. Carried.

TWENTY-SEVENTH DAY.

HALL OF REPRESENTATIVES, }
AUSTIN, TEXAS, October 6, 1875. }

Convention met pursuant to adjournment; roll called; quorum present; prayer by Rev. R. H. Willenberg, of the Cumberland Presbyterian Church at Austin.

Journal of yesterday read and adopted.

Mr. Ramey submitted a communication from J. G. Hazlewood on the subject of organizing the judiciary.

Referred to the Judiciary Committee.

Also a communication from M. Youngblood on the subject of the election of sheriffs and assessors in certain cases.

Referred to Judiciary Committee.

On motion of Mr. Martin, of Hunt, Mr. Nunn was added to the Committee on Frontier Affairs.

Mr. Erhard submitted the following minority report:

COMMITTEE ROOM, }
AUSTIN, October 4, 1875. }

To the Hon. E. B. Pickett, President of the Convention:

The undersigned, a member of your Committee on Immigration, to which committee were referred certain resolutions, memorials, etc., relating to and concerning the establishment and maintenance of a Bureau of Immigration, would submit that he can not concur in the report as made by a majority of said committee. He does not believe that the report above referred to is an expression of what he believes to be the wishes and opinions of a large majority of the people of this State upon this most important subject.

Said report, under the pretext of declining to impose upon the people of this State any additional burden in the way of taxation, in effect, by the present abolition of the present system of immigration, and its recommendation that no other system be inaugurated, by decreasing the number of immigrants, will cause an increase of taxation.

But it is contended that many immigrants, attracted by the salubrious climate, fertile soil, and the many advantages which attend a residence in Texas, will come within our borders without the outlay upon the part of the State of any money, and without receiving from the people thereof any assistance in coming hither.

The undersigned would submit that although moved by various considerations as above, many immigrants in the course of time may become citizens of the State, yet he regards it as a most mistaken and short-sighted policy upon the part of this Convention to refuse to provide for the establishment and efficient maintenance of an immigration bureau, for the reasons that although much may be accomplished in the building up of the fortunes of our State by individual efforts, yet it is an incontrovertable fact that a well sustained and efficient effort inaugurated and carried out under the supervision of the State inevitably accomplishes much more in attaining the desired end.

By individual effort we may perhaps partially carry out the wishes of the people; by combined effort we *most certainly* will.

It is presumed that no member of said committee seriously believes that it would not greatly redound to the interests of our State, and the interests of every individual citizen thereof, if an efficient bureau of immigration could be maintained. Believing that no one will seriously dispute this to be the fact, the undersigned insists that, therefore, the grounds of objection to such an establishment and maintenance must be those which are presented by a mistaken idea of economy and the inefficiency of former systems.

As to the argument of economy, the undersigned believes that to put in immediate and practical operation an immigration bureau would require a present outlay with no immediate prospect of reimbursement, yet that eventually the fruits of the industry of the numerous immigrants thereby induced to become citizens of our State would, in the matter of taxable property alone, largely repay to the people of this State the advances made. He submits that the plea of poverty, as advanced by the majority report, is one *unworthy* of the important subject concerning which said report is made.

That by increasing our population we increase our wealth; that the idea that immigrants will fill our broad prairies and till the thousands of acres which as yet are contributing nothing to the support of our State, is a mistaken one, if no effort is made to induce their coming; he believes the argument of poverty to be untenable, in view of the great good to be accomplished by a moderate outlay.

In so far as it is agreed that the failure or partial failure of former systems to carry out the ideas of the advocates of an immigration bureau should warn us that no practical good can arise from an immigration bureau, the undersigned would submit, that the fact that any given idea or proposition may have been abused, does not alone and can not constitute a fair argument against its use. He insists that a fair trial of an immigration bureau has never been had in this State.

It is further contended that, by offers of homsteads, etc., a better class of people will be induced to come among us than would come under the aid-system sought to be devised. The argument is not a good one in view of the fact that, in order to obtain these homes, so generously offered by the State, the immigrant must take up his abode on the frontier, (if he wishes lands fertile,) and live in daily, hourly danger of losing his property, his or his family's lives, because of hostile forays by savages.

That no sufficient number can be induced thus to expose themselves to such immient peril, to render assistance to each other, or induce any feeling of security.

By the establishing of an aid-system, the hard-working and oppressed toilers of Europe could be induced to pour themselves into our State, and along our exposed frontier, in such numbers that our frontier would soon be the boundary line of our State.

The immigrants we may possibly receive from older States in the Union will necessarily be few in number, because those States have also inducements to go to the far West, and because those States have, comparatively to Europe, but a small surplus of population.

Therefore, it is to the old world that we must look for the people who, in the future, are to rebuild the State and place her in the rank of the States, in that position to which, by virtue of her vast area, she is justly entitled.

The undersigned believes that it is contrary to the true policy of this State to discourage immigration, in view of the fact that every other State government of the West has established, and still maintains, an efficient system, to which is due their present prosperity; and he believes that Texas *can not*, in justice to herself, fail in this important particular.

The undersigned, in view of the above, respectfully differing with the majority of said committee, submits the above as a minority report in the premises, and urges the adoption of the accompanying article.   C. ERHARD.

"ARTICLE —.

"IMMIGRATION.

"Section 1. There shall be a bureau known as the "Bureau of Immigration," which shall have supervision and control of all matters connected with immigration. The head of this bureau shall be styled the "Superintendent of Immigration." He shall be appointed by the Governor, by and with the consent of the Senate. He shall hold office for four years; and, until otherwise provided by law, shall receive a salary of two thousand dollars per annum. He shall have such powers and duties connected with immigration as may be required by law.

"Sec. 2. The Legislature shall have power to appropriate part of the ordinary revenue of the State for the purpose of promoting and protecting immigration, and for the maintenance of said bureau, under such regulations as may be provided by law."

On motion of Mr. Erhard, one hundred copies of the report and article ordered printed.

Mr. Russell, of Wood, offered the following resolution:

WHEREAS, The history of men and nations prove that the credit system has been the cause of bankruptcy and financial ruin;

AND WHEREAS, The Judiciary Department of our State government has been grievously oppressive, partly by taxing honest, prompt paying citizens to support courts to litigate suits between men who are not governed by principle:

AND WHEREAS, A very large and respectable portion of the citizens of Texas demand that the credit system be abolished, and that the prompt payment system be established; therefore,

Be it ordained by the people of Texas, in Convention assembled, That no debts contracted two years after the ratification of this constitution shall be collected by law.

Referred to the Committee on State Affairs.

The Convention then proceeded to consider unfinished business, viz: Article —, "Executive Department."

Mr. Ramey called up his motion to reconsider the vote referring to increase the salary of Secretary of State.

The motion was lost.

Mr. Graves moved to strike out section 26.

Lost.

Mr. Nugent proposed to amend by inserting after "compensation" the words "and mileage."

Adopted.

Mr. Moore proposed to amend by adding to the end of section 1, after the words "Attorney General," "and the Legislature may provide for the election of Superintendent of Public Instruction whenever there may be established a system of free public schools."

Lost by the following vote:

YEAS—Ballinger, Brady, Crawford, Cook of Gonzales, Cline, Cooley, Cardis, Dillard, DeMorse, Dohoney, Davis of Brazos, Erhard, Ferris, Flanagan, Gaither, Henry of Smith, Henry of Limestone, King, Kilgore, Lockett, Martin of Navarro, Martin of Hunt, Morris, Mitchell, McKinney of Denton, McKinney of Walker, McCormick, Moore, Nunn, Pauli, Reynolds, Rentfro, Robeson of Fayette, Stockdale, Stayton, Sansom, Whitehead, West, Waelder—38.

NAYS—Allison, Abernathy, Arnim, Abner, Blake, Blassingame, Barnett, Burleson, Bruce, Chambers, Cooke of San Saba, Douglas, Darnell, Flournoy, Fleming, German, Graves, Holt, Holmes, Haynes, Johnson of Franklin, Johnson of Collin, Killough, Lacy, Lynch, McLean, Mills, Murphy, Norvell, Nugent, Reagan, Ramey, Robertson of Bell, Ross, Russell of Wood, Spikes, Scott, Sessions, Wade, Weaver—41.

Mr. Sansom offered the following amendment:

Section 24, line 216, strike out "may be required by the Governor under oath," and insert "shall be given under oath."

Lost.

Mr. Sansom moved to reconsider the vote just taken.

Lost.

Mr. Mills offered the following amendment:

"Sec. 2. There shall be a Superintendent of Public Instruction, who, after the first term of office, shall be elected by the people; the first term of office shall be filled by appointment of the Governor, by and with the advice and consent of the Senate. The Superintendent shall hold his office for the term of two years; he shall receive an annual salary of $2500 until otherwise provided by law."

Laid on the table by the following vote:

YEAS—Abernathy, Arnim, Blake, Blassingame, Barnett, Burleson, Bruce, Chambers, Cook of Gonzales, Cooke of San Saba, Cardis, Douglas, Dillard, Darnell, Davis of Brazos, Flournoy, Fleming, German, Gaither, Graves, Holt, Henry of Limestone, Holmes, Haynes, Johnson of Franklin, Johnson of Collin, Lynch, McLean, Martin of Navarro, Martin of Hunt, McKinney, Murphy, Norvell, Nugent, Reagan, Ramey, Robertson of Bell, Robeson of Fayette, Ross, Russell of Wood, Spikes, Scott, Sessions, Stockdale, Sansom, Wade, Whitehead, Weaver, Whitfield—49.

NAYS—Allison, Brown, Ballinger, Brady, Crawford, Cline, Cooley, DeMorse, Dohoney, Davis of Wharton, Erhard, Ferris, Flanagan, Henry of Smith, King, Kilgore, Lockett, Lacy, Morris, Mills, Mitchell, McCormick, Moore, Nunn, Pauli, Reynolds, Rentfro, Smith, Stayton, West, Waelder—32.

Mr. Douglas proposed to strike out "may" and insert "shall," in section 24, line 216.

Adopted.

The article was ordered to be engrossed and read third time.

UNFINISHED BUSINESS.

The reports of the majority and minority of Committee on Suffrage were taken up.

Mr. Weaver offered the following amendment:

Amend section 2, line 21, by adding: "and provided that female heads of families may vote in all elections for district school officers."

Lost.

Mr. Chambers proposed to strike out all in lines 13 and 14 from the word "vote" in line 13 to the word "election" in line 14.

Mr. Sansom offered the following as a substitute for Mr. Chambers' amendment:

Amend section 2 by inserting after the word "county," in line 14, the words "for school purposes," and by inserting same words after the word "county," in line 21.

On motion of Mr. Allison, the Convention adjourned, pending the amendment and substitute.

EVENING SESSION—2½ o'clock.

Convention met pursuant to adjournment; roll called; quorum present.

Question pending on adjournment—viz., Mr. Chambers' amendment to section 2, lines 13 and 14, article —, "Suffrage," with the substitute offered by Mr. Sansom—again taken up.

Mr. Reagan offered the following as a substitute for both propositions, viz:

Amend section 2 by striking out of lines 13 and 14 the words "all poll taxes" and inserting "the last poll taxes." And amend section 3 by striking out of lines 24 and 25 the words "all taxes" and inserting "the last taxes."

[Mr. Brown in the chair.]

On motion of Mr. McKinney, of Walker, the Convention adjourned until 9 o'clock A. M. to-morrow.

TWENTY-EIGHTH DAY.

HALL OF REPRESENTATIVES, }
AUSTIN, TEXAS, October 7, 1875. }

Convention met pursuant to adjournment; roll called; quorum present; prayer by Rev. Mr. Groety, of Austin.

On motion of Mr. Martin, of Navarro, Mr. McCormick was excused from attendance on the Convention for two days.

On motion of Mr. Reynolds, Mr. Abner was excused from attendance on the Convention for one week from to-morrow.

On motion of Mr. Cook, of Gonzales, Mr. Haynes was excused from attendance on the Convention until Tuesday next.

Mr. McKinney, of Walker, at his request, was excused from attendance on the Convention for three days, commencing to-morrow.

Journal of yesterday read and adopted.

Mr. Russell, of Wood, offered the following amendment to the rules:

Amend the last clause of rule 11 by striking out "fifteen minutes" and inserting "five minutes."

Unfinished business again taken up, viz: "Article —, Suffrage," with pending amendments.

Mr. Wade offered the following amendment:

20

Add to section 2 the following:

"*Provided,* said tax shall never exceed two dollars per annum; and shall be applied exclusively to school purposes."

[Mr. Darnell in the chair.]

Mr. Sansom withdrew his amendment.

Mr. Moore offered the following amendment:

Strike out all after the word "vote," in line 13, down to and including the word "election," in line 14, and insert therefor the following:

"And who, in addition thereto, shall, three months before said election, have paid all poll taxes due by him to the State and county six months immediately preceding; *provided,* however, that no receipt therefor shall be required as a precedent to vote."

Lost.

Mr. Flanagan moved to lay Mr. Reagan's amendment on the table.

Carried by the following vote:

YEAS—Abernathy, Arnim, Abner, Brown, Blake, Ballinger, Blassingame, Barnett, Burleson, Brady, Bruce, Chambers, Cook of Gonzales, Cooke of San Saba, Cline, Cooley, Cardis, Douglas, DeMorse, Darnell, Davis of Brazos, Davis of Wharton, Ford, Flournoy, Ferris, Flanagan, German, Henry of Limestone, Johnson of Franklin, Johnson of Collin, Lockett, McLean, Martin of Navarro, Martin of Hunt, Morris, Mills, Mitchell, McKinney of Denton, McKinney of Walker, Norvell, Pauli, Ramey, Reynolds, Rentfro, Russell of Wood, Spikes, Scott, Sessions, Sansom, Whitehead, Weaver, West—52.

NAYS—Allison, Crawford, Dillard, Dohoney, Erhard, Fleming, Gaither, Graves, Holt, Henry of Smith, Holmes, King, Kilgore, Killough, Lacy, Lynch, Moore, Murphy, Nugent, Reagan, Robertson of Bell, Robeson of Fayette, Smith, Stockdale, Stayton, Wade, Whitfield, Waelder—28.

Upon calling the roll, Mr. Ross stated that he had paired off with Mr. McCormick, Mr. Ross voting yea and Mr. McCormick nay.

Mr. Waelder offered the following amendment:

Insert in line 13 the word "vote," then following, "and who in addition thereto shall have paid all State and county taxes assessed against him for the year preceding said election."

A motion to lay the amendment on the table was carried by the following vote:

(Mr. Ross again paired off with Mr. McCormick, Mr. Ross voting yea and Mr. McCormick nay.)

YEAS—Allison, Abernathy, Arnim, Abner, Brown, Blake,

Blassingame, Barnett, Burleson, Brady, Bruce, Chambers, Cook of Gonzales, Cooke of San Saba, Cooley, Cardis, Douglas, De-Morse, Dohoney, Darnell, Davis of Brazos, Davis of Wharton, Ford, Flournoy, Ferris, German, Gaither, Henry of Limestone, Johnson of Franklin, Johnson of Collin, Lockett, Lacy, Lynch, McLean, Martin of Hunt, Mills, Mitchell, McKinney of Denton, McKinney of Walker, Moore, Norvell, Ramey, Reynolds, Rent-fro, Russell of Wood, Spikes, Scott, Sessions, Sansom, White-head, Weaver, West—52.

NAYS—Ballinger, Crawford, Cline, Dillard, Erhard, Fleming, Flanagan, Graves, Holt, Henry of Smith, Holmes, King, Kil-gore, Killough, Martin of Navarro, Morris, Murphy, Nugent, Pauli, Reagan, Robertson of Bell, Robeson of Fayette, Smith, Stockdale, Stayton, Wade, Whitfield, Waelder—28.

Mr. Dohoney offered the following:

Amend section 2, line 14, by striking out the words "before said election," and insert the words "which have accrued since the adoption of the present constitution."

Also in line 21, strike out the words "before said election," and insert "which have accrued since the adoption of the present constitution."

On motion of Mr. Johnson, of Collin, laid on the table.

Mr. Kilgore moved to adjourn until 9 o'clock A. M. to-morrow. Lost.

Mr. Flanagan moved the previous question.

The President ruled that the previous question was the en-grossment of the article.

Mr. Flanagan then withdrew his motion for the previous question.

Mr. Norvell offered the following as a substitute for section 2:

"Section 2. Every male person subject to none of the fore-going disqualifications, who shall have attained the age of twenty-one years, and who shall be a citizen of the United States, and shall have resided in this State for one year next preceding an election, and the last six months within the dis-trict or county in which he offers to vote, shall be deemed a qualified elector; and every male person of foreign birth subject to none of the foregoing disqualifications, who, six months before an election, shall have declared his intention to become a citizen of the United States in accordance with the Federal naturaliza-tion laws, who shall have resided in this State one year next preceding such election, and the last six months in the district or county in which he offers to vote, shall also be deemed a qualified elector. Should any qualified elector happen to be in any other county than that of his residence, situated in the district in which he resides at the time of an election, he shall be permitted to vote for district officers; *provided,* that the qualified electors shall be permitted to vote anywhere in the State for State officers.

Adopted by the following vote:

YEAS—Allison, Abernathy, Arnim, Abner, Brown, Blake, Ballinger, Blassingame, Barnett, Burleson, Brady, Bruce, Crawford, Chambers, Cooke of San Saba, Cooley, Cardis, Douglas, Dillard, DeMorse, Darnell, Davis of Brazos, Davis of Wharton, Erhard, Ford, Flournoy, Ferris, Flanagan, German, Gaither, Graves, Holt, Henry of Limestone, Johnson of Franklin, Johnson of Collin, Lockett, Lacy, McLean, Martin of Navarro, Martin of Hunt, Morris, Mills, Mitchell, McKinney of Denton, McKinney of Walker, Moore, Norvell, Pauli, Ramey, Reynolds, Rentfro, Ross, Russell of Wood, Spikes, Scott, Sessions, Smith, Sansom, Whitehead, Weaver, West—61.

NAYS—Cook of Gonzales, Cline, Dohoney, Fleming, Henry of Smith, Holmes, King, Kilgore, Killough, Lynch, Murphy, Nugent, Reagan, Robertson of Bell, Robeson of Fayette, Stockdale, Stayton, Wade, Whitfield, Waelder—20.

On motion of Mr. West, the Convention adjourned until 2¼ o'clock.

EVENING SESSION—2½ o'CLOCK.

Convention met pursuant to adjournment; roll called; quorum present.

The question pending on adjournment, viz: Mr. Whitfield's amendment, taken up:

Amend section 2, line 16, by striking out "six months" and inserting the words "who at any time."

Mr. Cook, of Gonzales, offered the following as an amendment to the pending amendment:

"The Legislature may, nevertheless, pass laws requiring every voter, before voting at any election, to produce to the officers of the election satisfactory evidence of his having paid all such poll taxes as may be due by him, for such time before such election as may be prescribed by law, and prescribe the rules of evidence of such payment."

Mr. Whitfield's amendment adopted.

Mr. Russell, of Wood, moved to lay Mr. Cook's (of Gonzales) amendment on the table.

The yeas and nays being called, the amendment was laid on the table by the following vote:

YEAS—Abernathy, Arnim, Abner, Blake, Ballinger, Blassingame, Barnett, Brady, Bruce, Chambers, Cooke of San Saba, Cooley, Cardis, DeMorse, Darnell, Davis of Wharton, Flournoy, Ferris, Flanagan, German, Graves, Henry of Limestone, Johnson of Franklin, Johnson of Collin, Killough, Lockett, Lacy, McLean, Martin of Navarro, Martin of Hunt, Mitchell, McKinney of Denton, McKinney of Walker, Norvell, Pauli, Ramey, Reynolds, Rentfro, Ross, Russell of Wood, Scott, Sessions, Sansom, Whitehead, Weaver—44.

NAYS—Allison, Burleson, Crawford, Cook of Gonzales, Douglas, Dillard, Dohoney, Erhard, Fleming, Gaither, Henry of Smith, Holmes, Kilgore, Lynch, Morris, Moore, Murphy, Nunn, Nugent, Reagan, Robertson of Bell, Robeson of Fayette, Smith, Stockdale, Stayton, Wade, Whitfield, Waelder—28.

Mr. Kilgore offered the following amendment:

Strike out the word "Federal" in line 18, section 2.

Lost by the following vote:

YEAS—Allison, Abernathy, Crawford, Dillard, DeMorse, Ford, Fleming, Kilgore, Killough, Lynch, Murphy, Reagan, Robertson of Bell, Ross, Scott, Stockdale, Whitfield—17.

NAYS—Arnim, Abner, Blake, Blassingame, Barnett, Burleson, Brady, Bruce, Chambers, Cook of Gonzales, Cooke of San Saba, Cooley, Douglas, Dohoney, Darnell, Davis of Wharton, Flournoy, Ferris, Flanagan, German, Gaither, Graves, Holt, Henry of Smith, Henry of Limestone, Holmes, Johnson of Franklin, Johnson of Collin, Lockett, McLean, Martin of Navarro, Martin of Hunt, Morris, Mills, Mitchell, McKinney of Denton, Moore, Norvell, Nunn, Nugent, Pauli, Ramey, Reynolds, Rentfro, Robeson of Fayette, Russell of Wood, Sessions, Smith, Stayton, Sansom, Wade, Whitehead, West, Waelder—55.

Mr. Stockdale proposed to amend as follows:

Amend by striking out all that refers to voting out of the county of the residence of the voter.

Lost.

Mr. Crawford offered the following amendment to section 1:

Amend section 1 by adding: " All persons between the ages of twenty-one and fifty years, who shall have failed to pay a poll-tax of two dollars, which shall have been levied and assessed for educational purposes in a manner prescribed by law, for six months and within two years next before the election at which he offers to vote."

Mr. Martin, of Navarro, moved to lay the amendment 'on the table.

Carried by the following vote:

Yeas—Abernathy, Arnim, Abner, Blake, Ballinger, Blassingame, Barnett, Burleson, Brady, Bruce, Chambers, Cook of Gonzales, Cooke of San Saba, Cline, Cooley, Cardis, Douglas, DeMorse, Darnell, Davis of Wharton, Flournoy, Flanagan, German, Gaither, Graves, Holt, Henry of Smith, Henry of Limestone, Johnson of Franklin, Johnson of Collin, Lockett, Lacy, McLean, Martin of Navarro, Martin of Hunt, Morris, Mills, Mitchell, McKinney of Denton, Norvell, Pauli, Reagan, Ramey, Reynolds, Rentfro, Ross, Russell of Wood, Spikes, Scott, Sessions, Smith, Sansom, Wade, Whitehead, Weaver, West—56.

Nays—Allison, Crawford, Dillard, Dohoney, Erhard, Fleming, Ferris, Holmes, King, Kilgore, Killough, Lynch, Moore, Murphy, Nunn, Nugent, Robertson of Bell, Robeson of Fayette, Stockdale, Stayton, Whitfield, Waelder—22.

Mr. Crawford offered the following amendment:

Amend section 1, line 4, sub-division 4, by striking out all after the word "bribery," and insert "perjury, forgery, arson, rape, or robbery."

Adopted.

Mr. Abernathy offered the following amendment:

Amend section 3, in line 24, by striking out all after the word "city," in line 24, to the word "shall," in line 26.

Mr. Flournoy offered the following as a substitute for section 3:

"Every qualified elector in this State, who shall have resided for twelve months next preceding any election at which he may offer to vote, in any incorporated town or city, shall be entitled to vote at elections held in such incorporated town or city."

The question on the adoption of the substitute being submitted, the yeas and nays were called, and the substitute adopted by the following vote:

Yeas—Arnim, Abner, Brown, Blake, Blassingame, Barnett, Brady, Bruce, Crawford, Chambers, Cooley, Cardis, Dillard, Darnell, Davis of Brazos, Davis of Wharton, Ford, Flournoy, Ferris, Flanagan, Graves, Henry of Smith, Henry of Limestone, Holmes, Johnson of Franklin, Johnson of Collin. Kilgore, Lockett, Lacy, Lynch, Martin of Navarro, Martin of Hunt, Mills, Mitchell, McKinney of Denton, McKinney of Walker, Norvell, Pauli, Ramey, Reynolds, Rentfro, Russell of Wood, Scott, Sessions, Whitehead, Weaver—46.

Nays—Allison, Abernathy, Ballinger, Burleson, Cook of Gonzales, Cooke of San Saba, Cline, Douglas, DeMorse, Dohoney, Erhard, Fleming, Gaither, Holt, King, McLean, Morris, Moore, Murphy, Nunn, Nugent, Reagan, Robertson of Bell,

Robeson of Fayette, Ross, Spikes, Smith, Stockdale, Stayton, Sansom, Wade, Whitfield, West, Waelder—34. . .

Mr. Crawford offered the following amendment:

Amend section 2, line 12, by adding after the word "county" the words "city or town," and in line 19, by adding after the word "county" the words "city or town," and strike out all of section 3.

Mr. West offered the following substitute for Mr. Crawford's amendment:

"*Provided,* That in elections for the creation of debt for the improvement of such town or city, or for other purposes, taxpayers only shall vote."

Mr. DeMorse offered the following substitute for the amendment and substitute:

"*Provided,* that in elections for the creation of debt for the improvement of such town or city, or for other purpose, freeholders and householders and tax-payers on property only shall vote."

Lost, and Mr. West's and Mr. Crawford's amendments lost.

Mr. Moore offered the following amendment:

Strike out in line 3, section 1, "all inmates of State asylums."

Adopted.

Mr. Ballinger offered the following amendment:

Section 3, add: "*Provided* that all elections by which any tax shall be imposed, or debt incurred, shall be confined to electors who are assessed for a tax imposed on property, or for a license in said city."

Mr. Waelder offered the following substitute for the last amendment:

Add to section 3: "*Provided* that in elections for the creation of debt for the improvement of such town or city, or for other purposes, such electors only as pay a tax upon city property, or a license tax upon some regular business, shall vote."

Lost by the following vote:

YEAS—Allison, Abernathy, Blake, Cook of Gonzales, Cooke of San Saba, Douglas, Davis of Brazos, Erhard, Ford, Fleming, Gaither, Holt, Henry of Limestone, Holmes, Killough, Lacy, McLean, Murphy, Nugent, Reagan, Stockdale, Sansom, Wade, Whitfield, West, Waelder—26.

NAYS—Arnim, Abner, Brown, Ballinger, Blassingame, Barnett, Burleson, Brady, Bruce, Crawford, Chambers, Cline, Dillard, DeMorse, Darnell, Flournoy, Ferris, Flanagan, German, Graves, Henry of Smith, Johnson of Franklin, Johnson of Collin, Kilgore, Lockett, Lynch, Martin of Navarro, Martin of

Hunt, Morris, Mills, Mitchell, McKinney of Walker, Moore, Norvell, Nunn, Pauli, Ramey, Reynolds, Rentfro, Robertson of Bell, Robeson of Fayette, Ross, Russell of Wood, Spikes, Scott, Sessions, Smith, Stayton, Whitehead, Weaver — 50.

The question then recurring upon the adoption of Mr. Ballinger's amendment, Mr. Flanagan moved to lay it upon the table.

Carried by the following vote:

YEAS—Allison, Abernathy, Arnim, Abner, Brown, Blake, Blassingame, Barnett, Burleson, Brady, Bruce, Crawford, Chambers, Cook of Gonzales, Cooley, Cardis, Dillard, Darnell, Davis of Brazos, Davis of Wharton, Ford, Ferris, Flanagan, Graves, Henry of Smith, Henry of Limestone, Holmes, Johnson of Franklin, Johnson of Collin, Kilgore, Killough, Lockett, Lacy, Lynch, Martin of Navarro, Martin of Hunt, Mills, Mitchell, McKinney of Denton, Norvell, Pauli, Ramey, Reynolds, Rentfro, Robertson of Bell, Robeson of Fayette, Ross, Russell of Wood, Scott, Sessions, Smith, Wade, Whitehead, Weaver—54.

NAYS — Ballinger, Cooke of San Saba, Cline, DeMorse, Dohoney, Erhard, Flournoy, Fleming, German, Gaither, Holt, King, McLean, Morris, McKinney of Walker, Moore, Murphy, Nunn, Nugent, Reagan, Spikes, Stockdale, Stayton, Sansom, Whitfield, West, Waelder — 27.

On motion of Mr. Cardis, the Convention adjourned until 9 o'clock A. M. to-morrow.

TWENTY-NINTH DAY.

HALL OF REPRESENTATIVES,   }
AUSTIN, TEXAS, October 8, 1875. }

Convention met pursuant to adjournment; roll called; quorum present; prayer by the Rev. Mr. J. S. Groety, of Austin.

Journal of yesterday read and adopted.

Mr. Sansom presented the memorial of the citizens of Lampasas county, relative to the sale of liquor.

Referred to the Committee on General Provisions.

Mr. Blassingame submitted the memorial of the citizens of Denison, asking that Justices of the Peace in Denison be empowered to issue writs of sequestration and attachment.

Referred to Judiciary Committee.

Mr. Reagan submitted the following report:

COMMITTEE ROOM,
AUSTIN, October 7, 1875.

To the Hon. E. B. Pickett, President of the Convention:

The Committee on the Judiciary have instructed me to report to the Convention that in the discharge of their duties in preparing their report on the Judiciary article, they were brought to the consideration of a section providing for the removal from office of Judges of the Supreme and District Courts, and in this connection, in some measure, to the consideration of the subject of impeachment.

The subject of impeachment is provided for in the present and former constitutions of Texas in a separate article in these constitutions, and the Judiciary Committee suppose that the duty of preparing this article was not intended to be devolved upon it. Nor does it appear that this subject or the subject of the division of the powers of government, has been referred to the consideration of any one of the standing committees. And the Judiciary Committee instruct me to suggest these facts, and to recommend that an additional standing committee be appointed to take into consideration the subjects of the division of the powers of government and of impeachments and removals from office.

To this end, under the instruction of the committee, I submit the accompanying resolution, and recommend its passage.

JOHN H. REAGAN, Chairman.

Resolved, That a standing committee of five be appointed to take into consideration and report on an article in relation to the division of the powers of government, and another in relation to impeachments and removals of the higher officers of the State from office.

Report and resolution adopted.

Mr. Fleming submitted for Mr. McKinney, of Walker, the following:

"AN ARTICLE TO REGULATE THE RESIDENCE OF CONVICTS TO THE PENITENTIARY.

"Article —. The Legislature may provide by law that convicts to the penitentiary shall not reside within the county in which the penitentiary is located in which they may have served their term of imprisonment, after the expiration of said term, unless such convicts resided in said county at the time of their conviction and sentence."

Referred to Committee on Penitentiary.

Mr. Brown offered the following resolution:

WHEREAS, There is reason to believe that many and dangerons frauds and forgeries have been committed within the past few years in relation to headright certificates, bounty warrants and other claims to land; therefore,

Resolved, That the Committee on the Judicial Department be instructed to inquire if there should not be such a modification in the rules of evidence as to guarantee greater assurance of justice in the trial of such cases; and that, in this connection, they are also requested to make inquiry into the manner and authority by which bounty warrant No. 2692, for 1250 acres, issued to Charles Baker, was withdrawn from the General Land Office in the year 1871.*

Referred to the select committee of seven on land titles.

On motion of Mr. McCabe, Mr. Reynolds was excused for two days, commencing to-morrow.

Unfinished business again taken up, viz: "Article —, Suffrage."

Mr. Norvell offered the following amendment:

Substitute for section 1.

"Section 1. The following persons shall not be allowed to vote in this State, to-wit: Persons under twenty-one years of age, idiots, lunatics, paupers supported by any county, persons convicted by bribery, perjury, forgery, rape or robbery, soldiers, seamen or marines in the army or navy of the United States.

Lost.

Mr. Dohoney offered the following amendment:

Section 1, line 6, insert "seamen" after "marines."

Adopted.

Mr. West offered the following as a substitute for section 4:

"Sec. 4. In all elections by the people the vote shall be by ballot, and the Legislature shall provide for the numbering of tickets, and make such other regulations as may be necessary to detect and punish frauds and preserve the purity of the ballot-box; and in elections by the Senate and House of Representatives, jointly or separately, the vote shall be given *viva voce,* except in the election of their officers."

Mr. Crawford proposed to amend the amendment by adding: "But no law shall ever be enacted requiring a registration of the voters of this State."

Accepted by Mr. West as a part of his amendment.

The hour having arrived for consideration of the special order, viz: "Article —. Education"—

Mr. Dohoney moved to postpone the consideration of the special order to 10 o'clock, Wednesday next.

Lost.

Mr. Flanagan moved to postpone the special order until the pending question was disposed of.

Carried.

Mr. Reagan proposed to amend the pending amendment by adding: "Except in cities of ten thousand inhabitants or more."

Mr. Crawford proposed to amend Mr. Reagan's amendment by adding: "But no registration law shall be enacted for any city, except upon the consent or request of a majority of the voters of said city."

Accepted by Mr. Reagan.

Mr. Reagan's amendment adopted.

Mr. West's amendment adopted.

Mr. Norvell offered to amend by striking out all that part which referred to elections by the two houses of the Legislature.

Adopted.

Mr. DeMorse offered the following amendment:

Substitute for the third section:

"Sec. 3. All qualified electors of the State, as hereinbefore described, who shall have resided for six months immediately preceding an election within the limits of any city or corporate town, shall have the right to vote for Mayor and all other elective officers; but in all elections to determine the expenditure of money or the assumption of debt, only those shall be qualified to vote who pay taxes on property in said city or incorporated town; *provided,* that no poll tax for the payment of debts thus incurred shall be levied upon the class thus debarred from voting in relation thereto."

Mr. Kilgore moved to lay the amendment on the table.

Lost by the following vote:

YEAS—Allison, Arnim, Blassingame, Barnett, Burleson, Bruce, Cooley, Flournoy, Flanagan, Graves, Henry of Limestone, Kilgore, Martin of Navarro, Martin of Hunt, Norvell, Russell of Wood, Sessions, Whitehead, Weaver—19.

NAYS—Abernathy, Brown, Ballinger, Brady, Crawford, Chambers, Cook of Gonzales, Cooke of San Saba, Cline, Douglas, Dillard, DeMorse, Dohoney, Darnell, Davis of Brazos, Davis of Wharton, Erhard, Ford, Fleming, Ferris, German, Gaither, Holt, Henry of Smith, Holmes, Johnson of Franklin, Johnson of Collin, King, Killough, Lockett, Lacy, Lynch, McLean, Morris, McKinney of Denton, Moore, Murphy, Nunn, Nugent, Pauli, Reagan, Rentfro, Robertson of Bell, Robeson of Fayette, Ross, Spikes, Scott, Smith, Stayton, Wade, Whitfield, West, Waelder—53.

Mr. Kilgore offered the following amendment to the substitute:

Strike out "city or town" in the substitute and insert "State."

Lost.

Mr. Crawford proposed to amend the substitute as follows:

"But no city or town shall incur, assume, or authorize, any debt, except upon the consent of a majority of the qualified voters, representing a majority of the taxable property of said city or town, to be ascertained in a manner prescribed by law."

Mr. German moved the previous question.

Lost.

Mr. Crawford's amendment lost.

Mr. Flournoy offered the following amendment:

"And in State elections, no persons shall vote in such election, whether for State officers or members of the Legislature, which may result in the expenditure of public money."

Lost.

The yeas and nays were then called upon the adoption of Mr. DeMorse's amendment, and the amendment adopted by the following vote:

YEAS—Allison, Abernathy, Brown, Blake, Ballinger, Blassingame, Burleson, Chambers, Cook of Gonzales, Cooke of San Saba, Cline, Douglas, Dillard, DeMorse, Dohoney, Darnell, Davis of Brazos, Erhard, Ford, Fleming, Ferris, German, Gaither, Holt, Henry of Smith, Henry of Limestone, Holmes, Johnson of Franklin, Johnson of Collin, King, Lacy, Lynch, McLean, Martin of Navarro, Morris, McKinney, Moore, Murphy, Nunn, Nugent, Reagan, Ramey, Rentfro, Robertson of Bell, Ross, Spikes, Scott, Sessions, Smith, Stockdale, Stayton, Sansom, Wade, Weaver, Whitfield, West, Waelder—57.

NAYS—Arnim, Barnett, Brady, Bruce, Crawford, Cooley, Davis of Wharton, Flournoy, Flanagan, Graves, Kilgore, Killough, Lockett, Martin of Hunt, Mitchell, Norvell, Pauli, Russell of Wood, Whitehead—19.

Mr. Whitfield offered the following amendment:

Provided that every qualified elector shall vote in the precinct where he resides.

Mr. Kilgore offered the following substitute for the amendment:

Strike out all after the word "election" in substitute for section 2, and insert "shall vote in the precinct of his residence."

Accepted by Mr. Whitfield.

The question on the adoption of the amendment was put, and the amendment adopted by the following vote:

YEAS—Abernathy, Arnim, Brown, Ballinger, Blassingame,

Barnett, Burleson, Crawford, Chambers, Douglas, Dillard, De-
Morse, Davis of Brazos, Erhard, Ford, Fleming, Gaither, Graves,
Holt, Henry of Smith, Johnson of Franklin, Johnson of Collin,
Kilgore, Killough, Lacy, Lynch, McLean, Martin of Navarro,
Martin of Hunt, Morris, Moore, Murphy, Nunn, Nugent, Reagan,
Rentfro, Robertson of Bell, Robeson of Fayette, Ross, Spikes,
Scott, Sessions, Smith, Stockdale, Stayton, Whitfield—45.

NAYS—Allison, Blake, Brady, Bruce, Cook of Gonzales,
Cooke of San Saba, Cline, Cooley, Dohoney, Darnell, Davis of
Wharton, Flournoy, Ferris, Flanagan, German, Henry of Lime-
stone, Holmes, Lockett, Mitchell, McKinney, Norvell, Pauli,
Ramey, Reynolds, Russell of Wood, Sansom, Wade, Whitehead,
Weaver, West, Waelder—32.

Mr. West offered the following as an additional section:

"Sec. 6. The Legislature shall make provision for taking the
votes of electors of this State who may be temporarily absent
from the county or State in the actual military service of the
United States, or of the State, during a time of war or invasion;
provided, however, that citizens of Texas who are regular
soldiers, sailors or marines in the army or navy of the United
States, shall not be allowed to vote."

On motion of Mr. Johnson, of Collin, laid on the table.

The article was then ordered engrossed.

The special order then taken up, viz: "Article—, Education."

On motion of Mr. Brown the Convention adjourned till 2½
o'clock P. M.

EVENING SESSION—2½ o'CLOCK.

Convention met pursuant to adjournment; roll called; quorum present.

Article on Education again taken up.

By leave, Mr. Martin, of Navarro, offered the following resolution, which was referred to the Committee on General Provisions:

Resolved, That all drawbacks and rebatements of freight
transportation, carriage, wharfage, storage, compressing, baling,
repairing, or for any other kind of labor or service of or to any
cotton, grain, or any other produce or article of commerce in
this State, paid or allowed or contracted for to any other common carrier, shipper, merchant, commission merchant, factor,
agent, or middle men of any kind, not the true and absolute
owner thereof, are forever prohibited, and it shall be the duty of
the Legislature to pass effective laws, punishing as felonies all
corporations, companies or persons in this State who pay, receive,
contract for, or respect the same.

Mr. Cline, of the Committee on Education, presented the following minority report:

COMMITTEE ROOM,
AUSTIN, October 8, 1875.

To the Hon. E. B. Pickett, President of the Convention:

The undersigned, member of your Committee on Education, has not been able to concur in either of the two reports submitted. He believes the time has now come which the fathers of Texas contemplated when they created our magnificent school fund, for the organization of education in Texas. He, therefore, recommends the adoption of the accompanying ordinance.

Very respectfully submitted.

HENRY CLINE.

" ARTICLE —.
" EDUCATION.

·" Sec. 1. A general diffusion of knowledge and intelligence being essential to the preservation of the rights and liberties of the people, the Legislature shall establish a thorough and efficient system of public instruction, and shall maintain public schools during not less than four months in every year, for the free education of all children in this State between the ages of nine and fifteen years, and other children may attend said schools upon conditions prescribed by law.

" Sec. 2. The supervision of said system and schools shall be vested in the Superintendent of Public Instruction, the Board of Education, County and City Superintendents, and such other officers as may be provided by law.

" Sec. 3. The Superintendent of Public Instruction shall be elected for .... years, and shall receive an annual salary of $ ...., until otherwise provided by law, and shall perform all duties that may be prescribed by law. A vacancy may be filled by appointment for the unexpired term by the Board of Education.

" Sec. 4. The Board of Education shall consist of the Superintendent of Public Instruction, the Governor, Attorney General and Secretary of State, who shall prescribe rules and regulations for the organization and government of the schools, and perform all other duties prescribed by law.

Sec. 5. County and City Superintendents, and other officers, may be elected or appointed, with such term of office, compensation, powers and duties as may be prescribed by law. The Board of Education may remove any of such officers for cause, and fill any vacancy by appointment for the unexpired term.

" Sec. 6. All lands, bonds and other property heretofore set apart for schools by the Republic and State of Texas, or that may hereafter be so set apart, and the proceeds from sales of public lands, and the proceeds of escheats, shall constitute the permanent State school fund, and the income from said fund, together with not less than one-fourth of one per cent. tax upon all subjects of general taxation, shall annually be distributed among the several counties and cities, according to their scholastic population.

"Sec. 7. All lands granted or to be granted to the several counties and cities for educational purposes, proceeds from sales of estrays, also other requisitions for such purposes, shall constitute the permanent county or city school fund; and the income from such fund, and all taxes on dogs, polls and occupations, and the annual receipts from the permanent State school fund, together with such tax on other subjects of county or city taxation as may be authorized by law, shall be annually expended for the support and maintenance of free public schools.

"Sec. 8. The moneys that may at any time belong to the permanent fund of the State and of the several counties and cities, shall be invested in the bonds of the United States and of the State of Texas.

"Sec. 9. The State and county school lands, also the university and asylum lands, shall be sub-divided into 80 or 160 acre tracts, whereof the alternate tracts may be sold at public auction, under such regulations as may be prescribed by law, and the proceeds invested in United States and Texas State bonds, and the incomes severally applied to the support of said funds and asylums.

"Sec. 10. No grant shall be made from any public fund for the benefit of any institution, church or school controlled by any ecclesiastical body, nor in aid of any particular opinions of conscience, creed or church.

HENRY CLINE.

On motion of Mr. DeMorse, one hundred copies of the report and article were ordered printed.

The article—, "Education," reported by the majority, taken up.

Mr. Dohoney offered the following amendment:

Add to section 1: "For at least four months in each year, for the free instruction of all the scholastic population between the ages of nine and fifteen years."

Mr. Russell, of Wood, offered the article reported by the minority of the committee—viz., Messrs. Sansom, Holt, Cooke of San Saba, and Dunnam—as a substitute for the article reported by the majority.

[Mr. Reagan in the chair.]

Mr. Chambers moved to lay Mr. Dohoney's amendment to section 1 on the table:

Carried by the following vote:

YEAS—Allison, Abernathy, Arnim, Brown, Blake, Blassingame, Barnett, Burleson, Bruce, Chambers, Cooke of San Saba, Cardis, Douglas, Dillard, DeMorse, Darnell, Davis of Brazos, Flournoy, Fleming, Ferris, German, Gaither, Graves, Holt, Henry of Limestone, Holmes, Johnson of Franklin, Johnson of Collin, Kilgore, Killough, Lacy, Lynch, McLean, Martin of Navarro, Martin of Hunt, McKinney, Murphy, Norvell, Nugent, Reagan, Ramey, Robeson of Fayette, Ross, Russell of Wood, Spikes, Scott, Sessions, Stockdale, Stayton, Sansom, Wade, Weaver, Whitfield—53.

NAYS—Ballinger, Brady, Crawford, Cline, Dohoney, Davis of Wharton, Erhard, Ford, Flanagan, Henry of Smith, King, Lockett, Mitchell, Moore, Nunn, Pauli, Reynolds, Rentfro, Robertson of Bell, Smith, Waelder—21.

On motion of Mr. Dohoney, the Convention adjourned until 9 o'clock A. M. to-morrow.

THIRTIETH DAY.

HALL OF REPRESENTATIVES, ⎱
AUSTIN, TEXAS, October 9, 1875. ⎰

Convention met pursuant to adjournment; roll called; quorum present; prayer by Rev. Mr. Dodge, of Austin.

Journal of yesterday read and adopted.

The Chair announced the following committees, authorized by resolutions of yesterday.

Select Committee of Seven, to examine certain land titles and examine certain rules of evidence: Mr. Brown, chairman; Messrs. Robertson of Bell, Henry of Smith, Nugent, McLean, Murphy, and Cooke of San Saba.

Select Committee of Five, to examine and report an article relative to the divisions of the powers of government, and an article on the subject of impeachments and removals of the higher officers of the State from office: Mr. Stockdale, Chairman; Messrs. Reagan, Norvell, Ballinger, and Cook of Gonzales.

Mr. Martin, of Navarro, offered the following resolution:

Resolved, That the President appoint a special committee of seven, to inquire into the direct charges of the *Democratic States-man,* that all the Grangers, except nine, of this Convention have formed an alliance with the negroes and radicals of this Convention; and that the vote upon the suffrage question was the result of said alliance; and that no member of the Grange or radical party be appointed upon said committee.

Mr. Brown moved to lay the resolution on the table.

(Upon calling the roll, upon their own request, Messrs. Dillard, McCormick, Murphy, and Rentfro were excused from voting on the question).

Lost by the following vote:

YEAS—Arnim, Brown, Blake, Ballinger, Cooke of San Saba, Cline, Cooley, Cardis, DeMorse, Dohoney, Darnell, Davis of Brazos, Erhard, Fleming, Ferris, Flanagan, Gaither, Holt, Henry of Smith, Holmes, Kilgore, McLean, Morris, Moore, Norvell, Nunn, Pauli, Robertson of Bell, Smith, Sansom, Wade, Weaver, Waelder—33.

NAYS—Allison, Abernathy, Blassingame, Barnett, Burleson, Brady, Bruce, Crawford, Chambers, Cook of Gonzales, Douglas, Ford, German, Graves, Henry of Limestone, Johnson of Franklin, Johnson of Collin, Killough, Lockett, Lacy, Lynch, Martin of Navarro, Martin of Hunt, Mitchell, McKinney of Denton, Nugent, Reagan, Ramey, Russell of Wood, Spikes, Scott, Sessions, Stockdale, Stayton, Whitehead, Whitfield, West—37.

Mr. Stockdale moved to amend the resolution by striking out "negroes and radicals" and inserting "Republican."

Accepted by Mr. Martin.

Mr. Crawford offered the following amendment:

"That said committee be authorized to send for persons and papers, and to administer oaths and take testimony, and that the report of said committee contain simply a statement of the matters and things as they transpire in fact, and that all deductions and conclusions be left to the members of this Convention and the country."

Adopted.

Mr. Moore proposed to add, "and that in determining who are Grangers the President shall be governed by the usually accepted signs."

Ruled out of order.

On motion of Mr. Flournoy the whole subject was laid on the table.

Mr. West moved to reconsider the vote ordering the engross-

21

ment of the article on suffrage, and to pass the consideration of the motion for the present.

Carried.

Mr. Scott moved to reconsider the vote tabling Mr. Martin's (of Navarro) resolution as amended.

(Upon calling the roll, Messrs. Dillard and McCormick were excused from voting at their own request. Mr. Stockdale, when his name was called, stated that he had paired off with Mr. Waelder, who would have voted nay.)

Vote reconsidered by the following vote:

YEAS—Allison, Abernathy Arnim, Abner, Blassingame, Barnett, Burleson, Brady, Bruce, Crawford, Chambers, Cook of Gonzales, Douglas, DeMorse, Darnell, Davis of Wharton, Ford, Flournoy, Ferris, German, Graves, Henry of Limestone, Johnson of Franklin, Johnson of Collin, Killough, Lockett, Lacy, Lynch, Martin of Navarro, Martin of Hunt, Mitchell, McKinney of Denton, Nugent, Reagan, Ramey, Rentfro, Robertson of Bell, Ross, Russell of Wood, Spikes, Scott, Sessions, Stayton, Sansom, Wade, Whitehead, Whitfield, West—48.

NAYS—Ballinger, Cooke of San Saba, Cline, Cooley, Cardis, Dohoney, Davis of Brazos, Fleming, Flanagan, Gaither, Holt, Holmes, Kilgore, McLean, Morris, Norvell, Nunn, Pauli—18.

On motion of Mr. German, the main question was ordered.

The question then recurring upon the adoption of the resolution as amended, the yeas and nays were called, and the resolution adopted by the following vote:

(Upon calling the roll Mr. Murphy was excused from voting at his own request, and Mr. Stockdale was paired off with Mr. Waelder.)

YEAS—Allison, Abernathy, Arnim, Blassingame, Barnett, Burleson, Brady, Bruce, Crawford, Chambers, Cook of Gonzales, Cardis, Douglas, DeMorse, Darnell, Flournoy, German, Graves, Henry of Limestone, Johnson of Franklin, Johnson of Collin, Killough, Lockett, Lacy, Lynch, Martin of Navarro, Martin of Hunt, Mitchell, McKinney of Denton, Nugent, Pauli, Reagan, Ramey, Rentfro, Robertson of Bell, Ross, Russell of Wood, Spikes, Scott, Sessions, Stayton, Sansom, Wade, Whitehead, Whitfield, West—46.

NAYS—Brown, Blake, Ballinger, Cooke of San Saba, Cline, Cooley, Dohoney, Davis of Brazos, Davis of Wharton, Fleming, Ferris, Flanagan, Gaither, Holt, Holmes, Kilgore, McLean, Morris, Moore, Norvell, Nunn, Smith, Weaver—23.

Mr. Sansom presented the memorial of the citizens of Williamson county relative to an organized and uniform system of sanitary regulations.

Referred to the Committee on General Provisions.

Mr. Moore presented the memorial of the Texas State Medical Association on the same subject.

Referred to Committee on General Provisions.

Mr. Nunn presented the memorial of citizens of Houston county on the same subject.

Referred to Committee on General Provisions.

Mr. Martin, of Hunt, presented a petition from the citizens, farmers of Hunt county, asking an extension of the time for paying taxes.

Referred to Committee on Revenue and Taxation.

Mr. Brown presented the memorial of the citizens of Dallas county upon the subject of a uniform system of sanitary regulations.

Referred to Committee on General Provisions.

Mr. Lockett presented the memorial of the citizens of Washton county on the same subject.

Referred to Committee on General Provisions.

Mr. Cooke, of San Saba, presented the memorial of the citizens of Lampases county on the same subject.

Referred to Committee on General Provisions.

Mr. Martin, of Hunt, presented a communication from the Greenville bar, on the subject of the organization of the Judiciary.

Referred to Committee on Judiciary.

Mr. McLean offered the following amendment to the rules of the Convention:

"Rule —. When the Secretary has commenced calling the roll all remarks shall be out of order. Members, upon the call of their names, shall answer 'yea' or 'nay,' or be excused from voting."

Laid over under the rules.

Mr. Cardis offered the following resolution:

Resolved, That no city or town of less than three thousand inhabitants be permitted to be incorporated.

Referred to the Committee on General Provisions.

On motion of Mr. Rentfro the Convention adjourned to 2½ o'clock P. M.

EVENING SESSION—2½ o'clock.

Convention met; roll called; quorum present.

On motion of Mr. Gaither, Mr. Robeson, of Fayette county,

was excused from attendance on the Convention for seven days.

Mr. McCormick submitted the memorial of sundry citizens of Colorado county, asking for a uniform system of sanitary regulations throughout the State.

Referred to the Committee on General Provisions.

Mr. Cline submitted the memorial of sundry citizens of Harris county, asking for a uniform system of sanitary regulations throughout the State.

Referred to the Committee on General Provisions.

Mr. Stayton submitted the memorial of sundry citizens of Victoria county, asking for a uniform system of sanitary regulations throughout the State.

Referred to the Committee on General Provisions.

Mr. Killough submitted the memorial of sundry citizens of Robertson county, asking for a uniform system of sanitary regulations throughout the State.

Referred to the Committee on General Provisions.

Mr. Dohoney submitted a memorial on the same subject from sundry citizens of Lamar county.

Referred to Committee on General Provisions.

Mr. Burleson submitted a memorial on same subject from sundry citizens of Hays county.

Referred to Committee on General Provisions.

Mr. West submitted memorial on same subject from sundry citizens of Lampasas county.

Referred to Committee on General Provisions.

Mr. Lockett submitted a memorial on same subject from sundry citizens of Washington county.

Referred to Committee on General Provisions.

Mr. Brown submitted a memorial on same subject from sundry citizens of Dallas county.

Referred to Committee on General Provisions.

Mr. Sansom submitted a memorial on same subject from sundry citizens of Williamson county.

Referred to Committee on General Provisions.

Mr. Moore submitted a memorial on same subject from sundry citizens of Fayette county.

Referred to Committee on General Provisions.

Mr. Nunn submitted a memorial on same subject from sundry citizens of Houston county.

Referred to Committee on General Provisions.

Mr. Haynes submitted a memorial on same subject from sundry citizens of Caldwell county.

Referred to Committee on General Provisions.

The article on "Education" was then taken up, the pending question being the motion of Mr. Russell, of Wood, to substitute the report and article reported by the minority for the article reported by the majority of the committee, it was put, and lost by the following vote:

YEAS—Arnim, Blassingame, Barnett, Burleson, Bruce, Cooke of San Saba, Douglas, Flanagan, German, Holt, Henry of Limestone, Holmes, Killough, Norvell, Robertson of Bell, Russell of Wood, Spikes, Scott, Sansom—19.

NAYS—Allison, Abernathy, Ballinger, Brady, Chambers, Cook of Gonzales, Cooley, DeMorse, Dohoney, Darnell, Davis of Brazos, Davis of Wharton, Ford, Flournoy, Fleming, Ferris, Gaither, Graves, Johnson of Franklin, Johnson of Collin, Kilgore, Lockett, Lacy, Lynch, McLean, Martin of Navarro, Martin of Hunt, Morris, Mitchell, McKinney of Denton, McCormick, Murphy, Nugent, Pauli, Reagan, Ramey, Rentfro, Ross, Sessions, Smith, Stayton, Wade, Whitehead, Weaver, Whitfield, Waelder—46.

When Mr. Henry's (of Smith) name was called, he stated that he had paired off with Mr. Dunnam, who would vote yea, if present.

Mr. Dohoney offered the following amendment to section 6:

"And the proceeds of these lands, when sold, shall constitute a part of the public school fund of the county to which the land belonged."

Mr. Scott offered the following amendment:

"The Legislature shall provide for the sale of the county school lands of this State by the county courts, to actual settlers in lots of 80 acres or 160 acres, at a price to be fixed by commissioners, and the actual occupants of said lands shall have the refusal of said lands at the price fixed, and the said lands shall be valued without any regard to any improvement thereon.

[Mr. Stockdale in the chair.]

Mr. Ferris offered the following substitute for the amendment:

Section 6, line 36, after the word "grant" add "provided that such lands shall be sold under such regulations, at such times, and upon such terms, as may be prescribed by law, and proceeds of sale shall inure to the respective counties."

Mr. Ballinger moved to lay the amendments on the table until the report from the Committee on Counties and County Lands shall have been made.

Mr. Ferris withdrew his substitute, and the other amendments were laid temporarily on the table under Mr. Ballinger's motion.

Mr. Wade offered the following substitute for section 4:

"The lands herein set apart for public school purposes shall be utilized under a system of lease or sale, under such rules and regulations as the Legislature shall establish. The proceeds of all lands sold shall be invested in interest-bearing bonds of this or some other State. All interest accruing upon said bonds, and all money derived from leases, shall be annually distributed, *pro rata,* among the scholastic population of the State."

Mr. Weaver moved to postpone the subject until Monday next, 9½ o'clock, and that it be made special order for that hour.

Carried.

Mr. Ramey submitted the following report:

> COMMITTEE ROOM. }
> AUSTIN, October 9, 1875. }

To the Hon. E. B. Pickett, President of the Convention:

SIR—Your committee on Engrossed and Enrolled Ordinances would respectfully report that they have examined and compared article —, "Executive Department," and find the same correctly engrossed. Respectfully,

WM. NEAL RAMEY, Chairman.

On motion of Mr. German, two hundred copies of the article —, "Executive Department," as engrossed, were ordered printed for use of the Convention.

On motion of Mr. Flanagan, the Convention adjourned until 9¼ o'clock A. M. Monday.

THIRTY-FIRST DAY.

> HALL OF REPRESENTATIVES, }
> AUSTIN, TEXAS, October 11, 1875. }

Convention met pursuant to adjournment; roll called; quorum present; prayer by the Rev. W. H. D. Carrington, of Austin.

Journal of Saturday read and adopted.

Mr. McLean called up his resolution amending rules and the amendment was adopted.

Mr. Scott called up Mr. Russell's (of Wood) resolution restricting the time of delegates to five minutes in debate, and amendment adopted.

The chair announced the following committee to investigate the charges of the *Democratic Statesman* in relation to a combination between the Republicans and Grangers: Mr. Stockdale, Chairman; Messrs. Fleming, McCormick, Murphy, Henry of Smith, Stayton, Nugent.

Mr. West withdrew his motion to reconsider the vote engrossing the article on suffrage.

Messrs. Crawford, Ferris, Fleming and Whitfield presented memorials from their respective counties, asking an uniform system of sanitary regulations, which were all referred to the Committee on General Provisions.

Mr. King, as chairman of Committee on Counties and County Lands, reported as follows:

Committee Room,
Austin, October 8, 1875.

To the Hon. E. B. Pickett, President of the Convention:

Sir — Your Committee on Counties and County Lands, to whom were referred certain resolutions and memorials on the subject of county school lands, have had the same under consideration, and instruct me to report the following provision, which they recommend for adoption as a part of the constitution.

Respectfully, Henry C. King, Chairman.

"All lands heretofore, or hereafter, granted to the several counties of this State, for education or schools, are of right the property of said counties, respectively, to which they were granted, and title thereto is vested in said counties, and no adverse possession or limitation shall ever be available against the title of any county. Each county may sell and dispose of its lands, in whole or in part, in manner to be provided by the police court of the county. Actual settlers, now residing on said lands, shall be protected in the prior right of purchasing the same to the extent of their settlements, not to exceed one hundred and sixty acres, at the price fixed by said court, which price shall not include the value of existing improvements made thereon by such settlers. Said lands, and the proceeds thereof when sold, shall be held by said counties alone, as a trust for the benefit of public schools therein, said proceeds to be invested in bonds of the State of Texas, or of the United States, and only the interest thereof to be used and expended annually.

On motion of Mr. Moore, two hundred copies of the report and article were ordered printed.

Mr. Ford reported as follows:

Committee Room,
Austin, October 9th, 1875.

To the Hon. E. B. Pickett, President of the Convention:

The Committee on State Affairs, to which was referred a

memorial in favor of establishing "an effectively organized Department of Health and Vital Statistics," have maturely considered the same, and have instructed me to report it back, and recommend that the Convention reject the petition of said memorialists.

JOHN S. FORD, Chairman.

Also —

COMMITTEE ROOM, }
AUSTIN, October 9, 1875. }

To the Hon. E. B. Pickett, President of the Convention:

The Committee on State Affairs, to which was referred a resolution providing "that no debts contracted two years after the adoption of this constitution, shall be collected by law," have had the same under consideration, and have instructed me to report said resolution back and recommend that it be not adopted by the Convention.

JOHN S. FORD, Chairman.

Reports received to come up in their order.

Mr. Waelder offered the following resolution:

Resolved, That the Committee on Municipal Corporations inquire into the expediency of providing, that incorporated cities and towns shall not levy and collect higher license or occupation taxes than are levied and collected by the State.

BUSINESS ON THE TABLE.

"Article —, Bill of Rights," taken up.

Pending the reading of the report and article, the hour arrived for the special order, and the same was taken up, viz: "Article —, Education."

Mr. Sansom withdrew his substitute for section 3, offered on Saturday last, and offered the following as a substitute for the section:

And there shall be set apart annually not more than one-tenth of the anual revenue derivable from taxation for general purposes, and a poll tax not to exceed two dollars for the support of public free schools.

And no person shall be allowed to vote at any election to take place in this State unless he has paid said tax.

On motion of Mr. Johnson, of Collin, laid on the table by the following vote:

YEAS—Abernathy, Arnim, Brown, Blake, Ballinger, Blassingame, Barnett, Burleson, Brady, Bruce, Chambers, Cook of Gonzales, Cooke of San Saba, Cline, Cooley. Cardis, Dillard, DeMorse, Darnell, Davis of Brazos, Ford, Flournoy, Ferris,

Flanagan, German, Gaither, Henry of Limestone, Johnson of Franklin, Johnson of Collin, Killough, Lockett, Lacy, McLean, Martin of Navarro, Martin of Hunt; Morris, Mitchell, Mc. Kinney of Denton, Norvell, Pauli, Ramey, Rentfro, Ross, Russell of Harrison, Russell of Wood, Spikes, Scott, Sessions. Smith, Whitehead, Weaver, Waelder—52.

Nays — Allison, Crawford, Douglas, Dohoney, Erhard, Fleming, Graves, Holt, Henry of Smith, Holmes, King, Kilgore, Lynch, McCormick, Moore, Murphy, Nunn, Nugent, Reagan, Robertson of Bell, Stockdale, Stayton, Sansom, Wade, Whitfield, West — 26.

The substitute offered by Mr. Wade on Saturday last was then taken up and lost.

Mr. Ballinger offered the following substitute for section 3 :

"Sec. 3. The Legislature shall provide for the levy and collection annually of a tax of one-fourth of one per cent. on all the taxable property of this State, or so much of said tax as together with a poll tax of two dollars per annum on each qualified elector in the State, and the other funds provided for school purposes shall be sufficient to educate all the scholastic children specified in this article four months in each year; *and, provided further,* that the payment of such poll tax shall be a condition precedent to the exercise of the right of suffrage in this State."

Mr. Nugent proposed to amend the substitute as follows:

"Provided that said tax shall only be levied when voted by a majority of the freeholders of the several school districts."

Lost.

Mr. Kilgore proposed to strike out of the substitute "one-fourth," and insert "one-eighth."

Lost.

On motion of Mr. Dohoney the substitute was laid on the table by the following vote:

Yeas—Allison, Abernathy, Arnim, Brown, Blake, Blassingame, Barnett, Burleson, Bruce, Chambers, Cook of Gonzales, Cooke of San Saba, Cardis, Douglas, Dillard, DeMorse, Dohoney, Darnell, Davis of Brazos, Ford, Flournoy, Ferris, German, Gaither, Graves, Holt, Henry of Limestone, Johnson of Franklin, Johnson of Collin, Lacy, McLean, Martin of Navarro, Martin of Hunt, McKinney of Denton, Moore, Norvell, Nugent, Pauli, Ramey, Rentfro, Robertson of Bell, Ross, Russell of Harrison, Russell of Wood, Spikes, Scott, Sessions, Sansom, Whitehead, Weaver — 49.

Nays—Ballinger, Brady, Crawford, Cline, Cooley, Davis of Wharton, Erhard, Fleming, Flanagan, Henry of Smith, Holmes,

King, Kilgore, Killough, Lockett, Lynch, Morris, Mitchell, McCormick, Murphy, Nunn, Smith, Stockdale, Stayton, Wade, Whitfield, West, Waelder—29.

The hour having arrived for considering the special order, viz: "Article —, Legislative Department," on motion of Mr. Flournoy it was postponed until Wednesday next at 10 o'clock.

[Mr. Stockdale in the chair.]

Consideration of "Article —, Education," resumed.

Mr. Dohoney offered the following substitute for section 7.

"Section 7. The Governor, Comptroller of Public Accounts and Treasurer shall constitute a public school board, for the sole purpose and with the sole power of annually apportioning and distributing the available public school fund among the several counties according to their respective scholastic population. And if at any time the State fund apportioned to any given county, added to any county fund that may be existing, shall not be sufficient to provide public free schools in said county, for at least four months in the year, for the instruction of all the scholastic population between the ages of nine and fifteen years, the county court of said county shall have the power to supply the deficiency by levying a poll tax of one dollar on every male citizen over twenty-one years of age, to be supplemented by an ad valorem tax upon all the taxable property in the county; *provided,* that said ad valorem tax shall never exceed one-sixth of one per cent.; *and provided further,* that no part of the tax raised in any county shall ever be applied to any other purpose than the payment of teachers in said county."

Mr. DeMorse offered the following as a substitute for the substitute:

"It shall be the duty of the Legislature, by the use of the available school fund, including a poll tax of two dollars, which shall be levied for educational purposes, to establish and maintain free public schools for such period of each year as the fund may be sufficient to accomplish, and the Legislature may authorize each school district in every county to levy and collect such tax as the vote of a majority of the freeholders of the district may determine, not exceeding one-fourth of one per cent. The available school fund hereinbefore provided shall be distributed to the several counties of the State according to scholastic population, the distribution to be made by the Comptroller."

Additional section to come in as section 8:

"Sec. 8. Each county shall be laid off into school districts by the county commissioners thereof, and one county superintendent, who shall have the examination of teachers, shall be elected by all the qualified electors; and a board of school trustees for each school district shall be elected by the qualified voters of the district."

Mr. Johnson, of Collin, offered the following amendment to section 7:

Amend by striking out all of said section down to the word "year," in line 44, and insert "the Legislature shall establish free schools throughout the State as soon as practicable, and shall provide by law that the available school fund herein provided shall be equally distributed among all the school population of the State."

On motion of Mr. Brown, the Convention adjourned until 2½ o'clock P. M.

EVENING SESSION—2½ o'CLOCK.

Convention met pursuant to adjournment; roll called; quorum present.

Mr. Cook, of Gonzales, stated that he had a telegram, directed to Major Ed. Burleson, advising him of the illness of several members of his family, and asking for him an indefinite leave of absence.

Granted.

The pending business was then resumed, being article —, on "Education," with pending amendments thereto.

Mr. Ramey, chairman Committee on Enrolled and Engrossed Ordinances, submitted the following report:

COMMITTEE ROOM,
AUSTIN, TEXAS, October 11, 1875.

To the Hon. E. B. Pickett, President of the Convention:

Your Committee on Engrossed and Enrolled Ordinances would respectfully report that they have carefully examined and compared article —, on "Suffrage," and find the same correctly engrossed.

WM. NEAL RAMEY, Chairman.

On motion of Mr. Cook, of Gonzales, two hundred copies of the article on "Suffrage" were ordered printed as engrossed.

On motion of Mr. Graves, the debate on the pending amendments to article —, on "Education," was estopped, and the vote was taken on the pending amendment offered by Mr. Johnson, of Collin.

The amendment was lost by the following vote:

YEAS—Allison, Brown, Blake, Ballinger, Blassingame, Barnett, Crawford, Cline, Cooley, DeMorse, Dohoney, Darnell,

Davis of Brazos, Fleming, Ferris, German, Henry of Smith, Johnson of Franklin, Johnson of Collin, King, McLean, Martin of Navarro, Martin of Hunt, Morris, McCormick, Moore, Norvell, Nunn, Reagan, Ramey, Spikes, Sessions, Smith, Sansom, Whitehead, West—36.

NAYS—Abernathy, Arnim, Brady, Bruce, Chambers, Cook of Gonzales, Cooke of San Saba, Cardis, Douglas, Dillard, Davis of Wharton, Erhard, Ford, Flournoy, Flanagan, Gaither, Graves, Holt, Henry of Limestone, Holmes, Kilgore, Killough, Lockett, Lacy, Lynch, Mitchell, McKinney, Murphy, Nugent, Pauli, Rentfro, Robertson of Bell, Ross, Russell of Harrison, Russell of Wood, Scott, Stockdale, Stayton, Wade, Weaver, Whitfield, Waelder—42.

The vote was then taken on the substitute offered by Mr. DeMorse.

The substitute was lost by the following vote:

YEAS—Ballinger, Crawford, Cook of Gonzales, Cline, Cooley, Dillard, DeMorse, Davis of Brazos, Ford, Fleming, Ferris, Flanagan, Henry of Smith, Holmes, Johnson of Franklin, King, Kilgore, Lockett, McLean, Martin of Navarro, Martin of Hunt, Morris, Mitchell, McCormick, Nugent, Ross, Russell of Harrison, Sessions, Smith, Wade, Weaver, West, Waelder—33.

NAYS—Allison, Abernathy, Arnim, Brown, Blake, Blassingame, Barnett, Brady, Bruce, Chambers, Cooke of San Saba, Cardis, Douglas, Dohoney, Darnell, Erhard, Flournoy, German, Gaither, Graves, Holt, Henry of Limestone, Johnson of Collin, Killough, Lacy, Lynch, McKinney, Moore, Murphy, Norvell, Nunn, Pauli, Reagan, Rentfro, Robertson of Bell, Russell of Wood, Spikes, Scott, Stockdale, Sansom, Whitehead, Whitfield—42.

The vote was then taken on the substitute offered by Mr. Dohoney.

The substitute was lost by the following vote:

YEAS—Ballinger, Brady, Crawford, Cline, Cooley, Dohoney, Ford, Ferris, Flanagan, Henry of Smith, Johnson of Franklin, King, Kilgore, Lockett, McLean, Morris, Mitchell, McCormick, Nunn, Pauli, Rentfro, Ross, Russell of Harrison, Smith, Sansom, Wade, West, Waelder—28.

NAYS—Allison, Abernathy, Arnim, Brown, Blake, Blassingame, Barnett, Bruce, Chambers, Cook of Gonzales, Cooke of San Saba, Cardis, Douglas, Dillard, DeMorse, Darnell, Davis of Brazos, Erhard, Flournoy, Fleming, German, Gaither, Graves, Holt, Henry of Limestone, Holmes, Johnson of Collin, Killough, Lacy, Lynch, Martin of Navarro, Martin of Hunt, Mc-

Kinney, Moore, Murphy, Norvell, Nugent, Reagan, Ramey, Robertson of Bell, Russell of Wood, Spikes, Scott, Sessions, Stockdale, Stayton, Whitehead, Whitfield—48.

Mr. Whitfield moved the previous question.

Withdrawn.

Mr. Waelder then offered the following as a substitute for section 3:

"The Legislature shall provide for the levying and collection of an annual tax, of not more than one-sixth of one percentum upon the taxable property, real and personal, of this State, and also a poll-tax of two dollars on each voter of the State; and the taxes so levied and collected, as well as the income from the fund herein provided, shall be annually distributed for the education of all children between the ages of eight and fourteen years, among the several counties or school districts, according to their respective scholastic population."

Pending discussion of the amendment offered by Mr. Waelder, on motion of Mr. McCormick, the Convention adjourned until 9 o'clock A. M. to-morrow.

THIRTY-SECOND DAY.

HALL OF REPRESENTATIVES, }
AUSTIN, TEXAS, October 12, 1875. }

Convention met pursuant to adjournment; roll called; quorum present; prayer by the Rev. Mr. Lee, Rector of St. David's Church, Austin.

Journal of yesterday read and adopted.

Mr. Weaver submitted the following motion:

To the Honorable Members of the Constitutional Convention:

The undersigned does not believe that this Convention is actuated by a spirit of Jacobinism. He trusts that all men here wish to ascertain what is right and to do it. There are grave questions coming up that demand discussion. There are also legal questions to be settled, and there are in this body men who, by common consent, rank among the ablest lawyers of the State. He, for one, desires to hear their views, as well as those of other gentlemen. No man can define his position intelligibly, or give reasons for his vote on important questions, in five minutes. He does not believe it is the wish of this body to act hastily and unthinkingly on so grave a matter as making a constitution for a million and a half of people—an irrepealable law; and believing it is due to the people that important matters should be fully and freely discussed in a deliberative body of the gravity, magnitude and importance of a Constitutional Convention; and believing with Shelley, that "the man who dare not reason is a coward, the man who will not reason is a *bigot,* and the man who can not reason is a fool," he respectfully moves a reconsideration of the vote limiting debate to five minutes.

All of which is respectfully submitted.

W. S. WEAVER.

The motion to reconsider was carried by the following vote:

YEAS—Allison, Abernathy, Arnim, Brown, Ballinger, Blassingame, Barnett, Bruce, Crawford, Chambers, Cook of Gonzales, Cooke of San Saba, Cline, Cooley, Douglas, DeMorse, Dohoney, Darnell, Davis of Brazos, Erhard, Ford, Fleming, Ferris, Flanagan, Graves, Henry of Smith, Henry of Limestone, Holmes, Johnson of Franklin, King, Kilgore, Killough, Lockett, Lacy, McLean, Martin of Navarro, Martin of Hunt, McKinney of Denton, Moore, Norvell, Nunn, Nugent, Pauli, Reagan, Ramey, Robertson of Bell, Ross, Russell of Harrison, Sessions, Smith, Stockdale, Stayton, Sansom, Weaver, West—55.

NAYS—Dillard, Holt, Johnson of Collin, Lynch, Morris, Mills, McCormick, Murphy, Rentfro, Russell of Wood, Spikes, Scott, Whitehead—13.

Mr. Graves then moved to so amend the rules as to leave no limitation to the time of debate.

The question was then taken on the adoption of the proposed amendment limiting members to five minutes debate and the amendment was lost.

Mr. McCormick presented a memorial from Wm. B. Scates, of Colorado county, "relative to a pension."

Referred to Committee on General Provisions.

Mr. McCormick offered the following resolution:

Resolved, That this Convention will adjourn *sine die* on the 5th day of November next; *provided,* that should it be necessary to continue longer in session, that no *per diem* shall be drawn by any of the delegates after such date.

Mr. Mills moved to refer the resolution to the Committee on Printing and Contingent Expenses.

Lost.

The question then recurring on the adoption of the resolution, it was lost by the following vote:

YEAS—Brady, Dillard, Fleming, Flanagan, Graves, Holt, Henry of Limestone, Holmes, Johnson of Collin, Lockett, Lacy, Lynch, Morris, Mills, Mitchell, McCormick, Murphy, Nunn, Ross, Russell of Harrison, Russell of Wood, Scott, West, —23.

NAYS—Allison, Abernathy, Arnim, Brown, Blake, Ballinger, Blassingame, Barnett, Bruce, Crawford, Cook of Gonzales, Cooke of San Saba, Cline, Cooley, Cardis, Douglas, DeMorse, Dohoney, Darnell, Davis of Brazos, Davis of Wharton, Erhard, Ford, Flournoy, Ferris, Gaither, Henry of Smith, Johnson of Franklin, King, Kilgore, Killough, McLean, Martin of Navarro, Martin of Hunt, McKinney of Denton, Moore, Norvell, Nugent, Pauli, Reagan, Ramey, Rentfro, Robertson of Bell, Spikes, Sessions, Smith, Stockdale, Stayton, Sansom, Wade, Whitehead, Weaver—52.

Mr. Ramey offered the following resolution:

Resolved, That the Legislature shall authorize the different county courts in the State to establish such public roads in their respective counties as the public interest may demand, and require them to be kept up by the labor of all male persons between the ages of eighteen and forty-five, and that no person within those ages shall be exempt from working the public roads except for disability; *provided,* that any person may have the privilege to pay such equivalent for the time each person may be required to work the public roads as the Legislature may establish.

Referred to Committee on General Provisions.

Mr. King offered the following resolution:

Resolved, That the following provision be incorporated under its appropriate article as a section of the constitution:

"Sec. —. The Legislature shall make adequate provision for the equipment and maintenance of such of the militia forces of the State as the Governor may call out to protect the frontier from hostile incursions by Indians or other marauding bands."

Referred to Committee on General Provisions.

The unfinished business was then taken up, being the further consideration of article —, on education, with a pending amendment, offered by Mr. Waelder on yesterday.

Mr. Dohoney offered the following as an amendment to the amendment:

"Provided that the taxes raised under this provision shall be applied to the public schools in the county where they are collected."

Mr. Waelder amended the amendment offered by him, by

striking out the word "two," in regard to the number of dollars as a poll tax, and insert "one."

The amendment of Mr. Dohoney was lost.

Mr. Martin, of Navarro, offered the following as a substitute for the whole subject matter under consideration:

"Section 1. The principal of all funds arising from the sale or other disposition of lands and other property, granted or intrusted to the State for educational purposes, shall forever be preserved inviolate; and the income therefrom shall be faithfully applied to specific objects of the original grants and trusts.

"Sec. 2. The Legislature shall make such provision, whenever deemed practicable, by taxation or otherwise, as, with the income arising from the school trust-fund, will secure a thorough and efficient system of common schools throughout the State; and no religious, or other sect, shall ever have exclusive right to, or control of, any part of the school funds of the State.

"Sec. 3. All public lands which have been heretofore, or may hereafter be granted, to the various counties of this State, for public schools, are, of right, the property of said counties respectively to which they are granted and entitled thereto, is hereby vested in said counties; subject to the trust created in the grant.

"Sec. 4. The Legislature shall have power, whenever deemed advisable, to provide for the sale in part, or in whole, of all lands heretofore granted for the benefit of the Lunatic Asylum, the Blind Asylum, the Deaf and Dumb Asylum, and the Orphan Asylum, together with such donations as may have been, or may hereafter be made, to either, are hereby set apart to provide a permanent school fund for the support and maintenance and improvements of said asylums.

"Sec. 5. Separate schools shall be provided for the white and colored children, and impartial provision shall be made for both."

Mr. Nunn moved that the majority report, and all pending amendments, be referred to a select committee of seven.

Mr. Cook, of Gonzales, moved to reconsider the vote taken on yesterday, refusing to adopt the amendment offered by Mr. Johnson, of Collin, to the pending article.

On motion of Mr. Allison, the Convention adjourned to 2¼ o'clock P. M.

EVENING SESSION—2½ o'clock.

Convention met pursuant to adjournment, at 2½ P. M.; roll called; quorum present.

The pending business resumed, viz: the motion to refer the article on Education and pending amendments to a select committee of seven.

Mr. McLean moved to amend the motion by striking out "seven" and inserting "fifteen," and that the committee have their own time to report.

Lost.

The question then recurring on the original motion of Mr. Nunn to refer to a select committee of seven, was adopted by the following vote:

YEAS—Ballinger, Brady, Crawford, Cook of Gonzales, Cline, Cooley, Dillard, Dohoney, Darnell, Davis of Brazos, Davis of Wharton, Erhard, Ford, Fleming, Ferris, Flanagan, Henry of Smith, Holmes, Johnson of Franklin, King, Lockett, McLean, Martin of Navarro, Martin of Hunt, Morris, Mitchell, McCormick, Moore, Murphy, Nunn, Pauli, Reagan, Ramey, Rentfro, Ross, Russell of Harrison, Sessions, Smith, Stockdale, Stayton, Wade, Weaver, Waelder—43.

NAYS—Allison, Abernathy, Arnim, Blake, Blassingame, Barnett, Bruce, Chambers, Cooke of San Saba, Douglas, Flournoy, German, Gaither, Graves, Holt, Henry of Limestone, Johnson of Collin, Killough, Lacy, Lynch, McKinney of Denton, Norvell, Nugent, Robertson of Bell, Russell of Wood, Spikes, Scott, Sansom—28.

The next business in order was the consideration of "Bill of Rights."

On motion of Mr. Barnett, the Convention decided to consider section by section.

Mr. McCormick moved to strike out the first article.

Adopted.

Mr. Moore proposed to amend section 4 by striking out all of line 54 after the word "sentiment."

Lost.

Mr. Flournoy proposed to amend section 3, line 51, by striking out the words "but in consideration of public services."

Lost.

Mr. Ferris offered the following amendment to section 1:

Section 1, lines 39 and 40, strike out all to the word "and" in line 40, and insert the following: "Texas is a free and independent State, subject only to the Constitution of the United States."

Adopted.

Mr. Norvell offered the following amendment:

22

Amend by striking out all the section after the word "belief" in line 58, section 5, and insert the words "provided that no atheist shall be a competent witness."

On motion of Mr. Dillard, the motion was laid on the table.

Mr. Murphy offered an amendment to section 5, line 58, as follows:

Insert between the word "affirmation" and the word "shall" the words "in legal tribunals."

On motion of Mr. Russell, of Harrison, the amendment was laid on the table.

Mr. DeMorse offered the following as a substitute for section 1:

"Texas is one of the free and independent States of the United States of America, holding that independence in conformity with the Constitution of the United States, and that the maintenance of free institutions and the most enduring support of the Federal Union depend upon the preservation of the right of local self-government in all the States composing that Union."

Lost.

Mr. Norvell moved to amend by striking out section 5.

Lost.

Mr. Abernathy offered to amend section 6, line 61, by adding the word "Almighty" between the words "worship" and "God."

Mr. Russell, of Harrison, moved to lay the amendment on the table.

Lost and amendment adopted.

Mr. Cooley moved to amend section 6 by inserting after the word "protect," in line 68, the word "equally."

Adopted.

Mr. Holt moved to amend section 6 by adding: "provided, nothing in this section shall be so construed as to prohibit the Legislature from passing laws preventing ordinary work being done on Sunday."

On motion of Mr. Weaver, the amendment was laid on the table.

Mr. McLean moved to amend section 8, line 79, by adding after the word "matter" the words "is true and."

Mr. Moore offered the following as a substitute for the amendment offered by Mr. McLean:

In section 8, line 78, strike out all after the word "jury," and add the following words: "who shall have the right to determine the law and facts, under the direction of the court, as in other cases."

Mr. Reagan offered the following as a substitute for both the amendment and substitute:

"In prosecutions for the publication of papers investigating the conduct of officers, or men in public capacity, or when the matter published is proper for public information, the truth thereof may be given in evidence; and in all indictments for libels the jury shall have the right to determine the law and the facts, under the direction of the court, as in other cases."

Mr. McLean's amendment adopted.

Mr. Moore withdrew his amendment, and Mr. Reagan's substitute for the section was adopted.

On motion of Mr. Russell, of Harrison, the Convention adjourned until 9 o'clock A. M. to-morrow, pending section 9 of the Bill of Rights.

THIRTY-THIRD DAY.

HALL OF REPRESENTATIVES, }
AUSTIN, TEXAS, October 13, 1875. }

Convention met pursuant to adjournment; roll called; quorum present. Prayer by the Rev. Mr. Dodge.

The chair announced the following select committee, to which was referred the article on Education: Mr. Nunn chairman, Messrs. Norvell, Moore, Ross, Ballinger, Martin of Navarro, and Robertson of Bell.

The following communication was presented by Mr. Ballinger:

MATAGORDA COUNTY, October 6, 1875.

To the Hon. E. B. Pickett, President of the Convention:

SIR—In consequence of disasters resulting to me from the recent tornado, I find it impossible for me longer to attend as a delegate to the Convention from the Twelfth Senatorial District, and therefore tender my resignation. Hoping wise and harmonious action by the body over which you have the honor of presiding, I have the honor to be, with great consideration and respect, sir, your most obedient servant.

E. S. RUGELEY.

Mr. Ballinger offered the following resolution:

WHEREAS, The Hon. E. S. Rugeley has resigned his place as a delegate to the Constitutional Convention from the Twelfth District;

Resolved, That the Governor of this State is hereby authorized and requested forthwith to issue a writ of election to said district to fill said vacancy, by an election to be held on Saturday, 23d day of the present month, and return thereof made within five days thereafter.

Adopted.

Mr. Russell, of Harrison, offered the following resolution:

Resolved, That the following shall be incorporated in the Bill of Rights, under the proper article:

"Importations of persons under the name of 'coolies,' or any other name or designation, or the adoption of any system of peonage whereby the unfortunate and helpless may be reduced to practical bondage, shall never be authorized or tolerated by the laws of this State; and neither slavery nor involuntary servitude, except as a punishment for crime, whereof the party shall have been duly convicted, shall ever exist in this State."

Referred to Committee on Bill of Rights.

Mr. Erhard offered the following resolution:

Resolved, That no person shall be deprived by law of the right to indulge in public recreation or pleasure on any day of the week; *provided,* that any person availing himself of that right shall not thereby violate public decency in the respect due to public worship.

Referred to Committee on State Affairs.

Mr. Martin, of Navarro, submitted the proceedings of a public meeting of the citizens of Dresden, Navarro county, on the subject of taxing dogs and taking wolf scalps.

Referred to Committee on Revenue and Taxation.

Mr. Mills submitted the following article on the subject of Superintendent of Education:

"Section —. There shall be a Superintendent of Public Instruction, who shall be elected by the people. The Superintendent shall hold his office for the term of two years. He shall receive an annual salary of three thousand dollars.

"Sec. —. The Superintendent shall have supervision and control of the public free schools of the State. The Legislature shall lay off the State into convenient school districts, and shall provide for the formation of a Board of School Directors in each county, and for the purpose of taxation each county shall be a school district. It shall be the duty of the Superintendent of Public Instruction to recommend to the Legislature such provisions of law as may be found necessary, in the progress of time, to the establishment and perfection of a complete system of education adapted to the circumstances and wants of the people of the State. He shall, at each session of the Legislature, furnish that body with a complete report of all free schools in the State.

"Sec. —. The Legislature shall establish a uniform system of public free schools throughout the State.

"Sec. —. As a basis for the establishment and endowment of said public free school, all the funds, lands and other property heretofore set apart and appropriated, or that may hereafter be set apart and appropriated, for the support and maintenance of public schools, shall constitute the public school fund; and all sums of money that may come to this State hereafter from the sale of any portion of the public domain of Texas shall also constitute a part of the public school fund; and the Legislature shall appropriate all the proceeds resulting from sales of public lands of this State to such public school fund. And the Legislature shall set apart, for the benefit of public schools, not less than one-sixth of the annual revenue derivable from general taxation, and shall also cause to be levied and collected an annual poll tax of one dollar on all male persons in this State between the ages of twenty-one and sixty years, also a tax of one and one-half per cent. on the gross earnings of all railroads, steamship lines and insurance companies of this State, also all the fines collected for carrying concealed weapons and disturbances of the peace, also all money collected for license for selling malt and spirituous liquors, for the benefit of public schools. And said fund and the income derived therefrom, and the taxes and other moneys herein provided for school purposes, shall be a perpetual fund, to be applied as needed, exclusively for the education of all the scholastic inhabitants of this State, and no law shall ever be made appropriating such fund for any other use or purpose whatever.

"Sec. —. The public lands heretofore given to counties shall be under the control of the board of school directors of their respective counties, and may be leased or sold by them under such rules and regulations as the Legislature shall prescribe.

"Sec. —. The Legislature shall, at its first session, and from time to time thereafter. as may be necessary, provide all needful rules and regulations for the purpose of carrying into effect the provisions of this article. It is made the imperative duty of the Legislature to see to it that all the children in the State between the ages of (8) eight to (15) fifteen are, without delay, provided with ample means of education. The Legislature shall annually appropriate for school purposes, and to be equally distributed among all the scholastic inhabitants of the State, the interest accruing on the school fund and the income derived from taxation for school purposes; and shall, from time to time, as may be necessary, invest the principal of the school fund in the bonds of the State of Texas or of the United States; and all school moneys invested in the bonds of the State of Texas are hereby declared NOT to be of doubtful validity."

Referred to the Select Committee of Seven on Article —, Education.

Mr. Nugent submitted the following report:

COMMITTEE ROOM,
AUSTIN, October 12, 1875.

To the Hon. E. B. Pickett, President of the Convention:

The undersigned, constituting a majority of the special committee, appointed to inquire into the expediency of incorporating a provision in the constitution, setting apart public lands to certain sections of the State for the purpose of aiding in the construction of railroads, beg leave to submit the following report:

The policy of subsidizing railroads, notwithstanding it may seem to be sanctioned by the legislation of the State for nearly a quarter of century, is not, in our view, well founded in principle, and we fail to perceive that it has resulted in anything more than a mere speculative advantage to those corporations which have been made its beneficiaries. It seems clear to us from the experience of the past and the admonitions of the present, that the further construction of railroads in this State can not be predicated upon grants of this kind, which, so far as human foresight can determine, will not, for many years, sustain any appreciable value in the markets of the world. These lands, situated as they are on the distant frontier, remote from settlements, can never be made available as a fund for any practical purpose until they have been reclaimed from the savage by the hardy pioneers who stand ready to enter upon them whenever this Convention shall have placed it beyond the power of corporations to anticipate them in the occupancy of their rightful heritage. No policy is so hallowed in the traditions of Texas as that which has constantly guaranteed to actual settlers the right of selecting homes out of our unappropriated domain; no policy has proven so efficacious as this in peopling our vacant land with emigrants from other shores; and, in our humble opinion, no policy has contributed so largely as this to the productive wealth of the State, or commended itself so strongly to the beneficent spirit of the age. This policy should be fostered and liberalized; and we do not think its wise design can be effectuated if powerful corporations are permitted to preoccupy the ground upon which the immigrant would establish his home. To make land grants to railroads means that our pre-emption laws are to become nugatory; it means that the poor man shall continue to remain a homeless wanderer upon our soil, for the reason that his efforts to secure his western home are paralyzed when he contemplates the hopelessness of competition with these corporations, whose surveying partie are always enabled to keep a hundred miles ahead of him. It seems to us, then, a mere delusion when it is proposed to still subsidize railroads, and at the same time tender pre-emption privileges to actual settlers. In its last analysis, the proposition means that the public domain is to be the legitimate and exclusive prey of railroad corporations. Again, we do not perceive the force of the suggestion that the good faith of the State is pledged to the policy indicated in the resolution referred to us for consideraion. The policy itself, we submit, was wrong in its inception, and we can not understand why it should be continued. Private corporations, while they frequently contribute to the public good, are always formed for the enrichment of individuals; and we submit that the first principles of our government are at war with every policy which seeks to lavish the bounty of the State upon a few private citizens, as a mere bonus for their ultimate aggrandizement. Besides, if no principle were involved, the impolicy of endowing private corporations with wealth, beyond what may be acquired by the proper investment of their capital in legitimate pursuits, must, we submit, be apparent to every one. Already they have become an ordinary appendage of government; they have dictated the laws of the country for years past; they have organized conspiracies in the capitals of the States, and through them have so shaped the course of legislation that they enjoy a virtual immunity from civil restraint and burdens. And we can not see that a policy which has in no small degree contributed to these evils, and which is full of forebodings for the future of our country, should be persisted in for any reason of sentimental or imaginary justice. The land grants of the State have heretofore been made without regard to sectional boundaries; and in the single instance in which it was undertaken to loan the school fund, the general law on the subject distributed the bounty of the State with as much fairness as the condition of the country then permited; and surely no section has any reason to complain if it failed to reap the benefits of a law of which all could avail themselves alike. We think if good faith requires the adoption of the policy embodied in the resolution under consideration, it would equally demand a donation, or loan, of money to the sections named; for, unquestionably, these have never obtained loans of money equal to

those made to other portions of the State. For these, among
other reasons, we believe that no such policy as that indicated
in the resolution referred to should be perpetuated in the organic
law of the State. On the contrary, we think that the Legislature should be prohibited from making such grants in the future.
In no other way, it seems to us, can anticipated evils be ob-
viated; in no other way can the State government be placed in
an attitude in which it can curb those corporations, which are
rapidly growing beyond legislative restraints. We therefore
recommend that section 51 of the Legislative Department of the
constitution be so amended as to prohibit land grants in the
future.

All of which is respectfully submitted.

T. L. NUGENT,
WM. BLASSINGAME,
JOHN JOHNSON,
B. D. MARTIN.

Two hundred copies ordered printed.

COMMITTEE ROOM,
AUSTIN, October 12, 1875.

To the Hon. E. B. Pickett, President of the Convention.

The members of your Select Committee, appointed to inquire
into the expediency of setting apart a portion of the public domain of the State, to be donated to aid in the construction of
railways in the sections of the State that heretofore have not had
the benefits resulting from such donations, and thereby to equalize every part of the State in the benefits resulting from such
donations, have had the same under consideration, and being unable to agree in regard to the same, the undersigned, members
of said committee, believing it proper that such appropriation of
a portion of the public domain should be made, return herewith
an article which they recommend may be incorporated into the
constitution.

JOHN W. STAYTON,
CHARLES DEMORSE,
W. W. WHITEHEAD.

"ARTICLE —.

"Section 1. The Legislature shall have no power to make any
donation of any of the public lands of this State to any work of
internal improvement in this State except as is hereinafter provided.

"Sec. 2. It having been the policy of the State to encourage
the construction of railroads by donations of land, and that policy having resulted in the construction of such works in certain

portions of the State, while certain other portions, more remote, have to a great extent received no advantage as yet from said policy; therefore, in order to equalize the benefits of the State's bounty to all portions of its territory, it is hereby provided: That the Legislature shall hereafter encourage the construction of railways, by donations of land, in alternate sections, as follows:

"First. In the territory embraced in the following boundaries, to-wit:

"Beginning at the mouth of the Colorado river; thence up said river to the point where it intersects the 99th degree of longitude west from Greenwich; thence north, on the line of said degree of longitude to its intersection with the 32d degree of latitude north; thence with said degree of latitude west to the Rio Grande; thence down said Rio Grande to the Gulf of Mexico; thence with the margin of said Gulf to the place of beginning; to which territory there is hereby allotted twenty thousand sections of land, the same to be received by railways hereafter constructed in said territory, surveys being made by the owners of such railways alternately of an equal number of sections for the State.

"Second. In the territory embraced in the following boundaries, to-wit:

"Beginning at the point of the intersection of the 32d degree of north latitude with the 99th degree of west longitude; thence on the line of said degree of longitude north to the north-eastern corner of what is called the Pan Handle; thence west to the northwestern corner of said Pan Handle; thence south with the line of the 103d degree of west longitude (to its intersection with the 32d degree or north latitude); thence east with said degree of latitude to the place of beginning; to which territory there is hereby alloted ten thousand sections, to be received and surveyed as hereinbefore provided for the first division of territory.

"Third. In the territory embraced in the following boundaries, to-wit:

"Beginning at the point where the Galveston, Houston and Henderson railway strikes Galveston bay; thence with said railway to its intersection with the International and Great Northern railway; thence in a north-easterly direction along said railway to the point where the same intersects the Texas and Pacific railway; thence east to the eastern boundary of the State; thence with the eastern boundary of the State to the Gulf of Mexico; thence along the margin of the gulf to the entrance into Galveston bay; and thence to the place of beginning; to which territory there is hereby allotted three thousand three hundred sections, to be received and surveyed as hereinbefore provided for the first division of territory.

"Sec. 3. The alternate sections of land, provision for the survey of which is made in the preceding sections, and not to be donated to railways, are hereby set apart, donated, and declared to be a part of the public school fund of the State, and they shall never be otherwise used or appropriated; and the land authorized to be donated to railways shall never be appropriated to any other use by the State, except that the same may be sold to actual settlers, or located by land certificates which by failure to locate were rendered invalid by section 4 of article 10 of former constitution, which by this constitution may be validated if said lands are so sold or located before railways are constructed in the territory aforesaid, so as to entitle the owners of railways to the same."

Two hundred copies of the report and article ordered printed.

The Convention then proceeded to the consideration of unfinished business, viz: Section 9, Bill of Rights.

On motion of Mr. German, the vote taken yesterday striking out article 1, Bill of Rights, was reconsidered.

[Mr. Darnell in the chair.]

Mr. Stockdale moved to make "Bill of Rights" article 1, and "Boundaries" article 2.

Lost.

Mr. German moved to amend the Bill of Rights so as to make it read article 1; Boundaries article 2, Bill of Rights.

Carried.

Mr. Stayton proposed to amend article 1 by striking out all that precedes line 20.

Adopted.

Mr. Reagan offered the following amendment:

Strike out lines 22, 23 and 24, and to the word "thence" in line 25, and insert in lieu thereof the following: "Beginning in the Gulf of Mexico three marine leagues in front of the mouth of Sabine Pass, and running thence to the center of the mouth of Sabine Pass and up the middle of Sabine Pass bay and river to latitude 32 degrees north."

Adopted.

Mr. DeMorse offered the following amendment:

Sec. 10. After "favor," in line 92, insert "and shall have the right to make a declaration of his acts and the motives therefor, the truth and the weight of which may be considered by the jury in connection with other evidence."

The hour having arrived for considering the special order, viz:

"Art. —, Legislative Department," on motion of Mr. Mills the same was postponed until the pending business be disposed of. .

Mr. Stockdale offered the following as a substitute for Mr. DeMorse's amendment:

In civil causes, no party thereto, if he have an interest therein, shall testify unless called to testify by the opposite party; and in criminal cases no defendant shall testify.

On motion of Mr. Ballinger the amendment and substitute were laid on the table.

Mr. Moore offered the following amendment:

Sec. 11, line 103, strike out the words "the offenses committed," and insert the words "the prosecution is pending."

Adopted.

Mr. Stayton offered to amend by striking out all after the words "*habeas corpus,*" in line 102.

Lost.

Mr. Stockdale offered the following amendment:

In lines 101 and 102, section 11, strike out "other courts of record" and insert "or District Judge."

Mr. German offered to substitute for the amendment, strike out "or other court of record," and insert "or District Court."

Accepted by Mr. Stockdale.

Mr. Moore proposed to amend section 11, line 101, by adding after the word "record," in line 102, the words "having jurisdiction to try the offense."

Accepted by Mr. Stockdale.

Mr. McCormick offered the following as a substitute for the section.

"Sec. 11. All prisoners shall be bailable by sufficient security, unless for capital offenses, when the proof is evident or the presumption great; but this provision shall not prevent bail after indictment found upon the examination of the evidence by a Judge of the Supreme, District, or other court of this State, upon the return of a writ of *habeas corpus,* issued returnable, as may be provided by law."

Lost.

Mr. Moore's amendment, as accepted, adopted.

Mr. Kilgore offered the following amendment:

In section 12 insert in line 105, after the word "remedy" the words "by such writ."

Lost.

Mr. Norvell proposed to amend by striking out in line 106 the words "in all proper cases."

Adopted.

On motion of Mr. Stockdale, section 12 was passed over for the present.

Mr. Murphy offered to amend section 14, line 112, by adding after the word "guilty" the words "in a court of competent jurisdiction."

Adopted.

Mr. Rentfro proposed to amend section 15 by adding at the close thereof: "But no law shall be passed requiring any other qualification for jurors than those required of electors in this State."

On motion of Mr. Russell, of Wood, the amendment was laid on the table by the following vote:

YEAS—Allison, Abernathy, Arnim, Brown, Blake, Ballinger, Blassingame, Barnett, Bruce, Crawford, Chambers, Cook of Gonzales, Cooke of San Saba, Cooley, Douglas, DeMorse, Dohoney, Darnell, Davis of Brazos, Ford, Fleming, Ferris, German, Gaither, Graves, Holt, Henry of Smith, Henry of Limestone, Holmes, Haynes, Johnson of Franklin, King, Kilgore, Killough, Lacy, Lynch, McLean, Martin of Navarro, Martin of Hunt, Morris, McKinney, McCormick, Murphy, Norvell, Nunn, Nugent, Reagan, Robertson of Bell, Russell of Wood, Spikes, Scott, Smith, Stockdale, Stayton, Wade, Whitehead, Wright, Weaver, West, Waelder—60.

NAYS—Brady, Flanagan, Lockett, Mills, Mitchell, Pauli, Reynolds, Rentfro, Russell of Harrison—9.

Mr. Allison offered the following as a substitute for section 16:

"Sec. 16. No bail of attainder, *ex post facto* law, or law impairing the obligation of contracts, or retrospective in its operations, or making any irrevocable grants of special privilege or immunities, can be passed by the Legislature."

Withdrawn.

Mr. West proposed to add to section 16 the following:

"Nor shall any law be passed depriving a party of any remedy for the enforcement of a contract which existed when the contract was made."

Mr. Mills proposed to amend the amendment by adding: "Except usurious ones."

On motion of Mr. Dillard, the amendments were laid on the table.

On motion of Mr. Martin, of Hunt, the Convention adjourned to 2½ o'clock P. M.

EVENING SESSION — 2½ o'clock.

Convention met pursuant to adjournment; roll called; quorum present.

Convention resumed the consideration of Bill of Rights.

Mr. Reynolds offered the following as an additional section, to come in as section 17:

"No form of slavery shall ever exist in this State, and involuntary servitude of any character whatever is hereby forbidden, except as a punishment for crime, whereof the party shall have first been duly convicted."

On motion of Mr. Nugent, laid on the table by the following vote:

YEAS — Abernathy, Arnim, Blessingame, Barnett, Bruce, Chambers, Cook of Gonzales, Cooke of San Saba, Douglas, Dillard, Davis of Brazos, Flournoy, Fleming, Graves, Holt, Henry of Limestone, Holmes, Haynes, Johnson of Franklin, King, Kilgore, Killough, Lacy, Lynch, McLean, Martin of Navarro, McKinney of Denton, McCormick, Norvell, Nugent, Spikes, Sessions, Wade, Whitehead, Weaver — 35.

NAYS — Allison, Brown, Blake, Ballinger, Brady, Cardis, Dohoney, Darnell, Davis of Wharton, Ferris, Flanagan, German, Gaither, Johnson of Collin, Lockett, Martin of Hunt, Morris, Mitchell, Moore, Murphy, Pauli, Ramey, Reynolds, Rentfro, Robertson of Bell, Ross, Russell of Wood, Scott, Smith, Stockdale, Stayton, Wright — 32.

Mr. Scott proposed to amend section 17 by inserting after the word "Legislature" the words "or created under its authority."

Adopted.

Mr. McCormick proposed to amend lines 120 and 121 by striking out the words "except for the use of the State."

Lost.

Mr. Stayton proposed to amend by striking out the words "or secured by a deposit of money," in lines 121 and 122.

Lost.

Mr. Flournoy proposed to amend by inserting after the word "State," in line 121, as follows: "or for the use of some county or incorporated city or town within the State."

Lost.

Mr. Flournoy moved to reconsider the vote just taken.

Lost.

Mr. Waelder offered the following amendment:

Strike out the words "damaged, destroyed," in line 118, section 117.

Mr. Mills proposed to amend by inserting after " destroyed" the words " except to prevent conflagration."

Mr. Waelder's amendment lost.

Mr. Reagan proposed to amend Mr. Mill's amendment by adding the words " or in suppressing insurrection or repelling invasion."

Accepted.

[Mr. Brown in the chair.]

Mr. Nugent offered the following as a substitute for the amendment:

Insert " for " after the word " destroyed," in line 118, also " or " between " damaged " and " destroyed," in same line.

Messrs. Mills and Reagan withdrew their amendments.

Mr. Stockdale offered the following amendment:

Strike out all the section down to and including the word " money," in line 122, and insert " Private property shall not be taken except for public use; nor shall it be so taken without just compensation being made to the owner; if taken for public use to be applied by any corporation, except the State or a county, the compensation shall first be made therefor."

Mr. Robertson, of Bell, moved to strike out " county " from the amendment.

Carried.

Mr. Dillard moved to lay Mr. Stockdale's amendment on the table.

Mr. Nugent's amendment adopted.

On motion of Mr. Nunn, Mr. Dunnam was granted unlimited leave of absence on account of sickness in his family.

Mr. Ferris proposed to amend section 17 by inserting, in line 121, after the word " State," " or for public county roads."

Mr. Dillard moved to lay the amendment on the table.

Lost by the following vote:

Yeas—Ballinger, Blassingame, Crawford, Cook of Gonzales, Douglas, Dillard, Davis of Wharton, Erhard, Fleming, Flanagan, Gaither, Graves, Henry of Limestone, Holmes, Haynes, Lacy, Lynch, McKinney of Denton, Moore, Murphy, Norvell, Nugent, Reynolds, Robertson of Bell, Russell of Wood, Spikes, Scott, Sessions, Stayton, Wade, Whitehead, Wright, West—33.

Nays—Allison, Abernathy, Arnim, Brown, Blake, Barnett, Brady, Bruce, Chambers, Cooke of San Saba, DeMorse, Dohoney, Darnell, Ford, Flournoy, Ferris, Holt, Henry of Smith, Johnson of Franklin, King, Kilgore, Killough, Lockett, McLean, Martin of Navarro, Martin of Hunt, McCabe, Morris, Mills,

Mitchell, McCormick, Nunn, Pauli, Reagan, Ramey, Rentfro, Ross, Russell of Harrison, Smith, Stockdale, Waelder — 41.

The question on the adoption of Mr. Ferris's amendment was then put and amendment lost.

Mr. Allison proposed to amend by adding to section 18 the words "except for non-payment of fines and penalties imposed by law."

Lost.

Mr. McLean proposed to amend as follows:

Section 19, line 127, after the word "property" strike out "or," and insert after the word "privileges," "or immunities."

Mr. Holt offered the following as a substitute for section 19:

"The sole object and only legitimate end of government is to protect the citizen in life, liberty and property, and when government assumes other functions it is usurpation and oppression."

The chair ruled the substitute out of order.

Mr. McLean's amendment adopted.

Mr. Kilgore proposed to amend section 19 by striking out after the word "or," in line 127, the words "in any manner," and insert the word "be."

Lost.

Mr. Ballinger proposed to amend section 19 by striking out all after the word "disfranchised" and insert "except by due course of the law of the land."

Adopted.

On motion of Mr. Chambers, the Convention adjourned until 9 o'clock A. M. to-morrow.

THIRTY-FOURTH DAY.

HALL OF REPRESENTATIVES, }
AUSTIN, TEXAS, October 14, 1875. }

Convention met pursuant to adjournment; roll call; quorum present; prayer by the Rev. Mr. Wright, of Austin.

Mr. McKinney, of Walker, presented the memorial of the citizens of Grimes county, relative to legislative apportionment.

Referred to Committee on Legislative Apportionment.

Mr. Gaither offered the following resolution:

Resolved, That whereas, it being the duty of this Convention to frame a constitution that will aid in quieting the land titles of the State, and, whereas, the statute of limitations discriminating in favor of females and against males, is a source of much litigation in the courts of the State, therefore

Be it resolved, that the Committee on General Provisions be instructed to take the matter into consideration, and report a provision that will remedy the evil.

Referred to Committee on General Provisions.

Mr. Russell, of Wood, presented a memorial from Hon. Gustave Cooke.

Referred to Committee on General Provisions.

Mr. Henry, of Limestone, presented the memorial of the bar of Limestone county, on the subject of judicial apportionment.

Referred to Committee on Judicial Apportionment.

Mr. German offered the following resolution:

Resolved, That the following be a clause in the constitution:

" Sec. —. No corporation shall issue stock or bonds, except for money paid, labor done, or property actually received, and all fictitious increase of stock or indebtedness shall be void. The stock and bonded indebtedness of corporations shall not be increased, except in pursuance of general law, nor without the consent of the persons holding the larger amount in value of the stock first obtained at a meeting called for the purpose, first giving sixty days public notice, as may be provided by law."

Referred to Committee on Private Corporations.

Mr. Flournoy offered the following resolution:

Resolved, That the following be referred to the Committee on General Provisions, and that they consider the propriety of reporting, in substance, the following:

" That, to prevent litigation hurtful to the public interest, quiet title in the occupants, in good faith, of real estate, and discourage, as far as practicable, all disposition to discover defects in the claims of actual passessors, or speculation on the validity of unpresented and unknown outstanding titles;

" The Legislature shall define *champerty* and maintenance, and provide for the prevention and punishment thereof; and shall pass laws vacating the 'license' of any 'attorney-at-law' in this State who shall hereafter, as such, undertake the recovery of real estate for any 'plaintiff' upon the consideration in any respect contingent or conditional upon success, or upon a contract for any part, divided or undivided, of such real estate."

Referred to Committee on General Provisions.

Unfinished business taken up, viz: " Bill of Rights."

Mr. Nugent moved to reconsider the vote taken on yesterday, adopting an amendment to section 11, viz:

Add after the word "record," in line 102, the words "having jurisdiction to try the offense."

Carried.

Mr. Ballinger proposed to amend as follows:

Strike out all after the word "evidence," in line 101, and insert the words, "in such manner as may be prescribed by law."

The amendment, upon which the vote was reconsidered, was then lost, and Mr. Ballinger's amendment adopted.

Mr. Waelder offered the following amendment to section 29:

Strike out the words, "and no appropriation of money shall be made to aid immigrants to the State."

Mr. Erhard offered to amend as follows:

Section 29, line 155, insert after the word "prohibited," the words "but immigration shall be encouraged by the Legislature by all means within their power."

Mr. Russell, of Harrison, moved to strike out the entire section.

The question on the adoption of Mr. Waelder's amendment was then put, and the amendment lost by the following vote:

YEAS—Ballinger, Brady, DeMorse, Davis of Brazos, Erhard, Fleming, Flanagan, King, Lockett, Lynch, McLean, Martin of Navarro, McCabe, Morris, Mills, McKinney of Walker, McCormick, Pauli, Russell of Harrison, Stockdale, Stayton, Waelder—23.

NAYS—Allison, Abernathy, Arnim, Brown, Blake, Blassingame, Barnett, Crawford, Chambers, Cook of Gonzales, Cooke of San Saba, Cardis, Douglas, Dillard, Dohoney, Darnell, Davis, of Wharton, Flournoy, Ferris, German, Gaither, Graves, Holt, Henry of Smith, Henry of Limestone, Holmes, Haynes, Johnson of Franklin, Johnson of Collin, Kilgore, Killough, Lacy, Martin of Hunt, Mitchell, McKinney of Denton, Norvell, Nunn, Nugent, Reynolds, Robertson of Bell, Ross, Russell of Wood, Scott, Sessions, Smith, Wade, Whitehead, Wright, Weaver—49.

Mr. German moved to lay the amendments of Messrs. Erhard and Russell, of Harrison, on the table.

Carried by the following vote:

YEAS—Allison, Abernathy, Arnim, Blassingame, Barnett, Bruce, Chambers, Cooke of San Saba, Douglas, Dillard, Dohoney, Flournoy, German, Gaither, Graves, Holt, Henry of Smith, Henry of Limestone, Holmes, Haynes, Johnson of Franklin, Johnson of Collin, Kilgore, Killough, Lacy, McCabe, Morris, McKinney of Denton, Norvell, Nunn, Nugent, Robertson, of Bell, Russell of Wood, Spikes, Scott, Sessions, Wade, Whitehead, Wright, Weaver—40.

23

NAYS—Brown, Blake, Ballinger, Brady, Crawford, Cook of Gonzales, Cooley, Cardis, DeMorse, Darnell, Davis of Brazos, Davis of Wharton, Erhard, Ford, Fleming, Ferris, Flanagan, Lockett, Lynch, McLean, Martin of Navarro, Martin of Hunt, Mills, Mitchell, McKinney of Walker, McCormick, Murphy, Pauli, Reynolds, Rentfro, Ross, Russell of Harrison, Smith, Stockdale, Stayton, West, Waelder — 37.

Mr. Wade proposed to amend as follows:

Section 29, line 155, after "prohibited in" insert "immigration is invited, but."

On motion of Mr. Scott, it was laid on the table.

Mr. Waelder offered the following amendment:

Line 156, strike out the line and insert "money shall be paid to immigrants for coming to this State."

Mr. Scott proposed to substitute the amendment as follows:

"But we cordially invite all who desire to better their condition to make their homes among us."

On motion of Mr. Bruce, all the amendments were laid on the table.

Mr. Russell, of Harrison, offered the following amendment as an additional section:

"Sec. 30. Importation of persons under the name of coolies, or any other name or designation, or the adoption of any system of peonage, whereby the helpless and unfortunate may be reduced to practical bondage, shall never be authorized or tolerated by the laws of this State; and neither slavery, nor involuntary servitude, except as a punishment for crime, whereof the party shall have been duly convicted, shall ever exist in this State."

Mr. Brown offered the following as a substitute for the amendment:

"No form of compulsory servitude, except as a punishment for crime, shall ever be allowed in this State."

Mr. Crawford made the following point of order, viz: that under the rules the amendment and substitute were not properly before the house, but should be referred to a committee.

Pending discussion on the point of order, Mr. Martin, of Navarro, moved to lay both amendments on the table.

Lost by the following vote:

YEAS — Abernathy, Blassingame, Barnett, Bruce, Crawford, Chambers, Cook of Gonzales, Cooke of San Saba, Douglas, Dillard, Graves, Holt, Henry of Smith, Henry of Limestone, Holmes, Haynes, Killough, Lynch, Martin of Navarro, McCormick, Norvell, Nugent, Sessions, Whitehead — 24.

NAYS—Allison, Arnim, Brown, Ballinger, Brady, DeMorse,

Dohoney, Darnell, Ford, Flournoy, Fleming, Ferris, Flanagan, German, Gaither, Johnson of Franklin, Johnson of Collin, Kilgore, Lockett, Lacy, McLean, Martin of Hunt, McCabe, Mills, Mitchell, McKinney of Denton, McKinney of Walker, Murphy, Nunn, Pauli, Reagan, Reynolds, Rentfro, Robertson of Bell, Ross, Russell of Harrison, Russell of Wood, Spikes, Scott, Smith, Stockdale, Stayton, Wade, Wright, Weaver, West, Waelder—47.

The President ruled out of order that portion of Mr. Russell's (of Harrison) amendment which referred to slavery or involuntary servitude, as the Convention had acted on the same yesterday in laying Mr. Reynold's amendment on the same subject on the table.

Mr. Ballinger offered to amend the substitute by adding "except that of children to parents and lawful apprentices."

On motion of Mr. Russell, of Harrison, the main question on the amendments was ordered.

Mr. Ballinger's amendment to the substitute of Mr. Brown adopted by the following vote:

YEAS—Allison, Abernathy, Brown, Blake, Ballinger, Crawford, Chambers, Cook of Gonzales, Cardis, Douglas, Dillard, DeMorse, Dohoney, Darnell, Davis of Brazos, Erhard, Ford, Ferriss, Flanagan, German, Gaither, Holt, Henry of Smith, Henry of Limestone, Johnson of Collin, Killough, Lacy, McLean, Martin of Navarro, Martin of Hunt, Morris, McKinney of Denton, McKinney of Walker, McCormick, Moore, Norvell, Nunn, Nugent, Reagan, Ramey, Ross, Russell of Wood, Spikes, Sessions, Smith, Stockdale, Wade, Whitehead, West, Waelder—50.

NAYS—Arnim, Blassingame, Barnett, Brady, Bruce, Cooley, Davis of Wharton, Flournoy, Fleming, Graves, Holmes, Haynes, Johnson of Franklin, Kilgore, Lynch, Mills, Mitchell, Murphy, Pauli, Reynolds, Rentfro, Robertson of Bell, Russell of Harrison, Scott, Stayton, Wright, Weaver—27.

The question on the adoption of Mr. Brown's substitute as amended by Mr. Ballinger was put, and the substitute adopted by the following vote:

YEAS—Allison, Brown, Blake, Crawford, Chambers, Cook of Gonzales, Cooke of San Saba, Cardis, Douglas, Dillard, DeMorse, Dohoney, Darnell, Davis of Brazos, Erhard, Ford, German, Gaither, Graves, Henry of Smith, Henry of Limestone, Johnson of Franklin, Johnson of Collin, Killough, Lacy, McLean, Martin of Navarro, Martin of Hunt, Morris, McKinney, of Denton, McKinney of Walker, McCormick, Moore, Murphy, Norvell, Nunn, Ramey, Robertson of Bell, Russell of Wood, Spikes, Scott, Sessions, Smith, Stockdale, West, Waelder—46.

Nays—Abernathy, Arnim, Ballinger, Blassingame, Barnett, Brady, Bruce, Cooley, Davis of Wharton, Flournoy, Fleming, Ferris, Flanagan, Holt, Holmes, Haynes, Kilgore, Lynch, McCabe, Mills, Mitchell, Nugent, Pauli, Reagan, Reynolds, Rentfro, Ross, Russell of Harrison, Stayton, Wade, Wright, Weaver—32.

Mr. Norvell moved to strike out section 30.

Mr. Stockdale proposed to amend the section, when Mr. Scott made this point of order: that no motion or amendment could be entertained until the main question was exhausted, and that the main question was not exhausted until the vote was taken as to whether the substitute should be incorporated as a section to the article.

The Chair ruled the point well taken, and ordered the vote accordingly, which resulted in the refusal to adopt the substitute as a section of the article by the following vote:

Yeas—Allison, Brown, Ballinger, Chambers, Cooke of San Saba, Cooley, Cardis, Douglas, DeMorse, Dohoney, Erhard, Ford, Ferris, German, Henry of Smith, Henry of Limestone, Johnson of Franklin, Johnson of Collin, King, Killough, Lacy, McLean, Martin of Hunt, Morris, McKinney of Denton, McKinney of Walker, Moore, Murphy, Nunn, Ramey, Robertson of Bell, Russell of Wood, Scott, Sessions, Smith, Stockdale, Stayton, West, Waelder—39.

Nays—Abernathy, Arnim, Blake, Blassingame, Barnett, Burleson, Brady, Bruce, Crawford, Cook of Gonzales, Dillard, Darnell, Davis of Brazos, Davis of Wharton, Flournoy, Fleming, Flanagan, Gaither, Graves, Holt, Holmes, Haynes, Kilgore, Lockett, Lynch, Martin of Navarro, McCabe, Mills, Mitchell, McCormick, Norvell, Nugent, Pauli, Reagan, Reynolds, Rentfro, Ross, Russell of Harrison, Wade, Wright, Weaver—41.

On motion of Mr. Russell, of Wood, the vote taken yesterday, adopting an amendment to section 19, adding the word "immunities" to the section, was reconsidered, and the amendment again adopted.

Mr. Flournoy proposed to amend section 29 by adding: "But liberal pre-emption laws shall be passed, to encourage and protect actual settlers on the public domain."

Withdrawn.

Mr. McCormick moved to reconsider the vote refusing to strike out section 29.

Carried.

The question was then put upon the motion to strike out the section.

Mr. Johnson, of Franklin, moved to reconsider the vote refusing to adopt Mr. Reynolds' amendment, to add an additional section to the "Bill of Rights," to come in after section 16 as section 17, prohibiting slavery or involuntary servitude except for crime, etc.

Mr. Graves moved the main question on engrossing the "Article —. Bill of Rights."

Carried.

First question being the motion to strike out section 29, the same was put and section stricken out by the following vote:

YEAS—Brown, Blake, Ballinger, Brady, Crawford, Cook of Gonzales, Cooley, Cardis, Douglas, DeMorse, Davis of Brazos, Ford, Flournoy, Fleming, Ferris, Flanagan, Gaither, Henry of Limestone, King, Lockett, Lacy, Lynch, McLean, Martin of Navarro, Martin of Hunt, Morris, Mills, Mitchell, McKinney of Walker, McCormick, Moore, Murphy, Nunn, Pauli, Reagan, Reynolds, Rentfro, Ross, Russell of Harrison, Sessions, Smith, Stockdale, Stayton, Wade, Whitehead, Waelder—46.

NAYS—Allison, Abernathy, Arnim, Blassingame, Barnett, Burleson, Bruce, Chambers, Cooke of San Saba, Dillard, Dohoney, Darnell, Erhard, German, Graves, Holt, Henry of Smith, Holmes, Haynes, Johnson of Franklin, Johnson of Collin, Kilgore, McCabe, McKinney of Denton, Norvell, Nugent, Ramey, Robertson of Bell, Russell of Wood, Spikes, Scott, Wright. West—33.

The article, "Bill of Rights," was then ordered engrossed.

Mr. Nunn moved to reconsider the vote engrossing the article.

Lost.

On motion of Mr. Flanagan the Convention adjourned.

EVENING SESSION—2½ o'clock.

Convention met pursuant to adjournment; roll called; quorum present.

Special order taken up, viz: "Article —. Legislative Department."

Mr. Darnell moved to postpone until Monday next at 10 o'clock.

Carried.

"Article —, Lands and Land Office," taken up.

Mr. Stayton offered the following amendment:

Amend section 2 by adding "and any genuine land certificates which under former laws have been declared invalid, because located upon titled lands, or upon lands held by older location, are hereby revived and may be located on any of the vacant lands of the State."

Mr. Fleming moved to strike out section 2.

Mr. McLean proposed to amend as follows:

Section 2, line 7, after "certificates" insert "in the possesion or ownership of the original grantee, his or her heirs."

Mr. Dillard moved to lay the amendments offered by Messrs. Fleming and McLean on the table.

Carried by the following vote:

YEAS—Allison, Abernathy, Brown, Blake, Blassingame, Barnett, Burleson, Brady, Bruce, Chambers, Cook of Gonzales, Cooke of San Saba, Cooley, Cardis, Douglas, Dillard, DeMorse, Dohoney, Darnell, Davis of Brazos, Erhard, Ford, Ferris, Flanagan, German, Gaither, Graves, Henry of Smith, Henry of Limestone, Holmes, Haynes, Johnson of Collin, King, Kilgore, Killough, Lockett, Lynch, Martin of Navarro, Martin of Hunt, McCabe, Morris, Mills, Mitchell, McKinney of Denton, Murphy, Norvell, Nunn, Nugent, Pauli, Reagan, Ramey, Reynolds, Robertson of Bell, Ross, Russell of Harrison, Russell of Wood, Spikes, Scott, Smith, Stockdale, Stayton, Wade, Whitehead, Weaver, West, Waelder—66.

NAYS—Arnim, Crawford, Fleming, McLean, McKinney of Walker, McCormick, Moore, Rentfro, Wright, Whitfield—10.

Mr. Allison proposed to amend as follows:

Add to end of section 2 the words: "and returned to the Land Office by the 1st of January, 1880."

Mr. Barnett offered the following substitute for section 2:

"Sec. 2. All unsatisfied genuine soldier or headright land-certificates, barred by section 4, article 10, of the constitution of 1869, by reason of the holder or owner thereof failing to have them surveyed and returned to the Land Office by the 1st day of January 1875, are hereby revived, and may be located on any of the vacant lands in the State."

Mr. Kilgore moved to lay the substitute on the table.

The yeas and nays being demanded, the substitute was laid on the table by the following vote:

YEAS—Abernathy, Brown, Blake, Blassingame, Brady, Cooke of San Saba, Cooley, Dohoney, Darnell, Davis of Brazos, Erhard, Ford, Ferris, Flanagan, Holt, Henry of Smith, King, Kilgore, Killough, Lockett, Martin of Navarro, Morris, Mitchell, Moore, Murphy, Norvell, Nunn, Pauli, Ramey, Reynolds, Robertson of Bell, Russell of Harrison, Scott, Sessions, Smith, Stockdale, Stayton, Wade, West, Waelder—40.

NAYS—Allison, Arnim, Barnett, Burleson, Bruce, Crawford,

Chambers, Cook of Gonzales, Cardis, Douglas, Dillard, De-Morse, Fleming, German, Gaither, Graves, Haynes, Johnson of Collin, Lacy, Lynch, McLean, Martin of Hunt, McCabe, Mills, McKinney of Denton, McKinney of Walker, McCormick, Nugent, Reagan, Rentfro, Ross, Russell of Wood, Spikes, Whitehead, Weaver, Whitfield—36.

Mr. Stayton's amendment adopted.

Mr. Crawford offered the following substitute for section 2:

"Sec 2. All unsatisfied genuine land certificates barred by section 4, article 10, constitution of 1869, are hereby revived. All unsatisfied genuine land certificates now in existence shall be surveyed and returned to the general office within five years after the adoption of this constitution or be forever barred; and all genuine land certificates hereafter issued by the State shall be surveyed and returned to the General Land Office within five years after its issuance or be forever barred.

Mr. Allison's amendment was lost.

Mr. Gaither proposed to amend section 2 as follows:

Provided that none of the land certificates hereby revived shall ever be located, surveyed or patented on lands held under previous title or color of title from the soverignty.

Adopted.

Mr. Reagan moved to reconsider the vote just taken.

Carried.

Mr. Stockdale offered the following as a substitute for the amendment:

"No location or survey, by virtue of any genuine land certificate, shall hereafter be made upon any land which appears to be appropriated, deeded or patented, by the records of the county or the General Land Office."

Adopted.

On motion of Mr. Cardis, the Convention adjourned until 9 o'clock A. M. to-morrow.

THIRTY-FIFTH DAY.

HALL OF REPRESENTATIVES. }
AUSTIN, TEXAS, October 15, 1875. }

Convention met pursuant to adjournment; roll called; quorum present; prayer by Rev. A. C. Graves, member from Coryell.

Journal of yesterday read and adopted.

On motion of Mr. Cooke, of San Saba, Mr. Sansom was excused from attendance on the Convention until Wednesday evening next.

On motion of Mr. Weaver, Mr. Holmes was granted unlimited leave of absence on account of sickness in his family.

Mr. Russell, of Harrison, presented the memorial of the physicians of Harrison county asking that "occupation tax" on their profession be abolished.

Referred to Committee on Revenue and Taxation.

Mr. Morris offered the following resolution;

Resolved, That a legal voter in his district, not under thirty, or over sixty, years of age, who can hear, speak, read, and write the language of the court, shall constitute a competent juror.

Referred to Judiciary Committee.

Mr. West moved to reconsider the vote refusing to adopt a resolution increasing the pay of the pages.

Carried by the following vote:

Yeas—Abernathy, Arnim, Ballinger, Burleson, Brady, Crawford, Cooke of San Saba, Cooley, Cardis, Douglas, Darnell, Davis of Brazos, Davis of Wharton, Flournoy, Fleming, Ferris, Flanagan, Gaither, Henry of Limestone, Johnson of Franklin, Kilgore, Killough, Lynch, McLean, McKinney of Walker, Morris, Mills, Mitchell, McCormick, Murphy, Nunn, Rentfro, Ross, Russell of Harrison, Scott, Sessions, Smith, Stockdale, Stayton, Wade, Whitehead, Weaver, Whitfield, West, Waelder —45.

Nays—Allison, Brown, Blake, Blassingame, Barnett, Bruce, Chambers, Cook of Gonzales, Cline, Dillard, DeMorse, Dohoney, Erhard, Ford, German, Graves, Holt, Henry of Smith, Haynes, Johnson of Collin, Martin of Hunt, McKinney of Denton, Moore, Norvell, Nugent, Pauli, Reagan, Ramey, Robertson of Bell, Russell of Wood, Spikes—31.

On motion of Mr. Abernathy, the resolution was so amended as that the extra pay should commence from to-day.

The question on the adoption of the resolution was then put, and the resolution adopted by the following vote:

Yeas—Abernathy, Arnim, Ballinger, Burleson, Brady, Crawford, Cook of Gonzales, Cooke of San Saba, Cooley, Cardis, Douglas, Dohoney, Darnell, Davis of Brazos, Davis of Wharton, Flournoy, Fleming, Ferris, Flanagan, Gaither, Henry of Limestone, Johnson of Franklin, King, Kilgore, Killough, Lynch, McLean, McCabe, Morris, Mills, McKinney of Walker, McCormick, Murphy, Nunn, Nugent, Reynolds, Rentfro, Ross, Russell of Harrison, Scott, Smith, Stockdale, Stayton, Wade,

Whitehead, Wright, Weaver, Whitfield, West, Waelder—50.

NAYS—Allison, Brown, Blake, Blassingame, Barnett, Bruce, Chambers, Cline, Dillard, DeMorse, Erhard, Ford, German, Graves, Holt, Henry of Smith, Haynes, Johnson of Collin, Martin of Hunt, McKinney of Denton, Moore, Norvell, Pauli, Reagan, Ramey, Robertson of Bell, Russell of Wood, Spikes —28.

Mr. Kilgore moved to reconsider the vote just taken and to lay the motion on the table.

Carried.

Mr. Flournoy offered the following resolution:

Resolved, That the Committee on Public Lands and Land Office be instructed to inquire into the propriety of validating the patents heretofore issued on all locations of headright and other certificates in the reservation heretofore known as the Peters' Colony Reservation and the Mississippi and Pacific Railroad Reserve.

Referred to Committee on Public Lands and Land Office.

UNFINISHED BUSINESS, VIZ:

"Article —, Public Lands and Land Office," taken up.

Mr. Stockdale offered the following amendment to the substitute offered by Mr. Crawford on yesterday:

Strike out the words " all unsatisfied genuine land certificates barred by section 4, article 10, constitution of 1869, are hereby revived," and that the remainder of the substitute be made a part of the section as amended.

Mr. Gaither offered the following as an amendment to Mr. Crawford's substitute:

"*Provided,* That all land certificates, heretofore or hereafter issued, shall be located, surveyed or patented only upon vacant, unappropriated public domain, and not upon any land tilled or equitably owned under color of title from the sovereignty of the soil, evidence of the appropriation of which is on the county records or in the General Land Office."

Mr. Stockdale's amendment lost.

Mr. Kilgore moved to lay Mr. Gaither's amendment on the table.

Lost by the following vote:

YEAS—Abernathy, Arnim, Blassingame, Cline, Cooley, Dohoney, Ferris, Flanagan, Kilgore, Lockett, McLean, Martin of Hunt, Mitchell, Norvell, Pauli, Reynolds, Rentfro, Russell of Harrison, Stayton, Wright, West—21.

NAYS—Allison, Brown, Blake, Ballinger, Barnett, Burleson, Brady, Bruce, Crawford, Chambers, Cook of Gonzales, Cooke of

San Saba, Cardis, Douglas, Dillard, Darnell, Davis of Brazos, Erhard, Ford, Fleming, German, Gaither, Graves, Holt, Henry of Smith, Henry of Limestone, Haynes, Johnson of Franklin, Johnson of Collin, King, Killough, Lacy, Lynch, Martin of Navarro, Morris, Mills, McKinney of Denton, McKinney of Walker, Nunn, Nugent, Reagan, Ramey, Robertson of Bell, Russell of Wood, Spikes, Scott, Sessions, Smith, Stockdale, Wade, Whitehead, Weaver, Waelder—53.

Mr. Gaither's amendment adopted.

Mr. Crawford's substitute, as amended, also adopted.

Mr. Scott proposed to amend as follows:

Section 1, line 2, strike out the words, "be at the seat of government," and insert in lieu thereof the words, "be self-sustaining, and shall be kept at the seat of government."

Mr. German offered the following substitute for Mr. Scott's amendment:

"The Legislature shall, by appropriate legislation, at the earliest time practicable, make the Land Office self-sustaining."

Adopted as a substitute for the amendment.

The question then, upon adopting it as an amendment to the section, was put and carried by the following vote:

YEAS—Abernathy, Arnim, Blassingame, Barnett, Burleson, Brady, Bruce, Crawford, Chambers, Douglas, Dillard, DeMorse, Dohoney, Darnell, Davis of Wharton, Ford, Flournoy, Ferris, German, Gaither, Holt, Henry of Limestone, Haynes, Johnson of Franklin, Johnson of Collin, Kilgore, Lacy, Lynch, McLean, Martin of Nevarro, Martin of Hunt, Mills, Mitchell, McKinney of Denton, McKinney of Walker, McCormick, Murphy, Norvell, Nunn, Ramey, Reynolds, Rentfro, Russell of Harrison, Russell of Wood, Spikes, Scott, Sessions, Stayton, Wade, Whitehead, Wright, Weaver, Whitfield, Waelder—54.

NAYS—Allison, Blake, Ballinger, Cooke of San Saba, Cline, Cooley, Davis of Brazos, Erhard, Fleming, Flanagan, Graves, Henry of Smith, King, Lockett, McCabe, Nugent, Reagan, Smith, Stockdale, West—20.

[Mr. Brown in the chair.]

Mr. Reagan proposed the following as a substitute for the amendment just adopted:

"The Legislature may, by appropriate legislation, make the Land Office self-sustaining."

On motion of Mr. German laid on the table.

Mr. Brady proposed to amend section 1 by adding "*provided* no Land Office shall be established at all until such time as it shall be self-sustaining, and this the Legislature shall provide."

Laid on the table.

Mr. Stockdale moved to pass over the consideration of section 3 for the present.

Carried.

Mr. Nunn offered the following amendment:

Strike out all after the word "and" in line 20, and insert "shall accrue to the benefit of the general school fund of the State; and the Legislature shall provide for resuming control of the same."

Mr. Davis, of Brazos, moved to amend by striking out section 4.

Mr. Ballinger offered the following:

Insert in line 18, before the word "alienated," the words "or shall not hereafter be."

Mr. Stayton offered the following as a substitute for all the amendments, and the section:

"Sec. 4. It shall be the duty of the Attorney General to cause proceedings to be instituted for the purpose of having a forfeiture declared of all lands granted, or that may hereafter be granted, to railways which have not been alienated in conformity with the terms of their charters and the laws of the State under which the grants were or may be made; and after such forfeiture such lands shall be subject to location or sale as other vacant lands."

On motion of Mr. Reagan, the section and pending amendments were recommitted to Committee on Public Lands and Land Office.

On motion of Mr. Allison, Mr. Flournoy was added to Committee on Legislative Apportionment.

On motion of Mr. Fleming the Convention adjourned.

EVENING SESSION—2½ o'clock.

Convention met; roll called; quorum present.

Pending business resumed, viz: Consideration of Art. —, Public Lands and Land Office.

On motion of Mr. Weaver, the Secretary of the Convention was granted leave of absence for the remainder of the evening.

Mr. Brown moved to reconsider the vote recommitting "Sec. 4 of Art. —, Public Lands and Land Office."

Carried.

Mr. Reagan moved to recommit the whole article to the Committee on Public Lands and Land Office.

Carried.

Business on the table was then taken up.

On motion of Mr. Ford, the following report from Committee

on State Affairs was read and referred to Committee on General Provisions:

COMMITTEE ROOM,
AUSTIN, October 4th, 1875.

To the Hon. E. B. Pickett, President of the Convention:

The Committee on State Affairs, to whom was referred the memorial of the widow and heirs of the late W. A. Smith, have had the same under consideration, and instruct me to report the accompanying section and recommend that it be adopted by the Conventiotn as a part of the new constitution.

JOHN S. FORD, Chairman.

"Sec. —. The Legislature shall make provisions by law to have all claims and demands justly and lawfully due by the existing State government, or by any of its predecessors, and which shall be presented within one year from a date specified by law, and not thereafter, either adjudicated or audited; *provided,* that such claims and demands have not heretofore been either adjudicated or audited; *and provided also,* that said claims and demands originated prior to the 28th day of January, 1861, or subsequent to the 5th day of August, 1865, and that they are not in contravention of the constitution and laws of the United States; and all claims and demands not so presented shall be and remain forever barred."

The following resolution was taken from the table and read:

Resolved, That when, in considering any of the articles of the constitution as reported, amendments are offered which affect such articles as may not yet be reported by the suitable committee, said amendments shall be referred without debate to said committee.

The Convention refused to adopt the resolution.

The following report was taken up and read:

To the Hon. E. B. Pickett, President of the Convention:

The Committee on Revenue and Taxation, to which was referred a memorial from Bastrop county relative to pay of Rangers, long due, direct me to report the memorial back to the Convention, and suggest that the subject be referred to the first session of the Legislature under this constitution.

Respectfully,
CHARLES DeMORSE, Chairman.

The report was then adopted.

The following report and ordinance was then taken up.

Mr. DeMorse, Chairman of the Committee on Revenue and Taxation, submitted the following report:

COMMITTEE ROOM, }
AUSTIN, September 30, 1875. }

To the Hon. E. B. Pickett, President of the Convention:

The Committee on Revenue and Taxation, to whose consideration was referred a proposed ordinance to relieve certain counties from taxation, on account of damages resulting from flood and storm, direct me to report said ordinance back to the Convention, and express their opinion that the committee has no authority in the premises, and doubts the propriety of any action by the Convention in this direction.

ORDINANCE.

*   *   *   *   *   *   *   *

"WHEREAS, The late disastrous storm on the coast of the State of Texas ruined and placed in a condition of want and distress the people residing in the counties hereinafter named; and whereas, in their said condition they are totally unable at present to pay the State taxes due by them for the year 1875, and to exact of them said tax would be to further embarrass and distress them and impose upon them additional ills and burdens; therefore,

"*Be it ordained by the people of Texas in Convention assembled,* That the collection of the State tax levied for the year 1875, upon the property of the people residing in the counties of Chambers, Brazoria, Matagorda and Calhoun, be and the same is hereby restrained and enjoined, and that the Sheriffs and Tax Collectors of said counties are hereby forbidden and enjoined from the collection of said tax; and that the tax payers in said counties are hereby relieved and exempted from the payment of said tax due for the year 1875."

*   *   *   *   *   *   *

Mr. McCormick moved to refer the report and ordinance to a select committee of five.

Mr. DeMorse offered the following as a substitute for the ordinance:

Resolved, That the collectors of State taxes for the year 1875, for the counties of Calhoun, Matagorda, Brazoria, Harris, Galveston and Chambers be directed to remit the collection thereof from all sufferers by the late tornado, and that the collectors shall receive evidence of the actual necessity in each case, and that necessity resulting from the cause aforesaid, and that each collector. aforesaid, shall return upon his rolls a specific entry, indicating the remission and the cause, and that he shall make a separate report, aggregating all the cases thus relieved, to the Comptroller of the State, who shall make corresponding entry on the records in his office.

Mr. McCormick moved to amend Mr. DeMorse's substitute by adding "the county of Galveston."

Accepted.

Mr. Reagan moved to amend by inserting the word "State" before the word "tax."

Accepted.

The substitute of Mr. DeMorse, as amended, was accepted by Mr. Russell.

The question then recurring on the adoption of the substitute, it was adopted by the following vote:

YEAS—Abernathy, Arnim, Brown, Blassingame, Barnett, Burleson, Brady, Chambers, Cook of Gonzales, Cooke of San Saba, Douglas, DeMorse, Davis of Wharton, Erhard, Ford, Fleming, Gaither, Graves, Henry of Limestone, Haynes, King, Lockett, Lynch, Martin of Hunt, McCabe, Mitchell, McCormick, Pauli, Reagan, Reynolds, Rentfro, Ross, Russell of Harrison, Sessions, Weaver—33.

NAYS—Allison, Blake, Bruce, Crawford, Cardis, Dohoney, Darnell, Davis of Brazos, Ferris, Holt, Henry of Smith, Johnson of Franklin, Johnson of Collin, Kilgore, Lacy, McLean, Mills, McKinney of Walker, Moore, Norvell, Nugent, Ramey, Robertson of Bell, Russell of Wood, Spikes, Scott, Smith, Stayton, Wade, Whitehead, Wright, West, Waelder—35.

The following report and article were then taken up:

COMMITTEE ROOM,
AUSTIN, October 8, 1875.

To the Hon. E. B. Pickett, President of the Convention:

SIR—Your Committee on Counties and County lands, to whom were referred certain resolutions and memorials on the subject of county school lands, have had the same under consideration, and instruct me to report the following provision, which they recommend for adoption as a part of the Constitution.

Respectfully

HENRY C. KING, Chairman Committee.

"All lands heretofore or hereafter granted to the several counties of this State for education or schools, are of right the property of said counties respectively to which they were granted, and title thereto is vested in said counties, and no adverse possession or limitation shall ever be available against the title of any county. Each county may sell and dispose of its lands in whole or in part, in manner to be provided by the police court of the county. Actual settlers residing on said lands shall be protected in the prior right of purchasing the same to the extent of their settlements, not to exceed one hundred and sixty acres, at the price fixed by said court, which price shall not include the value of existing improvements made thereon by such settlers. Said lands, and the proceeds thereof when sold, shall be held by said counties alone as a trust for the benefit of public schools therein. Said proceeds to be invested in bonds of the State of Texas, or of the United States, and only the interest thereon to be used and expended annually."

The article was ordered engrossed.

Mr. Nugent moved to reconsider the vote just taken engrossnig the article.

Lost.

Mr. Erhard moved a reconsideration of the vote passing the substitute offered by Mr. DeMorse, exempting certain counties from taxation on account of the late flood.

Mr. Graves moved to lay the motion on the table.

The Convention refused to lay the motion on the table by the following vote:

YEAS—Abernathy, Arnim, Brown, Blassingame, Chambers, Cook of Gonzales, Cooke of San Saba, Cline, DeMorse, Ford, Fleming, Gaether, Graves, Haynes, King, Lynch, Martin of Hunt, Mills, Mitchell, McCormick, Reagan, Reynolds, Rentfro, Ross, Russell of Harrison, Stockdale, Weaver—27.

NAYS—Allison, Blake, Barnett, Burleson, Brady, Cooley, Dehoney, Darnell, Davis of Brazos, Davis of Wharton, Erhard, Ferris, German, Holt, Henry of Limestone, Johnson of Franklin, Johnson of Collin, Kilgore, Killough, Lockett, Lacy, McLean, McCabe, McKinney of Denton, Moore, Norvell, Nugent, Pauli, Ramey, Robertson of Bell, Russell of Wood, Spikes, Scott, Sessions, Smith, Stayton, Wade, Whitehead, Wright, West, Waelder—41.

The question then being on the reconsideration of the vote passing the substitute, the Convention reconsidered it by the following vote:

YEAS—Allison, Abernathy, Arnim, Blake, Barnett, Burleson, Bruce, Crawford, Cooke of San Saba, Cardis, Douglas, Dohoney, Darnell, Davis of Brazos, Erhard, Ferris, German, Holt, Henry of Smith, Henry of Limestone, Johnson of Franklin, Johnson of Collin, Kilgore, Killough, Lockett, Lacy, McLean, McKinney of Denton, Moore, Norvell, Nugent, Ramey, Rentfro, Robertson of Bell, Ross, Russell of Wood, Spikes, Scott,

Sessions, Smith, Stayton, Wade, Whitehead, Wright, West, Waelder — 46.

NAYS—Brown, Blassingame, Chambers, Cook of Gonzales, DeMorse, Davis of Wharton, Ford, Fleming, Gaither, Graves, Haynes, King, Lynch, Martin of Hunt, McCabe, Mitchell, McCormick, Pauli, Reagan, Reynolds, Russell of Harrison, Stockdale, Weaver, Whitfield — 24.

The question then recurred on the passage of the substitute.

Mr. Cardis moved to adjourn until to-morrow at 9 o'clock A. M. Lost.

Mr. Mills moved the previous question.

Previous question ordered, which was the passage of the substitute.

Mr. Mills and Mr. King paired off.

Mr. Mills would have voted "nay," and Mr. King "yea."

The Convention refused to adopt the substitute by the following vote:

YEAS — Blassingame, Burleson, Brady, Chambers, Cook of Gonzales, DeMorse, Davis of Wharton, Ford, Fleming, Gaither, Graves, Haynes, Lynch, Martin of Hunt, McCabe, McCormick, Pauli, Reagan, Reynolds, Rentfro, Russell of Harrison, Stockdale, Weaver, Whitfield — 24.

NAYS—Allison, Abernathy, Arnim, Blake, Barnett, Bruce, Crawford, Cooke of San Saba, Cardis, Douglas, Dohoney, Darnell, Davis of Brazos, Flournoy, Ferris, German, Holt, Johnson, of Franklin, Johnson of Collin, Kilgore, Killough, Lockett, Lacy, McLean, Mitchell, McKinney of Denton, Moore, Norvell, Nunn, Nugent, Ramey, Robertson of Bell, Ross, Russell of Wood, Spikes, Scott, Sessions, Smith, Stayton, Wade, Whitehead, Wright, West, Waelder — 44.

The question then recurred on the adoption of the original ordinance, introduced by Mr. Russell, of Harrison.

Mr. Mills paired off with Mr. King. Mr. Mills would have voted "nay," and Mr. King "yea."

The Convention then refused to pass the ordinance by the following vote:

YEAS—Blassingame, Brady, Davis of Wharton, Fleming, Graves, Lynch, Martin of Hunt, McCabe, McCormick, Pauli, Reagan, Reynolds, Rentfro, Russell of Harrison, Weaver and Whitfield — 16.

NAYS—Allison, Abernathy, Arnim, Blake, Barnett, Burleson, Bruce, Crawford, Chambers, Cook of Gonzales, Cooke of San Saba, Cardis, Douglas, DeMorse, Dohoney, Darnell, Davis of Brazos, Ford, Flournoy, Ferris, German, Gaither, Holt, Henry of Smith, Haynes, Johnson of Franklin, Kilgore, Killough, Lockett, Lacy, McLean, Mitchell, McKinney of Denton, Moore, Norvell, Nunn, Nugent, Ramey, Robertson of Bell, Ross, Russell of Wood, Spikes, Scott, Sessions, Smith, Stayton, Wade, Whitehead, Wright, West, Waelder — 52.

The following resolution, introduced by Mr. Mills, heretofore, was taken up under the head of unfinished business.

Resolved, That the Secretary of State be requested to furnish this Convention with a statement of the registered vote of the State by counties, as it now stands, and a hundred copies be printed for the use this body.

Lost.

On motion of Mr. Brady, the Convention adjourned until 9 o'clock A. M. to-morrow.

THIRTY-SIXTH DAY.

HALL OF REPRESENTATIVES, }
AUSTIN, TEXAS, October 16, 1875. }

Convention met pursuant to adjournment; roll called; quorum present; prayer by the Rev. B. Abernathy, member from Camp.

Journal of yesterday read and adopted.

Mr. Ramey presented the petition of E. A. Blount, on the subject of framing a constitution.

Mr. Flanagan offered the following resolution:

Resolved, That the Sergeant-at-arms be required to procure the necessary fuel for the use of the Convention, for the remainder of the session.

Adopted.

Mr. Allison offered the following resolution:

Resolved, That all titles to land acquired from Spain, Mexico or Coahuila and Texas, shall be recorded in the county in which the land lies, if not contested, and if contested, suit shall be entered in the county in which the land lies, before the first day of January, 1880, or they shall be forever barred, notwithstanding any disabilities from married women or minors.

Referred to Committee on Lands and Land Offices.

Mr. Erhard offered the following resolution:

From the tenor of the press and public opinion, it is evident that it is extremely doubtful whether the new constitution will be adopted; be it therefore

24

Resolved, That the Governor convene a session of the Legislature, thereby avoiding confusion and dissatisfaction.

Referred to Committee on State Affairs.

On motion of Mr. McLean, the vote adopting the resolution was reconsidered.

Mr. Russell, of Harrison, offered the following amendment to article on Public Lands and Land Office:

Amend the article on Public Lands and Land Office with the following:

" Sec. —.   That claimants to land lying between the Nueces and Rio Grande rivers, and in the counties of El Paso and Presidio, under inchoate or imperfect titles from the government formerly holding sovereignty over said territory, shall have two years from the adoption of this constitution to sue the State for establishment of such claims, according to the extent originally intended to be granted;

"Provided, that suits to establish such claims shall be commenced and prosecuted in the District Court of Travis county, and shall be defended by the Attorney General, and that each party shall have the right of appeal; and provided, further, the rights of claimants in such suits shall be decided according to equity and the original intent of the government making the grant."

Referred to special Committee on Spanish and Mexican Grants.

Mr. West, Chairman of Committee on General Provisions, reported back the following resolution, and recommended its reference to Committee on Taxation and Revenue:

Resolved, That the Legislature nor any county shall ever levy and collect, for county purposes, a tax which shall exceed in the aggregate, in any one year, one-fourth of the amount of the tax levied by the State; save an excess to build courthouses and jails, and to keep the same in repair; and all taxes so raised shall be levied alone on such subjects of taxation as may be levied by the State.

Referred to Committee on General Provisions.

Report adopted, and resolutions referred as asked.

Mr. Weaver offered the following resolution:

WHEREAS, Texas having an historic glory peculiarly her own, as a dependency struggling for liberty against Mexican despotism, and as an independent republican nationality, as well as a great State of the United States of America, and in order that her history, colonial, republican and State, may be compiled and preserved; therefore be it

Resolved, That it shall be the duty of the Legislature to provide for collecting, arranging and safely keeping such records, rolls, correspondence and other documents, civil and military, as may be now in the possession of parties willing to confide their care and preservation to the State.

Referred to Committee on General Provisions.

BUSINESS ON THE TABLE.

The report of Mr. Ford, as chairman of Committee on State Affairs, against the adoption of a resolution forbidding the collection of debts by law at the expiration of two years after the adoption of this resolution, was taken up and adopted.

Also the report against the memorial in favor of establishing "an effectively organized department of health and vital statistics," was taken up and adopted.

Mr. Ballinger presented the memorial of sundry citizens of Brazoria county, asking for an uniform system of sanitary regulations.

Referred to Committee on General Provisions.

"Article —, Executive Department," as engrossed, taken up.

Mr. Abernathy proposed to amend section 21, line 182, by inserting "twenty-five hundred" instead of "two thousand."

Lost by the following vote:

YEAS—Allison, Abernathy, Brown, Blake, Ballinger, Blassingame, Burleson, Brady, Crawford, Cook of Gonzales, Cooke of San Saba, Cline, Cooley, Cardis, DeMorse, Dohoney, Darnell, Davis of Brazos, Davis of Wharton, Ford, Fleming, Ferris, Gaither, Henry of Limestone, King, Kilgore, Killough, Lynch, McCormick, Moore, Nunn, Reagan, Ramey, Rentfro, Ross, Russell of Harrison, Smith, Stockdale, Stayton, Wade, Wright, Weaver, Whitfield, West, Waelder—45.

NAYS—Arnim, Abner, Barnett, Bruce, Chambers, Douglas, Dillard, Flournoy, Flanagan, German, Graves, Holt, Haynes, Johnson of Franklin, Lockett, Lacy, McLean, Martin of Navarro, Martin of Hunt, McCabe, Mills, McKinney of Denton, McKinney of Walker, Murphy, Norvell, Nugent, Pauli, Reynolds, Robertson of Bell, Russell of Wood, Spikes, Scott—32.

Mr. McLean proposed the following amendment to section 2, line 6:

Strike out the words "except Secretary of State," and in section 21, line 174, strike out all after the word "State" down to and including the word "elect" in line 176, and insert "who shall hold his office for two years and until his successor is duly qualified."

Mr. McLean's amendment lost by the following vote:

YEAS—Abner, Blassingame, Brady, Cooley, Cardis, Dillard, Davis of Wharton, Flanagan, German, Johnson of Franklin,

Lockett, McLean, Martin of Hunt, McCabe, Mills, Mitchell, McKinney of Denton, McKinney of Walker, Moore, Pauli, Reynolds, Rentfro, Russell of Harrison, Scott, Weaver, West—26.

NAYS—Allison, Abernathy, Arnim, Brown, Blake, Ballinger, Barnett, Burleson, Bruce, Crawford, Chambers, Cook of Gonzales, Cooke of San Saba, Cline, Douglas, DeMorse, Dohoney, Darnell, Davis of Brazos, Ford, Flournoy, Fleming, Ferris, Gaither, Graves, Holt, Henry of Smith, Henry of Limestone, Haynes, King, Kilgore, Killough, Lacy, Lynch, Martin of Navarro, McCormick, Murphy, Norvell, Nunn, Nugent, Reagan, Ramey, Robertson of Bell, Ross, Russell of Wood, Spikes, Sessions, Smith, Stockdale, Stayton, Wade, Wright, Whitfield, Waelder—54.

Mr. Weaver moved to reconsider the vote refusing to increase the salary of the Secretary of State to $2500.

Mr. Mills moved to lay the motion on the table.

Carried.

Mr. Waelder proposed to amend sec. 23, line 208, by striking out the word "article" and inserting "section."

Adopted.

Mr. King proposed to amend sec. 9, lines 55, 56 and 57:

Amend sec. 9 by substituting in lines 55, 56 and 57, beginning at the word "He" and ending with the word "vouchers," by substituting the following: "He shall account to the Legislature for all public moneys received and paid out by him from any funds subject to his order with vouchers, and shall accompany his message with a statement of the same."

Adopted.

Mr. Ferris proposed to amend sec. 23, line 207, by striking out the words, "or other compensations."

Adopted.

Mr. Dohoney proposed to amend sec. 4, line 28, by inserting after the word "installed:" "He shall not be eligible to election more than four years out of six successive years."

Lost.

Mr. Moore proposed to amend sec. 4, line 27, by striking out the word "two" and inserting "four."

Mr. Mills moved to lay the amendment on the table.

The Convention refused to lay on the table by the following vote:

YEAS—Allison, Abernathy, Abner, Brown, Blassingame, Barnett, Bruce, Chambers, Cook of Gonzales, Cooley, Douglas, Dillard, Dohoney, Darnell, Davis of Wharton, Ford, Flournoy,

Flanagan, German, Graves, Holt, Haynes, Johnson of Franklin, Martin of Navarro, Martin of Hunt, Mills, McKinney of Denton, Norvell, Nugent, Russell of Harrison, Russell of Wood, Spikes, Scott, Sessions, Wade, West—36.

NAYS—Arnim, Ballinger, Burleson, Brady, Crawford, Cooke, of San Saba, Cline DeMorse, Davis of Brazos, Erhard, Fleming, Ferris, Gaither, Henry of Smith, Henry of Limestone, Kilgore, Killough, Lockett, Lacy, Lynch, McLean, McKinney of Walker, McCormick, Moore, Murphy, Nunn, Pauli, Reagan, Ramey, Rentfro, Robertson of Bell, Ross, Smith, Stayton, Wright, Whitfield, Waelder—37.

Mr. Graves moved the previous question on the whole article. Lost.

The question then recurring on Mr. Moore's amendment, it was lost by the following vote:

YEAS—Arnim, Ballinger, Burleson, Cline, DeMorse, Davis of Brazos, Erhard, Fleming, Ferris, Gaither, Henry of Smith, Henry of Limestone, Kilgore, Lockett, Lynch, McCormick, Moore, Murphy, Reagan, Ramey, Robertson of Bell, Ross, Smith, Stayton, Weaver, Whitfield, Waelder—27.

NAYS—Allison, Abernathy, Abner, Brown, Blassingame, Barnett, Brady, Bruce, Crawford, Chambers, Cook of Gonzales, Cooke of San Saba, Cooley, Douglas, Dillard, Dohoney, Darnell, Davis of Wharton, Flanagan, German, Graves, Holt, Haynes, Johnson of Franklin, Killough, Lacy, McLean, Martin of Navarro, Martin of Hunt, Mills, Mitchell, McKinney of Denton, McKinney of Walker, Norvell, Nunn, Nugent, Pauli, Rentfro, Russell of Wood, Scott, Sessions, Wade, Wright, West—44.

Mr. Reagan proposed to amend section 5, line 32; Strike out the words "and no more."

Laid ont the table.

Mr. Ballinger proposed to amend section 24, line 218: Strike out "shall" and insert "may."

Lost.

Mr. Reagan proposed to amend section 11, line 65, and line 71, by inserting the words "of punishment" after the word "commutation."

Adopted.

Mr. Ferris offered the following amendment:

Amend section 14, line 112, by striking out the words "while approving" and inserting the words "and approve."

Adopted.

Mr. Brown offered the following amendment:

Insert after the word "public," in line 231, the words "having regard to the convenience of population, and not to exceed ten."

Adopted.

Mr. Waelder moved to reconsider the vote just taken.

Carried.

The question then recurring on the passage of the amendment, it was lost by the following vote:

[Mr. Reagan in the chair.]

YEAS—Brown, Blake, Chambers, Cline, Dillard, DeMorse, Erhard, Ford, Gaither, Graves, Henry of Limestone, Lockett, Lacy, Lynch, McLean, Mitchell, McKinney of Denton, Moore, Murphy, Reagan, Ramey, Rentfro, Robertson of Bell, Russell of Wood, Whitfield—25.

NAYS—Allison, Abernathy, Arnim, Abner, Ballinger, Blassingame, Barnett, Burleson, Bruce, Crawford, Cook of Gonzales, Cooke of San Saba, Cooley, Douglas, Dohoney, Darnell, Davis of Brazos, Fleming, Ferris, Flanagan, Holt, Henry of Smith, Johnson of Franklin, King, Kilgore, Killough, Martin of Navarro, Martin of Hunt, Mills, McKinney of Walker, McCormick, Norvell, Nunn, Nugent, Pauli, Ross, Russell of Harrison, Spikes, Scott, Smith, Stockdale, Stayton, Wade, Wright, Weaver, West, Waelder—47.

Mr. Ferris moved to strike out the words "they are," in section 3, line 51, and insert "it is."

Lost.

Mr. Dillard moved to amend section 5, line 32, by striking out the word "also."

Adopted.

Mr. Kilgore proposed to amend section 15, line 127, by striking out all after the word "vote" "to" and insert the word "in."

Lost.

Mr. Cline proposed to amend by adding to section 26 the words "and keep a record of original acts, with the signatures of the parties and witnesses, executed before them, and deliver same to their successors, or the county clerk."

Lost.

Mr. Fleming moved the previous question on the passage of the article.

The yeas and nays were ordered, and the ordinance passed by the following vote:

YEAS—Allison, Abernathy, Arnim, Abner, Brown, Blake, Ballinger, Blassingame, Barnett, Burleson, Bruce, Crawford, Chambers, Cook of Gonzales, Cooke of San Saba, Douglas, Dillard, DeMorse, Dohoney, Darnell, Davis of Brozos, Davis of Wharton, Ford, Fleming, Ferris, Flanagan, German, Gaither, Graves, Holt, Henry of Smith, Henry of Limestone, Haynes, Johnson of Franklin, Kilgore, Lacy, Lynch, McLean, Martin of Navarro, McCabe, McKinney of Denton, McKinney of Walker, McCormick, Moore, Murphy, Norvell, Nugent, Pauli, Reagan, Ramey, Reynolds, Robertson of Bell, Ross, Russell of Wood, Spikes, Scott, Sessions, Stockdale, Stayton, Wade, Wright, Weaver, Whitfield, West, Waelder—65.

NAYS—Brady, Cline, Lockett, Martin of Hunt, Mitchell, Nunn, Rentfro, Russell of Harrison—8.

The following was then taken from the table and read:

"Every member of the Legislature, before entering upon the duties of his position, shall have the following oath administered to him: 'I will faithfully represent the interests of my constituency, and the general interests of the State; I will observe and sustain the constitution of the State and the constitution of the United States; and I have not, since my election, received, and will not, during the continuance of my term of office, receive any gift, accommodation, free ticket, or compensation from any railroad or other corporate company other than shall be extended to citizens of the State generally; nor any unusual accommodation or compensation from any private individual.'"

Referred to Committee on General Provisions.

Report on suffrage taken up on its third reading.

Mr. McCormick proposed to amend section 1, line 6, after word "of," the words "murder, manslaughter, theft."

Mr. McKinney, of Walker, offered as a substitute the following:

Add to line 7 the words "or other felony."

Mr. McCormick accepted Mr. McKinney's amendment.

Mr. Dohoney proposed to amend section 1, line 6, by striking out all after the word "convicted," and inserting the words "of any felony."

Lost.

Mr. Nugent proposed as a substitute to amend section 1, line 7, by adding "murder or theft amounting to felony."

Mr. Flournoy proposed the following:

Insert the words "all persons convicted of any felony except manslaughter."

Accepted by Mr. Nugent.

Mr. McCormick proposed the following as a substitute for the fourth sub-division and amendments:

"No person, while kept in any asylum, or confined in any prison, or who has been convicted of a felony, or who is of unsound mind, shall be allowed to vote or hold any office in this State."

Mr. Nunn asked that the following be read for information:

In line 7, section 1, add "assault to commit rape, murder, assault to commit murder and theft, punished as a felony, embezzlement, swindling, an assault with intent to commit robbery, passing counterfeit money, assault with intent to maim, burglary, false swearing, sodomy, bigamy, abortion."

On motion of Mr. Allison, the Convention adjourned till 9 o'clock A. M. Monday.

THIRTY-SEVENTH DAY.

HALL OF REPRESENTATIVES,
AUSTIN, TEXAS, October 18, 1875.

Convention met pursuant to adjournment; roll called; quorum present.

Journal of Saturday read and adopted.

Mr. Ferris as chairman of Committee on Railroad Corporations, reported as follows:

COMMITTEE ROOM, }
AUSTIN, October 16, 1875. }

To the Hon. E. B. Pickett, President of the Convention.

The Committee on Railroad Corporations, to whom was referred various resolutions, beg leave to report that they have carefully considered the same, as well as the entire subject to which they relate, and now recommend that the following sections be adopted by the Convention, and incorporated into the constitution.

J. W. FERRIS, Chairman.

"RAILROADS.

"Sec. 1. Any railroad corporation or association, organized under the law for the purpose, shall have the right to construct and operate a railroad between any points within this State, and to connect at the State line with railroads of other States. Every railroad company shall have the right, with its road, to intersect, connect with or cross any other railroad, and shall receive and transport each the others passengers, tonnage and cars, loaded or empty, without delay or discrimination, under such regulations as shall be prescribed by law.

"Sec. 2. Railways heretofore constructed, or that may hereafter be constructed in this State, are hereby declared public highways, and railroad companies common carriers. The Legislature shall pass laws to correct abuses and prevent unjust discrimination and extortion in the rates of freight and passenger tariffs on the different railroads in this State, and shall, from time to time, pass laws establishing reasonable maximum rates of charges for the transportation of passengers and freight on said railroads, and enforce all such laws by adequate penalties.

"Sec. 3. Every railroad or other corporation, organized or doing business in this State, under the laws or authority thereof, shall have and maintain a public office or place in this State for the transaction of its business, where transfers of stock shall be made, and where shall be kept for public inspection books in which shall be recorded the amount of capital stock subscribed, the names of the owners of the stock, the amounts owned by them respectively, the amount of stock paid, and by whom, the transfer of said stock, with the date of the transfer, the amount of its assets and liabilities, and the names and places of residence of its officers. The directors of every railroad company shall hold one meeting annually in this State, public notice of which shall be given thirty days previously, and shall report annually under oath to the Comptroller, or some officer designated by law, all of their acts and doings, which report shall include such matters relating to railroads as may be prescribed by law. The Legislature shall pass laws enforcing, by suitable penalties, the provisions of this section.

"Sec. 4. The rolling stock and all other movable property belonging to any railroad company or corporation in this State, shall be considered personal property, and its real and personal property shall be liable to execution and sale in the same manner as the property of individuals, and the Legislature shall pass no law exempting any such property from execution and sale.

"Sec. 5. No railroad or other corporation, or the lessees, purchasers or managers of any railroad corporation shall consolidate the stock, property or franchises of such corporation with, or lease, or purchase the works or franchises of, or in any way control any railroad corporation owning or having under its control a parallel or competing line; nor shall any officer of such railroad corporation act as an officer of any other railroad corporation owning or having the control of a parallel or competing line.

Sec. 6. If any railroad company organized under the laws of this State, shall consolidate by sale or otherwise, with any railroad company organized under the laws of any other State, or of the United States, the same shall not thereby become a foreign corporation; but the courts of this State shall retain jurisdiction in all matters which may arise as if said consolidation had not taken place. In no case shall any consolidation take place, except upon public notice of at least sixty days to all stockholders, in such manner as may be provided by law.

Sec. 7. No law shall be passed by the Legislature granting the right to construct and operate a street railroad within any city, town, village, or on any public highway, without first acquiring the consent of the local authorities having control of the street or highway proposed to be occupied by such street railroad.

Sec. 8. No railroad corporation in existence at the time of the adoption of the constitution shall have the benefit of any future legislation, except on condition of complete acceptance of all the provisions of this constitution applicable to railroads.

On motion of Mr. Allison two hundred copies ordered to be printed.

Mr. Stayton submitted the following minority report:

COMMITTEE ROOM,
AUSTIN, October 18, 1875.

To the Hon. E. B. Pickett, President of the Convention:

The undersigned members of your Committee upon Railroad Corporations, while they believe that many of the recommendations contained in the report of the committee are proper and necessary for the protection of the people, yet they can not concur in the recommendations as an entirety.

JOHN W. STAYTON,
WEBSTER FLANAGAN.

On motion of Mr. Flournoy, Messrs. Johnson, of Franklin, Martin, of Navarro, and Crawford were added to Committee on Private Corporations.

Mr. DeMorse, chairman of Committee on Revenue and Taxation, made the following report:

To the Hon. E. B. Pickett, President of the Convention:

Your committee, to whom has been intrusted the consideration of the question of revenue and taxation, in the correct solution of which are involved the necessity of immediate relief to the ever-burdened tax-payers of the State, and at the same time the antagonistic requirements for increase of revenue and avoidance of further sale of State responsibilities, have endeavored to defne a system of taxation based upon consideration of natural rights and upon correct principles of political economy, limiting the assessment and expenditure strictly to legitimate objects of government and to so guard the definement as to prevent future variance and abuses.

With these objects in view, they have directed me to report the accompanying article and ask its consideration by the Convention as a portion of the constitution:

"ARTICLE —.

"REVENUE AND TAXATION.

"Section 1. Taxation in this State, as a rule, shall be equal and uniform, and this general principle shall only be departed from in cases of great public emergency, or for the purpose of repressing occupations deemed adverse to the god of society.

"Sec. 2. Occupation taxes, being in their nature an infringement upon natural rights of persons, shall be laid only to discourage pursuits immoral in their tendency or not strictly useful, or as a discrimination against itinerant traders.

"Sec. 3. Ad valorem taxation shall be the rule, and whenever it may be necessary to depart from it for extraordinary reasons, the extension shall first commence by taxation of incomes.

"Sec. 4. The legislative power to tax shall extend only to the levying of such an amount as shall suffice to pay the necessary expenses of the government of the State, the support of its asylums for the unfortunate; provision for the ordinary expenses of the courts (including cost of libraries) and the payment of their officers; the public defence; the maintenance of the peace; the arrest of criminals; the survey of the public lands or geological survey of any portion of the State; the maintenance of the public schools; the enforcement of the laws; the payment of the floating or unfunded debt; the maintenance of quarantine regulations; and to the payment of the principal and interest of the bonded public debt, and shall not extend to any system of public improvements, except the erection of necessary public buildings, and the improvement and ornamentation of the grounds attached thereto; and any proposition to appropriate public money for any purpose deemed of public benefit, and not herein stated, including the erection of any public building whose cost shall exceed a half million dollars, shall be referred by action of the Legislature to the people at a general election, and two-thirds of the popular vote approving, may be authorized by subsequent approval of a majority of the Legislature, for a levy not exceeding in amount two per cent. of the property in the State returned for taxation.

"Sec. 5. No taxes shall be levied for the construction or improvement of any roads.

"Sec. 6. *Ad valorem* taxation for State uses shall never exceed fifty cents upon the hundred dollars value of property; nor shall general county taxation (except for the support of the indigent) exceed one-half the general State tax; *provided,* that all counties shall have the right to levy tax for the payment of indebtedness already accrued and for the establishment of county poor-farms, first availing themselves of all convict labor which may be provided by this constitution.

"Sec. 7. The police of commissioner's court of any county desiring to build a courthouse, jail or other public building, or to establish a county farm for the maintenance of the poor, may, at any time, on sixty days' notice in the public prints of the county, or by posters in large type, at all public places, if there shall be no public prints, submit to the tax-payers of the county a proposition to authorize the work required, with responsible estimates of the cost thereof, and if at the election for that purpose a majority of the tax-payers of the county shall approve the erection or establishment of the proposed improvement, then the legal authorities may proceed to contract therefor, and provide for the completion of the proposed work, in the manner stated and authorized by the popular vote.

"Sec. 8. The municipal taxation of cities and incorporated towns shall be such amount as a majority of the tax-payers upon property may sanction by popular vote, to be taken at the general elections for municipal officers, upon submission of direct propositions, not to exceed annually two per cent. upon the property therein returned for taxation.

"Sec. 9. Taxes shall be levied upon all money belonging to individuals, associations, or corporate companies, in possession, on deposit, or loaned at interest; and on public or corporate bonds or stocks, or solvent individual responsibilities; and this tax shall not be evaded by temporary removal of such money, bonds or stocks beyond the limits of the State at the usual period of assessment or temporary conversion into other property, to be rescinded at will.

"Sec. 10. The Legislature may levy an income tax upon all agencies of foreign companies doing business within the State, and not otherwise to be reached for purposes of taxation, including transportation companies by steam or sailing vessels regularly engaged in transportation of passengers or freight to and from the ports of the State.

"Sec. 11. Municipal corporations and voting precincts shall have power to determine by a vote of the majority of the qualified electors, to be ascertained in some mode to be defined by law, whether the sale of spirituous liquors shall be permitted in their midst, and the action of any license law which may be passed by the Legislature shall be subject to this local option.

"Sec. 12.   The investment by treasures or other offiecers to whom the collection or safe-keeping of public money is intrusted, of any portion of said money for their own use or for profit, or the traffic in State or county warrants by such custodians of the public moneys, or comptrollers, or county clerks, having the issuance of such warrants, whether done directly or by collusion with other persons, shall be deemed a felony, and punished under the laws of the State as such.

"Sec. 13.   The State, nor any county, or city, or town thereof, shall ever subscribe stock to any enterprise, railroad, or other corporate body, nor shall any citizen ever be taxed either by the State, or any county, city, or other political division thereof, as a gratuity to any individual, corporate body or other association; nor shall the State, or any county, city or town thereof, loan its credit or in any manner become responsible for the indebtedness of any individual, association or corporate company.

"Sec. 14.   There shall be elected in each county of the State, an assessor of taxes, who shall, under the instruction of the Comptroller of the State, assess all taxable property situate in such county, and forward the rolls containing such assessment to the Comptroller, and keep a copy thereof in a bound book as a county record, in the office of the County Clerk, subject to the inspection of the Police Court, the Board of Equalization, and every citizen interested, and shall deliver to the collector of the county another full and complete copy, on all of which copies the names of the taxpayers shall be alphabetically arranged, and opposite to each name a continuous statement of the property rendered by each, or assessed against him, and its assessed value and the tax due thereon.

"Sec. 15.   The sheriff of each county shall be the collector of taxes therefor, and he shall, upon the rolls or record furnished him by the county assessor, and such additional information as he shall receive from the Comptroller of the State, proceed within the times fixed by law, to collect the taxes due from each individual in the county, and every corporate company or association reported to him as indebted for taxes, and he shall promptly, at the end of every month, pay over to the county treasurer such portion of his collections as may belong to the county, and remit to the Comptroller such portion of his collections as belong to the State, which payment shall be credited upon the record by the Comptroller, and the usual deposit certificate given to the sheriff or his representative, and the money remitted shall then be paid to the State Treasurer, who shall give his receipt therefor.

"Sec. 16. The Legislature shall, at its first session after the adoption of this constitution, determine by law the rate of compensation to be paid assessors of taxes and collectors of taxes, either by fixed salary, proportioned to amount of business, or by commissions upon amounts assessed or collected, in no case exceeding three thousand dollars in amount.

"Sec. 17. All real property rendered by any individual, or assessed against him by the county assessor, or the Comptroller of the State, shall be held liable for all his taxes, whether upon real or personal property, and no conveyance of real estate, after rendition for tax, and prior to the usual period for collection, shall relieve the purchaser from this lien in behalf of the State.

"Sec. 18. All the property of any railroad company, or any single proprietor of a railroad, shall be returned in the several counties in which said property lies, including so much of the roadbed as shall be in each county. The rolling stock may be reported in gross in the county where the principal office of the company is located, and the tax paid upon it shall be apportioned by the Comptroller, *pro rata,* among the several counties through which the road passes, as a part of their tax assets.

"Sec. 19. There shall be exempted from taxation only churches, public asylums, county property used for public purposes; the property used by universities, colleges and schools; libraries (except law and medical libraries); philosophical apparatus in use; the lands and other property used exclusively for agricultural fairs; clothing in use; and household and kitchen furniture to the value of two hundred and fifty dollars.

"Sec. 20. The Legislature at its biennial sessions shall make appropriations sufficient for the support of the State government for the ensuing two years, and provide for arrearages resulting from deficiency of previous appropriations, and shall levy a tax adequate to meet these requirements, and to prevent the creation of additional debt, and the consequent impairment of the credit of the State.

"Sec. 21. Landed property shall be assessed in the county where it lies, and the tax may be paid in that county or in the county where the owner is resident, or to the Comptroller of the State.

"Sec. 22. Lands not rendered for assessment by the owners shall be assessed by the assessor of each county, and in no case shall be valued at less than fifty cents per acre. All proceedings to enforce the collection of taxes thereon shall be *in rem.* without reference to the owner or claimant, and taxes on land are declared to be a special lien thereon.

"Sec. 23. The Legislature shall provide by law for summary proceedings in the District Courts to enforce collection of taxes by judgment and sale as fast as tax shall become due and be unpaid, all being proceeded against in gross, but judgments rendered in severalty, after publication; and each tract proceeded against being described unmistakably; and no proceedings which comply with these requisites to be held invalid for want of form; and the deed of conveyance made by the tax collector to the purchaser shall vest a perfect title, subject to impeachment only for fraud or want of jurisdiction, the former owner having the right of redemption for two years from date of deed to purchaser, upon payment of eight times the amount of purchase money paid.

"Sec. 24. Lands in unorganized counties shall be assessed and proceeded against in the counties to which such unorganized counties shall be attached for judicial purposes.

"Sec. 25. The sheriff, county clerk and chief justice shall compose a board of equalization in each county, to hear appeals by property holders and determine the just value of the property rendered for taxation.

"Sec. 26. The Comptroller of the State shall prepare a list of all lands, assessed or unassessed, for each separate county, and assess upon the portion unrendered all the present and back tax due thereon, and transmit to each collector of taxes the list prepared for his county; upon which list the collector shall proceed as herein prescribed.

"Sec. 27. The fiscal year shall commence the first of May, and end the last of April; assessments of taxes shall date from the first day of January of each year, and the collections shall commence on the first of December and shall be closed by the first day of April following, until otherwise provided by law."

On motion of Mr. Allison, 200 copies of the report and article were ordered printed.

UNFINISHED BUSINESS.

Article ——, "Suffrage," with pending amendments, taken up.

On motion of Mr. Scott, the pending amendments were laid on the table.

Mr. Allison offered the following amendment:

Section 1. Add "Provided pardons by the Governor shall restore the right of voting."

Mr. Kilgore offered the following as a substitute for the amendment:

Add to line 7, subdivision 4, the words, "unless pardoned by the Governor."

Accepted.

Mr. Ferris proposed to amend by adding the following to line 7:

"Unless relieved by a pardon or by act of the Legislature."

Lost.

Mr. DeMorse offered the following as a substitute for the amendment:

"*Provided,* That the privilege of franchise may at any time be restored by the Governor upon application by the party disfranchised, supported by the recommendation of citizens of good character residing in his own county."

Lost.

Mr. Reagan offered the following amendment to section 1:

Strike out lines 6 and 7, and add: "And the Legislature shall provide for the cases in which persons shall be excluded from voting on account of their having ben convicted of felonies."

Mr. Allison's amendment was lost.

Mr. Crawford called for a division of the question on Mr. Reagan's amendment.

Ruled out of order.

The hour having arrived for considering the special order, viz: "Article —, Legislative Department," on motion of Mr. Scott it was postponed until the pending business should be disposed of.

Mr. Reagan withdrew his amendment.

Mr. Dohoney moved to amend section 1 by striking out the words, "bribery, perjury, forgery, arson, rape or robbery," and insert, "all persons convicted of felony, subject to such exceptions as the Legislature may make."

Mr. Dohoney moved to reconsider the vote taken yesterday refusing to adopt his amendment to section 1 by striking out all of line 6 after the word "convicted," and inserting the words "of any felony."

On motion of Mr. Flanagan, the main question was ordered.

Mr. Dohoney's amendment was adopted by the following vote:

YEAS—Allison, Abernathy, Arnim, Abner, Brown, Blake, Ballinger, Barnett, Burleson, Bruce, Chambers, Cook of Gonzales, Cooke of San Saba, Douglas, Dillard, DeMorse, Dohoney, Dar-

nell, Davis of Brazos, Davis of Wharton, Erhard, Ford,
Flournoy, Fleming, Ferris, Flanagan, German, Gaither, Graves,
Holt, Henry of Smith, Henry of Limestone, Haynes, Johnson
of Franklin, King, Kilgore, Killough, Lacy, Lynch, McLean,
Martin of Navarro, Martin of Hunt, McCabe, McKinney of
Denton, McKinney of Walker, McCormick, Murphy, Norvell,
Nunn, Pauli, Reagan, Ramey, Robertson of Bell, Robeson of
Fayette, Ross, Russell of Harrison, Russell of Wood, Spikes,
Sessions, Smith, Stockdale, Stayton, Wade, Whitehead, Weaver,
Whitfield, West, Waelder—68.

NAYS—Crawford, Cline, Cooley, Lockett, Mills, Mitchell,
Reynolds, Rentfro, Scott, Wright—10.

Mr. Allison offered the following amendment:

Section 2, strike out line 22, and add: "Provided that electors in unorganized counties may vote in any county of the district to which their county is attached."

On motion of Mr. Fleming laid on the table.

Mr. Brown moved to strike out in line 29, section 2, the words "district or."

Carried.

Mr. Kilgore offered the following amendments:

Insert at the end of section 2 the words: "Provided that electors living in any unorganized county may vote at any election precinct in the county to which such county is attached."

Adopted.

Also amend section 2, line 31, by inserting after the word "the" the word "election."

Adopted.

Mr. Wade proposed to strike out "class" in line 30 and insert "persons."

Adopted.

The question then recurring upon the passage of the article, the yeas and nays were called and the article passed by the following vote:

YEAS—Mr. President, Allison, Abernathy, Arnim, Abner, Brown, Blake, Ballinger, Blassingame, Barnett, Bruce, Chambers, Cook of Gonzales, Cline, Douglas, Dillard, DeMorse, Darnell, Davis of Brazos, Davis of Wharton, Erhard, Ford, Flournoy, Ferris, Flanagan, German, Gaither, Graves, Holt, Henry of Smith, Henry of Limestone, Haynes, Johnson of Franklin, King, Killough, Lockett, Lacy, Lynch, McLean, Martin of Navarro, Martin of Hunt, McCabe, McKinney of Denton, McKinney of Walker, Murphy, Norvell, Nugent,

25

Ramey, Ross, Russell of Harrison, Russell of Wood, Spikes, Scott, Sessions, Smith, Stayton, Wade, Whitehead, Weaver, Whitfield, Waelder—61.

Nays—Brady, Crawford, Dohoney, Fleming, Kilgore, Mills, Mitchell, McCormick, Nunn, Pauli, Reagan, Reynolds, Rentfro, Robertson of Bell, Robeson of Fayette, Stockdale, Wright, West—18.

The special order, viz: "Article —, Legislative Department," was again taken up.

Mr. Abernathy offered the following as a substitute for the pending amendment and section 51:

"Sec. 51. The Legislature shall have no power to make any grant or authorize the making of any grant of public money or lands to any individual, association of individuals, municipal or other corporations whatever; *provided,* that this shall not be construed so as to prevent the actual settler from his home on public land, as provided by law; *and provided further,* that this shall not be so construed as to prevent the grant of aid in the case of public calamity."

Mr. Fleming moved to lay the substitute and pending amendment on the table.

Carried by the following vote:

Yeas—Allison, Abner, Blake, Ballinger, Burleson, Cook of Gonzales, Cline, Cooley, Cardis, Dohoney, Davis of Brazos, Davis of Wharton, Ford, Flournoy, Fleming, Flanagan, Gaither, Henry of Smith, Henry of Limestone, Haynes, Johnson of Franklin, King, Kilgore, Killough, Lockett, Lacy, Lynch, McLean, Martin of Navarro, McCabe, Mitchell, McKinney of Walker, McCormick, Murphy, Nunn, Pauli, Reagan, Reynolds, Ross, Russell of Harrison, Sessions, Smith, Stockdale, Stayton, Whitehead, Whitfield, Waelder—47.

Nays—Abernathy, Arnim, Brown, Blassingame, Barnett, Brady, Bruce, Crawford, Chambers, Cooke of San Saba, Douglas, DeMorse, Darnell, German, Graves, Holt, Martin of Hunt, Mills, McKinney of Denton, Norvell, Nugent, Ramey, Rentfro, Robertson of Bell, Robeson of Fayette, Russell of Wood, Spikes, Scott, Wade, Wright, Weaver, West—32.

Mr. Kilgore offered the following substitute for section 2 of the article:

"Sec. 2. The Senate shall consist of ...... members, and the House of Representatives of ...... members, until the first apportionment after the adoption of this constitution, when, or at any apportionment thereafter, the House of Representatives may be increased by a vote of two-thirds of the Legislature."

Mr. Martin, of Hunt, offered the following as a substitute for the substitute and section :

"Sec. 2. The Senate shall consist of thirty-one members, and shall never be increased above this unmber. The House of Representatives shall consist of ninety members until the first apportionment after the adoption of this constitution, when, or at any apportionment thereafter, the number of representatives may be increased by the Legislature upon the ratio of not more than one representative for every 15,000 inhabitants; *provided,* the number of representatives shall never exceed one hundred and fifty."

Mr. Chambers proposed to strike out "thirty" and insert "thirty-one," in the substitute.

Accepted by Mr. Martin, and substitute adopted.

Mr. Martin, of Navarro, offered the following substitute for the section :

"Sec. 2. The Senate shall consist of twenty-five members and the House of Representatives of seventy-five members until the first apportionment after the adoption of this constitution, when, or at any apportionment thereafter, both houses may be increased by the Legislature — the Senate not to exceed thirty-three members and the House of Representatives not to exceed one hundred members."

On motion of Mr. Mills laid on the table.

Mr. Brown moved to amend the section by inserting "ninety-three" instead of "ninety" members of the House of Representatives.

Adopted.

Mr. Robertson, of Bell, offered the following substitute for section 51 :

"Section 51. The Legislature shall have no power to make any grant, or authorize the making of any grant, of public money, public land or thing of value to any individual, association of individuals, municipal or other corporation whatsoever; *provided,* that this shall not be so construed as to prevent the grant of aid in case of public calamity or the grant of headrights to actual settlers on the public domain."

Ruled out of order, the substance of the same having been embodied in the amendment offered by Mr. Abernathy and voted down by the Convention. Yet the Chair submitted to the Convention the question as to whether the Convention would entertain the substitute.

Lost by the following vote:

Yeas—Allison, Abernathy, Arnim, Blassingame, Barnett, Brady, Bruce, Chambers, Cooke of San Saba, Douglas, Dillard,

DeMorse, Darnell, Ferris, German, Graves, Holt, Killough, McLean, Martin of Hunt, Mills, McKinney of Denton, Norvell, Nugent, Robertson of Bell, Robeson of Fayette, Russell of Wood, Spikes, Scott, Wade, Wright, Weaver—32.

NAYS—Abner, Brown, Blake, Ballinger, Burleson, Crawford, Cook of Gonzales, Cline, Cooley, Cardis, Dohoney, Davis of Wharton, Erhard, Ford, Flournoy, Fleming, Flanagan, Gaither, Henry of Limestone, Haynes, Johnson of Franklin, King, Kilgore, Lockett, Lacy, Lynch, Martin of Navarro, McCabe, Mitchell, McKinney of Walker, McCormick, Moore, Nunn, Pauli, Reagan, Reynolds, Rentfaro, Ross, Russell of Harrison, Sessions, Smith, Stockdale, Stayton, Whitehead, Whitfield, Waelder—46.

Mr. Waelder offered the following amendment:

In section 5 strike out the words "the first session under this constitution shall convene on the — day of — 1876."

Adopted.

Mr. DeMorse offered the following substitute for section 49:

"The Legislature shall have no power to create a public debt under any circumstances, exceeding in amount three hundred thousand dollars, and no debt whatever except in case of invasion."

Mr. McLean offered the following amendment to the amendment:

"Nor shall the county court of any county, or the municipal authority of any town or city, ever create any debt against such county, town or city; *provided,* that the towns or cities situated on the coast may incur debt in the erection of works for the safety and protection of life and property against storms, by the vote of those who pay taxes on property in such towns and cities."

[Mr. Stockdale in the chair.]

Mr. Dillard moved to lay the two amendments on the table.

Carried by the following vote:

YEAS—Abner, Blake, Ballinger, Burleson, Brady, Crawford, Cook of Gonzales, Cooke of San Saba, Cooley, Cardis, Dillard, Erhard, Flournoy, Fleming, Ferris, Flanagan, Graves, Holt, Haynes, King, Kilgore, Killough, Lockett, Lynch, Martin of Navarro, McCabe, McKinney of Walker, McCormick, Moore, Murphy, Norvell, Pauli, Reagan, Reynolds, Rentfro, Ross, Russell of Harrison, Spikes, Scott, Sessions, Smith, Stockdale, Stayton, Wade, Whitfield, West, Waelder—47.

NAYS—Allison, Abernathy, Arnim, Brown, Blassingame, Barnett, Bruce, Chambers, DeMorse, Dohoney, Darnell, German,

Gaither, Henry of Smith, Henry of Limestone, Johnson of Franklin, Lacy, McLean, Martin of Hunt, Mills, Mitchell, Nunn, Nugent, Robertson of Bell, Robeson of Fayette, Russell of Wood, Whitehead, Wright—28.

On motion of Mr. Nunn, the Convention adjourned.

EVENING SESSION—2½ o'clock.

Convention met; roll called; quorum present.

Pending question, viz: "Article —. Legislative Department," taken up.

Mr. Darnell offered the following additional section:

"Sec. —. No exclusive privileges shall ever be granted to any corporation organized for the purpose of constructing and running railroad or railroads, or to any other association of individuals for any purpose whatsoever that has heretofore been, or may be hereafter created over any of the public domain, but the said domain shall be held equally open to location by all who may have a just claim against the same."

Mr. Flournoy offered the following as a substitute for the section:

"Sec. —. The Legislature shall not hereafter have the power to reserve from location any particular part of the public domain for future location by any railroad or other incorporate company or any private person."

Mr. Wade offered the following amendment to the substitute:

"No reservation of public land shall hereafter be made, except the right of way in favor of any corporate company, and all such reservations heretofore made shall be void; *provided,* that no company shall be deprived of its rights in compliance of its charter."

Mr. Stockdale moved to refer the section, the substitute and the amendment to the Committee on Public Lands and Land Office.

Carried by the following vote:

YEAS—Allison, Abernathy, Abner, Brown, Ballinger, Burleson, Crawford, Cook of Gonzales, Cooley, Cardis, Dillard, DeMorse, Dohoney, Davis of Brazos, Erhard, Ford, Flournoy, Fleming, Ferris, Gaither, Henry of Smith, Henry of Limestone, Haynes, King, Lockett, Lynch, McLean, Martin of Navarro, McCabe, Mitchell, McKiney of Walker, McCormick, Moore, Murphy, Norvell, Pauli, Reagan, Ramey, Ross, Russell of Harrison, Sessions, Smith, Stockdale, Stayton, Wade, Whitehead, Wright, Whitfield, West, Waelder—50.

NAYS—Arnim, Blake, Blassingame, Barnett, Bruce, Chambers, Darnell, German, Graves, Holt, Lacy, Martin of Hunt, Mills, McKinney of Denton, Nugent, Robertson of Bell, Robeson of Fayette, Russell of ·Wood, Spikes, Scott, Weaver—21.

Mr. Ramey made the following report:

COMMITTEE ROOM,
AUSTIN, October 18, 1875.

To the Hon. E. B. Pickett, President of the Convention:

SIR—Your Committee on Engrossed and Enrolled Ordinances would respectfully report to your honorable body that they have carefully examined and compared " Article —, Bill of Rights," and find the same correctly engrossed. Respectfully,

WM. NEAL RAMEY, Chairman.

Mr. Mills proposed to amend section 25, line 126, by adding " or shall a county be entitled to a Senator, unless it has the requisite number of qualified electors."

Lost.

Mr. Brown proposed to amend as follows:

Strike out of section 28 " as follows," and insert " as provided by an ordinance of the Convention on that subject."

Adopted.

Mr. Nugent offered the following substitute for section 5:

" Sec. 5. The Legislature shall meet in regular session once only in every two years, at such time as may be provided by law; but the Governor may convene the same in extra session whenever he may deem it necessary for the public good."

Lost.

Mr. Waelder moved to strike out section 41.

Carried.

Mr. Waelder offered the following additional section:

" Sec. —. The Legislature may pass laws for the regulation of live stock and the protection of stock-raisers in the stock-raising portion of this State, and exempt from the operation of such laws other portions, sections, or counties, anything to the contrary contained in this constitution notwithstanding."

Withdrawn.

Mr. Crawford proposed to substitute section 47 by the following:

" Sec. 47. No lottery shall be authorized by this State, and the buying or selling of lottery tickets within this State is prohibited."

Mr. Waelder renewed his amendment.

Mr. Dohoney proposed to amend Mr. Waelder's amendment, as follows:

After the word " State " in line 4 add: " and also in reference to fencing for agriculture in the agricultural portions of the State."

Accepted by Mr. Waelder.

On motion of Mr. Kilgore, Mr. Waelder's amendment and amendments thereto were referred to Committee on General Provisions.

Mr. Crawford's substitute for section 47 was lost.

Mr. West proposed to amend, as follows:

Add the following section: "In all elections by the Senate and House of Representatives, jointly or separately, the vote shall be given *viva voce*, except in the elections of their officers."

Adopted.

Mr. Fleming proposed to amend section 56, line 287, by inserting between the words "not" and "pass," as follows: "Except as otherwise provided in this constitution."

Adopted.

Mr. Robertson, of Bell, offered the following amendment:

Section 48, in line 246, after the word "schools," insert the words, "not to exceed one-twentieth of the annual revenue."

On motion of Mr. Whitfield the amendment was laid on the table.

Mr. Brady moved to reconsider the vote refusing to adopt an amendment offered by Mr. Mills, section 26, line 126.

Lost.

Mr. Moore moved to strike out the words, "of the State has been," from section 2 of the attached article.

Carried.

Mr. McCormick offered the following section as substitute for section 43:

"Sec. 43. At the first session after the adoption of this constitution the Legislature shall appoint not less than three nor more than five persons learned in the law, whose duty it shall be to revise and arrange the statute laws of this State, both civil and criminal, so as to have but one law on any one subject, all of which shall be in plain English; who shall act at as early day as practicable and report their labors to the Legislature for their adoption and modification; and such revision may be made every ten years thereafter."

Adopted.

Mr. Wade moved to strike out the word "plain" before the word "English" in the amendment.

Adopted.

Mr. Scott moved to lay the amendment on the table.

Lost.

Mr. Ballinger moved to amend the amendment by striking out the words " all of which shall be in plain English."

Adopted.

Mr. Dohoney moved to reconsider the vote refusing to adopt a substitute offered by himself for section 1.

Mr. Cline proposed to strike out " so as to have but one law on one subject " from section 43.

Carried.

Mr. Ballinger proposed to amend by adding to section 43:

" And sections 35 and 36, herein, shall not limit the effect which may be given by law to such digest."

Adopted.

Mr. Brady proposed to amend section 25 by adding:

" And no senatorial district shall be formed having less than seven thousand qualified electors."

Mr. Dohoney offered the following amendment:

" Sec. 1. The Legislature may, at any regular session, pass a joint resolution, submitting the proposition to the qualified electors of the State, whether a constitutional convention shall be called, which proposition shall be voted on at the next general election, and if a majority of the votes cast at such election shall be in favor of such convention, the Legislature shall, at its next regular session, pass a joint resolution calling such constitutional convention. Any constitution framed by such constitutional convention shall be submitted to the qualified electors of the State for ratification or rejection."

On motion of Mr. Brown, the main question was ordered.

Question on the adoption of Mr. Dohoney's amendment was put and amendment lost by the following vote:

Yeas—Abernathy, Brown, Ballinger, Barnett, Chambers, Cooley, Curdis, DeMorse, Dohoney, Ford, Ferris, McLean, Mills, Robertson of Bell, Ross, Sessions, Smith, Wade, Wright, West, Waelder—21.

Nays—Arnim, Abner, Blake, Blassingame, Burleson, Brady, Bruce, Crawford, Cook of Gonzales, Cline, DiHard, Darnell, Davis of Brazos, Flournoy, Fleming, Flanagan, Germux, Gaither, Graves, Holt, Henry of Smith, Henry of Limestone, Haynes, Johnson of Franklin, Kilgore, Killough, Lockett, Lacy, Lynch, Martin of Navarro, Martin of Hunt, Mitchell, McKinney of Denton, McKinney of Walker, McCormick, Murphy, Norvell, Nunn, Nugent, Pauli, Reagan, Ramey, Robeson of Fayette, Russell of Harrison, Russell of Wood, Spikes, Scott, Stockdale, Stayton, Whitehead, Weaver, Whitfield—52.

Yeas—Abner, Brady, Crawford, Cline, Flanagan, Lockett.

The question on the adoption of Mr. Brady's amendment was then put and the amendment lost by the following vote:

Mills, Mitchell, Pauli, Reynolds, Russell of Harrison—11.

NAYS—Allison, Abernathy, Arnim, Brown, Blake, Ballinger, Blassingame, Barnett, Bruce, Chambers, Cook of Gonzales, Cardis, Dillard, Dohoney, Darnell, Davis of Brazos, Erhard, Flournoy, Fleming, Ferris, German, Gaither, Graves, Holt, Henry of Smith, Henry of Limestone, Haynes, Kilgore, Killough, Lacy, Lynch, McLean, Martin of Navarro, Martin of Hunt, McKinney of Denton, McKinney of Walker, McCormick, Murphy, Norvell, Nunn, Nugent, Reagan, Ramey, Robertson of Bell, Robeson, of Fayette, Ross, Russell of Wood, Spikes, Scott, Sessions, Smith, Stockdale, Stayton, Wade, Whitehead, Weaver, Whitfield, West, Waelder—59.

The question then recurring upon the engrossment of the article, the same was put and the article ordered engrossed by the following vote:

YEAS—Allison, Abernathy, Arnim, Brown, Blake, Ballinger, Blassingame, Barnett, Burleson, Bruce, Chambers, Cook of Gonzales, Douglas, Dillard, Dohoney, Darnell, Flournoy, Fleming, Ferris, German, Gaither, Graves, Holt, Henry of Smith, Henry of Limestone, Haynes, Johnson of Franklin, Killough, Lacy, Lynch, McLean, Martin of Navarro, Martin of Hunt, McKinney of Denton, McKinney of Walker, McCormick, Murphy, Norvell, Nunn, Nugent, Reagan, Ramey, Robeson of Fayette, Ross, Russell of Wood, Spikes, Scott, Sessions, Stockdale, Stayton, Wade, Whitehead, Wright, Weaver, Whitfield, West, Waelder—57.

NAYS—Abner, Brady, Crawford, Cline, DeMorse, Davis of Brazos, Davis of Wharton, Erhard, Flanagan, Lockett, Mills, Mitchell, Pauli, Robertson of Bell, Russell of Harrison, Smith—16.

On motion of Mr. Brown, the Convention adjourned until 9 o'clock A. M. to-morrow.

THIRTY-EIGHTH DAY.

HALL OF REPRESENTATIVES, ⎱
AUSTIN, TEXAS, October 19, 1875. ⎰

Convention met pursuant to adjournment; roll called; quorum present. Prayer by the Rev. T. B. Lee, Rector of St. David's Church at Austin.

Journal of yesterday read and adopted.

Mr. Ramey submitted the following report:

COMMITTEE ROOM, ⎱
AUSTIN, October 19, 1875. ⎰

To the Hon. E. B. Pickett, President of the Convention:

SIR—Your Committee on "Engrossed and Enrolled Ordinances" would respectfully report that they have carefully examined and compared a provision "On County School Lands," and find the same correctly engrossed. Respectfully,

WM. NEAL RAMEY, Chairman.

On motion of Mr. German, 200 copies of "Bill of Rights," as engrossed, was ordered to be printed.

On motion of Mr. Ramey, 200 copies of the article on "County School Lands," just reported by him, be printed.

Mr. Wright offered the following resolution:

WHEREAS, The Congress of the Republic of Texas, by an act passed on the 9th day of January in the year 1841, entitled an "Act to quiet the land titles within the frontier leagues bordering on the United States of the North," fixed the status of the titles of said lands to a certain extent; and,

WHEREAS, It becomes the duty of this Convention, so far as it has the power, to aid the settlers who have obtained patents from the State of Texas for lands situated within said border league country from being disturbed by suits on Mexican and Spanish titles, and to protect and quiet said settlers in the titles and possession of said lands; therefore,

Resolved, That all titles granted previous to the 17th day of March, in the year 1836, for one league and labor of land situated within the twenty frontier leagues bordering on the then "United States of the North," be and the same are hereby declared void and of no validity; unless the grantees in said titles actually resided at the time of said grants on the lands to which titles were made;

And on the trial of the validity of any of said grants the grantees shall be compelled to prove, outside of the statements and recitations in said grants, said facts, and shall also be compelled to prove a strict and literal compliance with all the conditions and requirements connected with said grants and that said grantees, at the time said grants were made, did take actual possession of said lands so granted in good faith, and have paid all dues and taxes as they have become due up to the time of the institution of said suits.

Mr. Wright, of Lamar, asked that it be referred to the Committee on Mexican and Spanish Land Titles and Claims.

Referred to Committee on Mexican Land Titles.

Mr. Ford offered the following resolution:

Resolved, That the Committee on General Provisions be instructed to inquire into the propriety of adopting the following as a section of the constitution:

"Section —. The Legislature may, when the public interests require it, provide for the creation of the office of Commissioner of Insurance, Statistics and History; and that the salary of said officer shall not exceed two thousand dollars per annum.

Referred to Committee on General Provisions.

Mr. Moore submitted the following report:

COMMITTEE ROOM, ⎱
AUSTIN, October 18, 1875. ⎰

To the Hon. E. B. Pickett, President of the Convention:

The undersigned members of the special committee of seven, to whom was referred the majority and two minority reports and pending amendments on the subject of public schools, beg leave to report that they have carefully investigated the subject; and, in view of the conflicting opinions of this body, have agreed on the following eight sections as the most practicable basis, under the circumstance, on which to organize the public free schools of this State.

They would further submit that they have also considered the subject of the asylums, and find no cause to change the majority report thereon, heretofore presented, but suggest that it be placed among the general provisions, as it does not appropriately pertain to the public free school system.

D. A. NUNN,
L W. MOORE,
L. NORVELL,
W. P. BALLINGER.
MARION MARTIN,
L. S. ROSS.

"PUBLIC FREE SCHOOLS.

"Section 1. A general diffusion of knowledge being essential to the preservation of the liberties and rights of the people, it shall be the duty of the Legislature of the State to establish and make suitable provision for the support and maintenance of an efficient system of public free schools.

"Sec. 2. All funds, lands, and other property heretofore set apart and appropriated for the support of public schools, all the alternate sections of land reserved by the State out of grants heretofore made, or that may hereafter be made, to railroad or other corporations, of any nature whatsoever, one-half of the public domain of the State, and all sums of money that may come to the State from the sale of any portion of the same, shall constitute a perpetual public school fund.

"Sec. 3. And there shall be set apart annually not more than one-fourth the general revenues of the State, and a poll tax of two dollars on all male inhabitants in this State between the ages of twenty-one and sixty years, for the benefit of the public free schools.

"Sec. 4. The lands herein set apart to the public free school fund shall be sold under such regulations, at such times, and on such terms, as may be prescribed by law; and the Legislature shall not have power to grant any relief to the purchasers thereof. The Comptroller shall invest the proceeds of such sale, and of those heretofore made, as may be directed by the Board of Education, herein provided for, in the bonds of this State, if the same can be obtained, otherwise in United States bonds; and the United States bonds now belonging to said fund shall likewise be invested in State bonds, if the same can be obtained on terms advantageous to the school fund.

"Sec. 5. The principal of all bonds or other funds, and the principal arising from the sale of the lands hereinbefore set apart to said school fund, shall be the permanent school fund; and all the interest derivable therefrom and the taxes herein authorized and levied shall be the available school fund, which shall be applied annually to the support of the public free schools. And no law shall ever be enacted appropriating any part of the permanent or available school fund to any other purpose whatever; nor shall the same or any part thereof ever be appropriated to or used for the support of any sectarian school. And the available school fund herein provided shall be distributed to the several counties according to their scholastic population, and applied in manner as may be provided by law.

"Sec. 6. All lands heretofore or hereafter granted to the seve-

ral counties of this State for education or schools, are of right
the property of said counties respectively to which they were
granted, and title thereto is vested in said counties, and no
adverse possession or limitation shall ever be available against
the title of any county.   Each county may sell and dispose of its
lands in whole or in part, in manner to be provided by the
police court of the county.   Actual settlers residing on said
lands shall be protected in the prior right of purchasing the
same to the extent of their settlement not to exceed one hundred
and sixty acres, at the price fixed by said court, which price
shall not include the value of existing improvements made
thereon by such settlers.   Said lands and the proceeds thereof
when sold, shall be held by said counties alone as a trust for the
benefit of public schools therein.   Said proceeds to be invested
in bonds of the State of Texas, or of the United States, and
only the interest thereon to be used and expended annually.

" Sec. 7.   Separate schools shall be provided for the white and
colored children, and impartial provision shall be made for both.

" Sec. 8.   The Governor, Comptroller and Secretary of State
shall constitute a Board of Education, who shall distribute said
fund to the several counties, and perform such other duties concerning public schools as may be provided by law.

" ASYLUMS.

" All lands heretofore granted for the benefit of the Lunatic,
Blind, Deaf and Dumb, and Orphan Asylums, together with
such donations as may have been or may hereafter be made to
either of them, are hereby set apart to them respectively, as
indicated in the several grants, to provide a permanent fund for
the support and maintenance and improvement of said asylums.

" And the Legislature may provide for the sale of the lands and
the investment of the proceeds in manner as provided for sale
and investment of school lands in section 4 of article —, on public schools."

On motion of Mr. Nunn two hundred copies of the report and
ordinance were ordered printed, and they were made special
order for Saturday next 10 o'clock A. M.

COMMITTEE ROOM,   }
AUSTIN, October 18, 1875. }

To the Hon. E. B. Pickett, President of the Convention:

The undersigned, one of the special committee to which was
referred the article reported by the majority of the standing Committee on Education, begs leave to dissent from the majority
report of said special committee for the following reasons:

That while he favors a general diffusion of knowledge, and

believes that it is the duty of individuals as well as governments to encourage and promote this object by all legitimate means in their power, he does not believe that a general system of free public schools can be adopted by Texas at the present time that will afford that efficiency to the desired end as will be satisfactory to the friends of free public education, without the levying of a tax upon all the values of the State of from one-third to one-half of one per cent.

That the report of the Superintendent of Public Instruction shows that the scholastic population, between the ages of six and eighteen, for the year 1874, was 313,061, and for 1875 it is 339,000, an increase of 26,000 in twelve months.

That there was distributed to the scholastic population of 1874, $499,959 05, and that for 1875, $498,330 00, or thereabouts.

That after levying a tax of one-fourth of the annual revenue, we find only one dollar and forty-seven and two-third cents *per capita*, to pay the tuition of the scholar for four months, leaving an additional tax (assuming that the tuition will only amount to six dollars for four months) of about four hundred per cent. to be collected from the taxable values of the county.

That with the rapid immigration to the State, we may safely calculate that the increase of scholastic population will amount to from twenty-five to thirty thousand annually, giving an annual increase in taxation for free public schools of from one hundred and eighty to two hundred thousand dollars.

That a large proportion of the immigration to the country that will aid in increasing the scholastic population of the State will add but little, if anything, for many years to the taxable values of the State.

That any system of public free schools will necessarily increase, even in old settled States and countries, beyond the increase in taxable values.

That in the city of Boston the tax for public free schools has increased from $389,829 in 1854–55 to $2,081,043 in 1874–75, an annual increase of $104,052, or nearly thirty per cent.

That while this increase of expense in Boston will probably fall far short of the increase of scholastic population in Texas, it the last four years, which may be assumed as a fair average, as follows:

Taxable property for 1872 . . . . $211,000,000
Taxable property for 1873 223,000,000
Taxable property for 1874 241,000,000
Probable amount for 1875 250,000,000

That it is evident, if I am correct in the above estimate, that no system of free public schools can be maintained without a practical confiscation of the property of the country, and the striking down of all her industries.

That the industrious farmer and mechanic can never rise, or accumulate property, if you levy an annual tribute on him for the education of the children of his less industrious neighbor.

That he does not believe that it ever was the intention of the founders of our republican form of government to take the entire control of the education of the children of the country out of hands of the parents or legal guardians.

That the history of the country, from the first landing of the Pilgrims down to the present time, will not warrant the conclusion that any species of compulsory education was intended or would be tolerated.

That the appointment of high officials or a commission by the government to select text books that shall be used for the study and training of the youth of the country, is at war with the laws of God, and is subversive of the principles of free speech, liberty of conscience and freedom of thought, as enunciated in 1776, by the authors of American liberty, and re-enunciated time and again since that time.

That as the forms and formulas prescribed in religion enslave thought and fetters conscience, so the minds of the youth of the country will be trained to look to government for all their wants and necessities, and finally to regard it as parent, and then as master, would prevent the development of that independent, self-reliant and chivalrous feeling that constitutes one of the best supports of our republican form of government.

That taxation for purposes other than the legitimate expenses of the government is in violation of right, where life, liberty and the pursuit of happiness is guaranteed, because it assumes to educate the child in a prescribed manner, contrary to the wish and desire of the parent—taxes him for a purpose that is contrary to right and revolting to his conscience, and compels him to support an institution never contemplated by the founders of a republic, because in no way necessary to its perpetuity.

That it was not—could not have been the intention of the men of 1836 or 1845 to declare that a system of free public schools should be maintained by a direct tax on the property and industries of the people throughout all time, with the standing invitation for immigration from all parts of the world.

They certainly did not intend to open the way for an uncertain annual increase of taxation upon the labor of the country, amounting to a probable increase of from twenty to thirty per cent.

I can not believe that they intended to fasten on themselves and their descendants a form of government that would guarantee an education to the children of all countries (as well as their own) that might think proper to avail themselves of it, without money and without price.

I can not believe that Texas did then, or is bound now, to conscript the industries of the country to support and maintain an institution, not only not essential to the maintenance of a free government, but absolutely subversive of both civil and religious liberty.

That it was not the intention, as it was not the policy of the framers of the constitutions of 1836 or 1845 to do more than to encourage education, and to aid the schools of the country that might be established by individual enterprise and money, by the donation of lands and a portion of the money received for the sale of our north-western territory, an amount sufficient to educate all the indigent orphans of the country.

The undersigned would, therefore, offer the following article as a substitute for the one offered by the majority of the committee.

All of which is respectfully submitted.

E. S. C. ROBERTSON.

"ARTICLE ——.

"Section 1. To promote the general diffusion of knowledge the lands heretofore set apart by the Republic or State of Texas, and the moneys, bonds and other property now owned by the State, which have been devoted to the use of public free schools, shall constitute the basis of a permanent fund, to be called the General Educational Fund;

"Provided, That the title to lands given to the State for the use and benefit of public free schools shall be surrendered to the donors at their option; but the right of the State to improvements put upon said lands by the State shall not be hereby affected.

"Sec. 2. The Legislature shall provide for the sale of all lands set apart in section 1 of this article as soon as practicable, which have been located, or which may hereafter be located, by railroad or other corporations, and for the sale of all other property therein set apart; and all moneys derived from the same shall be invested in bonds of the State of Texas.

"Sec. 3. The interest accruing on the General Educational Fund shall be distributed annually by the Comptroller of Public Accounts between the respective counties of the State, according to their scholastic population, as follows:

" 1. To the payment of tuition for four months in each year of all the indigent orphan children of the State between the ages of eight and sixteen years; the remainder to be applied *pro rata* to the payment of tuition of all children of the State within said ages; and the Legislature may set aside not more than one-twentieth of the annual revenues of the State in aid of said General Educational Fund."

On motion of Mr. Stockdale, 200 copies of this report and article were ordered printed, and made special order for Saturday at 10 o'clock A. M.

Mr. Darnell reported as follows:

COMMITTEE ROOM,
AUSTIN, October 19, 1875.

To the Hon. E. B. Pickett, President of the Convention:

The Committee on Public Lands and Land Office, to whom was referred the annexed resolution concerning Spanish land titles, beg leave to report that they have examined the same, and recommend that it be referred to the select committee on Mexican and Spanish Land Titles.   Respectfully submitted,

N. H. DARNELL, Chairman.

Report adopted, and resolution referred as indicated.

Mr. Haynes offered the following resolution:

Resolved, That Joseph Junker, the porter in charge of the State Library, in addition to his present duties, be required to do the engrossing and enrolling of the Convention, and that his pay be increased to five dollars per day, to commence from this date.

Adopted.

Mr. Cook, of Gonzales, offered the following resolution:

Resolved, That the Committee on General Provisions be, and they are hereby, instructed to inquire into the expediency of requiring the Legislature to meet next after the adoption of this constitution, to set apart and appropriate, out of the available school fund, for the current year, the sum of four hundred thousand dollars, or so much thereof as may be necessary to pay the teachers of public schools for services rendered prior to first day July, A. D. 1873, and report by ordinance or otherwise.

Referred to Committee on General Provisions.

BUSINESS ON THE TABLE.

Majority and minority reports on immigration taken up.

Mr. Russell, of Wood, offered the following resolution, to accompany the majority report:

26

Resolved, That the following provision be placed in the constitution, under the head of "General Provisions":

"Sec. —. The Legislature shall have no power to appropriate any of the public money for the establishment and maintenance of a Bureau of Immigration or for any purpose of bringing immigrants to this State."

[Mr. Darnell in the chair.]

Mr. Reagan offered the following amendment to section 1 of the article reported by the minority of the committee signed by Messrs. Waelder and Pauli:

Amend by striking out the proviso in lines 68, 69 and 70, and insert, "*provided,* that the moneys expended by this bureau shall be for the collection and dissemination of information on these subjects, and that no money shall be paid out for bringing immigrants to the State."

Accepted.

Mr. Whitfield proposed to amend the article of the minority report, as amended by Mr. Reagan, as follows:

Section 1, line 68, strike out all after the word "provided," and insert: "that the Legislature shall never make any appropriation to defray the expenses of immigrants to this State; *and provided further,* that said bureau shall not cost exceeding five thousand dollars per year."

On motion of Mr. Abernathy, the main question was ordered.

The question on the adoption of Mr. Whitfield's amendment was put and the amendment lost by the following vote:

YEAS—Allison, Blake, Crawford, Cook of Gonzales, De-Morse, Dohoney, Davis of Brazos, Ford, Henry of Smith, Henry of Limestone, Haynes, McCormick, Murphy, Nugent, Ross, Smith, Wade, Whitfield—18.

NAYS—Abernathy, Arnim, Abner, Ballinger, Blassingame, Barnett, Burleson, Brady, Bruce, Chambers, Cline, Cardis, Douglas, Dillard, Davis of Wharton, Erhard, Flournoy, Fleming, Ferris, Flanagan, German, Gaither, Graves, Holt, Johnson of Franklin, Johnson of Collin, King, Killough, Kilgore, Lockett, Lacy, Lynch, McLean, Martin of Navarro, Martin of Hunt, McCabe, Morris, Mills, Mitchell, McKinney of Walker, Norvell, Nunn, Pauli, Reagan, Ramey, Reynolds, Rentfro, Robertson of Bell, Robeson of Fayette, Russell of Harrison, Russell of Wood, Spikes, Scott, Sessions, Stockdale, Stayton, Sansom, Whitehead, Wright, Weaver, West, Waelder—62.

The question was then put on the adoption of the article reported by Messrs. Waelder and Pauli, as amended by Mr. Reagan.

The yeas and nays being called, the article was lost by the following vote:

YEAS—Blake, Ballinger, Burleson, Crawford, Cline, DeMorse, Erhard, Flanagan, Henry of Smith, Henry of Limestone, King, Kilgore, Lockett, Lynch, Martin of Navarro, McCabe, Morris, Mills, Mitchell, McKinney of Walker, McCormick, Murphy, Pauli, Reagan, Reynolds, Russell of Harrison, Sessions, Smith, Stockdale, Stayton, Whitfield, West, Waelder—33.

NAYS—Allison, Abernathy, Arnim, Abner, Brown, Blassingame, Barnett, Bruce, Chambers, Cook of Gonzales, Cooke of San Saba, Douglas, Dillard, Dohoney, Darnell, Davis of Brazos, Flournoy, Fleming, Ferris, German, Gaither, Graves, Holt, Haynes, Johnson of Franklin, Johnson of Collin, Killough, Lacy, McLean, Martin of Hunt, McKinney of Denton, Norvell, Nunn, Nugent, Ramey, Rentfro, Robertson of Bell, Robeson of Fayette, Ross, Russell of Wood, Spikes, Scott, Sansom, Wade, Whitehead, Wright, Weaver—47.

[President in the chair.]

The chair decided that the main question was not exhausted until a vote upon the engrossment of Mr. Russell's (of Wood) resolution offered this morning.

Mr. Stockdale made this point of order, viz.: that under the rules Mr. Russell's (of Wood) resolution should be referred to a committee, printed, and laid upon the desks of delegates before it could be engrossed.

The Chair ruled against this point, and ordered the vote upon the engrossment, which resulted in engrossing the resolution by the following vote:

YEAS—Allison, Abernathy, Arnim, Abner, Blassingame, Barnett, Bruce, Crawford, Chambers, Cooke of San Saba, Douglas, Dillard, Dohoney, Darnell, Davis of Brazos, Flournoy, Ferris, German, Gaither, Graves, Holt, Haynes, Johnson of Franklin, Johnson of Collin, Kilgore, Killough, Lacy, McLean, Martin of Hunt, McKinney of Denton, Norvell, Nugent, Ramey, Robertson of Bell, Robeson of Fayette, Russell of Wood, Spikes, Scott, Stockdale, Sansom, Wade, Whitehead, Wright, Weaver—44.

NAYS—Brown, Blake, Ballinger, Burleson, Brady, Cook of Gonzales, Cline, DeMorse, Davis of Wharton, Erhard, Ford, Fleming, Flanagan, Henry of Smith, Henry of Limestone, King, Lockett, Lynch, Martin of Navarro, McCabe, Morris, Mills, Mitchell, McKinney of Walker, McCormick, Murphy, Nunn, Pauli, Reagan, Reynolds, Rentfro, Ross, Russell of Harrison, Sessions, Smith, Stayton, Whitfield, West, Waelder—39.

Mr. McLean moved to reconsider the vote and to lay the motion on the table.

On motion of Mr. Mills, the Convention adjourned until 9 o'clock A. M. to-morrow.

THIRTY-NINTH DAY.

HALL OF REPRESENTATIVES,
AUSTIN, TEXAS, October 20, 1875.

Convention met pursuant to adjournment; roll called; quorum present. Prayer by the Rev. T. B. Lee, of St. David's Church.

Journal of yesterday read and adopted.

On motion of Mr. McKinney, of Walker, Mr. Ross was excused until Monday next.

On motion of Mr. Robeson, of Fayette, Mr. Moore was excused until Saturday next.

Mr. Russell, of Wood, submitted the following report of a majority of Committee on Revenue and Taxation:

COMMITTEE ROOM,
AUSTIN, October 18, 1875.

To the Hon. E. B. Pickett, President of the Convention:

The undersigned, constituting a portion of the Committee on Revenue and Taxation, regret that they can not concur in that portion of the report of said committee which provides that taxes on real and personal property due by non-residents may be paid at the Comptroller's Office in Austin or in the county where the non-resident tax-payer resides, instead of being paid to the collector of taxes in the county where the property is situated.

We believe that enormous wrongs have heretofore been perpetrated by non-resident tax-payers in not rendering their lands for taxation at all, and in inadequate valuation on property, both real and personal, and in the privilege heretofore granted that class of persons in allowing taxes to be paid elsewhere than in the county where the same are due, and that all other subjects of retrenchment and reform sink into comparative insignificance when compared to this.

We believe that the past history of the country shows that large land owners, many of whom reside beyond the limits of the State, under pre-existing laws, have been enabled to escape taxation in whole or in part, and the actual settlers owning far less property have been required to pay largely over a just proportion of the expenses of the State government, and that the only way to effect a permanent remedy for the evil is to require all taxes to be paid in the county where the property is situated.

We believe that taxation should be equal and uniform through the country, and that every citizen and property owner should bear his just proportion of the burthens of government; and that no man, or set of men should have exclusive privileges, and that law is best which affords the greatest good to the greatest number of persons. And while we would be willing that citizens of unorganized counties should be permitted to pay their taxes at the office of the Comptroller of Public Accounts at the capital of the State, we do, most earnestly, insist that all other persons should be required to pay taxes on property in the county where the property is situated, and that this can only be done by having the mode of collecting taxes made plain, direct and expeditious.

We are informed and believe that several million dollars are now due the State for back taxes, and notwithstanding frequent legislative enactments on the subject, some of which requiring landed property to be valued in the county where situated, more than 35,000,000 million acres of patented land in Texas, owned by non-residents, have heretofore escaped taxation entirely, whereby the country is annually being wronged out of a very large amount of money.

W. P. McLEAN,
J. RUSSELL,
ASA HOLT,
J. W. WHITFIELD,
J. R. FLEMING,
B. ABERNATHY,
G. B. COOKE,
JOHNSON, of Collin,
L. S. ROSS.

On motion of Mr. Allison one hundred copies of the report ordered printed.

On motion of Mr. Russell, of Harrison, Mr. Flanagan was excused indefinitely.

Mr. Holt offered the following resolution and ordinance:

Resolved, That the following ordinance be submitted to the people, to be voted on by them as a separate and distinct proposition, at the election upon the ratification of the constitution to be framed by his Convention; and if a majority of the votes cast at such election upon such ordinance shall be in favor thereof, the same shall be a part of the constitution of the State:

"ORDINANCE ON SUFFRAGE.

"No person who shall be twenty-two years of age or upwards, shall be permitted to vote at any election held in this State unless he shall have paid a State or county tax, which shall have been assessed at least two months and paid at least one month before the election."

On motion of Mr. Kilgore, the resolution and ordinance were referred to a select committee of five.

Mr. Dohoney offered the following resolution:

Resolved, That the Committee on Agriculture and Stock-raising be instructed to inquire into the expediency of reporting the following article, or something similar, as a provision in the constitution, to-wit:

"ARTICLE —.

"AGRICULTURE AND STATISTICS.

"Section 1. The Legislature shall provide for the establishment and support of a Bureau of Agriculture and Statistics, which bureau shall be charged with gathering and publishing correct statistical information as to the population, public lands, productions, agricultural, industrial and stock-growing, as well as the mineral and other resources of the different sections of the State."

Referred to Committee on Agriculture and Stock-raising.

To the Hon. E. B. Pickett, President of the Convention:

I am instructed by the majority of the Committee on Judiciary to report to the Convention the accompanying article as the result of their labors to present to the Convention an article on the "Judicial Department" in the constitution for the State to be framed by this Convention.

Diversity of opinion existed among the committee; and each member of the committee will feel himself at liberty to act upon his own views on the different sections of the article.

W. P. BALLINGER,
One of the Committee.

"ARTICLE —.

"JUDICIAL DEPARTMENT.

"Section 1. The judicial power of this State shall be vested in one Supreme Court, in District Courts, in County Courts, in Commissioners' Courts, in Courts of Justices of the Peace, and in such other courts as may be established by law. The Legislature may establish criminal district courts, with such jurisdiction as it may prescribe, but no such court shall be established unless the district includes a city containing at least fifteen thousand inhabitants, as ascertained by the census of the United States, or other official census.   The Criminal District Court of Galveston and Harris counties shall continue with the district jurisdiction and organization now existing by law, until otherwise provided by law.

" Sec. 2. The Supreme Court shall consist of five justices, three of whom shall constitute a quorum, and the concurrence of three judges shall be necessary to a decision by said court. The State shall be divided into five districts, as nearly equal in population as practicable, and the qualified voters of each district shall elect one of said justices at an election for members of the Legislature.   Each of said justices at the time of his election shall be a citizen of the United States, at least thirty years of age, and have been a practicing lawyer, or judge of a court of record, either or together, in this State seven years, and have resided two years next preceding his election in the district by which he may be elected.   They shall hold their office for eight years, and shall each receive an annual salary of four thousand dollars, which amount shall not be increased or diminished during their term of office.   They shall elect from among their number, from time to time as they may deem proper, a presiding judge, with reference to the dispatch of business in said court.

" Sec. 3. The Supreme Court shall have appellate jurisdiction only, which shall be co-extensive with the limits of the State. In criminal cases below the grade of felony, no appeal shall be allowed from the County Court, unless within such time and under such regulations as may be prescribed by law, upon inspection of a transcript of the record from the County Court, the district judge of said county, or a judge of the Supreme Court first applied to, and whose duty it shall be to indorse his action thereon, shall certify his belief that error therein has been committed by said County Court.   Appeals may be allowed from interlocutory judgments in such cases and under such regulations as may be provided by law.   The Supreme Court and the judges thereof shall have power to issue the writ of *habeas corpus,* and under such regulations as may be prescribed by law they may issue the writ of mandamus and all other writs necessary to enforce the jurisdiction of said court.   The Supreme Court shall have power upon affidavits, or otherwise, as by the court may be thought proper, to ascertain such matters of fact as may be necessary to the proper exercise of its jurisdiction. The Supreme Court shall sit for the transaction of business from the first Monday of October until the last Saturday of June of every year, at the seat of government, and at not more than two other places in the State.

"Sec. 4. The Supreme Court shall appoint a clerk for each place at which it may sit, and each of said clerks shall give bond in such manner as is now, or may hereafter, be required by law; shall hold his office for four years, and shall be subject to removal by the said court for good cause, entered of record on the minutes of said court.

"Sec. 5. On certificate from the Supreme Court that said court is unable to dispose of the business pending therein, together with the current business of said court, the Legislature shall provide for the organization of a commission for the determination of all cases pending in said Supreme Court, and which may be turned over to said commission by the Supreme Court.

"Sec. 6. The State shall be divided into . . . judicial districts, which may be increased or diminished by the Legislature. For each district there shall be elected by the qualified voters thereof, at a general election for members of the Legislature, a judge, who shall be at least twenty-five years of age, shall be a citizen of the United States, shall have been a practicing attorney in the courts of this State for the period of four years, shall reside in his district during his term of office, shall hold his office for the term of six years, shall receive an annual salary of three thousand dollars, which shall not be increased or diminished during his term of service, and shall hold the regular terms of court at one place in each county in the district twice in each year, in such manner as may be prescribed by law.

"The Legislature shall have power, by general act, to authorize the holding of special terms, when necessary for the dispatch of business, and shall provide for the holding of district courts, when the judge thereof is absent, or is, from any cause, disabled or disqualified from presiding.

"Sec. 7. The District Court shall have original jurisdiction of all criminal cases; of all suits in behalf of the State to recover penalties, forfeitures, and escheats; of all cases of divorce; of all suits to recover damages for slander or defamation of character; of all suits for the trial of title to land; of all suits for the enforcement of liens; of all suits for the trial of the right to property, levied on by virtue of any writ of execution, sequestration or attachment, when the property levied on shall be equal to or exceed in value one hundred dollars; and of all suits, complaints or pleas whatever, without regard to any distinction between law and equity, when the matter in controversy shall be valued at, or amounted to, one hundred dollars, exclusive of interest; and the said courts and the judges thereof shall have power to issue writs of injunction, certiorari, and all other writs necessary to enforce their own jurisdiction, and to give them a general superintendence and control over inferior tribunals. The District Courts shall have original and appellate jurisdiction and general control in probate matters over the County Court established in each county; for appointing guardians, granting letters testamentary and of administration; for settling the accounts of executors, administrators, and guardians, and for the transaction of business appertaining to estates; and original jurisdiction and general control over executors, administrators, guardians and minors, under such regulations as may be prescribed by the Legislature."

" Sec. 8. There shall be a clerk of the District Court for each county, who shall be elected by the qualified voters for State and county officers, and who shall hold his office for four years, subject to removal by information or by indictment of a grand jury, and conviction by a petit jury; in case of vacancy, the judge of the Distrit Court shall have the power to appoint a clerk who shall hold until the next general election.

" Sec. 9. In the trial of all causes in the District Courts the plaintiff or defendant shall, upon application made in open court, have the right of trial by jury, but no jury shall be empaneled in any civil case unless demanded by a party to the case, and a jury fee be paid by the party demanding a jury; for such sum and with such exceptions as may be prescribed by the Legislature.

" Sec. 10. No judge shall sit in any case wherein he may be interested, or where either of the parties may be connected with him by affinity or consanguinity, within such degree as may be prescribed by law, or where he shall have been of counsel in the case. When the Supreme Court, or any three of its members shall be thus disqualified to hear and determine any case or cases in said court, the same shall be certified to the Governor of the State, who shall immediately commission the requisite number of persons, learned in the law, for the trial and determination of said case or cases. When a judge of the District Court is disqualified, by any of the causes above stated, the parties may, by consent, appoint a proper person to try said case; or, upon their failing to do so, a competent person shall be appointed to try the cause in the county where it is pending, in such manner as may be prescribed by law; and the District Judges may exchange districts, or hold courts for each other, when they may deem it expedient, and shall do so when directed by law. The disqualification of judges of inferior tribunals shall be remedied and vacancies in their offices shall be filled as prescribed by law.

"Sec. 11. All judges of the Supreme and District Courts shall, by virtue of their offices, be conservators of the peace throughout the State. The style of all writs and process shall be, 'The State of Texas;' all prosecutions shall be carried on in the name and by the authority of 'The State of Texas,' and conclude 'against the peace and dignity of the State.'

"Sec. 12. Grand and petit juries in the District Courts shall be composed of twelve men; but nine members of a grand jury shall be a quorum to transact business and present bills. In trials of civil cases, and in trials of criminal cases below the grade of felony, in the District Courts, nine members of the jury, concurring, may render a verdict; but when the verdict shall be rendered by less than the whole number, it shall be signed by every member of the jury concurring in it. When, pending the trial of any case, one or more jurors may die or be disabled from sitting, the remainder of the jury shall have power to render a verdict; *provided,* that the Legislature may change or modify the rule authorizing less than the whole number of the jury to render a verdict.

"Sec. 13. There shall be established in each county in the State an inferior tribunal styled the County Court, which shall be a court of record; and there shall be elected by the qualified voters in each county a judge of the said County Court, who shall be well informed in the law of the State and a conservator of the peace, and shall hold his office for four years, and until his successor is qualified. He shall receive such compensation as may be prescribed by law, and shall be removed from office for neglect of duty, incompetency, malfeasance, or official misconduct, and the Legislature shall enact laws to regulate such removal.

"Sec. 14. The County Court shall have jurisdiction, with such exceptions as may be provided by law, of all misdemeanors and of civil cases when the matter in controversy shall exceed one hundred dollars and not exceed five hundred dollars, exclusive of interest, without regard to any distinction between law and equity; but shall not have jurisdiction of suits for the recovery of lands, nor to enforce liens on real estate. Said County Court shall have the general jurisdiction of a probate court; shall probate wills, appoint guardians of minors, idiots, lunatics, persons *non compos mentis,* and common drunkards; grant letters testamentary and of administration; settle the accounts of executors, administrators and guardians; transact all business appertaining to the etates of deceased persons, minors, idiots, lunatics, persons *non compos mentis,* and common drunkards, including the settlement, partition and distribution of such estates, and apprentice minors, as prescribed by law. It shall have jurisdiction of appeals from justices of the peace to such extent and in such manner as may be prescribed by law, but there shall be no further appeal to the District or Supreme Court in such cases. The Judge of said County Court shall have power to issue writs of mandamus, injunction and all other writs necessary to the enforcement of the jurisdiction of said court, and to issue writs of *habeas corpus* in cases where the offense charged is of a grade that said County Court or other inferior court is competent to try. The Legislature shall have power, by local law, for any county or counties having as many as ten thousand inhabitants, or by general law, to confer upon said County Courts further jurisdiction concurrent with the District Courts, of felonies, the punishment of which is not capital, and of civil cases where the matter in controversy shall not exceed in value one thousand dollars, and to regulate proceedings for the exercise of such jurisdiction, and for appeals therefrom. The County Court shall not have criminal jurisdiction in any county in which there is a Criminal District Court, unless expressly conferred by law.

"Sec. 15. The County Courts shall always be open for the trial of criminal cases, and shall hold a term for civil business at least once in every two months, and for probate business as prescribed by law. Prosecutions may be commenced therein by information, and as otherwise provided by law. Grand juries, empanneled in the District Courts, shall inquire into all crimes, including misdemeanors, and indictments therefor shall be returned into the District Court, and all indictments now pending, or hereafter returned into the District Court, for offenses of turned into the District Court, and all indictments now pending in the District Court, jurisdiction of which is given to the County Court, and in which the plaintiff may prefer removal thereto, and all probate business shall be transferred to the County Court, in all counties in which a County Court may have been organized. The jury in the County Court shall consist of six persons, but no jury shall be empaneled for the trial of civil cases, unless demanded by one of the parties, who shall pay such jury fee in advance as may be prescribed by law, unless he makes affidavit that he is unable to pay the same. The jury may be waived by agreement in all misdemeanors.

"Sec. 16. There shall be elected by the qualified voters in

each county four County Commissioners, whose term of office shall be two years from the date of their election, and until their successors are duly qualified, who, together with the County Judge, shall constitute the Commissioner's Court of the county, with jurisdiction over county revenue, police, roads, and public affairs of the county, and the powers, duties and mode of proceeding thereof shall be such as have been heretofore prescribed for Commissioner's and Police Courts in this State, until otherwise provided or regulated by law.

"Sec. 17. The Commissioner's Court of the county shall fix a convenient number of justices of the peace for each county, and divide the county into justice's precincts, in each of which a justice of the peace shall be elected by the qualified voters of such precinct. They shall have such jurisdiction as may be provided by law in civil cases where the matter in controversy shall not exceed one hundred dollars, exclusive of interest, and in misdemeanors where the punishment does not exceed a fine of one hundred dollars.

"Sec. 18. There shall be elected for each county, by the qualified voters, a County Clerk, who shall hold his office for two years, who shall be the clerk of the County and Commissioners' Courts, whose duties and perquisites and fees of office shall be prescribed by the Legislature, and a vacancy in whose office shall be filled by the judge of the County Court, until the next general election for county or State officers; provided, that in counties having a population of less than eight thousand persons the Legislature may provide for the election of a single clerk, who shall perform the duties of District and County Clerks.

"Sec. 19. A County Attorney shall be elected by the qualified voters of each county, who shall be commissioned by the Governor, and hold office for the term of two years. In case of vacancy the Commissioners' Court of the county shall have power to appoint a County Attorney until the next general election. The County Attorneys shall represent the State in all cases in the District Court, and inferior courts, in their respective counties; but if any county shall be included in a district in which there shall be a District Attorney, the respective duties of District Attorneys and County Attorneys shall in such counties be regulated by the Legislature. The Legislature may provide for the election of District Attorneys in such districts as may be deemed necessary, and make provision for the compensation of District Attorneys and County Attorneys.

"Sec. 20. There shall be elected by the qualified voters of

each county, a Sheriff, and by the qualified voters of each justices' precinct, one Constable, who shall hold their offices for the term of two years, whose duties and perquisites and fees of office shall be prescribed by the Legislature, and vacancies in whose offices shall be filled by the judge of the County Court, until the next general election for county or State officers.

"Sec. 21. County Judges, County Attorneys, Clerks of the District and County Courts, Sheriffs, Justices of the Peace, Constables, and other county officers, may be removed by the judges of the District Courts for incompetency, official misconduct, habitual drunkenness, or other causes defined by law, upon the cause therefor being set forth in writing, and the finding of its truth by a jury.

"Sec. 22. The Supreme Court shall have power to make rules and regulations for the government of said court and the other courts of the State, to regulate proceedings, and expedite the dispatch of business therein.

"Sec. 23. The State shall have no right of appeal in criminal cases."

COMMITTEE ROOM, ⎱
AUSTIN, October 20, 1875. ⎰

To the Hon. E. B. Pickett, President of the Convention:

The undersigned, members of the Committee on Judiciary, not being able to agree to all the sections of the "Judiciary Article," as reported by a majority of the committee, and especially disagreeing with the majority in the arrangement of the jurisdiction of the courts provided for, submit to the Convention the annexed sections, which they recommend as substitutes for the corresponding sections in the article reported by the majority of the committee.

The objections to the present judicial system, more probably than those to any other part of the present constitution, induced the people of the State to vote for the call of a Constitutional Convention. They are very clearly defined in the minds of the people, who look to us to remedy the evils complained of, to reduce, by a wise and judicious reorganization of our judicial system, the burdensome expenses imposed on them by the present system, and to relieve the industries of our people of the exhausting drain on them caused by it.

The principal grounds of objection to the present judicial system are:

1. That the District and Supreme Court dockets are so overcrowded with petty cases as to greatly impair the usefulness of

those courts, and delay justice, and, in many cases, to amount to almost a denial of justice.

2. The extension of the jurisdiction of the District Courts to almost every subject of litigation, however small and unimportant, and the right of appeal given to the Supreme Court from almost all judgments of the District Courts, has not only greatly impaired the usefulness of these courts and injured the interests of litigants to an extent which it would be difficult to estimate, but it has made it necessary that we should have about forty District Judges, including the judges of criminal districts, at a great expense to the public, which, it is believed, would not be necessary under a proper judicial system; but even with all these judges, and with this great and unnecessary expense, the District Court dockets are so crowded, and the business of these courts is so delayed, that it is not certain in many cases whether an injured party had not better abandon his claim for justice than attempt to secure his rights through the courts.

3. The present system of giving the District Courts original jurisdiction in all civil cases for sums of one hundred dollars and more, and over all criminal offences, even of the least and most trivial kinds, causes very great numbers of the people of all classes and conditions, and from every part of their counties, to be called away from their ordinary vocations at every term of the court, and, on account of the crowded condition of the dockets, to have to remain away from their business in attendance on the courts, at a ruinous cost to themselves, and to such an extent in the aggregate as to produce an exhausting drain on the industries of our people.

4. The same causes very greatly, and, it is believed, unnecessarily, increase the amount of jury service to be performed, and the cost of that service to the people. And this, with the various court costs and fees of officers, which form a part of these evils, has already bankrupted many of our counties, and is bankrupting many others.

The people all over the State see, and feel, and know these things, and earnestly look to this Convention for relief from them.

While the plan submitted by the majority of the committee is doubtless designed to furnish a partial remedy for these evils, by the creation of a County Court with civil and criminal and probate jurisdiction, we respectfully submit that it will not do so to the extent to which the people have just right to expect relief. It gives the District Courts concurrent jurisdiction with the County Courts and Justices' Courts over all misdemeanors, and will not, it is believed, operate to transfer the trial and determination of a very great number of these cases from the district to the inferior courts.

And, as to those misdemeanors which may be tried in the County Courts, the people, as parties, or witnesses, or jurors, will still have to be drawn from all parts of their counties to the county towns for their trial, and will thus be exposed to the same hardships, only some less in degree, than they are under the present system. And, in relation to cases of this kind, it is not to be forgotten that witnesses are never paid by the State, and very rarely by defendants; and yet, summoned possibly from the remote parts of a county to their county town, they must abandon their business, at whatever loss to them, and go and lose their time, and pay their bills, or camp out, as best they may; and all this because such cases are to be tried at the county towns, rather than in the precincts where the offenses may have been committed.

And, under the plan presented by the majority of the committee, jurisdiction is retained in the District Courts, in civil cases, over all sums of one hundred dollars or more. The District Courts having concurrent jurisdiction with the County Courts over all sums from one hundred to five hundred dollars, and all cases tried in the County Courts are liable, on appeal, to be re-tried *de novo* in the District Courts, and many of them will be so re-tried, and will thus, to this extent, perpetuate the existing evils of crowded District Court dockets.

And, under the plan of the majority a party, aggrieved by the decision of a County Court, in a civil case, before he can take his case to the District Court, must go to the expense of having a petition prepared for a *certiorari*, and then hunt up a judge and get his petition granted before his case can go up, it will be seen that the remedy is costly and inconvenient, and, we do not doubt, will be unsatisfactory.

And under the plan presented by the majority of the committee, appeals are allowed, in criminal cases, directly from the County Courts to the Supreme Court. The effect of this, if this right of appeal shall not be unduly embarrassed, will be to crowd the docket of the Supreme Court with petty cases, as it now is, and to render it impossible for that court to dispose of the business before it, and to involve litigants and the country in all the disasters arising from delays in its decisions, which we now experience. And besides this, in the plan presented by the majority of the committee, it is provided that no one can obtain such an appeal without first going to the expense of obtaining a copy of the whole record of the case, and of then getting the certificate of a District or Supreme Court Judge that the appeal ought to be granted. This can not fail to prove vexatious and unsatisfactory to the people. We believe that when appeals are allowed in criminal cases they should be allowed as a matter of right, and should not be encumbered with such expense and hindrances as to substantially deny the right in many cases, while professing to allow it.

The plan of jurisdiction which we present gives exclusive original jurisdiction to justices of the peace in civil cases, where the matter in controversy is two hundred dollars or less, with such exceptions as are provided in the section in relation to the jurisdiction of the District Courts. And it gives them exclusive jurisdiction over offenses in which the fine or penalty is not more than two hundred dollars, with such exceptions as are provided in the section in relation to the jurisdiction of the District Courts, with the right of appeal and trial, *de novo,* in all cases, civil and criminal, to the County Court, in which the judgment of the Justice's Court is for more than ten dollars, exclusive of costs. This will localize the trial of all petty cases within the precinct where the cause of action may originate, and will enable the parties, their witnesses, and the jurymen who try the case, to go from their homes in the morning, attend to the case, and return home at night, without a great waste of time, or material interruption to their ordinary pursuits, and will thus operate to relieve, in a large degree, the present excessive drain on the industrial interests of the country, which results under the present system from taking a large part of these cases away from the precincts to the county towns for trial.

The extensive jurisdiction thus given to this class of magistrates, allowing five of them only to each county, and giving them notarial powers, will, it is believed, secure to them, in most of the counties, such emoluments as to make it practicable to secure the services of good men, properly qualified for these important duties.

It is urged as a reason for not increasing the jurisdiction of justices of the peace, that we can not obtain persons of proper qualifications to fill these offices. We submit that it has been the fault of our system heretofore which has caused us to have incompetent men in so many instances in these offices; and that whenever we so arrange our system as to make the positions honorable, profitable, and important, we may reasonably expect them to be filled by respectable and competent men.

It is also sometimes objected that they can not be expected to perform such judicial duties well, because, generally, they are not lawyers. We submit that for the settlement of petty cases generally, such as occur between neighbors, an honest and sensible man, and six of the neighbors as jurymen, are more likely to get at the real merits and justice of the case, than an indifferent lawyer, with just enough of technical knowledge of the law to confuse him, would. And that the next best judge to a good lawyer for such cases, is an upright, sensible man.

It is also urged that the people can not be relied on to elect good justices of the peace. If we will but give business and emoluments enough to this class of officers to induce active business men to accept them, there is no just reason why the people may not be as successful in electing a good justice of the peace as in electing a good Governor or Supreme Judge.

By the sections we submit we give to the County Courts jurisdiction of all misdemeanors, the jurisdiction of which is not given to the justices of the peace, or conferred on the District Courts, embraces most of the more important cases of misdemeanor. And we give them jurisdiction, in civil cases, over sums from two hundred to five hundred dollars, with a few exceptional cases in which the jurisdiction is given to the District Courts. We also give them general probate jurisdiction.

And civil and criminal cases tried in this court may be taken by appeal to the District Courts; but the appeal goes up on the records of the County Courts, and is tried by the judge on the records, with but little consumption of time, and none of the expenses of a jury trial.

The original jurisdiction of the District Courts, under the sections we present, will extend to all felonies, and to a few classes of misdemeanors, which, it will be seen, is appropriately left with it; and to civil cases of five hundred dollars or more, and to a few exceptional classes of cases involving less than five hundred dollars, with the right of appeal to the Supreme Court in all of these cases, except those for gambling, which are not allowed to go beyond the District Courts.

By this system we shall relieve the Supreme Court docket of nearly all petty cases, and can make it practicable for a bench of five judges to dispose of the business of that court promptly and speedily, so as to meet the wants of the country for many years to come without the assistance of any other tribunal.

By this plan, and by the reduction of the terms of the District Courts to two a year, we so relieve the District Courts of the large mass of petty cases, as to enable us to greatly increase the

27

size of the districts and reduce the number of judges, and thereby save much of the past cost of the present judicial system, and secure a much cheaper judicial system than that presented by the majority of the committee, which gives the District Courts the same jurisdiction they have under the present system, only slightly relieved by the County Courts proposed, from which many litigants will be driven to the District Courts, where they can obtain a cheaper appeal to a higher court.

By the plan of the County Court we present, a considerable exclusive original jurisdiction is given to it, with trials not less than four times a year; and it is to be always open for the trial of criminal cases—fewer men (six) being required for its juries, and much expense, both to litigants and to the public, will be saved.

These advantages, with the great benefit it is believed will result from the large jurisdiction we propose to give justices of the peace, the localilzing of the administration of the law in petty cases, and the great saving of time and expense which it is believed will be made to individuals and the public, constitute the chief grounds on which we rest our recommendation of the plan of jurisdiction for our courts which we present.

And we think the plan we present will make our judicial system cheap, speedy, efficient and satisfactory to the people.

The great importance we attach to this subject, is our excuse for stating our reasons in favor of this plan at such great length.

JOHN H. REAGAN,
P. R. SCOTT,
C. B. KILGORE,
MARION MARTIN.

" Sec. ——. The Supreme Court shall consist of a Chief Justice and four Associate Justices, any three of whom shall constitute a quorum, and the concurrence of a majority of the judges sitting shall be necessary to the decision of a case.   No prison shall be eligible to the office of Chief Justice or Associate Justice of the Supreme Court unless he be, at the time of his election, a citizen of the United States, and of this State, and unless he shall have attained the age of thirty years, and shall have been a practicing lawyer, or judge of a court, in this State, or such lawyer and judge together, at least seven years.   Said Chief Justice and Associate Justices shall be elected by the qualified voters of the State, at a general election; shall hold their offices for eight years, and shall each receive an annual salary of four thousand dollars, which shall not be increased or diminished during his term of office.

" Sec. ——. The Supreme Court shall have appellate jurisdiction only, which shall be co-extensive with the limits of the State; but in criminal cases its appellate jurisdiction shall only extend to cases of felony, to cases of misdemeanor involving official misconduct, and to cases of violation of the laws in relation to insurance and banking, and in civil cases to suits involving sums of five hundred dollars or more, exclusive of interests, and to suits, without reference to the amount in controversy, in behalf of the State, to recover penalties, fines, forfeitures, and escheats; to cases of divorce: to suits for the recovery of dmages for slander and defamation of character; to suits for the trial of the title to land, and for the enforcement of liens on land; and to suits involving the constitutionality of a law, or the validity of a law imposing a tax. And it shall have such jurisdiction, by appeal, over interlocutory judgments of the District Courts, with such exceptions and under such regulations as may be prescribed by law. The Supreme Courts, and the judges thereof, shall have power to issue the writ of *habeas corpus,* and, under such regulation as may be prescribed by law, the said court, and the judges thereof, may issue the writ of *mandamus,* and such other writs as may be necessary to enforce its own jurisdiction. The Supreme Court shall also have power, upon affidavits or otherwise, as to the court shall seem proper, to ascertain such matters of fact as may be necessary to the proper exercise of its own jurisdiction. And it shall sit for the transaction of business from the first Monday in October until the last Saturday in June of every year, at the seat of government, and at not more than two other places.

" Sec. ——. The District Court shall have original jurisdiction in criminal cases of the grade of felony; in cases of misdemeanor involving official misconduct; in all cases of gambling, including betting on elections; and in all cases of violation of the laws in relation to insurance and banking. And they shall have jurisdiction in criminal cases, brought by appeal from the County Courts, in all cases of which the County Courts may have original jurisdiction which cases shall be tried on the record from the County Court, and without further right of appeal.

" In civil cases the District Courts shall have original jurisdiction of all suits in behalf of the State to recover penalties, fines, forfeitures and escheats; of all cases of divorce; of all suits to recover damages for slander and defamation of character; of all suits for the trial of the title to land, and to enforce liens on land; and of all suits involving the constitutionality of any law; or to test the validity of a law imposing a tax; and of all suits, complaints and pleas whatever, without regard to any distinction between law and equity, when the matter in controversy shall not be less than five hundred dollars, exclusive of interest; and the said courts and judges thereof shall have power to issue the writs of *habeas corpus, mandamus,* injunction, *certiorari,* and all other writs necessary to enforce their own jurisdiction, and to give them a general superintendence and control over inferior tribunals. And they shall have appellate jurisdiction of all civil cases originating in the County Courts, which cases shall be tried on the record of the County Courts, without further right of appeal. And the District Courts shall have original and appellate jurisdiction and general control over County Courts, sitting as probate courts, for appointing guardians, granting letters testamentary or of administration; for settling the accounts of executors, administrators and guardians, and for the transaction of business appertaining to estates; and such original jurisdiction and general control over executors, administrators, guardians and minors, and under such regulations as may be prescribed by law.

"Sec. ——. There shall be established in each county in this State a County Court, which shall be a court of record; and there shall be elected in each county, by the qualified voters, a County Judge, who shall be well informed in the law of the State; shall be a conservator of the peace, and shall hold his office for two years, and until his successor shall be elected and qualified. He shall receive as compensation for his services such fees and perquisites as may be precribed by law.

"Sec. ——. The County Court shall have exclusive original jurisdiction of all misdemeanors, for which the fine or penalty, shall be not less than two hundred nor more than five hundred dollars, as the same are now or may be hereafter prescribed by law, except in case of official misconduct; and they shall have jurisdiction concurrent with the District Courts in all cases of gambling, including betting on elections, and cases of the violation of the laws in relation to insurance and banking. And they shall have exclusive original jurisdiction in all civil cases, when the amount involved is not less than two hundred nor more than five hundred dollars, exclusive of interest, except in such cases as are otherwise provided for in this constitution; and they shall have such other jurisdiction as may be conferred on they by law. And they shall have appellate jurisdiction of all cases, evil and criminal, of which justices' courts shall have original jurisdiction, when the judgment of the court appealed from shall exceed the sum of ten dollars, exclusive of costs, under such regulations as may be prescribed by law, with such appellate jurisdiction from corporation courts, and other inferior tribunals, as may be prescribed by law. In all appeals from justices' courts, or corporation courts, or other inferior tribunals, the cases so appealed shall be tried *de novo* in the County Courts, and such trial shall be final, under such regulations, and with such exceptions, as may be provided by law.

The County Courts shall have the general jurisdiction of a probate court. They shall probate wills, appoint guardians of minors, idiots, lunatics, persons *non compos mentis,* and common drunkards; grant letters testamentary and of administration; settle the accounts of executors, administrators and guardians; transact all business appertaining to the estates of deceased person, minors, idiots, lunatics, persons *non compos mentis,* and common drunkards, including the settlement, partition and distribution of such estates, and to apprentice minors as provided by law. And the County Courts, or the judges thereof, shall have power to issue writs of mandamus, injunction, and all other writs necessary to the enforcement of the jurisdiction of said courts; and to issue writs of *habeas corpus* in cases where the offense charged is within the jurisdiction of the County Court, or any other court or tribunal inferior to said court.

The County Courts shall not have criminal jurisdiction in any county where there is a criminal District Court, unless expressly conferred by law, and in such counties appeals from Justices' Courts and other inferior courts and tribunals, shall be to the civil or criminal District Courts under such regulations as may be prescribed by law.

"Sec. —. There shall be not less than four terms of the County Court a year, as may be provided by law, for the trial of civil cases, and the Legislature may prescribe what probate orders may be made and business done in vacation, and said court shall always be open for the trial of criminal cases. Prosecutions may be commenced in said court by information filed by the county attorney, or by affidavit, as may be provided by law.

Grand juries, empannelled in the District Courts, shall inquire into misdemeanors, and all indictments therefor returned into the District Courts, shall forthwith be certified to the County Courts, or other inferior courts, having jurisdiction to try them, for trial, and if such indictments be quashed in the county, or other inferior courts, the person charged shall not be discharged, if there is probable cause of guilt, but may be held by such court or magistrate to answer an information or affidavit.

A jury in the County Court shall consist of six men, but no

jury shall be empannelled to try a civil case, unless demanded by one of the parties, who shall pay such jury fee therefor, in advance, as may be prescribed by law, unless he makes affidavit that he is unable to pay the same.

"Sec. ——. Each county shall be divided into five justice's precincts, for each of which precincts there shall be elected, by the qualified voters thereof, a Justice of the Peace, who shall hold his office for two years, and until his successor shall be elected and qualified, who shall exercise such jurisdiction, and perform such duties, and receive such compensation, as may be prescribed by law. Justices of the Peace shall have jurisdiction in criminal matters of all cases where the penalty or fine imposed on conviction shall be for two hundred dollars or less; and in civil matters of all cases where the amount in controversy is two hundred dollars or less, exclusive of interest, in which exclusive original jurisdiction is not given to the District or County Courts; and such other jurisdiction, criminal and civil, as may be provided by law. And the Justices of the Peace shall, *ex-officio*, be Notaries Public, and they shall hold their courts at such times and places as may be provided by law.

"Sec. ——. The Legislature shall, at its first session, provide for the transfer of all business, civil and criminal, pending in the District Courts, over which jurisdiction is given by this constitution to the County Courts or other inferior courts, to such county or inferior courts; and for the trial or disposition of all such cases by such county or other inferior courts.

[Mr. Brown in the chair.]

Messrs. Norvell and DeMorse gave notice of a minority report.

Mr. Stockdale moved to print two hundred copies of report.

Mr. Crawford moved to print five hundred copies.

Lost.

Two hundred copies ordered.

Mr. Fleming submitted the following report:

> COMMITTEE ROOM, }
> AUSTIN, October 20, 1875. }

To the Hon. E. B. Pickett, President of the Convention:

The undersigned, one of the Committee on Revenue and Taxation, not being able to concur with the majority of said committee in many of the sections submitted by them, begs leave to submit the following article as a substitute for the majority report, and ask that the same may be adopted.

J. R. FLEMING, Chairman.

"ARTICLE —.
" TAXATION AND REVENUE.

" Section 1. Taxation shall be equal and uniform throughout the State, and all property in the State shall be taxed in proportion to its value, to be ascertained as may be provided by law, except such property as two-thirds of both Houses of the Legislature may think proper to exempt from taxation.

" Sec. 2. Taxes shall be levied and collected by general laws and for public purposes only.

" Sec. 3. The power to tax corporations and corporate property shall not be surrendered or suspended by act of the Legislature.

" Sec. 4. All railroad corporations in this State, or doing business therein, shall be subject to taxation for State, county, school, municipal and other purposes on the real and personal property owned or used by them, and on their gross earnings, their net earnings, their franchises, and their capital stock.

" Sec. 5. The State tax on property, exclusive of the tax necessary to pay the public debt of the State, shall never exceed one-half of one per cent. on the one hundred dollars valuation.

" Sec. 6. No county, city, town, or other municipal corporation, nor the inhabitants thereof, nor the property therein, shall be released or discharged from their or its proportionate share of taxes to be levied for State purposes, nor shall commutation for such taxes be authorized in any form whatever.

" Sec. 7. The Legislature shall not impose taxes upon counties, cities, towns, or other municipal corporations, or upon the inhabitants or property thereof for county, city, town, or other municipal purposes, but may by general laws vest in the corporate authorities thereof the power to assess and collect taxes for such purposes.

" Sec. 8. All land, whether owned by persons or corporations, shall be assessed for taxation, and the taxes paid in the county where situated. Lands not rendered for assessment shall be assessed by the proper assessing officer, and in no case shall be valued at less than fifty cents per acre.

" Sec. 9. Lands in unorganized counties shall be assessed and the taxes paid in the counties to which such unorganized counties shall be attached for judicial purposes.

" Sec. 10. Provision shall be made by the first Legislature for the speedy condemnation and sale of all lands for the taxes due thereon, and every year thereafter for the sale of all lands upon which the taxes have not been paid, and the deed of conveyance to the purchaser for all lands thus sold shall be held to vest a good and perfect title in the purchaser thereof, subject to be impeached only for actual fraud; *provided,* the former owner shall, within two years from the date of the purchaser's deed, have the right to redeem the land upon the payment to the purchaser of three times the amount of money paid for the land.

"Sec. 11. There shall be an assessor of taxes in each county in this State, who shall be appointed or elected in such manner and under such regulations as the Legislature may direct.

"Sec. 12. The sheriff of each county, in addition to his other duties, shall be the collector of taxes therefor.

"Sec. 13. The specification of the objects and subjects of taxation shall not deprive the Legislature of the power to require other subjects or objects to be taxed in such manner as may be consistent with the principles of taxation fixed in this constitution.

"Sec. 14. The sheriff, county clerk, and chief justice shall compose a Board of Equalization in each county, to hear appeals by property holders, and determine the just value of the property rendered for taxation."

On motion of Mr. McCormick, one hundred copies of the report and article were ordered printed.

Mr. McLean withdrew his motion to reconsider and lay on the table the vote engrossing the article on the subject of immigration.

Mr. Stockdale moved to reconsider the vote engrossing the article on immigration.

[Mr. Brown in the chair.]

Mr. Pickett moved that the consideration of the motion be postponed to this day week, and that it be made the special order for 10 o'clock that day.

Carried.

On motion of Mr. Chambers, the Convention adjourned to 2½ P. M.

EVENING SESSION---2½ o'clock.

Convention met pursuant to adjournment; roll called; quorum present.

BUSINESS ON THE TABLE.

The reports of the majority and minority of the committee on the subject of granting and reserving lands to railroads were taken up.

Mr. Nugent moved to postpone the consideration of the reports until 10 o'clock Monday, and made the special order for that hour.

On motion of Mr. German, the rules were suspended and the report and article on railroads taken up, and read the second time.

Mr. Brown offered the following amendment, to come in as an additional section:

" Sec. 9. The Legislature shall pass no law retrospective in its operations, which may impose on the people of any town, county, or other municipal sub-division of the State, a new liability in respect to transactions or considerations already passed, nor to revive obligations to any individual, association, or corporation, which may have previously become void by default of such individual association or corporation."

Mr. Nugent offered the following amendment:

" The Legislature shall pass no law extending the time for the construction, in whole or in part, of railroads, beyond the period limited in the laws providing for their construction."

Withdrawn.

Mr. Wade moved to recommit the article and amendments to the Committee on Railroad Corporations.

Lost.

Mr. Nugent withdrew his amendment.

Mr. Waelder offered the following amendment:

Strike out in line 21 the words " for public inspection," and insert therefor " for inspection by the stockholders of such corporation."

Adopted.

Mr. McCormick offered the following amendment:

Amend line 35, section 4, by inserting after the word " property " the words " or any part thereof.".

Adopted.

Mr. Brown offered the following amendment:

Add as an additional section:

" Sec.——. No railroad hereafter constructed in this State shall pass within a distance of three miles of any county seat without passing through the same and establishing and maintaining a depot therein, unless prevented by natural obstacles, such as streams, hills, or mountains: *provided*, such town, or its citizens, shall grant the right of way through its limits, and sufficient ground for ordinary depot purposes."

Mr. Wade moved to amend the amendment by striking out the word " through " and inserting " within a half mile of the same."

Mr. Fleming moved the main question.

Lost.

Mr. Wade's amendment was lost.

Mr. Brown's amendment was adopted by the following vote:

YEAS—Allison, Abernathy, Arnim, Brown, Blassingame, Barnett, Burleson, Brady, Bruce, Crawford, Chambers, Cook of Gonzales, Cooke of San Saba, Dillard, DeMorse, Darnell, Davis of Wharton, Erhard, Ford, Fleming, German, Gaither, Graves, Henry of Smith, Henry of Limestone, Haynes, Johnson of Franklin, Johnson of Collin, Kilgore, Lacy, Lynch, McLean, Martin of Navarro, Martin of Hunt, Morris, Mills, McKinney of Denton, McKinney of Walker, McCormick, Murphy, Norvell, Nunn, Nugent, Pauli, Ramey, Rentfro, Robertson of Bell, Robeson of Fayette, Ross, Russell of Wood, Spikes, Scott, Sessions, Stockdale, Stayton, Sansom, Wade, Wright, Weaver—59.

NAYS—Abner, Blake, Cline, Cardis, Douglas, Dohoney, Davis of Brazos, Ferris, Holt, King, Killough, McCabe, Reagan, Reynolds, Russell of Harrison, Smith, Whitehead, Whitfield, West, Waelder—20.

Mr. Stockdale proposed to amend section 3, line 29, by striking out the word "all."

Adopted.

Mr. King proposed to amend section 3, line 28, after the word "and" insert "President or Superintendent."

Adopted.

Mr. Stayton offered to amend section 2, line 14, by striking out all after the word "State."

Mr. Sansom offered as a substitute for the amendment to strike out section 2.

Mr. Whitfield moved the previous question.

Carried.

The question on the adoption of Mr. Stayton's amendment was put and amendment lost by the following vote:

YEAS—Abner, Ballinger, Cline, Cardis, King, Lockett, McCabe, Morris, Reynolds, Russell of Harrison, Stockdale, Stayton, Sansom, West, Waelder—15.

NAYS—Allison, Abernathy, Arnim, Blake, Blassingame, Barnett, Burleson, Brady, Bruce, Crawford, Chambers, Cook of Gonzales, Cooke of San Saba, Douglas, Dillard, DeMorse, Dohoney, Darnell, Davis of Brazos, Davis of Wharton, Erhard, Flournoy, Fleming, Ferris, German, Gaither, Graves, Holt, Henry of Smith, Henry of Limestone, Haynes, Johnson of Franklin, Johnson of Collin, Kilgore, Killough, Lacy, Lynch, McLean, Martin of Navarro, Martin of Hunt, Mills, Mitchell, McKinney of Denton, McKinney of Walker, McCormick,

Murphy, Norvell, Nunn, Nugent, Pauli, Reagan, Ramey, Rentfro, Robertson of Bell, Bobeson of Fayette, Ross, Russell of Wood, Spikes, Scott, Sessions, Smith, Wade, Whitehead, Wright, Weaver, Whitfield—66.

The question on the adoption of Mr. Sansom's amendment was put, and amendment lost by the following vote:

YEAS—Cline, Cardis, Lockett, McCabe, Reynolds, Russell of Harrison, Stockdale, Sansom, West, Waelder—10.

NAYS—Allison, Abernathy, Arnim, Abner, Blake, Ballinger, Blassingame, Barnett, Burleson, Brady, Bruce, Crawford, Chambers, Cook of Gonzales, Cooke of San Saba, Douglas, Dillard, DeMorse, Dohoney, Darnell, Davis of Brazos, Davis of Wharton, Erhard, Flournoy, Fleming, Ferris, German, Gaither, Graves, Holt, Henry of Smith, Henry of Limestone, Haynes, Johnson of Franklin, Johnson of Collin, King, Kilgore, Killough, Lacy, Lynch, McLean, Martin of Navarro, Martin of Hunt, Morris, Mills, Mitchell, McKinney of Denton, McKinney of Walker, McCormick, Murphy, Norvell, Nunn, Nugent, Pauli, Reagan, Ramey, Rentfro, Robertson of Bell, Robeson of Fayette, Ross, Russell of Wood, Spikes, Scott, Sessions, Smith, Stayton, Wade, Whitehead, Wright, Weaver, Whitfield—71.

The question recurring upon the engrossment of the article, the same was put and the article ordered engrossed by the following vote:

YEAS—Allison, Abernathy, Arnim, Abner, Blake, Blassingame, Barnett, Burleson, Bruce, Crawford, Chambers, Cook of Gonzales, Cooke of San Saba, Douglas, Dillard, DeMorse, Dohoney, Darnell, Davis of Brazos, Erhard, Flournoy, Fleming, Ferris, German, Gaither, Graves, Holt, Henry of Smith, Henry of Limestone, Haynes, Johnson of Franklin, Johnson of Collin, Kilgore, Killough, Lacy, Lynch, McLean, Martin of Navarro, Martin of Hunt, Morris, Mitchell, McKinney of Denton, McKinney of Walker, McCormick, Murphy, Norvell, Nunn, Nugent, Reagan, Ramey, Robertson of Bell, Robeson of Fayette, Ross, Russell of Wood, Spikes, Scott, Sessions, Smith, Stockdale, Wade, Whitehead, Wright, Weaver, Whitfield—64.

NAYS—Ballinger, Brady, Cline, Cardis, Davis of Wharton, Lockett, McCabe, Pauli, Reynolds, Rentfro, Russell of Harrison, Stayton, Sansom, West, Waelder—15.

On motion of Mr. Stockdale the Convention adjourned to 9 o'clock A. M. to-morrow.

FORTIETH DAY.

HALL OF REPRESENTATIVES, ⎱
AUSTIN, TEXAS, October 21, 1875. ⎰

Convention met pursuant to adjournment; roll called; quorum present. Prayer by the Rev. T. B. Lee, Rector of St. David's Church at Austin.

On motion of Mr. Scott, Mr. Norvell was excused for to-day.

Mr. Mills presented the petition of sundry citizens of Huntsville, in Walker county, on the subject of ex-convicts from the penitentiary, prohibiting them from remaining in Walker county after release.

Referred to Committee on Penitentiary.

Mr. McKinney presented the petition of Dugald McAlpine on the subject of public schools.

Referred to Committee on Education.

Also, the petition of same person on the subject of wills.

Referred to Committee on Judiciary.

The Chair announced the following select committee on the ordinance of Mr. Martin, of Hunt, on the subject of poll-tax:

Messrs. Kilgore, Holt, Darnell, Chambers and Burleson.

Mr. Abernathy offered the following resolution:

Resolved, That weights and measures shall be uniform throughout this State, and a standard of the same may be established anywhere that application may be made.

Referred to Committee on General Provisions.

Mr. Darnell submitted the following report:

COMMITTEE ROOM, ⎱
AUSTIN, October 20, 1875. ⎰

To the Hon. E. B. Pickett, President of the Convention:

. A majority of your Committee on Public Lands and Land Office, to whom was referred the article previously reported by them on the subject of public lands and land office, and various amendments offered to the same, together with various other resolutions, beg leave to say that they have considered the subject, and instruct me to report the accompanying article.

Respectfully submitted,

N. H. DARNELL, Chairman.

" ARTICLE —.

" Sec. 1. There shall be one General Land Office in the State, which shall be at the seat of government, where all land titles which have emanated, or may hereafter emanate from the State, shall be registered, except those titles the registration of which may be prohibited by this constitution. It shall be the duty of the Legislature, at the earliest practicable time, to make the Land Office self-sustaining, and from time to time the Legislature may establish such subordinate offices as may be deemed necessary.

" Sec. 2. All unsatisfied genuine land certificates barred by section 4, article 10 of the constitution of 1869, by reason of the holders or owners thereof failing to have them surveyed and returned to the Land Office by the first day of January, 1875, are hereby revived. All unsatisfied genuine land certificates now in existence shall be surveyed and returned to the General Land Office within five years after the adoption of this constitution or be forever barred; and all genuine land certificates hereafter issued by the State shall be surveyed and returned to the General Land Office within five years after issuance, or be forever barred; *provided*, that all land certificates heretofore or hereafter issued shall be located, surveyed or patented only upon vacant and unappropriated public domain, and not upon any land titled or equitably owned under color of title from the sovereignty of the State, evidence of the appropriation of which is on the county records or in the General Land Office.

" Sec. 3. The Legislature shall have no power to grant any of the public lands of this State to any railway company, except upon the following restrictions and conditions: First, that there shall never be granted to any such corporation more than sixteen sections of land to the mile, and no reservation of any part of the public domain for the purpose of satisfying such grant shall ever be made; Secondly, that no land certificates shall be issued to such company until they have equipped, constructed and in running order, at least twenty-five miles of road, and on the failure of such company to comply with the terms of its charter, or to alienate its land at a period to be fixed by law, in no event to exceed twelve years from the issuance of the patent, all said land shall be forfeited to the State and become a portion of the public domain, and liable to location and survey, and the Legislature shall have no power to extend the time or grant relief to any company obtaining a grant of land or land certificates, after the adoption of this constitution.

" Sec. 4. No certificate for land shall be sold at the Land Office except to actual settlers upon the same, and in lots not to exceed one hundred and sixty acres.

" Sec. 5. All lands heretofore or hereafter granted to railway companies, where the charter or law of the State required, or shall hereafter require, their alienation within a certain period, on pain of forfeiture, or is silent on the subject of forfeiture, and which lands have not been, or shall not hereafter be, alienated in conformity with the terms of their charters and the laws under which the grants were made, are hereby declared forfeited to the State and subject to pre-emption, location and survey, as other vacant lands. All lands heretofore granted to said railway companies to which no forfeiture was attached on their failure to alienate are not included in the foregoing clause, but in all such last named cases it shall be the duty of the Attorney General, in every instance where alienations have been or hereafter may be made, to inquire into the same, and if such alienation has been made in fraud of the rights of the State, and is colorable only, the real and beneficial interest being still in such corporation, to institute legal proceedings in the county where the seat of government is situated, to forfeit such lands to the State, and if such alienation be judicially ascertained to be fraudulent and colorable as aforesaid, such lands shall be forfeited to the State and become a part of the vacant public domain, liable to pre-emption, location and survey.

" Sec. 6. To every head of a family without a homestead there shall be donated one hundred and sixty acres of public land, upon the condition that he will select and locate said land, occupy the same three years and pay the office fees due thereon. To all single men eighteen years of age and upwards, shall be donated eighty acres of public land, upon the terms and conditions prescribed for heads of families.

" Sec. 7. The State of Texas hereby releases to the owner or owners of the soil all mines and minerals that may be on the same, subject to taxation as other property.

" Sec. 8. Persons residing between the Nueces river and the Rio Grande, and owning grants for lands which emanated from the Government of Spain or that of Mexico, which grants have been recognized and validated by the State by acts of the Legislature, approved February 10, 1852, August 15, 1870, and other acts, and who have been prevented from complying with the requirements of said acts by the unsettled condition of the country or by other causes, shall be allowed until the first day of January, 1880, to complete their surveys, and the plots thereof, and to return their field notes to the General Land Office; and all claimants failing to do so will be forever barred; *provided*, nothing in this section shall be so construed as to validate any titles not already valid, or to interfere with the rights of third persons."

On motion of Mr. Darnell two hundred copies of the report and article were ordered printed.

Mr. Brown offered the following resolution:

Resolved, That the Secretary of State, so far as he can, is requested to furnish to the Convention a list of all railroad charters granted since the commencement of the Legislature of 1866, under which no road has been built.

Resolved further, That he is requested to transmit to the Convention a list of all companies, of whatsoever nature or kind, incorporated under the act "Concerning Private Corporations," approved December 2, 1871, and the various acts amendatory of or supplementary thereto.

Adopted.

BUSINESS ON THE TABLE.

Report and article on Revenue and Taxation taken up, and, on motion of Mr. Fleming, was postponed to, and made special order for, 10 o'clock to-morrow.

Mr. Russell, of Wood, moved to reconsider the vote engrossing the article on railroads.

Mr. Graves moved to lay the motion on the table.

Lost.

The motion of Mr. Russell, of Wood, was carried.

Mr. Mills proposed to amend line 29, section 3, by striking out the words, "or some officer designated by law," and insert "Governor."

Adopted.

Mr. Crawford offered the following amendment:

"No railroad company organized under the laws of this State, shall consolidate by private or judicial sale, or otherwise, with any railroad company organized under the laws of any other State, or of the United States."

Offered as a substitute for section 6.

On motion of Mr. Mills, the main question was ordered.

Question on the substitute of Mr. Crawford for section 6 was put, and substitute adopted.

The article was then ordered engrossed.

Mr. Graves moved to reconsider the vote, and lay the motion on the table.

Carried.

[Mr. Stockdale in the chair.]

Separate section on "County School Lands," on its third reading, was taken up and read the third time.

Mr. Darnell offered the following amendment:

After the word "settlers" in line 11, insert: "Said lands shall be sold on a credit of not less than ten years, the purchaser paying interest at the rate of not more than ten per cent. per annum, and the proceeds thereof when sold shall be held by such county alone as a trust fund for the benefit of schools; said proceeds, when collected in money, to be invested in bonds of the State of Texas, or of the United States, and only the interest thereof to be used and expended annually."

Mr. Gaither offered the following proviso to the amendment:

"*Provided,* That a payment of one-fifth of the purchase money be required on all sales of said lands."

Mr. Scott offered the following as a substitute for the two amendments:

After the word "part," in line 6, insert "to actual settlers on ten years credit, with ten per cent. interest."

Mr. Robertson, of Bell, offered the following amendment to Mr. Scott's substitute:

"*Provided,* That the principal may be paid by the foreclosure at any time, and the amount invested in State or United States bonds, as hereinbefore provided."

Accepted by Mr. Scott as a part of his substitute.

Mr. Chambers moved to refer the article and several amendments to a select committee of five.

Mr. Chambers withdrew his motion to refer.

Mr. Reagan offered the following:

Amend by inserting after the word "settlers," in line 11, the words: "said lands shall be sold on a credit, and payment made in ten equal annual installments, with interest on such sums as may be due, at the rate of eight per cent. per annum, secured by a lien on such lands."

Mr. Scott accepted this as a substitute for his substitute.

Mr. Fleming moved to lay the amendments and substitutes on the table.

Carried by the following vote:

YEAS—Allison, Abernathy, Arnim, Blake, Ballinger, Barnett, Burleson, Cook of Gonzales, Douglas, Davis of Brazos, Davis of Wharton, Erhard, Ford, Flournoy, Fleming, Ferris, German, Gaither, Graves, Holt, Henry of Smith, Henry of Limestone, Haynes, King, Kilgore, Killough, Lockett, Lacy, Lynch, McLean, Martin of Navarro, Martin of Hunt, McCabe, Morris, Mills, Mitchell, McCormick, Murphy, Nunn, Ramey, Reynolds, Rentfro, Robeson of Fayette, Spikes, Sessions, Smith, Stayton, Wade, Whitehead, Wright, Waelder—52.

NAYS—Brown, Blassingame, Bruce, Crawford, Chambers, Cooke of San Saba, Cline, Dillard, DeMorse, Darnell, Johnson of Franklin, McKinney of Denton, Nugent, Pauli, Reagan, Russell of Harrison, Russell of Wood, Scott, Weaver, Whitfield —20.

Mr. Nugent proposed to amend by striking out of line 6 the words " in whole or in part," and insert " in tracts not exceeding three hundred and twenty acres;" also strike out "one hundred and sixty," line 9, and insert "three hundred and twenty."

Mr. Wade offered the following as a substitute for the amendment:

Strike out all from the word "county," in line 7, to the word "said," in line 11.

On motion of Mr. Dillard, the amendment and substitute were laid on the table.

Mr. Cline offered the following amendment:

Strike out the sentence beginning in line 5 and ending in line 7, and insert the following:

"The county school lands shall be sub-divided into equal portions, not exceeding one hundred and sixty acre tracts, whereof the alternate tracts may be sold at public auction, on such terms and conditions as may be prescribed by law. The Commissioners' Court of the county owning said lands may lease said tracts on such conditions as may be authorized by law. When any such tract may be sold, one-fourth the price shall be paid cash, and the balance in six equal annual payments, with ten per cent. from date of sale, and secured by lien on the land."

On motion of Mr. Mills the amendment was laid on the table.

On motion of Mr. Dillard the main question was ordered.

The question on the final passage of the section was then put, and the same passed by the following vote:

YEAS—Allison, Abernathy, Arnim, Brown, Blake, Ballinger, Barnett, Burleson, Bruce, Chambers, Cook of Gonzales, Douglas, Dillard, Dohoney, Davis of Brazos, Davis of Wharton, Erhard, Ford, Flournoy, Fleming, Ferris, German, Gaither, Graves, Holt, Henry of Smith, Henry of Limestone, Haynes, Johnson of Franklin, Johnson of Collin, King, Kilgore, Killough, Lockett, Lacy, Lynch, McLean, Martin of Navarro, Martin of Hunt, McCabe, Morris, Mills, Mitchell, McKinney of Denton, McKinney of Walker, McCormick, Murphy, Nunn, Nugent, Reagan, Ramey, Reynolds, Robeson of Fayette, Russell of Wood, Spikes, Scott, Sessions, Smith, Stayton, Whitehead, Wright, Weaver, Whitfield, Waelder—65.

NAYS—Abner, Blassingame, Cooke of San Saba, Cline, Cardis, DeMorse, Darnell, Pauli, Rentfro, Russell of Harrison, Wade—10.

28

On motion of Mr. Brown, the Convention adjourned to 2:30 o'clock P. M.

EVENING SESSION—2½ o'clock.

Convention met pursuant to adjournment; roll called; quorum present.

Mr. Abernathy moved to reconsider the vote passing the section on county school lands, and to lay the motion on the table. Carried.

Article ——, "Bill of Rights," on its third reading and final passage, taken up and read third time.

Mr. Waelder moved to strike out section 1, "Boundaries." Carried.

Mr. McCormick moved to reconsider the vote just taken, and to lay the motion on the table. Carried.

Mr. Dohoney offered the following amendment:

Amend section 8 by inserting before the word "in," in line 40, the words "every citizen shall be at liberty to speak, write, or publish his opinions on any subject, being responsible for the abuse of that privilege; and no law shall ever be passed curtailing the liberty of speech or of the press." Adopted.

Mr. Stockdale offered the following as a substitute for section 12:

"Sec. 12. The writ of *habeas corpus* is a writ of right. The right to have this writ, from the proper court or judge, shall never be suspended, except by act of the Legislature. The Legislature shall never suspend this right, except there be such hostile invasion of the State, by organized, armed force, as shall put in peril the safety of the State, or such rebellion within the State as shall make it necessary in order to preserve the authority of the State government; and only in these cases, in reference to arrests upon charges, made upon oath, of treason, conspiracy to commit treason, or some other offense, defined by law, against the authority of the government. Nor shall any person be held in arrest upon a charge of offense against the authority of the government, except upon a judicial warrant. When the right is suspended in accordance with the foregoing condition, then a person in arrest under judicial warrant, may be held in a place of safety, and removed, as circumstances may require, by the Executive or under his authority, and shall be so safely held without the benefit of trial, bail, or mainprize until the act suspending the right shall be repealed or shall expire by its own limitation.

"Every suspension of the right to the writ of *habeas corpus* by act of the Legislature shall be for a time certain, not to exceed ...... months."

On motion of Mr. Dillard, it was laid on the table.

Mr. Ballinger offered the following amendment:

Section 23, line 105, next before the word "regulate" insert "prohibit and."

On motion of Mr. Nugent, laid on the table.

Mr. Stockdale offered the following as a substitute for section 28:

"Sec. 28. No law or laws of this State shall be suspended except by the Legislature, which may only suspend in the same manner as laws are made or repealed. Whenever a law is suspended it shall be for a time certain."

Mr. Wade proposed to amend the amendment by inserting after "Legislature" the words, "by a two-thirds vote."

Lost.

Mr. Stockdale's substitute was lost.

Mr. Cline proposed to amend by striking out of section 21 the words, "and the estates of those who destroy their own lives shall descend or vest, as in case of natural death."

Lost.

Mr. King proposed to amend as follows:

Amend section 1, line 3, by striking out the words, "subject only to," and insert in lieu thereof, "limited only by."

Mr. Sansom offered the following substitute for the amendment:

At the end of line 3, section 1, insert "limitations imposed by."

Mr. Crawford offered section 1 of the original article, as it was reported by the committee, for section 1 of the engrossed article.

Mr. Gaither moved to adjourn.

Lost.

On motion of Mr. Fleming, the main question was ordered.

Mr. Sansom's substitute lost.

Mr. King's amendment lost.

The question then, on Mr. Crawford's substitute, was put and substitute lost by the following vote, it requiring a two-thirds vote to amend:

YEAS—Allison, Abernathy, Barnett, Burleson, Crawford, Cook of Gonzales, Cardis, Dillard, DeMorse, Darnell, Davis of Brazos, Henry of Limestone, Haynes, Kilgore, Killough, Lynch, Martin of Hunt, McKinney of Denton, McKinney of Walker, Norvell, Nunn, Reagan, Robertson of Bell, Spikes, Scott, Whitehead, Wright, Whitfield—28.

NAYS—Arnim, Abner, Brown, Ballinger, Blassingame, Bruce, Chambers, Cooke of San Saba, Cline, Douglas, Dohoney, Davis of Wharton, Erhard, Ford, Flournoy, Fleming, Ferris, Gaither, Graves, Holt, Henry of Smith, Johnson of Franklin, Johnson of Collin, King, Lockett, Lacy, McLean, Martin of Navarro, McCabe, Morris, Mills, Mitchell, McCormick, Murphy, Nugent, Pauli, Reynolds, Robeson of Fayette, Russell of Harrison, Russell of Wood, Sessions, Smith, Stockdale, Stayton, Sansom, Weaver, Waelder—47.

The article —, "Bill of Rights," was then finally passed by the following vote:

YEAS—Allison, Abernathy, Arnim, Brown, Ballinger, Blassingame, Barnett, Burleson, Crawford, Chambers, Cook of Gonzales, Cooke of San Saba, Cardis, Douglas, Dillard, DeMorse, Dohoney, Darnell, Davis of Brazos, Davis of Wharton, Erhard, Ford, Flournoy, Fleming, Ferris, German, Gaither, Graves, Henry of Smith, Henry of Limestone, Haynes, Johnson of Franklin, Johnson of Collin, King, Kilgore, Killough, Lacy, Lynch, McLean, Martin of Navarro, McCabe, Morris, McKinney of Denton, McKinney of Walker, McCormick, Murphy, Norvell, Nunn, Nugent, Reagan, Robertson of Bell, Robeson of Fayette, Russell of Wood, Spikes, Scott, Sessions, Smith, Stockdale, Stayton, Sansom, Wade, Whitehead, Wright, Weaver, Whitfield, Waelder—66.

NAYS—Abner, Cline, Lockett, Mills, Mitchell, Pauli, Reynolds, Rentfro, Russell of Harrison—9.

On motion of Mr. King, the Convention adjourned until 9 o'clock A. M. to-morrow.

FORTY-FIRST DAY.

HALL OF REPRESENTATIVES,   }
AUSTIN, TEXAS, October 22, 1875. }

Convention met pursuant to adjournment; roll called; quorum present. Prayer by the Rev. T. B. Lee, of St. David's Church, at Austin.

Journal of yesterday read and adopted.

Mr. Wright presented the petition of the Paris bar asking the passage of an ordinance validating certain acts of justices of the peace in Lamar county.

Referred to Committee on Ordinances.

Mr. DeMorse submitted the following minority report and article:

To the Hon. E. B. Pickett, President of the Convention:

The undersigned, a member of the Committee on the Judicial Department, being unable to agree with the majority of said committee in many of their recommendations, begs leave to submit to the Convention the accompanying plan of judicial administration.

He believes that the greatest relief to be afforded to the people by a new constitution, is to be found in a radical change of the judicial system, and a great reduction of its cost, and such a thorough reorganization as will make it largely self-sustaining, leave masses of the people, now forcibly drawn from their homes for weeks at a time (and most wrongfully at their own expense), to continue at their occupations, and eradicate as near as may be, that wrong of all systems heretofore—making the peaceful and uncontesting and laborious bear the burthens imposed by the litigious—in effect, forcing the best citizens to bear burdens they have not created, by changing wholly also that system by which the jails are kept full, and the counties are taxed to feed the inmates (the honest people being punished in order to punish the criminals), by providing prompt trial for offenders, and when they are convicted and adjudged to punishment, forcing them to labor in the service of the counties where the wrong is committed, and which have been burdened with their trial and punishment; and in pursuance of this object, so constituting the Supreme Court, that all appeals in criminal cases can be promptly responded to, instead of a delay of several months, during which the honest laborers of the country are taxed for food for the criminal drone. As a part of this system of reorganization and retrenchment, the undersigned proposes to give the trial of all petty criminal cases to the magistrates, and in all cases except those involving extreme punishment, avoiding cost of transportation to the Penitentiary, and placing the labor which now brings no compensation whatever to the State at the service of the counties, which can profitably employ it, under the direction of a county overseer, and may, by the use of that labor, keep the public roads always in good order, and establish county poor-farms, upon which paupers, by the aid of this labor, may become self-sustaining. In addition to this, the convict force may be employed upon any other character of labor beneficial to the counties, or be placed at the service of individuals for hire, as is now successfully and profitably done by the lessees of the State Penitentiary; the proceeds of such hire to go into the county treasury. Arrangements can be made for the security of the prisoners while at labor and their confinement at night.

There is another object to be held in view not less in magnitude—the preservation of the purity of adjudication and the preservation of life, liberty and property, by constituting juries only of intelligent citizens of good character, and, secondarily, the reduction of cost, by reducing the useless number composing them. The undersigned believes that it can not be demonstrated by reasoning that twelve intelligent men are more likely to give a correct verdict than five of that same number.

In fact, it is clear to him that the ponderous jury system heretofore in use, however reasonable it may have been when the masses of the people where it prevailed were ignorant, and its security to life and property lay in the hope that in that mass of ignorance a grain of intelligence could be found to direct the mass, or of stubborn honesty to resist corrupt tendencies, neither of these considerations is valuable now, if we will constitute intelligent juries, composed exclusively of persons of good character, and permitting lack of intelligence, as bounded by a knowledge of reading and writing, or a lack of good character, to constitute a right of peremptory challenge. Finally, by a small docket fee, the State can be largely reimbursed for the salaries paid to judges, by compelling those who desire the service of the courts to repay in some measure the cost.

All of which is respectfully submitted.

CHARLES DeMORSE,
One of the Committee.

"The Judicial Department of the State shall consist of a Supreme Court of two divisions; of twenty District Judges, having a convenient jurisdiction, to be defined by the Legislature; of a County Court for each organized county in the State; of such municipal courts as the Legislature may create, and a magistracy, of number to suit extent of territory within each county, and sufficient for the convenience of the people; and all of these officers shall be elective by the people.

"The Supreme Court shall be of two divisions, one known as the Supreme Court of Civil Jurisdiction, and the other as the Supreme Court of Criminal Jurisdiction; and the judges thereof shall be voted for with reference to the division to which they are to be assigned.

"The Supreme Court shall be an appellate court, but either branch shall have the power to issue writs of *habeas corpus, man-*

damus and injunction, and shall have a general controlling superintendence over inferior courts.

" The criminal division shall take cognizance of all appeals from the District and County Courts, and the civil division shall hear all appeals from the District Court, and by *certiorari,* approved by a district judge, from the County Courts.

" The Supreme Court shall have power, upon affidavit or otherwise, to ascertain facts necessary to the just exercise of its jurisdiction.

" The civil division of the Supreme Court shall sit at stated periods, to be determined by the Legislature, at the seat of government, at ......, and at ......, unless, from reasons of public necessity, the Legislature shall provide otherwise.

" The criminal division shall sit continuously throughout the year, at the seat of government, with such interruptions only as may be created by ill health of the judges, or a recess in midsummer, nor exceeding two months.

" There shall be a clerk for each division of the Supreme Court, including one for each locality at which the civil division shall hold its sessions; which clerks shall be appointed by a majority of the judges in each division, and shall give such bonds as may be required by the court, and shall hold their offices during good behavior.

" Each division of the Supreme Court shall be composed of three judges, and each division shall elect its own chief justice, and in case of inability to agree, the Governor shall determine by appointment.

" The salaries of the Supreme Judges shall be $3500 each per annum, and shall be paid by the State upon stated claims to be approved by the Comptroller, and they shall hold their offices for the period of six years; and no citizen shall be eligible to a Supreme Judgship unless he shall have been engaged in the practice of law in this State for at least ten years, or shall have been a judge of a State court for that length of time, or shall have been ten years occupied by legal pursuits either in one capacity or both.

"A judge of the Supreme Court may be presented for impeachment, by either branch of that tribunal, upon charges of official misconduct, and that presentation being indorsed by the Governor, shall be tried by the Senate, the Attorney General acting as prosecutor in behalf of the State.

" The style of all writs and process shall be ' The State of Texas.' All prosecutions shall be carried on in the name, and by the authority of 'The State of Texas,' and shall conclude, 'against the peace and dignity of the State.'

" The District Courts shall have jurisdiction in such counties as may be assigned to each district by the Legislature, and the judges thereof may authorize the issue of remedial process in adjoining districts whenever upon a sworn statement of facts and application for relief, they shall deem such action essential to the enforcement of equity.

" No Judge of a District Court shall be of bad moral character, less than thirty years of age; or shall be eligible to the station unless he shall have been engaged in the practice of the law in the State of Texas not less than five years prior to his entrance upon the duties of his office; and for any deficiency of any of these qualifications, or for misconduct in office, he may be impeached by presentation of two-thirds of the attorneys of the court residing in his district, and upon such impeachment indorsed by the Supreme Court of civil jurisdiction, he may be tried by the Supreme Court of criminal jurisdiction, and upon recognition and indorsement of the charges by the civil Supreme Court, the Governor shall suspend the exercise of his functions, and appoint a judge *pro tem.* for his district; and if the Criminal Supreme Court shall declare the charges proven, and an adequate cause for removal, the Governor shall, without delay, give thirty days' notice by proclamation, that a vacancy exists, and authorize an election to be held in the district at the termination of that time to fill the unexpired term.

" The District Court shall have two terms in each year, at such times as the Legislature shall direct, and may, by authorization of the Legislature, hold special terms.

" The District Court shall have original jurisdiction in suits for assumpsit for above five hundred dollars, and concurrent jurisdiction with the County Court for all sums not less than two hundred dollars, exclusive of interest, and all cases of breach of contract, fraud, slander, divorce, trial of title to land, for enforcement of liens, trial of right of property, either under levy or fraudulent seizure, where the amount involved exceeds two hundred dollars, and of all suits of whatever character involving the rights of the State, and of all suits, complaints or pleas whatever where the value in controversy exceeds five hundred dollars, having no regard to any distinction between law and equity, and of all criminal offenses of which the punishment is death or confinement for life, shall issue all remedial writs for the benefit of individuals, or writs of right to enforce its own jurisdiction, decide appeals from the County Courts, and shall have general supervision over all inferior tribunals.

" The District Judges shall hold their offices for four years, and shall receive an annual salary, paid by quarterly installments out of the State Treasury, of two thousand dollars, which may be increased by the Legislature at its second session, or thereafter, to twenty-five hundred dollars.

" There shall be elected by the qualified voters of each county, every four years, a Clerk of the District Court, who shall keep the records of said court, and issue all writs and other processes. and who may be removed from official misconduct or incapacity, by presentment of a grand jury, and trial by a petit jury, and, in case of removal, his place may be temporarily filled by the judge until such time as his place may be filled by election, upon an order issued by the County Commissioners.

" There shall be elected by the qualified voters of each county a Judge of the County Court, who shall have the same qualifications as a Judge of the District Court, the same tenure of office, and who shall be removable for similar causes, upon presentment of two-thirds of the attorneys of good character, residing in his county, which presentment being indorsed and approved by the District Judge of his district, shall be presented to the Governor, who shall indicate four District Judges outside of the district of the accused, who shall sit upon his case, and may decree his removal, either from failure of prescribed qualifications, incompetency or misconduct ; and upon certificate of their decision of removal, the Governor shall declare a vacancy, and proceed as in the case of a removal of a District Judge ; *provided,* that in all cases where such a court can not, from any cause, be organized, the class of business herein assigned to it may be done in the District Court.

" The Judge of the County Court shall open it on the first Monday of every month, and keep it open on every day, except Sunday, as long as there shall be cases ready for trial, and criminal cases shall always have precedence ; and it shall be the duty of the judge thereof to assign certain days in each month for the trial and investigation of probate business.

" The pay of a judge of a County Court shall be one thousand dollars, to be paid in quarterly installments out of the State Treasury ; five hundred dollars to be paid quarterly out of the county treasury, upon warrants issued by the County Commissioners, and such fees for the administration of probate business as shall be defined by the Legislature ; *provided,* that in counties where the fees of office are equal to the compensation allowed a judge of the District Court, there shall be no compensation paid out of either the State or the county treasury; and in no case shall any judge of the County Court receive more pay than the judge of a District Court.

"The County Court shall have jurisdiction of all such matters of controversy as are defined in the jurisdiction of the District Court, not exceeding in amount claimed five hundred dollars, exclusive of interest, except that it shall not grant divorces, or try suits for title of land, or suits for defamation of character. It shall have control and guardianship of the estates of deceased persons, and control of the persons and estates of minors and insane persons, persons *non compos mentis,* and common drunkards; it shall hear appeals from magistrates' courts in all civil cases above ten dollars in value, and in all trials by magistrates for misdemeanors or thefts, and shall have revisory power over magistrates' courts by *certiorari* or *mandamus;* shall have concurrent jurisdiction with magistrates of all assumpsits and claims for trespass or damages for over one hundred dollars, and over all thefts and misdemeanors; and shall have original jurisdiction of all criminal cases under the grade of capital, or whose punishment may be confinement for life; but an appeal from its judgments shall lie, either to the District Court or to the Criminal Supreme Court, at the option of the defendant, for all criminal offences charged, and in all removals to the District Court, the case shall be tried *de novo;* but in no case shall the State have a right of appeal in criminal cases. Appeals shall also lie of right, in civil cases, to either the District Court or the Civil Supreme Court.

"The Judges of the Supreme, the District, and the County Courts shall be conservators of the peace.

"There shall be a Clerk of the County Court, elected by the qualified electors of the county, every two years, who shall also be County Recorder, and *ex officio* Notary Public. He shall give bond in a sum to be determined by the County Judge, commensurate with his trust; shall keep the records of the county, and affix the seal to process and certificates; and he shall receive fees of office as prescribed by law, and in no case to exceed in the aggregate $3000 per annum; and he shall keep a fee-book, and enter daily, under the responsibilities of his oath, all fees received by him, which shall be examined by the County Commissioners at every regular meeting; and they shall require that whenever his fees, at the end of every year, from the commencement of his term as County Clerk and County Recorder, shall have exceeded the allowance above specified, the surplus, after deducting actual and necessary cost of assistance for recording, shall be paid into the county treasury; *provided,* that in counties with less than 8000 population, the offices of Clerk of the District Court, and Clerk of the County; may, by authority of the County Commissioners, be vested in one person, who shall receive the fees of both offices, and retain them, to an amount not exceeding that herein specified.

" There shall be elected in each county of the State, a Board of County Commissioners, which shall be composed of five persons, and shall meet on the first Monday of every second month, and which, when necessary to the public interest, may provide for extraordinary meetings, or may be convened in extraordinary session by the Judge of the County Court, and who shall receive for their services two dollars per day, while in session, to be paid out of the county treasury. And they shall keep their own records, in a bound book, to be kept in the office of the County Clerk, at all times subject to general inspection. And they shall have a general control of the county finances, and authorize the County Clerk to issue warrants upon the county treasury for the payment of county indebtedness, including the quarterly payment of the Judge of the County Court; and warrants for their own pay shall be issued by the County Clerk, after each meeting, upon calculation of time, as shown by their own records.

" There shall be elected every two years, by each county, a County Attorney, who shall represent the State in the District Court and in the County Court, and whose duty it shall be to prosecute all offenses charged by indictment or by information sustained by probable evidence, and to be vigilant in the obtainment of information; and where the offenses charged are within the scope of a magistrate's jurisdiction to prosecute before a magistrate, without delay, unless it shall be desirable for purposes of justice to have trial of the case by the County Court.

" The County Attorney shall receive a salary of three hundred dollars per annum, one-half to be paid by the State upon quarterly accounts approved by the Comptroller, and one-half by the county upon quarterly warrants issued by the County Clerk, approved by the County Commissioners; and the County Attorney shall receive such fees as may be allowed by the Legislature for all convictions procured by him.

" The County Commissioners of each county shall define the magistrate's precincts and voting precincts of the county, and shall authorize the election of not more than two magistrates for each precinct, who shall hold their courts monthly for determination of civil causes, and for examination and trial of persons charged with crime, on any day of the week except the Sabbath, and who shall be conservators of the peace, and shall make inquiry into all offenses committed within their cognizance, or reported upon testimony deemed reputable, and shall have power to summon persons and compel evidence of all offenses committed in their vicinage, and shall try all criminal offenses of a grade not exceeding theft to the value of twenty dollars, including thefts from a house, and all misdemeanors, including simple and aggravated assaults, assumpsits on note or open account, trespass and other suits for damages, where the damage alleged is not in excess of his civil jurisdiction, which is hereby fixed at two hundred dollars.

" Executions from magistrate's courts for amounts exceeding fifty dollars shall not be returnable under sixty days, and for amounts exceeding one hundred dollars not under four months. Appeals shall lie to the County Court in all judgments for money for more than ten dollars, and by *certiorari* for all amounts, and in all cases of removal the trial in the County Court shall be *de novo*.

" Cases of vagrancy charged may be tried before the nearest magistrate, or before the County Court, and decisions by magistrates in this class of cases may be revised by the County Court.

" There shall be elected by the qualified voters of each county one Sheriff, whose official term shall be two years, who shall be re-eligible but once successively, and who shall be removable by action of the District Court, on trial before jury, upon charges of official misconduct presented by the County Commissioners or by a grand jury; and in case of vagrancy, the Judge of the District Court shall appoint a Sheriff, who shall serve until a special election can be held under direction of the County Commissioners.

" The Legislature shall provide for the election of one Constable for each magistrate's precinct, who shall be removable for official misconduct by the County Court, upon trial by jury, upon complaint signed by twelve freeholders of the precinct, or by indictment found by a grand jury.

" The County Commissioners shall annually select from a list of the freeholders of the county, to be prepared by the County Assessor, a grand jury of twelve citizens of reliable intelligence, to serve as grand jurors, for the period of one year, who shall sit at each semi-annual term of the District Court, and at every third term of the County Court not held while the District Court is in session, and shall act as a grand inquest for the county, and shall find bills for all offenses against the law, with the assistance and information given by the county attorney, and with power to send for persons and papers; and nine grand jurors concurring, shall be sufficient to find a bill of indictment.

"Petit jurors for the trial of all causes, civil and criminal, before any of the courts of the State, shall be composed exclusively of intelligent citizens of good character, who can read and write, and a list of such citizens of good moral character shall be made out by the Clerk of the County Court from the Assessor's rolls, and he shall select from such prior to the sitting of each District and County Court a number presumably adequate for petit jury duty at each term, and shall not, if the number of qualified jurors in the county is sufficient, select one citizen twice in any one year; and if the parties so designated by him and summoned by the Sheriff, shall in any event prove insufficient, then the Sheriff shall summon talismen sufficient to complete the juries, always adhering to the rule of qualification herein prescribed, and no citizen shall be subject to jury duty who has attained the age of sixty years.

"Any party who shall bring suit in either the District or the County Court shall, before process shall issue thereon, pay a docket fee of not less than three dollars, which shall be retained by the clerk on deposit, and three days before the first term the clerk thereof shall remit the aggregate of such fees, by postal order or otherwise, to the Comptroller of the State, who shall return a certificate therefor, and, making an entry showing the source of payment and the amount, shall then pay it into the State Treasury, to the credit of the judicial fund, and shall be subject to appropriation by the Legislature.

"If after any day of trial in any court, the fees paid by litigants for jury service shall be more than sufficient to pay the jurors their prescribed compensation, then, at the close of the day, the clerk of the court or the magistrate, as may be, shall return the excess, *pro rata,* to the several litigants who have paid in the money.

"In all criminal offenses the punishment for which has heretofore been confinement in the State Penitentiary for a period not exceeding five years, the convict shall hereafter be sentenced to labor in the county where the offense was committed, upon the public roads and bridges, the county poor-farm, or such other labor as the County Commissioners shall direct, and the convict shall be in the same duress as heretofore when laboring for the State.

"Juries for the trial of all civil cases shall be composed of five citizens; and juries for the trial of all criminal cases, the punishment of which is not death or confinement or assignment to labor for life, shall be composed of seven persons; jurors for the trial of all cases the punishment of which is death or life-long labor or confinement, shall be composed of twelve persons; and persons subject to trial for any grade of offense, or being a party to a civil cause, shall have a peremptory challenge against all persons who can not read and write, or are not of good moral character; *provided,* that all persons are not challenged for disqualification or consanguinity or peremptory right under the law, shall be good jurors in criminal cases, who will swear that they entertain no bias or prejudice, and have not formed any previous opinion which may not be removed by hearing the evidence; *provided,* that after hearing the evidence any one juror shall from sickness be unable to continue the performance of his duties, he may be excused by the presiding judge, and the remaining jurors shall be competent to render a valid verdict.

"All parties bringing civil actions, who shall desire trial by jury, shall so state in their petitions, or when before magistrates, orally, and in such case shall deposit the jury fee for one day in advance; and all parties responding to actions shall state in their answers if they desire jury service, and if they do not, they shall not be taxed therefor; and if the defendant shall desire a jury, then he shall deposit the cost thereof for one day; and if he shall make good defense, the cost thereof shall be taxed against the plaintiff; and in the trial of all causes those in which juries are demanded shall be first tried; *provided,* that in all criminal cases involving more than ten dollars penalty, the party complained of shall have a right of trial by jury, without payment of fee; *and provided,* that in no case shall the county pay the cost of jury service, except for convictions in criminal cases.

"Every Board of County Commissioners shall have power to elect a county overseer, to superintend the labor of convicts, by work upon roads and bridges, county poor-farms, or any other labor beneficial to the county, under the general control of the said commissioners; and shall fix the compensation and prescribe the duties of said overseer, and shall provide for the payment of his salary out of the county treasury."

On motion of Mr. McLean, two hundred copies of the report and article were ordered printed.

Mr. Robertson, of Bell, submitted the following report:

COMMITTEE ROOM,
AUSTIN, October 22, 1875

To the Hon. E. B. Pickett, President of the Convention:

The undersigned, one of the minority of the Committee on

Public Lands and Land Office, begs leave to dissent from the report of the majority of said committee, upon the subject of granting lands to railroads in the future, for the following reasons:

1. That the policy of Texas from the earliest settlement has been to get her domain settled with tillers of the soil. That she gave at first one league and one labor of land to heads of families, and one-fourth of a league to single men. That this policy was continued down to the present day, lessening the quantity as the county progressed in settlement, until it has been reduced to one hundred and sixty acres for heads of families and eighty acres for single men, always carrying as a condition to the various grants the condition of settlement and cultivation, and permanent residence in the country.

2. That the policy inaugurated in 1854, known as the general railroad law, had for its avowed object the more speedy settlement of the country than could be accomplished under the former policy; the introduction of foreign capital into the country; the defense and settlement of the wild and unoccupied lands along the entire length of the parallel of thirty-two degrees north latitude, embracing the finest country in Texas.

3. That intersecting roads should connect with the coast, bays and bayous of the Gulf of Mexico.

4. That to carry out the first proposition the Southern Pacific was chartered, running laterally through the State on the parallel of 32 degrees, north latitude, in the direction of New Mexico and California.

That sixteen sections to the mile was granted along the line of said road.

That within twelve years, these lands were to be alienated, carrying with the grant the idea that sixteen families to the mile would be settled along the line of 32 degrees for a distance of over seven hundred miles, or eleven thousand two hundred families, actual occupants and tillers of the soil, who would not only afford protection to the trans-continental commerce conducted on and over this great highway through Texas, but would have afforded ample protection to all of the country south of the said parallel of 32 degrees.

5. That this highway of the world would be intersected at various points by roads running from the coast, say four or five, averaging four hundred miles in length each, receiving sixteen sections to the mile, assuring also the actual settlement of twenty-five thousand six hundred families, tillers of the soil. And reserving to the government, free from location or preemption along the line of the Southern Pacific, eleven thousand

two hundred sections, or seven millon nine hundred and seventy-nine thousand two hundred acres of land, and along the lines of the intersecting roads from the seaboard twenty-five thousand six hundred sections, or sixteen million four hundred and nine thousand six hundred acres.

There can be no question that this policy was conceived in wisdom, and sound, far-seeing statemanship and eminently worthy of the great minds of Houston, Rusk, and other eminent men of Texas, who mapped it out.

6. There is no doubt that the framers of the railroad law of 1854, contemplated that its provisions should be carried out in good faith.

That the roads chartered under its provisions should be built with foreign capital within twelve years, and all the railroad lands, sixteen sections to the mile, alienated within the contract time, and occupied by actual settlers, assuring complete protection to all Texas from the inroads and depredations of the hostile Indians on the country south of thirty-two degrees.

7. That Texas would thereby have been relieved from a large tax that has been, and is still, levied annually upon the values and general industries of the country to defend the line of thirty-two degrees across the entire length of the State.

That with this and the intersecting roads from the coast, every portion of Texas would have been completely built up long since.

That the charters carried on their face the fact that they were all to terminate in twelve years from their respective dates, and were not to be extended beyond that time.

That the history of the Southern Pacific and other railroads for the last twenty years shows that failure after failure to comply with their engagements has followed.

That instead of introducing foreign capital as an equivalent for the large bodies of land donated, and the privilege of operating railways in the State, that in less than two years from the date of the first charter, they secured the passage of the act of August 13, 1856 (article 1682, Oldham & White), *requiring* the loan of the school fund to railroads for the term of ten years, at the low rate of six per cent., when it could have been loaned at ten per cent.

That the Legislatures, instead of enforcing a compliance by the railroads with the terms of their charters, as they ought to have done in justice to the country, granted one extension after another, one gratuity after another, until now they base a claim of vested right, not by virtue of any contract, but upon the grace heretofore shown to them.

They now claim as a vested right what was only intended as, and was in truth, a gratuity.

They aim to control in future, as they have done in the past, the Legislatures of the country. Their appetites are as keen as ever. They demand not only a further extension of their contracts, but demand that the constitution *shall* be left open to further railroad grants by the Legislature.

The undersigned would not destroy, or assent to the destruction of any vested right, of any character whatever, that is based on the laws of the country, but feels bound to enter his solemn protest against the policy of leaving the Legislature authorized to continue the donation of the public domain of the State to railroads—a policy that has absorbed nearly one-fourth of the entire area of Texas, the rightful inheritances of, and should have been held for the use and occupation of the descendants of the men who paid for it with their money and their lives; a policy that has taken its own time to pass through the most densely populated sections of the State, destroying the value, in a great degree, of all the towns along its route, built at great trouble and expense by the pioneers of the country; a policy that has fastened on many of the towns and counties of the State a debt that will not only absorb all the profits from the industries of the present generation, but holds a lien on the children of the country for many succeeding generations; a policy that has done more to demoralize legislation, and destroy confidence in the minds of the people toward their Legislatures, than any other question that has ever come before the country, and should now be closed.

The undersigned further believes that if there is still left any public domain that has not been heretofore appropriated, that it should be left for actual settlers, as pre-emptions, and for sale, the proceeds applied to the payment of the debt of the State.

All of which is respectfully submitted.

E. S. C. ROBERTSON, Chairman.

On motion of Mr. Cline two hundred copies were ordered to be printed.

Mr. Ramey offered the following:

COMMITTEE ROOM, ⎫
AUSTIN, October 22, 1875. ⎭

To the Hon. E. B. Pickett, President of the Convention:

Your Committee on Engrossed and Enrolled Ordinances begs leave to report to your honorable body that they have carefully

29

examined and compared Article —, "Legislative Department," and find the same correctly engrossed.

Respectfully,   WM. NEAL RAMEY, Chairman.

On motion of Mr. German, two hundred copies of the engrossed ordinance were ordered printed.

Mr. West submitted the following report:

COMMITTEE ROOM,
AUSTIN, October 21, 1875.

To the Hon. E. B. Pickett, President of the Convention:

The Committee on General Provisions, to whom was referred a memorial of Dr. L. G. Lincecum, of Travis county, calling the attention of the Convention to the propriety of inserting in the constitution a clause making it the duty of the Legislature to pass a law placing the practitioners of the different schools of medicine on an equality, and providing for the establishment of medical colleges in the State, open alike to all students of medicine, have carefully considered the same, and have instructed me to report, that while we recognize the importance of the subjects treated of in the memorial, they deem it best to leave the Legislature free to act on the matter as they may deem best, and that it is not expedient or proper to insert in the constitution any clause on the subject.

They therefore instruct me to return the memorial, and recommend that its prayer be not granted.

Respectfully submitted,
C. S. WEST, Chairman.

Mr. McLean offered the following sections:

" Sec. ——. In all civil or criminal actions for slander or libel, the truth of the words spoken, published, or written, may be given in evidence to the jury; and if it shall appear that the alleged slanderous or libellous speech, publication, or writing, is true, and was proper for public information, and was spoken, published, or written, with good motives and for justifiable ends, it shall be a sufficient defense."

Referred to Committee on General Provisions.

" Sec. ——. The Legislature shall, at its first session after the ratification of this Constitution, provide pensions for the disabled and indigent surviving soldiers of the revolution, by which the independence of Texas was achieved in the year 1836."

Referred to Committee on State Affairs.

The hour having arrived, the special order, viz: the majority and minority reports of the Committee on Revenue and Taxation, with accompanying articles, were taken up.

[Mr. Brown in the chair.]

Mr. Reagan offered the following as a substitute for the article reported by the majority:

"Taxation shall be equal and uniform throughout the State. All property in the State shall be taxed in proportion to its value, to be ascertained as directed by law, except such class or classes of property as two-thirds of both Houses of the Legislature may think proper to exempt from taxation.

"The Legislature shall have power to levy an income tax, and to tax all persons pursuing any occupation, trade, or profession; *provided,* that the term occupation shall not be construed to apply to pursuits either agricultural or mechanical.

"Assessors and collectors of taxes shall be appointed in such manner and under such regulations as the Legislature may direct."

Mr. Waelder proposed to amend the substitute by adding the following sections:

"Section 1. The Legislature shall provide for the appointment of a Board of Appraisers in each county, who shall appraise for taxation all property in the county, whether owned by residents or non-residents, according to its value; and all taxes levied or assessed upon the property so appraised may be paid to the collector of taxes of the county or the Comptroller of the State.

"Sec. 3. All railroads and other corporations of this State, or doing business therein, shall be subject to taxation for State, county, or municipal and other purposes on the real and personal property owned or used by them.

"Sec. 4. There shall be a collector of taxes in each county in this State, who shall be elected in such manner and receive such compensation as may be provided by law.

"Sec. 5. The Legislature shall provide for the collection of taxes and for the sale of property upon which taxes remain unpaid, and that sale, made under such proceedings as may be provided, shall vest title in the purchaser at such sale.

"Sec. 6. The State tax on property, exclusive of the tax necessary to pay the public debt and the interest thereon, shall never exceed fifty cents on the one hundred dollars valuation."

Mr. McLean raised the point of order, that the article accompanying the report of a minority of the committee was not before the Convention; that it must be presented separately by a member, and not come in with a report of a minority of the committee. [Barkley, p. 62.]

On motion of Mr. Cook, of Gonzales, the Convention adjourned to 2½ o'clock, P. M.

EVENING SESSION—2½ o'clock.

Convention met pursuant to adjournment; roll called; quorum present.

Question pending when the Convention adjourned—viz., "Revenue and Taxation"—again taken up, with pending amendment.

On motion of Mr. McKinney, of Walker, Mr. Lynch was excused from attendance on the Convention on account of sickness.

Mr. Ramey made the following report:

Committee Room, ⎱
Austin, October 22, 1875. ⎰

To the Hon. E. B. Pickett, President of the Convention:

Sir—Your Committee on Engrossed and Enrolled Ordinances beg leave to report to your honorable body that they have carefully examined and compared "Article —, On Railroads," and find the same correctly engrossed. Respectfully,

Wm. Neal Ramey, Chairman.

The following communication was taken from the President's desk and read:

Department of State, ⎱
Austin, October 22, 1875. ⎰

To the Hon. E. B. Pickett, President of the Convention:

Sir—I have the honor to acknowledge the receipt of a certified copy of a resolution adopted by the Convention, October 21, 1875, of which the following is a copy:

"*Resolved,* That the Secretary of State, so far as he can, is requested to furnish to the Convention a list of all railroad charters granted since the commencement of the Legislature of 1866, under which no road has been built.

"*Resolved, further,* That he is requested to transmit to the Convention a list of all companies, of whatever nature or kind, incorporated under the act "Concerning Private Corporations," approved December 2, 1871, and the various acts amendatory of or supplementary thereto."

Austin, Texas, October 22, 1875.

"I certify that the above resolution was adopted by the Constitutional Convention, on the 21st day of October, 1875.

[Signed.]   "Leigh Chalmers,
"Secretary Convention.

In response to said resolution I beg leave to state that there is nothing in this office to show what railroads have *not been* built. All that appears on that subject is this: when a railroad company completes a section of its road according to its charter, application is made to the Governor to appoint an engineer to inspect the section completed; when the report of the engineer is received by the Governor it is filed in this office. Whether or not, all the work that has been completed has thus been inspected, it is impossible to determine from any records or papers in this office. I find upon examination of the special laws, passed since the commencement of the Legislature in 1866, that eighty-three railroad charters have been granted by the Legislature since that time. It would require several days to make a list of all of these, giving the caption of the acts (which is the shortest method). I therefore give the pages on the index of the special laws of 1866, 1870, 1871, first and second session 1873, 1874 and 1875.

Special laws 1866, eleventh Legislature, index page 3.

Special laws 1870, twelfth Legislature, index page 340.

Special laws, first session 1871, twelfth Legislature, index p. 554.

Special laws, second session 1871, twelfth Legislature, index p. 274.

Special laws, 1873, thirteenth Legislature, index page 826.

Special laws, 1874, fourteenth Legislature, index page 108.

Special laws, 1875, fourteenth Legislature, index page 158.

Where a list of all railroad charters granted since the war can be found, and which, it is hoped, will answer the purposes of the Convention.

I find that under the act concerning private corporations, approved December 2, 1871, and the acts amendatory of, and supplementary thereto, five hundred and sixty charters have been filed in this office up to this date. The printed reports of the Secretary of State contain lists of all those filed prior to December 1, 1874, but do not include those filed since that date, of which there are two hundred and forty-five. To make this list complete will require several days. This list, as well as a list of all charters granted to railroads since the commencement of the Legislature in 1866, will be furnished as soon as they can be prepared if the information herein furnished is not sufficient for the purpose of the Convention.

I have the honor to be, very respectfully,

Your obedient servant.

A. W. DeBerry,

Secretary of State.

Mr. Graves moved to lay the substitute and amendment on the table.

Lost by the following vote:

YEAS—Abernathy, Arnim, Brown, Blassingame, Barnett, Bruce, Chambers, Cardis, Dillard, DeMorse, Flournoy, Fleming, Ferris, Gaither, Graves, Holt, Henry of Limestone, Johnson of Franklin, Johnson of Collin, Killough, McLean, Martin of Navarro, Martin of Hunt, Mills, Mitchell, McKinney of Denton, McKinney of Walker, Nugent, Ramey, Rentfro, Russell of Wood, Wade, Whitehead, Whitfield—34.

NAYS—Allison, Abner, Blake, Ballinger, Burleson, Crawford, Cook of Gonzales, Cooke of San Saba, Cline, Douglas, Dohoney, Darnell, Davis of Brazos, Davis of Wharton, Erhard, Henry of Smith, Haynes, King, Kilgore, Lockett, Lacy, Morris, Norvell, Nunn, Pauli, Reagan, Reynolds, Robertson of Bell, Robeson of Fayette, Spikes, Scott, Sessions, Smith, Stockdale, Stayton, Sansom, Weaver, West, Waelder—39.

The question on the adoption of Mr. Waelder's amendment was put, and the amendment lost.

On motion of Mr. Nunn, Mr. Douglas was excused for ten days from Monday next.

Mr. Dohoney offered the following amendment to Mr. Reagan's substitute:

"Section 1. The *ad valorem* taxation for State revenue shall never exceed one-half of one per cent. And no higher rate of taxation than that levied for State purposes shall ever be levied by any county town or city; *provided,* that in cities of over ten thousand population, a higher rate of taxation may be imposed, not to exceed .... per cent.; *and provided further,* that counties may levy and collect sufficient taxes to meet their present indebtedness.

"Sec. 2. All property, real and personal, in organized counties, whether belonging to individuals or corporations, shall be assessed and the taxes paid in the county where the property is situate. Property situate in unorganized counties may be assessed and the taxes paid thereon in such manner and under such regulations as the Legislature may prescribe.

"Sec. 3. There shall be elected in each county, at the general elections, every two years, an assessor and collector of taxes, who shall hold his office for two years, and until his successor is qualified, and whose compensation and whose duties shall be prescribed by law."

Accepted by Mr. Reagan.

Mr. Fleming offered the article reported by him as one of the

Committee on Taxation and Revenue, as a substitute for the substitute of Mr. Reagan, and the article reported by the majority of said committee.

Adopted by the following vote:

YEAS—Allison, Abernathy, Arnim, Abner, Brown, Ballinger, Blassingame, Barnett, Burleson, Bruce, Crawford, Chambers, Cook of Gonzales, Cooke of San Saba, Cardis, Douglas, Dillard, Darnell, Davis of Wharton, Erhard, Ford, Flournoy, Fleming, Ferris, German, Graves, Holt, Henry of Smith, Haynes, Johnson of Franklin, Johnson of Collin, Killough, Lacy, Martin of Navarro, Martin of Hunt, McCabe, Morris, Mitchell, McKinney of Denton, McKinney of Walker, McCormick, Norvell, Nunn, Nugent, Pauli, Reagan, Reynolds, Rentfro, Russell of Wood, Spikes, Scott, Stockdale, Stayton, Sansom, Wade, Whitehead, Weaver, Waelder—58.

NAYS—Cline, DeMorse, Dohoney, Gaither, King, Kilgore, Lockett, McLean, Mills, Ramey, Robertson of Bell, Robeson of Fayette, Sessions, Wright, Whitfield, West—16.

Upon calling the roll, Mr. Henry of Limestone stated that he had paired off with Mr. Ross, who was absent; that Mr. Ross would have voted yea, and Mr. Henry nay.

On motion of Mr. Ballinger, the rule was suspended, and "Article —, Judiciary," was taken up and made the special order for Tuesday next at 10 o'clock.

On Motion of Mr. Brown, the rule was suspended, and "Article —, Railroads," was taken up and one hundred copies ordered printed.

On motion of Mr. Fleming the Convention adjourned till 9 o'clock A. M. to-morrow.

FORTY-SECOND DAY.

HALL OF REPRESENTATIVES, ⎱
AUSTIN, TEXAS, October 23, 1875. ⎰

Convention met pursuant to adjournment; roll called; quorum present. Prayer by the Rev. T. B. Lee, Rector of St. David's Church, at Austin.

Journal of yesterday read and adopted.

On motion of Mr. Lacy, Mr. Davis, of Brazos, was excused until Tuesday next.

Mr. Cooke, of San Saba, presented the memorial of sundry citizens of Lampasas county, on the subject of local option.

Referred to Committee on General Provisions.

Mr. Norvell submitted the following minority report on article .... "Judiciary":

To the Hon. E. B. Pickeett, President of the Convention:

The undersigned members of the Committee on the Judiciary Department are not satisfied that the article reported by the majority of the committee adequately provides for the administration of justice in the State. It does not provide, they submit, for the permanent relief of the Supreme Court from the constantly increasing pressure of business upon it. Neither does it, in their opinion, afford the desired relief to the District Courts, which, in many counties, are likewise overburdened with business.

While the article proposed by the majority of the committee would fail, it is feared, to accomplish these essential ends, and, while it restricts appeals in some cases, and imposes onerous conditions upon them in others, it would probably swell the expenses of this department of the government much beyond what it at present costs.

The said article proposes dangerous innovations, it is conceived, in the trial by jury, and in the grand jury system, which, if engrafted into the organic law of the State, will endanger the existence of these time-honored institutions, upon the preservation of which, intact, it is believed, depend the continued existence of the American system of free government and the security of the liberties of the people.

Without further enumerating their objections to the article reported by the majority of the committee, the undersigned desire to call attention to the subjoined article, which, in their opinion, contains a more efficient plan for the judiciary of the State.

It is believed that the system here proposed would completely obviate the difficulties and hindrances which at present surround and encumber the administration of justice.

The Court of Appeals provided for, would, it is submitted, effectually and permanently relieve the Supreme Court of its accumulating mass of cases; while the Probate Court and Chief Justice's Court, by cutting off a large portion of the present jurisdiction of the District Court, would relieve the overburdened District Courts, and make it practicable to reduce the number of Judicial Districts.

These results would be obtained, it is thought, without either denying appeals in cases of any considerable importance, or allowing them only upon compliance with burdensome conditions, amounting frequently to a practical denial thereof.

The system here proposed, while it will, as is confidently believed, prove entirely adequate to the wants of the country, will cost the State nearly seventy thousand dollars less than the present judicial system.

The undersigned therefore beg leave to report the following article as a substitute for that submitted by the majority of the committee, and recommend its adoption.

Respectfully submitted,
Lipscomb Norvell,
Joe. P. Douglas.

I concur in the foregoing plan, except as to the salaries of the judges, which, in my opinion, are too low to secure an independent judiciary.   J. B. Murphy.

"Article —.

"JUDICIAL DEPARTMENT.

" Section 1. The judicial power of this State shall be vested in one Supreme Court, in a Court of Appeals, in District Courts, in Probate Courts, in County Courts, in Justices' Courts, and in such corporation and other inferior courts as the Legislature may from time to time ordain and establish ; *provided,* that no judge of any court, except those of the Supreme Court, the Court of Appeals, and the District Courts, shall receive a salary from the State or from any county.

" Sec. 2. The Supreme Court shall consist of a Chief Justice and two Associate Justices, any two of whom shall constitute a quorum. They shall be elected by the qualified voters of the State at a general election for State or county officers ; they shall have arrived at the age of thirty years at the time of election ; shall hold their offices for a term of six years, and each of them shall receive an annual salary of at least three thousand five hundred dollars, which shall not be increased or diminished during his term of office.

" Sec. 3. The Supreme Court shall have appellate jurisdiction only, from the Court of Appeals, which shall embrace all cases determined in said court; *provided, however,* that the Supreme Court shall have and retain jurisdiction to try and determine the cases which shall remain on its dockets at the time of the organization of the Court of Appeals under this constitution. The Supreme Court, and the judges thereof, shall have power to issue the writ of *habeas corpus;* and, under such regulations as may be prescribed by law, the said court and the judges thereof may issue the writ of *mandamus,* and such other writs as may be necessary to enforce its own jurisdiction. The Supreme Court shall also have power, upon affidavits or otherwise, as by the

court may be thought proper, to ascertain such matters of fact
as may be necessary to the proper exercise of its jurisdiction.
The Supreme Court shall sit, for the transaction of business,
from the first Monday of October until the last Saturday of
June of every year, at the capital, and at not more than two
other places in the State.

" Sec. 4. The Supreme Court shall appoint its own clerks,
who shall give bonds in such manner as may be required by law;
shall hold their offices for two years, and shall be subject to removal by the said court, for good cause, entered of record on the
minutes of said court.

" Sec. 5. The Court of Appeals shall consist of a Presiding
Judge and two Associate Judges, any two of whom shall constitute a quorum. They shall be elected by the qualified voters of
the State at a general election for State or county officers; they
shall have arrived at the age of thirty years at the time of election; shall hold their offices for a term of six years, and each of
them shall receive an annual salary of at least $3500, which
shall not be increased or diminished during his term of office.

" Sec. 6. The Court of Appeals shall have appellate jurisdiction only, which shall be co-extensive with the limits of the
State. The Court of Appeals and the judges thereof shall have
power to issue the writ of *habeas corpus;* and, under such regulations as may be prescribed by law, the said court and the judges
thereof may issue the writ of *mandamus,* and such other writs
as may be necessary to enforce its own jurisdiction. The Court
of Appeals shall also have power, upon affidavits, or otherwise,
as by the court may be thought proper, to ascertain such matters of fact as may be necessary to the proper exercise of its
jurisdiction. The Court of Appeals shall sit, for the transaction
of business, from the first Monday of October until the last
Saturday of June of every year, at the capital, and at not more
than two other places in the State, at which the Supreme Court
shall hold its sessions. The Court of Appeals shall not be required to deliver opinions in writing.

" Sec. 7. The Court of Appeals shall appoint its own clerks,
who shall give bond in such manner as may be prescribed by law;
shall hold their offices for two years, and shall be subject to removal by the said court, for good cause, entered of record on the
minutes of said court.

" Sec. 8. The State shall be divided into convenient judicial
districts. For each district there shall be elected, by the qualified voters thereof, at a general election for State or county
officers, a judge, who shall reside in the same; shall hold his

office for the term of four years; shall receive an annual salary of not less than $2500, which shall not be increased or diminished during his term of service; and shall hold the courts at one place in each county in the district, at least twice in each year, in such manner as may be prescribed by law.

"Sec. 9. The District Court shall have original jurisdiction of all criminal cases; of all suits in behalf of the State to recover penalties, forfeitures and escheats; of all cases of divorce; of all suits to recover damages for slander or defamation of character; of all suits for the trial of title to land; of all suits for the enforcement of liens; of all suits for the trial of the right of property, levied on by virtue of any writ of execution, sequestration or attachment, when the property levied on shall be equal to, or exceed in value five hundred dollars; and of all suits, complaints or pleas whatever, without regard to any distinction between law and equity, when the matter in controversy shall be valued at, or amount to, five hundred dollars, exclusive of interest; and the said courts and the judges thereof shall have power to issue writs of injunction, *certiorari,* and all other writs necessary to enforce their own jurisdiction, and to give them a general superintendence and control over inferior tribunals.   All indictments for offenses below the grade of felony returned to, and all informations filed in the District Court shall be transferred to the court of the Chief Justice of the county, in such manner as may be prescribed by law, there to be tried or disposed of.   The District Court shall have appellate jurisdiction in cases originating or tried in inferior courts, under such regulations, limitations and restrictions as the Legislature may prescribe, and original and appellate jurisdiction and general control over the probate court established in each county, for appointing guardians, granting letters testamentary and of administration; for settling the accounts of executors, administrators and guardians, and for the transaction of business appertaining to estates, and original jurisdiction and general control over executors, administrators, guardians and minors, under such regulations as may be prescribed by law.

"Sec. 10.   There shall be a Clerk of the District Court for each county, who shall be elected by the qualified voters, and who shall hold his office for two years, subject to removal by information or by indictment of a grand jury, and conviction by a petit jury.   In case of vacancy the Judge of the District Court shall have the power to appoint a clerk until a regular election can be held.   The Clerk of the District Court shall be recorder for the county, and *ex-officio* Clerk of the Probate, County and Chief Justices' Courts.

" Sec. 11. All Judges of the Supreme Court, Court of Appeals and District Courts shall, by virtue of their office, be conservators of the peace throughout the State. The style of all writs and process shall be ' The State of Texas.' All prosecutions shall be carried on in the name and by the authority of the ' State of Texas,' and conclude ' against the peace and dignity of the State.'

" Sec. 12. In case of a vacancy in the offices of Justice of the Supreme Court, Judge of the Court of Appeals, Judges of the District Courts and District Attorneys, the Governor of the State shall have power to fill the same by appointment, which shall continue in force until the office can be filled at the next general election for State or county officers, and the successor duly qualified.

" Sec. 13. The Judges of the Supreme Court, Court of Appeals and District Courts shall be removed by the Governor, on the address of a majority of each house of the Legislature, for willful neglect of duty, misconduct, habits of drunkenness, oppression in office, incompetency, or other reasonable cause, which shall not be sufficient ground for impeachment; *Provided, however,* that the causes or cause for which such removal shall be required shall be stated at length in such address, and entered on the journals of each house; and, *provided further,* that the cause or causes shall be notified to the judge so intended to be removed, and he shall be admitted to a hearing in his own defense before any vote for such address shall pass; and in all such cases the vote shall be taken by yeas and nays, and entered on the journals of each house respectively.

" Sec. 14. No judge shall sit in any case wherein he may be interested, or where either of the parties may be connected with him by affinity or consanguinity within such degree as may be prescribed by law, or where he shall have been of counsel in the case. When the Supreme Court, or any two of its members, shall be thus disqualified to hear and determine any case or cases in said court, or when no judgment can be rendered in any case or cases in said court, by reason of the equal division of opinion of said judges, the same shall be certified to the Governor of the State, who shall immediately commission the requisite number of persons, learned in the law, for the trial and determination of said case or cases. When the Court of Appeals, or any two of its members, shall be thus disqualified to hear and determine any case or cases in said court, or when no judgment can be rendered in any case or cases in said court, by reason of the equal division of opinion of said judges, the same shall, in like manner, be certified to the Governor of the State, who shall immediately commission the requisite number of persons learned in the law for the trial and determination of said case or cases. When a Judge of the District Court is thus disqualified, the parties may, by consent, appoint a proper person to try the said case; or upon their failing to do so, a competent person shall be appointed to try the same in the county where it is pending, in such manner as may be prescribed by law. And the District Judges may exchange districts, or hold courts for each other, when they may deem it expedient, and shall do so when directed by law. The disqualification of judges of inferior tribunals shall be remedied as may be prescribed by law.

"Sec. 15. There shall be a District Attorney for each Judicial District in the State, elected by the qualified voters of the district, who shall reside in the district for which he shall be elected; shall hold his office for two years, and, together with the perquisites prescribed by law, shall receive an annual salary of not more than five hundred dollars, which shall not be increased or diminished during his term of office.

"Sec. 16. Each county shall be divided into five justices' precincts. There shall be elected in each county by the qualified voters thereof, as may be directed by law, five Justices of the Peace, one of whom shall reside, after his election, at the county seat, and shall be the Chief Justice; and no two of said justices shall reside in the same justice's precinct. They shall hold their offices for two years, be commissioned by the Governor; and should a vacancy occur, an election shall be held for the unexpired term.

"Sec. 17. There shall be established in each county in the State an inferior tribunal, styled the Probate Court, one term of which shall be holden by the Chief Justice, at the county seat, in each month, as may be prescribed by law. The Probate Court shall have jurisdiction to probate wills, to appoint guardians of minors, idiots, lunatics, and persons *non compos mentis;* to grant letters testamentary and of administration; to settle the accounts of executors, administrators, and guardians; to transact all business appertaining to the estates of deceased persons, minors, idiots, lunatics, and persons *non compos mentis,* including the settlement, partition, and distribution of such estates; and to apprentice minors under such regulations as may be prescribed by law.

"Sec. 18. The justices of the peace in each county, or any

three of them, shall constitute the County Court, with such jurisdiction over the local affairs, interests and police matters in the county as the Legislature may prescribe.

" Sec. 19.   The Chief Justice shall have original jurisdiction of all misdemeanors and petty offenses, as the same are now or may hereafter be defined by law, of such civil cases, where the matter in controversy shall not exceed five hundred dollars, exclusive of interest, under such regulations, limitations, and restrictions as may be prescribed by law, without regard to any distinction between law and equity, and appellate jurisdiction in cases originating in the other Justices' Courts in the county, under such regulations, limitations and restrictions as may be prescribed by law.   The Legislature may provide for the election of a County Attorney, to represent the State and county in the Chief Justice's Court, whose term of office, duties and compensation, to consist of fees and commissions only, shall be such as may be prescribed by law.   The other justices of the peace shall have such civil and criminal jurisdiction as shall be provided by law.   The justices of the peace shall be *ex-officio* Notaries Public. They shall also perform the duties of Coroner, except such as may, by law, be devolved upon Constables.

" Sec. 20.   There shall be elected in each county, by the qualified voters, one Sheriff; also one Constable for each justice's precinct, to be elected by the qualified voters of the precinct or county as the Legislature may direct, who shall hold their offices for two years, and should a vacancy occur, an election shall be held for the unexpired term.   The Sheriff shall be commissioned by the Governor.

" Sec. 21.   In all cases of law or equity, where the matter in controversy shall be valued at or exceed twenty dollars, the right of trial by jury shall be preserved."

On motion of Mr. Whitehead, two hundred copies of the report and article were ordered printed.

Mr. West submitted the following report:

COMMITTEE ROOM,
AUSTIN, October 23, 1875.

To the Hon. E. B. Pickett, President of the Convention:

The Committee on General Provisions, to whom was referred a number of memorials from the Texas State Medical Association, endorsed and approved by a large number of citizens in different parts of the State, recommending the insertion in the constitution of a clause making it the duty of the Legislaure to provide for an uniform system of sanitary regulations throughout the State, instruct me to report:

That they have given the subject that careful consideration that its importance demands. It appears to them that it is as much the duty of the State to protect the lives and promote the health of its citizens as it is to protect their property, and that the organization of a department of health and of vital statistics would be productive of the most beneficial results. They do not, however, believe it necessary or expedient to insert any clause on that subject in the organic law. In time, no doubt, such a law, when required, will be passed, and all the important objects sought to be attained by the memorialists will be reached through the ordinary legislative channels.

Respectfully submitted.   C. S. WEST, Chairman.

Mr. McCormick submitted the following resolution:

Resolved, That the Committee on General Provisions be requested to inquire into the propriety of incorporating the following section in the proposed constitution:

" Section —. The Legislature may establish a Bureau of Health and Vital Statistics, under such regulations and with such duties as may be provided by law."

Referred to the Committee on General Provisions.

Mr. Cook, of Gonzales, offered the following resolution:

Resolved, That the Committee on Printing and Contingent Expenses be, and they are hereby authorized, to audit and approve the claim of the *State Gazette* for furnishing one hundred copies of the paper, per day, to the Convention, for the first eight days of its session; and that the same be paid as other contingent expenses of the body.

Mr. Blassingame offered the following amendment:

Amend by adding, "Galveston *News,* Houston *Telegraph,* and all other publications that were laid on our desks."

On motion of Mr. Dillard, the main question was ordered.

Mr. Blassingame's amendment lost.

The question then recurring on the adoption of the main question, the yeas and nays were called, and the resolution adopted by the following vote:

YEAS—Allison, Abernathy, Arnim, Abner, Brown, Blake, Burleson, Crawford, Chambers, Cook of Gonzales, Cline, Dillard, DeMorse, Darnell, Erhard, Ford, Flournoy, Fleming, German, Gaither, Henry of Limestone, Johnson of Franklin, Johnson of Collin, King, Killough, Lockett, Lynch, McLean, Martin of Navarro, Martin of Hunt, McCabe, Mills, McKinney of Denton, McKinney of Walker, McCormick, Murphy, Nunn, Reagan, Ramey, Reynolds, Robertson of Bell, Robeson of Fayette,

Russell of Harrison, Scott, Sessions, Stockdale, Stayton, White-head, Wright, Weaver, Whitfield, West, Waelder—53.

Nays—Ballinger, Blassingame, Bruce, Cooke of San Saba, Cardis, Douglas, Dohoney, Graves, Holt, Haynes, Lacy, Morris, Mitchell, Moore, Norvell, Nugent, Pauli, Rentfro, Russell of Wood, Spikes, Smith, Sansom, Wade—23.

Mr. Mills offered the following:

The following shall be a section of the constitution:

"Sec. ——. After the first day of January, 1877, no deed shall be received for filing and record by the clerk of the District Court, or whoever shall be made the recorder of deeds, unless accompanied by the tax receipt for the previous year, and for all years succeeding up to the time of offering such paper for record. The word deed shall apply to mortgages, deeds of trust, deeds of partition, or decrees of partition of lands, and deeds of sale."

Referred to Committee on General Provisions.

Mr. Russell, of Wood, offered the following resolution:

Resolved, That the Commissioner of the General Land Office be requested to furnish this Convention with a statement of all lands granted to each and every railroad in the State and the number of miles completed by each railroad.

Adopted.

Mr. Scott offered the following substitute for "Rule 4 of the Amended Rules:"

"Rule 4. Whenever any article of the constitution shall be passed upon its third reading, under the foregoing rules, it shall be, as of course, referred to the Committee on Style and Arrangement; when the whole constitution shall be presented to the Convention by said committee it shall not be subject to any amendment that will change the meaning or intent, except by a two-thirds vote."

Laid over under the rules.

The hour having arrived, the special order, viz: "Public Schools," was taken up, and, on motion of Mr. Nunn, postponed to Thursday next at 10 o'clock.

The Convention then proceeded to consider the unfinished business of yesterday, viz: "Article ——, Taxation and Revenue."

Mr. Dohoney offered the following amendment:

Amend section 1 by adding the words, "The Legislature shall have power to impose advalorem, occupation, income and poll taxes."

Mr. Russell, of Harrison, moved to lay the amendment on the table.

Lost by the following vote:

YEAS—Barnett, Bruce, Crawford, Cline, Cardis, Dillard, De Morse, Flournoy, Fleming, Gaither, Holt, Johnson of Collin, Killough, Martin of Navarro, Martin of Hunt, McCabe, Mills, Mitchell, McKinney of Denton, McCormick, Murphy, Nugent, Pauli, Reynolds, Russell of Harrison, Russell of Wood, Spikes, Smith, Wade, Wright, Weaver, Whitfield—32.

NAYS—Allison, Abernathy, Arnim, Blake, Ballinger, Burleson, Chambers, Cook of Gonzales, Cooke of San Saba, Douglas, Dohoney, Darnell, Erhard, Ford, Ferris, German, Henry of Smith, Henry of Limestone, Haynes, Johnson of Franklin, King, Kilgore, Lockett, Lacy, Lynch, McLean, McKinney of Walker, Morris, Moore, Norvell, Nunn, Reagan, Rentfro, Robertson of Bell, Robeson of Fayette, Scott, Sessions, Stockdale, Stayton, Sansom, West, Waelder—42.

Mr. Sansom offered the following as a substitute for the article and amendment:

"Section 1. Taxation shall be equal and uniform throughout the State. All property shall be rendered for taxation, and the taxes paid thereon in the county where it is situated, and shall be taxed in proportion to its value, to be ascertained as directed by law, except such property (not to exceed two hundred and fifty dollars to each head of a family, and all property belonging to churches, institutions of learning, charitable institutions and cemeteries, and used only for such purposes) as may be exempted by the Legislature.

"Sec. 2. It shall be the duty of the Legislature to provide by law for the speedy and certain collection of taxes upon all property, whether real or personal, subject to taxation, by condemnation and sale; and that the title made by the State to lands sold for the payment of taxes shall not be attacked, except for fraud, after four years from the date of the sale; *provided,* the original owners may redeem said lands at any time within said four years, by the payment of the taxes and interest, and four times the amount paid by the purchaser at the tax sale."

Mr. Dohoney withdrew his amendment, and offered the following in its stead:

"The Legislature shall have power to impose *ad valorem* and poll taxes, and also occupation or income taxes, except on agricultural or mechanical pursuits."

On motion of Mr. McCormick, a call of the Convention was ordered.

ABSENT—Messrs. Burnett, Brady, Cook of Gonzales, Cooley, Cardis, Davis of Wharton, Ford, Flournoy, Ferris, McCabe,

30

Reynolds, Rentfro, Sessions, Sansom, Whitehead, Wright, and West.

On motion of Mr. Allison the call was suspended, and the Convention proceeded with the consideration of the pending question.

Mr. Allison moved to adjourn to $2\frac{1}{2}$ o'clock P. M.

Mr. Cline moved to adjourn to 9 o'clock Monday morning, whereupon the yeas and nays were called, and the Convention refused to adjourn by the following vote:

YEAS—Ballinger, Barnett, Burleson, Crawford, Cline, Cardis, DeMorse, Darnell, Davis of Wharton, Ford, Gaither, Henry of Limestone, King, Kilgore, Moore, Pauli, Rentfro, Robeson of Fayette, Russell of Harrison, Stockdale, Weaver, West—22.

NAYS—Allison, Abernathy, Arnim, Abner, Brown, Blake, Blassingame, Bruce, Chambers, Dillard, Dohoney, Flournoy, Fleming, Ferris, German, Graves, Holt, Johnson of Franklin, Johnson of Collin, Killough, Lockett, Lacy, Lynch, McLean, Martin of Navarro, Martin of Hunt, McCabe, Morris, Mills, Mitchell, McKinney of Denton, McKinney of Walker, McCormick, Murphy, Norvell, Nugent, Reagan, Ramey, Reynolds, Robertson of Bell, Russell of Wood, Spikes, Scott, Sessions, Sansom, Wade, Whitehead, Wright, Whitfield, Waelder—50.

The question on Mr. Allison's motion to adjourn to $2\frac{1}{2}$ P. M., was put and lost.

Mr. Scott moved the previous question.

On motion of Mr. West, the Convention adjourned to $2\frac{1}{2}$ o'clock P. M.

EVENING SESSION—$2\frac{1}{2}$ o'clock.

Convention met pursuant to adjournment; roll called; quorum present.

The question pending, when the Convention adjourned, was resumed.

Mr. Scott moved to close debate upon the pending amendments, and bring the Convention to a vote.

Carried.

Question on Mr. Dohoney's amendment put, and amendment adopted by the following vote:

YEAS—Allison, Abernathy, Arnim, Abner, Blake, Ballinger, Blassingame, Burleson, Cook of Gonzales, Cooke of San Saba, Douglas, Dillard, Dohoney, Darnell, Erhard, Flournoy, Ferris, Graves, Holt, Henry of Smith, Henry of Limestone, Haynes, Johnson of Franklin, Kilgore, Killough, Lockett, Lacy, Lynch,

McLean, Morris, McKinney of Walker, Moore, Murphy, Norvell, Reagan, Ramey, Scott, Sessions, Sansom, Whitfield, West, Waelder—42.

NAYS—Barnett, Brady, Bruce, Crawford, Chambers, Cline, DeMorse, Davis of Wharton, Fleming, German, Johnson of Collin, Martin of Navarro, Martin of Hunt, McCabe, Mitchell, McKinney of Denton, McCormick, Nugent, Pauli, Reynolds, Rentfro, Robertson of Bell, Russell of Harrison, Russell of Wood, Spikes, Stayton, Wade, Whitehead, Wright, Weaver—30.

The question on Mr. Sansom's substitute was then put, and substitute lost by the following vote:

YEAS—Cooke of San Saba, Davis of Wharton, McLean, Mitchell, McKinney of Denton, Moore, Pauli, Rentfro, Sansom, West—10.

NAYS—Allison, Abernathy, Arnim, Abner, Blake, Ballinger, Blassingame, Barnett, Burleson, Brady, Bruce, Crawford, Chambers, Cook of Gonzales, Cline, Douglas, Dillard, DeMorse, Dohoney, Darnell, Erhard, Flournoy, Fleming, Ferris, German, Graves, Holt, Henry of Smith, Henry of Limestone, Haynes, Johnson of Franklin, Johnson of Collin, Kilgore, Killough, Lockett, Lacy, Lynch, Martin of Navarro, Martin of Hunt, McCabe, Morris, McKinney of Walker, McCormick, Murphy, Norvell, Nugent, Reagan, Ramey, Reynolds, Robertson of Bell, Russell of Harrison, Russell of Wood, Spikes, Scott, Wade, Whitehead, Wright, Weaver, Whitfield, Waelder—60.

Mr. Wade proposed to amend as follows:

Section 1. After the word "taxation," line 8, insert "not to exceed two hundred and fifty dollars worth of household and kitchen furniture."

Mr. McKinney, of Walker, proposed to amend the amendment by adding "and property used for religious and charitable purposes exclusively."

Lost.

Mr. Martin, of Navarro, proposed to amend section 1 by striking out all after the word "law," in fifth line.

Mr. Wade's amendment lost.

Mr. Martin's (of Navarro) amendment adopted.

Mr. Martin, of Navarro, offered the following section:

"Section 1. All taxes shall be uniform and upon the same class of subjects within the limits of the authority levying the tax. But the Legislature may, by general laws, exempt from taxation public property used for public purposes, actual places of religious worship, places of burial not used or held for private or corporate profit, and institutions of purely public charity, and all laws exempting property from taxation other than the property above enumerated shall be void."

Mr. Whitfield proposed to amend the amendment as follows:

Provided, there shall be exempt from taxation household and kitchen furniture to the value of two hundred and fifty dollars.

Adopted by the following vote:

YEAS—Allison, Abner, Ballinger, Blassingame, Barnett, Burleson, Brady, Bruce, Chambers, Cook of Gonzales, Cline, Douglas, Dillard, DeMorse, Dohoney, Darnell, Davis of Wharton, Erhard, Fleming, Ferris, German, Graves, Henry of Smith, Henry of Limestone, Haynes, Johnson of Franklin, Johnson of Collin, Kilgore, Killough, Lockett, Lacy, Lynch, Martin of Navarro, Martin of Hunt, McCabe, Morris, Mitchell, McKinney of Denton, McKinney of Walker, McCormick, Moore, Murphy, Nugent, Ramey, Reynolds, Rentfro, Robertson of Bell, Russell of Wood, Spikes, Scott, Stockdale, Stayton, Wade, Whitehead, Wright, Weaver, Whitfield, West, Waelder—59.

NAYS—Abernathy, Arnim, Blake, Crawford, Cooke of San Saba, Flournoy, Holt, McLean, Norvell, Pauli, Reagan, Russell of Harrison, Sessions, Sansom—14.

Mr. Reagan proposed to amend as follows:

Add to the end of section 12 the words, "but the Legislature may provide that in counties of more than fifteen thousand inhabitants (the number of inhabitants to be ascertained by the census of the United States, or other lawful census) for the election of collectors of taxes."

Mr. Abernathy offered the following as a substitute for section 12:

"Sec. 12. There shall be one tax collector elected in each county, who shall hold his office for two years, whose duty it shall be to collect all taxes, both State and county."

Mr. German offered the following as a substitute for sections 11 and 12:

"Sec. —. In each and every organized county in the State there shall be an assessor and collector of taxes elected by the people at the next ensuing general election, and every two years thereafter, who shall assess the property and collect the taxes so assessed in conformity to law."

Mr. Scott proposed to amend Mr. Reagan's amendment by striking out "15,000" and inserting "10,000."

Adopted.

Mr. Whitfield proposed to strike out "shall" and insert "was," in Mr. Reagan's amendment.

Carried.

Mr. Reagan's amendment as amended was adopted.

Mr. Abernathy's substitute for section 12 was lost by the following vote:

YEAS—Abernathy, Arnim, Dillard, DeMorse, Holt, Johnson of Franklin, Rentfro, Russell of Harrison, Russell of Wood, Spikes—10.

NAYS—Allison, Abner, Blake, Ballinger, Blassingame, Barnett, Burleson, Brady, Bruce, Crawford, Chambers, Cook of Gonzales, Cooke of San Saba, Cline, Douglas, Dohoney, Darnell, Davis of Wharton, Erhard, Fleming, Ferris, German, Graves, Henry of Smith, Henry of Limestone, Haynes, Johnson of Collin, Kilgore, Killough, Lockett, Lacy, Lynch, McLean, Martin of Navarro, Martin of Hunt, McCabe, Morris, Mitchell, McKinney of Denton, McKinney of Walker, McCormick, Murphy, Norvell, Nugent, Pauli, Reagan, Ramey, Robertson of Bell, Scott, Stockdale, Stayton, Sansom, Wade, Whitehead, Weaver, Whitfield, West, Waelder—58.

The question on Mr. German's substitute was put and lost.

On motion of Mr. Martin, of Navarro, Mr. Sessions was excused for ten days, commencing Monday next.

Mr. Robertson, of Bell, proposed to amend by striking out the words " appointed or," of section 11, lines 3 and 4.

Adopted.

Mr. McLean moved to reconsider the vote just taken.

Lost.

Mr. Scott proposed to amend section 9 by striking out " land," in line 1, and insert " all property subject to taxation."

Adopted.

Mr. Ferris offered the following section:

" Sec. —. No money shall be drawn from the treasury but in pursuance of specific appropriation made by law; nor shall any appropriation of money be made for a longer time than two years."

Adopted.

Mr. Norvell proposed to amend section 8 by striking out all the section after the word " office," in the seventh line.

Mr. McCormick offered the following substitute for the amendment:

In section 8, amend by inserting before and after the word " lands," in line five, the following: " all lands and other property not rendered for taxation by the owners thereof shall be assessed at its fair value by the proper officer."

Adopted.

Mr. West offered the following:

" Sec. —.   While taxes should be equal and uniform, they should also be just, and the Legislature shall by proper laws guard against the levy upon the same values of duplicate taxes; and the payment of tax upon the same value shall be a satisfaction of all taxes due thereon."

Lost.

Mr. Martin of Hunt proposed to amend section 4, line third, by striking out the words " be subject to taxation," and insert the words " be taxed."

On motion of Mr. Ferris the Convention adjourned to 9 o'clock A. M. Monday, pending the amendment offered by Mr. Martin, of Hunt.

FORTY-THIRD DAY.

HALL OF REPRESENTATIVES, }
AUSTIN, TEXAS, October 25, 1875. }

Convention met pursuant to adjournment; roll called; quorum present.   Prayer by the Rev. Horatio V. Philpott, of the M. E. Church, South, at Austin.

Mr. Allison, chairman of the Committee on Senatorial and Representative Apportionment, made the following report:

COMMITTEE ROOM, }
AUSTIN, October 23, 1875. }

To the Hon. E. B. Pickett, President of the Convention:

SIR—The undersigned majority of the committee of thirty (being one from each Senatorial District) to divide the State into Senatorial and Representative Districts, are pleased to report that after long and patient investigation, having in view the best interests of the State, a due regard for special feelings and interests in some localities, and keeping in view the leading idea of local representation—a principle dear to an overwhelming majority of the people of Texas—have agreed upon the accompanying ordinance, and recommend its passage by the Convention.

THOS. G. ALLISON, Chairman.   JOHN HENRY BROWN,
B. H. DAVIS,   L. S. ROSS,
JOHN R. HENRY,   ED. BURLESON,
ASA HOLT,   JOEL W. ROBISON,

W. W. WHITEHEAD,
B. D. MARTIN,
GEO. MCCORMICK,
ED. CHAMBERS,
GEORGE FLOURNOY,
JOHN S. FORD,
E. S. C. ROBERTSON,
JOE P. DOUGLAS,

JOHN W. STAYTON,
R. SANSOM,
C. B. KILGORE,
W. W. DILLARD,
JO. W. BARNETT,
W. T. G. WEAVER,
J. F. JOHNSON,
HENRY C. KING.

AN ORDINANCE,
To divide the State of Texas into Senatorial and Representative Districts.

Section 1.   *Be it ordained by the people of Texas in Convention assembled,* That until after the first apportionment of Senators and Representatives, as provided in this constitution, after the census of the United States shall have been taken in 1880, the State shall be divided into Senatorial and Representative Districts, as follows:

SENATORIAL DISTRICTS.

First District—The counties of Liberty, San Jacinto, Hardin, Tyler. Jefferson, Jasper, Orange, Newton and Polk shall elect one senator; Tyler to be the returning county.

Second District—The counties of Houston, Angelina, Nacogdoches, San Augustine and Sabine shall elect one senator; Nacogdoches shall be the returning county.

Third District—The counties of Rusk, Panola and Shelby shall elect one senator; Panola being the returning county.

Fourth District—The county of Harrison shall elect one senator.

Fifth District — The counties of Marion, Cass, Bowie and Morris shall elect one senator; Cass to be the returning county.

Sixth District—The counties of Red River, Titus, Franklin and Hopkins shall elect one senator; Titus to be the returning county.

Seventh District—The counties of Camp. Upshur, Gregg and Smith shall elect one senator; Gregg to be the returning county.

Eighth District—The counties of Cherokee, Anderson and Henderson shall elect one senator; Anderson to be the returning county.

Ninth District—The counties of Lamar, Fannin and Delta shall elect one senator; Lamar to be the returning county.

Tenth District—The counties of Wood, Van Zandt, Kaufman, Rains, Rockwell and Hunt shall elect one senator; Kaufman to be the returning county.

Eleventh District—The counties of Grayson and Cook shall elect one senator; Grayson to be the returning county.

Twelfth District—The counties of Collin and Denton shall elect one senator; Collin to be the returning county.

Thirteenth District—The counties of Dallas and Ellis shall elect one senator; Ellis to be the returning county.

Fourteenth District—The counties of Navarro, Limestone and Freestone shall elect one senator; Limestone to be the returning county.

Fifteenth District—Leon, Robertson and Brazos shall elect one senator; Robertson to be the returning county.

Sixteenth District—Grimes, Madison, Walker and Trinity counties shall elect one senator; Walker to be the returning county.

Seventeenth District—Montgomery, Waller, Fort Bend and Wharton counties shall elect one senator; Montgomery to be the returning county.

Eighteenth District—The counties of Harris and Chambers shall elect one senator; Harris to be the returning county.

Nineteenth District—The counties of Galveston, Brazoria and Matagorda shall elect one senator; Galveston to be the returning county.

Twentieth District—Austin, Washington and Burleson counties shall elect one senator; Washington to be the returning county.

Twenty-first District—The counties of Falls, Milam and Bell shall elect one senator; Milam shall be the returning county.

Twenty-second District—The counties of Johnson, Hill and McLennan shall elect one senator; McLennan to be the returning county.

Twenty-third District—The counties of Tarrant, Parker, Wise, Montague, Clay, Jack and Young, with the unorganized counties west of them shall elect one senator; Tarrant to be the returning county.

Twenty-fourth District—The counties of Coryell, Bosque, Hamilton, Brown, Coleman, Comanche, Erath, Somerville, Hood, Palo Pinto, Eastland and Shackelford, with the unorganixed counties of Runnels, Baylor, Callahan, Jones and Stephens shall elect one senator; Comanche to be the returning county.

Twenty-fifth District—The counties of Travis, Williamson, Burnet and Lampasas shall elect one senator; Williamson to be the returning county.

Twenty-sixth District—The counties of Fayette, Bastrop and Lee shall elect one senator; Fayette to be the returning county.

Twenty-seventh District—The counties of Colorado, Lavaca and Gonzales shall elect one senator; Lavaca to be the returning county.

Twenty-eighth District—The counties of Calhoun, Victoria, DeWitt, Aransas, Refugio, Bee, Goliad, Karnes, Wilson, Jackson and Atascosa shall elect one senator; Victoria to be the returning county.

Twenty-ninth District—The counties of Cameron, Hidalgo, Starr, Webb, Maverick, Kinney, Uvalde, Medina, Nueces, San Patricio, Live Oak and Frio, with the unorganized counties of Duval, Encinal, McMullen, La Salle, Dimmit and Zalala, shall elect one senator; Nueces to be the returning county.

Thirtieth District—The counties of Bexar, Comal, Bandera, Kendall, Kerr, Gillespie, Mason, Menard, Tom Green, Pecos, Presidio and El Paso, with the unorganized counties of Concho and Crockett, shall elect one senator; Bexar to be the returning county.

Thirty-first District—The counties of Guadalupe, Caldwell, Hays, Blanco, Llano and San Saba, and the unorganized county of McCulloch, shall elect one senator; Hays to be the returning county.

REPRESENTATIVE DISTRICTS.

Sec. 2. *Be it further ordained,* That until said apportionment, after the census of 1880, representatives shall be elected as follows:

First District—The counties of Liberty, Hardin and Jefferson shall elect one representative; Liberty to be the returning county.

Second District—The counties of San Jacinto, Polk and Tyler shall elect one representative; Tyler to be the returning county.

Third District—The counties of Jasper, Newton and Orange shall elect one representative; Jasper to be the returning county.

Fourth District—The counties of San Augustine and Sabine shall elect one representative; San Augustine to be the returning county.

Fifth District—The county of Houston shall elect one representative.

Sixth District—The counties of Nacogdoches and Angelina shall elect one representative; Nacogdoches to be the returning county.

Seventh District—The county of Rusk shall elect one representative.

Eighth District—The counties of Panola and Shelby shall elect one representative; Panola to be the returning county.

Ninth District—The counties of Rusk, Panola and Shelby shall elect one representative; Panola to be the returning county.

Tenth District—The county of Harrison shall elect one representative.

Eleventh District—The counties of Marion, Cass, Bowie and Morris shall elect three representatives; Cass to be the returning county.

Twelfth District—The county of Red River shall elect one representative.

Thirteenth District—The counties of Titus and Franklin shall elect one representative; Titus to be the returning county.

Fourteenth District—The county of Hopkins shall elect one representative.

Fifteenth District—The counties of Smith, Gregg, Upshur and Camp shall elect three representatives; Gregg to be the returning county.

Sixteenth District—The county of Lamar shall elect one representative.

Seventeenth District—The county of Fannin shall elect one representative.

Eighteenth District—The counties of Lamar, Fannin and Delta shall elect one representative; Lamar to be the returning county.

Nineteenth District—The counties of Hunt and Rockwall shall elect one representative; Hunt to be the returning county.

Twentieth District—The counties of Kaufman, Rains, Wood and Van Zandt shall elect two representatives; Kaufman to be the returning county.

Twenty-first District—The county of Henderson shall elect one representative.

Twenty-second District—The county of Anderson shall elect one representative.

Twenty-third District—The county of Cherokee shall elect one representative.

Twenty-fourth District—The county of Leon shall elect one representative.

Twenty-fifth District—The county of Robertson shall elect two representatives.

Twenty-sixth District—The county of Brazos shall elect one representative.

Twenty-seventh District—The county of Grimes shall elect one representative.

Twenty-eighth District—The counties of Grimes and Madison shall elect one representative; Grimes to be the returning county.

Twenty-ninth District—The counties of Walker and Trinity shall elect one representative; Walker to be the returning county.

Thirtieth District—The county of Montgomery shall elect one representative.

Thirty-first District—Harris county shall elect two representatives.

Thirty-second District—The counties of Harris and Chambers shall elect one representative; Harris to be the returning county.

Thirty-third District—The county of Galveston shall elect two representatives.

Thirty-fourth District—The counties of Brazoria, Galveston and Matagorda shall elect one representative; Galveston to be the returning county.

Thirty-fifth District—The counties of Wharton, Fort Bend and Waller shall elect two representatives; Waller to be the returning county.

Thirty-sixth District—Austin county shall elect one representative.

Thirty-seventh District—Washington county shall elect one representative.

Thirty-eighth District—Washington and Burleson counties shall elect one representative; Burleson to be the returning county.

Thirty-ninth District—The counties of Falls, Milam and Bell shall elect three representatives; Bell to be the returning county.

Fortieth District—The county of Limestone shall elect one representative.

Forty-first District—The county of Freestone shall elect one representative.

Forty-second District—The county of Navarro shall elect one representative.

Forty-third District—The county of Ellis shall elect one representative.

Forty-fourth District—The county of Dallas shall elect two representatives.

Forty-fifth District—The county of Collin shall elect one representative.

Forty-sixth District—The county of Grayson shall elect two representatives.

Forty-seventh District—The counties of Grayson and Collin shall elect one representative; Grayson to be the returning county.

Forty-eighth District—The county of Cook shall elect one representative.

Forty-ninth District—The county of Denton shall elect one representative.

Fiftieth District—The counties of Clay, Montague and Wise, with the unorganized counties west of Clay, shall elect one representative; Wise to be the returning county.

Fifty-first District—The county of Tarrant shall elect one representative.

Fifty-second District—The counties of Parker, Jack and Young, with the unorganized counties west of them, shall elect one representative; Parker to be the returning county.

Fifty-third District—The county of Johnson shall elect one representative.

Fifty-fourth District—The county of Hill shall elect one representative.

Fifty-fifth District—The county of McLennan shall elect one representative.

Fifty-sixth District—The counties of Jackson, Calhoun, Victoria, DeWitt, Aransas, Refugio, Bee and Goliad shall elect two representatives; Victoria to be the returning county.

Fifty-seventh District—The counties of Colorado and Lavaca shall elect two representatives; Lavaca to be the returning county.

Fifty-eighth District—The county of Gonzales shall elect one representative.

Fifty-ninth District—The county of Fayette shall elect one representative.

Sixtieth District—The county of Bastrop shall elect one representative.

Sixty-first District—The counties of Fayette and Lee shall elect one representative; Fayette to be the returning county.

Sixty-second District—The counties of Caldwell, Guadalupe and Hays shall elect two representatives; Hays to be the returning county.

Sixty-third District—Travis county shall elect one representative.

Sixty-fourth District—Travis and Blanco counties shall elect one representative; Travis to be the returning county.

Sixty-fifth District—Williamson and Lampasas counties shall elect one representative; Williamson to be the returning county.

Sixty-sixth District—The counties of Coryell, Hamilton, Brown and Coleman, and the unorganized county of Runnells, shall elect one representative; Coryell to be the returning county.

Sixty-seventh District—The counties of Bosque, Somerville and Wood shall elect one representative; Bosque to be the returning county.

Sixty-eighth District—The counties of Erath, Comanche, Palo Pinto, Eastland and Shackleford, with the unorganized counties of Stephens, Jones, Callahan and Taylor, shall elect one representative; Comanche to be the returning county.

Sixty-ninth District—The county of Bexar shall elect one rep-representative.

Seventieth District—The counties of Bexar and Comal shall elect one representative; Bexar to be the returning county.

Seventy-first District—The counties of Uvalde, Medina, Bandera, Kendall, Kerr, Gillespie and Menard, with the unorganized counties of Edwards and Kimball, shall elect one representative; Gillespie to be the returning county.

Seventy-second District—The counties of Llano, Mason, San Saba, McCulloch and Concho shall elect one representative; San Saba to be the returning county.

Seventy-third District—The counties of El Paso, Presidio, Pecos, Tom Green and Crockett shall elect one representative; El Paso to be the returning county.

Seventy-fourth District—The counties of Cameron, Hidalgo, Starr, Zapata and Webb shall elect one representative; Cameron to be the returning county.

Seventy-fifth District—The counties of Nueces, Frio, Maveric k and Kinney, with the unorganized counties of Duval, Encinal, McMullen, La Salle, Dimmit and Zavala, shall elect one representative; Nueces to be the returning county.

Seventy-sixth District—The counties of San Patricio, Live Oak, Karnes, Wilson and Atascosa, shall elect one representative; Karnes to be the returning county.

Seventy-seventh District—The counties of Cherokee, Rusk, Panola, Shelby and Harrison shall elect one representative; Rusk to be the returning county.

"Sec. 3. *Be it further ordained,* That for all purposes connected with the first election provided for by this Convention, this ordinance shall take effect and be in force from and after its passage, and should the constitution be ratified by the people, this ordinance shall be and remain in force until the first apportionment after the census of 1880; but should the constitution be rejected by the people, this ordinance shall thereafter be and remain of no force and effect."

Mr. Rentfro gave notice of a minority report.

On motion of Mr. Norvell, two hundred copies of the report and ordinance were ordered printed for the use of the Convention.

Mr. Burleson offered the following resolution:

Resolved, That from and after the adoption of this constitution no paper which pretends to convey title to land and which was issued under the authority of Spain or Mexico, shall be received in evidence by any court in the State unless the same has been heretofore filed in the General Land Office, and the survey delineated on the map of the county in which the land is claimed to be.

Referred to the Committee on Spanish Land Titles.

Mr. Johnson, of Franklin, offered the following resolution:

Resolved, That the committee on General Provisions be instructed to inquire into the expediency of inserting a clause in the constitution requiring the publication in a newspaper for judicial sales and other legal notices.

Referred to the Committee on General Provisions.

Mr. Russell, of Wood, offered the following resolution:

Resolved, That the Comptroller of Public Accounts be requested to furnish this Convention with the amount of money loaned to each and every railroad, and out of what fund loaned, at what rate of interest, and as to whether the interest on said loans are promptly paid or not; if not, what roads are defaulters.

Adopted.

Mr. Kilgore offered the following resolution:

WHEREAS, The Convention did on last Saturday vote to pay the *State Gazette* for copies furnished the Convention the first eight days of the session, therefore, in order not to be partial, but to do justice to all who furnished papers for the same length of time, be it

Resolved, That the Committee on Printing and Contingent Expenses be authorized to allow payment for all papers furnished by the *Democratic Statesman* the first eight days of the session.

Mr. Flournoy proposed to amend, as follows:

That the Committee on Printing be instructed to inquire into the facts and report the proper and just measure.

Mr. Wade proposed to add the Houston *Telegraph,* and *Evening News,* and Galveston *News,* and such other papers as may have been furnished, and that each member pay out of his own money.

On motion of Mr. Ramey, the subject was referred to the Committee on Printing.

Mr. Rentfro submitted the following minority report:

COMMITTEE ROOM,
AUSTIN, October 25, 1875. }

To the Hon. E. B. Pickett, President of the Convention:

The undersigned, members of your Committee on Senatorial and Representative Apportionment, would respectfully submit that they concur in the report made by a majority of your said committee. While recognizing and admitting the fact that it would be an impossiblity so to apportion the State as to escape an expressed dissatisfaction on the part of a large minority of the citizens of each district so constituted; while in the main indorsing, or rather not protesting against, the action of the said majority in the premises, yet we must be permitted most earnestly to protest against the indorsement by the Convention of said report in many particulars. In the "Article on Legislative Department," which, by the vote of a large majority of the members of the Convention has been adopted, and which, in so far as the power in this Convention vested could so do, has been incorporated in the proposed constitution, as a part of the organic law, we find as relating to the duties of your Committee on Senatorial and Legislative Apportionment, sections 25 and 26, and we submit that under these sections and by virtue of the instructions therein given, your Committee on Senatorial and Legislative Apportionment are to be guided and governed.

These sections are in the following order, to-wit:

"Sec. 25. The State shall be divided into senatorial districts of contiguous territory, according to the number of qualified electors, as nearly as may be, and each district shall be entitled to elect one senator, and no single county shall be entitled to more than one senator.

"Sec. 26. The members of the House of Representatives shall be apportioned among the several counties according to the number of population of each, as near as may be, on a ratio obtained by dividing the population of the State, as ascertained by the most recent United States census, by the number of members of which the house is composed; *provided,* that whenever a single county has sufficient population to be entitled to a representative, such county shall be formed into a separate representative district, and when two or more counties are required to make up the ratio of representation, such counties shall be contiguous to each other, and when any one county has more than sufficient population to be entitled to one or more representatives, such representative or representatives shall be apportioned to such county, and for any surplus of population it may be joined in a representative district with any other contiguous county or counties."

The undersigned insist that while it may be claimed with some degree of plausibility that sections 25 and 26 are inoperative in so far as regards the present temporary apportionment, as provided for in ordinance accompanying majority report, and further, that said ordinance is proposed under and by virtue of section 28 of said article on " Legislative Department," yet they believe that said apportionment, though so termed, is not temporary in its character, and that, to extent of the contiguity and compactness of territory, as required by section 28, and amount of population, as provided for in section 26, the said sections 25 and 26 should and do contain the guide to a proper and equitable apportionment. We insist that the Convention derives whatever power it may possess in regard to apportioning the State into senatorial and representative districts from the very fact that its action in framing a constitution has rendered such apportionment necessary. Hence we argue that if such power exists at all, it only exists in accordance with and by virtue of sections 25 and 26, as hereinbefore set forth, and that if said apportionment be proper and just, it can only so be because of the necessity of apportionment, created by said article on " Legislative Department," and by sections 25 and 26 thereof. And further, we believe that any variance from the terms of such sections would not only be improper and void, but would very properly raise a suspicion as to the motives by which we might be actuated in the premises. We hold that the Convention having laid down a rule by which said Committee on Apportionment are to be guided, that said committee can not depart from such rule, and in the event they do so, their action in such particular can not be approved by the Convention, unless such rule of action be first reconsidered or set aside.

We deem it needless to urge the self-evident proposition that the Convention was not called for the purpose alone of re-districting the State; that it has been convened for the purpose of setting forth a declaration of rights and establishing a frame of government, and that such power to re-district, if it at all exists, is an incidental power, the exercise of which, if necessary at all, is so rendered necessary by the action of this Convention in altering and changing *in toto* the heretofore existing method of representation; therefore, if such proposition to re-district is entertained, and such re-districting is done by the Convention, it must be done in accordance with sections of the proposed constitution which have rendered a re-districting necessary. Hence we conclude that any portion of the said majority report, which is not in accordance with sections 25 and 26, hereinbefore referred to, is not correct and proper, and can not be adopted by the Convention.

Said section 25 provides that each senatorial district shall be composed of contiguous territory; and further, that each district must contain an equal amount of population, as near as may be. Under this we maintain that if any proposed district shall be found at variance with the foregoing provisions, the same can not be approved, as to that extent said majority report will be incorrect.

We call especial attention to the following portions of said majority report, waiving for the present the discussion of the question as to the power which the Convention may have, to give effect to said apportionment in its present form, before the same has been voted upon and adopted by the electors of this State.

It will be perceived that a great and remarkable difference exists as to the amount of population in the respective districts, and this difference is the more remarkable for the reason that many districts contiguous to each other differ to a great and unnecessary degree in said matter of population. The undersigned believe that, in many instances, a more equitable apportionment might be made, and respectfully submit the following, as a few of the most remarkable, and, in the opinion of the undersigned, uncalled-for deviations from the rule to which reference has heretofore been made.

For example, we find by referring to said majority report, that the county of Harrison is constituted a senatorial district, with right to elect one senator.

Premising that the basis of representation for senator, as agreed upon by your Committee on Senatorial and Representative Apportionment is and stands at 7500 electors, that is to say, that any county or counties having that number of registered electors shall be entitled to elect one senator, we necessarily come to the conclusion that the creation of Harrison county into a separate senatorial district, must be upon the part of the majority of said committee an unintentional mistake, as it must be known to each of the members signing such majority report that the registered vote of Harrison county does not exceed 5000, and that according to certificate of Registrar of said county, which said certificate is now on file in office of Secretary of State, the said vote is actually 4980. Hence, we conclude that the crea-

31

tion of such district is either a mistake upon the part of such majority, or if intentional, is an unequitable proceeding; in either event, the Convention, in our opinion, should correct. In contrast to the above, we would present for consideration the district composed of the counties of Brazos, Robertson and Leon. We find from data furnished by the Secretary of State that the registered electors of said counties number as follows: Brazos, 2500; Robertson, 5392; Leon, 2123—aggregating 10,015 votes. The great difference existing between said districts will at once appear to the Convention.

In order more fully to show the injustice of the apportionment proposed by the majority, we would again call attention to the vote of Harrison county, in connection with the vote of the county of Harris. We find that the list of electors for Harris county contains 7204 votes, being greater than the vote of Harrison county by 2224 voters. Yet to complete said district, the county of Chambers, with an estimated vote of about 600, is added. Whether the political complexion of the counties of Harris and Chambers, as associated together has aught to do in causing such union, we leave it to the Convention to decide. We refer to these variances from the rule as a few of the most glaring instances of unequitable apportionment, and earnestly request that a careful examination be made of that portion of proposed ordinance which regards senatorial apportionment, and confidently assert that it will be found to abound with many such instances.

Again, referring to that portion of said ordinance which proposes to divide the various counties of the State into legislative districts, we find still less to approve, and much more to condemn. The undersigned believe it to be the wish of the people of this State to return to that system of local representation which has heretofore obtained, and as a sufficient proof that the Convention so interprets the wishes of the people upon this subject, we have but to refer to section 26 of article on Legislative Department, in which said section we believe said doctrine of local representation to be incorporated. Believing then that this fact can not successfully be disputed, we find that to a great degree the idea of local representation has been carried out in the legislative apportionment referred to, yet we can not but add that in many cases this doctrine has been departed from, and to so great a degree that the conclusion forces itself upon the minds of the minority of your committee that such departure is an intentional one, and therefore the more inexcusable. The basis of representation in the proposed House of Representatives has been fixed by your committee at 2500 electors to each representative. Since the number of representatives has been increased by vote of the Convention from ninety to ninety-three members, it is believed that the basis will not exceed 2400. By referring to the hereinbefore incorporated section 26, we find it therein enunciated that whenever any one county shall have a sufficiency of electors to entitle it to one representative (which we conclude to mean 2400 electors) it shall be formed into a separate representative district. We believe that the Convention is to be guided by this provision in forming such districts.

In general the majority report does conform to this rule, yet we find that *Marion* county, with a list of electors amounting in the aggregate to 3077 voters, is formed into a representative district with the counties of Cass, Bowie and Camp, with an aggregate vote of 7275. We ask if the rule of local representation is here adhered to, and whether Marion county, with a vote of 3077, is not entitled to be formed into a separate representative district? Yet even if this apportionment obtains, we maintain that it is unjust, for the reason that it gives to the counties just named, with an aggregate vote of 7275, the right to elect *three* representatives, while to Harris county, with a vote of 7204, it only accords the right to elect *two* representatives. The injustice of this is manifest. Still further examining said majority report, we find that the county of *Colorado,* with a vote of 2923, is attached, for purposes of representation, to Lavaca county, which has a registered vote of 2002. We maintain this also to be unjust, as well as a direct violation of the doctrine of local representation, and that it deprives the people of Colorado county of that right which is extended to many other counties of this State: the right of local representation, for the reason that the registered vote of said Colorado county is largely in excess of the number required for local representation, to wit: 500 in excess. We submit that the apportionment would be more just and correct if Colorado county should be permitted to elect its own representative, and then for its surplus vote elect a second, in common with Lavaca county.

We find yet another instance of injustice: To Leon county, with a vote of 2123, is extended the right of electing one representative, while Walker county, with a vote of 2126, is added for purposes of representation to Trinity county, which has a vote of 762.

To Robertson county, which has a registered vote of 5,392, is accorded *two* representatives, while to Harris county, with a vote of 7,204, is accorded but *two* likewise. These instances are so frequent and so remarkable, that we would conceive ourselves derelict in our duty should we fail to direct to them the attention of the Convention. Necessarily it can not be that these differences are made for the purpose of increasing *Democratic* representation; yet, the undersigned would respectfully invite attention to the fact that in every case as noted in which the apportionment is incorrectly made, the counties named have decided Republican majorities; whether or no the action of the majority is influenced by this fact, we leave it to the Convention to decide. As to the question of the power of the Convention to give force and effect from and after passage to the proposed "ordinance," we deem it a subject worthy of a careful examination by each member of the Convention. We do not doubt that if said apportionment therein proposed should be incorporated in the constitution as a part thereof, if accepted by the people it would be of full force and effect, but we greatly doubt the power of the Convention to legalize the proposed ordinance from and after passage. If the proposed apportionment be presented in the form of an ordinance, in order to prevent sections 25 and 26 from ruling in the premises, we contend that not only would such action be unworthy of this Convention, but that it would meet the unqualified condemnation of the conservative people of this State, who always frown upon any unjust attempt to maintain party supremacy and who have repeatedly pronounced against the very system which the majority report seeks to perpetuate.

But we maintain that even in the shape of an "ordinance" the apportionment must conform to the terms in such sections set out. If district representation be sought, then let the system be universal. If local representation is desired, it should be general. In view of the premises, we earnestly ask that the apportionment proposed, which in the one place provides for *local*, and in the other for district representation, and the provisions of which force the conclusion that it is intended for party purposes, be not indorsed by the Convention. We admit that there has been established in times past a bad precedent, forced by circumstances, yet as delegates of the people, we earnestly hope that the time has arrived when the assembled representatives of the people of Texas, will not permit the engrafting upon our organic law of a provision so ruinous, so subversive of party morals, and which has so universally been condemned by the electors of Texas.

Believing that the majority report will not be sanctioned by the Convention, we confidently submit our protest and report in the premises.

R. B. RENTFRO,
E. W. BRADY,
WM. REYNOLDS,
T. J. LOCKETT.

Mr. Brady moved to have two hundred copies of the report printed.

Mr. Fleming moved to lay the motion on the table.

Withdrawn, and Mr. Brady's motion adopted.

[Mr. Brown in the chair.]

The hour having arrived for the special order, on motion of Mr. Scott the same was postponed until "Taxation and Revenue" shall be disposed of.

Unfinished business, viz: "Article ——, Revenue and Taxation," with pending amendment by Mr. Martin, of Hunt, taken up.

Mr. Martin, of Hunt, withdrew his amendment, and moved to strike out section 4.

Carried.

Mr. Flournoy proposed to amend by adding to section 3 the words, "but they and their property shall be taxed as other individuals."

Adopted.

Mr. Fleming proposed to amend section 5 by striking out "one-half of one per cent.," and insert "fifty cents."

Adopted.

Mr. Dohoney moved to amend by striking out section 7.

Mr. Robertson, of Bell, proposed to amend section 7 by adding in last line, after the word "purposes," the following: "by a majority vote of the freeholders of such county, city, town or other municipal government."

Withdrawn, and Mr. Dohoney's amendment adopted.

Mr. Stayton offered the following as a substitute for section 6:

"Sec. 6. The Legislature shall have no power to release the inhabitants or property of any county, city or town from the payment of taxes levied for State purposes."

Adopted.

Mr. McLean offered the following as section 7:

"Sec. 7. The County Courts of the several counties, and the municipal authorities of the towns and cities of the State, are prohibited from creating any debt against such counties, cities or towns; *provided,* that towns and cities situated on the coast may incur debt in the erection of works for the safety and protection of life and property against storms, by the vote of those who pay taxes on property in such towns and cities."

Withdrawn.

Mr. Ferris offered the following:

"Sec. 4. The Legislature shall not have power to borrow, or in any manner to divert from its purpose any special fund that may or ought to come into the treasury, and shall make it penal for any person or persons to borrow, withhold, or in any manner to divert from its purpose any special fund, or any part thereof."

Adopted.

Mr. Nunn proposed to strike out section 8.

Mr. Gaither offered the following amendment to section 8:

"All landed property shall be assessed in the county where it lies, and the tax may be paid by the non-resident in that county, or to the Comptroller of the State."

Mr. Fleming moved to lay both amendments on the table.

The question to lay on the table Mr. Nunn's motion to strike out section 8, was put and carried by the following vote:

YEAS—Allison, Abernathy, Arnim, Abner, Brown, Blassingame, Barnett, Brady, Bruce, Chambers, Cook of Gonzales, Cooke of San Saba, Cardis, Dillard, Dohoney, Darnell, Erhard, Fleming, Ferris, German, Graves, Holt, Haynes, Johnson of Franklin, Johnson of Collin, Lacy, Lynch, McLean, Martin of Hunt, Mills, Mitchell, McKinney of Denton, McKinney of Walker, McCormick, Murphy, Nugent, Pauli, Reynolds, Rentfro, Russell of Wood, Spikes, Scott, Wade, Weaver, Waelder—46.

NAYS—Blake, Ballinger, Burleson, Crawford, Cooley, De-Morse, Gaither, Henry of Smith, Kilgore, Killough, Lockett, Martin of Navarro, Morris, Moore, Norvell, Nunn, Reagan, Robertson of Bell, Robison of Fayette, Smith, Stockdale, Slayton, Whitehead, Wright, West—25.

Upon calling the roll, Mr. Henry, of Limestone, stated that he was paired off with Mr. Ross, but for which fact he would vote "no."

Mr. Fleming withdrew that part of his motion that proposed to lay Mr. Gaither's amendment on the table.

On motion of Mr. Whitfield, the Convention adjourned to 2:30 o'clock P. M.

EVENING SESSION—2½ o'CLOCK.

Convention met; roll called; quorum present.

Mr. Brown, by leave, introduced the following ordinance:

" AN ORDINANCE

"To provide for submitting the Constitution to a Vote of the People and for a General Election under its provisions.

"Section 1. *Be it ordained by the people of Texas in Convention assembled,* That by way of schedule to the constitution, and that no inconvenience shall arise in superseding the constitution of 1870 with the constitution adopted by this Convention, it is hereby ordained that an election shall be held throughout the State, on the .... day of ...., 1876, at which the voice of the electors of the State shall be taken on the ratification or rejection of the new constitution and the several ordinances adopted by this Convention. Those voting in favor of ratifying the same shall write or print on their respective tickets the word "ratification," or other word of similar import. Those opposed to their ratification shall write or print on their respective tickets the word "rejection," or other word of similar import, so as to express the wish of the elector. If a majority of all the votes cast at said election, as returned to the Secretary of State, shall be in favor of ratification, the Governor shall, within five days next succeeding the return day, issue his proclamation declaring the fact, and thereafter the said constitution and ordinances shall become and remain the fundamental, organic law of the State. Ordinances, however, of a temporary character shall not be reprinted or considered as permanent parts of the constitution after the accomplishment of their objects. But should a majority of all the votes so cast and returned be against ratification, the Governor shall, in like time and manner, proclaim the fact, after which neither said constitution, nor any ordinance passed by this Convention, shall have either force or effect in this State.

"Sec. 2. *Be it further ordained,* That at the same time and places there shall be a general election throughout the State for such precinct, county, district and State officers as are made elective by the new constitution. The election, as far as practicable, shall be conducted as now provided by law; but no registration of voters shall be required, and every elector shall vote in the precinct of his residence; *provided,* that electors residing in unorganized counties may vote in any precinct of the county to which their respective counties may be attached for judicial purposes. The qualifications of electors shall be as defined in the article regulating suffrage in the new constitution.

"Sec. 3. *Be it further ordained,* That the County Courts now existing shall assemble at their respective county seats within twenty days after the adjournment of this Convention, or as soon thereafter as practicable, and when assembled re-divide

their respective counties into the number of precincts provided
for by the new constitution, and make immediate proclamation
thereof for the information of the people.   Said courts shall
establish at least one voting place in each of such precincts, and
whenever deemed necessary for public convenience, they shall
establish two or more such voting places in any one precinct.

"Sec. 4. *Be it further ordained,* That the returns of said election shall be made as now provided by law, to the presiding justice of each county, or to the returning officer of each senatorial, representative or judicial district, as the case may be, and
in all cases provided by law, to the Secretary of State.   In all
cases the returns shall be made, opened, counted, and the result
recorded and declared as provided by law.

"Sec. 5. *Be it further ordained,* That in case the constitution shall be ratified at said election, the Lieutenant Governor,
Senators and Representatives then chosen shall assemble as the
Fifteenth Legislature, at the seat of government, on Tuesday,
the ...... day of ......, 1876.

"Sec. 6. *Be it further ordained,* That after the first election
as herein provided, until otherwise provided by law, the regular
biennial elections of this State for precinct, county, district and
State officers, including members of Congress, after the year
1876, and President and Vice President of the United States in
the year of their election, shall take place on the .... Tuesday
of November every second year, commencing with November,
1878.   All officers elected at the election herein provided for
shall hold over as though they had been elected in November,
1876, until their successors shall have been elected and qualified, whether the tenure of their offices be for two, four, six or
eight years.

"Sec. 7. *Be it further ordained,* That all county, precinct
and district officers elected in accordance with the provisions of
this ordinance, shall be installed into office on the .... day of
...... 1876; *provided,* that persons so elected who may be prevented from qualifying by reason of illness or absence shall
have ten additional days in which to do so.   The Governor, and
all other State officers, so elected, shall be installed on the first
Tuesday after the assemblage of the first Legislature elected
as herein provided.   As each newly elected officer may be qualified, his predecessor, if any, shall cease his functions, and deliver to his successor all books, papers, archives and records, and
all property, of whatsoever nature or kind, pertaining to his
office, or under his official charge.

"Sec. 8. *Be it further ordained,* That for all purposes herein mentioned, the same being incidental to the formation and ratification of the new constitution, this ordinance shall take effect and be in force from and after its passage."

Referred to the Committee on Ordinances.

Mr. Gaither, by leave, withdrew his amendment and offered the following:

"All property shall be assessed in the county where situated, but the taxes due by parties not residing in the county may be paid in the county where assessed, or at the office of the Comptroller of Public Accounts."

Mr. Fleming moved the main question on Mr. Gaither's amendment.

Lost.

Mr. Fleming moved to table the amendment.

Lost by the following vote:

YEAS — Abernathy, Arnim, Abner, Brown, Blassingame, Barnett, Bruce, Chambers, Cook of Gonzales, Cooke of San Saba, Cardis, Dillard, Darnell, Davis of Wharton, Fleming, Ferris, German, Graves, Holt, Haynes, Johnson of Franklin, Johnson of Collin, Lacy, McLean, Martin of Hunt, Mills, Mitchell, McKinney of Denton, McCormick, Nugent, Pauli, Reynolds, Russell of Wood, Spikes, Scott, Wade, Weaver — 37.

NAYS—Allison, Blake, Ballinger, Burleson, Brady, Crawford, Cline, Cooley, DeMorse, Dohoney, Ford, Flournoy, Gaither, Henry of Smith, ·King, Kilgore, Killough, Lockett, Lynch, Martin of Navarro, Morris, Moore, Murphy, Norvell, Nunn, Reagan, Ramey, Rentfro, Robertson of Bell, Robinson of Fayette, Russell of Harrison, Smith, Stockdale, Stayton, Whitehead, Wright, Whitfield, West, Waelder — 39.

Upon calling the roll, Mr. Henry, of Limestone, stated that he was paired off with Mr. Ross, but for which he would vote "no."

The question being the adoption of the resolution, on motion of Mr. Mills, a call of the Convention was ordered.

Absentees: Messrs. Erhard, McCabe, Sansom and McKinney of Walker.

Mr. Whitfield moved to suspend the call.

Lost.

Messrs. McKinney of Walker, and McCabe appeared and answered to their names.

The pending amendment was laid upon the table temporarily, and Mr. Flournoy offered the following amendment to section 1:

"Sec. 1. The Legislature may also, in its discretion, provide for levying a tax on the gross earnings and franchises, or either, of all corporations, or of any class of corporations."

Mr. Cline made the point of order that the amendment was not in order, the same subject matter having been definitely acted on by the Convention in striking out section 4 of the article.

The question on the adoption of the amendment was then put, and the amendment adopted by the following vote:

YEAS—Allison, Abernathy, Arnim, Brown, Blassingame, Barnett, Burleson, Brady, Bruce, Crawford, Chambers, Cook of Gonzales, Cooke of San Saba, Cardis, Dillard, Dohoney, Darnell, Flournoy, Fleming, German, Graves, Henry of Smith, Henry of Limestone, Haynes, Johnson of Franklin, Johnson of Collin, Lacy, Lynch, McLean, Martin of Navarro, Martin of Hunt, Mills, McKinney of Denton, McKinney of Walker, McCormick, Moore, Nugent, Ramey, Robertson of Bell, Robison of Fayette, Russell of Wood, Scott, Wade, Wright, Weaver, Whitfield — 46.

NAYS — Abner, Blake, Ballinger, Cline, Cooley, DeMorse, Davis of Wharton, Ford, Ferris, Gaither, Holt, King, Kilgore, Killough, Lockett, McCabe, Morris, Mitchell, Murphy, Norvell, Nunn, Pauli, Reagan, Reynolds, Rentfro, Russell of Harrison, Spikes, Smith, Stockdale, Stayton, Whitehead, West, Waelder — 33.

Mr. Russell, of Wood, offered the following amendment:

" All property of railroad companies shall be assessed and the taxes collected in the several counties in which said property is situated, including so much of the road-bed and fixtures as shall be in each county. The rolling stock may be reported in gross in the county where the principal office of the company is located, and the tax paid upon it shall be apportioned by the Comptroller (*pro rata*) among the several counties through which the road passes, as a part of their tax assets."

Adopted by the following vote:

YEAS—Allison, Arnim, Abner, Brown, Blassingame, Barnett, Burleson, Brady, Bruce, Crawford, Chambers, Cook of Gonzales, Cooke of San Saba, Cardis, Dillard, DeMorse, Darnell, Davis of Wharton, Ford, Flournoy, Fleming, Ferris, German, Gaither, Graves, Henry of Smith, Henry of Limestone, Haynes, Johnson of Franklin, Johnson of Collin, Killough, Lockett, Lacy, Lynch, McLean, Martin of Navarro, McCabe, Mills, Mitchell, McKinney of Denton, McKinney of Walker, McCormick, Moore, Murphy, Nunn, Nugent, Pauli, Ramey, Reynolds, Robertson of Bell, Robison of Fayette, Russell of Wood, Spikes, Scott, Weaver, Whitfield — 56.

NAYS—Abernathy, Blake, Ballinger, Cline, Cooley, Dohoney, Holt, King, Kilgore, Martin of Hunt, Morris, Norvell, Reagan,

Rentfro, Russell of Harrison, Smith, Stockdale, Stayton, Sansom, Wade, Whitehead, Wright, West, Waelder — 24.

Mr. Russell, of Wood, moved to suspend the call.

Lost.

Mr. Waelder offered the following as a substitute for section 9:

" Sec. 9. All property subject to taxation in, and owned by residents of unorganized counties, shall be assessed, and the taxes thereon paid in the counties to which such unorganized counties shall be attached for judicial purposes, and lands owned by non-residents of unorganized counties and lands lying in territory not laid off into counties, shall be assessed, and the taxes collected thereon at the office of the Comptroller of the State."

Mr. Waelder moved to reconsider the vote taken on Saturday, refusing to consolidate the offices of assessor and collector.

On motion of Mr. Kilgore, the Convention adjourned to 9 o'clock A. M. to-morrow.

FORTY-FOURTH DAY.

HALL OF REPRESENTATIVES, }
AUSTIN, TEXAS, October 26, 1875. }

Convention met pursuant to adjournment; roll called; quorum present. Prayer by the Rev. H. V. Philpott, of the M. E. Church, South, at Austin.

Journal of yesterday read and adopted.

Mr. Johnson, of Collin, offered the following resolution:

WHEREAS, The labors of the several committees have about closed, and reports made; therefore, be it

Resolved, That the Convention will hold night sessions until its labors are completed.

Mr. Russell, of Wood, moved to postpone the consideration of the resolution until to-day week, and that it be made special order for 10 o'clock that day.

Mr. Rentfro raised the point of order, viz: that the resolution being amendatory of the rule, should lay over one day for consideration, and that it would take a two-third vote to adopt it..

Chair ruled against the point.

Mr. Russell's (of Wood) motion to postpone was adopted.

Mr. McLean offered the following resolution:

Resolved, That the County Courts of the several counties and the municipal authorities of the towns and cities of the State, are prohibited from creating any debt against such counties, towns, and cities; *provided,* that towns and cities situated on the coast may incur debt in the erection of works for the safety and protection of life and property against storms, by the vote of those who pay taxes on property in such towns and cities.

Referred to Committee on Municipal Corporations.

On motion of Mr. Flournoy, Mr. McLean and Mr. Mills were added to the Committee on Municipal Corporations.

Mr. Martin, of Navarro, offered the following resolution:

Resolved, That the making of profit out of the public moneys, or using the same for any purpose not authorized by law, by any officer of the State, or member or officer of the Legislature, shall be a misdemeanor, and shall be punished as may be provided by law, but part of such punishment shall be disqualification to hold office for a period of not less than five years.

Referred to Committee on Crimes and Punishments.

UNFINISHED BUSINESS.

"Article —, Revenue and Taxation," with pending amendment offered by Mr. Gaither, taken up and amendment lost by the following vote:

YEAS—Allison, Abernathy, Blake, Ballinger, Cline, DeMorse, Dohoney, Davis of Brazos, Flournoy, Gaither, Henry of Smith, Henry of Limestone, King, Kilgore, Killough, Lockett, Lynch, Martin of Navarro, Morris, Moore, Murphy, Norvell, Nunn, Reagan, Ramey, Reynolds, Rentfro, Robertson of Bell, Robison of Fayette, Russell of Harrison, Smith, Stockdale, Stayton, Whitehead, Wright, Whitfield, West, Waelder—38.

NAYS—Arnim, Abner, Brown, Blassingame, Barnett, Burleson, Bruce, Crawford, Chambers, Cook of Gonzales, Cardis, Dillard, Darnell, Ford, Fleming Ferris, German, Graves, Holt, Haynes, Johnson of Franklin, Johnson of Collin, Lacy, McLean, Martin of Hunt, Mills, Mitchell, McKinney of Denton, McKinney of Walker, McCormick, Nugent, Pauli, Ross, Russell of Wood, Spikes, Scott, Sansom, Wade, Weaver — 39.

Mr. Mills moved to reconsider the vote just taken, and to lay the motion on the table.

On motion of Mr. Stockdale, a call of the Convention was ordered.

Absent — Messrs. Brady, Cooley, Erhard and Wade.

Mr. Moore moved to excuse Mr. Erhard.

Lost.

Pending question passed to the table pending the call, and the following communication was taken from the President's desk and read:

AUSTIN, October 25, 1875.

To the Hon. E. B. Pickett, President of the Convention:

SIR—In obedience to a resolution adopted by the honorable body of which you are president, I have the honor herewith to submit as accurate a statement as it is possible to be made from the records of this office. The number of certificates issued is accurately given, but the length of each road can only be ascertained by reference to the various inspection reports, only a part of which have been filed in this office, the balance in the offices of Secretary of State and Comptroller.

Very respectfully, your obedient servant,

J. J. GROOS, Commissioner.

GENERAL LAND OFFICE, AUSTIN, October 25, 1875.

Statement of Number of Certificates issued to and Quantity of Land granted to each Road in the State, and Length of each Road as nearly as can be ascertained.

NAME OF RAILROAD.	CERTIFICATES ISSUED.	NO. OF ACRES.	LENGTH OF ROAD COMPLETED.
Buffalo Bayou B. & C. R. R.	1,401	896,640	Consolidated with G. H. & S. A. R. R.
San Antonio & M. G. R. R.	373	238,720	Consolidated with G. W. T. & P. R. R.
Houston T. C. R. R.	7,452	4,769,280	501 47-100 miles.
Houston Tap & B. R. R.	800	512,000	Consolidated with Int'l & G. N. R. R.
Washington County R. R.	383	245,120	Consolidated with H. & T. C. R. R.
Texas & N. O. R. R. (Texas Div.)	1,920	1,228,800	108 miles.
East Texas R. R.	448	287,720	Length unknown.
Memphis E. P. & P. R. R.	502	321,280	Now Texas & Pacific.
Southern Pacific R. R.	576	368,640	Now Texas & Pacific.
Texas & Pacific R. R.	2,756	1,763,840	321 8-100 miles.
Galveston, Houston & H. R. R.	956	611,840	59 miles.
Houston & G. N. R. R.	3,611	2,311,040	Now I. & G. N. R. R.
International & G. N. R. R.	4,020	2,572,800	410 miles (approximate).
Waco & N. W. R. R.	752	481,280	No means of ascertaining length.
Galveston, Houston & S. A. R. R.	1,355	867,200	154 25-100 miles.
Indianola R. R.	281	179,840	Now G. W. T. & P. R. R.
Rusk Tramway	124	79,360	15¼ miles.
Columbus Tap	77	49,280	Now G. H. & S. A. R. R.
Gulf, W. T. & P. R. R.	473	302,720	68 8-10 miles.
Total	28,260	18,086,400	

Two hundred copies ordered printed.

Mr. Waelder's substitute for section 9, offered yesterday, was taken up and adopted.

Mr. Dohoney offered the following as a substitute for the section 9, as substituted by Mr. Waelder:

"Sec. 9. All property subject to taxation in unorganized counties shall be assessed and the taxes paid in such manner and under such regulations as the Legislature may prescribe."

Lost.

Mr. Fleming offered the following additional section:

"Sec. ——. The annual assessment made upon landed property shall be a special lien thereon."

Adopted.

Mr. Murphy offered the following section:

"Sec. ——. All lands, whether owned by persons or corporations, upon which no tax has been paid, in whole or in part, since the formation of this State, shall be relieved from the same upon the payment to the proper county officer of such back taxes as the Legislature may designate."

The hour having arrived for the special order, viz: "Article ——, Judiciary," on motion of Mr. Wright it was postponed to 2½ o'clock to-morrow.

Mr. Mills asked leave to withdraw his motion to reconsider and lay on the table.

Refused.

Messrs. Brady, Cooley, Erhard and Wade having appeared and answered to their names, the call was exhausted, and the question on the motion of Mr. Mills to reconsider and lay on the table was put and carried by the following vote:

YEAS—Arnim, Abner, Brown, Blassingame, Barnett, Burleson, Brady, Bruce, Crawford, Chambers, Cook of Gonzales, Cooke of San Saba, Cardis, Dillard, Darnell, Davis of Wharton, Ford Fleming, Ferris, German, Graves, Holt, Haynes, Johnson of Franklin, Johnson of Collin, Lacy, McLean, Martin of Hunt, McCabe, Mills, Mitchell, McKinney of Denton, McKinney of Walker, McCormick, Nugent, Pauli, Reynolds, Russell of Wood, Spikes, Scott, Sansom, Wade, Weaver—43.

NAYS—Allison, Abernathy, Blake, Ballinger, Cline, Cooley, DeMorse, Dohoney, Davis of Brazos, Erhard, Flournoy, Gaither, Henry of Smith, Henry of Limestone, King, Kilgore, Killough, Lockett, Lynch, Martin of Navarro, Morris, Moore, Murphy, Norvell, Nunn, Reagan, Ramey, Rentfro, Robertson of Bell, Robison of Fayette, Ross, Russell of Harrison, Smith, Stockdale, Stayton, Whitehead, Wright, Whitfield, West, Waelder—40.

The question upon Mr. Murphy's amendment recurring, Mr.

Murphy withdrew his amendment, and it was referred to the Committee on Back Taxes.

Mr. Dohoney proposed to amend section 8 by striking out the words " all lands," and insert " all property."

Carried.

Mr. Ballinger offered the following amendment:

Section 10, line 3, strike out the words " condemnation and."

Mr. Graves moved to close debate upon the amendment and bring the Convention to a vote on it.

Carried, and amendment lost by the following vote:

YEAS—Abernathy, Ballinger, Crawford, Chambers, Cook of Gonzales, Cooley, Davis of Brazos, Ford, Gaither, Henry of Smith, Henry of Limestone, Killough, Lynch, Morris, Norvell, Nunn, Scott, Sansom, Wright, West, Waelder—21.

NAYS—Allison, Arnim, Abner, Brown, Blassingame, Barnett, Burleson, Brady, Bruce, Cooke of San Saba, Cline, Cardis, Dillard, DeMorse, Dohoney, Darnell, Davis of Wharton, Fleming, Ferris, German, Graves, Holt, Haynes, Johnson of Franklin, Johnson of Collin, Kilgore, Lockett, Lacy, McLean, Martin of Navarro, Martin of Hunt, McCabe, Mills, Mitchell, McKinney of Denton, McKinney of Walker, McCormick, Moore, Murphy, Nugent, Pauli, Reagan, Ramey, Reynolds, Rentfro, Robertson of Bell, Robison of Fayette, Ross, Russell of Harrison, Russell of Wood, Spikes, Smith, Stockdale, Stayton, Wade, Whitehead, Weaver, Whitfield—58.

Mr. Ferris offered the following substitute for section 14:

" Sec. 14. The Legislature shall provide for equalizing, as near as may be, the valuation of all property subject to or rendered for taxation, by creating a board or boards of equalization, and it may also provide for the classification of all lands with reference to their value in the several counties."

Mr. Pauli proposed to amend section 14 by striking out the words " the Sheriff, County Clerk and Chief Justice shall compose," and insert " the Commissioners' Court in open session shall act as," also insert after the word " property holders " the words " or the Assessor."

Adopted.

Mr. Ferris's substitute was adopted.

Mr. Reagan offered the following amendment:

Amend section 10 by adding after the word " fraud," where it occurs before the proviso, the words " or because the taxes had been paid as required by law."

On motion of Mr. West, the Convention adjourned to 2¼ o'clock P. M.

EVENING SESSION—2¼ o'clock.

Convention met pursuant to adjournment; roll called; quorum present.

On motion of Mr. Russell, of Harrison, Mr. Abner was excused for the evening on account of sickness.

On motion of Mr. Moore, Mr. Erhard was excused on account of sickness.

Mr. Cook, of Gonzales, offered the following amendment to section 10 of pending article.

Amend section 10; next to last line strike out "three times" and insert the word "double."

Mr. Reagan's amendment pending an adjournment lost.

Mr. Cook's amendment adopted.

Mr. Reagan offered the following amendment:

Amend by striking out the first four lines of section 8 and inserting: "All property, whether owned by persons or corporations, shall be assessed for taxation in the county where it is situated, but the taxes may be paid in the county where the property is situated, or in the county where the owner may live, or at the Comptroller's office."

Mr. Russell, of Wood, made this point of order, viz.: that the amendment was out of order, the substance of the amendment having been contained in Mr. Gaither's amendment, which was voted down this morning.

The Chair ruled against the point.

Mr. McCormick moved to recommit the article and pending amendments to a select committee of five.

Mr. Fleming moved the main question.

Carried.

The question of referring the article and amendments to a select committee of five was then put and lost by the following vote:

YEAS—Abernathy, Brown, Ballinger, Cline, Cooley, DeMorse, Dohoney, Darnell, Davis of Brazos, Ford, Flournoy, Gaither, Henry of Smith, Henry of Limestone, Kilgore, Killough, Lockett, Lynch, Morris, McCormick, Murphy, Norvell, Nunn, Reagan, Robertson of Bell, Russell of Harrison, Smith, Stockdale, Stayton, Whitehead, Wright, Whitfield, West, Waelder—34.

NAYS—Allison, Arnim, Abner, Blassingame, Barnett, Burleson, Brady, Bruce, Crawford, Chambers, Cook of Gonzales, Cooke of San Saba, Cardis, Dillard, Davis of Wharton, Fleming, Ferris, German, Graves, Holt, Haynes, Johnson of Franklin, Johnson of Collin, Lacy, McLean, Martin of Navarro,

32

Martin of Hunt, McCabe, Mills, Mitchell, McKinney of Denton, McKinney of Walker, Moore, Nugent, Pauli, Ramey, Reynolds, Rentfro, Robison of Fayette, Ross, Russell of Wood, Spikes, Scott, Sansom, Wade, Weaver—46.

On motion of Mr. Graves, debate was closed on Mr. Reagan's amendment, and a vote was taken and the amendment lost by the following vote:

Yeas—Abernathy, Ballinger, Cline, Cooley, DeMorse, Dohoney, Davis of Brazos, Gaither, Kilgore, Killough, Lockett, Morris, Moore, Norvell, Nunn, Reagan, Robertson of Bell, Robison of Fayette, Smith, Stockdale, Stayton, Whitehead, Wright, West, Waelder—25.

Nays—Allison, Arnim, Abner, Brown, Blassingame, Barnett, Burleson, Brady, Bruce, Crawford, Chambers, Cook of Gonzales, Cooke of San Saba, Cardis, Dillard, Darnell, Davis of Wharton, Ford, Flournoy, Fleming, Ferris, German, Graves, Holt, Henry of Smith, Henry of Limestone, Haynes, Johnson of Franklin, Johnson of Collin, Lacy, Lynch, McLean, Martin of Navarro, Martin of Hunt, McCabe, Mills, Mitchell, McKinney of Denton, McKinney of Walker, McCormick, Murphy, Nugent, Pauli, Ramey, Reynolds, Rentfro, Ross, Russell of Harrison, Russell of Wood, Spikes, Scott, Sansom, Wade, Weaver, Whitfield—55.

Mr. Whitfield moved to postpone the consideration of the article until Saturday next at 10 o'clock; that it be made the special order for that hour, and that one hundred copies be printed.

Carried.

Mr. Dillard moved to reconsider the vote refusing to adopt Mr. Ballinger's amendment to section 10, taken this morning.

On motion of Mr. West, the Convention adjourned to 9 o'clock A. M. to-morrow.

FORTY-FIFTH DAY.

Hall of Representatives,
Austin, Texas, October 27, 1875.

Convention met pursuant to adjournment; roll called; quorum present. Prayer by the Rev. Horatio V. Philpott, of the M. E. Church, South, at Austin.

Journal of yesterday read and adopted.

The following communication was taken from the President's desk and read:

COMPTROLLER'S OFFICE,
AUSTIN, October 26, 1875.

To the Hon. E. B. Pickett, President of the Convention:

SIR—In compliance with an ordinance of your honorable body, passed October 25, 1875, viz: "That the Comptroller of Public Accounts be requested to furnish this Convention a statement with the amount of money loaned to each and every railroad, and amount of what fund loaned, at what rate of interest, and as to whether the interest on said loans are promptly paid or not; if not, what roads are defaulters"—I beg leave to submit the following statement of amounts loaned to railroads, all of which was from the Common School fund, viz:

Houston and Texas Central Railroad			$450,000
Washington County	"	"	66,000
Buffalo Bayou, Brazos and Colorado Railroad			420,000
Houston Tap and Brazoria	"		300,000
Texas and New Orleans	"		430,500
Southern Pacific	"		150,000

Total amount of aid given........ $1,816,500

For this amount the State took the bonds of the several railroad companies, bearing interest at the rate of six per cent. per annum. Under an act approved February 13, 1860, $63,183 of these bonds were liquidated, leaving in the possession of the State at this date bonds of railroad companies amounting to $1,753,317. Under an act approved August 13, 1870, it was provided that to the principal due from each company should be added all interest due on the first day of May, 1870, and upon the amounts so obtained six months interest and one per cent. sinking fund shall be paid on the first day of May and November of each year. Railroad companies are now operating under this law. The amounts upon which interest and sinking fund is due by railroad companies November 1, 1875, is as follows, viz:

Houston and Texas Central Railroad Company.	$594,472	38
Washington County	93,910	98
Southern Pacific	200,885	90
Texas and New Orleans	588,871	47
Galveston, Harrisburg and San Antonio	588,625	47

Total........................ $2,066,766 20

The interest and sinking fund required by law has been promptly paid by each company.

I have the honor to be, very respectfully,

STEPHEN H. DARDEN, Comptroller.

On motion of Mr. Allison, two hundred copies were ordered printed.

Mr. Russell, of Harrison, presented the memorial of sundry citizens of Brazoria county asking the prohibition of occupation tax.

Referred to Committee on Revenue and Taxation.

Mr. Blassingame presented the petition of the citizens of Sherman on the subject of railroad taxation.

Referred to Committee on Revenue and Taxation.

Mr. Martin, of Hunt, offered the following resolution:

Resolved, That the Legislature shall not hereafter create any office, except as provided in this constitution.

Referred to Committee on General Provisions.

Mr. Gaither offered the following resolution:

Resolved, That the President of the Convention be authorized to appoint a committee of six, one from each Congressional District, to prepare a brief address to the people of the State, setting forth the leading principles of the new constitution, the reforms provided for by it, and its claims to the approbation of the freemen of Texas.

Adopted.

Mr. Johnson, of Franklin, offered the following resolution:

Resolved, That the following provision be incorporated into the constitution:

"Sec. ——. The Legislature may provide, through the Agricultural and Mechanical College of Texas, for the collection, gathering and publication of agricultural, geological and geographical statistics and information in regard to this State, and for the distribution of such publications as shall be made, both at home and abroad.

Referred to Committee on Education.

Mr. West offered the following resolution:

Resolved, That the Governor be requested to furnish this Convention, if compatible with the public interest, a brief statement showing the amount of bonds sold during the term of Governor Davis, their character, the date of the law under which they were issued, the price for which they were sold, and the amount of commissions and other expenses attending the sale, so as to show the precise amount realized from the sale of such bonds. And that he also furnish this Convention information as to the number and amount of bonds sold during his administration up to date, showing the character of the bonds, their denomination, bearing what interest, and in what the principal and interest are payable, and when due, and under what law issued, the price paid for the bonds and the names of the purchasers, and dates of purchase, and what commissions, expenses and charges have attended the sale, so as to show the amount of money and its character received by the State, and whether there are any other bonds now offered for sale.   Also, what amount of bonds, if any, have been issued in liquidation of treasury warrants, the character of the warrants so taken up, to whom and when the bonds were issued, at what interest, when payable and in what character of funds.   And also, what amount of money, if any, has been paid out of the treasury for which there was no appropriation; on what claim or account it was paid, and to whom.

Adopted.

Mr. Scott called up his amendment to the rules, submitted on Saturday, viz:

"Whenever any article of the constitution shall be passed upon its third reading, under the foregoing rules, it shall be, as of course, referred to the Committee on Style and Arrangement. When the whole constitution shall be presented to the Convention by said committee, it shall not be subject to any amendment that will change its meaning or intent, except by a two-thirds vote."

The hour having arrived for the consideration of the special order, viz: to reconsider the vote adopting the resolution on the subject of immigration, it was taken up.

On motion of Mr. Crawford, the consideration of the special order was postponed until the final passage of the article on Legislative Department.

The question then recurring on the adoption of Mr. Scott's amendment to the rules, the yeas and nays were called for, and the amendment carried by the following vote, it requiring two-thirds to adopt:

YEAS—Allison, Abernathy, Arnim, Abner, Brown, Blassingame, Barnett, Burleson, Bruce, Chambers, Cook of Gonzales, Cooke of San Saba, Cardis, Dillard, DeMorse, Darnell, Erhard, Ford, Flournoy, Fleming, Ferris, German, Gaither, Graves, Holt, Henry of Limestone, Haynes, Johnson of Franklin, Johnson of Collin, Killough, Lockett, Lacy, McLean, Martin of Navarro, Martin of Hunt, Mills, McKinney of Denton, Moore, Murphy, Norvell, Ramey, Robertson of Bell, Robison of Fayette, Ross, Russell of Harrison, Russell of Wood, Spikes, Scott, Wade, Whitehead, Weaver, Whitfield, West—53.

NAYS—Ballinger, Brady, Crawford, Cline, Cooley, Dohoney, Davis of Brazos, Davis of Wharton, Henry of Smith, Kilgore, Lynch, Morris, McKinney of Walker, McCormick, Nunn, Nugent, Pauli, Reagan, Reynolds, Rentfro, Smith, Stockdale, Stayton, Sansom, Wright, Waelder—26.

Mr. Dohoney introduced the following ordinance:

WHEREAS, The Legislature passed an act, approved on the 10th day of March, 1875, entitled "An act to encourage the construction of canals and ditches for navigation and irrigation," which act fails to require any canal or ditch therein provided for, to be supplied with water; and which act has been construed to permit parties to avail themselves of its benefits, on canals and ditches, existing prior to the passage of said act; and,

WHEREA:, Many thousand acres of land certificates have been issued under the aforesaid act, and delivered to parties and companies on old canals and ditches, existing before the date of the passage of said act, and also on imaginary dry land ditches, which do not exist at all, and never will, and this without any compensation or benefit whatever to the State; and,

WHEREAS, No canals or ditches have actually been constructed under the aforesaid act and in accordance with its provisions; therefore,

Be it declared and ordained by the Constitutional Convention of the State of Texas, That all grants of land certificates under the aforesaid act of the Legislature, being without consideration to the State, are hereby declared void; all patents issued on any of said certificates are hereby declared canceled; and all lands patented, located or reserved bv virtue of said certificates, or under the provisions of the aforesaid act, shall revert to the State and constitute a part of the public domain.

Referred to Committee on Ordinances.

Mr. McCormick offered the following resolution:

WHEREAS, It is evident that the session of the Convention is being prolonged by the criticisms of the press, and the publication by the members of the same of their speeches; therefore, be it

Resolved, That in the opinion of this body the only object to be attained is a good constitution for the people of Texas, not the aggrandisement of individual members; that hereafter the Convention sit with closed doors, and that no one be admitted but the delegates and officers.

Laid over under the rules.

Mr. Burleson offered the following resolution:

Resolved, That all claimants to ancient land grants (save minor heirs whose disabilities are not barred) which are now occupied by citizens holding under color of title in good faith, be required to pay all taxes on said lands due from the date of their claim of title to the time of the institution of suit to try the title thereto.

Referred to the Committee on Spanish Land Titles.

The hour having arrived, the special order was taken up, viz: Reports of the majority and minority of a select committee to consider the propriety of setting apart a portion of the public domain for the benefit of railroads in Southeastern, Western and Northwestern Texas, the minority reporting an ordinance to that effect.

Mr. Dohoney moved to postpone the consideration of the same until 10 o'clock Monday next.

Mr. Stayton moved to amend by including "Article — on Public Lands and Land Office."

Carried.

BUSINESS ON THE TABLE.

"Article —, Legislative Department," on its third and final reading, was taken up and read a third time.

Mr. Reagan offered the following amendment:

Sec. 28, line 227, add: "And before the meeting of the next succeeding Legislature."

Adopted.

Mr. Waelder offered the following amendment:

Strike out the three first lines of section 3, to and including the word "classes," and insert:

"Sec. 3. The Senators shall be chosen by the qualified electors, for the term of four years, but a new Senate shall be chosen after every apportionment, and the Senators elected after each apportionment shall be divided by lot into two classes."

Adopted.

Mr. Waelder proposed to strike out the word "appoint," in line 197, section 43, insert "provide for the appointment of."

Mr. Moore offered the following as a substitute for the amendment:

Amend section 43; strike out in line 197 the word "appoint," and insert after the word "shall" the words "provide by law for the appointment of," and strike out all of the section after the word "criminal," in line 199.

On motion, of Mr. Martin, of Hunt, the Convention adjourned to 2½ o'clock P. M., pending Mr. Moore's amendment.

EVENING SESSION—2½ o'clock.

Convention met pursuant to adjournment; roll called; quorum present.

This being the hour set for considering "Article —, Judiciary," it was taken up.

Mr. Ramey moved to postpone the consideration of the article until the article "Legislative Department" shall be disposed of.

Carried, and the Convention resumed the consideration of the article "Legislative Department."

Mr. Moore's amendment, pending an adjournment, taken up.

Mr. Waelder, by leave, withdrew his amendment pending, and offered the following as a substitute for the entire section:

"Sec. 43. The first session of the Legislature under this constitution shall provide for revising, digesting and publishing the laws, civil and criminal, and a like revision, digest and publication may be made every ten years thereafter; *provided,* that in the adoption of, and giving effect to, any such digest or revision the Legislature shall not be limited by sections 35 and 36 of this article."

Mr. Moore's amendment lost.

Mr. Waelder's substitute adopted.

Mr. Dohoney moved to strike out section 43.

Lost.

Mr. Stayton moved to strike out the proviso from section 43.

Lost.

Mr. Ballinger offered the following amendment to section 48: insert in lieu of the words added by Mr. Reagan, "and before the next Legislature can provide for its payment."

Withdrawn.

Mr. Stockdale proposed to amend by striking out all after the word "State," in section 47, line 246.

Adopted.

Mr. McKinney, of Walker, proposed to amend section 56 by inserting after the word "civil," in line 320, the words "or criminal."

Adopted.

Mr. Dohoney proposed to amend section 49, line 245, by striking out the word "two," and insert "one."

Mr. DeMorse proposed to amend section 49, line 243, after the word "created," by inserting "shall never exceed at any time five hundred thousand dollars."

Mr. Brown moved to lay both amendments on the table.

Carried.

Mr. Crawford offered the following amendment: add to sec. 48, line 238, the words, "the State cemetery and her public grounds."

Adopted.

Mr. Weaver proposed to amend section 48, line 236, by adding, " nor shall the Legislature create any office not authorized by this constitution."

On motion of Mr. Martin, of Navarro, laid on the table.

Mr. Crawford offered the following amendment to section 48: add " the erection and repairs of public buildings."

Adopted.

Mr. Crawford also proposed to amend section 48 by adding the following:

" The establishment and support of a Bureau of Geological, Agricultural, Industrial, Scientific and Historical Statistics, for the collection, preservation and dissemination of useful information among the people of this State."

Lost by the following vote:

YEAS—Ballinger, Blake, Brown, Cline, Cooley, Crawford, Davis of Brazos, DeMorse, Dohoney, Erhard, Ford, Henry of Limestone, Henry of Smith, Johnson of Franklin, Kilgore, King, Lockett, Martin of Hunt, McCormick, McKinney of Walker, McLean, Moore, Morris, Murphy, Reagan, Russell of Harrison, Smith, Stayton, Stockdale, Wade, Waelder, West, Whitfield—33.

NAYS—Abernathy, Abner, Allison, Arnim, Barnett, Blassingame, Brady, Bruce, Burleson, Chambers, Cook of Gonzales, Cooke of San Saba, Darnell, Dillard, Ferris, Fleming, Flournoy, Gaither, German, Graves, Haynes, Holt, Johnson of Collin, Killough, Lacy, Lynch, Martin of Navarro, McKinney of Denton, Mills, Norvell, Nugent, Nunn, Pauli, Ramey, Rentfro, Robertson of Bell, Robison of Fayette, Russell of Wood, Scott, Spikes, Weaver, Whitehead, Wright—44.

Mr. Cline offered the following amendment:

In section 3, line 147, strike out the word " purpose " and insert the word " subject."

Mr. Brown moved the previous question.

Lost.

Mr. Cline's amendment lost.

Mr. Ferris proposed to insert in line 230, section 48, " including matured bonds, for the payment of which the sinking fund is inadequate."

Adopted.

Mr. McLean offered the following amendment:

Line 339, after the word " Legislature," insert " at the next general election," and in line 341, after the word " before," strike out " an," and insert the word " such."

Lost.

Mr. King proposed to amend section 32, line 153, by writing

after the word "preamble" the following: "or in the body of the bill."

Adopted.

Mr. Brady proposed to amend as follows:

Amend section 24 by striking out the word "session," in line 117, and by striking out the letter "a," in line 108, and inserting the word "per."

Adopted.

Mr. West moved to reconsider the vote refusing to adopt Mr. McLean's amendment to lines 339 and 341.

Lost by the following vote:

YEAS—Brady, Brown, Chambers, Cook of Gonzales, Cooke of San Saba, Darnell, DeMorse, Dillard, Fleming, Flournoy, Ford, Gaither, German, Holt, Johnson of Collin, Johnson of Franklin, Lacy, McCabe, McKinney of Denton, McLean, Mitchell, Murphy, Ramey, Rentfro, Reynolds, Robertson of Bell, Robison of Fayette, Russell of Harrison, Russell of Wood, Sansom, Scott, Spikes, Wade, West, Whitehead, Whitfield—36.

NAYS—Abernathy, Abner, Allison, Arnim, Ballinger, Barnett, Blake, Blassingame, Bruce, Burleson, Cline, Cooley, Crawford, Davis of Brazos, Dohoney, Erhard, Ferris, Graves, Haynes, Henry of Limestone, Henry of Smith, Kilgore, Killough, Lockett, Lynch, Martin of Hunt, Martin of Navarro, McCormick, McKinney of Walker, Mills, Moore, Morris, Norvell, Nugent, Nunn, Pauli, Reagan, Ross, Smith, Stayton, Stockdale, Waelder, Wright—43.

Mr. Flournoy offered the following amendment to section 48: insert in line 231, after the word "schools," the words "to the extent specially authorized in this constitution."

On motion of Mr. Graves, the main question was ordered.

Mr. Flournoy's amendment lost by the following vote:

YEAS—Allison, Arnim, Barnett, Blassingame, Bruce, Burleson, Chambers, Cook of Gonzales, Cooke of San Saba, Dillard, Fleming, Flournoy, Gaither, German, Graves, Haynes, Henry of Limestone, Holt, Johnson of Collin, Johnson of Franklin, Lacy, Lynch, Martin of Navarro, McKinney of Denton, McLean, Nugent, Robertson of Bell, Robison of Fayette, Russell of Wood, Sansom, Scott, Spikes, Wright—33.

NAYS—Abernathy, Abner, Ballinger, Blake, Brown, Cline, Crawford, Darnell, Davis of Brazos, DeMorse, Dohoney, Erhard, Ferris, Ford, Henry of Smith, Kilgore, Killough, Lockett, Martin of Hunt, McCabe, McCormick, McKinney of Walker, Mills, Mitchell, Moore, Morris, Norvell, Nunn, Pauli,

Ramey, Reagan, Rentfro, Reynolds, Ross, Smith, Stayton, Stockdale, Wade, Waelder, West, Whitehead, Whitfield—42.

The question recurring on the final passage of the article, the same was put, and the article passed by the following vote:

YEAS—Abernathy, Abner, Allison, Ballinger, Barnett, Blassingame, Brown, Bruce, Burleson, Chambers, Cline, Cook of Gonzales, Cooke of San Saba, Crawford, Darnell, Davis of Brazos, Dillard, Dohoney, Erhard, Ferris, Fleming, Flournoy, Ford, Gaither, German, Graves, Haynes, Henry of Limestone, Henry of Smith, Johnson of Collin, Johnson of Franklin, Kilgore, Killough, Lacy, Lockett, Lynch, Martin of Hunt, Martin of Navarro, McCormick, McKinney of Denton, McKinney of Walker, Moore, Murphy, Norvell, Nugent, Nunn, Ramey, Reagan, Robison of Fayette, Ross, Russell of Wood, Smith, Spikes, Stayton, Stockdale, Wade, Waelder, Whitehead, Whitfield, Wright—60.

NAYS—Arnim, Blake, Brady, DeMorse, Holt, McLean, Mills, Mitchell, Morris, Pauli, Rentfro, Reynolds, Robertson of Bell, Russell of Harrison, Sansom, Scott, West—17.

On motion, the Convention adjourned to 9 o'clock A. M. to-morrow.

FORTY-SIXTH DAY.

HALL OF REPRESENTATIVES, ⎱
AUSTIN, TEXAS, October 28, 1875. ⎰

Convention met pursuant to adjournment; roll called; quorum present. Prayer by the Rev. H. V. Philpot, of the M. E. Church, South, at Austin.

Journal of yesterday read and adopted.

On motion of Mr. Blassingame, Mr. Latimer, Assistant Secretary, was excused on account of sickness.

On motion of Mr. Weaver, Mr. Martin, of Hunt, was excused on account of sickness.

Mr. DeMorse made the following reports:

COMMITTEE ROOM, ⎱
AUSTIN, October 27, 1875. ⎰

To the Hon. E. B. Pickett, President of the Convention:

The Committee on Revenue and Taxation, to which was referred the memorial of the Patrons of Husbandry, of Hunt county, through their County Council, asking immediate relief by ordinance deferring the collection of taxes for the present year, instruct me to report that in conformity with the suggestions of this memorial, they had, prior to this time, reported to the Convention the following section, changing the periods of the fiscal year, on which the Convention has not yet acted, and which they again recommend to its consideration, as not only having the approval of their judgment, but that of the Comptroller of the State.

They refer the question of *immediate* relief, by special ordinance, to the judgment of the Convention itself, with the suggestion that the committee doubt the propriety of the exercise of such power by this Convention.   CHARLES DeMORSE,
Chairman of the Committee.

Resolution recommended by the committee, as a section of the article on Revenue and Taxation:

"Sec. ——. The fiscal year shall commence the first of May, and end the last of April following. Assessments of taxes shall date from the first day of January of each year, and the collections shall commence on the first of December, and shall be closed by the first day of April following, until otherwise provided by law."

COMMITTEE ROOM, ⎫
AUSTIN, October 27, 1875. ⎰

To the Hon. E. B. Pickett, President of the Convention:

Your Committee on Revenue and Taxation, to which was referred the memorial of the City Council of the city of Sherman, relative to municipal taxation of the property of railroad companies lying within the limits of cities and incorporated towns, instruct me to report that they have carefully considered the subject, and deem that the subjoined clauses, which they recommend to the consideration of the Convention, as constituent sections of the article on taxation, will remedy in the future the evils complained of, and reach the case of default alluded to, wherein no report has been made of property lying within the corporation properly subject to taxation. The entire scope of relief asked, by retroactive legislation by this body they deem unwise, and therefore can not recommend, although they are satisfied that the city which the memorialists represent has been wronged. We return the memorial to the Convention herewith, that it may be read for the information of the Convention, and enable it to judge of the equities of the case, and the proprieties of its action.

All of which is respectfully submitted.
CHARLES DeMORSE, Chairman.

Clauses recommended for article on Taxation:

" Sec. —.   The Comptroller of the State shall annually prepare a list of all lands assessed or unassessed for each separate county, and assess upon the portion unrendered all the present and back tax due thereon, and transmit to each collector of taxes the list prepared for his county; upon which list the collector shall proceed as by law prescribed."

" Sec. —. All property of railroad companies, of whatever description, lying or being within the limits of any city or incorporated town within this State shall bear its proportionate share of municipal taxation; and if any such property shall not have been heretofore rendered, the authorities of the city or town within which it lies shall have power to require its rendition and collect the usual municipal tax thereon, as on other property lying within said municipality."

COMMITTEE ROOM, ⎫
AUSTIN, October 27, 1875. ⎰

To the Hon. E. B. Pickett, President of the Convention:

Your Committee on Revenue and Taxation, to whom was referred the memorial of citizens of Brazoria county against any license law discriminating against occupations and professions, and urging the imposition only of equal and uniform taxation, report the memorial back to the Convention, with the suggestion that your committee have previously stated their opinions upon this subject, in the form of a section in the majority report, which expresses their decided conviction that all such taxation on commendable occupations is eminently unjust, and not sustainable upon enlightened principles of political economy, except in the gravest emergencies; but the Convention having overruled them, and authorized such taxation, they can only repeat their own nearly unanimous views upon the question, and defer to the superior judgment of the Convention.

All which is respectfully submitted.

The memorial is herewith returned.

CHARLES DeMORSE, Chairman.

Mr. Ramey moved to increase the number of the select committee authorized by Mr. Gaither's resolution to thirteen.

Carried.

Mr. Weaver offered the following resolution:

WHEREAS, The Supreme Court of the State has decided the law levying one per cent. school tax unconstitutional; be it therefore,

Resolved, That the amount of said tax paid by each taxpayer heretofore, be ascertained and placed to the credit of said tax-payer against the amount heretofore assessed.

Referred to Committee on Revenue and Taxation.

Mr. Moore offered the following resolution:

Resolved, That there shall be elected, by the qualified voters of each county in this State, a County Treasurer, who shall reside at the county site, hold his office for four years and until his successor shall be qualified, and shall have such compensation as may be provided by law.

Referred to Committee on General Provisions.

The special order of the hour, viz: motion to reconsider the vote engrossing the resolution of Mr. Russell, of Wood, on the subject of immigration, was taken up and motion lost by the following vote:

YEAS—Ballinger, Blake, Brown, Cardis, Cline, Cooley, Crawford, Davis of Brazos, DeMorse, Erhard, Ferris, Ford, Henry of Limestone, Henry of Smith, King, Lockett, McCabe, McKinney of Walker, Moore, Morris, Murphy, Nunn, Pauli, Reagan, Reynolds, Russell of Harrison, Smith, Stayton, Stockdale, West, Whitfield—31.

NAYS—Abernathy, Abner, Allison, Arnim, Barnett, Blassingame, Bruce, Burleson, Chambers, Cook of Gonzales, Cooke of San Saba, Darnell, Davis of Wharton, Dillard, Dohoney, Fleming, Flournoy, Gaither, German, Graves, Haynes, Holt, Johnson of Franklin, Johnson of Collin, Kilgore, Killough, Lacy, Lynch, Martin of Navarro, McKinney of Denton, McLean, Mills, Mitchell, Norvell, Rentfro, Robertson of Bell, Robison of Fayette, Ross, Russell of Wood, Scott, Spikes, Wade, Weaver, Whitehead, Wright—45.

" Article —, Judiciary," taken up, with three several reports from minorities.

Mr. Whitfield moved to postpone the article until the article on Public Free Schools shall be disposed of, and that the article on Free Schools be taken up.

Lost.

The Convention proceeded to consider the "Article —, on Judiciary."

The hour having arrived for the special order, viz: " Article —, Public Schools," was taken up.

Mr. Dohoney moved to postpone the same until Saturday at 9½ o'clock, and that it be made the special order for that hour.

Mr. Cline moved to postpone it to Tuesday, and make it the special order for 10 o'clock that day.

Carried by the following vote:

YEAS—Abernathy, Arnim, Ballinger, Barnett, Blassingame, Brady, Brown, Bruce, Burleson, Cardis, Cline, Cook of Gonzales, Cooley, Darnell, Davis of Wharton, Dohoney, Erhard, Flournoy, German, Graves, Henry of Limestone, Henry of Smith, Holt, Johnson of Collin, King, Lockett, Lynch, Martin of Navarro, McCabe, Mitchell, Morris, Nugent, Nunn, Pauli, Reagan, Rentfro, Reynolds, Ross, Russell of Harrison, Scott, Spikes, Stayton, Stockdale, Wade, Waelder, Weaver, West, Wright—48.

NAYS—Abner, Allison, Chambers, Cooke of San Saba, Crawford, Davis of Brazos, DeMorse, Dillard, Fleming, Ford, Gaither, Haynes, Johnson of Franklin, Kilgore, Killough, Lacy, McKinney of Denton, McLean, Mills, Murphy, Norvell, Ramey, Robertson of Bell, Robison of Fayette, Russell of Wood, Sansom, Smith, Whitehead, Whitfield—29.

Mr. Stockdale moved to reconsider the vote just taken.

Carried.

"Article —, Judicial Department," passed to the table for the present, and the Convention proceeded to the consideration of "Article —, Public Free Schools."

[Mr. Flournoy in the chair.]

Mr. Reagan offered the following amendment:

Sec. 3, line 14, strike out the word "two" and insert the word "one."

Mr. Johnson, of Franklin, offered the following substitute for the section:

"Sec. 3. And there shall be set apart not less than one-tenth of the annual revenue of the State derivable from taxation, and a poll tax of one dollar on all male inhabitants in this State between the ages of twenty-one and sixty years, for the benefit of the public free schools."

Mr. Reagan's amendment adopted by the following vote:

YEAS—Abner, Allison, Arnim, Barnett, Blake, Blassingame, Brown, Bruce, Cardis, Chambers, Cooke of San Saba, Cooley, Darnell, Fleming, Flournoy, German, Graves, Henry of Limestone, Holt, Johnson of Collin, Johnson of Franklin, Killough, Lynch, McKinney of Denton, McLean, Mills, Murphy, Nugent, Ramey, Reagan, Robertson of Bell, Robison of Fayette, Russell of Harrison, Russell of Wood, Sansom, Scott, Spikes, Stockdale, Weaver, West, Whitehead, Whitfield, Wright—43.

NAYS—Abernathy, Ballinger, Brady, Burleson, Cline, Cook ·of Gonzales, Crawford, Davis of Brazos, Davis of Wharton, DeMorse, Dillard, Dohoney, Ferris, Ford, Gaither, Haynes, Henry of Smith, Kilgore, King, Lacy, Lockett, Martin of Navarro,

McKinney of Walker, Mitchell, Moore, Morris, Norvell, Nunn, Pauli, Rentfro, Reynolds, Ross, Smith, Stayton, Wade, Waelder—36.

Mr. Johnson's (of Franklin) substitute.

On motion of Mr. Mills, the Convention adjourned to 2½ o'clock P. M.

EVENING SESSION—2½ o'clock.

Convention met pursuant to adjournment; roll called; quorum present.

Convention resumed consideration of pending question.

Mr. Wright, by leave, offered the following resolution:

Resolved, That the Convention tender this hall to Bishop George F. Pierce to hold divine service in this evening; and that the Sergeant-at-Arms be, and he is hereby, instructed to notify him of the fact.

Adopted.

Mr. Whitfield offered the following as a substitute for the article pending:

"ARTICLE —.

"EDUCATION.

"Section 1. A general diffusion of knowledge being essential to the preservation of liberties of the people, it shall be the duty of the Legislature of this State to make suitable provisions for the support and maintenance of public schools.

"Sec. 2. All funds, lands and other property heretofore set apart and appropriated, or that may hereafter be set apart and appropriated for the support of public schools, all the alternate sections of land reserved by the State out of grants heretofore made or that may hereafter be made to railroads or other corporations of any nature whatever, one-half of the public domain of the State, and all sums of money that may come to the State from the sale of any portion of the same, shall constitute a perpetual public school fund.

"Sec. 3. And there shall be set apart, annually, not more than one-tenth of the annual revenue derivable from taxation for general purposes, and such poll tax as may be by law levied under the provisions of this constitution, which shall also constitute a part of the public school fund.

"Sec. 4. The lands herein set apart to the public school fund shall be sold under such regulation, at such time, and upon such terms as may be prescribed by law, and the Legislature shall not have power to grant any relief to the purchasers thereof. The Comptroller shall invest the proceeds of such sale, and of those heretofore made, in the bonds of this State, if the same can be obtained, otherwise in United States bonds, and the United States bonds now belonging to said fund shall likewise be invested in State bonds, if the same can be obtained.

" Sec. 5. The principal of all bonds or other funds, and the principal arising from the sales of lands herein before set apart to said school fund, shall be the permanent school fund, and all the interest derivable therefrom, and the taxes herein provided shall be the available school fund, which shall be applied annually to the support of public schools, and no law shall ever be made appropriating any part of the permanent or available school fund to any other purpose whatever, except as hereinafter provided.

" Sec. 6. All public lands which have been heretofore, or may be hereafter granted to the various counties of this State for public schools, are of right the property of said counties respectively to which they are granted and entitled thereto, is hereby vested in said counties, subject to the trust created in the grant.

" Sec. 7. So soon as the available school fund may be sufficient, the Legislature shall establish and maintain " Free Public Schools " throughout the State for a period of not less than four months in each year, and may authorize any county to establish public schools in such county whenever the available fund apportioned to such county, as herein provided, together with the fund realized from the sale of the lands of the county, shall be sufficient to maintain public schools in such county for not less than four months in each year. But until such time the available school fund hereinbefore provided shall be distributed to the several counties of the State, according to the scholastic population, the distribution to be made by the Governor, the Comptroller and the Treasurer, who, for this duty, shall constitute a " School Board." The fund shall be distributed to the counties and applied in aid of private schools in such mode as the Legislature may provide.

" Sec. 8. All lands heretofore granted for the benefit of the Lunatic Asylum, the Blind Asylum, the Deaf and Dumb Asylum, and the Orphan Asylum, together with such donations as may have been, or may hereafter be made to either of them, are hereby set apart to provide a permanent school fund for the support and maintenance and improvement of said asylums; but the Legislature shall have the power, whenever deemed advisable, to provide for the sale, in part or in whole, of said lands. The proceeds of said lands, when realized, together with all moneys severally donated to such asylums, or either of them,

33

shall be invested in bonds of the State of Texas, if obtainable; if not, in bonds of the United States, in such manner as the Legislature may provide.   And the proceeds of the interest thereon shall be a several available fund for each of said asylums, and for no other purpose.

"Sec. 9. Separate schools shall be provided for the white and colored children, and impartial provision shall be made for both."

Mr. Moore moved to reconsider the vote adopting Mr. Reagan's amendment to section 3, line 14, to strike out "two" and insert "one."

On motion of Mr. Flournoy, the Convention adjourned to 9 o'clock A. M. to-morrow.

FORTY-SEVENTH DAY.

HALL OF REPRESENTATIVES, ⎞
AUSTIN, TEXAS, October 29, 1875. ⎠

Convention met pursuant to adjournment; roll called; quorum present.   Prayer by the Rev. H. V. Philpott, of the M. E. Church, South, at Austin.

The chair announced the following select committee, authorized by Mr. Gaither's resolution: Mr. Brown, Chairman; Messrs. Reagan, Ross, Whitfield, Ford, Ramey, Wright, Gaither, Chambers, Ballinger, Moore, Stockdale and McLean.

On motion of Mr. Martin, of Navarro, Mr. Weaver was excused from attendance on the Convention, on account of sickness.

Mr. Ford submitted the following report:

COMMITTEE ROOM, ⎞
AUSTIN, October 28, 1875. ⎠

To the Hon. E. B. Pickett, President of the Convention:

The Committee on State Affairs, to which was referred the following:

"Sec. —. The Legislature shall at its first session, after the ratification of this constitution, provide pensions for the disabled and indigent surviving soldiers of the revolution by which the independence of Texas was achieved, in the year 1836," have had the same under consideration, and have directed me to report as follows:

The revolution caused by the violation of the principles of the Mexican Constitution of 1834, the centralization of the powers of government in Gen. Santa Anna, the determination of the Supreme Government of Mexico to disarm the people of Texas and to reduce them to a state of vassalage, was a movement sustained by the principles of civil and religious liberty.

In this memorable contest the people of Texas, numbering about 50,000, threw down the gauntlet to a nation of 8,000,000 of people. They did this with a full knowledge that the penalty of failure was death. The decree declaring those participating in the revolution pirates and affixing the punishment of death therefor, the massacre of prisoners of war by order of President Santa Anna, leave no doubt that the policy of Mexico was to exterminate every man in Texas who had dared to assert his rights, and expel every American from its soil. It was the inauguration, by Mexico, of a war of races.

It would be useless to mention the fall of the Alamo, the surrender of Fannin, and the glorious victory of San Jacinto—they are matters of history. But it is not, perhaps, appreciated, that the Texas revolution effected grand results. It opened a country larger than France to the world, and added it to the United States.

The war between Mexico and the United States followed as a sequence of annexation. The acquisition of California, with its golden treasures, of New Mexico, of Arizona, and changes which have effected the destinies of a mighty people, and the commerce of the world, were assured by our final triumph on the plains of San Jacinto.

The history of the past furnishes no parallel to that achievement of 700 poorly armed Texans. It ranks with the decisive battles which have overthrown governments, and changed dynasties.

It was a victory on the side of freedom, and enlarged the area of representative republican government.

It would be a pleasant task to trace the progress of a State which exhibited so much strength in its infancy, and which is now fast attaini.. proportions. Men who aided the young Hercules to strangle the serpent of oppression yet live to see him a robust youth. They can contemplate his growth, and look out upon the great improvements which have been made. They see the little colonies expanded into a million and a half of people, and are lost in admiring the changes which have occurred.

What shall we do to reward men to whom we owe so much? Shall we lavish honors upon them? Many of them are indigent, maimed, and too feeble to work for a livelihood.

It is but an act of justice that we should lend a helping hand to those noble old veterans who struck for liberty upon the breasts of their oppressors, and gave to liberty " a local habitation and a name."   We owe them a debt of gratitude which we must pay, and let them feel that the blessings of their labors have followed them. It would be a dark spot upon the escutcheon of Texas should those heroes be suffered to drag out a miserable existence in want and misery, while we are enjoying the rich fruits of their labors.

For these and other reasons the adoption of the section by the Convention is cordially recommended.

> JOHN S. FORD, Chairman,
> ED. CHAMBERS,
> ROBT. LACEY,
> W. W. DILLARD,
> JOHNSON, of Franklin.
> JO. W. BARNETT.

Mr. Norvell offered the following resolution:

WHEREAS, J. D. Logan & Co. having failed to comply with their contract to do the printing for the Convention; therefore

Resolved, That the said contract be, and the same is hereby rescinded, and that the Committee on Printing and Contingent Expenses be, and they are hereby authorized to enter into new contracts for the printing of the Convention.

On motion of Mr. Scott, referred to Committee on Printing.

Mr. McKinney, of Denton, offered the following resolution:

Resolved, That there shall be at the next general election, a County Surveyor elected in each organized county in this State, who shall hold his office for two years, and receive such fees and compensations as may be prescribed by law.

Referred to Committee on General Provisions.

[Mr. Brown in the chair.]

Unfinished business, viz: " Article —, Public Free Schools," again taken up, the pending question being Mr. Johnson's (of Franklin) substitute for section 3, which was lost by the following vote:

YEAS—Ballinger, Brown, Cooley, Crawford, Darnell, Davis of Brazos, Dillard, Dohoney, Ferris, Fleming, Henry of Limestone, Johnson of Franklin, Kilgore, Killough, Lacy, Martin of Navarro, McCormick, McKinney of Walker, Mitchell, Moore, Nunn, Ross, Smith, Stayton, Waelder, West, Whitfield—27.

NAYS—Abernathy, Abner, Allison, Arnim, Barnett, Blassingame, Brady, Bruce, Burleson, Chambers, Cook of Gonzales, Cooke of San Saba, Davis of Wharton, DeMorse, Flournoy, Ford, Gaither, German, Graves, Haynes, Holt, Johnson of Collin,

Lockett, Martin of Hunt, McCabe, McKinney of Denton, Mc-Lean, Morris, Murphy, Norvell, Nugent, Pauli, Ramey, Reagan, Rentfro, Reynolds, Robertson of Bell, Robison of Fayette, Russell of Harrison, Russell of Wood, Sansom, Scott, Spikes, Stockdale, Wade, Whitehead, Wright—47.

Mr. Whitfield, by leave, withdrew his substitute, and offered the following in its stead:

" Article —.
" education.

" Section 1. A general diffusion of knowledge being essential to the preservation of liberties of the people, it shall be the duty of the Legislature of this State to make suitable provisions for the support and maintenance of public schools.

" Sec. 2. All funds, lands and other property heretofore set apart and appropriated, or that may hereafter be set apart and appropriated for the support of public schools, all the alternate sections of land reserved by the State out of grants heretofore made or that may hereafter be made to railroads or other corporations of any nature whatever, one-half of the public domain of the State, and all sums of money that may come to the State from the sale of any portion of the same, shall constitute a perpetual public school fund.

" Sec. 3. And there shall be set apart, annually, not more than one-tenth of the annual revenue derivable from taxation for general purposes, and such poll-tax as may be by law levied under the provisions of this constitution, which shall also constitute a part of the public school fund.

" Sec. 4. The lands herein set apart to the public school fund shall be sold under such regulation, at such time and upon such terms as may be prescribed by law, and the Legislature shall not have power to grant any relief to the purchasers thereof. The Comptroller shall invest the proceeds of such sale, and of those heretofore made, in the bonds of this State, if the same can be obtained, otherwise in United States bonds, and the United States bonds now belonging to said fund shall likewise be invested in State bonds, if the same can be obtained.

" Sec. 5. The principal of all bonds or other funds, and the principal arising from the sales of lands hereinbefore set apart to said school fund, shall be the permanent school fund, and all the interest derivable therefrom, and the taxes herein provided shall be the available school fund, which shall be applied annually to the support of public schools, and no law shall ever be made appropriating any part of the permanent or available school fund to any other purpose whatever, except as hereinafter provided.

" Sec. 6. All public lands which have been heretofore, or may be hereafter granted to the various counties of this State for public schools, are of right the property of said counties respectively to which they are granted and entitled thereto, is hereby vested in said counties, subject to the trust created in the grant.

" Sec. 7. The Legislature, as soon as practicable, shall establish public free schools throughout the State, and shall provide by law, that the available public free school fund herein provided, shall be distributed among all the scholastic population of the State. But, until otherwise provided, the available school fund hereinbefore provided shall be distributed to the several counties of the State, according to the scholastic population— the distribution to be made by the Governor, the Comptroller, and the Treasurer, who, for this duty shall constitute a " School Board." The fund shall be distributed to the counties and applied in aid of common schools in such mode as the Legislature may provide.

" Sec. 8. All lands heretofore granted for the benefit of the Lunatic Asylum, the Blind Asylum, the Deaf and Dumb Asylum, and the Orphan Asylum, together with such donations as may have been or may hereafter be made to either of them, are hereby set apart to provide a permanent school fund for the support and maintenance and improvement of said asylums; but the Legislature shall have the power, whenever deemed advisable. to provide for the sale, in part or in whole, of said lands. The proceeds of said lands, when realized, together with all moneys severally donated to such asylums, or either of them, shall be invested in bonds of the State of Texas, if obtainable; if not, in bonds of the United States, in such manner as the Legislature shall provide. And the proceeds of the interest thereon shall be a several available fund for each of said asylums, and for no other purpose.

" Sec. 9. Separate schools shall be provided for the white and colored children, and impartial provision shall be made for both."

Mr. Russell, of Harrison, offered the following amendment to section 3 :

" Sec. 3. And there shall be set apart annually not less than one-fourth the general revenue of the State, and a poll tax of one dollar on all male inhabitants in this State. between the ages of twenty-one and sixty years; and the Legislature shall provide for the levying and collecting annually of not less than one-sixth of one per cent. upon all taxable property in this State, for the benefit and support of public free schools, for a period of not less than four months in each year."

Lost by the following vote:

YEAS—Abner, Brady, Cline, Davis of Wharton, Erhard, Lockett, McCormick, Mills, Mitchell, Morris, Pauli, Rentfro, Reynolds, Russell of Harrison—14.

NAYS—Abernathy, Allison, Arnim, Ballinger, Barnett, Blassingame, Brown, Bruce, Burleson, Chambers, Cook of Gonzales, Cooke of San Saba, Darnell, Davis of Brazos, DeMorse, Dillard, Dohoney, Ferris, Fleming, Flournoy, Gaither, German, Graves, Haynes, Henry of Limestone, Henry of Smith, Holt, Johnson of Collin, Johnson of Franklin, Kilgore, Killough, Lacy, Martin of Hunt, Martin of Navarro, McCabe, McKinney of Denton, McKinney of Walker, McLean, Moore, Norvell, Nugent, Nunn, Ramey, Reagan, Robertson of Bell, Robison of Fayette, Ross, Russell of Wood, Sansom, Scott, Spikes, Stayton, Stockdale, Wade, West, Whitehead, Whitfield, Wright—59.

Mr. Dohoney offered the following amendment:

" Sec. 9. It shall be the duty of the County Court of each county to divide the county into school districts of proper size, and, under such regulations as the Legislature may prescribe, provide for the organization of public schools in such districts, by additional taxation or otherwise; *provided,* that no taxes shall be so levied in any school district, except upon a majority vote of the qualified electors therein, and all taxes so raised shall be applied exclusively to the payment of teachers in said district; and *provided, further,* that no *ad va lorem* tax so levied shall ever exceed one-quarter of one per cent. And whenever any such public school has been so organized in any school district, and provision made to keep up the same for at least four months in the year, and the number of scholastic population in said district is ascertained, it shall be the duty of the County Court to distribute to such district its proportion of the public school fund. The fund due school districts which fail to provide for public schools at least four months in the year shall remain in the county treasury for the benefit of the scholastic population to whom it belongs."

Mr. Russell, of Wood, moved to close debate upon the amendment, and bring the Convention to a vote.

On motion of Mr. Sansom, the Convention adjourned to 2:30 o'clock P. M.

EVENING SESSION—2½ o'clock.

Convention met; roll called; quorum present.

Mr. Russell, of Wood, renewed his motion to close the debate upon the amendment of Mr. Dohoney, and the substitute of Mr. Whitfield, and to bring the Convention to a direct vote.

Carried.

Mr. Dohoney's amendment lost.

Mr. Whitfield's substitute lost by the following vote:

YEAS—Abernathy, Allison, Arnim, Barnett, Blake, Blassingame, Bruce, Cardis, Chambers, Cook of Gonzales, Cooke of San Saba, Darnell, Flournoy, Gaither, German, Graves, Henry of Limestone, Holt, Johnson of Collin, Johnson of Franklin, Killough, Lacy, Lynch, Martin of Hunt, McKinney of Denton, Nugent, Reagan, Robertson of Bell, Robison of Fayette, Russell of Wood, Sansom, Scott, Spikes, Whitehead, Whitfield, Wright —36.

NAYS—Abner, Ballinger, Brady, Burleson, Cline, Cooley, Crawford, Davis of Brazos, Davis of Wharton, DeMorse, Dohoney, Ferris, Fleming, Ford, Haynes, Henry of Smith, Lockett, Martin of Navarro, McCabe, McCormick, McKinney of Walker, McLean, Mills, Mitchell, Moore, Morris, Murphy, Norvell, Nunn, Pauli, Ramey, Rentfro, Reynolds, Ross, Russell of Harrison, Smith, Stayton, Wade, Waelder, West—40.

Mr. Whitfield offered the following as a substitute for section 3:

"Sec. 3. The Legislature may provide for the levying of a tax for educational purposes. Said fund shall be annually distributed for educational purposes among the several counties, according to the population in each."

Mr. Waelder proposed to amend the substitute as follows:

Strike out all after the word "levying," in second line, and insert: "and collection annually of not less than one-tenth of one per cent. on all taxable property in the State, and a poll tax of not more than two dollars on all male inhabitants between the ages of twenty-one and sixty years, for the benefit and support of public free schools; but, if at any time hereafter a tax of less than one-tenth of one per cent. should be sufficient to maintain an efficient system of free public schools, the Legislature may reduce the tax accordingly."

On motion of Mr. Graves, the debate on the pending substitute and amendment was closed and a vote ordered.

The question on Mr. Waelder's amendment was put, and the amendment lost by the following vote:

YEAS—Abner, Ballinger, Brady, Cline, Crawford, Davis of Brazos, Davis of Wharton, Dohoney, Erhard, Ferris, Fleming, Ford, Haynes, Henry of Smith, Lockett, Martin of Hunt, Martin of Navarro, McCabe, McCormick, Mills, Mitchell, Moore, Morris, Nunn, Pauli, Rentfro, Reynolds, Ross, Russell of Harrison, Smith, Wade, Waelder, West—33.

NAYS—Abernathy, Allison, Arnim, Barnett, Blake, Blassingame, Bruce, Burleson, Chambers, Cook of Gonzales, Cooke of San Saba, Darnell, DeMorse, Dillard, Flournoy, Gaither, German, Graves, Henry of Limestone, Holt, Johnson of Collin, Johnson of Franklin, Kilgore, Killough, Lacy, Lynch, McKinney of Denton, McLean, Murphy, Norvell, Nugent, Ramey, Reagan, Robertson of Bell, Robison of Fayette, Russell of Wood, Sansom, Scott, Spikes, Stayton, Stockdale, Whitehead, Whitfield—43.

The question on Mr. Whitfield's substitute for section 3 was then put, and the substitute lost by the following vote:

YEAS—Abner, Ballinger, Brady, Cline, Cook of Gonzales, Crawford, Davis of Brazos, Dillard, Erhard, Fleming, Ford, Henry of Smith, Kilgore, Lockett, Martin of Hunt, Martin of Navarro, McCabe, McCormick, Mills, Mitchell, Moore, Morris, Norvell, Pauli, Rentfro, Reynolds, Ross, Russell of Harrison, Smith, Wade, Waelder, West, Whitehead, Whitfield—34.

NAYS—Abernathy, Allison, Arnim, Barnett, Blake, Blassingame, Bruce, Burleson, Cardis, Chambers, Cooke of San Saba, Darnell, Davis of Wharton, DeMorse, Dohoney, Ferris, Flournoy, Gaither, German, Graves, Haynes, Henry of Limestone, Holt, Johnson of Collin, Johnson of Franklin, Killough, Lacy, Lynch, McLean, Murphy, Nugent, Nunn, Ramey, Reagan, Robertson of Bell, Robison of Fayette, Russell of Wood, Sansom, Scott, Spikes, Stayton, Stockdale—42.

Mr. West moved to reconsider the vote adopting Mr. Reagan's amendment to section 3, line 14, striking out "two" and inserting "one," as poll tax.

On motion of Mr. Reagan, the Convention adjourned.

FORTY-EIGHTH DAY.

HALL OF REPRESENTATIVES, }
AUSTIN, TEXAS, October 30, 1875. }

Convention met pursuant to adjournment; roll called; quorum present. Prayer by the Rev. H. V. Philpott, of the M. E. Church, Austin.

Journal of yesterday read and adopted.

On motion of Mr. Kilgore, Mr. Henry, of Smith, was excused for ten days.

On motion of Mr. Flournoy, Mr. W. H. Stewart, delegate elect to fill the vacancy occasioned by the resignation of Mr. Rugely, came forward, presented his credentials, took the prescribed oath and his seat as a delegate to the Convention.

On motion of Mr. Cline, Mr. Morris was excused from attendance on the Convention for three days.

Mr. West, chairman of the Committee on General Provisions, made the following reports:

COMMITTEE ROOM, }
AUSTIN, October 29, 1875. }

To the Hon. E. B. Pickett, President of the Convention:

The Committee on General Provisions, to whom was referred a memorial of the Hon. Gustave Cook, of Harris county, asking that certain provisions be placed in the constitution regulating the manner in which the Governor of the State shall proceed in suppressing domestic violence, and prescribing his course of procedure when he makes application to the Federal authorities for troops to suppress insurrection, beg leave to report that they have given the subject matter careful consideration, and they do not deem it advisable to insert in the constitution the clauses suggested. They believe that the subject, without any constitutional injunction to that effect, would be, to a considerable extent, within the control of the Legislature, and that body could, by appropriate legislation, guard against the evils so clearly pointed out in the memorial.

Respectfully submitted,
C. S. WEST, Chairman.

COMMITTEE ROOM, }
AUSTIN, October 30, 1875. }

To the Hon. E. B. Pickett, President of the Convention:

The Committee on General Provisions, to whom was referred a series of resolutions providing for a clause in the constitution to limit the powers of private corporations, beg leave to report that they have examined the subject, and have instructed me to return them and recommend that they be referred to the Committee on Private Corporations. Respectfully submitted,
C. S. WEST, Chairman.

Report received, to come up in its order.

On motion of Mr. Brown, Mr. Stewart was added to the Committees on General Provisions, Education, Suffrage, and Style and Arrangement.

Unfinished business taken up, viz: "Article —, Public Schools."

Mr. Ferris offered the following amendment as an additional section:

"Sec. —. Until the available school fund, including the fund derivable from taxation, shall appear sufficient for the maintenance of a system of free schools, such fund may be used for the encouragement or support of public schools, which shall afford free tuition to pupils whose parents or guardians are unable to pay for tuition, in such manner and under such regulations as may be provided by law."

The hour having arrived for considering the special order, viz: "Revenue and Taxation," on motion of Mr. Crawford, it was postponed until the pending question shall have been disposed of.

Mr. Ferris also offered the following amendment to section 7:

"And in the counties where such schools exist, the available school fund to which each county is entitled shall be apportioned to such separate schools, according to the relative scholastic population of white and colored children in the county."

On motion of Mr. Scott, the main question was ordered.

Mr. Ferris's amendments were both lost.

The question recurring upon the engrossment of the article, it was carried by the following vote:

YEAS—Abernathy, Allison, Ballinger, Barnett, Blake, Brown, Burleson, Chambers, Cline, Cook of Gonzales, Cooke of San Saba, Crawford, Davis of Brazos, Dillard, Dohoney, Erhard, Ferris, Fleming, Flournoy, Gaither, German, Graves, Haynes, Henry of Limestone, Henry of Smith, Johnson of Collin, Johnson of Franklin, Killough, King, Lacy, Martin of Hunt, Martin of Navarro, McCormick, McKinney of Denton, McKinney of Walker, Moore, Norvell, Nugent, Nunn, Ramey, Reagan, Rentfro, Robertson of Bell, Robison of Fayette, Ross, Russell of Wood, Sansom, Scott, Smith, Spikes, Stewart, Waelder, West, Whitehead, Wright—55.

NAYS—Abner, Arnim, Blassingame, Brady, Bruce, Cardis, Cooley, Darnell, Davis of Wharton, DeMorse, Ford, Holt, Kilgore, Lockett, Lynch, McLean, Mills, Mitchell, Murphy, Pauli, Reynolds, Russell of Harrison, Stockdale, Wade, Whitfield—25.

Mr. Graves moved to reconsider the vote just taken, and to lay the motion on the table.

Carried by the following vote:

YEAS—Abernathy, Allison, Ballinger, Barnett, Blake, Brown, Burleson, Chambers, Cook of Gonzales, Cooke of San Saba, Davis of Brazos, Dillard, Ferris, Flournoy, Gaither, German, Graves, Henry of Limestone, Johnson of Collin, Johnson of Franklin, Killough, Lacy, Martin of Hunt, Martin of Navarro, McCormick, McKinney of Denton, Moore, Norvell, Nugent, Nunn, Ramey, Reagan, Robertson of Bell, Robison of Fayette, Ross, Russell of Wood, Sansom, Scott, Spikes, Stewart, Whitehead, Wright—42.

NAYS—Abner, Arnim, Blassingame, Brady, Bruce, Cardis, Cline, Cooley, Crawford, Darnell, Davis of Wharton, DeMorse, Dohoney, Erhard, Fleming, Ford, Haynes, Holt, Kilgore, King, Lockett, Lynch, McKinney of Walker, McLean, Mills, Mitchell, Murphy, Pauli, Rentfro, Reynolds, Russell of Harrison, Smith, Stayton, Stockdale, Wade, Waelder, West, Whitfield—38.

The Convention then proceeded to consider the special order, viz: "Art. —, Revenue and Taxation," on its second reading.

On motion of Mr. Murphy, the article was considered section by section.

Mr. Gaither moved to recommit the article to a select committee of five.

Mr. Holt moved to lay the motion on the table.

Both motions withdrawn, and the Convention proceeded to consider the article, section by section.

Mr. Ramey proposed to amend section 1, line 6, after "furniture," by adding, "belonging to each family in this."

Adopted.

Mr. Russell, of Harrison, offered the following amendment: Strike out all after the word "dollars," in section 1, line 7.

The question as to whether the amendment was in order having arisen, the chair submitted the same to a vote of the Convention, by which the amendment was declared in order.

Mr. McCormick offered the following substitute for the section and amendment:

"Section 1. Taxation shall be equal and uniform throughout the State, and all property subject to taxation in this State shall be taxed in proportion to its value, to be ascertained as shall be prescribed by law; *provided,* there shall be forever exempt from all taxation, household and kitchen furniture, the property of citizens of this State, not to exceed in value the sum of two hundred and fifty dollars. The Legislature may also impose occupation and income taxes, upon such occupations and pursuits that it may deem to the interest of the State to tax;

provided, That the counties, cities and towns or other political sub-divisions of this State, nor the authorities thereof, shall in no case impose any tax upon occupations or pursuits. But the Legislature may provide by law that such occupation or income tax collected by the State, or any portion thereof may be returned to the county for the benefit of the general county fund; *provided,* that the fund thus returned shall always be returned to the county from which it was collected.

[Mr. McLean in the chair.]

Mr. Brown moved to adjourn to 2½ o'clock P. M.

Lost.

On motion of Mr. German, the Convention adjourned to 2½ o'clock P. M.

EVENING SESSION—2½ o'clock.

Convention met pursuant to adjournment; roll called; quorum present.

The "Article —, Revenue and Taxation," was taken up, the pending question being upon the amendment of Mr. Russell, of Harrison.

Mr. McCormick withdrew his substitute.

Mr. Stockdale then offered the following substitute for section 1:

"Section 1. Taxation shall be equal and uniform. All property in this State, whether owned by natural persons or corporations other than municipal, shall be taxed in proportion to its value, which shall be ascertained as may be provided by law. The Legislature may impose a poll tax. It may also impose occupation taxes, both upon natural persons and upon corporations other than municipal doing any business in this State. It may also tax incomes of both natural persons and corporations other than municipal, except that persons engaged in mechanical and agricultural pursuits shall never be required to pay an occupation tax; *provided,* that two hundred and fifty dollars worth of household and kitchen furniture belonging to each family in this State shall be exempt from taxation."

The substitute was adopted.

Mr. McKinney, of Walker, offered the following amendment to the section:

Add to section 1 the words:

"*Provided further,* That the occupation tax levied by any

county, city or town, for any year, on persons or corporations pursuing any profession or business, shall not exceed one-half of the tax levied by the State for the same period on such profession or business."

The amendment was then adopted.

Mr. Moore offered the following amendment to section 2:

Strike out lines 11 and 12, except the word "the" at the end of line 12.

Mr. Stockdale offered the following amendment:

Insert the word "occupation" before taxes in line 11.

Mr. Moore then withdrew his amendment.

Mr. Stockdale's amendment was adopted.

Mr. Sansom offered the following amendment:

Amend section 2 by inserting in line 15, after the word "profit," "school houses and their necessary furniture."

On motion of Mr. Waelder, Mr. King was excused for ten days.

On motion of Mr. Henry, of Smith, Mr. Nunn was excused for ten days.

On motion of Mr. Mills, Mr. McCabe was excused for ten days from next Tuesday.

Mr. Sansom's amendment was then adopted.

Mr. Crawford moved to insert the word "public" before "school houses," in Mr. Sansom's amendment.

Mr. Waelder offered the following amendment as a substitute for Mr. Sansom's amendment just adopted:

"All buildings used exclusively and owned by persons, or associations of persons, for school purposes, and the necessary furniture of all schools."

Mr. Ross moved to lay the amendments on the table.

A division of the question ordered.

The motion to lay Mr. Waelder's amendment on the table was lost by the following vote:

Yeas—Abernathy, Allison, Arnim, Ballinger, Fleming, Graves, Norvell, Nugent, Nunn, Ross, Sansom, Smith, Stockdale, Whitfield—14.

Nays—Abner, Barnett, Blake, Blassingame, Brady, Bruce, Burleson, Cardis, Chambers, Cline, Cook of Gonzales, Cooke of San Saba, Crawford, Darnell, Davis of Brazos, DeMorse, Dillard, Dohoney, Erhard, Ferris, Flournoy, Ford, Gaither, German, Haynes, Henry of Limestone, Henry of Smith, Holt, Johnson of Collin, Johnson of Franklin, Kilgore, Killough, Lacy, Lockett, Lynch, McCormick, McKinney of Denton, McKinney of Walker, McLean, Mills, Mitchell, Moore, Murphy, Martin of Navarro, Martin of Hunt, Pauli, Ramey, Reagan, Rentfro, Reynolds, Robertson of Bell, Robison of Fayette, Russell of Harrison, Russell of Wood, Scott, Spikes, Stayton, Stewart, Waelder, West, Whitehead, Wright—62.

Mr. Crawford's amendment was laid on the table.

Mr. Waelder's amendment was adopted.

Mr. Cline offered the following as a substitute for section 2:

" Sec. 2. The Legislature may exempt from taxation property used for worship, education, burial, halls of Turners, Masons, Odd Fellows, and similar societies; hospitals, and all property used for purely public charity, and all public property used for public purposes; and no other property."

Lost.

On motion of Mr. McCormick, the Convention adjourned to 9 o'clock A. M. Monday.

FORTY-NINTH DAY.

HALL OF REPRESENTATIVES,
AUSTIN, TEXAS, November 1, 1875.

Convention met pursuant to adjournment; roll called; quorum present. Prayer by the Rev. Dr. W. H. Dodge.

Journal of Saturday read and adopted.

On motion of Mr. Rentfro, Mr. Cline was excused for four days, commencing from to-day.

Mr. Ford presented the petition of the citizens of Hidalgo county on the subject of allowing one man to hold two offices in counties having less than two hundred and fifty voters.

Referred to Committee on General Provisions.

Mr. Fleming offered the following resolution:

Resolved, That the Committee on Public Lands and Land Office be requested to consider the propriety of setting apart five million acres of the public domain for the purpose of building a State Capitol, and to report by ordinance or otherwise.

Referred to Committe on Public Lands and Land Office.

Mr. Norvell moved to suspend the rules and take up " Article —, on Legislative Apportionment."

Lost.

Unfinished business taken up, viz: " Article —, Revenue and Taxation."

Mr. Allison moved to reconsider the vote taken Saturday on amending sections 1 and 2 of the article.

The first question, to reconsider the substitute of Mr. Stockdale to section 1, lost.

Second question, to reconsider Mr. Russell's (of Harrison) amendment, to strike out all after the word "dollars," in line 7, section 1, lost.

Third question, to reconsider Mr. Waelder's amendment exempting school houses and furniture from taxation, lost.

Mr. Martin, of Hunt, offered the following amendment to section 4:

"The power to tax all of the property, real and personal, of corporations shall never be surrendered or suspended by act of the Legislature, but the same shall always be taxed as other property."

[Mr. McLean in the chair.]

On motion of Mr. Martin, of Navarro, the amendment was laid on the table.

Mr. Martin, of Navarro, moved to strike out section 4.

Mr. Crawford proposed to amend the section by striking out all after the word, "Legislature," in line 21, and insert "by any contract or grant to which the State shall be a party."

Adopted.

Mr. Martin, of Navarro, withdrew his motion to strike out section 4.

Mr. Blassingame offered the following as an additional section:

Sec. ——. All property of railroad companies of whatever description, lying or being within the limits of any city or incorporated town within this State shall bear its proportionate share of municipal taxation; and if any such property shall not have been heretofore rendered, the authorities of the city or town within which it lies shall have power to require its rendition and collect the usual municipal tax thereon, as on other property lying within said municipality."

Adopted.

Mr. Allison offered the following amendment to section 3:

"The veterans of the revolution of 1836 shall be exempt from poll tax, and shall be allowed exemption from taxation on two thousand dollars worth of property, under such regulations as may be prescribed by law."

Withdrawn.

Mr. Wade offered the following amendment:

Section 4, line 20, after the word "corporations," insert "cities, counties, towns, and their."

The hour having arrived for considering the special order, viz:

"Granting Lands to Railroads, and Article —, Public Lands and Land Office," the same was taken up.

On motion of Mr. Dohoney, the special order was postponed to Saturday next, 10 o'clock, and made special order for that hour.

On motion of Mr. Martin, of Navarro, Mr. Wade's amendment was laid on the table.

Mr. Brown offered the following amendment:

Add to section 5 the words "except by the first Legislature to assemble under this constitution, which may make the necessary appropriations to carry on the government until the assemblage of the Sixteenth Legislature."

Adopted.

Mr. McCormick offered the following substitute for section 6:

"Sec. 6. The Legislature shall pass no law borrowing, diverting, or seeking to divert, or change from its original purpose any money or thing of value that may, or ought to be, placed in the State Treasury to the credit of any special State fund; and shall pass such general laws as may be necessary to protect special county funds, raised for any purpose, from being diverted or changed from the purposes for which such funds were raised."

Withdrawn by Mr. McCormick, and offered by Mr. Reagan, and lost.

Mr. Ferris proposed to strike out of section 6, lines 26 and 27, the words "borrow, or in any manner."

Lost.

Mr. Ballinger proposed to amend section 7, line 34, by striking out all after the word "county."

On motion of Mr. Dillard, debate was closed on the amendment, and the amendment lost by the following vote:

YEAS—Abner, Ballinger, Blake, Brady, Cooley, Davis of Wharton, Erhard, Ferris, Kilgore, McCormick, McLean, Norvell, Reagan, Rentfro, Reynolds, Russell of Harrison, Sansom, Smith, Wade, Waelder, West—21.

NAYS—Abernathy, Allison, Arnim, Barnett, Blassingame, Brown, Bruce, Burleson, Cardis, Chambers, Cook of Gonzales, Cooke of San Saba, Crawford, Darnell, DeMorse, Dillard, Dohoney, Fleming, Flournoy, Ford, Gaither, German, Graves, Haynes, Henry of Limestone, Holt, Johnson of Collin, Killough, Lacy, Lockett, Lynch, McKinney of Denton, McKinney of Walker, Mitchell, Moore, Martin of Navarro, Martin of Hunt, Nugent, Nunn, Pauli, Robertson of Bell, Robison of Fayette, Ross, Russell of Wood, Scott, Spikes, Stayton, Stewart, Stockdale, Whitehead, Whitfield, Wright—52.

34

Mr. Dohoney moved to strike out section 7.

Lost by the following vote:

YEAS—Abner, Ballinger, Blake, Brady, Cooke of San Saba, Cooley, Dohoney, Erhard, Norvell, Reagan, Rentfro, Reynolds, Russell of Harrison, Sansom, Smith, Waelder, West, Whitehead—18.

NAYS—Abernathy, Allison, Arnim, Barnett, Blassingame, Brown, Bruce, Burleson, Cardis, Chambers, Cook of Gonzales, Crawford, Darnell, Davis of Brazos, Davis of Wharton, De-Morse, Dillard, Ferris, Fleming, Flournoy, Ford, Gaither, German, Graves, Haynes, Henry of Limestone, Holt, Johnson of Collin, Kilgore, Killough, Lacy, Lockett, Lynch, McCormick, McKinney of Denton, McKinney of Walker, McLean, Mitchell, Moore, Murphy, Martin of Navarro, Martin of Hunt, Nugent, Nunn, Pauli, Robertson of Bell, Robison of Fayette, Ross, Russell of Wood, Scott, Spikes, Stayton, Stewart, Stockdale, Wade, Whitfield, Wright—57.

Mr. Stayton proposed to amend section 7, line 35, by inserting "county" between "and" and "tax."

Adopted.

Mr. Reagan offered the following amendment to section 7: Strike out the words "pro rata," and insert the words "in proportion to the distance such road may run through any such county."

Adopted.

Mr. Dohoney proposed to amend section 8, by adding "no higher rate of taxation shall ever be levied by the authorities of any county, town or city, than the rate of taxation for State purposes in force at the time, except as may be herein otherwise prescribed."

Mr. DeMorse offered the following substitute for section 8, and the amendment:

"Sec. 8. *Ad valorem* taxation for State uses shall never exceed fifty cents on the one hundred dollars value of property; nor shall general county taxation (except for the support of the indigent) exceed one-half of the general State tax; *provided,* that all counties shall have the right to levy tax for the payment of indebtedness already accrued, and for the establishment of county poor-farms, first availing themselves of all convict labor which may be provided by this constitution."

On motion of Mr. Martin, of Navarro, the substitute was laid on the table.

Mr. Dohoney's amendment was adopted.

On motion of Mr. Chambers, the Convention adjourned to 2¼ o'clock P. M.

EVENING SESSION—2¼ o'clock.

Convention met pursuant to adjournment; roll called; quorum present.

Pending question again resumed.

Mr. Martin, of Navarro, offered the following amendment to Mr. Dohoney's amendment:

Strike out all after the word "except," and insert "for the payment of debts already incurred, and for the erection of public buildings, or as in this constitution is otherwise provided."

Adopted.

Mr. Robertson, of Bell, offered the following as a substitute for the amendment:

Section 8, line 41, add at end of section the words "and no county shall levy more than one-half of all State tax, except to pay past indebtedness, and then not to exceed the amount of the State tax in any one year."

Adopted.

Mr. Murphy proposed to add in the amendment just adopted the words "city or town" after the word "county."

Adopted.

Mr. Ramey moved to reconsider the vote just taken.

Mr. Ramey reported as follows:

Committee Room, }
Austin, November 1, 1875. }

To the Hon. E. B. Pickett, President of the Convention:

Sir—Your Committee on Engrossed and Enrolled Ordinances beg leave to report that they have examined and compared a provision on "Immigration," and find the same correctly engrossed. Respectfully,

Wm. Neal Ramey, Chairman.

Mr. Abernathy offered the following amendment to section 9:

Add to section 9: "Except in cases of great public calamity, may extend the time."

Lost.

Mr. Brown offered the following amendment:

Add to section 9: "Unless in case of great public calamity in any such county, city or town, when such release may be made by a vote of two-thirds of each house of the Legislature; *provided,* that no tax shall be laid on lands and buildings owned and used for public purposes by counties, cities or towns, nor on school lands, nor on school lands held by such counties, cities or towns for public educational purposes."

Adopted.

On motion of Mr. Crawford, the proviso of the amendment just adopted was stricken out.

Mr. Russell, of Harrison, moved to strike out section 9.

Lost.

Mr. Waelder offered the following amendment:

Strike out " or property," in line 43.

Adopted.

Mr. Stewart proposed to add in line 44, after State, the word " county."

Adopted.

Mr. Moore moved to reconsider the vote adopting Mr. Brown's amendment.

Mr. Kilgore offered the following amendment:

Amend section 10 by striking out the words " and the taxes paid," in line 46.

Mr. Russell, of Wood, moved to reject the amendment.

Carried by the following vote:

YEAS—Abernathy, Abner, Arnim, Barnett, Blassingame, Brady, Brown, Bruce, Burleson, Cardis, Cook of Gonzales, Cooke of San Saba, Crawford, Darnell, Davis of Wharton, Dillard, Dohoney, Ferris, Fleming, Flournoy, German, Graves, Haynes, Holt, Johnson of Collin, Lacy, Lynch, McKinney of Denton, McLean, Mitchell, Martin of Hunt, Nugent, Pauli, Reynolds, Ross, Russell of Harrison, Russell of Wood, Sansom, Scott, Spikes, Wade, Whitfield—42.

NAYS—Ballinger, Blake, Cooley, Davis of Brazos, DeMorse, Erhard, Ford, Gaither, Henry of Limestone, Kilgore, Killough, Lockett, McCormick, Moore, Murphy, Martin of Navarro, Norvell, Nunn, Ramey, Reagan, Robertson of Bell, Robison of Fayette, Smith, Stayton, Stewart, Stockdale, Waelder, West, Whitehead, Wright—30.

Upon calling the roll Mr. Chambers stated that he was paired off with Mr. Cline, but for which fact he would vote " yea "; and Mr. McKinney, of Wharton, stated that he was paired off with Mr. Henry, of Smith, but for which fact he would vote " yea."

Mr. Rentfro stated that he was paired off with Mr. McCabe, but for which fact he would vote " nay."

Mr. Waelder offered the following amendment:

Add after the word " situated," in line 46, the following: " but non-residents of such counties may deposit the amount of taxes due from them with the Comptroller of the State, to the credit of the collector of the county to which such taxes are due."

Mr. Fleming moved to reject the amendment.

On motion of Mr. Graves, the debate was closed on the proposition to reject, and the Convention brought to a direct vote, which resulted in rejecting the amendment by the following vote :

Mr. McKinney, of Walker, declined to vote for reasons above stated.

YEAS—Abernathy, Abner, Arnim, Barnett, Blassingame, Brown, Bruce, Burleson, Cooke of San Saba, Crawford, Darnell, Davis of Wharton, Dillard, Ferris, Fleming, Flournoy, German, Graves, Haynes, Holt, Johnson of Collin, Lacy, Lynch, McCormick, McKinney of Denton, McLean, Mitchell, Martin of Navarro, Martin of Hunt, Nugent, Pauli, Rentfro, Reynolds, Ross, Russell of Wood, Sansom, Scott, Spikes, Wade, Whitfield—40.

NAYS—Allison, Ballinger, Blake, Brady, Cook of Gonzales, Cooley, Davis of Brazos, DeMorse, Dohoney, Gaither, Henry of Limestone, Kilgore, Killough, Lockett, Moore, Murphy, Norvell, Nunn, Ramey, Reagan, Robertson of Bell, Robison of Fayette, Russell of Harrison, Smith, Stayton, Stewart, Stockdale, Waelder, West, Whitehead, Wright—31.

Mr. Darnell offered the following amendment to come in after the word "situated," in section 10, line 46: "But the Legislature may by a two-thirds vote authorize the payment of taxes of non-residents to be made at the office of the Comptroller of Public Accounts."

On motion of Mr. Fleming, the Convention adjourned to 9 o'clock A. M. to-morrow.

FIFTIETH DAY.

HALL OF REPRESENTATIVES, ⎱
AUSTIN, TEXAS, November 2, 1875. ⎰

Convention met pursuant to adjournment; roll called; quorum present. Prayer by the Rev. W. H. Dodge, of the Baptist Church, at Austin.

Journal of yesterday read and adopted.

On motion of Mr. Dohoney, Mr. Wright was excused indefinitely.

On motion of Mr. Mitchell, Mr. Reynolds was excused for three days from to-day.

On motion of Mr. Waelder, Mr. Cooley was added to the Committee on Judicial Apportionment, in place of Mr. King, excused.

On motion of Mr. Burleson, Mr. Haynes was excused for to-day on account of sickness.

On motion of Mr. Fleming, Mr. McKinney, of Walker, was added to the Committee on Judicial Apportionment.

Mr. Ballinger presented a memorial signed by the Mayor and Board of Aldermen of Galveston, the Chief Justice and Justices of the Peace of Galveston county, the president and officers of the Chamber of Commerce of Galveston, by the Cotton Exchange of Galveston, and over twelve hundred citizens of Galveston county, asking authority for counties and cities and towns on the coast to issue bonds and levy taxes to construct breakwaters and other improvements, and asking State aid in the same.

Referred to Committee on Municipal Corporations.

Mr. Ramey made the following report:

COMMITTEE ROOM,
AUSTIN, November 2, 1875.

To the Hon. E. B. Pickett, President of the Convention:

SIR—Your Committee on Engrossed and Enrolled Ordinances would respectfully report to your honorable body that they have carefully examined and compared " Article ——, The Public Free Schools," and find the same correctly engrossed.

Respectfully,   WM. NEAL RAMEY, Chairman.

Mr. Cook, of Gonzales, reported as follows:

COMMITTEE ROOM,
AUSTIN, November 2, 1875.

To the Hon. E. B. Pickett, President of the Convention:

Your Committee on Printing and Contingent Expenses, to whom was referred resolution with regard to the inefficiency of the printers employed to do the current printing of the Convention, and recommending that the contract be rescinded, have had the same under consideration and instruct me to report : That owing to the large amount of printing coming to the hands of the printers the past few days, the work was somewhat delayed, and mistakes occurred.   This delay was unavoidable, and the errors only such as are likely to occur with any printers under the circumstances.   The printers are now well up with their work, and your committee feel assured that the work will, in the future, be well and promptly done.

Your committee can see no sufficient cause for rescinding the printing contract in the premises, and ask to be discharged from further consideration of the subject.

W. D. S. COOK, Chairman.

Adopted.

Mr. Sansom offered the following resolution :

Resolved, That it shall be the duty of the State to provide for the custody and maintenance of indigent lunatics.

Referred to Committee on General Provisions.

Mr. McKinney, of Denton, offered the following resolution:

Resolved, That the Committee on General Provisions inquire into the propriety of inserting a clause in the constitution requiring any person who shall maliciously prosecute and indict another before a grand jury in this State, or shall, in any way corruptly procure the same, shall pay all costs and damages resulting from such malicious indictment, and be subject to such other penalties as may be prescribed by law.

Referred to Committee on General Provisions.

Mr. Ferris offered the following resolution:

Resolved, That the following section be made a part of the constitution:

" Sec. ——. The Legislature may from time to time establish new counties for the convenience of the inhabitants of such new county or counties; *provided,* that no new county shall be established which shall reduce the county or counties, or either of them, from which it shall be taken, to a less area than nine hundred square miles, unless by consent of two-thirds of the Legislature; nor shall any county be organized of less contents; *provided further,* that all counties heretofore created are hereby declared to be legally constituted counties. Every new county, as to the right of suffrage and representation, shall be considered as part of the county or counties from which it was taken, until the next apportionment of representation thereafter; *provided also,* that no new county shall be laid off, when less than one hundred and seventy-five qualified jurors are at the time resident therein; nor where the county or counties from which the new county is proposed to be taken, would thereby be reduced below that number of qualified jurors."

Referred to Committee on Counties and County Lands.

Mr. Mills offered the following resolution:

Resolved, that the following shall be a section of the constitution:

" Sec. ——. The Legislature shall provide by law for the exemption from garnishment of the wages of laborers for hire who are heads of families; and may also provide such for single persons, under such limitations and regulations as may be prescribed by law."

Referred to Committee on General Provisions.

On motion of Mr. Russell, of Harrison, Mr. Abner was excused until Thursday morning.

On motion of Mr. Whitfield, Mr. Arnim was excused for five days.

On motion of Mr. Martin, of Navarro, Mr. Abernathy was added to the Committee on Judicial Apportionment.

UNFINISHED BUSINESS.

"Article —, Revenue and Taxation," again taken up.

Mr. Darnell's amendment, pending on adjournment, being under consideration, Mr. Russell, of Harrison, proposed to add to the amendment, after the words "non-residents," the words "of counties."

Accepted, and the amendment as amended adopted by the following vote:

YEAS—Abernathy, Allison, Ballinger, Barnett, Brady, Brown, Burleson, Cardis, Chambers, Cook of Gonzales, Cooke of San Saba, Cooley, Crawford, Darnell, Davis of Brazos, Davis of Wharton, DeMorse, Dohoney, Erhard, Ferris, Flournoy, Gaither, German, Henry of Limestone, Johnson of Collin, Kilgore, Killough, Lacy, Lockett, Lynch, McCormick, McLean, Moore, Murphy, Martin of Navarro, Martin of Hunt, Norvell, Nunn, Pauli, Ramey, Reagan, Robertson of Bell, Robison of Fayette, Russell of Wood, Sansom, Scott, Sessions, Smith, Spikes, Stayton, Stewart, Wade, Waelder, West, Whitehead, Whitfield—55.

NAYS—Arnim, Blassingame, Bruce, Dillard, Fleming, Graves, Holt, Mills, Mitchell, Nugent, Ross—11.

Mr. Russell, of Harrison, on roll call, stated that he would vote yea but for having paired off with Mr. Abner.

The hour having arrived, the special order was taken up, viz: Mr. Johnson's (of Collin) resolution to have night sessions.

Mr. Darnell moved to postpone the consideration of the resolution until Monday next at 10 o'clock.

Carried.

Pending business resumed, Mr. Moore offered the following amendment as a substitute for Sec. 8:

"Sec. 8. The State tax on property, exclusive of the tax necessary to pay the public debt, shall never exceed fifty cents on the one hundred dollars valuation, and no county, city or town shall levy more than one-half of said State tax, except for the payment of debt already incurred, and for the erection of public buildings, not to exceed fifty cents on one hundred dollars valuation, in any one year, and except as in this constitution is otherwise provided."

Adopted.

Mr. Russell, of Harrison, offered the following substitute for section 9:

"Sec. 9. No property liable to taxation in any county, city

or town, shall be released from the payment of taxes levied for State or county purposes, except in cases of public calamity."

[Mr. Stockdale in the chair.]

Mr. Russell, of Harrison, withdrew his substitute.

Mr. Waelder proposed to amend section 9, line 43, by inserting after the word "of" the words "or property in."

Adopted.

Mr. DeMorse offered the following additional section to come in after section 10:

"Sec. —. The Comptroller of the State shall prepare a list of all lands assessed or unassessed, for each separate county, and assess upon the portion unrendered all the present and back tax due thereon, and transmit to each collector of taxes the list prepared for his county, upon which list the collector shall proceed as provided by law."

On motion of Mr. Fleming, the amendment was laid on the table.

Mr. Stayton offered the following as a substitute for section 12:

"Sec. 12. Laws shall be enacted by the Legislature, at the first session thereof after the adoption of this constitution, providing for the speedy judicial condemnation by a proceeding *in rem* and sale of lands for the taxes due thereon, and the deed to the purchaser at such sale, when made in accordance with the decree of the court authorizing the sale to be made, shall be held to vest title in him to such lands, subject to impeachment only for such causes as would render the decree of the court directing the sale void, or for fraud upon the part of the officer selling—of the buyer, or of the collector of taxes; *provided, however,* that the former owner shall have the right within two years after the decree confirming the sale, to redeem the land so sold by the payment to the purchaser of the amount of money paid for the land, together with such sum as the purchaser of the land has paid as taxes thereon after his purchase, with interest on such sums from the time of payment, at the rate of twenty per cent. per annum."

On motion of Mr. Pickett, the substitute was laid on the table.

Mr. Waelder offered the following substitute for section 12:

"Sec. 12. The Legislature shall, at its first session after the adoption of this constitution, provide for the sale of all lands upon which taxes remain unpaid, and for a like sale in each year; and it shall also provide for the vesting of title in the purchaser at such sale, and for the right of redemption by the owners of land so sold."

On motion of Mr. Fleming, laid on the table.

Mr. Stewart offered the following additional section:

" Sec. ——. The Legislature may authorize counties, cities and towns, by a vote of the freeholders thereof, to levy and collect a special tax for the support of public common free schools."

Upon the question of the adoption of the amendment, the yeas and nays were called, and the amendment lost by the following vote:

Yeas—Ballinger, Brown, Cook of Gonzales, Cooley, Crawford, Darnell, DeMorse, Dohoney, Fleming, Ford, Kilgore, Lockett, McCormick, McLean, Mitchell, Morris, Martin of Navarro, Martin of Hunt, Nunn, Pauli, Reagan, Smith, Stewart, Waelder, West, Whitfield—26.

Nays—Abernathy, Allison, Arnim, Barnett, Blake, Blassingame, Bruce, Burleson, Chambers, Cooke of San Saba, Davis of Brazos, Dillard, Erhard, Flournoy, Gaither, German, Graves, Henry of Limestone, Holt, Johnson of Collin, Killough, Lacy, Lynch, McKinney of Denton, McKinney of Walker, Moore, Murphy, Norvell, Nugent, Robertson of Bell, Robison of Fayette, Ross, Russell of Harrison, Russell of Wood, Sansom, Scott, Spikes, Stayton, Stockdale, Wade, Whitehead—41.

Mr. Brown offered the following as a substitute for sections 13 and 15:

" Sec. 13. There shall be elected in each county of the State an assessor of taxes and a collector of taxes, each of whom shall hold his office for two years, and until his successor shall be elected and qualified; *provided,* that in counties having less than two thousand qualified electors, the duties of collector shall be performed by the sheriff of each county respectively. In the first election provided for by this Convention the fact shall be determined by the number of qualified voters in each county. In all succeeding elections the fact shall be determined by the whole number of votes cast at the last preceding general election in each county."

Mr. Ballinger called up the motion to reconsider the vote to strike out the words "condemnation and" from section 12, line 56.

Carried.

Mr. Sansom offered the following amendment:

Strike out the words "condemnation and," and after the word "sale" insert "by levy, as in cases of personal property."

Lost.

Mr. Ballinger's amendment to strike out the words "condemnation and" was adopted.

Mr. Crawford offered the following substitute for the section:

" Sec. —. Provision shall be made by the Legislature for the sale of all lands for the taxes due thereon."

Mr. Murphy offered the following as a substitute for the substitute and section:

" Sec. —. The Legislature shall at its first session after the adoption of this constitution provide for the manner of enforcing liens on real estate incurred for non-payment of taxes."

Mr. Fleming moved to lay both substitutes on the table.

A division of the question was ordered.

Mr. Murphy's substitute was laid on the table.

On motion of Mr. Cook, of Gonzales, the Convention adjourned to 2½ P. M., pending Mr. Crawford's substitute.

EVENING SESSION—2½ o'clock.

Convention met pursuant to adjournment; roll called; quorum present.

Question pending on adjournment, viz: Mr. Crawford's substitute was taken up.

Mr. Ballinger offered the following as a substitute of the section and substitute:

" Sec. —. The Legislature, at its first session, shall provide for the speedy and effective collection of taxes in this State, and for the sale of any property, real or personal, for the payment of all taxes of any taxpayer; and the Legislature shall have full power to declare the effect of a tax deed in favor of the purchaser; and to regulate the time and terms for the redemption of property purchased at tax sales."

Mr. Russell, of Wood, moved to close debate on the amendment.

Carried.

Mr. Crawford, by leave, withdrew his substitute.

Mr. Ballinger's substitute was lost.

Mr. Russell, of Harrison, proposed to amend section 12, line 56, by adding after the word " land," the words " and other property."

Adopted.

Mr. Stewart offered the following amendment:

In lines 59 and 60 strike out all between the words " held " and " provided " and insert "to be *prima facie* evidence of title, and that all the prerequisites to the sale have been complied with."

[Mr. Brown in the chair.]

On motion of Mr. Fleming, the main question on the amendment was ordered, and amendment lost.

Mr. Ferris proposed to amend section 12 by inserting after the word "thereon," in line 56, the following: "upon the order or judgment of some court of record."

Mr. Russell, of Wood, moved the previous question on the engrossment of the article.

Carried.

Mr. Ferris's amendment lost.

Mr. Waelder's motion to reconsider the vote refusing to adopt Mr. German's amendment providing for the election of an assessor and collector in each organized county, was taken up and lost by the following vote:

YEAS—Abernathy, Ballinger, Blake, Brady, Cooke of San Saba, Cooley, Darnell, Davis of Brazos, Davis of Wharton, Dillard, Dohoney, Erhard, Ferris, Ford, German, Graves, Kilgore, Lockett, Mills, Mitchell, Moore, Morris, Murphy, Munn, Russell of Harrison, Sansom, Waelder, West—28.

NAYS—Allison, Barnett, Blassingame, Bruce, Burleson, Chambers, Crawford, DeMorse, Fleming, Flournoy, Gaither, Holt, Johnson of Collin, Killough, Lacy, Lynch, McCormick, McKinney of Denton, McLean, Martin of Navarro, Martin of Hunt, Norvell, Nugent, Pauli, Ramey, Reagan, Robertson of Bell, Ross, Russell of Wood, Scott, Smith, Spikes, Stayton, Stewart, Stockdale, Wade, Whitehead, Whitfield—38.

Mr. Brown, by leave, withdrew his substitute.

Mr. Martin, of Navarro, offered the following substitute for section 13:

"Sec. 13. There shall be elected by the qualified electors of each county, at the same time and under the same law regulating the election of State and county officers, an assessor of taxes, who shall hold his office for two years, and until his successor is elected and qualified."

Adopted.

Mr. Stewart offered the following amendment:

Amend section 7, lines 35 and 36, strike out the words "paid upon it," and insert "shall be paid to the Comptroller," who shall apportion the same.

Lost.

Mr. McCormick offered the following amendment:

Add after the word "thereon," in line 68, section 14, the following: "And all the property, both real and personal, belonging to any delinquent taxpayer, shall be liable to seizure and sale for the payment of all the taxes and penalties due by such delinquent, and such property may be sold for the payment of the taxes and penalties due by such delinquent, under such regulations as the Legislature may provide."

Adopted.

The question on the engrossment of the article was then put, and the article engrossed by the following vote:

YEAS—Mr. President, Abernathy, Allison, Arnim, Barnett, Blassingame, Brown, Bruce, Burleson, Chambers, Cooke of San Saba, Darnell, Ferris, Fleming, Flournoy, German, Graves, Holt, Johnson of Collin, Killough, Lacy, Lynch, McCormick, Martin of Navarro, Martin of Hunt, Nugent, Ramey, Ross, Russell of Wood, Sansom, Scott, Spikes, Wade, Whitfield—34.

NAYS—Ballinger, Blake, Brady, Cooley, Crawford, Davis of Brazos, Davis of Wharton, DeMorse, Dillard, Dohoney, Erhard, Ford, Gaither, Kilgore, Lockett, McLean, Mitchell, Moore, Morris, Murphy, Norvell, Nunn, Pauli, Reagan, Robertson of Bell, Russell of Harrison, Smith, Stayton, Stewart, Stockdale, Waelder, West, Whitehead—33.

" Article —, Judicial Department," taken up.

On motion of Mr. Flournoy, the Convention adjourned to 9 o'clock A. M. to-morrow.

Pending— " Article —, Judicial Department."

FIFTY-FIRST DAY.

HALL OF REPRESENTATIVES, }
AUSTIN, TEXAS, November 3, 1875. }

Convention met pursuant to adjournment; roll called; quorum present.   Prayer by the Rev. W. H. Dodge, of the Baptist Church, at Austin.

Journal of yesterday read and adopted.

On motion of Mr. Murphy, Mr. Cardis was excused for four days.

Mr. Fleming presented the petition of the citizens of Hamilton county, asking for a local option law.

Referred to Committee on General Provisions.

Mr. Ramey offered the following resolution:

RESOLUTION WITH REGARD TO PRISONS, ETC.

WHEREAS, The barbarities and cruelties practiced on the inmates of the penitentiary have been generally condemned; and

WHEREAS, the plan of scattering the convicts sent to the penitentiary promiscuously over the country has produced general complaint, and shown the necessity of more prisons; and

WHEREAS, The great number of youthful criminals demands the erection of another class of prisons; and

WHEREAS, The great majority of the county prisons are almost equal to the famous *Calcutta Hole*—seats of filth and disease—affording but little security to the prisoners, either by securing them from escape on the one hand, or mob violence on the other; and

WHEREAS, In most of the weak or frontier counties, where desperadoes most abound, the citizens are not able to erect safe and suitable prisons; therefore,

Be it resolved, That the Committee on General Provisions be requested to consider the propriety of reporting a clause in the constitution requiring the Legislature to enact laws regulating the kind and manner of erecting prisons, State, district and county, requiring them to be erected in a manner to secure the prisoners from escape and mob violence on the one hand, and with due regard to the laws of health and so forth on the other, and also laws with regard to the treatment of prisoners confined therein, imposing penalties for their violation; and in those counties in which the citizens are too poor to erect safe and suitable prisons, and where violators of the laws abound, to require the erection of at least one safe and suitable prison in each judicial district, and in such manner as they may prescribe.

Referred to Committee on General Provisions.

On motion of Mr. Allison, two hundred copies of article on education ordered printed.

On motion of Mr. Ramey, two hundred copies of the article on immigration were ordered printed.

Unfinished business, viz: "Article —, Judiciary," taken up.

Mr. Ballinger, by leave, offered the following resolution:

Resolved, That the order of considering the article on the "Judicial Department" in the constitution shall be as follows:

"Each entire article reported by a minority may in turn be presented as the substitute to be adopted by the Convention, in the discussion of which the merits of all reports may be considered. The sections reported by Mr. Reagan and others may be then presented, together, or severally, as substitutes for corresponding sections. After that, the article thus far arrived at as the basis for the action of the Convention, shall be considered, section by section, in their order until completed."

On motion of Mr. Ballinger, the rule was suspended, and the resolution taken up and adopted.

The question being upon the engrossment of the article reported by the majority, Mr. Norvell offered the following as a substitute for the pending article:

" ARTICLE —,

" JUDICIAL DEPARTMENT.

" Section 1. The judicial power of the State shall be vested in one Supreme Court, in a Court of Appeals, in District Courts, in Probate Courts, in County Courts, in Justices' Courts, and in such corporations and other inferior courts as the Legislature may from time to time ordain and establish; *provided,* that no judge of any court, except those of the Supreme Court, the Court of Appeals, and the District Courts shall receive a salary from the State, or from any county.

" Sec. 2. The Supreme Court shall consist of a Chief Justice and two Associate Justices, any two of whom shall constitute a quorum. They shall be elected by the qualified voters of the State at a general election for State or county officers; they shall have arrived at the age of thirty years at the time of election; shall hold their offices for a term of six years, and each of them shall receive an annual salary of at least three thousand five hundred dollars, which shall not be increased or diminished during his term of office.

" Sec. 3. The Supreme Court shall have appellate jurisdiction only from the Court of Appeals, which shall embrace all cases determined in said court; *provided, however,* that the Supreme Court shall have and retain jurisdiction to try and determine the cases which shall remain on its dockets at the time of the organization of the Court of Appeals under this constitution. The Supreme Court, and the judges thereof shall have power to issue the writ of *habeas corpus,* and, under such regulations as may be prescribed by law, the said court and the judges thereof may issue the writ of *mandamus* and such other writs as may be necessary to enforce its own jurisdiction. The Supreme Court shall also have power, upon affidavits or otherwise, as by the court may be thought proper, to ascertain such matters of fact as may be necessary to the proper exercise of its jurisdiction. The Supreme Court shall sit for the transaction of business from the first Monday of October until the last Saturday of June of every year, at the capital, and at not more than two other places in the State.

" Sec. 4. The Supreme Court shall appoint its own clerks, who shall give bond in such manner as may be required by law; shall hold their offices for two years, and shall be subject to removal by the said court, for good cause, entered of record on the minutes of said court.

Sec. 5. The ourt of Appeals shall consist of a Presiding Judge and two Associate Judges, any two of whom shall constitute a quorum. They shall be elected by the qualified voters of the State at a general election for State or county officers; they shall have arrived at the age of thirty years at the time of election; shall hold their offices for a term of six years, and each of them shall receive an annual salary of at least three thousand five hundred dollars, which shall not be increased or diminished during his term of office.

" Sec. 6. The Court of Appeals shall have appellate jurisdiction only, which shall be co-extensive with the limits of the State. The Court of Appeals and the judges thereof shall have power to issue the writ of *habeas corpus;* and, under such regulations as may be prescribed by law, the said court and the judges thereof may issue the writ of *mandamus,* and such other writs as may be necessary to enforce its own jurisdiction. The Court of Appeals shall also have power, upon affidavits, or otherwise, as by the court may be thought proper, to ascertain such matters of fact as may be necessary to the proper exercise of its jurisdiction. The Court of Appeals shall sit, for the transaction of business, from the first Monday of October until the last Saturday of June of every year, at the capital, and at not more than two other places in the State, at which the Supreme Court shall hold its sessions. The Court of Appeals shall not be required to deliver opinions in writing.

" Sec. 7. The Court of Appeals shall appoint its own clerks, who shall give bond in such manner as may be prescribed by law, shall hold their offices for two years, and shall be subject to removal by the said court for good cause, entered of record on the minutes of said court.

" Sec. 8. The State shall be divided into convenient judicial districts. For each district there shall be elected, by the qualified voters thereof, at a general election for State or county officers, a judge, who shall reside in the same, shall hold his office for the term of four years, shall receive an annual salary of not less than two thousand five hundred dollars, which shall not be increased or diminished during his term of service, and shall hold the courts at one place in each county in the district at least twice in each year, in such manner as may be prescribed by law.

" Sec. 9. The District Court shall have original jurisdiction of all criminal cases; of all suits in behalf of the State to recover penalties, forfeitures and escheats; of all cases of divorce; of all suits to recover damages for slander or defamation of character; of all suits for the trial of title to land; of all suits for the enforcement of liens; of all suits for the trial of the right of property levied on by virtue of any writ of execution, sequestration or attachment, when the property levied on shall be equal to, or exceed in value five hundred dollars; and of all suits, complaints or pleas whatever, without regard to any distinction between law and equity, when the matter in controversy shall be valued at, or amount to five hundred dollars, exclusive of interest; and the said courts, and the judges thereof shall have power to issue writs of injunction, *certiorari,* and all other writs necessary to enforce their own jurisdiction, and to give them a general superintendence and control over inferior tribunals. All indictments for offenses below the grade of felony returned to, and all informations filed in the District Court, shall be transferred to the Court of the Chief Justice of the County, in such manner as may be prescribed by law, there to be tried or disposed of. The District Courts shall have appellate jurisdiction in cases originating or tried in inferior courts, under such regulations, limitations and restrictions as the Legislature may prescribe, and original and appellate jurisdiction and general control over the Probate Court established in each county for appointing guardians, granting letters testamentary and of administration, for settling the accounts of executors, administrators and guardians, and for the transaction of business appertaining to estates, and original jurisdiction and general control over executors, administrators, guardians and minors, under such regulations as may be prescribed by law.

"Sec. 10. There shall be a Clerk of the District Court for each county, who shall be elected by the qualified voters, and who shall hold his office for two years, subject to removal by information or by indictment of a grand jury, and conviction by a petit jury. In case of vacancy, the Judge of the District Court shall have the power to appoint a clerk, until a regular election can be held. The Clerk of the District Court shall be recorder for the county and *ex-officio* Clerk of the Probate, County and Chief Justice's Courts.

"Sec. 11. All Judges of the Supreme Court, Court of Appeals and District Courts, shall, by virtue of their offices, be conservators of the peace throughout the State. The style of all writs and process shall be 'the State of Texas.' All prosecutions shall be carried on in the name and by the authority of the 'State of Texas,' and conclude 'against the peace and dignity of the State.'

35

"Sec. 12. In case of a vacancy in the offices of Justices of the Supreme Court, Judge of the Court of Appeals, Judges of the District Court, and District Attorneys, the Governor of the State shall have power to fill the same by appointment, which shall continue in force until the office can be filled at the next general election for State or county officers, and the successor duly qualified.

"Sec. 13. The Judges of the Supreme Court, Court of Appeals and District Courts shall be removed by the Governor, on the address of a majority of each House of the Legislature, for willful neglect of duty, misconduct, habits of drunkenness, oppression in office, incompetency, or other reasonable cause, which shall not be sufficient ground for impeachment; *provided, however,* That the cause, or causes, for each such removal shall be required, shall be stated at length in such address, and entered on the journals of the House; *and provided further,* That the cause or causes shall be notified to the judge so intended to be removed; and he shall be admitted to a hearing in his own defense, before any vote for such address shall pass. And in all such cases the vote shall be taken by yeas and nays, and entered on the journals of each House respectively.

"Sec. 14. No judge shall sit in any case wherein he may be interested, or where either of the parties may be connected with him by affinity or consanguinity, within such degree as may be prescribed by law, or where he shall have been of counsel in the case. When the Supreme Court, or any two of its members shall be thus disqualified to hear and determine any case or cases in said court, or when no judgment can be rendered in any case or cases in said court, by reason of the equal division of opinion of said judges, the same shall be certified to the Governor of the State, who shall immediately commission the requisite number of persons learned in the law for the trial and determination of said case or cases. When the Court of Appeals, or any two of its members shall be thus disqualified to hear and determine any case or cases in said court, or when no judgment can be rendered in any case or cases in said court by reason of the equal division of opinion of said judges, the same shall in like manner be certified to the Governor of the State, who shall immediately commission the requisite number of persons learned in the law for the trial and determination of said case or cases. When a judge of the District Court is thus disqualified, the parties may, by consent, appoint a proper person to try the said case; or upon their failing to do so, a competent person shall be appointed to try the same in the county where it is pending, in such manner as may be prescribed by law. And the District Judges may exchange districts, or hold courts for each other, when they may deem it expedient, and shall do so when directed by law. The disqualification of judges of inferior tribunals shall be remedied as may be prescribed by law.

"Sec. 15. There shall be a District Attorney for each Judicial District in the State, elected by the qualified voters of the district, who shall reside in the district for which he shall be elected; shall hold his office two years; and, together with the perquisites prescribed by law, shall receive an annual salary of not more than five hundred dollars, which shall not be increased during his term of office.

"Sec. 16. Each county shall be divided into five justices' precincts. There shall be elected in each county, by the qualified voters thereof, as may be directed by law, five Justices of the Peace, one of whom shall reside, after his election, at the county seat, and shall be the Chief Justice; and no two of said justices shall reside in the same justice's precinct. They shall hold their offices for two years, be commissioned by the Governor, and should a vacancy occur an election shall be held for the unexpired term.

"Sec. 17. There shall be established in each county in the State an inferior tribunal, styled the Probate Court, one term of which shall be holden by the Chief Justice, at the county seat, in each month, as may be prescribed by law. The Probate Court shall have jurisdiction to probate wills, to appoint guardians of minors, idiots, lunatics, and persons *non compos mentis;* to grant letters testamentary and of administration; to settle accounts of executors, administrators and guardians; to transact all business appertaining to the estates of deceased persons, minors, idiots, lunatics, and persons *non compos mentis,* including the settlement, partition, and distribution of such estates; and to apprentice minors, under such regulations as may be prescribed by law.

"Sec. 18. The Justices of the Peace of each county, or any three of them, shall constitute the County Court, with such jurisdiction over the local affairs, interests, and police matters in the county, as the Legislature may prescribe.

"Sec. 19. The Chief Justice shall have original jurisdiction of all misdemeanors and petty offenses, as the same are now, or may hereafter be defined by law; of such civil cases where the matter in controversy shall not exceed five hundred dollars, exclusive of interest, under such regulations, limitations and restrictions as may be prescribed by law, without regard to any distinction between law and equity; and appellate jurisdiction in cases originating in the other Justices' Courts in the county, under such regulations, limitations and restrictions as may be prescribed by law. The Legislature may provide for the election of a County Attorney to represent the State and county in the Chief Justice's Court, whose term of office, duties and compensation, to consist of fees and commissions only, shall be such as may be prescribed by law. The other Justices of the Peace shall have such civil and criminal jurisdiction as shall be provided by law. The Justices of the Peace shall be *ex officio* Notaries Public. They shall also perform the duties of Coroner, except such as may, by law, be devolved upon Constables.

"Sec. 20. There shall be elected in each county, by the qualified voters, one Sheriff; also one Constable for each Justice's precinct, to be elected by the qualified voters of the precinct, or county, as the Legislature may direct; who shall hold their offices for two years; and should a vacancy occur, an election shall be held for the unexpired term. The Sheriff shall be commissioned by the Governor.

"Sec. 21. In all cases of law or equity, where the matter in controversy shall be valued at or exceed twenty dollars, the right of trial by jury shall be preserved."

Lost by the following vote:

YEAS—Allison, Cooke of San Saba, Crawford, Davis of Wharton, Douglas, Flanagan, Henry of Limestone, Lacy, McKinney of Denton, Murphy, Norvell, Reagan—12.

NAYS—Abernathy, Abner, Ballinger, Barnett, Blake, Blassingame, Brown, Bruce, Burleson, Chambers, Cooley, Darnell, Davis of Brazos, DeMorse, Dillard, Dohoney, Ferris, Fleming, Graves, Haynes, Holt, Kilgore, Killough, Lockett, Lynch, McCormick, McKinney of Walker, Mills, Mitchell, Martin of Navarro, Martin of Hunt, Nugent, Nunn, Pauli, Robison of Fayette, Ross, Russell of Harrison, Russell of Wood, Scott, Spikes, Stayton, Stewart, Stockdale, Wade, Waelder, West—46.

Mr. Robertson, of Bell, at his request, was excused from voting.

Mr. Reagan offered the following amendments to the article reported by the majority:

Substitute the following for section 2:

"Sec. 2. The Supreme Court shall consist of a Chief Justice and four Associate Justices, any three of whom shall constitute a quorum, and a concurrence of a majority of the judges sitting shall be necessary to the decision of a case. No person shall be eligible to the office of Chief Justice or Associate Justice of the

Supreme Court, unless he be at the time of his election a citizen of the United States and of this State, and unless he shall have attained the age of thirty years, and shall have been a practicing lawyer or judge of a court in this State, or such lawyer and judge together, at least seven years. Said Chief Justice and Associate Justices shall be elected by the qualified voters of the State, at a general election, shall hold their offices for eight years, and shall each receive an annual salary of four thousand dollars, which shall not be increased or diminished during his term of office."

Substitute the following for section 3:

" Sec. 3. The Supreme Court shall have appellate jurisdiction only, which shall be co-extensive with the limits of the State; but in criminal cases its appellate jurisdiction shall only extend to cases of felony, to cases of misdemeanor involving official misconduct, and to cases of the violation of the laws in relation to insurance and banking; and in civil cases to suits involving sums of five hundred dollars or more, exclusive of interest; and to suits, without reference to the amount in controversy, in behalf of the State, to recover penalties, fines, forfeitures and escheats; to cases of divorce; to suits for the recovery of damages for slander and defamation of character; to suits for the trial of the title to land, and for the enforcement of liens on land; and to suits involving the constitutionality of a law, or the validity of a law imposing a tax. And it shall have such jurisdiction by appeal over interlocutory judgments of the District Courts, with such exceptions and under such regulations as may be prescribed by law. The Supreme Court, and the judges thereof, shall have power to issue the writ of *habeas corpus,* and, under such regulations as may be prescribed by law, the said court, and the judges thereof, may issue the writ of *mandamus,* and such other writs as may be necessary to enforce its own jurisdiction. The Supreme Court shall also have power, upon affidavits or otherwise, as to the court shall seem proper, to ascertain such matters of fact as may be necessary to the proper exercise of its own jurisdiction. And it shall sit for the transaction of business from the first Monday in October until the last Saturday in June of every year, at the seat of government, and at not more than two other places.

Substitute for section 7 as follows:

" Sec. 7. The District Court shall have original jurisdiction in criminal cases of the grade of felony; in cases of misdemeanor involving official misconduct; in all cases of gambling, including betting on elections; and in all cases of violation of the laws in relation to insurance and banking. And they shall have jurisdiction in criminal cases, brought by appeal from the County

Courts, in all cases of which the County Courts may have original jurisdiction, which cases shall be tried on the record from the County Court, and without further right of appeal.   In civil cases the District Courts shall have original jurisdiction of all suits in behalf of the State to recover penalties, fines, forfeitures and escheats; of all cases of divorce; of all suits to recover damages for slander and defamation of character; of all suits for the trial of the title to land, and to enforce liens on land; and of all suits involving the constitutionality of any law, or to test the validity of a law imposing a tax; and of all suits, complaints and pleas whatever, without regard to any distinction between law and equity, when the matter in controversy shall not be less than five hundred dollars, exclusive of interest; and the said court, and the judges thereof, shall have power to issue the writs of *habeas corpus, mandamus,* injunction, *certiorari,* and all other writs necessary to enforce their own jurisdiction, and to give them a general superintendance and control over inferior tribunals.   And they shall have appellate jurisdiction over all civil cases originating in the County Courts, which cases shall be tried on the record of the County Courts, without further right of appeal.   And the District Courts shall have original and appellate jurisdiction and general control over County Courts, sitting as Probate Courts, for appointing guardians, granting letters testamentary or of administration; for settling the accounts of executors, administrators and guardians, and for the transaction of business appertaining to estates; and such original jurisdiction and general control over executors, administrators, guardians and minors, and under such regulations as may be prescribed by law."

Substitute for section 13, as follows:

"Sec. 13. There shall be established in each county in this State a County Court, which shall be a court of record; and there shall be elected in each county, by the qualified voters, a County Judge, who shall be well informed in the law of the State, shall be a conservator of the peace, and shall hold his office for two years, and until his successor shall be elected and qualified.   He shall receive as a compensation for his services such fees and perquisites as may be prescribed by law."

Substitute sections 14 and 15, as follows:

"Sec. 14. The County Courts shall have exclusive original jurisdiction of all misdemeanors of which exclusive original jurisdiction is not given to the Justices' Courts, except in cases of official misconduct, and they shall have jurisdiction concurrent with the District Courts in all cases of gambling, including betting on elections, and cases of the violation of the laws in relation to insurance and banking. And they shall have exclusive original jurisdiction in all civil cases when the amount involved is not less than two hundred nor more than five hundred dollars, exclusive of interest, except in such cases as are otherwise provided for in this constitution; and they shall have such other jurisdiction as may be conferred on them by law. And they shall have appellate jurisdiction of all cases, civil and criminal, of which Justices' Courts shall have original jurisdiction, when the judgment of the court appealed from shall exceed the sum of ten dollars, exclusive of costs, under such regulations as may be prescribed by law, with such appellate jurisdiction from corporation courts, and other inferior tribunals, as may be prescribed by law. In all appeals from Justices' Courts, or corporation courts, or other inferior tribunals, the cases so appealed shall be tried *de novo* in the County Courts, and such trial shall be final under such regulations, and with such exceptions, as may be provided by law.

" The County Courts shall have the general jurisdiction of a probate court. They shall probate wills, appoint guardians of minors, idiots, lunatics, persons *non compos mentis,* and common drunkards; grant letters testamentary and of administrator; settle the accounts of executors, administrators and guardians; transact all business appertainining to the estates of deceased persons, minors, idiots, lunatics, persons *non compus mentis,* and common drunkards, including the settlement, partition and distribution of such estates; and to apprentice minors as provided by law. And the County Courts, or the judges thereof, shall have power to issue writs of *mandamus,* injunction, and all other writs necessary to the enforcement of the jurisdiction of said courts; and to issue writs of *habeas corpus* in cases where the offense charged is within the jurisdiction of the County Court, or any other court or tribunal inferior to said court. The County Courts shall not have criminal jurisdiction in any county where there is a Criminal District Court, unless expressly conferred by law; and in such counties appeals from Justices' Courts, and other inferior courts and tribunals, shall be to the Civil or Criminal District Courts, under such regulations as may be prescribed by law."

" Sec. 15. There shall not be less than four terms of the County Court, as may be provided by law, for the trial of civil cases; and the Legislature may prescribe what probate orders may be made and business done in vacation; and such court shall always be open for the trial of criminal cases. Prosecutions may be commenced in said court by information filed by the County Attorney, or by affidavit, as may be provided by law. Grand Juries impanneled in the District Courts shall inquire into misdemeanors, and all indictments therefor returned into the District Courts shall forthwith be certified to the County Courts, or other inferior courts, having jurisdiction to try them, for trial; and if such indictments be quashed in the county or other inferior court, the person charged shall not be discharged if there is probable cause of guilt, but may be held by such court or magistrate to answer an information or affidavit. A jury in the County Court shall consist of six men; but no jury shall be impanneled to try a civil case, unless demanded by one of the parties, who shall pay such jury fee therefor, in advance, as may be prescribed by law, unless he makes affidavit that he is unable to pay the same."

Substitute the following for section 17:

"Sec. 17. Each county shall be divided into five justices' precincts; for each of which precincts there shall be elected, by the qualified voters thereof, a Justice of the Peace, who shall hold his office for two years, and until his successor shall be elected and qualified, who shall exercise such jurisdiction, and perform such duties, and receive such compensation as may be prescribed by law. Justices of the Peace shall have jurisdiction in criminal matters of all cases where the penalty or fine imposed on conviction shall be two hundred dollars or less, with or without imprisonment; and in civil matters, of all cases where the amount in controversy is two hundred dollars or less, exclusive of interest, of which exclusive original jurisdiction is not given to the District or County Courts; and such other jurisdiction, criminal and civil, as may be provided by law. And the Justices of the Peace shall be *ex officio* Notaries Public. And they shall hold their courts at such times and places as may be provided by law."

Add the following section:

"Sec. ——. The Legislature shall at its first session provide for the transfer of all business, civil and criminal, pending in the District Court, over which jurisdiction is given by this constitution to the County Courts, or other inferior Courts, to such county or inferior courts; and for the trial or disposition of all such cases by such county or other inferior courts."

On motion of Mr. Stockdale, the Convention adjourned to 2½ o'clock P.M.

EVENING SESSION — 2½ o'clock.

Convention met pursuant to adjournment: roll called; quorum present.

Consideration of "Article — on Judiciary" resumed.

Mr. Darnell, by leave, withdrew from the papers returned by the Committee on Public Land and Land Office a resolution instructing said committee to inquire into the propriety of validating the patents heretofore issued, on all locations of headrights and other certificates in the reservation heretofore known as the Peters Colony Reservation and the Mississippi and Pacific Railroad Reservation.

On motion of Mr. Dohony, the Convention adjourned to 9 o'clock A. M., to-morrow.

FIFTY-SECOND DAY.

HALL OF REPRESENTATIVES, ⎱
AUSTIN, TEXAS, November 4, 1875. ⎰

Convention met pursuant to adjournment; roll called; quorum present. Prayer by the Rev. John M. Cochran, of the Presbyterian Church of Navasota.

Journal of yesterday read and adopted.

Mr. West, chairman of the Committee on General Provisions, made the following report:

COMMITTEE ROOM, ⎱
AUSTIN, November 3, 1875. ⎰

To the Hon. E. B. Pickett, President of the Convention:

The majority of the Committee on General Provisions instruct me to report the following article, and recommend its adoption.

Respectfully submitted.　　　C. S. WEST, Chairman.

"ARTICLE —.

" GENERAL PROVISIONS.

" Section 1. Members of the Legislature, and all officers, before they enter upon the duties of their offices, shall take the following oath or affirmation: 'I (A. B.), do solemnly swear (or affirm) that I will faithfully and impartially discharge and perform all the duties incumbent on me as . . . . , according to the best of my skill and ability, agreeably to the constitution and laws of the United States, and of this State; and I do futher solemnly swear (or affirm) that, since the adoption of this constitution by the Congress of the United States, I, being a citizen of this State, have not fought a duel with deadly weapons, within this State nor out of it, nor have I sent or accepted a challenge to fight a duel with deadly weapons, nor have I acted as second in carrying a challenge, or aided, advised or assisted, any person thus offending—so help me God. And I furthermore solemnly swear (or affirm) that I have not directly nor indirectly, paid, offered, or promised to pay, contributed nor promised to contribute, any money or other valuable thing, or promised any public office or employment, as a reward for the giving or with-holding a vote at the election at which I was elected (or appointed) to said office—so help me God.'

" Sec. 2. Laws shall be made to exclude from office, serving on juries, and from the right of suffrage, those who shall hereafter be convicted of bribery, perjury, forgery, or other high crimes. The privilege of free suffrage shall be protected by laws regulating elections, and prohibiting, under adequate penalties, all undue influence thereon, from power, bribery, tumult or other improper practice.

" Sec. 3. The Legislature shall make provision whereby persons convicted of misdemeanors and committed to the county jails in default of payment of fines and costs shall be required to discharge such fines and costs by manual labor on the public works of the county, under such regulations as may be prescribed by law.

" Sec. 4. Any citizen of this State who shall, after the adoption of this constitution, fight a duel with deadly weapons, or send or accept a challenge to fight a duel with deadly weapons, either within this State or out of it, or who shall act as second, or knowingly assist in any manner those thus offending, shall be deprived of the right of suffrage, or of holding any office of trust or profit under this State.

" Sec. 5. Every person shall be disqualified from holding any office of profit or trust in this State who shall have been convicted of having given or offered a bribe to procure his election or appointment.

" Sec. 6. No money shall be drawn from the treasury but in pursuance of specific appropriations made by law; nor shall any appropriation of money be made for a longer term than two years, except for purposes of education; and no appropriation for private or individual purposes shall be made without the concurrence of both houses of the Legislature. A regular statement, under oath, and on account of the receipts and expenditures of all public money shall be published annually, in such manner as shall be provided by law.

" Sec. 7. The Legislature shall, in no case, have power to issue " treasury warrants," " treasury notes," or paper of any description intended to circulate as money.

" Sec. 8. Each county in the State may provide, in such manner as may be prescribed by law, a manual labor poor-house and farm, for taking care of, managing, employing and supplying the wants of its indigent and poor inhabitants.

" Sec. 9. Absence on business of the State, or of the United States, shall not forfeit a residence once obtained, so as to deprive any one of the right of suffrage, or of being elected or appointed to any office, under the exceptions contained in this constitution.

" Sec. 10. The Legislature shall provide for deductions from the salaries of public officers who may neglect the performance of any duty that may be assigned them by law.

" Sec. 11. The legal rate of interest shall not exceed eight per cent. per annum, in the absence of any contract as to the rate of interest, and, by contract, parties may agree upon any rate not to exceed twelve per cent. per annum ; all interest charged above this last named rate shall be deemed usurious, and the Legislature shall, at its first session, provide, by appropriate pains and penalties, to prevent and punish usury.

" Sec. 12. No member of Congress, nor person holding or exercising any office of profit or trust under the United States, or either of them, or under any foreign power, shall be eligible as a member of the Legislature, or hold or exercise any office of profit or trust under this State.

" Sec. 13. The Legislature shall provide, at its first session, by law, for a change of venue in civil and criminal cases.

" Sec. 14. It shall be the duty of the Legislature to pass such laws as may be necessary and proper to decide differences by arbitration, when the parties shall elect that method of trial.

" Sec. 15. All civil officers shall reside within the State, and all district and county officers within their districts or counties, and shall keep their offices at such places therein as may be required by law.

" Sec. 16. General laws regulating the adoption of children, emancipation of minors, and the granting of divorces, shall be made ; but no special law shall be enacted relating to particular or individual cases.

" Sec. 17. All property, both real and personal, of the wife, owned or claimed by her before marriage, and that acquired afterward by gift, devise or descent, and the increase of the same, shall be her separate property ; and laws shall be passed clearly defining the rights of the wife in relation as well as to her separate property, as that held in common with her husband.

Laws shall be passed providing for the registration of the wife's separate property.

"Sec. 18. No corporate body shall hereafter be created, renewed or extended with banking or discounting privileges.

"Sec. 19. All officers within this State shall continue to perform the duties of their offices until their successors shall be duly qualified.

"Sec. 20. The rights of property and of action, which have been acquired under the constitution and laws of the Republic or State of Texas, shall not be divested; nor shall any rights or actions which have been divested, barred or declared null and void by the constitution of the Republic or State be reinvested, revived or reinstated by this constitution; but the same shall remain precisely in the situation which they were before the adoption of this constitution, unless otherwise herein provided.

"Sec. 21. The Legislature shall prescribe by law the qualication of grand and petit jurors.

"Sec. 22. The Legislature shall, at its first session, enact a law, whereby the qualified voters of any county, justice's precinct, town, or city, may by a majority vote, from time to time, determine whether the sale of intoxicating liquors, except for medicinal purposes, shall be prohibited within the prescribed limits.

"Sec. 23. All stationery, printing, paper and fuel used in the legislative and other departments of government, shall be furnished, and the printing, binding and distributing of the laws, journals, department reports, and all other printing and binding, and the repairing and furnishing the halls and rooms used for the meetings of the Legislature and its committees, shall be performed under contract, to be given to the lowest responsible bidder, below such maximum price, and under such regulations as shall be prescribed by law. No member or officer of any department of the government shall be, in any way, interested in such contracts; and all such contracts shall be subject to the approval of the Governor, Secretary of State and Comptroller.

"Sec. 24. The Legislature shall pass general laws, authorizing any county in the State, by a vote of two-thirds of the qualified voters, voting at any general election, to adopt a fence system in such county, for the protection of farmers and stock-raisers.

"Sec. 25. The Legislature shall make provision for laying out and working public roads, for the building of bridges, and for utilizing fines, forfeitures, and convict labor to all these purposes.

"Sec. 26. That all drawbacks and rebatement of insurance, freight, transportation, carriage, wharfage, storage, compressing, bailing, repairing, or for any other kind of labor or service of or to any cotton, grain, or any other produce or article of commerce, in this State paid or allowed, or contracted for, to any common carrier, shipper, merchant, commission merchant, factor, agent, or middle-man, of any kind, not the true and absolute owner thereof, are forever prohibited, and it shall be the duty of the Legislature to pass effective laws punishing as felons all persons in this State who pay, receive, or contract for, or respect the same.

"Sec. 27. Every person, corporation or company that may commit a homicide through willful act or omission, shall be responsible, in exemplary damages, to the surviving husband, widow, heirs of his or her body, or such of them as there may be, without regard to any criminal proceeding that may or may not be had in relation to the homicide.

"Sec. 28. The Legislature may provide that in counties bordering on the Rio Grande river, in which two-thirds of the resident population do not speak or understand the English language, that the proceedings in the trial of causes in the District Court may be conducted in the Spanish language; but shall in every instance be entered in English on the minutes of the court; the fact as to two-thirds of the population being ignorant of the English language to be ascertained or shall be prescribed by law.

"Sec. 29. No current wages for personal services shall ever be the subject of garnishment.

"Sec. 30. The Legislature shall provide by law for defining and punishing barratry, champerty and maintenance.

"Sec. 31. The duration of all offices, not fixed by this constitution, shall never exceed two years as the period of office.

"Sec. 32. The accounting officers of this State shall neither draw nor pay a warrant upon the treasury, in favor of any person, for salary or compensation as agent, officer or appointee, who holds, at the same time, any other office or position of honor, trust or profit under the State or United States, except as prescribed in this constitution.

"Sec. 33. The Legislature shall, at its first session, pass laws to protect laborers on public buildings, streets, roads, railroads, canals and other similar public works, against the failure of contractors and sub-contractors to pay their current wages when due, and to make the corporation, company or individual for whose benefit the work is done responsible for their ultimate payment.

"Sec. 43. The Legislature shall, at its first session, provide for the payment or funding, as they may deem best, of the amounts found to be justly due to the teachers in the public schools, for services rendered prior to the first day of July, A. D. 1873.

"Sec. 35. Mechanics and artisans of every class have a lien upon the articles manufactured or repaired by them, for the value of their labor done thereon, or materials furnished therefor; and the Legislature shall provide by law for the speedy and efficient enforcement of said liens.

"Sec. 36. The Legislature may, at such time as the public interest may require, provide for the office of Commissioner of Insurance, Statistics and History, whose terms of office, duties and salary may be prescribed by law.

"Sec. 37. Treason against this State shall consist only in levying war against it, or in adhering to its enemies, giving them aid and comfort; and no person shall be convicted of treason, unless on the testimony of two witnesses to the same overt act, or his own confession in open court.

"Sec. 38. The Legislature may, from time to time, make appropriations for preserving and perpetuating memorials of the history of Texas, by means of monuments, statues, paintings, and documents of historical value.

"Sec. 39. No person shall hold or exercise, at the same time, more than one civil office of emolument, except that of Justice of the Peace, Notary Public, and Postmaster, unless otherwise specially provided herein.

"Sec. 40. Any person who shall, directly or indirectly, offer, give, or promise any money, or thing of value, testimonial, privlege, or personal advantage, to any executive or judicial officer or mumber of the Legislature, to influence him in the performance of any of his public or official duties, shall be guilty of bribery, and be punished in such manner as shall be provided by law.   And any member of the Legislature, or executive or judicial officer, who shall solicit, demand, or receive, or consent to receive, directly or indirectly, for himself or for another, from any company, corporation, or person, any money, appointment, employment, testimonial, reward, thing of value or enjoyment, or of personal advantage, or promise thereof, for his vote or official influence, or for withholding the same, or with any understanding, expressed or implied, that his vote or official action shall be in any way influenced thereby; or who shall solocit or demand and receive any such money or other advantage, matter or thing, aforesaid, for another as the consideration of his vote or official influence, in consideration of the payment or promise of such money, advantage, matter, or thing to another, shall be held guilty of bribery, within the meaning of this constitution, and shall incur the disabilities provided for said offenses, with a forfeiture of the office or position they may hold, and such other additional punishment as is or shall be provided by law.

" Sec 41. The Legislature may establish an Inebriate Asylum for the cure of drunkenness and reform of inebriates.

" Sec 42. No man or set of men shall ever be exempted, relieved or discharged from the performance of any public duty or service imposed by general law by any special law; exemptions from the performance of such public duty or service shall only be made by general law.

" Sec. 43. The Legislature shall prescribe the duties, and provide for the election, by the qualified voters of each county in this State, a County Treasurer, who shall reside at the county seat, and hold his office for two years and until his successor is qualified, and shall have such compensation as may be provided by law.

" Sec. 44. It shall be the duty of the Legislature to provide for collecting, arranging, and safely keeping such records, rolls, correspondence and other documents, civil and military, relating to the history of Texas, as may be now in the possession of parties willing to confide them to the care and preservation of the State.

" Sec. 45. The Legislature shall provide by law for organizing and disciplining the militia of this State in such manner as they shall deem expedient, not incompatible with the constitution and laws of the Unted States.

" Sec. 46.　Any person who conscientiously scruples to bear arms shall not be compelled to do so, but shall pay an equivalent for personal service.

" Sec. 47. All laws and parts of laws now in force in the State of Texas, which are not repugnant to the constitution of the United States or to this constitution, shall continue and remain in force as the laws of this State until they expire by their own limitation, or shall be amended or repealed by the Legislature.

" Sec. 48. The Legislature shall have power, and it shall be its duty to protect by law from forced sale a certain portion of the personal property of all heads of families, and also of unmarried adults, male and female.

" Sec. 49. The homestead of a family shall be, and is hereby protected from forced sale for the payment of all debts, except for the purchase money thereof, or a part of such purchase money, the taxes due thereon, or for work and material used in constructing improvements thereon, and in this last case only when the work and material are contracted for in writing, with the consent of the wife given in the same manner as is required in making a sale and conveyance of the homestead; nor shall the owner, if a married man, sell the homestead without the consent of the wife, given in such manner as may be prescribed by law, but he shall have the power, with the consent of the wife, to mortgage or execute a deed of trust on the same.

" Sec 50. The homestead, not in a town or city, shall consist of not more than two hundred acres of land, which may be in one or more parcels; the homestead in a city, town, or village shall consist of lot or lots not to exceed in value five thousand dollars at the time of their designation as a homestead, without reference to the value of any improvements thereon.

" Sec. 51. On the death of the husband or wife, or both, the homestead shall descend and vest in like manner as other real property of the deceased, and shall be governed by the same laws of descent and distribution, but it shall not be partitioned among the heirs of the deceased during the lifetimes of the surviving husband or wife, or so long as the survivor may elect to use or occupy the same as a homestead, or so long as the guardian of the minor children of the deceased may be permitted, under the order of the proper court having jurisdiction, to use and occupy the same.

" Sec. 52. The Legislature shall, at its first session, provide for the registration and designation of the homestead, and after such designation, in accordance with the law, to be passed for that purpose, no claim of homestead shall be entertained, unless the homestead be registered or occupied by the owner in person, or by agent or tenant, and any property claimed and registered as a homestead shall be liable to forced sale to satisfy any lien or mrotgage that may have been created thereon prior to its designation as such.

" Sec. 53. That no inconvenience may arise from the adoption of this constitution, it is declared that all process and writs of all kinds which have been or may be issued and not returned or executed when this constitution is adopted, shall remain valid, and shall not be in any way affected by the adoption of this constitution.

" Sec. 54. It shall be the duty of the Legislature to provide for the custody and maintenance of indigent lunatics, at the expense of the State, under such regulations and restrictions as the Legislaure may prescribe.

" Sec. 55. The Legislature may provide annual pensions, not to exceed one hundred and fifty dollars per annum, to surviving soldiers and volunteers in the war between Texas and Mexico, from the commencement of the revolution in 1835 until the 1st of January, 1837, and also to the surviving signers of the declaration of the independence of Texas; *provided,* that no such pension be granted except to those in indigent circumstances, proof of which shall be made before the County Court of the county where the applicant resides, in such manner as may be provided by law."

On motion of Mr. West, two hundred copies of the report and article were ordered printed.

Mr. Darnell gave notice of a counter report on that part of the article allowing homesteads to be mortgaged.

On motion of Mr. Fleming, Mr. Kilgore was added to Committee on Judicial Apportionment.

On motion of Mr. German, Mr. Dohoney was added to said committee.

On motion of Mr. McCormick, Mr. Blassingame was added to the same committee.

Mr. Dohoney moved to reconsider the vote taken yesterday refusing to adopt Mr. Norvell's substitute for the article on judiciary pending.

Unfinished business—"Art. —, Judiciary," was taken up.

[Mr. Stockdale in the chair.]

Mr. Regan's amendments being under consideration, Mr. McCormick moved to close debate on the amendments, and bring the Convention to a direct vote.

On motion of Mr. Regan, a call of the Convention was ordered.

On motion of Mr. Mills, Mr. Brady was excused, on account of sickness.

On motion of Mr. Moore, Mr. Erhard was excused.

On motion of Mr. Flanagan, Mr. Russell, of Harrison, was excused for three days from to-day.

The roll was then called.

Absent—Messrs. Blake, Johnson of Collin, and Cook of Gonzales.

On motion of Mr. Burleson, Mr. Cook, of Gonzales, was excused, on account of sickness.

Mr. McCormick moved to suspend the call.

Lost.

The pending question went to the table temporarily, and "Art. —, Legislative Apportionment," was taken up and read a second time.

36

Mr. Martin, of Hunt, moved to dispense with the reading of the article.

Lost.

Mr. Allison offered the following amendments:

1. In line 6, after the word "Liberty," insert the word "Chambers."

2. In line 40 strike out the word "Montgomery."

3. In line 41 strike out the word "Montgomery," and insert the word "Waller."

4. In line 42 strike out the word "Chambers," and insert "Montgomery."

5. In line 84, after the word "Liberty," insert the word "Chambers."

6. In line 15 strike out the word "Chambers," and insert the word "Montgomery."

Messrs. Johnson, of Collin, and Blake having appeared, the call was exhausted, and the Convention resumed consideration of "Article —, Judiciary."

Mr. McCormick's motion to close debate was carried.

The question on the adoption of Mr. Reagan's amendments was put and amendments adopted by the following vote:

YEAS—Abernathy, Allison, Barnett, Blassingame, Brown, Bruce, Burleson, Chambers, Cooke of San Saba, Darnell, Davis of Wharton, Flournoy, Gaither, German, Graves, Haynes, Henry of Limeston, Holt, Johnson of Collin, Johnson of Franklin, Killough, Lacy, Lynch, McKinney of Denton, Mills, Martin of Navarro, Ramey, Reagan, Robertson of Bell, Ross, Russell of Wood, Sansom, Scott, Sessions, Spikes, Wade, Weaver, Whitehead—38.

NAYS—Abner, Ballinger, Blake, Cline, Cooley, Crawford, Davis of Brazos, DeMorse, Dillard, Dohoney, Douglas, Ferris, Flanagan, Fleming, Ford, Lockett, McCormick, McKinney of Walker, McLean, Mitchell, Moore, Morris, Murphy, Martin of Hunt, Norvell, Nugent, Nunn, Pauli, Robinson of Fayette, Smith, Stayton, Stewart, Stockdale, Waelder, West, Whitfield—36.

Mr. Kilgore stated that he was paired off with Mr. Henry, of Smith, but for which fact he would vote "yea."

Mr. Murphy asked to be excused from voting. The Convention refused to excuse him.

On motion of Mr. Sansom, the Convention adjourned to 2½ o'clock P. M.

EVENING SESSION—2½ o'clock.

Convention met pursuant to adjournment; roll called; quorum present.

"Article —, on Judiciary," again taken up.

Mr. McCormick offered the following as a substitute for section 2 of the Article:

"Sec. 2. The Supreme Court shall consist of six Justices, who shall be elected by the qualified voters of this State, at a general election held for members of the Legislature. Each of said Justices, at the time of his election, shall be a citizen of the United States, at least thirty years of age, and a practicing attorney-at-law, in this State, of at least seven years standing; they shall hold their offices for a term of .... years from the date of their election, unless sooner removed, as may be provided by law, or until their successors are qualified, and a vacancy in said court may be filled as is now or may hereafter be provided by law. At the first session of the Supreme Court after the election thereof, the said Justices shall elect one of their own number to the office of Chief Justice, who shall be the presiding justice of said court; and said Chief Justice, at each term of said court, shall assign three of said court to the hearing and determining of the civil causes pending therein, and three of said court to the hearing and determining of the criminal causes pending therein, and the concurrence of all three of said court thus assigned to either branch of said court shall be necessary to the determination of any cause pending before them; but should the Justices so assigned fail to agree upon any cause submitted to them, in such case, the Chief Justice shall convene the court in *banc* for a decision of said cause, and whenever, in the opinion of three Justices of said court, it is necessary or proper, in the decision of any cause, to take the opinion of the whole court, the Chief Justice shall convene the court in *banc,* and take their opinion upon the cause; and the opinion of the majority shall be the judgment of the court. The Chief Justice shall not assign any Justice of said court, either to the civil or criminal department thereof, for more than one term in succession, without the consent of said Justice. The Justices of the Supreme Court shall each receive an annual salary of four thousand dollars, which shall be paid by the State."

Lost.

Mr. Whitfield offered the following substitute for sections 2 and 6:

"Sec. 2. The State shall be divided into five judicial departments, as nearly equal in population as conveniently may be. There shall be elected in each of these departments, by the qualified voters thereof, one Justice of the Supreme Court, and five District Judges, at elections held for members of the Legislature. Each Justice of the Supreme Court, at the time of his election, shall be a citizen of the United States, at least thirty years of age, and have been a practicing lawyer or judge of the court of record, either or both, for at least seven years in this State, and have resided two years next preceding his election in the department in which he is elected. He shall receive a salary of .... dollars per annum, which amount shall not be increased or diminished during his term of office. The term of the Justices of the Supreme Court shall be eight years. The Justices of the Supreme Court shall select from their number from time to time, with reference to a dispatch of business, a presiding justice.

"Sec. 6. Each judicial department of this State shall be divided into five judicial districts. One of the five judges of the District Court elected in each department shall be chosen from each of said districts. Each District Judge shall be at least twenty-five years of age, shall be a citizen of the United States, shall have been a practicing attorney in the courts of this State for five years, and a resident of the district from which he comes for one year; he shall receive an annual salary of .... dollars, which shall not be increased or diminished during his term of office. The District Court shall be held at one place in each county in the State regularly, at least twice in each year, in such manner as may be prescribed by law. The Legislature may provide by general law for the holding of special terms of the District Court, when necessary for the dispatch of business, and shall provide for the holding of the District Court when the judge thereof is absent, or is from any cause disabled or disqualified. The term of the District Judges shall be six years."

On motion of Mr. Allison, the Convention adjourned to 9 o'clock A. M. to-morrow.

FIFTY-THIRD DAY.

HALL OF REPRESENTATIVES, }
AUSTIN, TEXAS, November 5, 1875. }

Convention met pursuant to adjournment; roll called; quorum present. Prayer by the Rev. W. H. Dodge, of the Baptist Church, at Austin.

Journal of yesterday read and adopted.

On motion of Mr. Haynes, Mr. Burleson was excused until Monday morning.

On motion of Mr. Stockdale, Mr. Nunn was added to Committee on Impeachment.

On motion of Mr. Norvell, Mr. Henry, of Limestone, was added to Committee on Judicial Apportionment.

UNFINISHED BUSINESS.

"Article ——, Judicial Department," taken up.

Mr. Flournoy offered the following substitute for the entire article:

"ARTICLE ——.
" JUDICIAL DEPARTMENT.

" Section 1. The judicial power of this State shall be vested in one Supreme Court, in District Courts, and in such inferior courts as the Legislature may from time to time ordain and establish, and such jurisdiction may be vested in corporation courts as may be deemed necessary, and be directed by law.

" Sec. 2. The Supreme Court shall consist of a Chief Justice and .... Associate Justices, any three of whom shall form a quorum.

" Sec. 3. The Supreme Court shall have appellate jurisdiction only, which shall be co-extensive with the limits of the State, but in criminal cases only those of the grade of felony, and in civil cases only when the amount involved, exclusive of interest and costs, shall exceed the sum of two hundred dollars; and in appeals from interlocutory judgments, with such exceptions and under such regulations as the Legislature shall make. And the Supreme Court and Judges thereof shall have power to issue the writ of *habeas corpus,* and, under such regulations as may be prescribed by law, may issue writs of *mandamus,* and such other writs as shall be necessary to enforce its own jurisdiction, and also compel a Judge of the District Court to proceed to trial and judgment in a cause. And the Supreme Court shall hold its sessions once every year, between the months of October and June, inclusive, at not more than three places in the State.

" Sec. 4. The Supreme Court shall appoint its own clerks, who shall hold their offices for four years, and be subject to removal by the said court for neglect of duty, misdemeanor in office, and such other causes as may be prescribed by law.

" Sec. 5. The Judges of the Supreme Court shall be elected by the qualified electors of the State at a general election, and shall hold their offices for the period of six years, and shall receive a salary of not more than four thosuand dollars annually.

"Sec. 6. The State shall be divided into convenient judicial districts, and for each district there shall be elected a judge, who shall reside in the same, and who shall receive as a salary not more than .... dollars annually, and who shall hold courts at one place in each county, and at least twice in each year, in such manner as may be prescribed by law, and may be required by law to hold terms of their court more than twice annually in any county, should the Legislature so direct.

"Sec. 7. Salaries of Supreme or District Judges shall not be increased or diminished during the term of office for which they may have been elected.

"Sec. 8. The Judges of the Supreme and District Courts shall be removed by the Governor, on the address of two-thirds of each house of the Legislature, for willful neglect of duty, or other reasonable cause which shall not be sufficient ground for impeachment; *provided, however,* that the cause or causes for which such removal shall be required shall be stated at length in such address, and entered on the journals of each house; *and provided, further,* that the cause or causes shall be notified to the judge so intended to be removed, and he shall be admitted to a hearing in his own defense before any vote for such address shall pass; and in all such cases the vote shall be taken by yeas and nays, and entered on the journals of each house respectively.

"Sec. 9. All Judges of the Supreme and District Courts shall, by virtue of their offices, be conservators of the peace throughout the State. The style of all writs and process shall be 'The State of Texas.' All prosecutions shall be carried on in the name and by the authority of the 'State of Texas,' and conclude 'against the peace and dignity of the State.'

"Sec. 10. The District Court shall have original jurisdiction of all cases of felony, of all suits in behalf of the State to recover penalties, forfeitures, and escheats, and of all cases of divorce, and of all suits, complaints and pleas whatever, without regard to and distinction between law and equity, when the matter in controversy shall be valued at or amount to two hundred dollars, exclusive of interest; and the said courts, or the judges thereof, shall have power to issue all writs necessary to enforce their own jurisdiction, and to give them a general superintendence and control over inferior jurisdictions. And in the trial of all criminal cases the jury trying the same shall find and assess the amount of punishment to be inflicted or fine imposed, except in capital cases, and where the punishment or fine imposed shall be specifically imposed by law; and shall have general supervision and power after judgment to remove, by *certiorari,* all causes from the Justices' Court and hear the same *de novo,* but no cause shall be removable from the Justice to the District Court until the party desiring to remove the same shall have first paid all the costs of such Justice Court, or made affidavit of inability to pay the same. And the same rule shall apply in all cases of appeal or writ of error from the District to the Supreme Court.

"Sec. 11. There shall be elected in each county five Justices of the Peace (the number to be increased in any county as the County Court, under the direction of the Legislature, may provide), one Sheriff, one Coroner, and a sufficient number of Constables, who shall hold their offices for two years. Justices of the Peace, Sheriffs and Coroners shall be commissioned by the Governor.

"The Sheriff shall not be eligible for more than four years in every six.

"Sec. 12. No Judge shall sit in any case wherein he may be interested, or where either of the parties may be connected with him by affinity or consanguinity, within such degrees as may be prescribed by law, or where he shall have been of counsel in the cause. When the Supreme Court or any two of its members shall be thus qualified to hear and determine any cause or causes in said court, or when no judgment can be rendered in any case of cases in said court, by reason of equal division of opinion of said judges, the same shall be certified to the Governor of the State, who shall immediately commission the requisite number of persons, learned in the law for the trial and determination of said case or cases. When judges of the District Courts are thus disqualified, the parties may, by consent, appoint a proper person to try said case; and the judges of the said courts may exchange districts, or hold courts for each other when they may deem it expedient, and *shall* do so when directed by law. The disqualification of judges of inferior tribunals shall be remedied as may hereafter be by law prescribed.

"Sec. 13. Inferior tribunals shall be established in each county for appointing guardians, granting titles testamentary and of administration; for settling the accounts of executors, administrators and guardians, and for the transaction of business appertaining to estates, and for the transaction of such other business as the Legislature may provide. And the District Courts shall have original and appellate jurisdiction and general control over the said inferior tribunals, and original jurisdiction and control over executors, administrators, guardians and minors, under such regulations as may be prescribed by law.

"Sec. 16. In the trial of all causes in equity in the District

Court, the plaintiff or defendant shall, upon application made in open court, have the right of trial by jury, to be governed by the rules and regulations prescribed in trials at law.

"Sec. 17. Justices of the Peace shall have original jurisdiction to try all misdemeanors, and all civil causes when the matter (not involving the title to real estate) involved shall not exceed the sum of two hundred dollars, and such other civil and criminal jurisdiction as the Legislature may provide.

"Sec. 18. In all cases arising out of a contract before any inferior judicial tribunal, when the amount in controversy shall exceed ten dollars, the plaintiff or defendant shall, upon application to the presiding officer, have the right of trial by jury.

"Sec. 19. In all criminal cases before Justices of the Peace the accused shall be entitled to demand a trial by a jury of six competent jurors, and six jurors shall always be a full panel on trials in the Justices' Courts.

BURGLARY OR ROBBERY.

"Sec. 20. Theft of property of the value of thirty dollars, unless accompanied by threats, shall never reach the grade of felony.

"Sec. 21. It shall be the duty of the Legislature to provide, at it first session after the adoption of this constitution, for the working of convicts, sentenced to the jail, in such mode as may be prescribed by law."

The substitute was received, and two hundred copies ordered printed for use of the Convention.

[Mr. Brown in the chair.]

Mr. Scott moved to have two hundred copies of the pending article as amended, and pending amendments, printed for use of the Convention; and that a further consideration of the article be postponed until to-morrow morning, at 10 o'clock.

Carried by the following vote:

YEAS—Abernathy, Abner, Allison, Ballinger, Barnett, Blassingame, Brown, Bruce, Chambers, Cline, Cooke of San Saba, Darnell, Davis of Brazos, DeMorse, Douglas, Ferris, Flanagan, Fleming Flournoy, Ford, Gaither, Graves, Haynes, Henry of Limestone, Holt, Johnson of Collin, Killough, Lacy, Lockett, Lynch, McCormick, McKinney of Denton, McKinney of Walker, McLean, Mills, Moore, Morris, Martin of Navarro, Martin of Hunt, Norvell, Nugent, Ramey, Reagan, Robertson of Bell, Robison of Fayette, Ross, Russell of Wood, Sansom, Scott, Sessions, Smith, Spikes, Stewart, Stockdale, Wade, Waelder, West, Whitehead, Whitfield—59.

NAYS—Cooley, Dohoney, Kilgore, Murphy, Nunn, Pauli—6.

Mr. Darnell submitted the following report:

COMMITTEE ROOM, }
AUSTIN, November 5, 1875. }

To the Hon. E. B. Pickett, President of the Convention:

SIR—The undersigned, members of the Committee on General Provisions, avail themselves of the notice given yesterday by the delegate from Tarrant, to place upon the journals of the Convention our objections to that clause in the report of the committee in relation to homestead exemptions, in so far as it fails to guard the homestead against incumbrance by way of mortgtge or deed of trust. The committee at one time inserted such a clause in the section, whereby no lien by way of mortgage or deed of trust, except for the purchase money, material furnished or labor performed, could be created; but, at its last meeting, in the absence of several members, that provision was stricken out.

We hold that, after thirty years experience, the homestead exemption is a principle cherished by the people of Texas. We believe it to be of essential value to the State in securing an industrious and law-abiding population. Its origin in the constitution of 1845, its very birth, was in the noblest sentiment of the human heart. It sought, first, to encourage the struggling husband and wife to secure by honest industry a homestead, and, when secured, to protect the wife and children in their shelter, thus acquired, against the calamities of whatsoever kind, even the death of the husband and father. It has proven a shield to thousands and tens of thousands of widowed mothers and their children, and has in cases without number saved the fathers of families from absolute penury. The theory of the homestead exemption is, that no one has any right to grant credit to the head of a family on the faith of the homestead. The creditor must know that it is sacred and beyond his reach. Being forewarned, he can not complain. Besides, it is not the policy of Texas to encourage the credit system, which has periodically engulphed in disaster almost every State in the South and West. On the contrary, sound public policy, based upon demonstrated experience, demands that government should rather restrict than encourage the system of credits in the business of life.

Such being the case and the principles of homestead exemption resting on the highest principles of governmental beneficence, it follows as a part of the life of the system, that no creditor should be allowed, or even tempted, to credit the unfortunate or failing husband on the faith of a lien, mortgage, or deed of trust on the homestead. Experience shows that in case innumerable unfortunate but honorable husbands tempt their confiding wives to sign such liens, guaranteeing extravagant interest, and in nine cases out of ten disappointment and domestic ruin is the result. The essence of the exemption being an act of beneficence, we protest against its destruction in the only cases where it is a real act of protection to the wife and children.

Beyond all this, we hold as a primary truth of inestimable value, that the principle of homestead exemption is the grandest foundation yet conceived, upon which to build up in our State an industrious, independent, self-sustaining and land-holding yeomanry, who shall forever be the great pillars of the State.

We therefore recommend the adoption of the accompanying amendment to the section.

N. H. DARNELL,
JOHN HENRY BROWN,
CHARLES DeMORSE,
MARION MARTIN,
GEO. FLOURNOY,
J. S. MILLS,
F. S. STOCKDALE,
A. T. McKINNEY,
JONATHAN RUSSELL,
WM. H STEWART,
J. F. JOHNSON,
A majority of the Committee.

Strike out the last sentence of section 49, and insert "all mortgages, deeds of trust and other liens created on the homestead, after the adoption of this constitution, shall be null and void, except as in section — provided."

On motion of Mr. Darnell, two hundred copies of the report and amendment were ordered printed.

"Article—, Legislative Apportionment," taken up.

The amendment offered by Mr. Allison on yesterday, adopted

Mr. Kilgore moved to consider the article section by section.

Mr. Whitfield moved the previous question on the engrossment of the article. Carried.

Mr. Kilgore's motion to consider the article section by section was lost.

The question on the engrossment of the article was put, and articlle ordered engrossed by the following vote:

YEAS—Abernathy, Allison, Ballinger, Barnett, Blake, Blassingame, Brown, Chambers, Cline, Cook of San Saba, Darnell, Dillard, Douglas, Fleming, Flournoy, Ford, Gaither, Graves, Haynes, Henry of Limestone, Holt, Johnson of Collin, Johnson of Franklin, Lacy, Lynch, McCormick, McKinney of Denton, McKinney of Walker, Moore, Morris, Murphy, Martin of Navarro, Norvell, Nugent, Ramey, Robertson of Bell, Robison of Fayette, Ross, Sansom, Scott, Sessions, Smith, Spikes, Stewart, Stockdale, Wade, Weaver, Whitehead, Whitfield—50.

NAYS—Abner, Brady, Bruce, Cooley, DeMorse, Dohoney, Flanagan, German, Kilgore, Lockett, McLean, Mills, Mitchell, Martin of Hunt, Pauli, Russell of Wood, Stayton, West—18.

"Article —, Immigration," on its third and final reading, taken up. Read third time.

Mr. Stewart offered the following amendment:

Strike out the words "Bureau of Immigration."

Mr. Dillard moved to lay the amendment on the table.

Carried by the following vote:

YEAS—Abernathy, Allison, Barnett, Blassingame, Bruce, Chambers, Cooke of San Saba, Darnell, Dillard, Dohoney, Douglas, Flournoy, Gaither, German, Graves, Haynes, Holt, Johnson of Collin, Johnson of Franklin, Killough, Lacy, McKinney of Denton, McLean, Mills, Murphy, Martin of Navarro, Martin of Hunt, Norvell, Nugent, Ramey, Robertson of Bell, Robison of Fayette, Ross, Russell of Wood, Sansom, Scott, Sessions, Spikes, Wade, Weaver, Whitehead—41.

NAYS—Abner, Ballinger, Blake, Brady, Brown, Cline, Cooley, Davis of Wharton, DeMorse, Ferris, Flanagan, Fleming, Ford, Henry of Limestone, Kilgore, Lockett, Lynch, McCormick, McKinney of Walker, Mitchell, Moore, Morris, Nunn, Pauli, Reagan, Smith, Stayton, Stewart, Stockdale, Waelder, West—31.

A message was received from his Excellency, the Governor.

The question then recurring on the passage of the "Article on Immigration," it was passed by the following vote:

YEAS—Abernathy, Abner, Allison, Barnett, Blassingame, Bruce, Chambers, Cooke of San Saba, Crawford, Dillard, Dohoney, Douglas, Ferris, Gaither, German, Graves, Haynes, Holt, Johnson of Collin, Johnson of Franklin, Kilgore, Killough, Lacy, McKinney of Denton, McLean, Murphy, Martin of Navarro, Martin of Hunt, Norvell, Nugent, Ramey, Robertson of Bell, Robison of Fayette, Ross, Russell of Wood, Sansom, Scott, Sessions, Spikes, Wade, Weaver, Whitehead—42.

NAYS—Ballinger, Blake, Brady, Brown, Cline, Cooley, Davis of Wharton, DeMorse, Flanagan, Fleming, Ford, Henry of Limestone, Lockett, Lynch, McCormick, McKinney of Walker, Mills, Mitchell, Moore, Morris, Nunn, Pauli, Reagan, Smith, Stayton, Stewart, Stockdale, Waelder, West, Whitfield—30.

The article on "Railroads," on its third reading, was then taken up.

Mr. Pickett prepared to amend section 2 by striking out all of the section down to and including the word "carries," in line 11.

Mr. Stockdale propsed to amend section 2 by inserting after "highways," in line 10, the words "to the extent provided in the constitution and the laws of this State."

Mr. DeMorse offered the following amendment to section 2:

Strike out "declared public highways" and insert "declared to be subject to public use."

Mr. Pickett's amendment lost by the following vote:

YEAS—Abner, Allison, Barnett, Brady, Bruce, Chambers, Cline, Cooke of San Saba, Crawford, Davis of Brazos, DeMorse, Dohoney, Flanagan, Ford, Kilgor, Lockett, McLean, Mills, Mitchell, Murphy, Martin of Hunt, Norvell, Nugent, Nunn, Ramey, Sansom, Scott, Spikes, Stayton, Stewart, Stockdale, Wade, Waelder, West, Whitehead—35.

NAYS—Abernathy, Ballinger, Blassingame, Brown, Darnell, Dillard, Douglas, Ferris, Fleming, Flournoy, Gaither, German, Graves, Haynes, Henry of Limestone, Holt, Johnson of Collin, Johnson of Franklin, Lynch, McKinney of Walker, Moore, Morris, Martin of Navarro, Pauli, Reagan, Robertson of Bell, Robison of Fayette, Ross, Russell of Wood, Sessions, Smith, Weaver, Whitfield—33.

Mr. Pickett offered the following as a substitute for both pending amendments:

Amend section 2 by inserting after the word "highways," in line 10, the words "so far only as to authorize the State to regulate and control them."

Lost.

Mr. Stockdale's amendment lost.

The following communication from the Governor was read:

EXECUTIVE OFFICE, STATE OF TEXAS,
AUSTIN, November 5, 1875.

To the Hon. E. B. Pickett, President of the Convention:

SIR—I have the honor to hand you herewith a detailed statement made to this office by the Comptroller of Public Accounts, giving the information with reference to the public debt of the State, asked by resolution of the Honorable Convention passed on the 27th day of October. Very respectfully.

RICHARD COKE, Governor.

COMPTROLLER'S REPORT.

Austin, October 29, 1875. }
Comptroller's Office, }

To His Excellency, Richard Coke, Governor:

Sir:—In response to your communication of the 27th instant, enclosing a copy of a resolution passed by the honorable Convention, requesting certain information, I beg leave to hand you the following statements, made from data in this office.

Very respectfully,   Stephen H. Darden, Comptroller.

Statement showing the amount, etc., of State bonds

DATE OF SALE.	NO. SOLD.	DENOMINATION.	UNDER WHAT LAW ISSUED.	RATE OF INTEREST.	AT WHAT PRICE SOLD.	TO WHOM SOLD.
1871.......	82	$1000	Act May 19,'71	10 per cent.	90c....	....
	5	"	"	"	92c....	
1872 Jan 2	88	"	"	"	90& int	Schuyler, Hartly & Graham
1871 Dec 80	86	"	"	"	95c....	Eugene Bremond
80	88	"	"	"	95& int	B. M. Odom
80	15	"	"	"	95& int	Sampson & He'ks
1872 Jan 2	50	"	"	"	90c....	Raym'd & Whitis
2	8	"	"	"	95c....	Wm. H. Sinclair
1871 Ap'l 26	6	"	Act Aug. 5, '70	7 per ct. gld	90c....	Geo. S. Bowdoin
May 20	100	"	"	"	90c....	Texas A. & M. Col
Ap'l 27	51	"	"	"	90c....	Rhodius & Co.
May 29	6	"	"	"	90c....	Geo. S. Bowdoin
May 28	18	"	"	"	90c....	S Antonio Na B'k
July 28	68	"	"	"	90c....	Texas A. & M. Col
July 26	7	"	"	"	90c....	Rhodius & Co.
Sept. 8	42	"	"	"	86c....	Winchester Repeating Arms Co.
Sept. 28	25	"	"	"	90c....	Raym'd & Whitis
July 26	1	"	"	"	90c....	Brown & Martin.
Dec. 21	6	"	"	"	90c....	Texas A. & M. Col
Dec. 9	12	"	"	"	90c....	Raym'd & Whitis
Dec. 9	8	"	"	"	90c....	J. T. Breckenridge
	607					

Recapitulation.

Bonds Sold.	Amount of Bonds sold.	Gross am't Rec'd.	Expenses.	Net am't Rec'd.
607	$607,000 00	$549,170 94	$7,595 00	$541,575 94

sold during Governor Davis's administration.

GROSS AMOUNT RECEIVED	EXPENSES OF SALE	NET AMOUNT RECEIVED	
			Interest and principal payable in cur.
$78,432 50			" " " " "
29,757 78			" " " " "
34,200 00			" " " " "
31,360 66			" " " " "
14,250 00			" " " " "
45,000 00			" " " " "
2,850 00	$6475 00	$229,375 94	Of this amount, $156,433.47 was received in State Warrants.
5,400 00	60 00	5,340 00	Interest and principal payable in gold.
90,000 00	1000 00	89,000 00	" " " " "
45,900 00		45,900 00	In payment for supplies furnished the frontier for defence.
5,400 00	60 00	5,340 00	In payment of claims for supplies furnished the frontier for defence.
16,200 00		16,200 00	
61,200 00		61,200 00	In payment of claims for supplies furnished the frontier for defence.
6,300 00		6,300 00	
36,120 00		36,120 00	For arms furnished for frontier defence.
22,500 00		22,500 00	In payment of claims for supplies, etc., furnished for frontier defence.
900 00		900 00	In payment of claims for supplies, etc., furnished the frontier for defence.
5,400 00		5,400 00	In payment of claims for supplies, etc., furnished for frontier defence.
10,800 00		10,800 00	
7,200 00		7,200 00	In payment of claims for supplies, etc., furnished for frontier defence.
$549,170 94	$7595 00	$541,575 94	

NOTE — One hundred bonds of act of May 19, 1871, of $1000 each, and three hundred and fifty bonds of August 5, 1870, were hypothecated with Messrs. Williams & Guion, of New York, for $327,074 70. Upon the settlement with Messrs. Williams & Guion, by Governor Coke, these bonds were relieved, and the three hundred and fifty of act of August 5, 1870, sold—per statement of Governor Coke's sales. Of the one hundred bonds of act of May 19, 1871, twenty were sold to Messrs. Williams & Guion, in settlement, and the remaining eighty returned to the State treasury.

DATE OF SALE.	NO. SOLD.	UNDER WHAT LAW ISSUED.	WHEN DUE.	AT WHAT PRICE SOLD.
1874—Aug. 6	500	Act Mar. 4, 1874	In 30 years.	85c. Flat.
" 18	150	" "	"	do
Sept. 3	50	" "	"	85c. and 15 days int.
" 10	300	" "	"	85c. and 23 days int.
Nov. 13	4	Act Dec. 2, 1871	In 20 years.	85c. and 4½ mos. int.
Dec. 30	10	" "	"	85c. less 3 days int.
" 31	5	" "	"	85c. flat
1875—Jan. 2	150	" "	"	85c. less 4 mos. int.
" 2	10	" "	"	90c. flat.
" 1	6	" "	"	85c. flat.
" 25	1	" "	"	90c. and 25 days int.
Mar. 5	22	" "	"	90c. and 60 days int.
April 9	20	" "	"	93c. flat
" 13	5	" "	"	92½c. and 102 days int.
" 14	1	" "	"	93c. flat.
" 23	5	" "	"	93c. and 112 days int.
" 29	2	" "	"	94½c. flat.
May 3	5	" "	"	95c. flat.
" 14	2	" "	"	94½c. flat.
" 27	24	" "	"	94c. flat
" 27	50	" "	"	94½c. flat.
" 28	178	" "	"	94½c. flat.
1874—Aug. 29	50	August 5, 1870	In 40 years.	87¾c. flat.
Sept. 5	75	" "	"	85c. flat.
" 30	20	" "	"	do
Oct. 3	30	" "	"	do
" 3	5	" "	"	do
" 8	14	" "	"	do
" 9	3	" "	"	do
" 19	21	" "	"	85c. flat.
" 21	1	" "	"	85c. and 27 days int.
" 27	5	" "	"	85c. and 58 days int.
" 28		" "	"	85½c. flat.
" 30	13	" "	"	85c. and 1 month int.
" 30	2	" "	"	85c. and 41 days int.
Nov. 10	2	" "	"	85c. and 9 days int.
" 18	1	" "	"	85c. and 15 days int.
" 18	21	" "	"	85c. and 49 days int.
Dec. 7	2	" "	"	85c. and 67 days int.
" 9	10	" "	"	85c. and 2 mos int
" 21	5	" "	"	85c. and 81 days int.
" 22	5	" "	"	85c. and 82 days int.
" 29	1	" "	"	85c. and 89 days int.
1875—Feb. 4	30	" "	"	90c. and 126 days int.
" 24	10	" "	"	90c. and 146 days int.
" 24	1	" "	"	90c. and 176 days int.
Mar. 6	25	" "	"	92½c. and 7 days int.
" 30	46	" "	"	92c. flat.
	1900			

The above bonds are all of the denomination of $1000. The rate of RECAPITULATION.—Number of bonds sold, 1800; amount of bonds sold paid in currency, $33,022 72; net amount received in currency, $1,618,114 20. Commissions of 2 per cent. fixed by law, act of March 4, 1874, were paid

NAME OF PURCHASER.	GROSS AMOUNT REALIZED. CURRENCY.	COMMISSIONS PAID. CURRENCY.	NET AMOUNT REALIZED. CURRENCY.
Charles Morgan	$425,000 00	$8,500 00	416,500 00
James B. Colgate	127,500 00	2,550 00	124,950 00
James B. Colgate	42,623 96	852 48	41,771 48
James B. Colgate	256,341 67	5,126 83	251,214 84
J. M. Jones	3,498 00	69 96	3,428 04
G. K. Sistare	8,494 17	169 88	8,324 29
Woodward & Stillman	4,250 00	85 09	4,165 00
Charles Morgan	124,390 14	2,657 80	130,722 34
Charles Morgan	9,000 00		
W. A. Miller	5,100 00	102 00	4,998 00
Nettur & Co.	904 79	18 09	886 70
Dr. James M. Miner	20,053 15	401 07	19,652 08
J. J. Cisco & Son	18,600 09	372 00	18,228 00
Ware, Murphy & Co.	4,722 80	94 45	4,628 35
W. C. Robards	930 00	18 60	911 40
H. Portman	4,757 40	95 15	4,662 25
G. K. Sistare	1,890 00	37 80	1,852 20
Ware, Murphy & Co.	4,750 00	95 00	4,655 00
Julia C. T. Randolph	1,890 00	37 80	1,852 20
D. A. Moran	22,560 00	451 20	22,108 80
John J. Cisco & Son	47,250 00	945 00	46,305 00
C. P. Leverich	168,210 00	3,364 20	164,845 80
A. J. Nicolay	41,950 00	839 00	41,111 00
Moses Taylor	63,750 00	1,275 00	62,475 00
A. C. Downing	17,000 00	340 00	16,660 00
C. H. Mallory & Co.	25,500 00	510 00	24,990 00
John W. Lawrence	4,250 00	85 00	4,165 00
J. Rintoul	11,900 00	238 00	11,662 00
H. Gildersleeve	2,572 74	51 45	2,521 29
J. J. Hendleif	17,911 25	358 23	17,553 02
J. Rintoul	850 00	17 00	833 00
J. H. Watkinson	4,276 27	86 53	4,190 74
H. Gildersleeve	1,722 54	24 45	1,688 08
George K. Sistare	11,115 00	222 50	10,892 70
J. H. Watkinson	1,711 67	44 23	1,677 43
J. H. Brower	1,715 94	34 32	1,681 62
J. H. Brower	859 53	17 19	842 34
Ware, Murphy & Co.	18,050 08	361 00	17,689 08
J. H. Brower	1,726 04	34 52	1,691 52
M. Kopperl	8,616 67	172 33	8,444 34
Ware, Murphy & Co.	4,328 85	86 58	4,242 27
Ware, Murphy & Co.	4,329 72	86 59	4,243 13
J. H. Brower	867 30	17 35	849 95
C. H. Mallory & Co.	27,724 93	554 49	27,170 44
C. H. Mallory & Co.	9,280 00	185 60	9,094 40
William Brady	933 75	18 67	915 08
George K. Sistare	23,158 56	463 17	22,695 39
C. H. Mallory &Co.	42,320 00	846 40	41,472 60
	$1,651,136 92	$33,022 72	$1,618,114 20

interest is 7 per cent. Principal and interest payable in gold.
$1,900,000; gross amount received in currency $1,651,136 92; commissions

W. L. Moody, agent for the sale of above bonds.
37

Richard Coke, Governor, in bond

Dr.

		CURRENCY.
To amount realized as above from the sale of bonds	$1,618,114 20	
To interest, 179 days at 3 per cent. on $15,000 deposited with United States Trust Company, of New York, subject to the decision of the arbitrators in the disagreement between W. L. Moody, Financial Agent of the State of Texas, and Messrs. Williams & Guion	222 50	$1,618,336 70

account with the State of Texas.

Cr.

DATE.			CURRENCY.
1874.			
August	15	By amount paid into the Treasury per deposit No. 953.........................	$415,000 00
August	29	By amount paid into the Treasury per deposit No. 1093........................	127,500 00
September	15	By amount paid Williams & Guion per their receipt...........................	101,645 02
September	18	By amount paid into the Treasury per deposit Nos. 22, 38.....................	298,965 63
October	7	By amount paid Williams & Guion per their receipt...........................	45,815 00
October	27	By amount paid Williams & Guion per their receipt...........................	.36,247 19
October	31	By amount paid Williams & Guion per their receipt...........................	14,258 22
November	19	By amount paid Williams & Guion per their receipt...........................	5,109 66
November	30	By amount paid Williams & Guion per their receipt...........................	18,531 42
Dec.	8, 22	By amount paid Williams & Guion per their receipt...........................	18,621 26
1875.			
January	4	By amount paid Williams & Guion per their receipt...........................	100,000 00
January	25	By amount paid into the State Treasury per deposit No. 509...................	27,761 67
February	20	By amount paid into the State Treasury per deposit No. 608...................	28,000 00
March	8, 22	By amount paid into the State Treasury per deposits 672, 735, 764..............	52,356 95
April	6, 24	By amount paid into the State Treasury per deposits 845, 846, 903.............	65,241 35
May	11, 19	By amount paid into the State Treasury per deposits 960, 975.................	11,169 45
June	8	By amount paid into the State Treasury per deposit 1007.....................	235,111 80
September	25	By amount paid Arthur Phelps, Knowles and Ransom, N. Y., in matter of settlement with Williams & Guion...........	1,000 00
		By amount paid Williams & Guion to balance their account, per their receipt.....	14,334 59
		By amount paid Davis and Coffin, in case of Williams vs. E. J. Davis, et al..........	512 86
September	25	By amount of express charges paid in bringing money from New York..............	1,150 00
October	30	By amount paid into the State Treasury per deposit No. 98....................	4 63
			$1,618,336 70

No money has been paid out of the State Treasury except upon a specific appropriation, or by authority of a general law, made under the constitution, requiring the same to be paid—which is an appropriation.

There are a number of special accounts created by law, and the disbursement of the funds belonging to the same, is regulated by the law creating them—for example: the amounts due the several counties, from non-residents, is required by law, when collected, to be paid into the State treasury. The manner of the payment of the same to the different counties is prescribed in an act approved June 15, 1870.

For the payment of the interest and sinking fund on the public debt, the constitution and the laws are full and positive. (See article 11, section 23, of the constitution; sections 4 and 7 of act August 5, 1870.) "The proper officers of the State shall cause the interest on said bonds to be paid semi-annually and promptly as the same becomes due and payable." (See sections 6 and 7 of the act of December 2, 1871; section 5 act of May 19, 1871; sections 7 and 8 act of March 4, 1874.) These laws require an amount sufficient to meet the interest and sinking fund on State bonds, to be set aside for that purpose, and which can not be used in any other manner.

The same manner of payment is prescribed for interest and sinking fund on bonds of counties and municipalities. In pursuance of the laws requiring the payment of interest and redemption of bonds, twenty bonds of the denomination of $1,000, gold, each, of act of August 5, 1870, were redeemed by the present administration, at 81¼c. on the dollar, in currency. The interest has been promptly paid upon all bonded debt of the State; the result of which is that the class of bonds which were redeemed at 81¼c. on the dollar are now selling near par, and other bonds, which at the time could not be sold even at a discount of 15 per cent., are now commanding a premium.

It will be observed from the statement of bonds sold during the administration of Governor Davis, that but a small amount of cash was realized, the bonds having been, for the most part, exchanged for State warrants and for claims against the State for supplies furnished for frontier defense.

The State is offering no bonds for sale. There is yet in the hands of the State Treasurer bonds issued under an act, approved May 2, 1874, for pending State warrants, amounting to $81,300.

Statement of ten per cent. bonds issued in lieu of State War-rants under an act approved May 30, 1873.

DATE OF ISSUE.	NO. OF BONDS.	TO WHOM ISSUED.
1873, Sept. 17....	1 to 97	E. M. Pease.
17....	98 to 117	T. J. Durant.
18....	118 to 129	E. M. Pease.
20....	130 to 131	E. Potoski.
22....	132 to 156	John G. Spence.
Oct. 1....	157 to 169	A. Dittman.
3....	170 to 176	W. H. Crain.
9....	177 to 190	R. Bertram.
16....	191 to 209	R. P. Tendick.
20....	210 to 221	P. B. Turpin.
20....	222 to 246	Mrs. C. F. McClane.
28....	247	J. W. Ferris.
29....	248 to 251	Ira H. Evans.
Nov. 1....	252 to 326	E. M. Pease.
12....	327 to 349	Mary M. Lane.
18....	350 to 351	Forster, Ludlow & Co.
21....	352 to 355	Miss Julia Avery.
21....	356 to 366	Sanford Mason.
21....	367 to 376	A. T. McKinney.
24....	377 to 383	E. M. Pease.
26....	384 to 386	W. H. Crain.
28....	387	J. H. Phillips.
Dec. 8....	388 to 403	E. M. Pease.
15....	404 to 417	J. K. McCreary.
18....	418 to 422	C. G. Douglass.
18....	423 to 432	E. R. Lane.
20....	433 to 474	E. M. Pease.
20....	475 to 479	Carrie A. Pease.
31....	480 to 481	J. H. Phillips.
31....	482 to 505	G. S. Smith.
1874, Jan. 6....	506 to 515	E. M. Pease.

Total issued during the term of Governor Davis......$51,500

Statement of ten per cent. bonds issued in lieu of State Warrants, under an act approved May 30, 1873—Continued.

DATE OF ISSUE.	NO. OF BOND.	TO WHOM ISSUED.
1874, Feb. 19....	1501 to 1561	E. M. Pease.
19....	1562 to 1583	A. Faulkner.
	1584 to 1586	C. R. Johns & Co.
	1587 to 1590	Hugh A. Haralson.
23....	1591 to 1594	Eugene Bremond.
	1595 to 1599	E. T. Eggleston.
24....	1600 to 1606	Thomas P. Hughes.
	1607 to 1608	Irving Eggleston.
25....	1609 to 1628	J. H. Phillips.
	1629 to 1637	L. M. Openheimer.
	1638 to 1642	Eugene Bremond.
March 4....	1643 to 1645	A. T. McKinney.
	1646 to 1650	Ed. Dougherty.
11....	1651 to 1780	Raymond & Whitis.
12....	1781 to 1782	Eugene Bremond.
	1783 to 1787	C. R. Johns & Co.
	1788 to 1789	J. W. McLaughlin.
14....	1790 to 1805	Eugene Bremond.
	1806 to 1812	C. R. Johns & Co.
	1813 to 1817	Sampson & Henricks.
	1818	Mary M. Lane.
23....	1819 to 1820	C. R. Johns & Co.
	1821	A. Faulkner.
April 8....	1822	E. R. Lane.
16....	1823 to 1837	J. B. Walker.
	1838 to 1872	Home Ins. and Banking Co.
20....	1873 to 1875	E. R. Lane.
May 11....	1876 to 1883	Eugene Bremond.

Amount issued under present administration..........$38,300
Amount issued under late administration............ 51,500

                                                   $89,800
Amount exchanged for coupon bonds under an act approved May 2d, 1874 85,400

Amount outstanding ....$ 4,400

Statement of ten per cent. coupon bonds issued in lieu of regis-tered bonds and State warrants under an act approved May 2, 1874.

$1000 bonds.

DATE OF ISSUE.	NO. OF BOND.	TO WHOM ISSUED.
September 21, 1874.	1301	E. M. Pease.
"	1302	"
"	1303	"
"	1304	"
"	1305	"
"	1306	"
"	1307	"
"	1308	"
"	1309	"
"	1310	"
"	1311	"
"	1312	"
"	1313	"
"	1314	"
"	1315	"
"	1316	"
"	1317	"
"	1318	"
"	1319	"
"	1320	"
"	1321	"
"	1322	"
"	1323	"
"	1324	"
"	1325	"
"	1326	"
"	1327	"
"	1328	"
"	1329	"
"	1330	"
"	1331	"
"	1332	"
"	1333	"
"	1334	"

*Statement of ten per cent. coupon bonds issued in lieu of regis-
tered bonds and State warrants, under an act approved May
2, 1874—Continued.*

$1000 bonds.

DATE OF ISSUE.	NO. OF BOND.	TO WHOM ISSUED.
1874—September 21	1335	E. M. Pease.
November 1	1336	M. Kopperl.
December 7	1337	W. H. Crain.
December 15	1338	J. K. McCreary.
1875—February 4.	1339	A. Faulkner.
4.	1340	"
April 1....	1341	J. B. Walker.
3....	1342	Canceled.
9....	1343	Forster, Ludlow & Co.
22....	1344	C. R. Johns & Co.
22....	1345	"
22....	1346	"
22....	1347	"
22....	1348	"
23....	1349	Forster, Ludlow & Co.
23....	1350	"
23....	1351	"
23....	1352	"
23....	1353	"
23....	1354	E. R. Lane.
23....	1355	"
23....	1356	"
23....	1357	"
23....	1358	"
30....	1359	C. R. Johns & Co.
30....	1360	"
30....	1361	"
30....	1362	"
30....	1363	"
May 3....	1364	Forster, Ludlow & Co.
3....	1365	"
3....	1366	"
3....	1367	"
3....	1368	"

Statement of ten per cent. coupon bonds issued in lieu of registered bonds and State warrants, under an act approved May 2, 1874—Continued.

$1000 bonds.

DATE OF ISSUE.	NO. OF BOND.	TO WHOM SOLD.
May 6....	1369	Forster, Ludlow & Co.
6....	1370	"
6....	1371	"
6....	1372	"
6....	1373	"
7....	1374	C. R. Johns & Co.
7....	1375	"
7....	1376	"
7....	1377	"
7....	1378	"
15....	1379	Sampson & Henricks.
15....	1380	"
15....	1381	"
15....	1382	"
15....	1383	"
15....	1384	C. R. Johns & Co.
15....	1385	"
15....	1386	"
15....	1387	"
18....	1388	Forster, Ludlow & Co.
18....	1389	"
18....	1390	"
18....	1391	"
18....	1392	J. P. Richardson.
24....	1393	Raymond & Whitis.
25....	1394	"
25....	1395	"
25....	1396	"
25....	1397	"
25....	1398	"
25....	1399	"
25....	1400	"
25....	1401	"
25....	1402	"

Statement of ten per cent. coupon bonds issued in lieu of registered bonds and State warrants, under an act approved May 2, 1874—Continued.

$1000 bonds.

DATE OF ISSUE.	NO. OF BOND.	TO WHOM ISSUED.
May 25....	1403	Raymond & Whitis.
27....	1404	"
27....	1405	"
June 28....	1406	Sampson & Herricks.
7....	1407	Forster, Ludlow & Co.
7....	1408	"
7....	1409	"
7....	1410	"
7....	1411	"
10....	1412	"
10....	1413	"
10....	1414	"
10....	1415	"
10....	1416	"
12....	1417	Duval Beal.
12....	1418	"
12....	1419	"
12....	1420	"
12....	1421	"
12....	1422	"
12....	1423	"
12....	1424	"
12....	1425	Forster, Ludlow & Co.
15....	1426	"
15....	1427	"
15....	1428	"
15....	1429	"
15....	1430	"
19....	1431	First National Bank Austin.
21....	1432	C. R. Johns & Co.
21....	1433	"
21....	1434	"
21....	1435	"
21....	1436	"

Statement of ten per cent. coupon bonds issued in lieu of registered bonds and State warrants, under an act approved May 2, 1874—Continued.

$1000 bonds.

DATE OF ISSUE.	NO. OF BOND.	TO WHOM ISSUED.
1874, June 22....	1437	Raymond & Whitis.
22....	1438	Forster, Ludlow & Co.
22....	1439	" "
22....	1440	" "
22....	1441	" "
22....	1442	" "
22....	1443	" "
22....	1444	" "
22....	1445	" "
22....	1446	" "
22....	1447	" "
23....	1448	C. R. Johns & Co.
23....	1449	" "
23....	1450	" "
23....	1451	" "
23....	1452	" "
24....	1453	Forster, Ludlow & Co.
24....	1454	" "
24....	1455	" "
24....	1456	" "
24....	1457	" "
25....	1458	C. R. Johns & Co.
26....	1459	Forster, Ludlow & Co.
28....	1460	C. R. Johns & Co.
28....	1461	" "
28....	1462	" "
29....	1463	Forster, Ludlow & Co.
29....	1464	" "
29....	1465	" "
29....	1466	C. R. Johns & Co.
July 2....	1467	Forster, Ludlow & Co.
2....	1468	" "
2....	1469	" "
2....	1470	" "

Statement of ten per cent. coupon bonds issued in lieu of regis-
tered bonds and State warrants, under an act approved May
2, 1874—Continued.

$1000 bonds.

DATE OF ISSUE.	NO. OF BOND.	TO WHOM ISSUED.
1874, July 2....	1471	Forster, Ludlow & Co.
2....	1472	C. R. Johns & Co.
2....	1473	" "
2....	1474	" "
2....	1475	" "
5....	1476	Forster, Ludlow & Co.
5....	1477	" "
5....	1478	" "
5....	1479	" "
5....	1480	" "
6....	1481	1st National Bank of Austin.
6....	1482	" "
6....	1483	" "
6....	1484	" "
9....	1485	C. R. Johns & Co.
13....	1486	Forster, Ludlow & Co.
13....	1487	" "
13....	1488	" "
13....	1489	" "
13....	1490	" "
16....	1491	C. R. Johns & Co.
16....	1492	" "
16....	1493	" "
19....	1494	" "
19....	1495	" "
20....	1496	" "
22....	1497	" "
22....	1498	" "
26....	1499	Raymond & Whitis.
26....	1500	" "
26....	1501	" "
26....	1502	" "
26....	1503	C. R. Johns & Co.
27....	1504	Forster, Ludlow & Co.

Statement of ten per cent. coupon bonds issued in lieu of registered bonds and State warrants, under an act approved May 2, 1874—Continued.

$1000 bonds.

DATE OF ISSUE.	NO. OF BOND.	TO WHOM ISSUED.
1874—July 29	1505	C. R. Johns & Co.
29	1506	Raymond & Whitis.
29	1507	"
• 29	1508	"
29	1510	"
29	1509	"
29	1511	"
29	1512	"
29	1513	"
29	1514	"
29	1515	"
29	1516	"
29	1517	"
29	1518	"
29	1519	"
29	1520	"
29	1521	"
29	1522	"
29	1523	"
30	1524	C. R. Johns & Co.
30	1525	Forster, Ludlow & Co.
31	1526	Raymond & Whitis.
31	1527	"
31	1528	"
31	1529	"
31	1530	"
31	1531	"
31	1532	"
31	1533	"
31	1534	Forster, Ludlow & Co.
31	1535	"
31	1536	"
31	1537	"
31	1538	"

*Statement of ten per cent. coupon bonds issued in lieu of regis-
tered bonds and State warrants, under an act approved May
2, 1874*—Continued.

$1000 bonds.

DATE OF ISSUE.	NO. OF BOND.	TO WHOM ISSUED.
1874—July 31....	1539	C. R. Johns & Co.
31....	1540	"　　　"
31....	1541	"　　　"
31....	1542	"　　　"
31.....	1543	"　　　"
31....	1544	"　　　"
31.....	1545	"　　　"
31....	1546	"　　　"
31.....	1547	"　　　"
31....	1548	"　　　"
31....	1549	"　　　"
31.....	1550	"　　　"
	$500 **BONDS.**	
1874—Sept. 10....	1001	Forster, Ludlow & Co.
10...	1002	"　　　"
10...	1003	"　　　"
10...	1004	"　　　"
10...	1005	"　　　"
10...	1006	"　　　"
10...	1007	"　　　"
10...	1008	"　　　"
10...	1009	"　　　"
10...	1010	"　　　"
10...	1011	"　　　"
10...	1012	"　　　"
10...	1013	"　　　"
10...	1014	"　　　"
10...	1015	"　　　"
10...	1016	"　　　"
10...	1017	"　　　"

Statement of ten per cent. coupon bonds issued in lieu of regis-
tered bonds and State warrants, under an act approved May
2, 1874—Continued.

$500 Bonds.

DATE OF ISSUE.	NO. OF BOND.	TO WHOM ISSUED.
1874. Sept. 10....	1018	Foster, Ludlow & Co.
10....	1019	" "
10....	1020	" "
10....	1021	" "
10....	1022	" "
10....	1023	" "
10....	1024	" "
10....	1025	" "
10....	1026	" "
10....	1027	" "
10....	1028	" "
10....	1029	" "
10....	1030	" "
10....	1031	" "
10....	1032	" "
10....	1033	" "
10....	1034	" "
10....	1035	" "
10....	1036	" "
10....	1037	" "
10....	1038	" "
10....	1039	" "
10....	1040	" "
10....	1041	" "
10....	1042	" "
10....	1043	" "
10....	1044	" "
10....	1045	" "
10....	1046	" "
10....	1047	" "
1874. Sept. 17....	1048	A. T. McKinney.
17....	1049	" "
1874. Sept. 21....	1050	E. M. Pease.
21....	1051	Hugh A. Haralson.

Statement of ten per cent. coupon bonds issued in lieu of registered bonds and State warrants, under an act approved May 2, 1874—Continued.

$500 Bonds.

DATE OF ISSUE.	NO. OF BOND.	TO WHOM ISSUED.
1874—Sept. 21...	1052	Sanford Mason.
21...	1053	" "
21...	1054	Ed. Dougherty.
Dec. 8...	1055	Walter Gresham.
1875—Jan'y 7...	1056	J. H. Phillips.
7...	1057	" "
7...	1058	" "
7...	1059	" "
7...	1060	Peter Tumlinson.
7...	1061	" "
March 18...	1062	O. M. Jackson.
April 1...	1063	J. B. Walker.
April 24...	1064	R. Bertram.
April 24...	1065	" "
April 26...	1066	E. R. Lane.
April 26...	1067	" "
May 7...	1068	Sampson & Hendricks.
May 10...	1069	Forster, Ludlow & Co.
10...	1070	" "
10...	1071	" "
10...	1072	" "
10...	1073	" "
10...	1074	" "
10...	1075	" "
10...	1076	" "
May 20...	1077	C. F. McClane.
20...	1078	" "
20...	1079	" "
20...	1080	" "
20...	1081	" "
20...	1082	G. G. Smith.
20...	1083	" "
20...	1084	" "
20...	1085	" "

Statement of ten per cent. coupon bonds issued in lieu of registered bonds and State warrants, under an act approved May 2, 1874—Continued.

$500 bonds.

DATE OF ISSUE.	NO. OF BOND.	TO WHOM ISSUED.
1875—May 20	1086	G. G. Smith.
" 20	1087	A. Dittmar.
" 20	1088	"
" 24	1089	J. P. Richardson.
" 27	1090	C. R. Johns & Co.
June 12	1091	Duvall Beall.
" 19	1092	J. K. McCreary.
" 19	1093	First National Bank.
" 22	1094	C. R. Johns & Co.
" 22	1095	"
" 26	1096	Foster, Ludlow & Co.
" 29	1097	"
July 3	1098	First National Bank.
" 6	1099	"
" 8	1100	"
" 9	1101	D. Beall.
" 22	1102	Foster, Ludlow & Co.
" 22	1103	"
" 22	1104	"
" 22	1105	"
" 22	1106	"
" 31	1107	"
" 31	1108	"
" 31	1109	"
" 31	1110	"
" 31	1111	"
Aug. 2	1112	C. R. Johns & Co.
" 2	1113	"
" 2	1114	"
" 2	1115	"
" 2	1116	"
" 2	1117	"
" 2	1118	Foster, Ludlow & Co.
" 2	1119	"

Statement of ten per cent. coupon bonds issued in lieu of regis-
tered bonds and State warrants under an act approved May
2, 1874—Continued.

$500 bonds.

DATE OF ISSUE.	NO. OF BOND.	TO WHOM ISSUED.
1875—Aug. 2....	1120	Forster, Ludlow & Co.
" 3....	1121	John G. Spence.
" 3....	1122	"
" 3....	1123	"
" 3....	1124	"
" 3....	1125	"
" 3....	1126	Forster, Ludlow & Co.
" 3....	1127	"
" 3....	1128	"
" 3....	1129	"
" 3....	1130	"
" 3....	1131	"
" 3....	1132	"
" 3....	1133	"
" 3....	1134	"
" 3....	1135	"
" 3....	1136	"
" 3....	1137	"
" 3....	1138	"
" 4....	1139	"
" 4....	1140	"
" 4....	1141	"
" 4....	1142	"
" 5....	1143	Raymond & Whitis.
" 5....	1144	"
" 5....	1145	"
" 5....	1146	"
" 5....	1147	Forster, Ludlow & Co.
" 5....	1148	"
" 5....	1149	C. R. Johns & Co.
" 5....	1150	"
" 5....	1151	"
" 5....	1152	"
" 5....	1153	"

Statement of ten per cent. coupon bonds issued in lieu of registered bonds and State warrants under an act approved May 2, 1874—Continued.

$500 bonds.

DATE OF ISSUE.	NO. OF BOND.	TO WHOM ISSUED.
1875—Aug. 5....	1154	C. R. Johns & Co.
5....	1155	"
5....	1156	"
5....	1157	"
5....	1158	"
5....	1159	"
5....	1160	"
5....	1161	"
5....	1162	"
5....	1163	"
5....	1164	"
5....	1165	"
5....	1166	"
5....	1167	"
5....	1168	"
6....	1169	Forster, Ludlow & Co.
6....	1170	"
6....	1171	"
6....	1172	"
6....	1173	"
6....	1174	"
6....	1175	"
6....	1176	"
6....	1177	"
6....	1178	"
6....	1179	"
7....	1180	"
7....	1181	"
7....	1182	"
7....	1183	"
10....	1184	"
10....	1185	"
10....	1186	"
10....	1187	"

Statement of ten per cent. coupon bonds issued in lieu of regis-
tered bonds and State warrants under an act approved May
2, 1874—Continued.

$500 bonds.

DATE OF ISSUE.	NO. OF BOND.	TO WHOM ISSUED.
1875—Aug. 10...	1188	Forster, Ludlow & Co.
11...	1189	"
11...	1190	"
11...	1191	"
11...	1192	"
11...	1193	"
11...	1194	"
12...	1195	"
12...	1196	"
12...	1197	M. D. Miller.
12...	1198	"
13...	1199	Forster, Ludlow & Co.
13...	1200	"
13...	1201	"
13...	1202	"
16...	1203	C. R. Johns & Co.
16...	1204	"
16...	1205	"
18...	1206	"
18...	1207	Forster, Ludlow & Co.
19...	1208	"
19...	1209	"
19...	1210	"
19...	1211	C. R. Johns & Co.
20...	1212	Forster, Ludlow & Co.
20...	1213	"
20...	1214	C. R. Johns & Co.
20...	1215	"
20...	1216	"
20...	1217	"
20...	1218	"
20...	1219	"
21...	1220	"
21...	1221	"

*Statement of ten per cent. coupon bonds issued in lieu of regis-
tered bonds and State warrants under an act approved May
2, 1874—Continued.*

$500 bonds.

DATE OF ISSUE.	NO. OF BOND.	TO WHOM ISSUED.
1875—August 25..	1222	Forster, Ludlow & Co.
25..	1223	"
26..	1224	John B. Jones.
28..	1225	Forster, Ludlow & Co.
28..	1226	"
28..	1227	"
31..	1228	C. R. Johns & Co.
31..	1229	"
31..	1230	"
31..	1231	"
31..	1232	"
31..	1233	"
31..	1234	"
31..	1235	"
31..	1236	"
31..	1237	"
31..	1238	"
31..	1239	"
31..	1240	"
31..	1241	"
31..	1242	"
31..	1243	"
31..	1244	"
31..	1245	"
31..	1246	"
31..	1247	"
31..	1248	"
31..	1249	"
31..	1250	"
31..	1251	"
31..	1252	"
31..	1253	"
31..	1254	"
31..	1255	"

*Statement of ten per cent. coupon bonds issued in lieu of regis-
tered bonds and State warrants under an act approved May
2, 1874—Continued.*

$500 bonds.

DATE OF ISSUE.	NO. OF BOND.	TO WHOM ISSUED.
1875—August 31..	1256	C. R. Johns & Co.
31..	1257	"
31..	1258	"
31..	1259	"
31..	1260	Raymond & Whitis.
31..	1261	"
31..	1262	"
31..	1263	"
31..	1264	"
31..	1265	Forster, Ludlow & Co.
31..	1266	"
31..	1267	"
31..	1268	"
31..	1269	"
31..	1270	"
31..	1271	"
31..	1272	"
September 1..	1273	"
1..	1274	"
1..	1275	"
1..	1276	C. R. Johns & Co.
1..	1277	"
1..	1278	"
1..	1279	"
1..	1280	"
1..	1281	"
1..	1282	"
2..	1283	Forster, Ludlow & Co.
2..	1284	"
3..	1285	"
3..	1286	"
3..	1287	"
3..	1288	"
3..	1289	"

Statement of ten per cent. coupon bonds issued in lieu of registered bonds and State warrants under an act approved May 2, 1874—Continued.

$500 bonds.

DATE OF ISSUE.	NO. OF BOND.	TO WHOM ISSUED.
1875—Sept.　4...	1290	Forster, Ludlow & Co.
4...	1291	"　　　　"
4...	1292	"　　　　"
4...	1293	"　　　　"
4...	1294	"　　　　"
4...	1295	C. R. Johns & Co.
4...	1296	"　　　"
4...	1297	"　　　"
4...	1298	"　　　"
4...	1299	"　　　"
7...	1300	E. W. Shands.

$100 BONDS.

DATE OF ISSUE.	NO. OF BOND.	TO WHOM ISSUED.
1874—Sept. 17...	1	A. T. McKinney.
17...	2	"　　　"
17...	3	"　　　"
17...	4	Hugh A. Haralson.
17...	5	Sanford Mason.
Nov. 14...	6	M. Kopperl.
14...	7	"
14...	8	Walter Gresham.
Dec. 10...	9	A. M. P. Hurlbut.
10...	10	"　　　"
10...	11	"　　　"
10...	12	"　　　"
10...	13	"　　　"
10...	14	"　　　"
10...	15	"　　　"
10...	16	"　　　"
10...	17	"　　　"
10...	18	"　　　"

*Statement of ten per cent. coupon bonds issued in lieu of regis-
tered bonds and State warrants under an act approved May
2, 1874—Continued.*

$100 bonds.

DATE OF ISSUE.	NO. OF BOND.	TO WHOM SOLD.
1874—Dec. 10....	19	A. M. P. Hurlbut.
10....	20	"
10....	21	"
10....	22	"
10....	23	"
10....	24	Eugene Bremond.
10....	25	"
10....	26	"
10....	27	"
10....	28	"
15....	29	J. K. McCreary.
15....	30	"
15....	31	"
15....	32	"
15....	33	J. H. Phillips.
15....	34	"
15....	35	"
15....	36	A. Faulkner.
15....	37	"
15....	38	"
1875—Mar. 18....	39	Peter Tumlinson.
18....	40	"
18....	41	"
April 24....	42	R. Bertram.
24....	43	"
24....	44	"
24....	45	"
29....	46	E. R. Lane.
30....	47	J. W. Ferris.
May 20....	48	Julia Avery.
20....	49	"
20....	50	"
20....	51	"

*Statement of ten per cent. coupon bonds issued in lieu of regis-
tered bonds and State warrants under an act approved May
2, 1874—Continued.*

$100 bonds.

DATE OF ISSUE.	NO. OF BOND.	TO WHOM ISSUED.
1875—May 20....	52	G. G. Smith.
20....	53	A. Dittman.
20....	54	"
20....	55	"
27....	56	C. R. Johns & Co.
27....	57	"
June 12....	58	Duval Beall.
12....	59	"
19....	60	J. K. McCreary.
19....	61	"
19....	62	First National Bank.
19....	63	"
21....	64	Forster, Ludlow & Co.
21....	65	Duval Beall.
22....	66	Forster, Ludlow & Co.
22....	67	"
22....	68	"
22....	69	"
22....	70	"
22....	71	"
27....	72	"
30....	73	"
Aug.	74	D. Beall.
12....	75	"
12....	76	"
12....	77	"
18....	78	Forster, Ludlow & Co.
25....	79	A. J. Walker.
25....	80	"
Sept. 4....	81	C. R. Johns & Co.
4....	82	"
7....	83	John B. Jones.
7....	84	"
7....	85	"

Statement of ten per cent. coupon bonds issued in lieu of registered bonds and State warrants under an act approved May 2, 1874—Continued.

$100 bonds.

DATE OF ISSUE.	NO. OF BOND.	TO WHOM ISSUED.
1875—Sept. 7...	86	John B. Jones.
7...	87	"
7...	88	"
7...	89	E. W. Shands.
7...	90	"
7...	91	"
7...	92	"
7...	93	"
7...	94	C. R. Johns & Co.
7...	95	"
7...	96	"
7...	97	"
7...	98	"
7...	99	"
7...	100	"
7...	101	"
7...	102	"
7...	103	"
Sept. 10...	104	John B. Jones.
10...	105	"
10...	106	"
10...	107	"
10...	108	Forster, Ludlow & Co.
10...	109	"
13...	110	C. R. Johns & Co.
13...	111	"
13...	112	"
13...	113	"
13...	114	"
13...	115	"
13...	116	"
13...	117	"
13...	118	"
13...	119	"

Statement of ten per cent. coupon bonds issued in lieu of registered bonds and State warrants under an act approved May 2, 1874—Continued. $100 bonds.

DATE OF ISSUE.	NO. OF BOND.	TO WHOM ISSUED.
1875. Sept. 21....	120	O. R. Johns & Co.
21....	121	" "
21....	122	" "
21....	123	" "
21....	124	" "
21....	125	" "
21....	126	" "
21....	127	" "
21....	128	" "
21....	129	" "
21....	130	" "
21....	131	" "
21....	132	" "
21....	133	" "
21....	134	" "
21....	135	" "
21....	136	" "
21....	137	" "
21....	138	" "
21....	139	" "
24....	140	E. W. Shands.
24....	141	" "
24....	142	" "
24....	143	" "
24....	144	" "
24....	145	" "
24....	146	" "
Oct. 4....	147	Forster, Ludlow & Co.
4....	148	" "
4....	149	" "
4....	150	" "
4....	151	" "
4....	152	" "
4....	153	" "
4....	154	" "
4....	155	" "
4....	156	" "

Statement of ten per cent. coupon bonds issued in lieu of regis-
tered bonds and State warrants under an act approved May
2, 1874—Concluded. $100 bonds.

DATE OF ISSUE.	NO. OF BOND.	TO WHOM ISSUED.
1875—Oct. 4.....	157	Forster, Ludlow & Co.
4.....	158	"
4.....	159	"
4.....	160	"
4.....	161	"
4.....	162	"
4.....	163	"
4.....	164	"
4.....	165	"
4.....	166	"
4.....	167	"
4.....	168	"
4.....	169	"
4.....	170	"
4.....	171	"
4.....	172	"
4.....	173	"
4.....	174	"
4.....	175	"
4.....	177	"
4.....	178	"
4.....	179	"
4.....	179	"
4.....	180	"
4.....	181	"
4.....	182	"
4.....	183	"
4.....	184	"
4.....	185	"
4.....	186	"
1875—Oct. 9.....	187	W. H. Crain.

RECAPITULATION.

250 $1000 bonds, less one cancelled........................	$249,000	00
300 $500 bonds	150,000	00
187 $100 bonds	18,700	00
Total ten per cent. coupon bonds issued....................	$417,700	00
Total ten per cent. registered bonds outstanding..........	4,400	00
Total funding bonds outstanding...........................	$422,100	00

ANDREW J. DORN, Treasurer.

On motion of Mr. Stockdale, five hundred copies were ordered printed.

Mr. German moved to reconsider the vote refusing to adopt Mr. Pickett's second amendment to section 2.

Mr. DeMorse's amendment lost by the following vote:

YEAS—Abernathy, DeMorse, McCormick, Ramey, Weaver—5.

NAYS—Abner, Ballinger, Barnett, Blassingame, Brown, Bruce, Chambers, Cline, Cooke of San Saba, Crawford, Darnell, Davis of Brazos, Davis of Wharton, Dillard, Dohoney, Douglas, Ferris, Flanagan, Fleming, Flournoy, Ford, Gaither, German, Graves, Haynes, Henry of Limestone, Holt, Johnson of Collin, Johnson of Franklin, Kilgore, Killough, Lacy, Lockett, McKinney of Denton, McKinney of Walker, McLean, Mills, Mitchell, Moore, Morris, Martin of Navarro, Martin of Hunt, Norvell, Nugent, Pauli, Reagan, Robertson of Bell, Robison of Fayette, Russell of Wood, Scott, Sansom, Smith, Spikes, Stayton, Stewart, Stockdale, Wade, Waelder, West, Whitehead, Whitfield—61.

Mr. Stockdale offered the following amendment:

Amend by striking out in section 14 the words, "from time to time pass laws establishing," and insert the following: "In the laws creating railway companies or authorizing the construction of railways prescribe."

On motion of Mr. Sansom the Convention adjourned to 2½ o'clock P. M.

EVENING SESSION—2½ o'CLOCK.

Convention met; roll called; quorum present. Pending question on adourmment resumed.

Mr. Stockdale's amendment to section 2, line 14, taken up and lost.

Mr. German called up his motion to reconsider the vote refusing to adopt the second amendment offered this morning by Mr. Pickett to section 2.

And the amendment was lost by the following vote, *it requiring a two-third vote to amend:*

YEAS—Abernathy, Abner, Allison, Barnett, Blassingame, Brown, Bruce, Chambers, Cooke of San Saba, Darnell, DeMorse, Dillard, Douglas, Ferris, Fleming, Flournoy, German, Graves, Henry of Limestone, Holt, Johnson of Collin, Killough, Lacy, McKinney, of Denton, McLean, Murphy, Martin of Navarro, Martin of Hunt, Norvell, Ramey, Russell of Wood, Scott, Sessions, Spikes, Stewart, Wade, Whitehead—37.

NAYS—Ballinger, Brady, Cline, Cooley, Davis of Brazos, Davis of Wharton, Dohoney, Flanagan, Gaither, Haynes, Kilgore, Lockett, McKinney of Walker, Mills, Moore, Morris, Nugent, Nunn, Pauli, Reagan, Robertson of Bell, Robison of Fayette, Sansom, Smith, Stayton, West, Whitfield—27.

Mr. Martin, of Navarro, offered the following amendment:

Section 1, line 4, strike out after the word "State," and insert "and every railroad in this State shall receive and transport the passengers, tonnage and cars, loaded or empty, without delay or discrimination, of every other railroad connected with it, directly or through other railroad or railroads, for reasonable compensation, to be ascertained by agreement of said railroad companies, or in manner provided by law."

Lost by the following vote:

YEAS—Abernathy, Ballinger, Blassingame, Brown, Bruce, Crawford, Darnell, Davis of Wharton, DeMorse, Dillard, Dohoney, Douglas, Ferris, Flanagan, Fleming, Flournoy, Gaither, German, Graves, Haynes, Henry of Limestone, Johnson of Collin, Johnson of Franklin, Kilgore, Killough, Lynch, McKinney of Walker, McLean, Murphy, Martin of Navarro, Martin of Hunt, Nugent, Nunn, Ramey, Robison of Fayette, Ross, Russell of Wood, Sessions, Stayton, Stewart, Stockdale, Wade—42.

NAYS—Abner, Allison, Barnett, Brady, Chambers, Cline, Cooke of San Saba, Cooley, Davis of Brazos, Holt, Lacy, McCormick, Mills, Mitchell, Moore, Norvell, Pauli, Reagan, Robertson of Bell, Sansom, Smith, Spikes, Waelder, West, Whitehead, Whitfield—26.

Mr. Abernathy moved the previous question on the final passage of the article.

Carried by the following vote:

YEAS—Abernathy, Allison, Barnett, Blassingame, Bruce, Chambers, Cooke of San Saba, Crawford, Davis of Brazos, DeMorse, Dillard, Douglas, Fleming, Flournoy, Gaither, German, Graves, Haynes, Henry of Limestone, Holt, Johnson of Collin, Johnson of Franklin, Killough, Lacy, Lynch, Moore, Murphy, Martin of Navarro, Norvell, Nugent, Ramey, Reagan, Robertson of Bell, Robison of Fayette, Ross, Russell of Wood, Sansom, Scott, Sessions, Smith, Spikes, Wade, Whitehead, Whitfield—44.

Nays—Abner, Ballinger, Brady, Brown, Cline, Cooley, Darnell, Davis of Wharton, Dohoney, Ferris, Flanagan, Kilgore, Lockett, McCormick, McKinney of Walker, McLean, Mills, Mitchell, Martin of Hunt, Nunn, Pauli, Stewart, Stockdale, Waelder, West, Whitfield—24.

The question being the final passage of the article, it passed by the following vote:

Yeas—Abernathy, Allison, Barnett, Blassingame, Brown, Bruce, Chambers, Cooke of San Seba, Crawford, Darnell, Davis of Brazos, DeMorse, Dillard, Dohoney, Douglas, Ferris, Fleming, Flournoy, Gaither, German, Graves, Haynes, Henry of Limestone, Holt, Johnson of Collin, Johnson of Franklin, Kilgore, Killough, Lacy, Lynch, McCormick, McKinney of Walker, McLean, Moore, Martin of Navarro, Martin of Hunt, Norvell, Nugent, Nunn, Ramey, Reagan, Robertson of Bell, Robison of Fayette, Ross, Russell of Wood, Scott, Sessions, Smith, Spikes, Stewart, Whitehead—51.

Nays—Abner, Ballinger, Brady, Cline, Cooley, Davis of Wharton, Flanagan, Lockett, Mills, Mitchell, Murphy, Pauli, Sansom, Stayton, Stockdale, Waelder, West, Whitfield—18.

On motion of Mr. Flournoy, the convention adjourned until 9 o'clock A. M. to-morrow.

FIFTY-FOURTH DAY.

Hall of Representatives, }
Austin, Texas, September 13, 1875. }

Convention met pursuant to adjournment; roll called; quorum present. Prayer by the Rev. Dr. W. H. Dodge, of the Baptist Church of Austin. Journal of yesterday read and adopted.

On motion of Mr. Cook, of Gonzales, Mr. West was excused for to-day.

On motion of Mr. Stayton, Mr. Lynch was granted indefinite leave from Monday next.

Mr. Darnell offered the following resolution:

Whereas, The Texas and Pacific Railway Company, a corporation, chartered by the Congress of the United States, has received certain grants from this State, and has acquired by purchase from or through the Southern Pacific Railroad Company, and the Southern Trans-Continental Railway Company, certain grants, property, rights and franchises, subject to certain legislative limitations and restrictions, as to the commencement and prosecution of the work, and as to the time of its completion to certain points in the State; and,

Whereas, After completing 265 miles of new road, and grading, bridging and tieing, ready for the iron rails, 118 additional miles of roadway, the financial panic of 1873, and the distrust and embarrassment that followed, paralyzing every industrial and commercial enterprise, has forced a temporary suspension of the work of construction, thereby occasioning a heavy loss to the company from causes against which it was powerless to protect itself; therefor,

Resolved, That none of the legislative grants made to or acquired by said company, in respect to the commencement and prosecution of the work, or as to the date of completion of any portion of its lines in Texas, shall be held to have lapsed; and that the said company shall have eighteen months from the passage of this ordinance, in which to complete 120 miles of its lines between Eagle Ford and Fort Worth, and between Brookston and Texarkana; and seven addition years in which to complete 695 miles additional of its road, upon the route as heretofore designated by legislative authority to the Rio Grande, at or near El Paso; this extension to be in lieu of the restrictions and limitations of time, and manner of prosecuting the work, heretofore fixed by legislative authority.

Mr. Darnell moved to refer the resolution to a select committee of fifteen.

Mr. German moved to refer it to the Committee on Railroad Corporations.   Lost, and the resolution referred to a select committee of fifteen.

Mr. Barnett offered the following resolution:

Resolved, That this Convention adjourn *sine die* at 12 o'clock, Monday, 22d instant.

Adopted.

Mr. Murphy moved to reconsider the vote adopting the resolution.

Mr. Ramey reported as follows:

COMMITTEE ROOM, ⎱
AUSTIN, TEXAS, November 5, 1875. ⎰

To the Hon. E. B. Pickett, President of the Convention:

SIR—Your Committee on Engrossed and Enrolled Ordinances would respectfully report to your honorable body that they have carefully examined and compared " Article —, Taxation and Revenue," and find the same correctly engrossed.

Respectfully,   WM. NEAL RAMEY, Chairman.

On motion of Mr. Fleming, two hundred copies of the article were ordered printed.

" Article —, Public Free Schools," taken up and read third time.

Mr. German offered the following amendment:

Amend section 4 by striking out lines 17, 18 and 19, down to the word " law," and insert " the lands herein set apart to the

public free school fund, which are located in any county now
organized, and whenever any new county may be organized,
shall be placed upon the market and sold under such regulations
and on such terms as may be prescribed by law.

Mr. Russell, of Wood, proposed to amend the amendment as
follows:

" Provided said lands shall not be disposed of at a less price
than one dollar per acre.

Adopted.

Amendment as amended lost by the following vote:

YEAS—Barnett, Blassingame, Brown, Bruce, Chambers,
Cooke of San Saba, Flournoy, German, Henry of Limestone,
Johnson of Collin, Johnson of Franklin, Lynch, Nugent, Russell
of Wood, Spikes—15.

NAYS—Abernathy, Abner, Allison, Ballinger, Brady, Cline,
Crawford, Darnell, Davis of Brazos, Davis of Wharton, DeMorse,
Dillard, Dohoney, Douglas, Flanagan, Fleming, Ford, Gaither,
Graves, Haynes, Holt, Kilgore, Killough, Lacy, Lockett, McCor-
mick, McKiney of Denton, McKinney of Walker, McLean,
Mills, Mitchell, Moore, Morris, Murphy, Martin of Hunt, Nor-
vell, Nunn, Pauli, Ramey, Reagan, Rentfro, Reynolds, Rob-
ertson of Bell, Robison of Fayette, Ross, Scott, Sessions, Smith,
Stayton, Stewart, Stockdale, Wade, Waelder, Whitehead—55.

Mr. Haynes offered the following amendments:

In line 13, section 3, strike out the word " more " and insert
" less."

In line 14 strike out the word " one " and insert " two."

Mr. Moore asked for a division of the question.

Mr. Scott moved to lay the first amendment on the table.

Carried by the following vote:

YEAS—Allison, Barnett, Blassingame, Brown, Bruce, Cham-
bers, Cooke of San Saba, DeMorse, Dillard, Dohoney, Douglas,
Ferris, Flournoy, Gaither, German, Graves, Henry of Lime-
stone, Holt, Kilgore, Killough, Lacy, Lynch, McKinney of Den-
ton, McLean, Moore, Murphy, Martin of Navarro, Norvell,
Nugent, Ramey, Reagan, Robertson of Bell, Robison of Fayette,
Russell of Wood, Sansom, Scott, Sessions, Spikes, Stayton,
Stockdale, Whitehead—41.

NAYS—Abner, Ballinger, Brady, Cline, Cooley, Crawford,
Darnell, Davis of Brazos, Davis of Wharton, Flanagan, Flem-
ing, Ford, Haynes, Johnson of Franklin, Lockett, McCormick,
McKinney of Walker, Mills, Mitchell, Morris, Martin of Hunt,
Nunn, Pauli, Rentfro, Reynolds, Ross, Smith, Stewart, Wade,
Waelder, Whitfield—31.

39

The hour having arrived for considering the special order, the same was taken up, viz: "Section ——, Granting Lands to Railroads," and "Article ——, Public Lands and Land Office."

On motion of Mr. Darnell, the special order was postponed until the pending business is disposed of.

"Article ——, Judiciary," was then taken up as the special order for this hour, and on motion of Mr. Dohoney was postponed to 10 o'clock, Monday.

The Convention resumed the consideration of the article on public free schools.

Mr. Kilgore offered the following amendment to Mr. Haynes' second amendment:

Amend the amendment by inserting before the word "two" the words "not to exceed."

Mr. Whitfield moved to lay both amendments on the table.

Carried by the following vote:

YEAS—Abernathy, Allison, Barnett, Blassingame, Brown, Bruce, Chambers, Cooley, Darnell, Ferris, Fleming, Flournoy, Gaither, German, Graves, Henry of Limestone, Holt, Johnson of Franklin, Killough, Lacy, Lynch, McCormick, McKinney of Denton, McLean, Murphy, Martin of Navarro, Nugent, Ramey, Reagan, Robertson of Bell, Robison of Fayette, Ross, Russell of Wood, Sansom, Scott, Sessions, Spikes, Stockdale, Whitehead, Whitfield—40.

NAYS—Abner, Ballinger, Brady, Cline, Cooke of San Saba, Crawford, Davis of Brazos, Davis of Wharton, DeMorse, Dohoney, Douglas, Flanagan, Ford, Haynes, Kilgore, Lockett, McKinney of Walker, Mills, Mitchell, Moore, Morris, Martin of Hunt, Norvell, Nunn, Pauli, Rentfro, Reynolds, Smith, Stayton, Stewart, Wade, Waelder—32.

Mr. Wade offered the following amendment:

"The Legislature shall have power to levy an *ad valorem* tax upon all property in this State of not less than one-tenth nor more than one-fourth of one per cent., and a poll tax of one dollar on all male citizens between the ages of twenty-one and sixty years."

Mr. Scott moved the previous question on the passage of the article.

On motion of Mr. Kilgore a call of the Convention was ordered.

Absent—Messrs. Blake, Johnson of Collin, and Weaver.

On motion of Mr. McKinney, of Denton, Mr. Johnson, of Collin, was excused.

On motion of Mr. Ramey, Mr. Blake was excused.

On motion of Mr. Haynes, Mr. Weaver was excused.

Mr. Scott, by leave, withdrew his motion for the previous question.

Mr. German offered the following amendment:

Amend section 4, line 18, by inserting the word "such" before the word "regulations."

Mr. Wade's amendment lost by the following vote:

YEAS—Ballinger, Brady, Cline, Cooley, Crawford, Davis of Wharton, Flanagan, Fleming, Ford, Haynes, Johnson of Franklin, Kilgore, Lockett, McCormick, McKinney of Walker, Mills, Mitchell, Morris, Martin of Hunt, Nunn, Pauli, Rentfro, Reynolds, Ross, Smith, Stewart, Wade, Whitfield—28.

NAYS—Abernathy, Allison, Barnett, Blassingame, Brown, Bruce, Chambers, Cooke, of San Saba, Darnell, Davis of Brazos, DeMorse, Dilllard, Douglas, Ferris, Flournoy, Gaither, German, Graves, Henry of Limestone, Holt, Killough, Lacy, Lynch, McKinney of Denton, McLean, Moore, Murphy, Martin of Navarro, Norvell, Nugent, Ramey, Reagan, Robertson of Bell, Robison of Fayette, Russell of Wood, Sansom, Scott, Sessions, Spikes, Stayton, Stockdale, Whitehead—42.

Mr. German's amendment adopted.

Mr. McCormick offered the following amendment:

Amend by adding the following after the word "annually," in line 54, section 6: "And said bonds shall be deposited with the State Treasurer for safe keeping, subject only to the order of the proper authorities."

Lost.

Mr. Brown offered the following amendment:

Amend section 4, line 20, by inserting after the word "thereof" the words *"provided,* that actual settlers on said lands shall have the same prior right of purchase, as is provided in section 6 of this article in relation to actual settlers on county school lands."

[Mr. Reagan in the chair.]

The question on Mr. Brown's amendment was put, and adopted by the following vote:

YEAS—Abernathy, Allison, Barnett, Blassingame, Brown, Bruce, Chambers, Cooke of San Saba, Crawford, Darnell, Davis, of Brazos, DeMorse, Dillard, Douglas, Ferris, Fleming, Flournoy, Ford, Gaither, German, Graves, Haynes, Henry of Limestone, Holt, Kilgore, Killough, Lacy, Lynch, McCormick, McKinney of Denton, McLean, Moore, Morris, Murphy, Martin of Navarro, Martin of Hunt, Nugent, Reagan, Robertson of Bell, Robison of Fayette, Ross, Russell of Wood, Sansom, Scott, Sessions, Smith, Stewart, Stockdale, Whitfield—49.

Nays—Ballinger, Brady, Cline, Cooley, Davis of Wharton, Dohoney, Flanagan, Lockett, McKinney of Walker, Mills, Mitchell, Norvell, Nunn, Pauli, Rentfro, Spikes, Stayton, Waelder, Whitehead—19.

Mr. Kilgore proposed to amend section 5, line 35, by inserting after the word "school" the following: "But the Legislature may provide for the instruction of the scholastic population in private schools not sectarian, where public schools can not be organized."

Lost by the following vote:

Yeas—Abernathy, Allison, Barnett, Blassingame, Brown, Bruce, Chambers, Cooke of San Saba, Darnell, Dillard, Dohoney, Douglas, Fleming, Flournoy, Gaither, German, Graves, Haynes, Henry of Limestone, Holt, Kilgore, Killough, Lacy, Lynch, McCormick, McKinney of Denton, McKinney of Walker, Murphy, Martin of Navarro, Martin of Hunt, Reagan, Robertson of Bell, Robison of Fayette, Ross, Russell of Wood, Sansom, Scott, Sessions, Spikes, Stewart, Stockdale, Whitehead, Whitfield—43.

Nays—Ballinger, Brady, Cline, Cooley, Crawford, Davis of Brazos, Davis of Wharton, DeMorse, Ferris, Flanagan, Ford, Lockett, McLean, Mills, Mitchell, Moore, Morris, Norvell, Nugent, Nunn, Pauli, Ramey, Rentfro, Smith, Stayton, Wade, Waelder—27.

Mr. Martin, of Hunt, offered the following amendment:

Sec. 2. Amend by striking out in line 10 the words "one-half," and insert the word "all."

Mr. Stayton offered the following as a substitute for the amendment:

Amend section 2 by striking out the words "one-half of the public domain of the State," in line 10.

Mr. Kilgore moved to lay the amendment and substitute on the table.

A division on the question was ordered, when Mr. Stayton's substitute was tabled by the following vote:

Yeas—Abernathy, Abner, Allison, Ballinger, Barnett, Blassingame, Brown, Bruce, Chambers, Cline, Cooke of San Saba, Darnell, Davis of Brazos, Dohoney, Douglas, Ferris, Flournoy, Gaither, German, Graves, Henry of Limestone, Holt, Kilgore, Killough, Lacy, McCormick, McKinney of Denton, McKinney of Walker, McLean, Mills, Mitchell, Moore, Martin of Navarro, Martin of Hunt, Nugent, Nunn, Ramey, Rentfro, Reynolds, Robertson of Bell, Russell of Wood, Scott, Sessions, Spikes, Stewart, Wade, Whitfield—47.

NAYS—Brady, Cooley, Crawford, Davis of Wharton, De-Morse, Dillard, Flanagan, Fleming, Ford, Lockett, Lynch, Morris, Murphy, Norvell, Pauli, Reagan, Robison of Fayette, Stayton, Stockdale, Waelder, Whitehead—21.

The question then recurring upon laying Mr. Martin's (of Hunt,) amendment on the table, the same was put, and amendment tabled by the following vote:

YEAS—Abernathy, Abner, Allison, Ballinger, Barnett, Brady, Brown, Cline, Cooke of San Saba, Cooley, Darnell, Davis of Brazos, Davis of Wharton, DeMorse, Dillard, Dohoney, Douglas, Ferris, Flanagan, Fleming, Ford, Gaither, Graves, Haynes, Henry of Limestone, Holt, Kilgore, Killough, Lockett, Lynch, McCormick, McKinney of Walker, McLean, Mitchell, Morris, Murphy, Martin of Navarro, Norvell, Nunn, Pauli, Ramey, Reagan, Rentfro, Reynolds, Robertson of Bell, Robison of Fayette, Scott, Sessions, Smith, Spikes, Stayton, Stewart, Stockdale, Wade, Waelder, Whitehead, Whitfield—57.

NAYS—Blassingame, Crawford, German, Lacy, McKinney of Denton, Mills, Martin of Hunt, Russell of Wood—8.

Mr. Bruce stated that he was paired off with Mr. Nugent, but for which fact he would have voted against laying the amendmenment on the table.

Mr. Moore stated that he would vote "yea," but was paired off with Mr. Arnim.

Mr. Kilgore moved to adjourn to 2½ P. M.

Lost.

Mr. Kilgore offered the following amendment:

Amend section 5 by striking out the word "manner," line 38, and inserting the words "to the education of such population, in public or private schools, in such manner and under such regulations."

Mr. Dillard moved the previous question.

Mr. Flanagan moved a call of the Convention.

Call ordered.

Mr. Kilgore moved to adjourn till 2½ o'clock.

Lost.

Absentees—Messrs. Davis of Wharton, Johnson of Franklin, Sansom.

Mr. Stewart moved to excuse the absentees.

Mr. Stockdale made the point of order that no member could ask that another be excused without it being at the request of the absent member.

Point sustained.

Mr. Ballinger moved to adjourn to 2½ o'clock.   Lost.

Mr. McCormick moved to suspend the call.

Lost.

Mr. Ferris moved to adjourn to 2½ o'clock P. M.

Ruled out of order.

The chair submitted to the Convention the question as to whether or not they would take up the special order for the hour.

The Convention refused to take up the special order.

Mr. Flourney moved to suspend the call.

Lost.

Mr. McCormick moved to excuse absent members.

The chair ruled the motion out of order; that delegates could not be excused without their request.

Mr. McLean appealed from the decision of the chair.

Mr. Flanagan moved a call of the Convention upon the appeal.

The chair ruled that the call upon the appeal was out of order.

The question upon Mr. McLean's appeal was then put, and the Convention sustained the chair by the following vote:

YEAS—Abernathy, Abner, Allison, Ballinger, Barnett, Blassingame, Brady, Brown, Bruce, Chambers, Cline, Cooke of San Saba, Cooley, Crawford, Darnell, Davis of Brazos, Davis of Wharton, DeMorse, Dohoney, Douglas, Ferris, Flanagan, Fleming, Flournoy, Ford, Gaither, Graves, Haynes, Henry of Limestone, Holt, Kilgore, Killough, Lacy, Lockett, Lynch, McCormick, McKinney of Denton, McKinney of Walker, Mills, Mitchell, Morris, Murphy, Martin of Hunt, Norvell, Nugent, Pauli, Ramey, Rentfro, Reynolds, Robertson of Bell, Robison of Fayette, Ross, Russell of Wood, Scott, Sessions, Smith, Spikes, Stayton, Stewart, Stockdale, Wade, Waelder, Whitehead, Whitfield—64

NAYS—Dillard, McLean, Moore, Nunn—4.

Mr. Stewart moved to suspend the call.

The Sergeant-at-arms reported that he had learned that Mr. Sansom had gone home.

On the question on Mr. Stewart's motion to suspend the call, the yeas and nays were called, and call suspended by the following vote:

YEAS—Allison, Ballinger, Barnett, Bassingame, Brown, Bruce, Chambers, Cooke of San Saba, Crawford, Darnell, Davis of Brazos, Dillard, Dohoney, Douglas, Ferris, Fleming, Flournoy, Ford, Gaither, German, Graves, Haynes, Henry of Limestone, Holt, Kilgore, Killough, Lacy, Lynch, McCormick, McKinney of Denton, McKinney of Walker, McLean, Moore, Morris, Murphy, Martin of Navarro, Martin of Hunt, Norvell, Nugent, Nunn, Ramey, Regan, Robertson of Bell, Ross, Russell of Wood, Scott,

Sessions, Smith, Spikes, Stewart, Wade, Waelder, Whitehead, Whitfield—54.

NAYS—Abner, Brady, Cline, Davis of Wharton, Flanagan, Lockett, Mills, Mitchell, Pauli, Rentfro, Reynolds, Stayton, Stockdale—13.

The previous question on the passage of the article was then ordered.

The question on Mr. Kilgore's pending amendment was then put, the yeas and yeas called, and amendment lost by the following vote:

YEAS—Abernathy, Allison, Barnett, Blassingame, Brown, Bruce, Chambers, Cooke of San Saba, Dohoney, Douglas, Flournoy, Gaither, German, Graves, Haynes, Henry of Limestone, Holt, Kilgore, Killough, Lacy, Lynch, McKinney of Denton, McKinney of Walker, Murphy, Martin of Navarro, Martin of Hunt, Nugent, Reagan, Robertson of Bell, Robison of Fayette, Russell of Wood, Scott, Sessions, Spikes, Stayton, Stockdale, Whitehead—37.

NAYS—Abner, Ballinger, Brady, Cline, Cooley, Crawford, Darnell, Davis of Brazos, Davis of Wharton, DeMorse, Dillard, Ferris, Flanagan, Fleming, Ford, Lockett, McCormick, McLean, Mills, Mtchell, Moore, Morris, Norvell, Nunn, Pauli, Ramey, Rentfro, Reynolds, Ross, Smith, Stewart, Wade, Waelder—33.

Mr. German's amendment—viz.: Amend section 2, line 10, by inserting after the word "whatsoever" "all lands forfeited to the State by railroad companies"—was then lost by the following vote:

YEAS—Ballinger, Barnett, Blassingame, Brady, Bruce, Chambers, Cline, Cooley, Davis of Brazos, Davis of Wharton, DeMorse, Dillard, Ferris, Fleming, Ford, German, Graves, Haynes, Kilgore, Lacy, Lockett, McKinney of Walker, Mills, Mitchell, Moore, Morris, Martin of Hunt, Nugent, Robertson of Bell, Robison of Fayette, Ross, Russell of Wood, Scott, Sessions, Smith, Spikes, Stewart, Waelder, Whitfield—39.

NAYS—Abernathy, Abner, Allison, Brown, Cooke of San Saba, Crawford, Darnell, Dohoney, Douglas, Flanagan, Flournoy, Gaither, Henry of Limestone, Holt, Killough, Lynch, McCormick, McKinney of Denton, McLean, Murphy, Martin of Navarro, Norvell, Nunn, Pauli, Ramey, Reagan, Rentfro, Reynolds, Stayton, Stockdale, Waelder, Whiefield—32.

The question then recurring upon the final passage of the article, the same was put and the article passed by the following vote:

YEAS—Abernathy, Allison, Ballinger, Barnett, Brown, Bruce,

Chambers, Cooke of San Saba, Crawford, Darnell, Davis of Brazos, Dillard, Dohoney, Douglas, Ferris, Fleming, Flournoy, Gaither, German, Graves, Haynes, Henry of Limestone, Killough, Lacy, McKinney of Denton, McLean, Moore, Martin of Navarro, Martin of Hunt, Norvell, Nugent, Nunn, Ramey, Reagan, Robertson of Bell, Robison of Fayette, Ross, Russell of Wood, Scott, Sessions, Spikes, Stewart, Waelder, Whitehead —44.

NAYS—Abner, Blassingame, Brady, Cline, Cooley, Davis of Wharton, DeMorse, Flanagan, Ford, Holt, Kilgore, Lockett, Lynch, McCormick, McKinney of Walker, Mills, Mitchell, Morris, Murphy, Pauli, Rentfro, Reynolds, Smith, Stayton, Stockdale, Wade, Whitfield—27.

Mr. Nugent moved to adjourn until 9 o'clock Monday morning.

Mr. Crawford submitted the following substitute for "Article —, Granting Lands to Railroads:"

"Section 1. No lands shall ever be granted, except in a manner prescribed by general law, and no law shall be passed granting to any citizen or class of citizens any of the public lands of the State, or privileges therein which, upon the same terms, shall not equally belong to all citizens.

"Sec. 2. The public domain of the State shall be appropriated as follows:

"First. For the use of the State proper, in such manner as the Legislature shall prescribe.

"Second. For homes for actual settlers.

"Third. For the creation of a perpetual fund for the education of the youth of the State.

"Fourth. For the encouragement of, and to aid in the construction of railroads.

"Sec. 3. There shall be two classes of railroads which shall be entitled to receive the State's aid, as follows:

"First. Broad guage roads of the first class shall receive sixteen sections of land, of 640 acres each, for every mile of road constructed and put into actual operation, to be issued upon completed sections of ten miles, and not otherwise.

"Second. Narrow guage roads, or roads of the second class, shall receive twelve sections of land, of 640 acres each, for every mile of road constructed and put into actual operation, to be issued upon completed sections of ten miles, and not otherwise.

"Sec. 4. All certificates issued to railway companies shall be located by the company to which they were issued, and in alternate sections, one for the railway company and one for the State, for the use and benefit of the perpetual school fund.

" Sec. 5. All lands granted to railway companies and held by them shall be open to and may be occupied by actual settlers, in lots of their option, of not less than eighty acres and not more than three hundred and twenty acres, at a price not to exceed one dollar per acre, and the railway companies shall be compelled to alienate to such settlers in fee, without the reservation of any privilege in said land; and the Legislature shall enact such laws as may be needed to give full force and effect to this section.

" Sec. 6. All railway companies shall be compelled to alienate the lands received from the State, one-fourth in every five years, so that the whole shall be sold in good faith within twenty years; and said railway companies shall annually furnish to the Commissioner of the General Land Office, in a manner to be prescribed by law, an abstract of all sales of land made the previous year, showing to whom sold, his residence, quantity of land sold, terms of sale, and price received; and all lands granted by the State, and not sold in good faith within the prescribed time, shall revert to and become the property of the State, and shall be open to occupation and settlement, or other disposition, as in the first instance.

" Sec. 7. To secure a just and uniform system of internal improvements, and to promote the settlements of the State, we declare that no land shall be granted to any railway company heretofore chartered by the State, or to any foreign company having any demand upon the State, except upon an exact compliance with the conditions of their charter or other contract under which the lands are claimed from the State; and the Legislature shall never grant an extension of time to any railway company heretofore chartered; nor shall any charter be renewed in any wise inconsistent with this constitution. The Legislature shall provide for the speedy enforcement of all forfeitures against defaulting companies.

" Sec. 8. All railway companies now in existence may accept the provisions of this constitution, upon a renouncement of all the provisions of their charters inconsistent herewith; and upon a full and complete acceptance of the provisions herein contained, and all railway companies so renouncing and accepting shall be entitled to a speedy and equitable adjustment of all demands against the State upon completed roads affecting reservations, exemption and immunities granted by the State. All reservations opened and lands restored to the State by this means, or by forfeitures, shall be disposed of as in the first instance.

" Sec. 9. No exclusive privileges shall ever be granted to any corporation organized for the purpose of constructing and running a railroad or railroads, or to any other association of individuals for any purpose whatever, that has heretofore been or may be hereafter created over any of the public domain, but the said domain shall be held equally open to location by all who may have a just claim against the same.

" Sec. 10. No foreign corporation or company (other than a commercial copartnership) shall ever acquire, hold or transmit lands in this State, except in such limited quantities as may be necessary for the conduct of a legitimate business in the State, conducted by permission of the State.

" Sec. 11. The lands reserved for the perpetual school fund may be sold in such manner and upon such conditions as the Legislature may prescribe."

One hundred copies ordered printed.

The question on adjournment was then put, and the Convention adjourned by the following vote:

Yeas—Abner, Allison, Ballinger, Brady, Brown, Cline, Cooke of San Saba, Cooley, Crawford, Darnell, Davis of Brazos, Davis of Wharton, DeMorse, Ferris, Flanagan, Fleming, Ford, Gaither, Kilgore, Killough, Lockett, Lynch, McCormick, Mills, Mitchell, Moore, Martin of Hunt, Nugent, Nunn, Pauli, Reagan, Rentfro, Reynolds, Stayton, Stockdale—35.

Nays—Abernathy, Barnett, Blassingame, Bruce, Chambers, Dillard, Dohoney, Douglas, Flournoy, German, Graves, Haynes, Henry of Limestone, Holt, Lacy, McKinney of Denton, McKinney of Walker, Morris, Murphy, Martin of Navarro, Norvell, Ramey, Robertson of Bell, Robison of Fayette, Ross, Scott, Sessions, Spikes, Stewart, Wade, Waelder, Whitehead, Whitfield—32.

FIFTY-FIFTH DAY.

Hall of Representatives,
Austin, Texas, November 8, 1875.

Convention met pursuant to adjournment; roll called; quorum present. Prayer by the Rev. Dr. A. P. Smith, pastor of the Southern Presbyterian Church, at Dallas.

Journal of yesterday read and adopted.

The President announced the following committee on **Mr.** Darnell's resolution, offered Saturday morning:

Mr. Darnell, Chairman; Messrs. Crawford, Waelder, Dohoney, Kilgore, West, Ford, Cardis, Nugent, Wade, McKinney of Denton, DeMorse, Norvell, Blassingame and Flanagan.

On motion of Mr. West, Mr. Sansom was excused indefinitely.

The following communication was then taken from the President's desk and read:

AUSTIN, TEXAS, November 8, 1875.

To the Hon. E. B. Pickett, President of the Convention:

At a meeting of the board of directors of the Capital Fair Association, a resolution was adopted, inviting the members of the Convention to attend the fair, commencing on the 9th and continuing until the 13th of November.

In pursuance of that action, I ask you to notify the Convention of their invitation, and to inform them that complimentary tickets for them have been placed in the hands of Major W. L. Chalmers, the Secretary of the Convention, who will distribute them to the members.   Respectfully yours,

C. S. WEST, President.

Mr. McLean moved to accept the invitation, and that the President of the Convention return the thanks of the body to the association.

Carried.

On motion of Mr. DeMorse, Mr. McLean was added to the Committee on Judicial Apportionment.

On motion of Mr. Ferris, Mr. Davis, of Brazos, was added to the same committee.

Mr. Brown presented the petition of sundry citizens of Dallas on the subject of judicial apportionment.

Mr. Ferris presented a petition from the same county on the same subject.

Both referred to Committee on Judicial Apportionment.

On motion of Mr. Cline, Mr. Morris was excused for two days.

Mr. Russell, of Wood, offered the following resolution:

WHEREAS, It is of great importance that the sons and daughters of Texas should be provided with institutions of learning sufficient to complete their education within the borders of the State; therefore be it

Resolved, That the following ordinance compose a part of the constitution:

"ARTICLE —.

"Section 1.   *Be it ordained,* That, in addition to the lands heretofore set apart for the erection and endowment of State universities, there be and is hereby set apart one million acres more of the unappropriated public domain, for the same purpose, to wit: for the erection, endowment and support of two State universities; and it shall be the duty of the Legislature, at its first session after the adoption of this constitution, or as soon thereafter as they may think expedient, to provide by law for the establishment, endowment, etc., of said universities.

Referred to the Committee on Education.

On motion of Mr. West, the article on General Provisions was taken up out of its order, and made special order for 10 o'clock Thursday next.

UNFINISHED BUSINESS.

"Section —, granting lands to railroads," and "Public Lands and Land Office," taken up, with Mr. Crawford's substitute pending.

Mr. Nugent offered the following amendment to section 3, Article —, Public Lands and Land Office: Strike out all after the word "company."

The hour having arrived for the special order, viz: resolution on night sessions, it was taken up.

Mr. Kilgore proposed to amend the resolution as follows:

Add the words, "Provided that no vote shall be taken on any pending question before the Convention at such night sessions."

Mr. Flournoy offered the following as a substitute for the resolution and amendment.

"That the Convention meet in night session on Monday, Wednesday, Thursday and Saturday nights.

Mr. Mitchell moved to lay the resolution and amendment on the table.

Carried by the following vote:

YEAS—Abner, Ballinger, Barnett, Brady, Cline, Crawford, Darnell, Davis of Brazos, Davis of Wharton, DeMorse, Ferris, Flanagan, Fleming, Ford, Gaither, Kilgore, Lockett, McCormick, Mitchell, Moore, Martin of Hunt, Norvell, Nugent. Pauli, Reagan, Rentfro, Reynolds, Robertson of Bell, Smith, Stayton, Stewart, Stockdale, Waelder, West, Whitfield—35.

NAYS—Abernathy, Allison, Blassingame. Bruce, Burleson, Chambers, Cooke of San Saba, Dillard, Dohoney, Douglas. Flournoy, German, Graves, Haynes, Henry of Limestone, Johnson of Collin, Johnson of Franklin, Lacy, McKinney of Denton. McKinney of Walker, McLean, Murphy, Martin of Navarro, Nunn, Ramey, Robison of Fayette, Ross, Russell of Wood. Scott, Sessions, Spikes, Wade, Whitehead—33.

On motion of Mr. Spikes, Mr. Holt was excused on account of sickness.

The hour having arrived for considering the special order, viz. : " Article —, Judiciary," it was taken up.

Mr. Reagan moved to postpone it until 2½ o'clock P. M. Carried.

Mr. Stayton offered the following as a substitute for the amendment and section 3 of the article:

" The Legislature shall have no power to make any donation of any of the public lands of this State to any work of internal improvement in this State, except as is hereinafter provided.

" It having been the policy of the State to encourage the construction of railroads by donations of land; and that policy having resulted in the construction of such words in certain portions of the State, while certain other portions, more remote, have to a great extent received no advantage, as yet, from said policy; therefore, in order to equalize the benefits of the State's bounty to all portions of its territory, it is hereby provided that the Legislature shall hereafter encourage the construction of railways by donations of land in alternate sections, as follows:

" First—In the territory embraced in the following boundaries, to-wit: Beginning at the mouth of the Colorado river, thence up said river to the point where it intersects the 99th degree of longitude west from Greenwich, thence north on the line of said degree of longitude to its intersection with the 32d degree of latitude, north; thence with the said degree of latitude west to the Rio Grande; thence down said Rio Grande to the Gulf of Mexico; thence with the margin of said Gulf to the place of beginning; to which territory there is hereby allotted twenty thousand sections of land, the same to be received by railways hereafter constructed in said territory, surveys being made by the owners of such railways alternately of an equal number of sections for the State.

" Second—In the territory embraced in the following boundaries, to-wit: Beginning at the point of the intersection of the 32d degree of north latitude, with the 99th degree of west longitude; thence on the line of said degree of longitude north to the north-eastern corner of what is called the Panhandle, thence west to the north-western corner of said Panhandle; thence south with the line of the 103d degree of west longitude, to its intersection with the 32d degree of north latitude; thence east with said degree of latitude to the place of beginning; to which territory there is hereby alloted ten thousand sections, to be re-

ceived and surveyed as hereinbefore provided for the first
division of territory.

"Third—In the territory embraced in the following boundaries, to wit: Beginning at the point where the Galveston,
Houston and Henderson Railway strikes Galveston Bay; thence
with said railway to its intersection with the International and
Great Northern Railway; thence in a north-easterly direction
along said railway to the point where the same intersects the
Texas and Pacific Railway; thence east to the eastern boundary
of the State; thence with the eastern boundary of the State to
the Gulf of Mexico; thence along the margin of the Gulf to the
entrance into Galveston Bay, and thence to the place of beginning; to which territory there is hereby allotted three thousand
three hundred sections, to be received and surveyed as hereinbefore provided for the first division of territory.

"Sec. 3. The alternate sections of land, provision for the survey of which is made in the preceding sections, and not to be
donated to railways, are hereby set apart, donated and declared
to be a part of the public school fund for the State, and they
shall never be otherwise used or appropriated; and the land authorized to be donated to railways shall never be appropriated to
any other use by the State, except that the same may be sold to
actual settlers, or located by land certificates which by failure to
locate were rendered invalid by the 4th section of article 10 of
former constitution, and which by this constitution may be validated, if said lands are so sold or located, before railways are
constructed in the territory aforesaid, as to entitle the owners
of railways to the same."

[Mr. Darnell in the chair.]

Pending the discussion, Mr. Reagan was called to the chair.

Mr. McCormick offered the following amendment to Mr.
Stayton's substitute, which was accepted by Mr. Stayton:

Amend by striking out all of the section from the words, to-
wit, in line 26, to and including line 36, and insert: "Beginning
at the point where the 97th degree of west longitude crosses the
Colorado river; thence north with said degree of longitude to
where it crosses Red river; thence up said river to where the
100th degree of north latitude crosses the same; thence north
with said degree to the north-east corner of what is known as the
Panhandle; thence west to the 103d degree of north longitude;
thence south with said line to where it crosses the 32d degree of
north latitude; thence east with said line to where it crosses the
Colorado river; thence down said river to the place of beginning; to which territory there is hereby allotted fifteen thousand

sections, to be received and surveyed as hereinbefore provided for the first division of territory."

Mr. Ford moved to grant the use of the hall to the chairman and members of the Democratic State Committee, and members of the Democratic party on Wednesday night next, 10th instant. Carried by the following vote:

YEAS—Abernathy, Abner, Allison, Ballinger, Barnett, Blassingame, Bruce, Burleson, Chambers, Cline, Cooke of San Saba, Crawford, Darnell, Davis of Brazos, DeMorse, Dillard, Doboney, Douglas, Ferris, Flanagan, Fleming, Ford, Gaither, German, Graves, Haynes, Henry of Limestone, Johnson of Collin, Johnson of Franklin, Kilgore, Killough, Lacy, McCormick, McKinney of Walker, McLean, Moore, Murphy, Martin of Navarro, Martin of Hunt, Norvell, Nugent, Nunn, Pauli, Ramey, Reagan, Reynolds, Robertson of Bell, Ross, Russell of Wood, Smith, Stayton, Stewart, Stockdale, Wade, Waelder, Whitehead, Whitfield—56.

NAYS—Brady, Mitchell, Rentfro—3.

On motion, the Convention adjourned to 2½ o'clock P. M.

EVENING SESSION—2½ o'clock.

Convention met pursuant to adjournment; roll called; quorum present.

Pending question resumed.

Mr. Ramey made the following report:

COMMITTEE ROOM, } AUSTIN, November 8, 1875. }

To the Hon. E. B. Pickett, President of the Convention:

SIR—Your Committee on Engrossed and Enrolled Ordinances beg leave to report that they have carefully examined and compared "An ordinance to divide the State of Texas into Senatorial and Representative Districts," and find the same correctly engrossed. Respectfully,

WM. NEAL RAMEY, Chairman.

On motion of Mr. Allison, 100 copies of the article were ordered printed.

The hour having arrived for considering the special order, "Article ——, Judiciary," was taken up, and on motion of Mr. Darnell, postponed until the pending business shall be disposed of.

Mr. German moved to close debate on pending amendments, and bring the question to a vote.

Carried.

Mr. Stayton's substitute lost by the following vote:

YEAS—Burleson, Cline, Cooke of San Saba, DeMorse, Fleming, Ford, Gaither, Haynes, McCormick, Murphy, Norvell, Ramey, Rentfro, Reynolds, Ross, Sansom, Stayton, Stockdale, Waelder, West, Whitehead, Whitfield—23.

NAYS—Abernathy, Allison, Ballinger, Barnett, Blassingame, Brady, Bruce, Chambers, Crawford, Darnell, Davis of Brazos, Dillard, Dohoney, Douglas, Ferris, Flournoy, German, Graves, Henry of Limestone, Johnson of Collin, Johnson of Franklin, Killough, Lacy, Lockett, McKinney of Denton, McKinney of Walker, Moore, Martin of Navarro, Nugent, Nunn, Reagan, Robertson of Bell, Robison of Fayette, Russell of Wood, Scott, Sessions, Smith, Spikes, Stewart, Wade—39.

Mr. Flanagan, when his name was called, stated that he would vote for the substitute, but that he was paired off with Mr. Holt.

Mr. Martin, of Hunt, stated that he was paired off with Mr. King, but for which he would vote no.

Mr. Nugent's amendment lost by the following vote:

YEAS—Barnett, Blassingame, Bruce, Burleson, Chambers, DeMorse, Fleming, German, Graves, Haynes, Johnson of Collin, Johnson of Franklin, Lacy, McCormick, McKinney of Denton, McLean, Murphy, Norvell, Nugent, Robertson of Bell, Russell of Wood, Scott, Stayton, Stockdale—24.

NAYS—Abernathy, Allison, Ballinger, Brady, Cline, Cooke of San Saba, Crawford, Darnell, Davis of Brazos, Davis of Wharton, Dillard, Dohoney, Douglas, Ferris, Flournoy, Ford, Gaither, Henry of Limestone, Kilgore, Killough, Lockett, McKinney of Walker, Martin of Navarro, Nunn, Ramey, Reagan, Rentfro, Reynolds, Robison of Fayette, Ross, Sansom, Sessions, Smith, Spikes, Stewart, Wade, Waelder, West, Whitehead, Whitfield—40.

Mr. Moore was paired off with Mr. Erhard, but would have voted "no."

Mr. Martin, of Hunt, was paired off with Mr. King, but for which would have voted "yea."

Mr. Kilgore would vote "no," but was paired off with Mr. Holt.

Mr. Crawford's substitute was lost by the following vote:

YEAS—Barnett, Blassingame, Bruce, Crawford, DeMorse, Dillard, Douglas, Fleming, Flournoy, Gaither, Graves, Johnson of Collin, Kilgore, Killough, McLean, Martin of Navarro, Norvell, Nugent, Ramey, Rentfro, Reynolds, Russell of Wood, Sansom—23.

NAYS—Abernathy, Abner, Ballinger, Brady, Burleson, Chambers, Cline, Cooke of San Saba, Darnell, Davis of Brazos, Dohoney, Ferris, German, Haynes, Henry of Limestone, Lacy, Lockett,

McCormick, McKinney of Denton, McKinney of Walker, Moore, Martin of Hunt, Nunn, Reagan, Robertson of Bell, Robison of Fayette, Ross, Sessions, Smith, Spikes, Stayton, Stewart, Stockdale, Wade, Waelder, West, Whitehead, Whitfield—38.

Mr. Flanagan stated that he was paired off with Mr. Holt, but for which fact he would vote "no."

Mr. Dohoney proposed to amend section 2 by striking out all after the word "barred," in line 18.

[Mr. Brown in the chair.]

On motion of Mr. Whitfield, the Convention adjourned until 9 o'clock A. M. to-morrow.

FIFTY-SIXTH DAY.

HALL OF REPRESENTATIVES, }
AUSTIN, TEXAS, November 9, 1875. }

Convention met pursuant to adjournment; roll called; quorum present. Prayer by the Rev. R. H. Willenburg, of the Cumberland Presbyterian Church, at Austin. Journal of yesterday read and adopted.

Mr. Nunn submitted the resignation of Mr. Dunnam, as follows:

CENTRALIA, TEXAS, Nov. 2, 1875.

To the Hon. E. B. Pickett, President of the Convention:

Having got leave of absence from the Convention on the thirteenth to visit my sick family, I arrived at my home only in time to be with a dying wife during her last moments. This calamity befalling me under such peculiar circumstances, I felt for the time unable to take any action as regards my membership in the Convention, my first impulse being to resign, but by the advice of friends both at home and in the Convention, I was induced to postpone any definite course until I could think more deliberately upon the matter; and now, after due thought, I conceive it my duty to my constituency, my family, and myself, that I offer my resignation to the Convention. My mind is not in a proper frame for those grave duties devolving upon me as a member of your honorable body, nor can I in justice leave my unhappy home for the present. For myself, I need that quiet that may restore me to the performance of those duties that are yet left to me. With these considerations, I offer my resignation,

40

hoping that the Convention may frame an organic law for the State worthy of its talent and time.

Yours respectfully,

A. J. C. DUNNAM.

Unfinished business, viz: "Public Lands and Land Office," with Mr. Dohoney's pending amendment to section 2, by striking out all after the word "barred," in line 18, taken up.

On motion of Mr. Fleming, the amendment was tabled by the following vote:

YEAS—Abernathy, Abner, Allison, Ballinger, Barnett, Blassingame, Brown, Bruce, Burleson, Cardis, Chambers, Cooke of San Saba, DeMorse, Dillard, Douglas, Ferris, Fleming, Flournoy, Gaither, German, Graves, Haynes, Henry of Limestone, Johnson of Collin, Killough, Lacy, McCormick, McKinney of Denton, Murphy, Martin of Navarro, Martin of Hunt, Nugent, Ramey, Robertson of Bell, Ross, Russell of Wood, Sessions, Smith, Spikes, Stayton, Stewart, Stockdale, Wade, Waelder, Whitfield—45.

NAYS—Cline, Crawford, Darnell, Kilgore, Lockett, McKinney of Walker, Moore, Norvell, Nunn, Pauli, Reagan, Rentfro, Robison of Fayette, Whitehead—15.

Mr. Dohoney, when his name was called, stated that he was paired off with Mr. Scott, but for which fact he would vote yea.

Mr. Reagan offered the following amendment:

[Mr. McLean in the chair.]

Amend section 2 by striking out all after the word "State," in line 21.

Mr. Stewart offered the following substitute for the amendment:

Between the words "records" and "or," in line 22, insert "or county map."

Mr. Flournoy offered the following as a substitute for the substitute and amendment:

After the word "barred," in line 18, insert: "No constructive notice of title to real estate shall be held good as against a *bona fide* purchaser for valuable consideration, or a *bona fide* locator thereon, unless the evidence of the same shall have heretofore been of record in the county, or on file in the County Surveyor's office."

Mr. Reagan, by leave, withdrew his amendment.

Mr. Gaither moved to lay the substitute and amendment on the table.

Mr. Flournoy, by leave, withdrew his substitute.

Mr. Stewart's amendment laid on the table by the following vote:

YEAS—Abernathy, Ballinger, Barnett, Blassingame, Brown, Bruce, Burleson, Chambers, Crawford, Darnell, Davis of Brazos, Davis of Wharton, Dillard, Douglas, Ferris, Fleming, Gaither, German, Graves, Haynes, Henry of Limestone, Johnson of Collin, Johnson of Franklin, Killough, Lacy, McCormick, McKinney of Walker, Moore, Martin of Hunt, Nugent, Nunn, Pauli, Reagan, Reynolds, Robertson of Bell, Robison of Fayette, Russell of Wood, Sansom, Sessions, Smith, Spikes, Stayton, Stockdale, Waelder, Whitehead, Whitfield—46.

NAYS—Allison, Cline, DeMorse, Dohoney, Flournoy, Ford, Lockett, McLean, Murphy, Martin of Navarro, Norvell, Rentfro, Stewart, West—14.

Mr. Stewart offered the following amendment:

In line 18, between the words "all" and "land," insert "genuine."

Adopted.

Mr. Reagan offered the following amendment:

Strike out section 8.

On motion of Mr. Fleming, debate was closed on the amendment, and it was lost by the following vote:

YEAS—Allison, Barnett, Chambers, Cline, Dohoney, Flanagan, Flournoy, Lacy, McKinney of Walker, McLean, Martin of Hunt, Norvell, Pauli, Reagan, Ross, Sansom, Sessions, Spikes—18.

NAYS—Abernathy, Ballinger, Blassingame, Bruce, Burleson, Cooke of San Saba, Crawford, Darnell, Davis of Brazos, DeMorse, Dillard, Douglas, Ferris, Fleming, Ford, Gaither, German, Graves, Haynes, Henry of Limestone, Johnson of Collin, Kilgore, Lockett, McCormick, McKinney of Denton, Moore, Murphy, Martin of Navarro, Nugent, Nunn, Ramey, Rentfro, Reynolds, Robertson of Bell, Robison of Fayette, Russell of Wood, Smith, Stayton, Stewart, Stockdale, Wade, Waelder, West, Whitehead —44.

Mr. Kilgore offered the following amendment:

Amend section 3 by adding at the end of the section the words, "the Legislature shall pass general laws only to give effect to the provisions of this section."

Mr. German proposed to strike out section 3.

Mr. Kilgore's amendment adopted by the following vote:

YEAS—Abernathy, Allison, Ballinger, Blassingame, Brown, Bruce, Crawford, Davis of Brazos, DeMorse, Dillard, Dohoney, Fleming, Flournoy, Gaither, German, Graves, Haynes, Henry of Limestone, Johnson of Collin, Kilgore, Killough, Lacy, Mc-

Cormick, McKinney of Denton, McKinney of Walker, McLean, Moore, Martin of Navarro, Martin of Hunt, Nugent, Ramey, Reagan, Robertson of Bell, Robison of Fayette, Ross, Russell of Wood, Sansom, Sessions, Stewart, Wade—40.

Nays—Abner, Barnett, Burleson, Chambers, Cline, Cooke of San Saba, Darnell, Douglas, Ferris, Flanagan, Ford, Lockett, Mitchell, Murphy, Norvell, Nunn, Pauli, Rentfro, Reynolds, Smith, Spikes, Stayton, Stockdale, Waelder, Whitehead—25.

Mr. Crawford offered the following substitute for section 3:

" Sec. 3. no lands shall ever be granted except in an manner prescribed by general law, and no law shall be passed granting to any citizen or class of citizens any of the public lands of the State, or privileges therein, which upon the same terms shall not equally belong to all citizens. The public domain shall be appropriated as follows:

" First—For the State proper, and to satisfy genuine unappropriated land certificate, in such manner as the Legislature shall prescribe.

" Second—For homes for actual settlers.

" Third—For the creation of a perpetual fund for the education of the youth of the State.

" Fourth—For the encouragement of and to aid in the construction of railroads.

" There shall be two classes of railroads which shall be entitled to receive the State's aid, as follows:

" First—Broad gauge roads of the first class shall receive sixteen sections of land, of 640 acres each, for every mile of road constructed and put into actual operation, to be issued upon completed sections of ten miles, and not otherwise.

" Second—Narrow gauge roads, or roads of the second class, shall receive twelve sections of land, of 640 acres each, for every mile of road constructed and put into actual operation, to be issued upon completed sections of ten miles, and not otherwise.

" All certificates issued to railroad companies shall be located by the company to which they were issued, and in alternate sections, one for the railroad company and one for the State, for the use and benefit of the perpetual school fund.

" All lands granted to railway companies and held by them shall be open to and may be occupied by actual settlers in lots, at their option, of not less than eighty acres and not more than three hundred and twenty acres, at a price not to exceed one dollar per acre; and the railway companies shall be compelled to alienate to such settlers in fee, without the reservation of any privilege in said land, as may be prescribed by law; and the

Legislature shall enact such laws as may be needed to give full force and effect to this section.

"All railway companies shall be compelled to alienate the lands received from the State, one-fourth in every five years, so that the whole shall be sold in good faith in twenty years, and said railroad companies shall annually furnish to the Commissioner of the General Land Office, in a manner to be prescribed by law, an abstract of all sales of land made the previous year, showing to whom sold, his residence, quantity of land sold, terms of sale and price received.

"And all laws granted by the State, and not sold in good faith within the time prescribed by law, shall revert to the State, and be open to occupation and settlement, or other disposition, as in the first instance."

On motion of Mr. Allison, the Convention adjourned to 2½ o'clock P. M.

EVENING SESSION---2½ o'clock.

Convention met; roll called; quorum present. Pending question on adjournment resumed, viz., Mr. Crawford's substitute.

On motion of Mr. McCormick, the main question was ordered.

Mr. Crawford's substitute adopted by the following vote:

YEAS—Barnett, Blassingame, Brown, Bruce, Burleson, Crawford, DeMorse, Dohoney, Douglas, Fleming, Flournoy, German, Graves. Haynes, Johnson of Collin, Johnson of Franklin, Kilgore, Killough, McKinney of Denton, McLean, Martin of Navarro, Martin of Hunt, Norvell, Nugent, Pauli, Ramey, Reagan, Reynolds, Ross, Russell of Wood, Sessions, Wade—33.

NAYS—Abernathy, Abner, Ballinger, Chambers, Cline, Cooke of San Saba, Darnell, Davis of Brazos, Davis of Wharton, Ferris, Flanagan, Ford, Gaither, Henry of Limestone, Lockett, McCormick, McKinney of Walker, Mitchell, Moore, Murphy, Nunn, Rentfro, Robertson of Bell, Robison of Fayette, Sansom, Smith, Spikes, Stayton, Stockdale, Waelder, Whitehead, Wright —32.

Mr. German's amendment to strike out "section 3," lost by the following vote:

YEAS—Abner, Ballinger, Blassingame, Bruce, Cline, Darnell, Dohoney, Ferris, Flanagan, Fleming, Ford, Gaither, Johnson of Collin, Lockett, McCormick, Mitchell, Murphy, Norvell, Nunn, Rentfro, Reynolds, Robison of Fayette, Ross. Russell of Wood, Sansom, Sessions, Smith, Stayton, Stewart, Stockdale, Waelder, West, Whitehead—33.

NAYS—Abernathy, Allison, Barnett, Brown, Burleson, Chambers, Cooke of San Saba, Crawford, Davis of Brazos, Davis of Wharton, DeMorse, Douglas, Flournoy, German, Graves, Haynes, Henry of Limestone, Johnson of Franklin, Kilgore, Killough, Lacy, McKinney of Denton, McKinney of Walker, McLean, Moore, Martin of Navarro, Martin of Hunt, Nugent, Pauli, Ramey, Reagan, Robertson of Bell, Spikes, Wade, Whitfield—35.

The question on the engrossment of the article was then put, on the yeas and nays call, the article was ordered engrossed by the following vote:

YEAS—Abernathy, Allison, Ballinger, Barnett, Blassingame, Brown, Burleson, Chambers, Cooke of San Saba, Crawford, Darnell, Davis of Brazos, DeMorse, Douglas, Ferris, Flournoy, Ford, Gaither, Graves, Haynes, Henry of Limestone, Johnson of Collin, Johnson of Franklin, Kilgore, Killough, Lacy, McKinney of Walker, McLean, Moore, Martin of Navarro, Nunn, Ramey, Reagan, Ross, Sansom, Sessions, Spikes, Stewart, West, Whitehead—40.

NAYS—Abner, Bruce, Cline, Davis of Wharton, Dohoney, Flanagan, Fleming, German, Lockett, McCormick, McKinney of Denton, Mitchell, Murphy, Martin of Hunt, Norvell, Nugent, Pauli, Rentfro, Reynolds, Robertson of Bell, Robison of Fayette, Russell of Wood, Smith, Stayton, Stockdale, Wade, Waelder, Whitfield—28.

"Article —, Judicial Department," was then taken up, Mr. Flournoy's substitute for the entire article being the pending question.

[Mr. Stockdale in the chair.]

Mr. Barnett moved to reconsider the vote of yesterday laying on the table the resolution to hold night sessions.

Mr. Kilgore moved to adjourn until 7½ P. M.

Mr. McCormick moved to adjourn until 9 o'clock A. M. to-morrow.

Carried.

FIFTY-SEVENTH DAY.

HALL OF REPRESENTATIVES, }
AUSTIN, TEXAS, November 10, 1875. }

Convention met pursuant to adjournment; roll called; quorum present. Prayer by the Rev. R. H. Willenberg, of the Cumberland Presbyterian Church at Austin.

Journal of yesterday read and adopted.

Mr. Blassingame moved to reconsider the vote engrossing the article on Public Lands and Land Office.

Mr. German moved to reconsider the vote adopting Mr. Crawford's substitute for section 3 of article on Public Lands and Land Office.

Mr. McLean moved to lay the motion on the table.

A call of the Convention was demanded.

Absent—Messrs. Arnim, Brady, Cooley, Flanagan, Johnson of Franklin, Mills, Morris, Ramey, Robertson of Bell, Scott, and West.

On motion of Mr. Russell, of Wood, Mr. Scott was excused on account of sickness.

On motion of Mr. Lockett, Mr. Mills was excused.

On motion of Mr. Sansom, Mr. West was excused for to-day.

On motion of Mr. Cline, Mr. Morris's leave of absence was extended for three days after to-day.

On motion of Mr. McCormick, Mr. Arnim's leave of absence was extended.

Mr. McLean moved to excuse all absent members.

Mr. Rentfro made the point of order that members could not be excused except at their own request.

Chair sustained the point.

Mr. Brady appeared and answered to his name.

Mr. Robertson, of Bell, was announced by the doorkeeper.

Mr. Whitfield offered the following resolution:

WHEREAS, The Convention received on yesterday a tender of the resignation of the Hon. A. J. C. Dunnam, member of this body from the Third district, induced by the death of his wife; therefore,

Resolved, That the resignation of Mr. Dunnam be not accepted, but that his name shall continue on the rolls of the Convention, with indefinite leave of absence.

Resolved further, That the sympathies of this body are hereby tendered to our afflicted associate in his sad bereavement, and that the Secretary is instructed to transmit to him a copy of these resolutions.

Unanimously adopted.

Mr. Flanagan and Mr. Ramey were announced by the doorkeeper.

Mr. Nunn offered the following resolution:

Resolved, That this Convention do hereafter hold night sessions, in addition to the two sessions now held daily, until the labor of this Convention are concluded.

Johnson of Franklin, Kilgore, Killough, Lacy, McKinney of Denton, McKinney of Walker, McLean, Murphy, Martin of Navarro, Martin of Hunt, Norvell, Nugent, Ramey, Reagan, Robertson of Bell, Robison of Fayette, Ross, Russell of Wood, Sansom, Sessions, Smith, Spikes, Stayton, Stewart, Stockdale, Wade, Waelder, Whitehead, Whitfield—52.

The question on adjourning to 2½ o'clock P. M. was then put and carried.

EVENING SESSION—2½ o'clock.

Convention met pursuant to adjournment; roll called; quorum present.

The Sergeant-at-arms reported that pending the call this morning all of the members were brought in, except Cooley, who was absent, at home, in Gillespie county.

"Article —, Public Lands and Land Office," taken up.

A call of the Convention was demanded.

Absent—Messrs. Brady, Cardis, Chambers, Cooley, Dillard, Flanagan, Fleming, Flournoy, Graves, Johnson of Collin, McCormick, McKinney of Denton, McLean and Whitfield.

Messrs. McKinney of Denton, Fleming, and Johnson of Collin, appeared and answered to their names.

On motion of Mr. Waelder, the call was suspended.

Mr. Walker offered the following amendment:

Strike out all after the word "survey," in line 37 of the third section of the original section.

Mr. Waelder moved the previous question.

Lost.

The question on the adoption of Mr. Robertson's (of Bell), amendment to the substitute was put, and the amendment lost by the following vote:

YEAS—Barnett, Blassingame, Bruce, DeMorse, German, Graves, Haynes, Johnson of Collin, Lacy, Norvell, Nugent, Robertson of Bell, Russell of Wood, Wade—14.

NAYS—Abernathy, Abner, Allison, Ballinger, Brady, Brown, Burleson, Cardis, Chambers, Cline, Cooke of San Saba, Crawford, Darnell, Davis of Brazos, Davis of Wharton, Dohoney, Douglas, Ferris, Fleming, Ford, Gaither, Henry of Limestone, Henry of Smith, Johnson of Franklin, Kilgore, Killough, King, Lockett, McCormick, McKinney of Denton, McKinney of Walker, Mitchell, Moore, Murphy, Martin of Hunt, Nunn, Pauli, Ramey, Reagan, Rentfro, Reynolds, Robison of Fayette, Ross, Sansom, Sessions, Smith, Spikes, Stayton, Stewart, Stockdale, Waelder, Whitehead—52.

The question then recurring on the adoption of Mr. Crawford's substitute, the same was put and the substitute lost by the following vote:

YEAS—Allison, Barnett, Brown, Crawford, Dohoney, Douglas, Fleming, Graves, Haynes, Johnson of Franklin, Kilgore, Killough, Martin of Hunt, Nugent, Pauli, Ramey, Reagan—17.

NAYS—Abner, Ballinger, Blassingame, Brady, Bruce, Burleson, Cardis, Chambers, Cline, Cooke of San Saba, Darnell, Davis of Brazos, Davis of Wharton, DeMorse, Ferris, Ford, Gaither, German, Henry of Limestone, Henry of Smith, Johnson of Collin, King, Lacy, Lockett, McCormick, McKinney of Denton, McKinney of Walker, Mitchell, Moore, Murphy, Norvell, Nunn, Rentfro, Reynolds, Robertson of Bell, Robison of Fayette, Ross, Russell of Wood, Sansom, Sessions, Smith, Spikes, Stayton, Stewart, Stockdale, Wade, Waelder, Whitehead—48.

Mr. Abernathy stated that he was paired off with Mr. Dillard, but for which he would vote "no."

Mr. Waelder's amendment to the original section being the pending question, on motion of Mr. Graves debate was closed, and the Convention brought to a vote, which resulted in the adoption of the amendment by the following vote:

YEAS—Abernathy, Abner, Allison, Ballinger, Barnett, Brady, Brown, Burleson, Cardis, Cline, Cooke of San Saba, Crawford, Darnell, Davis of Brazos, Davis of Wharton, Dohoney, Douglas, Ferris, Fleming, Ford, Gaither, Haynes, Henry of Limestone, Henry of Smith, Johnson of Franklin, Kilgore, Killough, King, Lockett, McCormick, McKinney of Walker, Mitchell, Moore, Murphy, Martin of Hunt, Nunn, Pauli, Ramey, Reagan, Rentfro, Reynolds, Robison of Fayette, Ross, Russell of Wood, Sansom, Sessions, Smith, Spikes, Stayton, Stewart, Stockdale, Waelder, Whitehead—53.

NAYS—Bruce, Chambers, DeMorse, German, Graves, Johnson of Collin, Lacy, McKinney of Denton, Norvell, Nugent, Robertson of Bell, Wade—12.

When Mr. Blassingame's name was called, he stated that he was paired off with Mr. Martin, of Navarro, but for which fact he would vote "no."

Mr. German offered the following amendment:

Strike out all after the word "State," in line 50, to the word "all," in line 51, and insert, "and shall become a part of the common free school fund."

Lost.

Mr. Sansom proposed to amend as follows:

Amend section 3 by striking out all of said section after the word "road," in line 33.

Lost.

Mr. Crawford offered the following amendment:

In section 3, line 33, strike out "25" and insert "10," and in line 35 strike out "12" and insert "20."

A division of the question was ordered, and the amendment to section 3, line 33, was adopted and the remainder of the amendment lost.

Mr. Stayton offered the following amendment:

Amend section 2 by adding the words, "or when the appropriation is evidenced by the occupany of the owner, or of some person holding for him."

Adopted.

Mr. Nugent offered the following new section:

"Sec. ——. All titles to lands situated in organized counties in this State shall, within one year after the adoption of this constitution, be recorded in the counties respectively in which such lands are situated, and titles to lands in counties which shall hereafter be organized shall be recorded in such last mentioned counties within one year after the organization thereof; and all titles not so recorded shall be held not to be notice as against a subsequent purchaser for a valuable consideration."

Lost.

On motion of Mr. McCormick, the main question was ordered on the engrossment of the article.

The yeas and nays were demanded and the article ordered engrossed by the following vote:

YEAS—Abernathy, Allison, Ballinger, Barnett, Brown, Burleson, Cardis, Chambers, Cooke of San Saba, Darnell, Davis of Brazos, DeMorse, Dohoney, Douglas, Ferris, Ford, Gaither, Graves, Haynes, Henry of Limestone, Johnson of Collin, Johnson of Franklin, Kilgore, Killough, King, Lacy, McKinney of Denton, McKinney of Walker, Moore, Murphy, Martin of Hunt, Nunn, Ramey, Reagan, Robison of Fayette, Ross, Sessions, Smith, Spikes, Stewart, Waelder, Whitehead—42.

NAYS—Abner, Blassingame, Brady, Bruce, Cline, Crawford, Fleming, German, McCormick, Mitchell, Norvell, Nugent, Pauli, Rentfro, Reynolds, Robertson of Bell, Russell of Wood, Sansom, Stayton, Wade—20.

"Article ——, Judicial Department," again taken up.

On motion of Mr. Stockdale, the Convention adjourned to 9 o'clock A. M. to-morrow.

FIFTY-EIGHTH DAY.

HALL OF REPRESENTATIVES,
AUSTIN, TEXAS, November 11, 1875. }

Convention met pursuant to adjournment; roll called; quorum present. Prayer by the Rev. R. H. Willenberg, of the Cumberland Presbyterian Church, at Austin.

Journal of yesterday read and adopted:

Mr. Reagan offered the following:

Amend the Article on General Provisions by inserting the following as a separate section:

"Sec. ——. That all the navigable waters of this State shall forever remain public highways, free to the citizens of the State, and of the United States, without tax, impost or toll; and that no tax, toll, impost or wharfage shall be demanded or received from the owners of any merchandise or commodity, for the use of the shores, or any wharf erected on the shores, or in, or over any of said waters, unless expressly authorized by law."

One hundred copies ordered printed.

[Mr. Brown in the chair.]

Mr. Rentfro offered the following resolution:

Resolved, That the following be and become one of the rules of this Convention:

"Rule ——. When under a call of the Convention any member shall be absent, it shall be the duty of the Sergeant-at-arms to bring said member into the presence of the Convention. Convention to hear excuse for absence, and judge of its sufficiency. In the event the member be not excused, he shall be fined one dollar, for the benefit of the State, and shall be debarred of his right of voting on any and all questions in said Convention until said fine shall have been paid."

Laid over one day under the rules:

Mr. Robertson, of Bell, offered the following resolution:

WHEREAS, It is the settled policy of this Convention that the Legislature may continue to grant landed subsidies to aid in the construction of railroads;

AND WHEREAS, The experience of the last twenty years has made it manifest that no railroad company that has ever been chartered in Texas has complied with the terms of its contract, thereby creating a necessity for an extension of time;

AND WHEREAS, It must be apparent that no railroad that may be chartered in the future can be built and put into running order in less time than fifty years;

And Whereas, The welfare of the people of Texas demands that they should be relieved from every unnecessary expense in the administration of their government;

And Whereas, The legislation so often demanded for the extension of time to railroad contracts is both expensive to the people and demoralizing in its operation, and demands a reformation, therefore, be it

Resolved, That the Committee on General Provisions be instructed to prepare an article prohibiting the Legislature from entering into any contract with any railroad, river, bayou, ditch or canal company in the future, that will require any of said companies to comply with the terms of their contracts under a period of fifty years.

Referred to the Committee on General Provisions.

Mr. Stewart offered the following resolution:

Resolved, That the Legislature, at its first and second general sessions, shall have power to provide for the annual assessment and collection of a special tax for the maintenance of public common free schools, the said tax not to exceed the general State tax, and when collected and paid into the State Treasury, to be by the Governor, Comptroller and Treasurer distributed to the several counties in this State, according to their respective scholastic population. And the said tax shall never be used by the State or counties for any other purpose than the maintenance of unsectarian public common free schools.

Referred to the Committee on Education.

Mr. Nunn moved to take up his resolution relative to night sessions.

The chair ruled that it required a two-thirds vote to take up the resolution out of its order.

Mr. Nunn appealed from the decision of the chair.

The Convention sustained the chair.

Mr. Stewart offered the following resolution:

Resolved, That three millions of acres of the public domain is hereby reserved and set apart for the purpose of building a State Capitol and other necessary public buildings at the seat of government, which lands shall not be sold within ten years from the adoption of this constitution.

Referred to Committee on State Affairs.

"Article —, Judicial Department," taken up.

Mr. Flournoy's substitute pending.

Mr. Whitfield moved to lay Mr. Flournoy's substitute on the table.

Whereupon the yeas and nays were called, and the Convention

refused to lay the substitute on the table by the following vote:

YEAS—Abernathy, Ballinger, Brown, Cardis, Cline, Davis of Brazos, Davis of Wharton, DeMorse, Dillard, Dohoney, Ferris, Fleming, Henry of Limestone, Henry of Smith, Kilgore, Killough, Lockett, McCormick, Mitchell, Moore, Murphy, Martin of Hunt, Nugent, Nunn, Reagan, Rentfro, Reynolds, Sansom, Smith, Stockdale, Waelder, Whitfield—32.

NAYS—Abner, Allison, Barnett, Blassingame, Bruce, Burleson, Crawford, Darnell, Douglas, Flournoy, Gaither, German, Graves, Haynes, Johnson of Collin, Johnson of Franklin, Lacy, McKinney of Denton, McKinney of Walker, McLean, Martin of Navarro, Norvell, Pauli, Ramey, Robertson of Bell, Robison of Fayette, Ross, Russell of Wood, Sessions, Spikes, Stayton, Wade, Whitehead—33.

The hour having arrived for considering the special order, viz: "Article —, General Provisions," it was taken up, and on motion of Mr. King, postponed until the pending business shall be disposed of.

Mr. Wade moved to close debate on the pending substitute. Carried by the following vote:

YEAS—Abernathy, Allison, Ballinger, Barnett, Blassingame, Brown, Bruce, Burleson, Cardis, Chambers, Cooke of San Saba, DeMorse, Dillard, Dohoney, Douglas, Ferris, Fleming, Flournoy, Gaither, Graves, Haynes, Henry of Limestone, Johnson of Collin, Johnson of Franklin, Kilgore, Killough, Lacy, McCormick, McKinney of Denton, McKinney of Walker, McLean, Moore, Murphy, Martin of Navarro, Martin of Hunt, Norvell, Nugent, Nunn, Pauli, Ramey, Reagan, Rentfro, Robison of Fayette, Ross, Sansom, Sessions, Spikes, Stewart, Stockdale, Wade, Waelder, Whitehead, Whitfield—53.

NAYS—Abner, Brady, Cline, Crawford, Darnell, Davis of Brazos, Davis of Wharton, Flanagan, Henry of Smith, King, Lockett, Mitchell, Reynolds, Robertson of Bell, Russell of Wood, Smith—16.

The question then recurring on the adoption of Mr. Flournoy's substitute, the same was put, and the substitute lost by the following vote:

YEAS—Allison, Barnett, Blassingame, Bruce, Cardis, Crawford, Flournoy, Johnson of Collin, Johnson of Franklin, McLean, Russell of Wood—11.

NAYS—Abernathy, Abner, Ballinger, Blake, Brady, Burleson, Chambers, Cline, Cooke of San Saba, Darnell, Davis of Brazos, Davis of Wharton, DeMorse, Dillard, Dohoney, Douglas, Ferris,

Flanagan, Fleming, Gaither, German, Haynes, Henry of Limestone, Henry of Smith, Kilgore, Killough, King, Lacy, Lockett, McCormick, McKinney of Walker, Mitchell, Moore, Murphy, Martin of Hunt, Norvell, Nugent, Nunn, Pauli, Reagan, Rentfro, Reynolds, Robertson of Bell, Robison of Fayette, Ross, Sansom, Sessions, Smith, Spikes, Stayton, Stewart, Stockdale, Wade, Wharton, Whitehead, Whitfield—56.

Mr. Graves was paired off with Mr. Scott, but for which he would have voted "no."

Mr. Nugent moved to reconsider the vote just taken, and to lay the motion on the table.

Carried.

Mr. Waelder offered the following amendment:

Insert after the word "court," in line 2, section 1, the words "in a Court of Appeals."

Adopted by the following vote:

YEAS—Abernathy, Ballinger, Barnett, Brown, Cline, Cooke of San Saba, Davis of Brazos, Davis of Wharton, Ferris, Fleming, Gaither, Henry of Limestone, Henry of Smith, Killough, King, Lacy, Lockett, McCormick, Moore, Murphy, Norvell, Nugent, Nunn, Pauli, Reagan, Rentfro, Robison of Fayette, Sansom, Sessions, Smith, Stayton, Stewart, Stockdale, Wade, Waelder, Whitehead, Whitfield—37.

NAYS—Allison, Blassingame, Bruce, Crawford, DeMorse, Dillard, Dohoney, Douglas, Flournoy, German, Graves, Haynes, Johnson of Collin, Johnson of Franklin, Kilgore, McKinney of Denton, McLean, Martin of Navarro, Martin of Hunt, Ramey, Ross, Russell of Wood, Spikes—23.

Mr. Russell, of Wood, offered the following amendment:

Strike out all of section 1 after the word "law," in fourth line.

Mr. Nugent moved to lay the amendment on the table.

Lost by the following vote:

YEAS—Ballinger, Barnett, Cooke of San Saba, Darnell, Davis of Brazos, Ferris, Gaither, Haynes, King, Murphy, Nugent, Nunn, Reagan, Sansom, Smith, Stewart, Stockdale, Waelder—18.

NAYS—Allison, Blassingame, Bruce, Burleson, Cardis, Chambers, Cline, Crawford, Davis of Wharton, DeMorse, Dillard, Dohoney, Fleming, Flournoy, German, Graves, Henry of Limestone, Henry of Smith, Johnson of Collin, Johnson of Franklin, Kilgore, Killough, Lacy, Lockett, McCormick, McLean, Moore, Martin of Navarro, Norvell, Pauli, Ramey, Rentfro, Robison of

Fayette, Ross, Russell of Wood, Sessions, Spikes, Stayton, Wade, Whitehead ,Whitfield—41.

Mr. Russell, of Wood, by leave withdrew his amendment.

Mr. Dohoney offered the following amendment:

Amend section 1, line 7, by striking out " fifteen " and insert " thirty."

On motion of Mr. Johnson, of Collin, the Convention ad-Wade, Whitehead, Whitfield—41.

EVENING SESSION—2½ o'clock.

Convention met pursuant to adjournment; roll called; quorum present.

The pending business was taken up, being the amendment of Mr. Dohoney to section 1 of article on Judiciary, to strike out the word " fifteen " before the word " thousand," and insert " thirty."

The amendment was adopted by the following vote:

Yeas—Abernathy, Allison, Bruce, Chambers, Cooke of San Saba, Davis of Wharton, DeMorse, Dohoney, Douglas, Fleming, Gaither, German, Graves, Haynes, Henry of Limestone, Henry of Smith, Johnson of Collin, Johnson of Franklin, Kilgore, Lacy, McCormick, McKinney of Denton, Mitchell, Moore, Martin of Navarro, Martin of Hunt, Norvell, Nugent, Nunn, Pauli, Ramey, Rentfro, Reynolds, Robison of Fayette, Ross, Russell of Wood, Sessions, Spikes, Stayton, Wade, Whitehead—41.

Nays—Ballinger, Barnett, Brown, Burleson, Cardis, Cline, Crawford, Darnell, Dillard, Ferris, Flournoy, Killough, King, McKinney of Walker, Murphy, Reagan, Sansom, Smith, Stewart, Stockdale, Waelder, Whitfield—22.

Mr. Russell, of Wood, offered the following as an amendment to be added to section 1, as amended:

" Provided, such town or city shall support said Criminal District Court, when established."

Adopted.

Mr. Cline offered the following amendment:

Strike out all of section 1, beginning with the words " such," in line 3, and insert the words " municipal courts."

Lost.

Mr. King offered the following amendment to section 1:

In lines 6 and 7 strike out the words " containing at least fifteen thousand inhabitants," and insert after the word " city " the words, " which, together with the county in which it may be situated, contains an aggregate population of thirty thousand."

Lost.

Mr. Waelder offered the following amendment:

In section 2, line 12, strike out "four" ad insert "two;" in line 13 strike out "three" and insert "two;" and in line 14 strike out "a majority of the" and insert "two;" and also strike out the word "sitting" in line 14.

Adopted.

Mr. Whitfield offered his substitute, heretofore presented, as a substitute for section 2; and also offered to amend his substitute by striking out the word "five," in line 4, and insert "and as many district judges as may be hereafter provided."

Lost by the following vote:

YEAS—Allison, Ballinger, Burleson, Cardis, Cooke of San Saba, Crawford, Davis of Brazos, Dillard, Fleming, Flournoy, Haynes, Henry of Limestone, Killough, King, McCormick, McKinney of Walker, Moore, Murphy, Nugent, Nunn, Reagan, Robison of Fayette, Sansom, Stayton, Stewart, Stockdale, Wade, Whitehead, Whitfield—29.

NAYS—Abernathy, Barnett, Blassingame, Brady, Brown, Bruce, Chambers, Cline, Darnell, Davis of Wharton, DeMorse, Dohoney, Douglas, Ferris, Gaither, German, Graves, Henry of Smith, Johnson of Collin, Johnson of Franklin, Kilgore, Lacy, Lockett, McKinney of Denton, Mitchell, Martin of Navarro, Martin of Hunt, Norvell, Pauli, Ramey, Rentfro, Reynolds, Ross, Russell of Wood, Sessions, Smith, Spikes, Waelder—38.

Mr. Bruce offered the following amendment:

In section 2, line 22, strike out "eight" and insert "six."

Mr. German offered the following amendment to the amendment:

Amend section 2, line 22, striking out the words "shall hold their offices for eight years," and insert "shall hold their offices for four years."

Mr. Barnett moved to lay the amendment on the table.

Carried, by the following vote:

YEAS—Abernathy, Abner, Allison, Ballinger, Barnett, Blassingame, Brady, Brown, Bruce, Burleson, Cardis, Chambers, Cline, Cooke of San Saba, Darnell, Davis of Brazos, Ferris, Fleming, Flournoy, Gaither, Graves, Haynes, Henry of Smith, Kilgore, Killough, King, Lacy, Lockett, McCormick, McKinney of Walker, Mitchell, Moore, Murphy, Martin of Navarro, Martin of Hunt, Nugent, Pauli, Ramey, Reagan, Reynolds, Robertson of Bell, Robison of Fayette, Ross, Russell of Wood, Sansom, Sessions, Smith, Spikes, Stayton, Stewart, Stockdale, Wade, Waelder, Whitehead—54.

NAYS—Crawford, Davis of Wharton, DeMorse, Dillard, Dohoney, Douglas, German, Henry of Limestone, Johnson of Collin, Johnson of Franklin, Norvell, Nunn, Rentfro—13.

Mr. Bruce offered the following amendment:

In section 2, line 23, strike out the words "four thousand," and insert "three thousand."

Mr. Sansom offered the following as a substitute for the amendment:

Strike out the words "four thousand," and insert "three thousand and five hundred."

Mr. Gaither moved to lay the amendments on the table.

Mr. Russell, of Wood, called for a division on the question.

The amendment of Mr. Bruce to strike out the word "eight," and insert "six," in section 2, line 22, was voted on.

The Convention then laid the motion on the table by the following vote:

YEAS—Abernathy, Abner, Allison, Ballinger, Brown, Burleson, Cline, Davis of Brazos, Ferris, Fleming, Flournoy, Gaither, Haynes, Henry of Smith, Kilgore, Killough, King, McCormick, McKinney of Walker, Moore, Murphy, Martin of Navarro, Martin of Hunt, Pauli, Reagan, Reynolds, Ross, Sessions, Stayton, Stewart, Stockdale, Wade, Waelder—33.

NAYS—Barnett, Blassingame, Brady, Bruce, Chambers, Crawford, Darnell, Davis of Wharton, DeMorse, Dohoney, Douglas, German, Graves, Henry of Limestone, Johnson of Collin, Johnson of Franklin, Lacy, Lockett, McKinney of Denton, Mitchell, Norvell, Nugent, Nunn, Ramey, Rentfro, Robertson of Bell, Robison of Fayette, Russell of Wood, Sansom, Spikes, Whitehead—31.

The Convention then laid the substitute offered by Mr. Sansom on the table by the following vote:

YEAS—Abernathy, Ballinger, Brady, Brown, Cline, Davis of Brazos, Davis of Wharton, Dohoney, Ferris, Flournoy, Gaither, Haynes, Henry of Limestone, Henry of Smith, Kilgore, King, McCormick, McKinney of Walker, Moore, Murphy, Martin of Navarro, Nunn, Pauli, Reagan, Reynolds, Ross, Sessions, Stayton, Stewart, Stockdale, Wade, Waelder, Whitfield—33.

NAYS—Abner, Allison, Barnett, Blassingame, Bruce, Burleson, Chambers, Crawford, Darnell, DeMorse, Douglas, Fleming, German, Graves, Johnson of Collin, Johnson of Franklin, Killough, Lacy, Lockett, McKinney of Denton, Mitchell, Martin of Hunt, Norvell, Nugent, Ramey, Rentfro, Robertson of Bell, Robison of Fayette, Russell of Wood, Sansom, Spikes, Whitehead—32.

The amendment offered by Mr. Bruce, to strike out "four

thousand " and insert "three thousand," was then laid on the table by the following vote:

YEAS—Abernathy, Abner, Ballinger, Brown, Burleson, Cline, Darnell, Davis of Brazos, Davis of Wharton, DeMorse, Dohoney, Douglas, Ferris, Flournoy, Gaither, Haynes, Henry of Smith, Kilgore, Killough, King, McCormick, McKinney of Walker, Moore, Murphy, Martin of Navarro, Martin of Hunt, Norvell, Nunn, Pauli, Reagan, Reynolds, Robison of Fayette, Ross, Sessions, Smith, Stayton, Stewart, Stockdale, Waelder, Whitfield —40.

NAYS—Allison, Barnett, Blassingame, Brady, Bruce, Chambers, Crawford, Fleming, German, Graves, Henry of Limestone, Johnson of Collin, Johnson of Franklin, Lacy, Lockett, Mitchell, Nugent, Ramey, Rentfro, Robertson of Bell, Russell of Wood, Sansom, Spikes, Wade, Whitehead—25.

Mr. Haynes offered the following amendment:

Section 2, strike out lines 12 and 13 to the word "and," in line 13, and insert the following: "The Supreme Court shall consist of three justices, who shall be elected for the term of twelve years, and after the first election after the adoption of this constitution shall be divided by lot into three classes. The term of the first class to expire at the end of four years; the term of the second class to expire at the end of eight years; and the term of the third class to expire at the end of twelve years."

Lost.

Mr. German offered the following amendment:

In section 2, line 23, strike out "four thousand dollars," and insert "not more than three thousand five hundred and fifty dollars."

Mr. McCormick moved to lay the amendment on the the table. Carried by the following vote:

YEAS—Abernathy, Ballinger, Barnett, Brady, Brown, Bruce, Burleson, Cline, Darnell, Davis of Brazos, Davis of Wharton, Dohoney, Ferris, Flournoy, Gaither, Graves, Haynes, Henry of Smith, Kilgore, Killough, King, McCormick, McKinney of Walker, Moore, Murphy, Martin of Navarro, Nunn, Pauli, Reagan, Reyonlds, Robison of Fayette, Ross, Sessions, Stayton, Stewart, Stockdale, Waelder, Whitfield—38.

NAYS—Abner, Allison, Blassingame, Chambers, Crawford, DeMorse, Douglas, Fleming, German, Henry of Limestone, Johnson of Collin, Johnson of Franklin, Lacy, Lockett, McKinney of Denton, Mitchell, Martin of Hunt, Norvell, Nugent, Ramey, Rentfro, Robertson of Bell, Russell of Wood, Sansom, Smith, Spikes, Wade, Whitehead—28.

Mr. Nunn moved to reconsider the vote just taken, and to lay the motion to reconsider on the table.

Lost by the following vote:

YEAS—Abernathy, Ballinger, Brady, Brown, Burleson, Darnell, Davis of Brazos, Davis of Wharton, Dohoney, Ferris, Flournoy, Gaither, Haynes, Henry of Smith, Kilgore, Killough, King, McCormick, McKinney of Walker, Moore, Murphy, Nunn, Pauli, Reagan, Rentfro, Reynolds, Ross, Sessions, Stayton, Stewart, Stockdale, Waelder, Whitfield—33.

NAYS—Abner, Allison, Barnett, Blassingame, Bruce, Chambers, Cline, Cooke of San Saba, Crawford, De Morse, Douglas, Fleming, German, Graves, Henry of Limestone, Johnson of Collin, Johnson of Franklin, Lacy, Lockett, McKinney of Denton, Mitchell, Martin of Navarro, Martin of Hunt, Norvell, Nugent, Ramey, Robertson of Bell, Robison of Fayette, Russell of Wood, Sansom, Smith, Spikes, Wade, Whitehead—34.

Mr. Graves moved to adjourn until 9 o'clock A. M. Saturday.

Carried, by the following vote:

YEAS—Abner, Allison, Ballinger, Barnett, Brady, Brown, Cline, Cooke of San Saba, Crawford, Darnell, Davis of Brazos, Davis of Wharton, DeMorse, Dohoney, Douglas, Fleming, Flournoy, Graves, Henry of Smith, Kilgore, Killough, King, Lockett, Mitchell, Moore, Murphy, Martin of Navarro, Martin of Hunt, Nugent, Pauli, Rentfro, Reynolds, Stayton, Stockdale, Whitehead—35.

NAYS—Abernathy, Blassingame, Bruce, Burleson, Chambers, Ferris, Gaither, German, Haynes, Henry of Limestone, Johnson of Collin, Johnson of Franklin, Lacy, McCormick, McKinney of Denton, McKinney of Walker, Norvell, Nunn, Ramey, Reagan, Robertson of Bell, Robison of Fayette, Ross, Russell of Wood, Sansom, Sessions, Smith, Spikes, Stewart, Wade, Waelder, Whitfield—32.

FIFTY-NINTH DAY.

HALL OF REPRESENTATIVES,
AUSTIN, TEXAS, November 13, 1875. }

Convention met pursuant to adjournment; roll called; quorum present. Prayer by the Rev. R. H. Willenburg, of the Cumberland Presbyterian Church, at Austin. Journal of yesterday read and adopted.

On motion of Mr. Whitfield, Mr. McCormick was excused until Wednesday morning.

On motion of Mr. Gaither, Mr. Robison, of Fayette, was excused until Monday morning.

On motion of Mr. Nugent, Mr. Haynes was excused until Wednesday morning.

On motion of Mr. Spikes, Mr. Russell, of Wood, was excused on account of sickness.

Mr. Norvell offered the following resolution:

WHEREAS, The time fixed for final adjournment is drawing near, and there yet remains a considerable amount of work to be done, therefore,

Resolved, That rule 11, of the Rules and Order of Proceeding, be amended so as to read as follows:

"Rule 11. No member shall speak more than once in any one debate, until every member desiring to do so shall have spoken; nor shall any member speak more than twice in any one debate, nor longer than five minutes at any one time."

Adopted.

Mr. Dohoney moved to amend by striking out the word "five," and inserting "ten."

Lost.

Mr. Fleming moved to suspend the rules, and act upon the resolution.

Motion sustained and resolution adopted.

UNFINISHED BUSINESS.

"Article —, Judicial Department," taken up, the pending question being the motion to reconsider the vote refusing to adopt Mr. German's amendment relative to salaries of judges.

A call of the Convention ordered.

Absent—Messrs. Brady, Bruce, Cooley, Davis of Wharton, Henry of Smith, King McLean, Waelder, and West.

On motion of Mr. Reagan, Mr. West was excused.

Mr. Stewart's amendment, pending an adjournment, was adopted.

Mr. Stewart offered the following amendment:

Amend section 2, by striking out all that portion of the section down to and including the word "case," in line 4, and inserting the following, viz.: "The Supreme Court shall consist of six justices, who shall elect a presiding officer from their own number, who shall be styled the Chief Justice; a majority of whom, when sitting in banc, shall constitute a quorum and be necessary to the decision of a cause; when sitting in bancs the Chief Justice shall, for the better dispatch of business, have power, as often as he may deem it necessary, to divide the court into two equal sections, and when sitting in sections the concurrence of all three of the judges of the section shall be necessary for a decision of any cause before it; and in case of disagreement in the section of the court, the cause shall be decided by the court in banc, and the Chief Justice may assemble the court to sit in banc at any time during the term thereof, for the trial of causes and the transaction of the business of the court."

Lost by the following vote:

YEAS—DeMorse, Flournoy, Robertson of Bell, Stayton, Stewart—5.

NAYS—Abernathy, Abner, Allison, Arnim, Ballinger, Blake, Blassingame, Brown, Burleson, Cardis, Chambers, Cline, Cooke of San Saba, Crawford, Darnell, Davis of Brazos, Davis of Wharton, Dillard, Dohoney, Douglas, Ferris, Fleming, Gaither, German, Graves, Henry of Limestone, Henry of Smith, Holt, Johnson of Collin, Kilgore, Killough, Lockett, McKinney of Denton, McKinney of Walker, Mills, Mitchell, Moore, Murphy, Martin of Navarro, Martin of Hunt, Norvell, Nugent, Nunn, Pauli, Ramey, Reagan, Rentfro, Reynolds, Ross, Sansom, Sessions, Smith, Spikes, Stockdale, Wade, Waelder, Whitehead—57.

Mr. Dohoney proposed to amend section 2, line 22, by striking out the word "eight" and inserting "six."

Adopted.

Mr. Norvell offered the following amendment:

Amend section 2 by striking out, after the word "State," in line 18, the words "and unless he shall have attained the age of thirty years, and have been a practicing lawyer or a Judge of a District Court in the State, or such lawyer and judge together, at least seven years."

Lost.

Mr. Mills moved to suspend the call.

Lost.

Mr. Mills, on his own motion, was excused.

Mr. Nunn asked leave to withdraw his motion to reconsider. Refused.

Mr. Barnett offered to amend section 3, lines 48 and 49, by striking out all after "government."

Lost by the following vote:

YEAS—Arnim, Barnett, Blassingame, Brady, Bruce, Burleson, Cline, Cooke of San Saba, Dohoney, Fleming, German, Graves, Henry of Limestone, Holt, Johnson of Collin, Lacy, McKinney of Denton, Moore, Martin of Hunt, Nugent, Pauli, Rentfro, Robertson of Bell, Sansom, Smith, Stayton, Stewart—27.

NAYS—Abernathy, Abner, Allison, Ballinger, Blake, Brown, Cardis, Chambers, Crawford, Darnell, Davis of Brazos, Davis of Wharton, DeMorse, Dillard, Douglas, Ferris, Flournoy, Ford, Gaither, Henry of Smith, Johnson of Franklin, Kilgore, Killough, Lockett, McKinney of Walker, Mitchell, Murphy, Martin of Navarro, Norvell, Nunn, Ramey, Reagan, Reynolds, Ross, Sessions, Spikes, Stockdale, Wade, Waelder, Whitehead—40.

Mr. Waelder offered the following substitute for section 3:

"Sec. 3. The Supreme Court shall have appellate jurisdiction only, which shall be co-extensive with the limits of the State, but shall only extend to civil cases, of which the District Courts have original or appellate jurisdiction. Appeals may be allowed from interlocutory judgments of the District Courts, in such cases and under such regulations as may be provided by law. The Supreme Court and the judges thereof shall have power to issue, under such regulations as may be prescribed by law, the writ of *mandamus* and all other writs necessary to enforce the jurisdiction of said court. The Supreme Court shall have power, upon affidavit, or otherwise, as by the court may be thought proper, to ascertain such matters of fact as may be necessary to the proper exercise of its jurisdiction. The Supreme Court shall sit for the transaction of business from the first Monday in October until the last Saturday of June of every year, at the seat of government, and at not more than two other places in the State."

Adopted.

Mr. Brown proposed to amend section 3 as follows:

Amend section 3, line 48, by striking out the words, "and not more than two other places," and inserting "until otherwise provided by law, at the cities of Dallas and Galveston."

Withdrawn.

Mr. Norvell offered the following amendment:

"Strike out section 5."

Carried.

Mr. Waelder offered the following substitute:

"Sec. 5. The Court of Appeals shall consist of three judges, any two of whom shall constitute a quorum, and the concurrence of two judges shall be necessary to a decision by said court. They shall be elected by the qualified voters of the State, at a general election; they shall be citizens of the United States, and of this State; shall have arrived at the age of thirty years at the time of election, and shall have been a practicing lawyer or a judge of a court in this State, or such lawyer and judge together, for at least seven years. Said judges shall hold their offices for a term of .... years, and each of them shall receive an annual salary of ......, which shall not be increased nor diminished during their terms of office."

Adopted.

"Sec. 6. The Court of Appeals shall have appellate jurisdiction co-extensive with the limits of the State in all criminal cases of whatever grade, and in all civil cases, unless hereafter otherwise provided by law, of which the County Courts have original and appellate jurisdiction. In civil cases the court shall not deliver opinions in writing. The Court of Appeals and the judges thereof shall have power to issue the writ of *habeas corpus;* and, under such regulations as may be prescribed by law, issue such writs as may be necessary to enforce its own jurisdiction. The Court of Appeals shall also have power, upon affidavits or otherwise, as by the court may be thought proper, to ascertain such matters of fact as may be necessary to the proper exercise of its jurisdiction. The Court of Appeals shall sit, for the transaction of business, from the first Monday of October until the last Saturday of June of every year, at the capitol, and at not more than two other places in the State, at which the Supreme Court shall hold its sessions. The court shall appoint a clerk for each place at which it may sit, and each of said clerks shall give bond in such manner as is now, or may hereafter be required by law; shall hold his office for four years, and shall be subject to removal by the said court for good cause, entered of record on the minutes of said court."

Adopted.

Mr. Waelder offered the following amendment:

"Sec. 7. All cases now pending in the Supreme Court of which the Court of Appeals has appellate jurisdiction under the provisions of this article, shall, as soon as practicable after the establishment of said Court of Appeals, be certified, and the records transmitted to the Court of Appeals, and shall be decided by such Court of Appeals, as if the same had been originally appealed to such court."

Adopted.

Mr. Norvell offered the following amendment:

Amend section 6 by filling the blank with the word "six."

Adopted by the following vote:

YEAS—Allison, Barnett, Blake, Blassingame, Brady, Burleson, Cardis, Chambers, Cooke of San Saba, Crawford, Darnell, DeMorse, Dillard, Dohoney, Douglas, Fleming, Flournoy, Gaither, German, Graves, Henry of Limestone, Holt, Johnson of Collin, Johnson of Franklin, Killough, Lockett, McKinney of

Denton, McKinney of Walker, Mitchell, Martin of Navarro, Martin of Hunt, Norvell, Nugent, Nunn, Pauli, Ramey, Rentfro, Reynolds, Robertson of Bell, Sansom, Sessions, Smith, Spikes, Stockdale, Wade, Whitehead—46.

Nays—Abernathy, Arnim, Ballinger, Brown, Cline, Davis of Brazos, Davis of Wharton, Ferris, Henry of Smith, Kilgore, King, Lacy, Moore, Murphy, Reagan, Stayton, Waelder—17.

Mr. Johnson, of Collin, proposed to amend section 6, line 69, by striking out the words "three thousand" and inserting "two thousand five hundred, and no more."

Mr. Waelder offered the following substitute:

"Sec. 8. The State shall be divided into convenient Judicial Districts, which may be increased or diminished by the Legislature; each district shall have a judge, who shall reside in the same, and receive an annual salary of .... dollars, and who shall hold courts at one place in each county, and at least twice in each year, as may be prescribed by law, and said judges may be required to hold terms of their courts more than twice annually in any county, should the Legislature so direct. The judges of the several districts shall be elected by the qualified electors thereof, at a general election for members of the Legislature; each judge shall be at least twenty-five years of age; shall be a citizen of the United States; shall have been a practicing attorney or judge of a court, in the courts of this State, for at least fuor years, and shall hold his office for the term of .... years."

Lost.

Mr. Brown offered the following amendment:

Amend section 6 by inserting after the word "Legislature" the words, "and when any judge may be deprived of office by the abolition of his district, he shall receive no further salary."

Adopted.

Mr. McKinney, of Walker, offered the following amendment to section 6:

Amend by inserting after the word "years," "and shall have resided in the district in which he is elected for two years next before his election."

Mr. Barnett moved to excuse Mr. Cooley.

Mr. Rentfro made the point of order, viz: that no member could be excused without his consent.

Mr. Waelder moved to excuse Mr. Cooley by his request.

Carried.

Mr. Flournoy moved to excuse Mr. Flanagan.

Lost.

Mr. Fleming, proposing to pair off with Mr. Flanagan, moved to excuse him.

Lost.

Mr. McKinney's (of Walker) amendment adopted.

Mr. Waelder's substitute lost.

Mr. Whitfield offered the following amendment:

Amend section 6 by adding the following: "Provided, that the District Judges for the first term, under this constitution, shall be appointed by the Governor, by and with the advice and consent of the Senate; after which they shall be elected as in this section provided."

Lost by the following vote:

YEAS—Ballinger, Blake, Brown, Cooke of San Saba, Douglas, Ferris, Henry of Smith, King, Lacy, McKinney of Walker, Moore, Reagan, Sansom, Stayton, Stewart, Waelder, Whitfield —17.

NAYS—Abernathy, Abner, Allison, Arnim, Barnett, Blassingame, Brady, Bruce, Burleson, Cardis, Chambers, Cline, Crawford, Darnell, Davis of Wharton, DeMorse, Dohoney, Fleming, Flournoy, Ford. Gaither, German, Graves, Henry of Limestone, Holt, Johnson of Collin. Kilgore, Killough, Lockett, McKinney of Denton, McLean, Mills, Mitchell, Murphy, Martin of Navarro, Martin of Hunt, Norvell, Nugent, Nunn, Pauli, Ramey, Rentfro, Reynolds, Robertson of Bell, Ross, Sessions, Smith, Spikes, Stockdale, Wade. Whitehead—51.

Mr. Waelder proposed to amend by adding after the word "necessary," in line 74. the words "and to provide for holding more than two terms of the court in any county."

Adopted.

Mr. Martin, of Navarro, proposed to amend line 66, by inserting after the words "practicing attorney," the words "or a judge of a court in this State."

Adopted.

Mr. Stewart proposed to amend section 6, line 63, by striking out the word "thereof," and insert "of the State."

Lost.

Mr. Waelder offered the following substitute for section 7:

"Sec. 7. The District Court shall have original jurisdiction of all criminal cases of the grade of felony; of all suits in behalf of the State to recover penalties, forfeitures and escheats; of all cases of divorce; in cases of misdemeanor involving official misconduct; of all suits to recover damages for slander or defamation of character; of all suits for the trial of title to land, and to enforce liens on land; of all suits for the trial of right to property levied on by virtue of any writ of execution, sequestration or attachment, when the property levied on shall be equal to, or exceed in value, five hundred dollars; and of all suits, complaints or pleas whatever, without regard to any distinction between law and equity, when the matter in controversy shall be valued at or amount to five hundred dollars, exclusive of interest; and the said courts and the judges thereof shall have power to issue writs of *habeas corpus* in felony cases, *mandamus,* injunction, *certiorari,* and all writs necessary to enforce their jurisdiction. The District Courts shall have appellate jurisdiction and general control in probate matters over the County Court established in each county for appointing guardians, granting letters testamentary and of administration; for settling the accounts of executors, administrators and guardians, and for the transaction of business appertaining to estates; and original jurisdiction and general control over executors, administrators, guardians and minors, under such regulations as may be prescribed by the Legislature."

Adopted by the following vote:

YEAS—Abernathy, Abner, Arnim, Ballinger, Barnett, Blake, Blassingame, Brown, Bruce, Burleson, Cardis, Chambers, Cline, Cooke of San Saba, Darnell, Davis of Brazos, Dohoney, Douglas, Ferris, Fleming, Ford, Graves, Henry of Limestone, Henry of Smith, Holt, Johnson of Collin, Johnson of Franklin, Kilgore, Killough, King, Lacy, McKinney of Denton, Moore, Murphy, Martin of Navarro, Martin of Hunt, Nugent, Nunn, Reagan, Robertson of Bell, Ross, Sansom, Sessions, Smith, Stayton, Stewart, Stockdale, Wade, Waelder—49.

NAYS—Allison, Brady, Crawford, Davis of Wharton, De-Morse, Dillard, Flournoy, Gaither, German, Lockett, McLean, Mills, Mitchell, Norvell, Pauli, Ramey, Rentfro, Reynolds, Whitehead—19.

Mr. Graves proposed to amend section 8, line 111, by striking out the word " four," and inserting " two."

Adopted by the following vote:

YEAS—Abner, Allison, Barnett, Blake, Blassingame, Brown, Bruce, Cardis, Chambers, Cooke of San Saba, Crawford, Darnell, Dillard, Dohoney, Douglas, Fleming, Flournoy, German, Graves, Henry of Limestone, Holt, Johnson of Collin, Johnson of Franklin, Killough, King, Lacy, McKinney of Denton, McKinney of Walker, McLean, Mills, Martin of Navarro, Norvell, Nugent, Nunn, Ramey, Reagan, Ross, Sansom, Sessions, Stewart—40.

NAYS—Abernathy, Arnim, Ballinger, Brady, Burleson, Cline, Davis of Brazos, Davis of Wharton, DeMorse, Ferris, Ford,

Gaither, Henry of Smith, Kilgore, Lockett, Mitchell, Moore, Murphy, Martin of Hunt, Pauli, Rentfro, Reynolds, Robertson of Bell, Smith, Spikes, Stayton, Stockdale, Wade, Waelder, Whitehead—30.

The Convention being full, on the appearance of absentees, the question on Mr. Nunn's motion to reconsider, upon which the Convention was called, was put and the motion carried by the following vote:

YEAS—Abner, Allison, Barnett, Blassingame, Brady, Bruce, Burleson, Chambers, Cooke of San Saba, Crawford, Davis of Wharton, DeMorse, Dillard, Douglas, Flanagan, Fleming, German, Henry of Limestone, Holt, Johnson of Collin, Johnson of Franklin, Lacy, Lockett, McKinney of Denton, McLean, Mills, Mitchell, Martin of Navarro, Martin of Hunt, Norvell, Nugent, Pauli, Ramey, Reynolds, Robertson of Bell, Sansom, Sessions, Smith, Spikes, Wade—40.

NAYS—Ballinger, Blake, Brown, Cardis, Darnell, Davis of Brazos, Dohoney, Ferris, Ford, Gaither, Henry of Smith, Kilgore, Killough, King, McKinney of Walker, Moore, Murphy, Nunn, Reagan, Rentfro, Ross, Stayton, Stewart, Stockdale, Waelder, Whitehead, Whitfield—27.

Mr. Arnim was paired off with Mr. Cooley, but for which he would vote "yea."

Mr. Abernathy was paired off with Mr. Scott, but for which he would vote "nay."

Mr. Cline was paired off with Mr. Robison, of Fayette, but for which he would vote "nay."

Mr. Flournoy was paired off with Mr. Russell of Wood, but for which he would vote "nay."

Mr. Graves was paired off with Mr. West, but for which he would vote "yea."

The vote having been reconsidered on the question on the adoption of the amendment, on motion of Mr. Wade debate was closed, and the amendment adopted by the following vote:

YEAS—Abner, Allison, Barnett, Blassingame, Brady, Bruce, Burleson, Chambers, Cooke of San Saba, Crawford, Davis of Wharton, DeMorse, Dillard, Douglas, Flanagan, German, Henry of Limestone, Holt, Johnson of Collin, Johnson of Franklin, Lacy, Lockett, McKinney of Denton, McLean, Mills, Mitchell, Martin of Hunt, Nugent, Ramey, Reynolds, Robertson of Bell, Sansom, Sessions, Smith, Spikes, Wade—36.

NAYS—Ballinger, Blake, Brown, Cardis, Darnell, Davis of Brazos, Dohoney, Ferris, Ford, Henry of Smith, Kilgore, Killough, King, McKinney of Walker, Moore, Murphy, Martin of

Navarro, Norvell, Nunn, Reagan, Rentfro, Ross, Stayton, Stewart, Stockdale, Waelder, Whitehead—27.

The same members were paired off as on the vote to reconsider.

Mr. Fleming was paired off with Mr. Whitfield, but for which he would vote "yea."

Mr. Abner moved to reconsider the vote just taken, and to lay the motion on the table.

Mr. Dohoney offered the following amendment:

Amend by adding after the word "years," at the end of line 22, of section 2, the words, "*provided,* that the terms of office of the justices elected at the first general election, shall be divided by lot into three classes; the term of the first class to be two years, the term of the second to be four years, and the term of the third to be six years, in order that a new justice may be elected at each general election thereafter, whose term of office shall be six years."

Lost.

Mr. Waelder moved to fill the blank salaries of Judges of Courts of Appeals by inserting $3550.

Adopted.

Mr. Bruce offered the following amendment:

Section 6, line 61, after the word "into," insert "twenty-five."

Adopted.

Mr. Bruce offered to amend section 6, lines 68 and 69, by striking out "six" and inserting "four years."

Adopted by the following vote:

YEAS—Allison, Barnett, Blassingame, Bruce, Chambers, Crawford, Darnell, Davis of Wharton, DeMorse, Dillard, Dohoney, Douglas, Flanagan, Flournoy, German, Henry of Limestone, Holt, Johnson of Collin, Johnson of Franklin, Lacy, McCabe, McKinney of Denton, McLean, Mills, Mitchell, Martin of Navarro, Martin of Hunt, Norvell, Nugent, Nunn, Pauli, Ramey, Rentfro, Reynolds, Robertson of Bell, Sansom, Sessions, Smith, Spikes, Stewart, Wade, Whitehead—42.

NAYS—Abernathy, Arnim, Ballinger, Brown, Burleson, Cline, Cooke of San Saba, Davis of Brazos, Ferris, Fleming, Ford, Gaither, Kilgore, Killough, King, McKinney of Walker, Moore, Murphy, Reagan, Ross, Stayton, Stockdale, Waelder—23.

Mr. Bruce offered the following amendment:

Section 6, line 69, strike out "$3000" and insert "$2000."

Mr. Barnett proposed to amend the amendment by inserting "$2500" instead of "$3000."

Adopted.

And amendment as amended was adopted by the following vote:

YEAS—Abernathy, Abner, Allison, Barnett, Blassingame, Brady, Bruce, Burleson, Chambers, Cooke of San Saba, Crawford, Davis of Wharton, DeMorse, Dillard, Dohoney, Douglas, Flanagan, Flournoy, Gaither, German, Henry of Limestone, Holt, Johnson of Collin, Johnson of Franklin, Lacy, Lockett, McCabe, McKinney of Denton, McLean, Mills, Mitchell, Martin, of Navarro, Martin of Hunt, Nugent, Nunn, Pauli, Ramey, Reynolds, Robertson of Bell, Sansom, Sessions, Smith, Spikes, Stewart, Wade—46.

NAYS—Ballinger, Davis of Brazos, Ferris, Ford, Henry of Smith, Kilgore, Killough, King, McKinney of Walker, Moore, Murphy, Norvell, Reagan, Rentfro, Ross, Stayton, Stockdale, Waelder, Whitehead—19.

The same members were paired off as on two former votes on subject of salaries.

Mr. Allison moved to reconsider the vote, and to lay the motion on the table.

Carried.

Mr. German proposed to amend by inserting after the word " of " in line 69, the words " not more than."

[Mr. Stockdale in the chair.]

On motion of Mr. Ramey, the Convention adjourned until 2¼ o'clock P. M.

EVENING SESSION—2¼ o'CLOCK.

Convention met; roll called; quorum present. Consideration of pending business resumed, viz., "Article —, Judicial Department."

Mr. Ramey reported, as follows:

COMMITTEE ROOM, }
AUSTIN, November 13, 1875. }

To the Hon. E. B. Pickett, President of the Convention:

Sir—Your Committee on Engrossed and Enrolled Ordinances would respectfully report to your honorable body, that they have examined and compared " Article —, Public Lands and Land Office," and find the same correctly engrossed.

WM. NEAL RAMEY, Chairman.

On motion of Mr. Graves, one hundred copies of the article were ordered printed.

Mr. German, by leave, withdrew his pending amendment.

Mr. Graves offered the following amendment:

Amend by striking out all after the word "hold," in line 114, and insert "until the office can be filled by an election."

Adopted.

Mr. Waelder moved to reconsider the vote just taken.

Lost by the following vote:

YEAS—Abernathy, Blake, Blassingame, Burleson, Cardis, Chambers, Coke of San Saba, Davis of Brazos, Dohoney, Gaither, Henry of Smith, Killough, Murphy, Martin of Hunt, Norvell, Nunn, Pauli, Reagan, Sansom, Spikes, Stewart, Waelder—22.

NAYS—Abner, Allison, Arnim, Barnett, Cline, Darnell, Davis of Wharton, DeMorse, Douglas, Fleming, Flournoy, German, Graves, Henry of Limestone, Holt, Johnson of Collin, Johnson of Franklin, Lacy, Lockett, McKinney of Denton, McKinney of Walker, Mitchell, Martin of Navarro, Ramey, Rentfro, Reynolds, Robison of Fayette, Sessions, Whitehead—29.

Mr. Reagan proposed to amend by adding to the end of section 9 the following: "And jurors shall receive no compensation for their services in criminal cases."

On motion of Mr. Johnson of Collin, laid on the table.

Mr. Norvell moved to strike out "section 9."

On motion of Mr. Graves, laid on the table.

Mr. Fleming proposed to amend section 10, as follows:

Section 10, line 126, strike out "three" and insert "two."

Mr. Reagan proposed to substitute the amendment, as follows:

Amend section 10 by striking out of line 26 the words "or any three," and insert "or the Court of Appeals, or any two of the members of either."

Adopted.

Also amend section 11 by inserting after the word "Supreme," in line 141, the words "Court of Appeals."

Adopted.

Mr. Cline proposed to amend section 10, line 133, by striking out "shall" and insert "may."

Adopted.

Mr. DeMorse offered the following amendment:

In line 147 strike out "petit and;" in line 148, after "twelve men," insert "and petit juries shall consist of six men in all civil cases, and in criminal cases below the grade of capital or involving imprisonment for ten years." Lost.

Mr. Norvell moved to strike out section 12.

Mr. Reagan proposed to amend the section by inserting after the word "jurors" the words "not exceeding three."

Adopted.

Mr. Waelder proposed to amend the section by striking out "and in trials of criminal cases below the grade of felony," in lines 149 and 150.

Lost.

Mr. Allison offered the following amendment:

Section 12, strike out all down to line 153, and insert: "Grand juries shall be composed of twelve men, and petit juries of twelve man, in all criminal cases, and six men or twelve men, as may be decided by the parties, in trials of civil cases and in trials of criminal cases below the grade of felony, in the District Courts, concurring, may render a verdict, but when the verdict shall be rendered by less than the whole number it shall be signed by every member of the jury concurring, to the number of nine."

Lost.

Mr. Stewart offered the following amendment:

Section 12, line 149, strike out the words "in trials of civil cases," and insert "in trials of civil cases the jury shall be composed of six men."

Lost.

Mr. Robertson, of Bell, offered the following amendment:

Section 12, line 149, strike out all after the word "bills," to "it," in line 153.

Lost.

Mr. Norvell's amendment to strike out section 12, lost by the following vote:

YEAS—Cline, Lockett, Norvell, Robertson of Bell, Smith, Whitehead—6.

NAYS—Abernathy, Abner, Allison, Arnim, Ballinger, Barnett, Blake, Blassingame, Brady, Bruce, Burleson, Chambers, Cooke of San Saba, Darnell, Davis of Brazos, Davis of Wharton, De-Morse, Dohoney, Douglas, Ferris, Fleming, Flournoy, Gaither, German, Graves, Henry of Limestone, Henry of Smith, Holt, Johnson of Collin, Johnson of Franklin, Killough, King, Lacy, McKinney of Denton, McKinney of Walker, Mitchell, Murphy, Martin of Navarro, Martin of Hunt, Nunn, Pauli, Ramey, Reagan, Reynolds, Sansom, Sessions, Spikes, Stayton, Stewart, Stockdale, Wade, Waelder—52.

Mr. Robertson, of Bell, offered to amend by striking out all after "bills," in line 149.

Lost.

Mr. Ballinger offered the following as an additional section:

"Sec. —. Any county may constitute a separate Judicial District, such county to pay the salary of the Judge of said Dis-

42

trict Court; *provided,* that the County Court of the county shall submit the questions of the establishment of such district and of the amount of such salary to a vote of the qualified voters of the county, and a majority shall vote therefor; such salary not to be increased or diminished during such term of office, and a county tax shall be duly assessed and collected for the payment of the same."

Adopted.

Mr. Dohoney offered the following amendment:

Amend section 14 by striking out all from the beginning of the section down to and including the word "law," in line 175, and insert as follows, to-wit:

"The County Court shall have exclusive jurisdiction (with such exceptions as may be provided by law) of all misdemeanors and all indictments for felony, less than capital, not disposed of at the adjournment of each term of the District Court, shall be transferred to the County Court for trial. The County Court shall also have exclusive jurisdiction in all civil cases when the amount in controversy, exclusive of interest, exceeds two hundred dollars (and does not exceed five hundred dollars), and shall have concurrent jurisdiction with the District Court in all civil cases when the amount in controversy, exclusive of interest, exceeds five hundred dollars, and does not exceed one thousand dollars, without any regard to any distinction between law and equity; and shall have power to foreclose mortgages and enforce liens of all kinds upon real and personal property, to the extent of the jurisdiction herein conferred, but shall not have jurisdiction of suits for the recovery of lands; and it shall have such other jurisdiction as may be conferred on it by law."

Mr. Waelder offered the following substitute in the nature of an amendment to the amendment and a part of section 14:

"The County Court shall have original jurisdiction of all misdemeanors, as the same are now or may be hereafter prescribed by law, and when the fine to be imposed shall exceed two hundred dollars; and they shall have exclusive original jurisdiction in all civil cases, when the matter in controversy shall exceed in value the sum of two hundred dollars, and not exceed five hundred dollars, exclusive of interest, concurrent jurisdiction with Justices' Courts in sums between one and two hundred dollars, and concurrent jurisdiction with the District Courts when the matter in controversy shall exceed five hundred and not exceed one thousand dollars, exclusive of interest; but shall not have jurisdiction of suits for the recovery of land, or to enforce liens upon real estate. They shall have appellate

jurisdiction in all cases, civil and criminal, of which Justices'
Courts shall have original jurisdiction, when the judgment of
the court appealed from shall exceed twenty dollars, exclusive of
costs, under such regulations as may be prescribed by law. In
all appeals from Justices' Courts there shall be a trial *de novo*
in the County Court, and when the judgment rendered or fine
imposed by the County Court shall not exceed one hundred
dollars, such trial shall be final; but if the judgment rendered
or fine imposed shall exceed one hundred dollars, as well as in
all cases, civil and criminal, of which the County Court has
exclusive or concurrent original jurisdiction, an appeal shall
lie to the Court of Appeals, under such regulations as may be
prescribed by law."

Mr. Dohoney made the point of order that the amendment
could not be entertained as an amendment to his amendment.

The chair ruled against the point.

Mr. Dohoney appealed, and the Convention sustained the
chair.

Mr. Waelder's amendment adopted by the following vote:

YEAS—Abner, Arnim, Ballinger, Barnett, Burleson, Cline,
Cooke of San Saba, Darnell, DeMorse, Douglas, Ferris, Flana-
gan, Fleming, Graves, Henry of Smith, Killough, King, Mc-
Cabe, McKinney of Walker, Mitchell, Murphy, Martin of Na-
varro, Nunn, Reagan, Rentfro, Reynolds, Robertson of Bell,
Sansom, Smith, Stayton, Stewart, Stockdale, Wade, Waelder—34.

NAYS—Abernathy, Blassingame, Bruce, Chambers, Dohoney,
Flournoy, Gaither, Henry of Limestone, Johnson of Collin,
Johnson of Franklin, Lacy, McKinney of Denton, Martin of
Hunt, Norvell, Pauli, Sessions, Spikes, Whitehead—18.

Mr. Flournoy offered the following as a substitute for section 13:

"Sec. 13. Inferior tribunals shall be established in each
county, for appointing guardians, granting letters testamentary
and of administration; for settling the accounts of executors,
administrators and guardians, and for the transaction of business appertaining to estates, and for the transaction of such
other business as the Legislature may provide. And the District Court shall have original and appellate jurisdiction and
general control over executors, administrators, guardians and
minors, under such regulations as may be prescribed by law."

Mr. Douglas moved to lay the substitute on the table, whereupon the yeas and nays were called, and the motion carried by
the following vote:

YEAS— Ballinger, Brady, Burleson, Cline, Cooke of San

Saba, Darnell, Davis of Brazos, Dohoney, Douglas, Ferris, Fleming, Henry of Limestone, Henry of Smith, Holt, Johnson of Collin, King, McKinney of Walker, Murphy, Martin of Navarro, Martin of Hunt, Nunn, Pauli, Reagan, Rentfro, Reynolds, Sansom, Sessions, Smith, Stayton, Stockdale, Wade, Waelder—32.

NAYS—Abernathy, Abner, Allison, Arnim, Barnett, Blassingame, Bruce, Chambers, DeMorse, Flanagan, Flournoy, Gaither, German, Graves, Killough, Lacy, Lockett, McCabe, McKinney of Denton, Mitchell, Norvell, Ramey, Robertson of Bell, Spikes, Stewart, Whitehead—26.

Mr. Abernathy proposed to amend section 13, line 158, by striking out the word " shall," and inserting " may."

Lost.

Mr. Nunn offered the following amendment:

Add to section 14 the following: "Any case pending in the County Court which the County Judge may be disqualified to try shall be transferred to the District Court of the same county, for trial; and where there exists any cause disqualifying the County Judge for the trial of a cause of which the County Court has jurisdiction, the District Court of such county shall have original jurisdiction of such cause."

Adopted.

Mr. King proposed to amend section 13, lines 163 and 164, by striking out all between the words " receive," in line 163, and " as," in line 164, and insert " such compensation for his services."

Adopted by the following vote:

YEAS—Abner, Ballinger, Barnett, Blake, Blassingame, Burleson, Cline, Darnell, Davis of Brazos, DeMorse, Ferris, Flanagan, Flournoy, Henry of Smith, Killough, King, Lacy, Lockett, McCabe, McKinney of Walter, Murphy, Martin of Navarro, Martin of Hunt, Nunn, Pauli, Rentfro, Sessions, Smith, Stayton, Stockdale, Waelder—31.

NAYS—Abernathy, Allison, Arnim, Brady, Bruce, Chambers, Cooke of San Saba, Davis of Wharton, Douglas, Fleming, Gaither, German, Graves, Henry of Limestone, Holt, Johnson of Collin, Johnson of Franklin, McKinney of Denton, Mitchell, Norvell, Ramey, Reagan, Reynolds, Robertson of Bell, Sansom, Spikes, Stewart, Wade, Whitehead—29.

Mr. McKinney, of Walker, offered the following amendment to section 14:

Amend by inserting after the word " jurisdiction," in line —, the words " and of all such civil cases."

Adopted by the following vote:

Yeas—Abner, Arnim, Ballinger, Barnett, Blake, Blassingame, Brady, Burleson, Chambers, Cline, Cooke of San Saba, Darnell, Davis of Wharton, DeMorse, Douglas, Flanagan, Fleming, Gaither, German, Graves, Henry of Limestone, Henry of Smith, Holt, Johnson of Collin, Killough, Lacy, Lockett, McCabe, McKinney of Walker, Mitchell, Martin of Hunt, Norvell, Nunn, Pauli, Ramey, Reagan, Rentfro, Reynolds, Robertson of Bell, Sansom, Smith, Spikes, Stayton, Stewart, Stockdale, Wade, Whitehead—47.

Nays—Allison, Dohoney, Ferris, Murphy, Martin of Navarro, Sessions, Waelder—7.

Mr. Stewart offered the following amendment:

Add to section 13: *"Provided,* that no part of the pay of the Judge of the County Court shall be made out of the State Treasury."

Lost by the following vote:

Yeas—Abernathy, Arnim, Barnett, Blake, Blassingame, Bruce, Burleson, Dohoney, Fleming, Flournoy, German, Graves, Henry of Limestone, Holt, Johnson of Collin, Johnson of Franklin, Lacy, McKinney of Denton, McKinney of Walker, Norvell, Ramey, Reagan, Robertson of Bell, Stewart, Wade—25.

Nays—Abner, Allison, Ballinger, Brady, Chambers, Cline, Cooke of San Saba, Darnell, Davis of Brazos, Davis of Wharton, DeMorse, Douglas, Ferris, Flanagan, Gaither, Henry of Smith, Killough, Lockett, McCabe, Mitchell, Murphy, Martin of Navarro, Marin of Hunt, Nunn, Pauli, Rentfro, Reynolds, Sansom, Sessions, Smith, Spikes, Stayton, Stockdale, Waelder, Whitehead—35.

Mr. Stewart proposed to amened by adding at the end of section 13, *"Provided,* that the pay of the Judge of the County Court may, by local law of the Legislature, be different in amount in different counties, and to be paid out of the county treasury, and by fees of office, either or both."

[Mr. Stockdale in the chair.]

Mr. Blassingame moved to reconsider the vote adopting Mr. King's amendment to section 13, lines 163 and 164.

On motion of Mr. Whitehead, Mr. Norvell was excused for six days from Monday next.

Mr. Stockdale submitted, by leave, the following report:

COMMITTEE ROOM, ⎫
AUSTIN, November 13, 1875. ⎭

To the Hon. E. B. Pickett, President of the Convention:

The Committee on the Division of the Powers of Government

have instructed me to report the following article, and to recommend the adoption of the same as a part of the Constitution.   Respectfully submitted,

F. S. STOCKDALE, Chairman.

"ARTICLE —.

"Section 1. The powers of the government of the State of Texas shall be divided into three distinct departments, each of which shall be confined to a separate body of magistracy, to-wit: Those which are legislature to one; those which are executive to another, and those which are judicial to another; and no person or collection of persons, being of one of these departments, shall exercise any power properly attached to either of the others, except in the instances herein expressly permitted."

One hundred copies orderd printed.

On motion of Mr. Ramey, the Convention adjourned until 9 o'clock, A. M., Monday.

SIXTIETH DAY.

HALL OF REPRESENTATIVES,
AUSTIN, TEXAS, November 15, 1875. }

Convention met pursuant to adjournment; roll called; quorum present.   Prayer by the Rev. J. S. Groety, of the Presbyterian Church at Austin.

Journal of Saturday read and adopted.

Journal of the evening session of November 11th read and adopted.

On motion of Mr. Roberston, of Bell, Mr. Gaither was granted unlimited leave of absence, to take effect from to-morrow.

Mr. Ballinger presented the petition of the bar of Galveston.

Referred to the Committee on Judicial Apportionment.

Mr. Blassingame's motion to reconsider the vote adopting Mr. King's amendment to section 13, lines 163 and 164, was called up, and the Convention reconsidered the vote by the following vote.

YEAS—Abernathy, Abner, Allison, Arnim, Ballinger, Barnett, Blake, Blassingame, Brady, Brown, Bruce, Burleson, Chambers, Cooke of San Saba, Darnell, Davis of Wharton, DeMorse, Dillard, Douglas, Fleming, Flournoy, Gaither, German, Graves, Henry of Limestone, Holt, Johnson of Collin, Kilgore, Killough, Lacy, Lockett, McKinney of Denton, McKinney of Walker, McLean, Martin of Navarro, Martin of Hunt, Mills, Moore,

Norvell, Nugent, Reagan, Rentfro, Reynolds, Robertson of Bell, Ross, Russell of Wood, Sansom, Scott, Sessions, Spikes, Stewart, Wade, Whitehead—53.

NAYS—Cline, Crawford, Davis of Brazos, Dohoney, Ferris, Flanagan, Henry of Smith, King, McCabe, Mitchell, Murphy, Nunn, Pauli, Russell of Harrison, Smith, Stayton, West—17.

Mr. Gaither offered the following substitute for the amendment:

" He shall receive fees and perquisites of office as may be prescribed by law, including a docket fee for each civil case tried in the court; and the Commissioner's Court of any county may allow him such other compensation as in their discretion they may deem proper."

Lost.

Mr. King's amendment was lost by the following vote:

YEAS—Ballinger, Blake, Cline, Crawford, Darnell, Davis of Brazos, Davis of Wharton, DeMorse, Dohoney, Ferris, Flanagan, Ford, Henry of Smith, King, Lockett, Murphy, Nunn, Pauli, Rentfro, Russell of Harrison, Smith, Stayton, Stockdale, Waelder, West—25.

NAYS—Abernathy, Abner, Allison, Arnim, Barnett, Blassingame, Brady, Brown, Bruce, Burleson, Chambers, Cooke of San Saba, Dillard, Douglas, Fleming, Flournoy, Gaither, German, Graves, Henry of Limestone, Holt, Johnson of Collin, Johnson of Franklin, Kilgore, Killough, Lacy, McCabe, McKinney of Denton, McKinney of Walker, McLean, Martin of Navarro, Martin of Hunt, Mills, Mitchell, Moore, Norvell, Nugent, Ramey, Reagan, Robertson of Bell, Ross, Russell of Wood, Sansom, Scott, Sessions, Spikes, Stewart, Wade, Whitehead, Whitfield—50.

Mr. Henry, of Smith, offered the following as a new section:

" Sec. —. The Legislature may, by local law, applicable to one or more counties, provide that the County Courts shall have jurisdiction in criminal cases below the grade of capital, and provide for the payment of a salary to the County Judge in such counties."

Lost by the following vote:

YEAS—Ballinger, Blake, Brown, Cline, Darnell, Davis of Brazos, Davis of Wharton, DeMorse, Dohoney, Douglas, Ferris, Henry of Smith, Kilgore, King, Lockett, McCabe, Mills, Mitchell, Nunn, Reynolds, Russell of Harrison, Smith, Stayton, Stockdale, Waelder, West, Whitfield—27.

NAYS—Abner, Allison, Arnim, Barnett, Blassingame, Brady, Bruce, Burleson, Chambers, Cook of Gonzales, Cooke of San

Saba, Crawford, Dillard, Flanagan, Fleming, Flonrnoy, Gaither, German, Graves, Henry of Limestone, Holt, Johnson of Collin, Johnson of Franklin, Killough, Lacy, McKinney of Denton, McLean, Martin of Navarro, Martin of Hunt, Moore, Murphy, Norvell, Nugent, Pauli, Reagan, Rentfro, Robertson of Bell, Ross, Russell of Wood, Sansom, Scott, Sessions, Spikes, Wade, Whitehead—45.

Mr. Reagan offered the following amendment:

Amend section 14 by inserting after the word "misdemeanor," in line 2, the words "of which exclusive original jurisdiction is not given to the Justices' Courts."

Adopted.

Mr. Waelder proposed to amend by adding to section 14, line 203, "and in all such cases an appeal shall lie from the District Court to the Court of Appeals."

Adopted.

Mr. Davis, of Brazos, proposed to amend section 13 by inserting between the words "perquisites" and "as," in line 164, the words "of office and such other compensation."

Lost by the following vote:

YEAS—Ballinger, Blake, Brady, Cline, Crawford, Darnell, Davis of Brazos, DeMorse, Dohoney, Ferris, Flanagan, Ford, Henry of Smith, Kilgore, King, Lockett, McCabe, Mills, Mitchell, Moore, Murphy, Nunn, Pauli, Rentfro, Reynolds, Russell of Harrison, Smith, Stayton, Stockdale, Waelder, West, Whitfield—32.

NAYS—Abernathy, Abner, Allison, Arnim, Barnett, Blassingame, Brown, Bruce, Burleson, Chambers, Cook of Gonzales, Cooke of San Saba, Dillard, Douglas, Fleming, Flournoy, Gaither, German, Graves, Holt, Johnson of Collin, Johnson of Franklin, Killough, Lacy, McKinney of Denton, McKinney of Walker, McLean, Martin of Navarro, Norvell, Nugent, Reagan, Robertson of Bell, Ross, Russell of Wood, Sansom, Scott, Sessions, Spikes, Stewart, Wade, Whitehead—41.

Mr. Allison offered the following substitute for sections 14 and 15:

"Sec. —. The County Court, for probate business, shall be holden by the Chief Justice, or County Judge, at the county seat once in each month, as may be prescribed by law, and shall have jurisdiction to probate wills, to appoint guardians of minors, idiots, lunatics, and persons *non compos mentis* (to grant letters testamentary and of administration, to settle the accouns of executors and administrators and guardians, to transact all business appertaining to the estates of deceased persons, minors, idiots, lunatics, and persons *non compos mentis*), including the settlement, partition, and distribution of estates, and to apprentice minors under such regulations as may be prescribed by law. And such County Court may have such other jurisdiction, both civil and criminal, as may hereafter be prescribed by law."

Mr. Reagan made the point of order that the amendment was out of order, containing the same subject matter of Mr. Flournoy's substitute, voted down on a former occasion by the Convention.

Chair ruled against the point.

Mr. Nugent moved to lay the substitute on the table.

Carried by the following vote:

YEAS—Abernathy, Abner, Ballinger, Brady, Brown, Burleson, Cline, Cooke of San Saba, DeMorse, Dohoney, Douglas, Ferris, Fleming, Flournoy, Ford, Gaither, Graves, Haynes, Henry of Limestone, Holt, Kilgore, Killough, Lockett, McKinney of Walker, Martin of Navarro, Martin of Hunt, Mills, Moore, Murphy, Nugent, Nunn, Pauli Reagan, Rentfro, Ross, Russell of Harrison, Sansom, Scott, Sessions, Smith, Spikes, Stayton, Wade, Waelder, West, Whitfield—45.

NAYS—Allison, Arnim, Barnett, Blake, Blassingame, Bruce, Chambers, Crawford, Darnell, Davis of Wharton, Dillard, Flanagan, German, Johnson of Collin, Johnson of Franklin, King, Lacy, McCabe, McKinney of Denton, McLean, Mitchell, Norvell, Ramey, Reynolds, Robertson of Bell, Russell of Wood, Stewart, Stockdale, Whitehead—29.

Mr. Henry, of Smith, moved to reconsider the vote refusing to adopt Mr. Flournoy's substitute for section 13, taken Saturday last.

Mr. Fleming moved to lay the motion to reconsider on the table.

Lost by the following vote.

YEAS—Ballinger, Brady, Brown, Burleson, Chambers, Cline, Cooke of San Saba, Dohoney, Douglas, Ferris, Fleming, Ford, Henry of Limestone, Holt, Lockett, McKinney of Walker, Martin of Hunt, Mills, Murphy, Reagan, Rentfro, Sansom, Scott, Smith, Spikes, Wade, Waelder, Whitfield—28.

NAYS—Abernathy, Abner, Allison, Arnim, Barnett, Blake, Blassingame, Bruce, Crawford, Darnell, Davis of Brazos, Davis of Wharton, DeMorse, Dillard, Flanagan, Flournoy, Gaither, German, Graves, Henry of Smith, Johnson of Collin, Johnson of Franklin, Kilgore, Killough, King, Lacy, McCabe, McKinney of Denton, Moore, Norvell, Nugent, Nunn, Ramey, Reynolds, Robertson of Bell, Ross, Russell of Harrison, Russell of

Wood, Sessions, Stayton, Stewart, Stockdale, West, Whitehead—42.

The question of reconsidering the vote was then put, and the yeas and nays being called, the motion to reconsider carried by the following vote:

YEAS—Abernathy, Abner, Allison, Arnim, Barnett, Blake, Blassingame, Bruce, Crawford, Darnell, Davis of Brazos, Davis of Wharton, DeMorse, Flanagan, Fleming, Flournoy, Gaither, German, Graves, Henry of Smith, Johnson of Collin, Kilgore, Killough, King, Lacy, McCabe, McKinney of Denton, Moore, Norvell, Nugent, Nunn, Ramey, Robertson of Bell, Ross, Russell of Wood, Stayton, Stewart, Stockdale, West, Whitehead—41.

NAYS—Ballinger, Brady, Brown, Burleson, Chambers, Cline, Cooke of San Saba, Dohoney, Douglas, Ferris, Ford, Henry of Limestone, Holt, Lockett, McKinney of Walker, Martin of Navarro, Martin of Hunt, Mills, Mitchell, Murphy, Reagan, Rentfro, Reynolds, Sansom, Sessions, Smith, Spikes, Wade, Waelder, Whitfield—31.

Mr. Henry, of Smith, offered the following amendment to the substitute just reconsidered:

Amend by inserting before the word "business" the words "civil and criminal," and between the words "as" and "business" the words "in one or more counties."

Adopted by the following vote:

YEAS—Abernathy, Allison, Ballinger, Barnett, Blake, Cline, Crawford, Darnell, Davis of Wharton, DeMorse, Dohoney, Ferris, Flanagan, Flournoy, Ford, German, Henry of Smith, King, Lacy, McCabe, McKinney of Walker, Mitchell, Moore, Murphy, Norvell, Nugent, Nunn, Ramey, Smith, Stayton, Stewart, Waelder, West, Whitehead—34.

NAYS—Arnim, Blassingame, Brady, Brown, Bruce, Burleson, Chambers, Cooke of San Saba, Douglas, Fleming, Gaither, Graves, Henry of Limestone, Holt, Johnson of Collin, Johnson of Franklin, Killough, Lockett, McKinney of Denton, Martin of Navarro, Martin of Hunt, Mills, Reagan, Rentfro, Reynolds, Ross, Russell of Harrison, Russell of Wood, Sansom, Scott, Sessions, Spike, Wade—33.

Mr. Nugent offered the following amendment to the substitute:

"*Provided*, that the judges of said tribunals shall only be compensated by fees and perquisites of office."

Adopted by the following vote:

YEAS—Abernathy, Allison, Arnim, Barnett, Blassingame, Bruce, Burleson, Chambers, Cooke of San Saba, Darnell, Dillard,

Douglas, Fleming, Flournoy, German, Graves, Henry of Limestone, Holt, Johnson of Collin, Johnson of Fronklin, Lacy, McKinney of Denton, McKinney of Walker, McLean, Martin of Navarro, Martin of Hunt, Mills, Norvell, Nugent, Ramey, Ross, Russell of Wood, Sansom, Scott, Sessions, Spikes, Stewart, Wade, Whitehead—39.

NAYS—Abner, Ballinger, Blake, Brady, Cline, Crawford, Davis of Brazos, Davis of Wharton, DeMorse, Dohoney, Ferris, Flanagan, Ford, Gaither, Henry of Smith, Killough, King, Lockett, McCabe, Mitchell, Moore, Murphy, Nunn, Reagan, Rentfro, Reynolds, Russell of Harrison, Smith, Stayton, Stockdale, Waelder, West, Whitfield—33.

The question then recurring on the adoption of the substitute, as amended, the yeas and nays were called, and substitute lost by the following vote:

YEAS—Abnernathy, Abner, Allison, Arnim, Barnett, Blake, Blassingame, Bruce, Chambers, Crawford, Darnell, Davis of Wharton, Dillard, Flanagan, Flournoy, German, Graves, Johnson of Collin, Lacy, McCabe, McKinney of Denton, McKinney of Walker, McLean, Norvell, Nugent, Ramey, Ross, Russell of Harrison, Russell of Wood, Stewart, Stockdale, Whitehead—32.

NAYS—Ballinger, Brady, Brown, Burleson, Cline, Cooke of San Saba, Davis of Brazos, DeMorse, Dohoney, Douglas, Ferris, Fleming, Ford, Gaither, Henry of Limestone, Henry of Smith, Holt, Kilgore, Killough, King, Lockett, Martin of Navarro, Martin of Hunt, Mills, Mitchell, Moore, Murphy, Nunn, Reagan, Rentfro, Reynolds, Sansom, Scott, Sessions, Smith, Spikes, Stayton, Wade, Waelder, West, Whitfield—41.

Mr. Wade offered the following new section, to follow section 14:

"The Legislature shall have power to relieve County Courts of civil an criminal jurisdiction in any county designated, and to increase or diminish the jurisdiction of Justices of the Peace."

Lost.

Mr. Scott offered the following amendment:

Amend the Waelder substitute for section 14 by striking out that portion of the substitute which gives the County Court concurrent jurisdiction with the Justice's Courts of all suits in which the amount involved is not less than one hundred dollars and not more than two hundred dollars.

Adopted by the following vote:

[Mr. Stockdale in the chair.]

YEAS—Abernathy, · Allison, Arnim, Barnett, Blassingame, Bruce, Burleson, Chambers, Cooke of San Saba, Dillard, Dohoney, Douglas, Ferris, Flournoy, Gaither, German, Graves, Henry of Limestone, Holt, Johnson of Collin, Johnson of Franklin, Kilgore, Killough, Lacy, Lockett, McKinney of Denton, McLean, Martin of Navarro, Martin of Hunt, Ramey, Robertson of Bell, Ross, Russell of Wood, Scott, Sessions, Spikes, Wade, Whitehead, Whitfield—39.

NAYS—Ballinger, Blake, Brady, Cline, Darnell, Davis of Brazos, Davis of Wharton, DeMorse, Fleming, Ford, Henry of Smith, McCabe, McKinney of Walker, Mills, Mitchell, Moore, Murphy, Norvell, Nugent, Nunn, Reagan, Rentfro, Reynolds, Sansm, Smith, Stayton, Stewart, Stockdale, Waelder, West—30.

Mr. Waelder offered the following as a substitute for section 15, from line 204 to the word "cares," in line 208:

"The County Court shall hold a term for civil business at least once in every two months, and shall dispose of probate business either in term time or vacation, as may be provided by law, and said court shall hold a term for criminal business once in every month, as may be provided by law."

Adopted.

Mr. Dohoney proposed to amend the following:

Amend section 15, line 212, by inserting before the word "misdemeanors" the word "such," and after the word "misdemeanors," the words "as may be authorized by law."

Withdrawn.

On motion of Mr. Mills, the Convention adjourned to 2½ o'clock P. M.

EVENING SESSION—2½ o'CLOCK.

Convention met pursuant to adjournment; roll called; quorum present.

Pending question, viz., "Article —, Judicial Department."

Mr. Kilgore moved to amend by striking out "section 16."

On motion of Mr. Nunn, the amendment was laid on the table.

Mr. Nunn offered the following amendment:

Strike out in lines 213 and 214, after the words "County Courts," "or other inferior courts having jurisdiction to try them."

Lost by the following vote:

YEAS—Ballinger, Blake, Cline, Cooke of San Saba, Davis of Wharton, DeMorse, Dohoney, Douglas, Ferris, Flanagan, Fleming, Henry of Smith, Johnson of Franklin, Lockett, McCabe, McKinney of Walker, Mitchell, Moore, Murphy, Norvell,

Nugent, Nunn, Pauli, Rentfro, Reynolds, Ross, Russell of Harrison, Smith, Stayton, Stockdale, Waelder—31.

Nays—Abernathy, Abner, Allison, Arnim, Barnett, Blassingame, Brown, Bruce, Burleson, Chambers, Darnell, Dillard, Gaither, German, Graves, Henry of Limestone, Holt, Johnson of Collin, Kilgore, Killough, Lacy, McKinney of Denton, Martin of Navarro, Martin of Hunt, Ramey, Reagan, Robertson of Bell, Sansom, Scott, Sessions, Spikes, Wade, Whitehead—33.

On motion of Mr. Dillard, Mr. Owens, Sergeant-at-arms, was excused for the evening.

Mr. Norvell offered to amend section 15, by striking out in line 219 the word "six" and inserting "twelve."

Lost.

Mr. Allison proposed to amend section 17, by inserting in line 232, between the words "unto" and "five," the words "not less than."

Mr. DeMorse offered the following substitute for the amendment:

Strike out all after "thereof," in line 234, down to line 237, and insert "one or more Justices of the Peace, as may be determined by the County Commissioners, who shall hold their offices for two years, or until such time as their successors may be qualified, who shall exercise such jurisdiction and perform such duties, and receive such compensation as may be prescribed by law."

Mr. Allison's amendment lost.

Mr. DeMorse's amendment lost.

Mr. Brown offered the following substitute for all of section 16 and the first paragraph of section 17:

"Sec. 16. Each organized county in the State, now or hereafter existing, shall be divided, from time to time, for the convenience of the people, into precincts, not less than four, and not more than eight. The present County Court shall make the first division. Subsequent divisions shall be made by the County Commissioners' Court provided for by this constitution. In each such precinct there shall be elected, at each biennial election, one Justice of the Peace, one Constable, and one County Commissioner, each of whom shall hold his office for two years, and until his successor shall be elected and qualified; *provided*, that in any precinct in which there may be a city of eight thousand or more inhabitants there shall be elected two Justices of the Peace. The County Commissioners so chosen, with the County Judge as presiding officer, shall compose the County Commissioners' Court, which shall exercise such powers and jurisdiction over all county business as is conferred by this constitution and the laws of the State, or as may be hereafter prescribed by law."

Adopted by the following vote:

YEAS—Abernathy, Allison, Arnim, Ballinger, Barnett, Blake, Blassingame, Brown, Bruce, Chambers Cline, Cooke of San Saba, Crawford, Darnell, Davis of Brazos, DeMorse, Dohoney, Douglas, Ferris, Gaither, German, Graves, Henry of Limestone, Johnson of Collin, Killough, King, Lacy, McLean, Martin of Navarro, Martin of Hunt, Nugent, Nunn, Pauli, Ramey, Robertson of Bell, Sansom, Smith, Stayton, Stockdale, West, Whitehead—41.

NAYS—Abner, Brady, Burleson, Davis of Wharton, Flanagan, Fleming, Henry of Smith, Holt, Johnson of Franklin, Kilgore, Lockett, McCabe, McKinney of Denton, McKinney of Walker, Mills, Mitchell, Moore, Murphy, Norvell, Reagan, Rentfro, Reynolds, Ross, Russell of Harrison, Scott, Sessions, Spikes, Stewart, Wade, Waelder—30.

Mr. Martin, of Navarro, offered the following amendment to the substitute just adopted:

Strike out "ten" and insert "eight."

Mr. Graves proposed to amend by striking out "one County Commissioner for each precinct," and insert "four County Commissioners, no two of which shall live in the same precinct."

Mr. Nugent moved to lay the amendment on the table. Lost.

Martin's (of Navarro) amendment adopted.

Mr. Graves' amendment lost.

Mr. Johnson, of Collin, offered the following amendment:

Section 17, strike out in line 241 "two," and insert "five."

Mr. Rentfro moved to lay the amendment on the table.

The yeas and nays being called, the motion to table was adopted by the following vote:

YEAS—Abernathy, Arnim, Ballinger, Blake, Cline, Crawford, Darnell, Davis of Wharton, DeMorse, Dillard, Dohoney, Douglas, Ferris, Fleming, Flournoy, Ford, Gaither, Graves, Henry, of Limestone, Henry of Smith, Killough, King, Lockett, McCabe, McKinney of Walker, Martin of Navarro, Martin of Hunt, Mills, Mitchell, Moore, Murphy, Norvell, Nugent, Nunn, Reagan, Rentfro, Reynolds, Robertson of Bell, Ross, Sessions, Smith, Spikes, Stewart, Stockdale, Waelder, Whitehead—46.

NAYS—Allison, Barnett, Blassingame, Brady, Brown, Bruce, Burleson, Chambers, Cooke of San Saba, Davis of Brazos, Flanagan, German, Holt, Johnson of Collin, Johnson of Franklin, Lacy, McKinney of Denton, Pauli, Ramey, Sansom, Scott, Wade, Whitfield—23.

Mr. Reagan offered the following amendment:

Amend by adding after the word "law," in line 244, the words "and appeals to the County Courts shall be allowed in all cases decided in Justice's Courts, where the judgment is for more than ten ($10) dollars, exclusive of costs."

Mr. Waelder moved to strike out "ten" and insert "twenty."

Adopted.

Amendment adopted.

Mr. Moore offered the following amendment:

In line 239 strike out the words "imposed in connection shall be" and insert the words "to be imposed by law may not be more than," and strike out "or less," in line 240.

Mr. Mills moved to reconsider the vote refusing to adopt Mr. Grave's amendment to Mr. Brown's substitute.

Carried, and amendment amended to read as follows:

Strike out "and County Commissioners," and insert "the county shall be divided into four Commissioner's precincts, in each of which shall be elected one Commisioner."

Adopted.

Mr. Reagan offered the following amendment:

Amend section 17 by adding before the word "and," in line 244, the words "under such regulations as may be prescribed by law."

Adopted.

Mr. McKinney of Walker offered the following amendment:

Add to section 17 the words "and in all criminal cases."

Adopted.

Mr. German proposed to amend section 18, in line 251, by inserting after the word "filled" the words "by an election to be ordered."

Lost.

Mr. Waelder proposed to insert after "courts," in line 249, the words "and recorder of the court."

Mr. Mills moved to lay the amendment on the table.

Lost, and the amendment adopted.

Mr. Nugent proposed to strike out "eight thousand" and insert "fifteen thousand" in line 254.

Lost.

Mr. —— offered the following:

In line 252 strike out "next general election" and insert "can be filled by election, as directed by law." Lost.

Mr. Murphy moved to strike out "and," after duties, in line 250.

Adopted.

Mr. Brown offered the following amendment:

In Section 18, lines 251 and 252, strike out "Judge of the County" and insert "County Commissioners."

Adopted.

Mr. Stayton moved to strike out "eight thousand" and insert "twelve thousand" in line 254.

Adopted.

Mr. Darnell moved to reconsider the vote just taken.

Mr. Kilgore moved to lay the resolution on the table.

Lost by the following vote.

YEAS—Ballinger, Barnett, Burleson, Cline, Dohoney, Fleming, Gaither, Holt, Kilgore, McKinney of Walker, Mills, Norvell, Nugent, Nunn, Ramey, Reagan, Russell of Harrison, Smith, Stayton, Stockdale, Waelder, Whitfield—22.

NAYS—Abernathy, Allison, Arnim, Blake, Blassingame, Brady, Brown, Bruce, Chambers, Cooke of San Saba, Crawford, Darnell, Davis of Brazos, Davis of Wharton, DeMorse, Dillard, Douglas, Ferris, Flanagan, Flournoy, German, Henry of Limestone, Johnson of Collin, Johnson of Franklin, Killough, King, Lacy, Lockett, McCabe, Martin of Navarro, Martin of Hunt, Mitchell, Moore, Murphy, Pauli, Rentfro, Reynolds, Robertson of Bell, Ross, Russell of Wood, Sansom, Sessions, Spikes, Stewart, Wade, West, Whitehead—47.

The question recurring upon the motion to reconsider, the same was put and the vote reconsidered by the following vote:

YEAS—Abernathy, Allison, Arnim, Blake, Blassingame, Brady, Brown, Chambers, Cooke of San Saba, Crawford, Darnell, Davis of Brazos, Dillard, Douglas, Ferris, Flanagan, Flournoy, German, Holt, Johnson of Collin, Johnson of Franklin, Killough, Lacy, Lockett, McCabe, Martin of Navarro, Pauli, Ramey, Rentfro, Reynolds, Robertson of Bell, Russell of Wood, Sansom, Scott, Sessions, Stewart, Whitehead—37.

NAYS—Abner, Ballinger, Barnett, Bruce, Burleson, Cline, Davis of Wharton, Dohoney, Fleming, Gaither, Graves, Henry of Limestone, Henry of Smith, Kilgore, King, McKinney of Walker, Martin of Hunt, Mills, Mitchell, Moore, Murphy, Norvell, Nugent, Nunn, Reagan, Ross, Russell of Harrison, Smith, Spikes, Stayton, Stockdale, Waelder, West, Whitfield—34.

Mr. Kilgore proposed to substitute the amendment by striking out "twelve thousand" and inserting "ten thousand."

Mr. Stayton's amendment lost by the folloing vote:

YEAS—Abner, Barnett, Bruce, Burleson, Cline, Dohoney, Fleming, Gaither, Graves, Henry of Limestone, Kilgore, King, Lacy, McCabe, McKinney of Walker, McLean, Martin of Hunt, all cases decided in Justice's Courts, where the judgment is for

Moore, Murphy, Norvell, Nugent, Reagan, Russell of Harrison, Smith, Spikes, Stayton, Wade, Whitfield—28.

NAYS—Abernathy, Arnim, Ballinger, Blassingame, Brady, Brown, Chambers, Cooke of San Saba, Crawford, Darnell, Davis of Brazos, DeMorse, Dillard, Douglas, Ferris, Flanagan, Flournoy, German, Holt, Johnson of Collin, Johnson of Franklin, Killough, Lockett, Martin of Navarro, Mills, Mitchell, Pauli, Ramey, Rentfro, Reynolds, Robertson of Bell, Ross, Russell of Wood, Sansom, Scott, Sessions, Stewart, West, Whitehead—39.

Mr. Kilgore's amendment lost.

Mr. Pauli proposed to amend section 18 by striking out the proviso.

Mr. Graves moved to lay the amendment on the table.

Carried by the following vote :

YEAS—Abner, Allison, Ballinger, Barnett, Blake, Blassingame, Bruce, Burleson, Chambers, Cline, Cooke of San Saba, Davis of Brazos, DeMorse, Dillard, Dohoney, Douglas, Ferris, Fleming, Flournoy, German, Graves, Henry of Limestone, Henry of Smith, Holt, Johnson of Franklin, Kilgore, Killough, King, Lacy, McKinney of Walker, Martin of Navarro, Martin of Hunt, Moore, Murphy, Norvell, Nugent, Nunn, Ramey, Reagan, Ross, Scott, Sessions, Smith, Spikes, Stayton, Stewart, Wade, Waelder, West, Whitehead, Whitfield—51.

NAYS—Abernathy, Arnim, Brady, Brown, Crawford, Darnell, Davis of Wharton, Flanagan, Gaither, Lockett, McKinney of Denton, Mills, Mitchell, Pauli, Rentfro, Reynolds, Robertson of Bell, Russell of Harrison, Russell of Wood, Sansom—20.

Mr. Russell, of Wood, offered to amend by adding to section 19 the words "by fees and perquisites of office."

Adopted.

Mr. Cline moved to reconsider the vote just taken.

Carried by the following vote :

YEAS—Abner, Ballinger, Blake, Brady, Cline, Crawford, Davis of Brazos, Davis of Wharton, Dillard, Dohoney, Ferris, Flanagan, Fleming, Gaither, Henry of Smith, Kilgore, Killough, King, Lacy, Lockett, McCabe, McKinney of Walker, Martin of Hunt, Mills, Mitchell, Moore, Murphy, Norvell, Nugent, Nunn, Pauli, Ramey, Rentfro, Reynolds, Ross, Russell of Harrison, Smith, Stayton, Stockdale, West, Whitehead—41.

NAYS—Allison, Arnim, Barnett, Blassingame, Brown, Bruce, Burleson, Chambers, Cooke of San Saba, Darnell, DeMorse, Douglas, Flournoy, German, Graves, Henry of Limestone, Holt, Johnson of Collin, Johnson of Franklin, McLean, Martin of Na-

43

varro, Reagan, Robertson of Bell, Russell of Wood, Sansom, Scott, Sessions, Spikes, Wade, Whitfield—30.

[Mr. Flanagan in the chair.]

Mr. Martin, of Navarro, proposed to amend the amendment by inserting the word "commissions," between "fees" "and," so as to read "fees, commissions and perquisites."

Accepted by Mr. Russell, of Wood.

On motion of Mr. Dillard, debate was closed, and the amendment lost by the following vote :

YEAS—Abernathy, Allison, Arnim, Barnett, Blassingame, Brown, Bruce, Burleson, Chambers, Cooke of San Saba, Davis of Wharton, DeMorse, Dillard, Douglas, Flournoy, German, Graves, Holt, Johnson of Collin, Johnson of Franklin, McKinney of Denton, McLean, Martin of Navarro, Nugent, Ramey, Reagan, Robertson of Bell, Russell of Wood, Sansom, Scott, Sessions, Spikes, Stewart, Wade, Whitehead, Whitfield—36.

NAYS—Abner, Ballinger, Blake, Brady, Cline, Crawford, Darnell, Davis of Brazos, Dohoney, Ferris, Flanagan, Fleming, Gaither, Henry of Limestone, Henry of Smith, Kilgore, Killough, Lacy, Lockett, McCabe, McKinney of Walker, Martin of Hunt, Mills, Mitchell, Moore, Murphy, Norvell, Nunn, Pauli, Rentfro, Reynolds, Ross, Russell of Harrison, Smith, Stayton, Stockdale, Waelder, West—38.

Mr. Dohoney moved to adjourn to 9 o'clock A. M. to-morrow. Carried.

SIXTY-FIRST DAY.

HALL OF REPRESENTATIVES,
AUSTIN, TEXAS, November 16, 1875.

Convention met pursuant to adjournment; roll called; quorum present.   Prayer by the Rev. J. S. Groety, of the Presbyterian Church.

Journal of yesterday read and adopted.

Mr. Chambers stated that in the several votes taken on salaries for judges he had agreed to pair off with Mr. McCormick, he (Chambers) voting for the lower salaries, and Mr. McCormick for the salaries reported by the committee.

The Secretary was instructed to make the necessary correction.

On motion of Mr. Reynolds, Mr. Davis, of Wharton, was indefinitely excused.

On motion of Mr. Cooke, of San Saba, Mr. West was excused for to-day.

On motion of Mr. Ford, Mr. Cardis was excused.

Mr. Reagan made the following report :

COMMITTEE ROOM,   }

AUSTIN, TEXAS, November 16, 1875. }

To the Hon. E. B. Pickett, President of the Convention:

The special committee to whom was referred various resolutions in relation to old Spanish and Mexican land titles, have had the same under consideration, and with a full appreciation of the importance of the subject, and after careful consideration, instruct me to report the following declarations, and to recommend their adoption as a separate article in the constitution.

JOHN H. REAGAN, Chairman.

" ARTICLE —.

"Sec. 1.   All fines, penalties, forfeitures and escheats which have heretofore accrued to the Republic and State of Texas, under their constitutions and laws, shall accrue to the State under this constitution; and the Legislature shall provide a method for determining what lands have been forfeited, and for giving effect to escheats; and all such rights of forfeiture and escheat to the State shall *ipso facto* enure to the protection of the holders of junior titles, as provided in sections 2, 3 and 4 of this article.

" Sec. 2. Any claim of title or right to land in Texas, issued prior to the 13th day of November, 1835, not duly recorded in the county where the land was situated at the time of such record, or not duly archived in the General Land Office, or not in the actual possession of the grantee thereof, or some person claiming under him, prior to the accruing of junior title or color of title thereto from the sovereignty of the soil, under circumstances reasonably calculated to give notice to said junior grantee, has never had, and shall not have, standing or effect against such junior tittle or color of title, acquired without such notice of such prior claim of title or right; and no condition annexed thereto has been, or ever shall be released or waived, but actual performance of all such conditions shall be proved by the person or persons claiming under such title or claim of right in order to maintain action thereon, and the holder of such junior title or color of title shall have all rights of the government which have heretofore existed, or now exist, arising from the non-performance of all such conditions.

" Sec. 3. Non-payment of taxes on any claim of title to land dated prior to the 13th day of November, 1835, up to the date of the adoption of this constitution, shall be held to be a presumption that the right thereto has reverted to the State, and that said claim is a State demand, which presumption shall only be rebutted by payment of all taxes on said lands, State, county, and city, to be assessed on the fair value of such lands by the Comptroller, and paid to him, without commutation or deduction for any part of the above period.

"Sec. 4. No claim of title or right to land, which existed prior to the 13th day of November, 1835, which has not been duly recorded in the county where the land was situated at the time of such record, or which has not been duly archived in the General Land Office, shall ever thereafter be deposited in the General Land Office, or recorded in this State, or delineated on the maps, or used as evidence in any of the courts of this State; and the same are State claims. But this shall not effect such rights or presumptions as arise from actual possession.

"Sec. 5. All claims, locations, surveys, grants and titles to land of any kind, which are declared null and void by the constitution of the Republic or State of Texas, are, and the same shall remain, forever null and void.

"Sec. 6. The Legislature shall pass stringent laws for the detection and conviction of all forgers of land titles, and may make such appropriations of money for that purpose as may be necessary.

"Sec. 7. Sections 2, 3, 4 and 5 of this article shall not be construed to set aside or repeal any law or laws of the Republic or State of Texas releasing the claimants of headrights of colonists of a league of land or less from compliance with the conditions on which their grants were made."

On motion of Mr. Dohoney, one hundred copies ordered printed and made special order for Saturday, 20th inst., at 10 o'clock A. M.

Mr. King made the following report :

COMMITTEE ROOM,
AUSTIN, TEXAS, November 14, 1875. }

To the Hon. E. B. Pickett, President of the Convention:

SIR—Your committee on Counties and County Lands, to whom were referred various resolutions and memorials, have carefully considered the same in connection with the whole subject, and beg leave to report the following article, and recommend its adoption as a part of the constitution.

Respectfully,   HENRY C. KING, Chairman.

"ARTICLE ——.

"COUNTIES.

" Section 1. The Legislature shall have power to create counties for the convenience of the people, subject to the following provisions:

" First—In the territory of the State exterior to all counties now existing, no new county shall be created with a less area than nine hundred square miles, in a square form, unless prevented by pre-existing boundary lines. Should the State lines render this impracticable in border counties, the area may be less. The territory referred to may, at any time, in whole or in part, be divided into counties in advance of population, and attached, for judicial and land surveying purposes, to the most convenient organized county or counties.

" Second—Within the territory of any county or counties now existing, no new county shall be created with a less area than four hundred and fifty square miles, nor shall any such county now existing be reduced to a less area than four hundred and fifty square miles. No new county shall be created so as to approach nearer than twelve miles of the county seat of any county from which it may in whole or in part be taken. Counties of a less area than nine hundred, but of four hundred and fifty or more square miles, within counties now existing, may be created by a vote of two-thirds of each house of the Legislature, taken by yeas and nays, and entered on the journals. Any county now existing may be reduced to an area of not less than four hundred and fifty square miles, by a like two-thirds vote. When any part of a county is stricken off and attached to another county, the part stricken off shall be holden for, and obliged to pay, its proportion of all the liabilities then existing of the county from which it is taken, in such manner as may be prescribed by law.

"Third—No part of any existing county shall be detached from it and attached to another existing county, until the proposition for such change shall have been submitted, in such manner as may be provided by law, to a vote of the electors of both counties, and shall have received a majority of those voting on the question in each.

"COUNTY SEATS.

" Sec. ——. The legislature shall pass laws regulating the manner of removing county seats, but no county seat situated within five miles of the geographical centre of the county shall be removed except by a vote of two-thirds of all electors voting on the subject. A majority of such electors, however, voting at such election, may remove a county seat from a point more than five miles from the geographical centre of the county to a point within five miles of such centre, in either case the centre being determined by a certificate from the Commissioner of the General Land Office."

On motion of Mr. Allison, one hundred copies were ordered printed.

Unfinished business, viz: "Art. —, Judicial Department."

Mr. Chambers offered the following amendment:

"*Provided,* District Attorneys shall receive an annual salary of $500, to be paid by the State, and such fees, commisisons and perquisites as may be provided by law. (County Attorneys shall receive as compensation only such fees, commissions and perquisites as may be prescribed by law)."

Adopted.

Mr. German offered the following amendment to section 19, line 270.

Strike out the words "the next general election," and insert "an election shall be held for the unexpired term."

Lost.

Mr. Stewart proposed to amend as follows:

After the word "attorney," in section 19, line 257, insert the words "for counties in which there is not a resident Criminal District Attorney."

Adopted.

Mr. Stewart offered the following additional section, to follow section 19 of printed bill:

"Sec. —. The Legislature, by a vote of two-thirds, shall have power by local law in any county to allow in all cases, civil and criminal, without regard to amount or nature of the judgment, to confer the right of appeal directly from the judgments and orders of County Courts and Justices of the Peace, and County Commissioners, to the District Court of such county or counties; *provided,* that the operation of such local laws shall not extend in all to more than one-tenth of the organized counties in this State."

Lost by the following vote:

YEAS—Arnim, Ballinger, DeMorse, Erhard, King, McCormick, Martin of Hunt, Reagan, Robertson of Bell, Spikes, Stewart—11.

NAYS—Abernathy, Allison, Barnett, Blake, Blassingame, Bruce, Burleson, Crawford, Darnell, Dillard, Dohoney, Douglas, Ferris, Flanagan, Fleming, Flournoy, German, Graves, Henry of Limestone, Holt, Johnson of Collin, Johnson of Franklin, Killough, Lacy, Lockett, Mills, Mitchell, Moore, Murphy, Martin of Navarro, Nugent, Nunn, Pauli, Rentfro, Reynolds, Ross, Russell of Harrison, Russell of Wood, Sansom, Scott, Sessions, Smith, Stockdale, Wade, Waelder, Weaver, Whitehead—47.

Mr. Sansom offered the following additional section:

"Sec. 20. The Legislature shall have the power, after two years from the adoption of this constitution, to make such modifications in the judicial system of the State as may be necessary to meet the wants of the people."

Mr. McKinney, of Walker, offered the following substitute for Mr. Sansom's amendment:

"The Legislature shall have power to increase, diminish or change the civil and criminal jurisdiction of the County Courts."

The yeas and nays being demanded, the amendment was adopted, as an amendment to the substitute, by the following vote:

YEAS—Abernathy, Arnim, Ballinger, Blake, Blassingame, Brown, Chambers, Cline, Darnell, Davis of Brazos, Douglas, Erhard, Flanagan, Fleming, Flournoy, German, Graves, Johnson of Collin, Johnson of Franklin, Killough, Lockett, McCormick, McKinney of Denton, McKinney of Walker, Martin of Navarro, Mills, Nugent, Robertson of Bell, Ross, Russell of Harrison, Russell of Wood, Smith, Spikes, Stayton, Stewart, Wade, Waelder—37.

NAYS—Allison, Barnett, Brady, Bruce, Burleson, Cooke of San Saba, Crawford, DeMorse, Dillard, Dohoney, Ferris, Henry of Limestone, Henry of Smith, Holt, Kilgore, King, Lacy, Martin of Hunt, Moore, Murphy, Nunn, Pauli, Reagan, Rentfro, Reynolds, Sansom, Scott, Sessions, Weaver, Whitehead—30.

Adopted as an amendment to the article.

Mr. Waelder proposed to amend the amendment as follows: Insert after "power" the words "by local or general law."

Adopted by the following vote:

YEAS—Abernathy, Allison, Arnim, Ballinger, Blake, Blassingame, Brown, Burleson, Chambers, Cooke of San Saba, Crawford, Darnell, Davis of Brazos, DeMorse, Dillard, Dohoney, Douglas, Erhard, Ferris, Flournoy, Graves, Henry of Smith, Holt, Johnson of Collin, Johnson of Franklin, Kilgore, Killough, McCormick, McKinney of Denton, McKinney of Walker, Martin of Navarro, Martin of Hunt, Moore, Nugent, Nunn, Ramey, Reagan, Ross, Russell of Wood, Sansom, Scott, Sessions, Smith, Spikes, Stayton, Stewart, Stockdale, Wade, Waelder, Weaver, Whitehead, Whitfield—52.

NAYS.—Barnett, Brady, Bruce, Cline, Flanagan, Fleming, German, Henry of Limestone, Lacy, Lockett, Mills, Murphy,

Pauli, Rentfro, Reynolds, Robertson of Bell, Russell of Harrison—17.

Mr. Flournoy proposed to amend the section just adopted as follows:

"And in case of any such change of jurisdiction the Legislature shall also conform the jurisdiction of the other courts to such change."

Adopted.

Mr. Davis, of Brazos, offered the following amendment:

Add to section — the following: "And after the first of January, 1880, the Legislature shall have power to make such changes and modifications in the organization and jurisdiction of any of the courts of this State as may be deemed necessary for the speedy, prompt and efficient administration of justice."

Lost.

Mr. Brown offered the following amendment:

Amend section 20, line 284, by striking out the words " judge of the county," and insert " County Commissioners."

Adopted.

Mr. German proposed to amend section 20, line 284, by striking out the words "until the general election for county or State officers," and insert the words "an election shall be held for the unexpired term."

Lost by the following vote:

YEAS—Allison, Arnim, Barnett, Blassingame, Bruce, Burleson, Crawford, DeMorse, Dohoney, Ferris, Flanagan, Flournoy, Ford, German, Graves, Henry of Limestone, Johnson of Collin, Lockett, McKinney of Denton, Martin of Hunt, Robertson of Bell, Russell of Harrison, Russell of Wood, Scott, Spikes, Wade, Weaver, Whitehead—28.

NAYS—Abernathy, Ballinger, Blake, Brady, Brown, Chambers, Cline, Cooke of San Saba, Darnell, Douglas, Erhard, Fleming, Henry of Smith, Holt, Johnson of Franklin, Kilgore, Killough, Lacy, McCabe, McCormick, McKinney of Walker, Martin of Navarro, Moore, Nugent, Nunn, Pauli, Reagan, Rentfro, Reynolds, Ross, Sessions, Smith, Stayton, Stewart, Stockdale, Waelder, Whitfield—37.

Mr. DeMorse offered the following amendment:

Add to section 20, "In no case shall the fees hereafter charged by district, county or precinct officers exceed those existent in 1860, until the meeting of the first Legislature; and it shall be the duty of the first Legislature under this constitution to revise and reduce the fees allowed to executive officers of the courts, exercising a judicious discretion therein."

Lost.

Mr. Brown offered the following amendment:

Amend section 20 as follows: Strike out all after the word "sheriff," in line 280, to the word "who," in line 281; also in line 281 strike out the words "their offices," and insert the words "his office."

Adopted.

Mr. Murphy offered the following amendment:

Amend section 22 by adding to the section the words, "Which may include the science of economy and the art of knowing how to live on the smallest possible fees and salaries."

The chair ruled the amendment out of order.

Mr. Murphy appealed, and the Convention sustained the ruling of the chair.

Mr. Sansom offered the following amendment:

"Sec. ——. The Legislature shall provide by law for the protection of counties against exorbitant charges for board of prisoners; for the compensation of jurors without charging the counties therefor, and for the enforcement of penal servitude upon persons who may become a charge upon counties by reason of the commission of crime."

Lost.

Mr. Ferris offered the following amendment to section 7, Waelder's substitute:

Strike out "$500" and insert "$200," so as to read "when the matter in controversy shall be valued at or amount to $200, exclusive of interest."

Lost by the following vote:

YEAS—Ballinger, Cline, Crawford, Davis of Brazos, De-Morse, Dillard, Dohoney, Ferris, Flanagan, Ford, Henry of Smith, Kilgore, McCormick, Moore, Murphy, Nugent, Nunn, Ramey, Smith, Stayton, Stockdale, Waelder—22.

NAYS—Abernathy, Arnim, Blassingame, Brady, Brown, Bruce, Burleson, Chambers, Darnell, Douglas, Fleming, German, Graves, Henry of Limestone, Holt, Johnson of Collin, Killough, Lacy, Lockett, McCabe, McKinney of Denton, Martin of Navarro, Martin of Hunt, Mills, Mitchell, Pauli, Reagan, Rentfro, Reynolds, Robertson of Bell, Ross, Russell of Harrison, Russell of Wood, Sansom, Scott, Sessions, Spikes, Wade, Weaver, Whitehead—40.

Mr. Waelder offered the following additional section:

"Sec. ——. Vacancies in the office of Judges of the Supreme Court, of the Court of Appeals and District Court shall be filled by the Governor, until the next succeeding general election; and vacancies in the office of County Judge and Justice of the Peace shall be filled by the County Commissioners' Court, until the next general election for such officers."

On motion of Mr. Reagan, the main question, on the engrossment of the article, was ordered.

Mr. Waelder's amendment adopted.

The yeas and nays being called on the engrossment of the article, it was ordered engrossed by the following vote:

Yeas—Abernathy, Allison, Arnim, Blassingame, Brown, Bruce, Burleson, Chambers, Cooke of San Saba, Darnell, Dillard, Dohoney, Douglas, Ferris, Fleming, Flournoy, German, Graves, Henry of Limestone, Holt, Johnson of Collin, Johnson of Franklin, Killough, Lacy, McCormick, McKinney of Denton, McKinney of Walker, Martin of Navarro, Nugent, Ramey, Reagan, Robertson of Bell, Ross, Russell of Wood, Sansom, Scott, Sessions, Spikes, Wade, Waelder, Weaver, Whitehead—43.

Nays—Ballinger, Brady, Crawford, Davis of Brazos, De-Morse, Flanagan, Ford, Henry of Smith, Kilgore, King, Lockett, McCabe, Mills, Mitchell, Moore, Murphy, Nunn, Pauli, Rentfro, Reynolds, Russell of Harrison, Smith, Stayton, Stewart, Stockdale—25.

Mr. Cline was paired off with Mr. Gaither, but would have voted "nay."

Mr. Martin, of Hunt, was paired off with Mr. Norvell, but would have voted "yea."

On motion of Mr. King, Mr. Waelder was granted indefinite leave of absence from to-morrow.

On motion of Mr. Stockdale, Mr. Stayton was granted indefinite leave of absence from to-morrow.

On motion of Mr. Whitfield, Mr. Ford was granted indefinite leave of absence from next Saturday.

On motion of Mr. Ford, Mr. Whitfield was granted indefinite leave of absence from Saturday next.

"Article —, General provisions," was then taken up and read second time.

[Mr. Brown in the chair.]

Mr. McCormick offered the following amendment:

Amend section 1 by striking out all of the section after the word "State," in line 7, down to and including line 14.

The yeas and nays being called on the adoption of the amendment it was lost by the following vote:

Yeas—Abernathy, Arnim, Barnett, Blake, Burleson, Dillard, Douglas, Erhard, King, Lockett, McCormick, Murphy, Reagan, Russell of Harrison, Stayton, Stockdale—16.

NAYS—Allison, Ballinger, Blassingame, Brown, Bruce, Chambers, Cline, Cooke of San Saba, Crawford, Darnell, Davis of Brazos, DeMorse, Dohoney, Ferris, Flanagan, Fleming, German, Graves, Henry of Limestone, Henry of Smith, Holt, Johnson of Collin, Johnson of Franklin, Killough, Lacy, McKinney of Denton, McKinney of Walker, Martin of Navarro, Martin of Hunt, Mills, Mitchell, Moore, Nugent, Nunn, Ramey, Roberston of Bell, Sansom, Scott, Sessions, Smith, Spikes, Stewart, Wade, Weaver, Whitehead—45.

Mr. Stockdale proposed to amend by striking out from line 9, section 1, the words "by the Congress of the United States."

Mr. Stewart proposed to amend the amendment as follows:

Add to Mr. Stockdale's amendment the words "by the legal voters of the State."

Laid on the table, and Mr. Stockdale's amendment adopted.

Mr. Ramey, by leave, offered the following resolution:

Resolved, That the Committee on Engrossed and Enrolled Ordinances be authorized to employ such assistance as may be necessary to keep the engrossing and enrolling up with the work of the Convention.

Adopted.

Mr. Cline proposed to amend by striking out all of section 1, line 15, to line 20, both inclusive.

Adopted.

Mr. Stockdale offered to amend as follows:

Strike out "or appointed," in line 19, and insert in the parenthesis "or if the office is one of appointment, to secure my appointment."

Adopted.

Mr. Nunn proposed to amend by inserting in line 22, after " who shall." " have been or may."

Mr. Crawford offered the following substitute for the amendment:

Section 2, line 26, after the word "office" insert "and ;" and in line 22 strike out the words "and from the right of suffrage."

Mr. Nunn's amendment adopted.

On motion of Mr. Flournoy, the Convention adjourned to 2½ o'clock P. M., pending Mr. Crawford's amendment.

EVENING SESSION—2½ o'clock.

Convention met pursuant to adjournment; roll called; quorum present.

Consideration of pending question resumed, viz : "Article —, General Provisions."

Mr. Waelder, this morning, in voting for the engrossment of the article on Judiciary, stated that he did so while protesting against the inadequate salaries provided for the judges.

Mr. Whitfield, in voting the affirmative, made the same protest.

Mr. Darnell, by leave, submitted the following report :

COMMITTEE ROOM,
AUSTIN, November 16, 1875.

To the Hon. E. B. Pickett, President of the Convention:

SIR—Your select committee of fifteen, to whom was referred an ordinance for an extension of time in favor of the Texas and Pacific Railroad Company, on certain parts of its lines in the State of Texas, would respectfully report that they have had the same under careful consideration, and the majority of said committee instruct me to report the accompanying ordinance back to the Convention, and recommend its passage, with the following amendment to be added at the end of said ordinance, to-wit :

"Provided, that nothing herein contained shall interfere with any contract heretofore made by said company with the citizens, or any of the them, of any county or town on the line or lines of its road, as to the completion of any part thereof. *And provided further,* that said road shall be constructed on its chartered line from Fort Worth to a point at or near the town of El Paso, on the Rio Grande river.   N. H. DARNELL, Chairman.

WHEREAS, The Texas and Pacific Railway Company, a corporation chartered by the Congress of the United States, has received certain grants from this State, and has acquired, by purchase from or through the Southern Pacific Railway Company, and the Southern Trans-Continental Railway Company, certain grants, property rights and franchises, subject to certain legislative limitations and restrictions as to the commencement and prosecution of the work, and as to the time of its completion to certain points in this State;

AND WHEREAS, After completing 265 miles of new road, and grading, bridging and tieing, ready for the iron rails, 118 additional miles of roadway, the financial panic of 1873, and the distrust and embarrassment that followed, paralizing every industrial and commercial enterprise, has forced a temporary suspension of the work of construction. thereby occasioning a heavy loss to the company, from causes against which it was powerless to protect itself ; therefore,

Resolved, That none of the legislative grants made to or acquired by said company, in respect to the commencement and prosecution of the work, or as to the date of completion of any portion of its lines in Texas, shall be held to have lapsed, and that the said company shall have eighteen months from the passage of this ordinance in which to complete 120 miles of its lines between Eagle Ford and Fort Worth, and between Brookston and Texarkana, and seven additional years in which to complete 695 miles additional of its road, upon the route as heretofore designated by legislative authority to the Rio Grande, at or near El Paso; this extension to be in lieu of the restrictions and limitations of time and manner of prosecuting the work heretofore fixed by legislative authority.

On motion of Mr. Darnell, one hundred copies of the ordinance and amendment were ordered to be printed.

Mr. Blassingame protested against the report as being a majority report of the committee.

Mr. Crawford's amendment, pending on adjournment, to article on General Provisions, was lost.

Mr. Nunn offered the following amendment :

In line 30, after the word "county," strike out and insert " or if there be no such public works, then in such other manner and under such regulations as may be prescribed by law."

Withdrawn.

Mr. Holt offered the following amendment :

After "labor," in line 30, strike out the words "on the public works of the county."

Adopted.

Mr. McCormick moved to strike out section 4.

On motion of Mr. Mills, laid on the table.

Mr. Nugent proposed to amend by striking out in lines 36 and 37 the words "of suffrage or."

Lost.

Mr. Roberston, of Bell, offered the following amendment :

Section 6, line 46, after the word "concurrence," insert "of two-thirds."

Adopted.

Mr. Bruce offered the following amendment :

Strike out "without the concurrence of both houses of the Legislature."

Adopted.

Mr. Flanagan proposed to amend as follows :

Amend section 11 by striking out all after "interest," in line 65.

Mr. Nugent moved to lay the amendment on the table.

Carried by the following votes :

YEAS—Abernathy, Allison, Arnim, Ballinger, Barnett, Blake, Blassingame, Bruce, Burleson, Cooke of San Saba, Crawford, Darnell, Dillard, Dohoney, Douglas, Erhard, Ferris, Fleming, Flournoy, German, Graves, Henry of Limestone, Henry of Smith, Johnson of Collin, Johnson of Franklin, Killough, Lacy, McCormick, McKinney of Walker, Martin of Hunt, Moore, Nugent, Nunn, Reagan, Ross, Russell of Wood, Sansom, Scott, Sessions, Smith, Spikes, Stewart, Wade, Weaver, West, Whitehead—46.

NAYS—Brady, Chambers, Flanagan, Holt, Kilgore, King, Lockett, McCabe, Martin of Navarro, Mills, Mitchell, Murphy, Pauli, Rentfro, Reynolds, Robertson of Bell, Russell of Harrison, Stockdale, Waelder—19.

Mr. Robertson, of Bell, offered the following amendment:

Section 11, line 66, strike out the word "twelve" and insert "ten."

Mr. Blassingame offered the following as an amendment to the amendment :

Line 64, strike out "eight" and insert "six." Line 66, strike out "twelve" and insert "ten."

Mr. Russell, of Wood, moved to lay both amendments on the table.

Carried by the following vote :

YEAS—Abernathy, Allison, Arnim, Ballinger, Blake, Cooke, of San Saba, Darnell, Davis of Brazos, Dillard, Douglas, Erhard, Ferris, Flournoy, Ford, German, Graves, Henry of Limestone, Henry of Smith, Holt, Johnson of Franklin, Killough, King, Lacy, Lockett, McCormick, McKinney of Denton, McKinney of Walker, Martin of Navarro, Martin of Hunt, Moore, Murphy, Nunn, Reagan, Ross, Russell of Wood, Sessions, Spikes, Stewart, Stockdale, Waelder, Weaver, Whitehead—42.

NAYS—Barnett, Blassingame, Brady, Bruce, Burleson, Chambers, Cline, Crawford, DeMorse, Dohoney, Flanagan, Fleming, Johnson of Collin, Kilgore, McCabe, Mitchell, Nugent, Pauli, Rentfro, Reynolds, Robertson of Bell, Russell of Harrison, Sansom, Scott, Smith, Wade—26.

Mr. Russell, of Harrison, offered the following substitute for section 11 :

"Sec. 11. The Legislature is forbidden from making laws limiting parties to contracts in the amount of interest they may agree upon for loans of money or other property; *provided*, this section is not intended to change the provisions of law fixing rate of interest in contracts where the rate of interest is not specified."

Lost by the following vote:

YEAS—Ballinger, Blake, Brady, Cline, Erhard, Flanagan, Holt, King, McCabe, Mitchell, Pauli, Rentfro, Reynolds, Russell of Harrison, Stockdale, Waelder—16.

NAYS—Abernathy, Allison, Arnim, Barnett, Blassingame, Bruce, Burleson, Chambers, Cooke of San Saba, Crawford, Darnell, Davis of Brazos, Dohoney, Douglas, Ferris, Fleming, Flournoy, Ford, German, Graves, Henry of Limestone, Henry of Smith, Johnson of Collin, Johnson of Franklin, Kilgore, Killough, Lacy, Lockett, McCormick, McKinney of Denton, McKinney of Walker, Martin of Navarro, Martin of Hunt, Mills, Moore, Murphy, Nugent, Nunn, Reagan, Robertson of Bell, Ross, Russell of Wood, Sansom, Scott, Sessions, Smith, Spikes, Stayton, Stewart, Wade, Weaver, Whitehead—52.

Mr. Rentfro moved to amend by striking out "section 11."·

Lost by the following vote:

YEAS—Ballinger, Blake, Brady, Cline, Erhard, Flanagan, Lockett, Murphy, Pauli, Rentfro, Reynolds, Russell of Harrison, Stockdale—13.

NAYS—Abernathy, Allison, Arnim, Barnett, Blassingame, Bruce, Burleson, Chambers, Cooke of San Saba, Crawford, Darnell, Davis of Brazos, DeMorse, Dillard, Dohoney, Douglas, Ferris, Fleming, Flournoy, Ford, German, Graves, Henry of Limestone, Henry of Smith, Johnson of Collin, Johnson of of Franklin, Kilgore, Killough, King, Lacy, McCabe, McCormick, McKinney of Denton, McKinney of Walker, Martin of Navarro, Martin of Hunt, Mills, Mitchell, Nugent, Nunn, Reagan, Robertson of Bell, Ross, Russell of Wood, Scott, Sessions, Smith, Spikes, Stewart, Wade, Waelder, Weaver, Whitehead—53.

Mr. Pauli moved the following amendment:

Strike out "section 12."

Mr. Dillard moved to lay the motion on the table.

Carried by the following vote:

YEAS—Abernathy, Allison, Arnim, Ballinger, Barnett, Blassingame, Bruce, Burleson, Chambers, Cline, Cooke of San Saba, Crawford, Darnell, Davis of Brazos, DeMorse, Dillard, Dohoney, Douglas, Erhard, Ferris, Flournoy, Ford, German, Graves, Henry of Limestone, Henry of Smith, Holt, Johnson of Collin, Johnson of Franklin, Kilgore, Killough, King, Lacy, McCormick, McKinney of Denton, Martin of Navarro, Martin of Hunt, Mills, Moore, Murphy, Nugent, Nunn, Reagan, Russell of Wood, Sansom, Scott, Sessions, Smith, Spikes, Stayton, Stewart, Stockdale, Wade, Waelder, Whitehead—55.

NAYS—Blake, Brady, Flanagan, Fleming, Lockett, McCabe,

Mitchell, Pauli, Rentfro, Reynolds, Robertson of Bell, Russell of Harrison—12.

Mr. Waelder moved to strike out " section 13."

Carried.

Mr. Sansom offered the following amendment, to fill the blank made by striking out " section 13:"

" Sec. 13. The counties of this State shall not pay for board of prisoners at a rate to exceed forty cents per day for each prisoner; and the Legislature is required to pass suitable laws to enforce this provision."

Laid on the table by the following vote:

YEAS—Abernathy, Arnim, Ballinger, Barnett, Blake, Blassingame, Bruce, Burleson, Cline, Crawford, Darnell, Davis of Brazos, DeMorse, Dohoney, Erhard, Ferris, Fleming, Ford, Graves, Henry of Limestone, Holt, Johnson of Franklin, Kilgore, Killough, King, Lacy, McCormick, McKinney of Walker, Martin of Navarro, Martin of Hunt, Mitchell, Moore, Murphy, Nugent, Reagan, Rentfro, Reynolds, Robertson of Bell, Ross, Sessions, Smith, Spikes, Stockdale, Waelder, Weaver—45.

NAYS—Allison, Brady, Chambers, Cooke of San Saba, Dillard, Douglas, Flanagan, Flournoy, German, Johnson of Collin, Lockett, McCabe, McKinney of Denton, Mills, Nunn, Pauli, Russell of Harrison, Russell of Wood, Sansom, Stewart, Whitehead—21.

Mr. Nunn offered the following amendment:

Add in line 83, " and failure to comply with this condition shall vacate the office so held."

Adopted.

On motion of Mr. Nunn, " section 16 " was stricken out.

Mr. McCormick moved to strike out " or claimed," in section 17, line 87.

Lost.

Mr. Cline moved to strike out of line 89, section 17, the words " and the increase of the same."

Mr. Stockdale moved to substitute the motion by inserting the word " natural " before " increase."

Mr. Russell, of Wood, moved to close debate on the pending amendments.

Lost.

Mr. Stockdale amended his amendment as follows:

Line 87, between " of " and " wife " " the husband;" line 88, read " their " for " her," and line 89, read " their " for " her."

Mr. DeMorse moved to lay both amendments on the table.

A division of the question was ordered.

The question to lay Mr. Stockdale's amendment on the table was put and carried by the following vote:

YEAS—Allison, Arnim, Barnett, Blassingame, Bruce, Burleson, Chambers, Cooke of San Saba, Darnell, Davis of Brazos, DeMorse, Douglas, Erhard, Ferris, Ford, Graves, Henry of Smith, Johnson of Collin, Johnson of Franklin, Killough, Lacy, McCormick, Martin of Navarro, Martin of Hunt, Moore, Murphy, Robertson of Bell, Russell of Harrison, Sessions, Smith, Spikes, Stewart, Wade, Weaver—34.

NAYS—Ballinger, Blake, Brady, Cline, Dillard, Dohoney, Flanagan, Fleming, Holt, King, Lockett, McCabe, McKinney of Denton, Mills, Mitchell, Nugent, Reagan, Rentfro, Reynolds, Ross, Russell of Wood, Stockdale, Waelder, Whitehead—24.

The question then recurring on laying Mr. Cline's amendment on the table, the same was put, and the Convention refused to lay the amendment on the table by the following vote:

YEAS—Arnim, Blassingame, Burleson, Darnell, DeMorse, Dohoney, Flanagan, Flournoy, Henry of Limestone, Johnson of Collin, Killough, King, Lacy, McCabe, Martin of Navarro, Martin of Hunt, Mills, Mitchell, Reynolds, Robertson of Bell, Ross, Russell of Harrison, Russell of Wood, Sessions, Smith, Spikes, Stewart, Stockdale, Wade, Weaver, Whitehead—31.

NAYS—Allison, Ballinger, Barnett, Blake, Brady, Bruce, Chambers, Cline, Cooke of San Saba, Crawford, Davis of Brazos, Dillard, Douglas, Erhard, Ferris, Fleming, Ford, Graves, Henry of Smith, Holt, Lockett, McCormick, McKinney of Denton, Moore, Murphy, Nugent, Nunn, Pauli, Ramey, Reagan, Rentfro, Scott—32.

On motion of Mr. Nugent debate was closed on the amendment, and a direct vote had, which resulted as follows:

YEAS—Allison, Ballinger, Barnett, Blake, Chambers, Cline, Crawford, Davis of Brazos, Dillard, Douglas, Erhard, Ferris, Flournoy, Ford, German, Graves, Henry of Limestone, Henry of Smith, Holt, Killough, Lockett, McCormick, McKinney of Denton, Moore, Murphy, Nugent, Pauli, Ramey, Reagan, Scott, Sessions, Wade, Waelder—33.

NAYS—Abernathy, Arnim, Blassingame, Brady, Brown, Bruce, Darnell, DeMorse, Dohoney, Flanagan, Fleming, Johnson of Collin, Johnson of Franklin, Lacy, McCabe, Martin of Navarro, Martin of Hunt, Mills, Mitchell, Nunn, Rentfro, Reynolds, Robertson of Bell, Ross, Russell of Harrison, Russell of Wood, Smith, Spikes, Stewart, Stockdale, Weaver, West, Whitehead, Whitfield—34.

So the amendment was lost.

44

Mr. Davis, of Brazos, proposed to amend as follows:

Add to the section as follows: "And all property owned, claimed or acquired in like manner by the husband shall be his separate property."

[Mr. Stockdale in the chair.]

Mr. Davis's (of Brazos) amendment adopted:

Mr. Dohoney moved to strike out section 18.

Lost.

Mr. Waelder offered the following additional section:

"Sec. ——. The Legislature may pass laws for the regulation of live stock and the protection of stock-raisers in the stock-raising portions of the State, and exempt from the operation of such laws other portions, sections or counties; *provided*, that any local laws thus passed shall be submitted to the freeholders of the section to be affected thereby, and approved by them, before it sholl go into effect."

Adopted.

Mr. Crawford offered the following as a substitute for section 17:

"Sec. 17. All property, both real and personal, of the wife, owned or claimed by her before marriage, and that acquired afterwards by gift, devise, or descent, shall be her separate property, and laws shall be passed more clearly defining the rights of the wife, in relation as well to her separate property as that held in common with her husband. Laws shall also be passed providing for the registration of the wife's separate property."

Adopted by the following vote:

YEAS—Abernathy, Allison, Arnim, Ballinger, Barnett, Blake, Brady, Brown, Bruce, Burleson, Chambers, Cline, Cooke of San Saba, Crawford, Darnell, Davis of Brazos, Dillard, Douglas, Erhard, Ferris, Fleming, Flournoy, Ford, German, Graves, Henry of Limestone, Henry of Smith, Holt, Johnson of Collin, Killough, Lacy, Lockett, McCormick, McKinney of Denton, McKinney of Walker, Murphy, Nugent, Pauli, Ramey, Reagan, Reynolds, Robertson of Bell, Ross, Russell of Wood, Sansom, Scott, Sessions, Spikes, Wade, West, Whitehead, Whitfield—52.

NAYS—DeMorse, Dohoney, Flanagan, Mitchell, Rentfro, Stockdale—6.

On motion of Mr. Chambers, the Convention adjourned to 9 A. M. to-morrow.

SIXTY-SECOND DAY.

HALL OF REPRESENTATIVES, ⎱
AUSTIN, TEXAS, November 17, 1875. ⎰

Convention met pursuant to adjournment; roll called; quorum present. Prayer by the Rev. J. S. Grasty, of the Cumberland Presbyterian Church, at Austin.

Journal of yesterday read and adopted.

On motion of Mr. Sansom, Mr. West was excused for to-day.

Mr. Whitfield reported as follows:

COMMITTEE ROOM, ⎱
AUSTIN, November 17, 1875. ⎰

To the Hon. E. B. Pickett, President of the Convention:

The Committee on Education, to whom was referred the resolution of the delegate from Wood, providing for the establishment and maintenance of two universities, having carefully considered the same, as well as several other resolutions upon the same subject referred to them, direct me to report the following in lieu thereof, and recommend its adoption:

J. W. WHITFIELD, Chairman.

" UNIVERSITY.

" WHEREAS, from the earliest period of Texas history the people have, through their representatives, repeatedly expressed a cherished purpose to establish within the State an institution of learning of the highest order, upon what is known as the 'university system,' and have, from time to time, illustrated a design to provide for the ample endowment of the same, in order to place within the reach of their sons, whether rich or poor, an opportunity of acquiring in Texas a thorough education in the classics, and in all the branches of the liberal arts and sciences; and

" WHEREAS, Beside other advantages, such an institution will bring together a large number of young Texans in a common field of continuous intellectual labor, thereby tending to encourage a love of Texas, her history and her institutions; and

" WHEREAS, To this end liberal appropriations have heretofore been made, but not utilized; and

" WHEREAS, In the opinion of your committee, the time has arrived to provide for the practical inauguration of the laudable work of establishing a State university, to this end your committee recommend the adoption of the following as a part of the constitution of the State:

" Section 1. The Legislature shall, as soon as practicable, establish, organize, and provide for the maintenance, support and direction of a university of the first class, to be located at or near the city of Austin, and styled ' The University of Texas,' for the promotion of literature and the arts and sciences, including an agricultural and mechanical department.*

"Sec. 2. In order to enable the Legislature to perform the duty set forth in the foregoing section, it is hereby declared that all lands and other property heretofore set apart and appropriated for the establishment and maintenance of ' The University of Texas,' together with all the proceeds of sales of the same, heretofore made or hereafter to be made, and all grants, donations and appropriations that may hereafter be made by the State of Texas, or from any other source, shall constitute and become a permanent university fund.   And the same, as realized and received into the treasury of the State (together with such sum belonging to the fund as may now be in the treasury), shall be invested in bonds of the State of Texas, if the same can be obtained, if not, then in United States bonds; and the interest accruing thereon shall be subject to appropriation by the Legislature to accomplish the purpose declared in the foregoing section; *provided,* that the one-tenth of the alternate sections of the land granted to railroads, reserved by the State, which were set apart and appropriated to the establishment of ' The University of Texas,' by an act of the Legislature, of February 11, 1858, entitled ' An act to establish the University of Texas,' shall not be included in or constitute a part of the permanent universtiy fund.

" Sec. 3. The lands herein set apart to the university fund shall be sold under such regulations, at such times, and on such terms, as may be provided by law; and the Legislature shall provide for the prompt collection, at maturity, of all debts due on account of university lands heretofore sold, or that may herafter be sold, and shall in neither event have the power to grant relief to the purchaser.

" Sec. 4. The 'Agricultural and Mechanical College of Texas,' established by an act of the Legislature passed April 17, 1871, located in the county of Brazos, is hereby made and constituted a branch of ' The University of Texas,' for instruction in Agriculture, the Mechanic Arts, and the Natural Sciences connected therewith.   And the Legislature shall, at its next session, make an appropriation, not to exceed forty thousand dollars, for the construction and completion of the buildings and improvements,

* The article as it reads is constitution except that " Austin " was stricken out.

and providing for the furniture necessary to put said college in immediate and successful operation.

" Sec. 5. The Legislature shall also, when deemed practicable , establish and provide for the maintenance of college or branch university, for the instruction of the colored youths of the State, to be located in or near the city of Austin; *provided,* that no tax shall be levied and no money appropriated out of the general revenue, either for this purpose or for the establishment and erection of the buildings of the University of Texas.

" Sec. 6. In addition to the lands heretofore granted to the University of Texas, there is hereby set apart and appropriated for the endowment, maintenance and support of said university and its branches one million acres of the unappropriated public domain of the State, to be designated and surveyed as may be provided by law; and said lands shall be sold under the same regulations, and the proceeds invested in the same manner, as is hereinbefore provided for the sale and investment of the permanent university fund. And the Legislature shall not have power to grant any relief to the purchasers of said lands."

Mr. McCormick moved to have two hundred copies printed. Lost.

Mr. Allison moved to have one hundred copies. Carried.

Mr. Flournoy reported as follows:

COMMITTEE ROOM.
AUSTIN, TEXAS, November 16, 1875.

To the Hon. E. B. Pickett, President of the Convention:

Your Committee on Municipal Corporations, having considered of the various matters referred to them, authorize me to report the following article for the action of the Convention.

GEORGE FLOURNOY, Chairman.

" Section 1. The several counties of this State are hereby recognized as legal subdivisions of the State.

" Sec. 2. The construction of jails, court-houses and bridges, the removal of county seats, and the establishment of county poor houses and farms, and the laying out, construction and repairing of county roads, shall be provided for by general laws.

" Sec. 3. No county, city, or other municipal corporation, shall hereafter become a subscriber to the capital stock of any private corporation or association, or make any appropriation or donation to the same, or in any wise loan its credit; but this shall not be construed to in any way affect any obligation heretofore undertaken pursuant to law.

"Sec. 4. Cities and towns having a population of ten thousand inhabitants, or less, may be chartered alone by general law; they may levy, assess and collect an annual tax to defray the current expense of their local government, but such tax shall never exceed, for any one year, one-fourth of one per cent., and shall be collectable only in current money.

"Sec. 5. Cities having a population of more than ten thousand inhabitants may have their charters granted or amended by special act of the Legislature, and may levy, assess and collect such taxes as may be authorized by law; but no tax for any purpose shall ever be lawful, for any one year, which shall exceed five per cent. of the taxable property of such city, and no debt shall ever be created by any city unless at the same time provision be made to assess and collect annually a sufficient sum to pay the interest thereon, and create a sinking fund of at least two per cent. thereon.

"Sec. 6. Counties, cities and towns are authorized, in such mode as may now or hereafter be provided by law, to levy, assess and collect the taxes necessary to pay the interest and provide a sinking fund to satisfy any indebtedness heretofore legally made and undertaken, but all such taxes shall be assessed and collected separately from that levied, assessed and collected for current expenses of municipal government, and shall, when levied, specify in the act of levying the purpose therefor, and such taxes may be paid in the coupons, bonds or other indebtedness, for the payment of which such tax may have been levied.

"Sec. 7. All counties and cities bordering on the coast of the Gulf of Mexico are hereby authorized, upon a vote of two-thirds of the tax-payers therein (to be ascertained as may be provided by law), to levy and collect such tax for construction of sea walls, breakwaters, or for sanitary purposes, as may be authorized by law, and may create a debt for such works, and issue bonds in evidence thereof; but no debt for any purpose shall ever be incurred, in any manner, by any city or county, unless provision is made at the time of creating the same, for levying and collecting a sufficient tax to pay the interest thereon and provide at least two per cent. as a sinking fund; and the condemnation of the right of way for the erection or construction of such works shall be fully provided for.

"Sec. 8. The counties and cities on the gulf coast being subject to calamitous overflows, and a very large proportion of the general revenue being derived from those otherwise prosperous localities, the Legislature is expressly authorized to aid, by donation of such portion of the public domain as may be deemed proper, and in such mode as may be provided by law, the construction of sea walls or breakwaters, such aid to be proportioned to the extent and value of the works constructed, or to be constructed, in any locality.

" Sec. 9. The property of counties, cities and towns, owned and held only for public purposes, such as public buildings and the sites therefor, fire engines and the furniture thereof, and all property used or intended for extinguishing fires, public grounds and all other property devoted exclusively to the use and benefit of the public, shall be exempt from forced sale.

" Sec. 10. The Legislature may authorize counties and cities to levy and collect occupation, income and license taxes by general law, except as to cities of more than five thousand inhabitants, in which case special laws may be provided. Counties and cities shall at all times have the right to levy and collect occupation, income and license taxes to the amount of one-half the State tax therefor.

" Sec. 11. The Legislature may constitute any city or town a separate and independent school district, and when the citizens of any city or town have a charter, authorizing the city authorities to levy and collect a tax for the support and maintenance of a public institution of learning, such tax may be hereafter levied and collected, if, at an election held for that purpose, a majority of the tax-payers of such city or town shall vote for such tax."

On motion of Mr. Flournoy, the reading of the report was dispensed with, and two hundred copies ordered printed.

Mr. DeMorse submitted the following minority report:

COMMITTEE ROOM,
AUSTIN, November 17, 1875

To the Hon. E. B. Pickett, President of the Convention:

The undersigned, a minority of the special committee to which was referred the question of extension by this Convention of certain railroad charters granted by this State, the stipulations of which required the completion of specified work by certain dates named in such extensions, desires to express his dissent to the action of the majority of said committee, for reasons herein stated.

First—That the majority recommend a further extension of eighteen months on the still incomplete work of the Texas Pacific road between Eagle Ford and Fort Worth, and on the section between Paris and Texarkana, on which the road bed has been constructed and the ties laying beside it for near two years; and propose to decree that the people of that section of the State, who have been deluded for years with a vain hope that at frequent successive periods the road was just about to be constructed *in fact,* shall be again taught the painful lesson that of all the uncertainties of life, nothing else is so wholly unreal as the promise of a railway company, and nothing else so deceptive as its contracts, subject to the interpretation of an average Legislature.

Second—The majority proposes to grant seven years for the completion of the road from Fort Worth to San Diego. It is apparent to the undersigned that with the indorsement of the Congress of the United States of the interest on the company's bonds, five years will be ample time to complete the work. Without such indorsement, it will not be built within the next ten years, perhaps not within twenty years. In other words, the present company will never build the road much beyond Fort Worth without such indorsement by Congress.

Third—The majority propose that the Convention shall pass an absolute ordinance with the force of law, granting the desired extension—not to be submitted to the people—and the argument for this extraordinary action is, that the Convention, early in its session, passed an ordinance deferring the usual election for members of the Legislature, and therefore it may properly do this act. The undersigned is unable to see any affinity between the two propositions. One had a political connection with the objects for which the people had called the Convention together, and on which they had given to the Convention the power to act. The other is a special act, for the benefit of a private corporation, and has no connection or affinity whatever for the objects contemplated by the people in creating the Convention.

In the contemplation of the undersigned, this Convention has no authority to give any more than temporary effect to *any* ordinance, until such time as the people shall have the opportunity to act upon it, and either approve or disapprove; nor did he conceive, when the ordinance deferring the election was adopted, that it had any other than temporary force, derivable from the assumed assent of the people, but he considered that in passing it we shouldered a responsibility warrantable by the apparent political necessity, only.

All of which is respectfully submitted.

CHARLES DEMORSE,
One of the Committee.

The undersigned members of the committee concur in the above.   W. BLASSINGAME,
S. A. McKINNEY.

Mr. Nugent gave notice of a minority report.

Mr. Kilgore submitted the following report :

COMMITTEE ROOM,
AUSTIN, November 16, 1875.

To the Hon. E. B. Pickett, President of the Convention:

SIR—The select committee to whom was referred a resolution on the subject of qualified suffrage, beg leave to report as a substitute therefor the subjoined ordinance, and recommend its adoption by the Convention.

C. B. KILGORE, Chairman,
ASA HOLT,
E. N. BURLESON.

Be it ordained, That at the next general election to be held for the adoption or rejection of the Constitution, the electors shall be permitted to vote on the following section, to be separately submitted to the qualified voters of the State, to-wit :

"Sec. —. The Legislature may regulate the right of suffrage, so as to require any elector to show by his own oath or otherwise that he has paid all or any portion of the State or county tax due from him and collectable more than six months preceding the election at which he proposes to vote; but if the payment of a poll tax shall ever be made a prerequisite to the right of suffrage, such poll tax shall never exceed the sum of two dollars in any one year."

And the ballot on this section shall be "For qualified suffrage," or "Against qualified suffrage," which words shall be written or printed on the same ballots cast on the adoption or rejection of the constitution; and if a majority of the votes cast shall be in favor of the section hereby separately submitted, then the same shall be and become a part of the constitution, and shall be section 6 in the article on suffrage.

Mr. McCormick moved to have one hundred copies of the report and article printed.

Carried by the following vote:

YEAS—Abernathy, Allison, Arnim, Ballinger, Blake, Brown, Burleson, Cooke of San Saba, Crawford, Darnell, Davis of Brazos, DeMorse, Dillard, Dohoney, Douglas, Erhard, Ferris, Fleming, Ford, German, Graves, Henry of Smith, Holt, Kilgore, Killough, King, Lacy, McCormick, Martin of Navarro, Martin of Hunt, Murphy, Nugent, Nunn, Pauli, Robertson of Bell, Robison of Fayette, Ross, Russell of Harrison, Sansom, Scott, Sessions, Smith. Spikes, Stockdale, Wade, Whitehead—46.

NAYS—Barnett, Blassingame, Bruce, Chambers, Cline, Flanagan, Haynes, Johnson of Collin, Lockett, McCabe, McKinney of

Walker, Mills, Mitchell, Rentfro, Reynolds, Russell of Wood, Stewart, Weaver—18.

On motion of Mr. German, one hundred copies of Mr. De-Morse's minority report were ordered printed.

Mr. Chambers submitted the following report :

COMMITTEE ROOM, }
AUSTIN, November 17, 1875. }

To the Hon. E. B. Pickett, President of the Convention:

SIR—The undersigned, one of your special committee charged with the duty of considering the propriety of submitting to the people the separate proposition that the right to the exercise of suffrage shall be conditioned upon the payment of a poll tax, begs leave to dissent from the majority, and would respectfully recommend the rejection of said majority report.

Respectfully,   ED. CHAMBERS.

One hundred copies ordered printed.

Mr. Ford submitted the following report:

COMMITTEE ROOM, }
AUSTIN, November 17, 1875. }

To the Hon. E. B. Pickett, President of the Convention:

The Committee on State Affairs to which was referred a resolution providing for the appropriation and setting apart of three millions of acres of the public lands for the purpose of erecting a new capitol and other necessary public buildings, and that said lands shall not be sold until ten years after the adoption of the new constitution, have had the same under consideration, and instruct me to report as follows:

It is evident that within a few years repairs and changes will be required to be made upon the capitol and other public buildings, and, in order to accomplish these objects, an outlay of money will be made. As a measure of economy, it may be proper and expedient to erect these buildings anew, so that they may more appropriately represent the augmented population of the State. In order to provide for these contingencies, and, at the same time, not increase the burden of taxation, your committee beg leave to report the following section, and ask the Convention to adopt it:

" Sec. —. Three million acres of the public domain are hereby appropriated and set apart for the purpose of erecting and constructing a new State capitol and other necessary public buildings, at the seat of government; said lands not to be sold until ten years after the adoption of this constitution; and the Legislature shall pass suitable laws to carry this section into effect."

All of which is respectfully submitted.

> JOHN S. FORD, Chairman,
> J. F. JOHNSON,
> ED. CHAMBERS,
> Jo. W. BARNETT,
> W. W. DILLARD,
> ROBT. LACEY.

One hundred copies ordered printed.

Mr. McCormick offered the following amendments to the rules:

Amend rule 38, by striking out the word "three," and inserting the word "ten."

Also amend rule 39, by striking out the word "three," in first line, and inserting the word "ten."

Laid over under the rule.

Unfinished business, viz: "Art. —, General Provisions."

Mr. Allison offered the following section :

"Sec. 20. In all elections to fill vacancies of offices in this State it shall be to fill the unexpired terms."

Adopted.

Mr. McCormick offered the following additional section, to follow section 21:

"Sec. —. The Legislature shall provide by law that all sales of real estate made under or by virtue of any writ or process issued out of the courts of this State shall be duly advertised in some newspaper published either in the county where the sale is made, or in the county where the judgment or decree is rendered; *provided,* that the owner of the property thus sold may waive the right to have such advertisement made."

Lost by the following vote:

YEAS—Arnim, Brown, Cline, Cook of Gonzales, DeMorse, Erhard, McCormick, Nugent, Ramey, Russell of Harrison—10.

NAYS—Abernathy, Allison, Ballinger, Barnett, Blake, Blassingame, Bruce, Burleson, Chambers, Cooke of San Saba, Crawford, Darnell, Davis of Brazos, Douglas, Ferris, Flanagan, Fleming, German, Graves, Haynes, Henry of Limestone, Holt, Johnson of Collin, Killough, King, Lacy, Lockett, McCabe, McKinney of Denton, McKinney of Walker, Martin of Navarro, Martin of Hunt, Mills, Moore, Murphy, Nunn, Pauli, Reagan, Rentfro, Reynolds, Robertson of Bell, Robison of Fayette, Russell of Wood, Sansom, Scott, Sessions, Smith, Spikes, Stewart, Wade, Weaver, Whitehead—52.

Mr. Rentfro moved to strike out section 21.

Lost by the following vote :

YEAS—Brady, Cline, Flanagan, Lockett, McCabe, Mills, Mitchell, Pauli, Rentfro, Reynolds, Russell of Harrison—11.

NAYS—Abernathy, Allison, Arnim, Ballinger, Barnett, Blake, Blassingame, Brown, Bruce, Burleson, Chambers, Cook of Gonzales, Cooke of San Saba, Crawford, Davis of Brazos, DeMorse, Dillard, Dohoney, Douglas, Erhard, Fleming, Graves, Haynes, Henry of Limestone, Henry of Smith, Holt, Johnson of Collin, Johnson of Franklin, Kilgore, Killough, King, Lacy, McCormick, McKinney of Denton, McKinney of Walker, Martin of Navarro, Martin of Hunt, Moore, Nugent, Nunn, Ramey, Reagan, Robertson of Bell, Robison of Fayette, Ross, Russell of Wood, Sansom, Scott, Sessions, Spikes, Stewart, Wade, Weaver, Wright—54.

[Mr. Reagan in the Chair.]

Mr. McCormick moved to strike out section 24 and insert the following :

"Sec. 24. The Legislature shall pass general laws authorizing any county, justice's precinct, or other sub-division of a county, by a vote of two-thirds of the qualified voters of such county voting at such election, or such sub-division of a county, to adopt a fence system for the protection of farmers and stock-raisers."

Mr. Robertson, of Bell, proposed to amend the amendment by striking out "two-thirds" and inserting "three-fourths."

On motion of Mr. Dillard, debate was closed, and Mr. Robertson's (of Bell) amendment lost by the following vote :

YEAS—Blake, Brady, Davis of Brazos, Killough, Lockett, McCabe, McKinney of Denton, Mills, Mitchell, Murphy, Rentfro, Reynolds, Robertson of Bell, Robison of Fayette, Russell of Harrison, Smith—16.

NAYS—Abernathy, Allison, Arnim, Ballinger, Barnett, Blassingame, Bruce, Burleson, Chambers, Cline, Cook of Gonzales, Cooke of San Saba, Darnell, DeMorse, Dillard, Dohoney, Douglas, Erhard, Ferris, Fleming, Graves, Haynes, Henry of Limestone, Holt, Johnson of Franklin, King, McCormick, McKinney of Walker, Martin of Navarro, Martin of Hunt, Moore, Nugent, Nunn, Reagan, Ross, Russell of Wood, Sansom, Scott, Sessions, Spikes, Stockdale, Wade, Weaver, Whitehead—44.

Mr. McCormick's amendment lost by the following vote :

YEAS—Barnett, Brown, Bruce, Burleson, Chambers, Cook of Gonzales, DeMorse, Dillard, Dohoney, Erhard, Flanagan, Graves, Haynes, Holt, Kilgore, McCormick, McKinney of Walker, Moore, Pauli, Reagan, Robison of Fayette, Ross, Sansom—23.

Nays—Abernathy, Allison, Arnim, Balinger, Blake, Blassingame, Brady, Cline, Cooke of San Saba, Darnell, Davis of Brazos, Douglas, Ferris, Ford, Henry of Limestone, Henry of Smith, Johnson of Collin, Killough, Lacy, Lockett, McCabe, McKinney of Denton, Martin of Navarro, Martin of Hunt, Mills, Mitchell, Morris, Nugent, Nunn, Ramey, Rentfro, Reynolds, Robertson of Bell, Russell of Wood, Scott, Sessions, Spikes, Stewart, Wade, Weaver, Whitehead—41.

Mr. Holt proposed to amend section 24 by striking out "two-thirds" and inserting "a majority."

Lost by the following majority:

Yeas—Abernathy, Barnett, Brown, Bruce, Burleson, Chambers, Cline, Cook of Gonzales, Dillard, Dohoney, Douglas, Erhard, Flanagan, Fleming, Graves, Haynes, Henry of Limestone, Holt, Kilgore, King, McCormick, Martin of Navarro, Moore, Nugent, Nunn, Pauli, Reagan, Russell of Harrison, Sansom, Sessions, Spikes, Stewart—32.

Nays—Allison, Arnim, Ballinger, Blake, Blassingame, Brady, Cooke of San Saba, Darnell, DeMorse, Ferris, Ford, Henry of Smith, Johnson of Collin, Killough, Lacy, Lockett, McCabe, McKinney of Denton, McKinney of Walker, Martin of Hunt, Mills, Mitchell, Murphy, Ramey, Rentfro, Reynolds, Robertson of Bell, Robison of Fayette, Ross, Russell of Wood, Scott, Smith, Wade, Weaver, Whitehead—35.

Mr. Sansom offered the following as a substitute for section 24:

"Sec. 24. The Legislature shall have the power to pass such fence laws, applicable to any sub-division of the State or counties, as may be needed to meet the wants of the people."

Adopted.

Mr. Cline proposed to amend section 26 by striking out of line 134 the words "as felons."

Adopted.

Mr. Flanagan moved to strike out section 26.

Mr. Martin, of Navarro, moved to lay the motion on the table. Carried.

Mr. Stewart moved to insert the words "or gross neglect" after "omission," in section 27, line 137.

Mr. Holt moved to strike out section 28.

Adopted by the following vote:

Yeas—Abernathy, Barnett, Blassingame, Bruce, Chambers, Crawford, Davis of Brazos, Dillard, Fleming, Flournoy, Graves, Haynes, Henry of Limestone, Holt, Johnson of Collin, Kilgore, Killough, Lacy, McCormick, Martin of Navarro, Martin of

Hunt, Moore, Nunn, Rentfro, Robison of Fayette, Russell of Wood, Scott, Sessions, Smith, Spikes, Stewart, Weaver, Whitehead, Wright—34.

NAYS—Allison, Arnim, Blake, Brown, Burleson, Cline, Cook of Gonzales, Cooke of San Saba, Darnell, DeMorse, Dohoney, Douglas, Erhard, Ferris, Flanagan, McCabe, McKinney of Walker, Mills, Murphy, Nugent, Reagan, Russell of Harrison, Sansom, Stockdale, Wade—25.

Mr. Nunn moved to strike out section 29.

Mr. Abernathy moved to lay the motion on the table.

Carried by the following vote:

YEAS—Abernathy, Arnim, Barnett, Blassingame, Brady, Brown, Bruce, Burleson, Chambers, Cooke of San Saba, Darnell, DeMorse, Dohoney, Ferris, Flanagan, Fleming, Flournoy, German, Graves, Haynes, Henry of Limestone, Johnson of Collin, Johnson of Franklin, Lacy, Lockett, McCabe, Martin of Navarro, Martin of Hunt, Mills, Moore, Nugent, Pauli, Reagan, Robertson of Bell, Ross, Russell of Harrison, Sansom, Sessions, Spikes, Stewart, Stockdale, Wade, Weaver, Whitehead, Wright—45.

NAYS—Allison, Cline, Crawford, Davis of Brazos, Dillard, Douglas, Holt, Killough, McCormick, McKinney of Walker, Nunn, Rentfro, Robison of Fayette, Russell of Wood, Scott, Smith—16.

Mr. Stockdale stated that the words "champerty" and "maintance" were incorrectly inserted in section 30.

Mr. Flournoy moved to re-insert the words.

Lost by the following vote:

YEAS—Allison, Arnim, Barnett, Blassingame, Brown, Bruce, Burleson, Chambers, Cooke of San Saba, Darnell, Dillard, Douglas, Erhard, Flournoy, Ford, Haynes, Henry of Limstone, Holt, Johnson of Collin, Johnson of Franklin, Lacy, Martin of Navarro, Mills, Mitchell, Reagan, Robertson of Bell, Robison of Fayette, Ross, Russell of Harrison, Russell of Wood, Sansom, Scott, Sessions, Spikes, Wade—35.

NAYS—Abernathy, Ballinger, Blake, Brady, Cline, Crawford, Davis of Brazos, DeMorse, Dohoney, Ferris, Flanagan, Fleming, Graves, Henry of Smith, Kilgore, Killough, King, Lockett, McCabe, McCormick, McKinney of Denton, McKinney of Walker, Martin of Hunt, Moore, Murphy, Nugent, Nunn, Pauli, Rentfro, Smith, Stewart, Stockdale, Weaver, Whitehead, Wright—35.

[Mr. Dohoney in the chair.]

Mr. Pickett moved to strike out section 30.

Lost by the following vote :

YEAS—Brady, Cline, Crawford, Douglas, Erhard, Ferris,

Flanagan, Henry of Smith, Kilgore, Lockett, McCormick, Mc-Kinney of Walker, Martin of Hunt, Moore, Nugent, Nunn, Pauli, Rentfro, Smith, Stockdale, Wright—21.

NAYS—Abernathy, Allison, Arnim, Ballinger, Barnett, Blassingame, Brown, Bruce, Burleson, Chambers, Cooke of San Saba, Darnell, DeMorse, Dillard, Dohoney, Fleming, Flournoy, Ford, Graves, Henry of Limestone, Johnson of Collin, Johnson of Franklin, Killough, Lacy, Martin or Navarro, Mills, Mitchell, Murphy, Reagan, Reynolds, Robertson of Bell, Robison of Fayette, Ross, Russell of Wood, Sansom, Scott, Sessions, Spikes, Stewart, Wade, Weaver—41.

On motion of Mr. Darnell, the Convention adjourned to 2½ o'clock P. M.

EVENING SESSION—2½ o'CLOCK.

Convention met pursuant to adjournment; roll called; quorum present.

Pending question resumed.

Mr. Barnett offered the following additional section:

"Sec —. The Legislature shall pass laws prescribing the qualifications of practitioners of medicine in this State, and to punish persons for malpractice, but no preference shall ever be given by law to any school of medicine."

Adopted.

Mr. McCormick offered the following additional section:

"Sec. 35. The Legislature may provide by law for the establishment of a Board of Health and Vital Statistics, under such rules and regulations as it may deem proper."

Adopted by the following vote:

YEAS—Abernathy, Allison, Arnim, Ballinger, Barnett, Blassingame, Brady, Bruce, Burleson, Chambers, Cline, Crawford, Darnell, Davis of Brazos, DeMorse, Fleming, Ford, Haynes, Henry of Limestone, Henry of Smith, Johnson of Franklin, Kilgore, Killough, Lacy, Lockett, McCormick, McKinney of Walker, Martin of Hunt, Mills, Nugent, Pauli, Reagan, Reynolds, Robertson of Bell, Robison of Fayette, Ross, Russell of Wood, Sansom, Scott, Sessions, Spike, Stockdale, Wade, Waelder, Weaver, Whitehead, Wright—47.

NAYS—Douglas, German, Graves, Holt, Johnson of Collin, McKinney of Denton—6.

Mr. Kilgore offered the following amendment to section 34:

Strike out the words "first day of July, A. D. 1873," and insert "15th day of March, 1875," in line 168.

Adopted.

Mr. Pauli proposed to amend section 34 by adding after word "teachers," in line 167, the words "and inspectors."

Lost.

Mr. Stewart offered the following amendment:

"And all material men furnishing to the owner, or builder, or contractor, materials for the construction or repair of buildings, or other improvements, shall have a lien on such buildings and improvements for the value of such materials so furnished," to be inserted between the words "therefor" and "and," in line 171.

Mr. Cline proposed to substitute the amendment by the following:

Strike out line 169 and line 170 to the word "manufactured," inclusive, and insert the words "mechanics, artisans, and material men of every class, shall have a lien upon the buildings and articles made."

Mr. Martin, of Navarro, moved to lay both amendments on the table.

A division of the question was ordered.

Mr. Stewart's amendment was laid on the table by the following vote:

YEAS—Abernathy, Allison, Arnim, Ballinger, Blake, Blassingame, Bruce, Burlison, Chambers, Cline, Cooke of San Saba, Crawford, Darnell, DeMorse, Dohoney, Flanagan, Fleming, German, Graves, Henry of Limestone, Henry of Smith, Holt, Johnson of Collin, Johnson of Franklin, Killough, Lacy, Lockett, McCabe, McKinney of Denton, Martin of Navarro, Martin of Hunt, Mitchell, Murphy, Nugent, Pauli, Reagan, Reynolds, Robertson of Bell, Ross, Russell of Wood, Sansom, Scott, Sessions, Smith, Spikes, Stockdale, Wade, Weaver, Whitehead, Wright—50.

NAYS—Brady, Douglas, McCormick, McKinney of Walker, Mills, Rentfro, Robison of Fayette, Stewart—8.

The question then recurring on laying Mr. Cline's amendment on the table, the same was put, and the Convention refused to lay it on the table by the following vote:

YEAS—Abernathy, Blake, Blassingame, Burleson, Crawford, Darnell, Graves, Henry of Smith, Holt, King, McCabe, Martin of Navarro, Robertson of Bell, Robison of Fayette, Ross, Scott, Sessions, Spikes, Wade, Whitehead, Wright—21.

NAYS—Ballinger, Barnett, Brady, Bruce, Chambers, Cline, Cooke of San Saba, DeMorse, Dohoney, Douglas, Erhard, Flanagan, Fleming, Ford, Johnson of Collin, Johnson of Franklin, Killough, Lacy, Lockett, McCormick, McKinney of Denton, Mc-

Kinney of Walker, Martin of Hunt, Mills, Mitchell, Murphy, Nugent, Pauli, Reagan, Rentfro, Russell of Wood, Stewart, Stockdale, Weaver—34.

Mr. McKinney, of Walker, offered the following substitute for section 35:

" Mechanics and artisans of every class shall have a lien on the articles and buildings manufactured, constructed or repaired by them, for the value of their labor done thereon, or materials furnished therefor ; and the Legislature shall provide by law for the speedy and efficient enforcement of such liens."

Mr. Cline's amendment adopted.

Mr. McKinney's substitute lost.

Mr. Brady offered the following section :

" Section —. The Legislature shall, at its first session after the ratification of this constitution by the people, provide for the payment of all outstanding deficiency warrants due, or which become due, to the teachers of public free schools from the various school districts into which the different counties of the State have been, are, or may hereafter be divided, on or before the 1st day of September, A. D. 1876; also for amounts due for leases and rentings of school-houses to same date."

Mr. Graves moved to lay the amendment on the table.

Carried by the following vote:

YEAS—Abernathy, Allison, Arnim, Barnett, Blake, Blassingame, Bruce, Burleson, Chambers, Cooke of San Saba, Dohoney, Douglas, Graves, Henry of Limestone, Henry of Smith, Holt, Lacy, McCormick, McKinney of Denton, Martin of Navarro, Moore, Nugent, Reagan, Robison of Fayette, Russell of Wood, Sansom, Scott, Sessions, Smith, Spikes, Stockdale, Wade, Whitehead, Wright—34.

NAYS—Brady, Cline, Crawford, Darnell, DeMorse, Erhard, Flanagan, Fleming, Ford, Johnson of Collin, Killough, Lockett, McCabe, McKinney of Walker, Mills, Mtchell, Pauli, Rentfro, Reynolds, Ross, Stewart, Weaver—23.

Mr. Reagan moved to reconsider the motion adopting Mr. Kilgore's amendment to section 34, striking out the words " July 1, 1873," and inserting " 15th March, 1875."

Carried.

The question on the adoption of the amendment was then put, and the amendment was lost by the following vote:

YEAS—Brady, Dunnam, Flanagan, Fleming, German, Graves, Haynes, Holt, Kilgore, King, Lockett, Mcormick, McKinney of Walker, Mills, Mitchell, Moore, Nugent, Nunn, Pauli, Rentfro, Reynolds, Wade—22.

45

NAYS—Abernathy, Allison, Arnim, Barnett, Blake, Blassingame, Bruce, Burleson, Chambers, Cooke of San Saba, Darnell, DeMorse, Dillard, Douglas, Erhard, Ford, Henry of Limestone, Johnson of Collin, Johnson of Franklin, Killough, Lacy, McKinney of Denton, Murphy, Ramey, Reagan, Robertson of Bell, Robison of Fayette, Russell of Wood, Sansom, Scott, Sessions, Spikes, Stockdale, Weaver, Whitehead, Wright—36.

Mr. Ramey made the following report:

CommitteeRoom,   }
Austin, Texas, November 17, 1875. }

To the Hon. E. B. Pickett, President of the Convention:

Sir—Your Committee on Engrossed and Enrolled Ordinances beg leave to report to your honorable body that they have examined and compared " Article —, Judicial Department," and find the same correctly engrossed.

Respectfully,   Wm. Neal Ramey, Chairman.

Two hundred copies of the article ordered printed.

Mr. McKinney, of Walker, offered the following amendments:

Amend section 34 by inserting in line 167, after the word "schools," the words "by the State;" add to line 168 "and for the payment by the school districts in this State of the amount justly due teachers of public schools by such districts to January, 1876.

Mr. Nugent proposed to amend as follows:

"*Provided*, that the Legislature shall authorize a tax to be levied in the several school districts of the State for the payment of balances due teachers for services rendered therein during the scholastic year ending the 31st day of August, 1875."

Lost by the following vote:

Yeas—Allison, Ballinger, Brady, Burleson, Crawford, Darnell, Davis of Brazos, DeMorse, Dohoney, Ferris, Flanagan, Ford, German, Haynes, Henry of Smith, Holt, Johnson of Franklin, King, McCabe, McCormick, Mills, Mitchell, Moore, Nugent, Nunn, Pauli, Rentfro, Reynolds, Smith, Stockdale—30.

Nays—Abernathy, Arnim, Barnett, Blake, Blassingame, Brown, Bruce, Chambers, Cline, Cooke of San Saba, Dillard, Douglas, Flournoy, Graves, Henry of Limestone, Johnson of Collin, Kilgore, Killough, Lacy, McKinney of Denton, McKinney of Walker, Martin of Navarro, Murphy, Reagan, Robertson of Bell, Robison of Fayette, Sansom, Scott, Sessions, Spikes, Weaver, Whitehead, Wright—33.

Mr. McKinney's (of Walker) amendment lost by the following vote:

YEAS—Allison, Arnim, Ballinger, Brady, Brown, Bruce, Burleson, Chambers, Cline, Crawford, Darnell, Davis of Brazos, DeMorse, Dillard, Dohoney, Erhard, Flanagan, Fleming, Ford, German, Graves, Haynes, Henry of Smith, Holt, Johnson of Collin, Johnson of Franklin, Kilgore, Killough, King, Lockett, McCabe, McCormick, McKinney of Walker, Martin of Hunt, Mills, Moore, Nugent, Nunn, Pauli, Rentfro, Reynolds, Scott, Spikes, Stewart, Stockdale, Weaver, Whitehead—47.

NAYS—Abernathy, Barnett, Blake, Blassingame, Cooke of San Saba, Douglas, Henry of Limestone, Lacy, McKinney of Denton, Martin of Navarro, Murphy, Reagan, Robertson of Bell, Robison of Fayette, Russell of Harrison, Russell of Wood, Sessions, Wright—18.

Mr. Erhard offered the following amendment:

Section 34, line 168: "and for school house leases, and for services of school superintendents, such as have been approved up to July 1, 1873."

Laid on the table.

Mr. Bruce moved to strike out section 36.

Lost by the following vote:

YEAS—Allison, Arnim, Barnett, Blassingame, Bruce, Chambers, Cooke of San Saba, Dillard, Douglas, Fleming, German, Graves, Henry of Limestone, Holt, Johnson of Collin, Lacy, McKinney of Denton, Mills, Mitchell, Pauli, Rentfro, Robertson of Bell, Robison of Fayette, Russell of Wood, Scott, Spikes, Whitehead, Wright—28.

NAYS—Abernathy, Ballinger, Blake, Brady, Brown, Burleson, Cline, Crawford, Darnell, Davis of Brazos, DeMorse, Dohoney, Erhard, Flanagan, Ford, Haynes, Henry of Smith, Johnson of Franklin, McCabe, McCormick, McKinney of Walker, Martin of Navarro, Martin of Hunt, Moore, Murphy, Nunn, Reagan, Reynolds, Sessions, Stewart, Stockdale, Weaver—32.

Mr. Bruce offered the following amendment:

Add to section 36 the following: "Until such office shall be created, the Comptroller shall perform the duties pertaining thereto, for which service he shall be allowed, out of the fees accruing from that source, such compensation as may be provided by law." Laid on the table.

On motion of Mr. Nugent, section 37 was stricken out.

Mr. Robertson, of Bell, offered the following amendment:

Section 39, in line 189, strike out the words "postmasters."

Lost.

Mr Cline proposed to add at the end of line 188 the words "County Commissioners."

Adopted.

Mr. Rentfro moved to adjourn to 9 o'clock A. M. to-morrow.
Lost.

Mr. Douglas moved to strike out section 41.
Lost.

Mr. Sansom offered the following amendment as a substitute for sections 48, 49, 50, 51 and 52:

"Sec. ——. The property of every head of a family, not to exceed in value fifteen hundred dollars, shall be exempt from forced sale, except for the purchase money of the same, or for the taxes due thereon to the State or county, or corporation, in which the same may be situated."

On motion of Mr. Mills, the Convention adjourned to 9 o'clock A. M. to-morrow.

SIXTY-THIRD DAY.

HALL OF REPRESENTATIVES,   }
AUSTIN, TEXAS, November 18, 1875. }

Convention met pursuant to adjournment; roll called; quorum present. Prayer by the Rev. J. S. Grasty, of the Presbyterian Church, at Austin.

Journal of yesterday read and adopted.

[Mr. Brown in the chair.]

On motion of Mr. Pauli, Mr. Reynolds was excused until day after to-morrow.

On motion of Mr. Scott, Mr. Russell, of Wood, was excused on account of sickness.

Mr. Darnell moved to take up the ordinance granting relief to the Texas and Pacific Railroad.

Carried, and the ordinance made special order, to be taken up as soon as the pending question, General Provisions, was disposed of.

Mr. Bruce moved to reconsider the vote adopting the amendment of Mr. Barnett relative to regulating the practice of medicine.

On motion of Mr. Dillard, the main question was ordered, and the vote was not reconsidered.

Mr. McCormick called up his resolution amending the rules, which was submitted on yesterday, and the resolution lost by the following vote:

YEAS—Abernathy, Arnim, Barnett, Blake, Cooke of San

Saba, Crawford, Davis of Brazos, Dillard, Douglas, Fleming, Flourney, Graves, Henry of Limestone, Holt, McCormick, Moore, Ross, Scott, Sessions, Spikes, Wade, Whitehead, Wright—23.

NAYS—Allison, Ballinger, Blassingame, Brown, Bruce, Chambers, Cline, Darnell, DeMorse, Dohoney, Erhard, Ferris, Flanagan, Ford, German, Haynes, Henry of Smith, Johnson of Collin, Kilgore, Killough, King, Lacy, Lockett, McCabe, McKinney of Denton, Martin of Navarro, Mills, Murphy, Nugent, Nunn, Ramey, Rentfro, Robertson of Bell, Robison of Fayette, Russell of Harrison, Sansom, Smith, Stewart, Stockdale, Weaver—40.

Mr. Rentfro moved to reconsider the vote just taken, and to lay the motion on the table.

Carried.

Unfinished business, viz: "General Provisions."

Mr. Sansom's substitute for sections 48, 49, 50, 51 and 52, pending on adjournment, was taken up.

On motion of Mr. Dillard, the substitute was laid on the table.

Mr. Darnell offered the following amendment:

Amend section 49 by striking out, in line 252, all after the word "law" to the end of the section, and insert "nor shall they or either of them ever have the power to mortgage or execute a deed of trust on the same; and all pretended sales of the homestead, involving any condition of defeasance, shall be void."

Mr. Nugent offered the following amendments:

Strike out all of section 51 after the word "as," in line 266, and insert the words "any of the children of the deceased are minors."

Strike out section 52.

Mr. Johnson, of Collin, offered the following as a substitute for Mr. Darnell's amendment:

In section 49, strike out all after the word "law," in line 252, and insert, "No mortgage, trust deed or other lien on the homestead shall ever be valid, except for purchase money therefor, or improvements thereon as hereinabove provided, whether such mortgage or trust deed, or other lien, shall have been created by the husband alone, or together with his wife; and all pretended sales of the homestead, involving any condition of defeasance, shall be void."

On motion of Mr. Wade, the debate was closed on Mr. Johnson's (of Collin) substitute, and adopted by the following vote:

YEAS—Abernathy, Allison, Arnim, Ballinger, Barnett, Blake, Blassingame, Brown, Bruce, Burleson, Chambers, Cook of Gonzales, Cooke of San Saba, Darnell, DeMorse, Erhard, Fleming, Flournoy, Graves, Haynes, Henry of Limestone, Johnson of Collin, Johnson of Franklin, Lacy, Lockett, McCormick, McKinney of Denton, McKinney of Walker, Martin of Navarro, Martin of Hunt, Mills, Nugent, Pauli, Ramey, Rentfro, Robertson of Bell, Ross, Russell of Harrison, Sessions, Stewart, Stockdale, Wade, Weaver, Whitehead—44.

Nays—Cline, Crawford, Davis of Brazos, Dillard, Dohoney, Douglas, Ferris, Flanagan, Henry of Smith, Holt, Kilgore, Killough, McCabe, Mitchell, Moore, Nunn, Reagan, Robison of Fayette, Sansom, Scott, Smith, Spikes, Wright—23.

Mr. Murphy was paired off with Mr. Waelder, but for which he would have voted " yea."

The question then recurring on the adoption of the amendment as a part of the article, the same was put and the amendment adopted, by the following vote:

Yeas—Abernathy, Allison, Arnim, Ballinger, Barnett, Blake, Blassingame, Brown, Bruce, Burleson, Chambers, Cook of Gonzales, Cooke of San Saba, Darnell, DeMorse, Erhard, Flournoy, Ford, Graves, Haynes, Henry of Limestone, Johnson of Collin, Johnson of Franklin, King, Lacy, McCormick, McKinney of Denton, McKinney of Walker, Martin of Navarro, Martin of Hunt, Mills, Mitchell, Nugent, Pauli, Ramey, Rentfro, Robertson of Bell, Ross, Russell of Harrison, Sessions, Spikes, Stewart, Stockdale, Wade, Weaver, Whitehead—46.

Nays—Cline, Crawford, Davis of Brazos, Dillard, Dohoney, Douglas, Ferris, Flanagan, Henry of Smith, Holt, Kilgore, Killough, Lockett, McCabe, Moore, Nunn, Reagan, Robison of Fayette, Sansom, Scott, Smith, Wright—22.

Mr. Murphy was again paired off with Mr. Waelder, but for which fact he would have voted " yea."

Mr. Mills moved to reconsider the vote just taken, and to lay the motion on the table.   Carried.

Mr. Stockdale offered the following amendments:

Amend section 50 by inserting in line 256, after the word " parcels," the following: " *Provided,* that the same shall be used for the purposes of a home, or for the raising of any crop or crops, and for preparing the same for market."

And the section further by adding at the end thereof the following: " *Provided,* that the same shall be used for the purposes of a home, or as a place to exercise the calling or business of the head of the family."

Mr. Haynes moved the main question on the engrossment of the article.

Mr. King made the point that the motion was out of order, as the Convention was considering the article section by section.

The chair ruled against the point, and the Convention refused to order the main question.

Mr. Robertson, of Bell, offered the following as an amendment to Mr. Stockdale's amendment :

Section 50, line 256, after the word "parcels," insert the words "with the improvements thereon."

Adopted.

Mr. Murphy offered the following amendment:

"*Provided, also,* that any temporary renting of the homestead shall not change the character of the same where no other homestead has been acquired."

Accepted.

Mr. Stockdale's amendment as amended was adopted.

Mr. Ballinger offered the following amendment:

Section 49, line 243, after the word "family," insert the words "not acquired by fraud."

On motion of Mr. Flanagan, the Convention adjourned to 2½ o'clock P. M.

EVENING SESSION—2½ o'clock.

Convention met pursuant to adjournment; roll called; quorum present.

Mr. Ballinger's amendment, pending on adjournment, on motion of Mr. Reagan, passed over for the present.

[Mr. Stockdale in the chair.]

Mr. Reagan offered the following amendment:

Amend section 50 by adding "*provided,* no homestead exemption shall exceed ten thousand dollars in value, and the Legislature shall provide for determining for the disposition of the excess over ten thousand dollars, for the benefit of creditors."

Lost by the following vote :

YEAS—Allison, Arnim, Blake, Cline, Cook of Gonzales, Crawford, Dillard, Dohoney, Erhard, Fleming, Henry of Limestone, Holt, Killough, Lockett, McCormick, Murphy, Martin of Navarro, Pauli, Reagan, Robison of Fayette, Ross, Sansom, Scott, Smith—24.

NAYS—Abernathy, Ballinger, Barnett, Blassingame, Brown, Bruce, Burleson, Chambers, Cooke of San Saba, Darnell, De-Morse, Douglas, Flanagan, Flournoy, Ford, German, Haynes, Johnson of Collin, Johnson of Franklin, King, Lacy, McCabe, McKinney of Denton, McKinney of Walker, Mills, Mitchell,

Moore, Martin of Hunt, Nugent, Rentfro, Robertson of Bell, Sessions, Spikes, Stewart, Stockdale, Wade, Weaver, Whitehead, Wright—39.

Mr. Ballinger's amendment was again taken up.

Mr. Graves moved to close debate on all pending amendments. Carried.

Mr. Ballinger's amendment lost by the following vote :

YEAS—Allison, Ballinger, Blake, Brady, Cline, Cooke of Gonzales, Crawford, Davis of Brazos, Dillard, Dohoney, Douglas, Erhard, Ferris, Flanagan, Henry of Smith, Holt, Kilgore, Killough, Lockett, McCabe, McCormick, Moore, Nunn, Pauli, Reagan, Robison of Fayette, Ross, Sansom, Scott, Smith, Spikes, Stockdale—32.

NAYS—Abernathy, Arnim, Barnett, Blassingame, Brown, Bruce, Burleson, Chambers, Cooke of San Saba, Darnell, DeMorse, Flournoy, Ford, German, Graves, Haynes, Henry of Limestone, Johnson of Collin, Johnson of Franklin, King, Lacy, McKinney of Denton, Martin of Navarro, Mills, Mitchell, Nugent, Rentfro, Robertson of Bell, Sessions, Stewart, Wade, Weaver, Whitehead, Wright—34.

Mr. Nugent's amendments lost.

Mr. King's amendment, to add to section 47, "*provided,* that the public free school law shall continue in full force and operation until the 1st of September, 1876," lost.

Mr. Nugent's amendment to strike out section 52 adopted, as follows:

YEAS—Allison, Arnim, Barnett, Blassingame, Brown, Bruce, Burleson, Chambers, Cooke of San Saba, Darnell, DeMorse, Erhard, Fleming, Ford, Graves, Haynes, Johnson of Collin, Johnson of Franklin, Kilgore, King, Lacy, McKinney of Denton, Martin of Hunt, Moore, Murphy, Nugent, Ramey, Reagan, Rentfro, Robertson of Bell, Ross, Smith, Stewart, Wade, Weaver, Whitehead—36.

NAYS—Abernathy, Ballinger, Blake, Brady, Cline, Cook of Gonzales, Crawford, Davis of Brazos, Dillard, Dohoney, Douglas, Ferris, Flanagan, Flournoy, Henry of Limestone, Henry of Smith, Holt, Killough, Lockett, Martin of Navarro, Mills, Mitchell, Nunn, Pauli, Robison of Fayette, Sansom, Scott, Sessions, Spikes, Stockdale, Wright—31.

Mr. Reagan offered the following additional section :

"Sec. —. That all the navigable waters of the State shall forever remain public highways, free to the citizens of the State and of the United States, without tax, impost or toll; and that no tax, toll, impost or wharfage shall be demanded or received from the owner of any merchandise or commodity, for the use of the shores, or any wharf erected on the shores, or in, or over any of said waters, unless expressly authorized by law."

Mr. Kilgore moved to reconsider the vote taken on yesterday adopting Mr. Sansom's substitute for section 24.

Lost.

Mr. Ford offered the following new sections:

"Sec. ——. The Legislature shall pass laws authorizing the Governor to lease or sell to the government of the United States a sufficient quantity of the public domain of this State necessary for the erection of forts, barracks, arsenals and military stations, or camps, and for other needful military purposes; and the action of the Governor therein shall be subject to the approval of the Legislature."

Adopted.

"Sec. ——. The Legislature shall pass laws to prevent interference in elections, other than their own, by judicial officers, and the same shall be cause for removal from office."

Lost.

Mr. DeMorse offered the following amendment:

"Every male citizen between the ages of seventeen and fifty years shall be subject to work upon the public roads and bridges not exceeding ten days in any one year, under direction of a road or county overseer, to be elected by the County Commissioners thereof, which labor may be substituted or compensated by the payment of one dollar per day; and no road tax shall ever be levied for work on roads; but a tax for the construction of bridges, when indispensable, not exceeding one-sixth of one per cent. on the taxable property in each county, may be levied by the County Commissioners of any county in the State."

Lost.

Mr. Cline offered the following amendment:

"Section ——. The rights of married women to their separate property, real and personal, shall be protected by law; and married women, infants, and insane persons shall not be barred of their rights of property by adverse possession or law of limitation of less than seven years from and after their age of majority, and the removal of each and all of their respective legal disabilities."

Lost by the following vote:

YEAS—Brady, Cline, DeMorse, Dohoney, Lockett, Mills, Pauli, Ramey, Rentfro, Stewart, Wade, Weaver—12.

NAYS—Abernathy, Allison, Arnim, Ballinger, Barnett, Blake, Blassingame, Brown, Bruce, Chambers, Cooke of San Saba,

Crawford, Darnell, Davis of Brazos, Dillard, Douglas, Ferris, Flanagan, Fleming, Flournoy, German, Graves, Haynes, Henry of Limestone, Henry of Smith, Holt, Johnson of Collin, Johnson of Franklin, Killough, King, Lacy, McCormick, Martin of Navarro, Martin of Hunt, Mitchell, Moore, Nugent, Nunn, Reagan, Robertson of Bell, Scott, Sessions, Spikes, Whitehead, Wright—45.

Mr. Ballinger offered the following section:

"Section —. The Legislature shall have power to pass general and special laws providing for the inspection of cattle, stock and hides, and for the regulation of brands."

Mr. Dillard moved the previous question.

Mr. King offered the following amendment:

Amend section 55 by striking out all after the word "pensions," in line 285, and add "to surviving soldiers or volunteers in the war between Texas and Mexico, the surviving signers of the declaration of the independence of Texas, and to such others who have rendered military service in behalf of the State, as may be deemed worthy of pension."

Mr. Reagan withdrew his amendment, and offered it as a distinct section, and it was made the special order for 10 o'clock A. M. to-morrow, under suspension of the rule.

On motion of Mr. Dillard, the main question was ordered.

Mr. Ballinger's amendment adopted.

Mr. King's amendment adopted.

Mr. Wright offered the following amendment:

Add to section 18, "*provided,* that insurance companies may be permitted to discount notes and bills." Lost.

The article was then ordered engrossed, by the following vote:

YEAS—Abernathy, Allison, Arnim, Ballinger, Barnett, Blassingame, Brown, Bruce, Burleson, Chambers, Cooke of San Saba, Crawford, Darnell, Davis of Brazos, DeMorse, Dillard, Dohoney, Douglas, Erhard, Ferris, Flanagan, Fleming, Flournoy, Ford, German, Graves, Haynes, Henry of Limestone, Henry of Smith, Holt, Johnson of Collin, Johnson of Franklin, Kilgore, Killough, King, Lacy, McCormick, McKinney of Denton, McKinney of Walker, Martin of Navarro, Martin of Hunt, Moore, Nugent, Nunn, Ramey, Reagan, Robertson of Bell, Robison of Fayette, Ross, Sansom, Scott, Sessions, Smith, Spikes, Stewart, Stockdale, Wade, Weaver, Whitehead, Wright—62.

NAYS—Brady, Cline, Lockett, McCabe, Mills, Mitchell, Murphy, Pauli, Rentfro—9.

On motion of Mr. Kilgore, two hundred copies of the article were ordered printed, after engrossment.

Mr. Darnell moved to adjourn to 7½ o'clock P. M.

On motion of Mr. Rentfro, the Convention adjourned to 9 o'clock A. M. to-morrow.

SIXTY-FOURTH DAY.

HALL OF REPRESENTATIVES, ⎱
AUSTIN, TEXAS, November 19, 1875. ⎰ ·

Convention met pursuant to adjournment; roll called; quorum present. Prayer by the Rev. J. S. Grasty, of the Presbyterian Church.

Journal of yesterday read and adopted.

Mr. Wright submitted the following report:

COMMITTEE ROOM, ⎱
AUSTIN, TEXAS, November 18, 1875. ⎰

To the Hon. E. B. Pickett, President of the Convention:

SIR—Your Committee on Private Corporations have considered the various matters referred to them, and have instructed me to submit the following article and recommend its adoption.

W. B. WRIGHT, Chairman.

"Section 1. No private corporation shall be created except by general laws.

"Sec. 2. General laws shall be enacted providing for the creation of private corporations, and shall therein provide fully for the adequate protection of the public and of the individual stockholders.

"Sec. 3. The right to authorize and regulate freight, tolls, wharfage or fares, levied and collected, or proposed to be levied and collected, by individuals, companies or corporations, for the use of highways, landings, wharves, bridges and ferries, devoted to public use, has never been, and shall never be relinquished or abandoned by the State, but shall always be under legislative control and depend upon legislative authority.

"Sec. 4. The first Legislature assembled after the adoption of this constitution shall provide a mode of procedure by the Attorney General and District or County Attorneys in the name and behalf of the State, to prevent and punish the demanding and receiving or collection of any and all charges as freight, wharfage, fares or tolls, for the use of property devoted to the public, unless the same shall have been specially authorized by law.

"Sec. 5. All laws granting the right to demand and collect freight, fares, tolls or wharfage shall at all times be subject to amendment, modification or repeal by the Legislature."

W. B. WRIGHT, Chairman,
GEORGE FLOURNOY,
GEO. McCORMICK,
ROBERT LACEY,
W. W. DILLARD,
MARION MARTIN,
W. L. CRAWFOD,
J. F. JOHNSON.

Mr. Murphy reported as follows:

COMMITTEE ROOM,
AUSTIN, November 18, 1875.

To the Hon. E. B. Pickett, President of the Convention:

The undersigned members of the Committee on Private Corporations can not concur in the report made by the chairman, nor in the article recommended to be adopted, in so far as it assumes in the article, as a right on the part of the State to regulate "freights, charges," etc., of companies heretofore chartered, for the reasons following:

1. The charters heretofore granted are executed contracts, and article 1, section 10, of the Constitution of the United States prohibits any State from passing any law impairing the obligation of contracts.

2. Because the effect of the article as to exesting charters would be to deprive the incorporators without due process of law of their property, which is prohibited by article 14 of the Constitution of the United States.

3. Because the State has no right to regulate the charges of incorporated companies unless reserved in the charters.

J. B. MURPHY,
T. L. NUGENT,
B. BLAKE.

One hundred copies of the reports and articles ordered printed.

Special order taken up, viz., "Ordinance for relief of the Texas and Pacific Railroad," with report of a select committee, recommending amendments, and a minority report of the committee.

Mr. German moved to postpone the consideration of the ordinance until the action on the articles on "Taxation and Revenue," "Judicial Department," and "General Provisions."

Lost.

Mr. Dohoney offered the following amendments to the committee's amendments:

In line 2 strike out the words "interfered with" and insert the word "affect."

In line 5, after the word "town" insert the words "or city."

Adopted.

The amendments of committee adopted.

Mr. Nugent offered the following amendment:

"*And provided, further,* that any reservation of public domain heretofore made for said railway shall be opened to actual settlement under the pre-emption laws of the State."

The yeas and nays being demanded, the amendment was adopted by the following vote:

YEAS—Abernathy, Allison, Arnim, Barnett, Blassingame, Brown, Bruce, Chambers, Cook of Gonzales, Crawford, De-Morse, Dillard, Fleming, Flournoy, German, Graves, Haynes, Johnson of Collin, Johnson of Franklin, Kilgore, Killough, Lacy, McCormick, McKinney of Denton, McKinney of Walker, Moore, Nugent, Nunn, Pauli, Ramey, Reagan, Robertson of Bell, Robison of Fayette, Ross, Russell of Wood, Scott, Sessions, Smith, Whitehead—39.

NAYS—Blake, Burleson, Cline, Cooke of San Saba, Darnell, Davis of Brazos, Dohoney, Erhard, Ferris, Flanagan, Ford, Henry of Limestone, Holt, King, Lockett, Lynch, McCabe, Martin of Navarro, Martin of Hunt, Mills, Murphy, Rentfro, Russell of Harrison, Sansom, Spikes, Stockdale, Wade, Weaver, Whitfield, Wright—30.

Mr. Nugent moved to reconsider the vote just taken, and to lay the motion on the table.

A call of the Convention was demanded.

Absentees—Messrs. Brady, Morris, McLean and West.

On motion of Mr. Dillard, Mr. McLean was excused.

Mr. Brady appeared and answered to his name.

Mr. McCormick moved to suspend the call.

Lost.

The hour having arrived for the special order, viz: Mr. Reagan's separate section relative to public highways, it was taken up.

Mr. Reagan offered the following amendment to the section:

Amend the section by inserting between the words "State" and "shall," in line 1, the following: "embracing those which form common boundaries between this State and other States or territories, and between this State and Mexico."

Mr. West appeared and answered to his name.

On motion of Mr. Reagan, the call was suspended.

Mr. Nugent's motion to reconsider and lay on the table was then put and lost by the following vote:

YEAS—Arnim, Blassingame, Bruce, DeMorse, Dillard, Fleming, German, Graves, Haynes, Johnson of Collin, Lacy, McCormick, Moore, Nugent, Pauli, Robertson of Bell, Robison of Fayette, Ross, Russell of Wood, Sansom, Scott—21.

NAYS—Abernathy, Ballinger, Barnett, Blake, Brady, Brown, Burleson, Chambers, Cline, Cook of Gonzales, Cooke of San Saba, Crawford, Darnell, Dohoney, Douglas, Erhard, Ferris, Flanagan, Flournoy, Ford, Henry of Limestone, Holt, Johnson of Franklin, Kilgore, Killough, King, Lockett, McCabe, Martin of Navarro, Mills, Mitchell, Murphy, Nunn, Ramey, Reagan, Rentfro, Russell of Harrison, Sessions, Smith, Spikes, Stockdale, Wade, Weaver, West, Whitehead, Whitfield, Wright—47.

On motion of Mr. Wright, the question under consideration, viz: Mr. Reagan's section on public highways over the waters of the State, was postponed and consolidated with the article on private corporations.

The Convention then proceeded with the consideration of the ordinance for the relief of the Texas Pacific Railroad, the question to reconsider the vote adopting Mr. Nugent's amendment being the pending question.

[Mr. Brown in the chair.]

Mr. Dillard moved the previous question. Carried.

The vote was then reconsidered by the following vote:

YEAS—Ballinger, Barnett, Blake, Brown, Burleson, Chambers, Cline, Cooke of San Saba, Crawford, Darnell, Dohoney, Douglas, Erhard, Ferris, Flanagan, Ford, Henry of Limestone, Holt, Johnson of Franklin, Kilgore, Killough, King, Lockett, Martin of Navarro, Martin of Hunt, Mills, Mitchell, Murphy, Reagan, Rentfro, Russell of Harrison, Sansom, Sessions, Smith, Spikes, Stockdale, Wade, Weaver, Waelder, West, Whitfield, Wright—41.

NAYS—Arnim, Blassingame, Bruce, DeMorse, Dillard, Fleming, Flournoy, German, Graves, Haynes, Johnson of Collin, Lacy, McCabe, McCormick, McKinney of Walker, Moore, Nugent, Pauli, Ramey, Robertson of Bell, Robison of Fayette, Ross, Whitehead—22.

Mr. Nugent's amendment was then lost by the following vote:

YEAS—Arnim, Blassingame, Bruce, Crawford, DeMorse, Dillard, Fleming, Flournoy, German, Graves, Haynes, Johnson of Collin, Lacy, McCabe, McCormick, McKinney of Walker, Moore, Nugent, Pauli, Ramey, Robertson of Bell, Robison of Fayette, Ross, Smith, Whitehead—25.

NAYS—Barnett, Blake, Brady, Brown, Burleson, Cline, Cooke of San Saba, Darnell, Davis of Wharton, Dohoney, Douglas, Erhard, Ferris, Flanagan, Ford, Henry of Limestone, Holt, Johnson of Franklin, Kilgore, Killough, King, Lockett, Martin of Navarro, Martin of Hunt, Mills, Murphy, Nunn, Reagan, Rentfro, Russell of Harrison, Sansom, Sessions, Spikes, Stockdale, Wade, Weaver, West, Whitfield, Wright—39.

Mr. Stockdale offered the following amendment:

" AND WHEREAS, said financial panic has had the same paralyzing effect on all other railway constructions in this State; therefore,

" *Be it further ordained,* that all railway companies in this State are hereby granted twelve months time, from the adoption of the constitution framed by this Convention, to comply with the requirements of their charters; and the time for the construction of any part and for the completion of the whole of the work to be done by any railway company as required by the charters thereof."

Mr. Ballinger offered the following amendment:

" *Provided,* that the express condition of this ordinance, and of all rights under the same, is, and it is hereby enacted and declared, that any railroad now or hereafter chartered by the State of Texas, whose line connects with or crosses the line of said Texas and Pacific Railway, may connect with the same, and shall have and receive all facilities for such connection in transportation and business, and for the receipt and transfer of cars and freight from one to the other, without breaking bulk, which can be afforded to connecting railways, and that the cars, passenger and freight, received from said connecting railroads, or carried over said Texas and Pacific Railway, or any part thereof, destined to any point on the gulf coast, or any of said connecting railroads, shall be transported and carried by said Texas and Pacific Railway Company at the same *pro rata* rates of freight and passage per mile, and at no higher rates than the through rates of freight and passage charged by said Texas and Pcific Railway Company to the extreme points of its own and all connecting railroads to their termini on the Atlantic or Pacific; the express intent and effect hereof being, that cars, passengers and freights to and from the gulf coast and other points on any of such connecting Texas railroads shall always be carried by said Texas and Pacific Railway Company, and bargained for by it, with all its other connecting roads and through lines, at the most favored rates of the through freight and passage on said railroad and its connections, and this right may always be enforced by any of said connecting railroad companies, and by any all persons interested in freight or passage thereon and no Legislature shall hereafter grant any relief to said Texas and Pacific Railway Company which does not recognize and secure the rights and privileges herein provided."

Mr. Nugent offered the following amendment to Mr. Stockdale's amendment:

"It is hereby further ordained that said companies shall file in the office of the Secretary of State a full and complete acceptance of all the provisions of this constitution, applicable to railroads, before the relief herein provided for shall take effect."

Adopted by the following vote:

YEAS—Allison, Arnim, Barnett, Blake, Blassingame, Burleson, Cooke of San Saba, Crawford, DeMorse, Dillard, Douglas, Fleming, Flournoy, German, Graves, Haynes, Henry of Limestone, Holt, Johnson of Collin, Johnson of Franklin, Lacy, McCormick, McKinney of Walker, Martin of Hunt, Moore, Nugent, Nunn, Pauli, Ramey, Reagan, Rentfro, Robertson of Bell, Robison of Fayette, Ross, Sessions, Spikes, Stewart, Wade, Whitehead—38.

NAYS—Ballinger, Brady, Brown, Cline, Darnell, Davis of Brazos, Dohoney, Erhard, Ferris, Flanagan, Kilgore, King, Lockett, McCabe, Martin of Navarro, Mills, Mitchell, Murphy, Russell of Harrison, Sansom, Smith, Stockdale, Weaver, Whitfield, Wright—25.

Mr. Flanagan moved to lay the whole subject matter on the table.

Lost by the following vote:

YEAS—Allison, Arnim, Barnett, Blassingame, Brady, Bruce, Crawford, Davis of Brazos, DeMorse, Dillard, Flanagan, Fleming, Flournoy, German, Graves, Haynes, Henry of Smith, Johnson of Collin, Kilgore, Lacy, McCabe, McCormick, McKinney of Walker, Moore, Nugent, Pauli, Robertson of Bell, Robison of Fayette, Ross, Smith, Stewart, Stockdale, Whitehead, Wright—34.

NAYS—Abernathy, Ballinger, Blake, Brown, Burleson, Cline, Chambers, Cooke of San Saba, Darnell, Dohoney, Douglas, Erhard, Ferris, Ford, Henry of Limestone, Holt, Johnson of Franklin, Killough, King, Lockett, Martin of Navarro, Martin of Hunt, Mills, Mitchell, Murphy, Nunn, Ramey, Reagan, Rentfro, Sansom, Sessions, Spikes, Wade, Weaver, West, Whitfield—36.

On motion of Mr. King, the Convention adjourned to 2½ o'clock P. M.

EVENING SESSION—2½ o'clock.

Convention met pursuant to adjournment; roll called; quorum present.

Pendng question resumed, viz: Mr. Stockdale's amendment as amended.

Mr. Abernathy moved to reconsider the vote refusing to table the whole subject taken up this forenoon.

Carried by the following vote:

YEAS—Abernathy, Arnim, Barnett, Blassingame, DeMorse, Dillard, Ferris, Flanagan, Flournoy, German, Graves, Johnson of Collin, Lacy, McCabe, McCormick, McKinney of Denton, McKinney of Walker, Murphy, Nugent, Pauli, Robertson of Bell, Robison of Fayette, Ross, Scott, Stewart, Stockdale, Whitehead—27.

NAYS—Blake, Cline, Cooke of San Saba, Darnell, Davis of Brazos, Dohoney, Douglas, Henry of Limestone, Johnson of Franklin, Kilgore, Killough, King, Lockett, Martin of Hunt, Mills, Mitchell, Russell of Harrison, Sansom, Sessions, Spikes, Wade, Weaver, Whitfield—23.

The question recurring on tabling the whole subject, on motion of Mr. Darnell a call of the Convention was demanded.

Absentees—Brady, Brown, Erhard, Ford, Henry of Smith, Holt, Nunn, Ramey, Rentfro, Russell of Wood, and Wright.

The pending question went to the table temporarily.

Messrs. Ford, Wright, Moore, Henry of Smith, and Holt appeared and answered to their names.

"Article ——, Taxation and Revenue," taken up and read third time.

Mr. Murphy offered the following amendment:

Section 11, line 82, strike out the words "by a two-thirds vote," and the word "vote" in line 83.

[Mr. Brown appeared, and was announced by the doorkeeper.]

The amendment was lost by the following vote:

YEAS—Abernathy, Allison, Ballinger, Blake, Burleson, Cline, Cook of Gonzales, Darnell, Davis of Brazos, DeMorse, Dohoney, Ferris, Flournoy, Henry of Limestone, Henry of Smith, Kilgore, Killough, King, Lockett, McCormick, Martin of Navarro, Moore, Murphy, Ramey, Reagan, Robertson of Bell, Robison of Fayette, Russell of Harrison, Sessions, Smith, Stewart, Stockdale, West, Whitehead, Whitfield, Wright—36.

NAYS—Arnim, Barnett, Blassingame, Brown, Bruce, Cooke of San Saba, Crawford, Dillard, Flanagan, Fleming, German, Graves, Haynes, Holt, Johnson of Collin, Johnson of Franklin,

46

Lacy, McCabe, McKinney of Denton, McKinney of Walker, Martin of Hunt, Mills, Mitchell, Nugent, Pauli, Ross, Sansom, Scott, Spikes, Wade, Weaver—31.

Mr. Pauli offered the following amendment as a substitute for section 18:

"Sec. 18. The County Commissioners' Court shall act as a Board of Equalization in each county to determine the just value of the property rendered for taxation."

Mr. Ballinger proposed to substitute the amendment by the following:

Add to the end of the section the words: "and the County Commissioners shall constitute said board."

Adopted.

Mr. Fleming offered to amend section 13, line 98, by inserting after the word "lands" the words "and other property;" and in line 100, after the word "lands," insert "and other property."

Adopted.

Mr. Brown offered the following amendment:

Amend section 16 by striking out all after the word "therefor," in line 119, and inserting: "but in counties having ten thousand inhabitants, to be determined by the last preceding census of the United States, a collector of taxes shall be elected, to hold office for two years and until his successor shall have been elected and qualified."

Adopted.

Mr. Cline proposed to amend section 13, lines 97 and 98, by inserting after the word "sale" the words "a sufficient portion."

Adopted.

Mr. Nugent offered the following amendment:

Add to section 15: "*Provided,* that the homstead exempt from forced sale shall only be liable for the taxes due thereon."

Messrs. Russell, of Wood, and Erhard appeared and answered to their names.

Mr. Nugent's amendment lost by the following vote:

YEAS—Abernathy, Arnim, Ballinger, Barnett, Blassingame, Brady, Brown, Bruce, Burleson, Chambers, Cook of Gonzales, Crawford, Darnell, Davis of Brazos, DeMorse, Dillard, Dohoney, Erhard, Ferris, Flournoy, Ford, Haynes, Killough, King, Lacy, Lockett, McCormick, McKinney of Denton, Mills, Moore, Murphy, Nugent, Pauli, Ramey, Reagan, Rentfro, Robertson of Bell, Ross, Russell of Harrison, Scott, Stayton, Wade, Weaver, Whitehead, Whitfield—45.

NAYS—Blake, Cline, Cooke of Son Saba, Douglas, Flanagan, Fleming, German, Graves, Henry of Limestone, Henry of Smith,

Holmes, Johnson of Collin, Johnson of Franklin, Kilgore, Mc-
Kinney of Walker, Martin of Navarro, Martin of Hunt, Mitchell,
Robison of Fayette, Russell of Wood, Sansom, Smith, Spikes,
Stockdale, West, Wright—26.

Mr. Crawford offered the following amendment:

Section 9, line 69, strike out all after the word "levy" down
to "except," and insert "an annual tax of not more than one-
half of one per cent."

On motion of Mr. Nugent, the main question on the final
passage of the article was ordered.

Mr. Crawford's amendment lost by the following vote:

YEAS—Abernathy, Ballinger, Brady, Brown, Cline, Cook
of Gonzales, Crawford, Darnell, Davis of Brazos, DeMorse, Dillard, Ferris, Flanagan, Haynes, Kilgore, King, Lockett, Mc-
Cable, Martin of Navarro, Martin of Hunt, Pauli, Ramey, Reagan, Rentfro, Russell of Harrison, Sansom, Smith, Spikes,
Wade, West, Whitehead, Wright—32.

NAYS—Allison, Arnim, Barnett, Blake, Blassingame, Bruce,
Burleson, Chambers, Cooke of San Saba, Dohoney, Douglas,
Erhard, Fleming, Henry of Limestone, Holt, Johnson of Col-
lin, Johnson of Franklin, Killough, Lacy, McCormick, McKin-
ney of Walker, Mills, Mitchell, Moore, Murphy, Nugent, Nunn,
Robertson of Bell, Robison of Fayette, Russell of Wood, Scott,
Stewart, Stockdale, Weaver, Whitfield—35.

Mr. King offered the following amendment:

Amend section 10 by adding: "*provided,* that the Legislature
may authorize counties with a population of less than two thousand inhabitants to use the State tax to build jails and court
houses in said counties."

Lost.

Mr. Dillard offered the following amendment:

Section 16, line 120, strike out "ten thousand" and insert
"eight thousand."

Lost.

The article passed by the following vote:

YEAS—Abernathy, Allison, Arnim, Barnett, Blassingame,
Bruce, Burleson, Chambers, Cook of Gonzales, Cooke of San
Saba, Dillard, Dohoney, Douglas, Ferris, Fleming, Flournoy,
German, Graves, Haynes, Holt, Johnson of Collin, Johnson of
Franklin, McCormick, McKinney of Denton, McKinney of
Walker, Murphy, Nugent, Ramey, Robison of Fayette, Ross,
Russell of Wood, Scott, Sessions, Spikes, Wade, Weaver, White-
head, Whitfield—40.

NAYS—Ballinger, Blake, Cline, Crawford, Darnell, Davis of

Brazos, DeMorse, Erhard, Flanagan, Ford, Henry of Limestone, Henry of Smith, Kilgore, Killough, King, Lacy, Lockett, McCabe, Martin of Navarro, Mills, Moore, Nunn, Pauli, Reagan, Rentfro, Robertson of Bell, Russell of Harrison, Sansom, Smith, Stewart, Stockdale, West, Wright—32.

Mr. Brady was paired off with Mr. Gaither, but for which he would vote "nay."

Mr. Martin, of Hunt, was paired off with Mr. Norvell, but for which he would vote "yea."

On motion of Mr. Flournoy, Mr. Russell, of Wood, was granted unlimited leave of absence.

Mr. Fleming moved to reconsider the vote just taken, and to lay the motion on the table.

Lost by the following vote:

YEAS—Abernathy, Allison, Arnim, Blassingame, Bruce, Burleson, Cooke of San Saba, Dillard, Dohoney, Douglas, Ferris, Fleming, Flournoy, Ford, German, Graves, Haynes, Henry of Limestone, Holt, Johnson of Collin, Johnson of Franklin, Lacy, McKinney of Denton, McKinney of Walker, Murphy, Nugent, Robison of Fayette, Russell of Wood, Scott, Spikes, Wade, Whitfield—32.

NAYS—Ballinger, Barnett, Blake, Brady, Brown, Chambers, Cline, Cook of Gonzales, Crawford, Darnell, Davis of Brazos, DeMorse, Erhard, Flanagan, Henry of Smith, Kilgore, Killough, King, Lockett, McCabe, McCormick, Martin of Navarro, Mitchell Moore, Nunn, Pauli, Ramey, Reagan, Rentfro, Robertson of Bell, Rose, Russell of Harrison, Sansom, Sessions, Smith, Stewart, Stockdale, Weaver, West, Whitehead, Wright—41.

The question then recurring on the motion to reconsider, the same was put and carried by the following vote:

YEAS—Allison, Ballinger, Barnett, Blake, Brady, Brown, Chambers, Cline, Cook of Gonzales, Crawford, Darnell, Davis of Brazos, DeMorse, Erhard, Flanagan, Henry of Smith, Kilgore, Killough, King, Lockett, McCabe, McCormick, Martin of Navarro, Martin of Hunt, Mitchell, Moore, Nunn, Pauli, Reagan, Rentfro, Russell of Harrison, Sansom, Smith, Stewart, Stockdale, West, Wright—37.

NAYS—Abernathy, Arnim, Blassingame, Bruce, Burleson, Cooke of San Saba, Dillard, Dohoney, Douglas, Ferris, Fleming, German, Graves, Haynes, Henry of Limestone, Holt, Johnson of Collin, Johnson of Franklin, Lacy, McKinney of Denton, Murphy, Nugent, Ramey, Robertson of Bell, Robison of Fayette, Ross, Russell of Wood, Scott, Sessions, Spikes, Wade, Weaver, Whitehead, Whitfield—34.

Mr. Crawford offered the following amendment:

Sec. 9, line 68, strike out the words "city or town."

Mr. Murphy moved to lay the amendment on the table.

Lost by the following vote:

YEAS—Blassingame, Burleson, Chambers, Cooke of San Saba, Dohoney, Henry of Limestone, Henry of Smith, Holt, Johnson of Collin, McKinney of Denton, Martin of Navarro, Mills, Mitchell, Murphy, Nugent, Robertson of Bell, Robison of Fayette, Russell of Harrison, Scott, Spikes, Stockdale, Wade, Whitfield—28.

NAYS—Abernathy, Allison, Arnim, Ballinger, Barnett, Blake, Brady, Brown, Bruce, Cline, Cook of Gonzales, Crawford, Darnell, Davis of Brazos, DeMorse, Dillard, Douglas, Erhard, Ferris, Flanagan, Fleming, Flournoy, Graves, Haynes, Kilgore, Killough, King, Lacy, Lockett, McCabe, McCormick, McKinney of Walker, Martin of Hunt, Moore, Nunn, Pauli, Ramey, Reagan, Rentfro, Ross, Russell of Wood, Sansom, Sessions, Smith, West, Whitehead—47.

The Convention being full by appearance of absentees, the call was exhausted, and the Convention again resumed the question on which the call was ordered, viz: the motion to lay on the table the ordinance for the relief of the Texas Pacific Railroad, and all pending amendments.

Yeas and nays called, and motion to table carried by the following vote:

YEAS—Abernathy, Allison, Arnim, Barnett, Blassingame, Brady, Bruce, Chambers, Crawford, DeMorse, Dillard, Flanagan, Fleming, Flournoy, German, Graves, Haynes, Henry of Smith, Johnson of Collin, Kilgore, Lacy, McCabe, McCormick, McKinney of Denton, McKinney of Walker, Martin of Navarro, Moore, Nugent, Pauli, Ramey, Rentfro, Robertson of Bell, Robison of Fayette, Ross, Russell of Wood, Scott, Sessions, Smith, Stewart, Stockdale—40.

NAYS—Brown, Burleson, Cline, Cook of Gonzales, Cooke of San Saba, Darnell, Davis of Brazos, Dohoney, Douglas, Ferris, Henry of Limestone, Holt, Johnson of Franklin, Killough, King, Lockett, Mills, Murphy, Nunn, Reagan, Russell of Harrison, Sansom, Spikes, Wade, West, Whitehead, Whitfield, Wright—28.

Convention again resumed consideration of taxation and revenue, Mr. Crawford's amendment pending.

Mr. Dohoney offered the following as a substitute for the amendment:

Amend section 9, line 69, by striking out the words "one-half of."

Mr. Stewart offered the following amendment:

Strike out all after the word "valuation," in line 68.

[Mr. Stockdale in the chair.]

Mr. Allison moved the previous question on the passage of the article.

Carried.

Mr. Stewart's amendment lost.

Mr. Dohoney withdrew his amendment.

Mr. Crawford's amendment lost by the following vote:

YEAS—Allison, Ballinger, Barnett, Blake, Brady, Brown, Bruce, Burleson, Cline, Cook of Gonzales, Cooke of San Saba, Crawford, Davis of Brazos, DeMorse, Dillard, Erhard, Ferris, Flanagan, Fleming, Ford, Graves, Johnson of Collin, Killough, King, Lacy, Lockett, McKinney of Walker, Martin of Navarro, Martin of Hunt, Moore, Nugent, Nunn, Pauli, Ramey, Reagan, Ross, Russell of Wood, Sansom, Sessions, Smith, Stewart, Wade, Whitehead—43.

NAYS—Abernathy, Arnim, Blassingame, Chambers, Dohoney, Douglas, German, Haynes, Henry of Limestone, Henry of Smith, Holt, Kilgore, McCormick, McKinney of Denton, Mills, Murphy, Rentfro, Robertson of Bell, Robison of Fayette, Scott, Spikes, Stockdale, Whitfield, Wright—24.

The article was then finally passed by the following vote:

YEAS—Abernathy, Allison, Arnim, Barnett, Blassingame, Brown, Bruce, Burleson, Chambers, Cook of Gonzales, Cooke of San Saba, Crawford, Dillard, Dohoney, Douglas, Ferris, Fleming, Flournoy, German, Graves, Haynes, Holt, Johnson of Collin, Johnson of Franklin, Lacy, McCormick, McKinney of Denton, McKinney of Walker, Martin of Navarro, Murphy, Nugent, Ramey, Robison of Fayette, Ross, Russell of Wood, Scott, Sessions, Wade, Whitehead, Whitfield—39.

NAYS—Ballinger, Blake, Cline, Darnell, Davis of Brazos, DeMorse, Erhard, Flanagan, Henry of Limestone, Henry of Smith, Kilgore, Killough, King, Lockett, McCabe, Mitchell, Moore, Nunn, Pauli, Reagan, Rentfro, Robertson of Bell, Sansom, Smith, Stewart, Stockdale, West, Wright—28.

Mr. Brady was paired off with Mr. Gaither, but for which he would vote "nay."

Mr. Martin, of Hunt, was paired off with Mr. Norvell, but for which he would vote "yea."

Resolution in relation to night sessions taken up and postponed until to-morrow.

"Article ——, Legislative Apportionment," taken up and read third time.

Mr. Kilgore offered the following amendment:

"—— District—The county of Smith shall elect one representative.

"—— District—The counties of Smith and Gregg shall elect one representative; Smith to be the returning county.

"—— District—The counties of Camp and Upshur shall elect one representative; Upshur to be the returning county."

Adopted.

Mr. Moore offered the following amendment as a substitute for lines 138 and 139, " Burleson county shall elect one representative."

Mr. Graves moved the main question.

Mr. Dillard moved to adjourn to 7½ o'clock to-night.

Mr. Brady moved to adjourn to 9 o'clock A. M. to-morrow.

Carried.

SIXTY-FIFTH DAY.

HALL OF REPRESENTATIVES,
AUSTIN, TEXAS, November 20, 1875.

Convention met pursuant to adjournment; roll called; quorum present. Prayer by the Rev. J. S. Grasty, of the Presbyterian Church, at Austin.

Journal of yesterday read and adopted.

Mr. McCormick reported as follows:

COMMITTEE ROOM,
AUSTIN, November 19, 1875.

To the Hon. E. B. Pickett, President of the Convention:

The majority of the Committee on Judicial Apportionment instruct me to report the accompanying ordinance, dividing the State into Judicial Districts, and recommend its adoption.

GEO. MCCORMICK, Chairman.

" AN ORDINANCE

" TO DIVIDE THE STATE OF TEXAS INTO JUDICIAL DISTRICTS.

" *Be it ordained by the people of the State of Texas in Convention assembled,* That until otherwise provided by law, the State of Texas shall be divided into twenty-five judicial districts, as follows, to-wit:

" Section 1. The First District shall be composed of the counties of Jefferson, Chambers, Liberty, Hardin, Polk, Tyler, Jasper, Newton, Orange and San Jacinto.

"Sec. 2. The Second District shall be composed of the counties of Harrison, Rusk, Panola, Shelby and Sabine.

"Sec. 3. The Third District shall be composed of the counties of San Augustine, Nacogdoches, Cherokee, Houston and Anderson.

"Sec. 4. The Fourth District shall be composed of the counties of Grimes, Walker, Madison, Leon, Trinity, Angelina and Montgomery.

"Sec. 5. The Fifth District shall be composed of the counties of Marion, Cass, Bowie, Titus, Morris, Franklin and Camp.

"Sec. 6. The Sixth District shall be composed of the counties of Red River, Lamar, Fannin and Grayson.

"Sec. 7. The Seventh District shall be composed of the counties of Gregg, Smith, Upshur, Wood, Rains, Van Zandt and Henderson.

"Sec. 8. The Eighth District shall be composed of the counties of Hunt, Hopkins, Collin, Rockwall, Kaufman and Delta.

"Sec. 9. The Ninth District shall be composed of the counties of Brazos, Robertson, Burleson and Milam.

"Sec. 10. The Tenth District shall be composed of the counties of Cooke, Denton, Montague, Wise, Clay, Parker, Tarrant, and the unorganized counties of Archer, Wichita, Baylor, Wilbarger, Knox, Hardeman, Greer and Wegefarth.

"Sec. 11. The Eleventh District shall be composed of the counties of Dallas and Ellis.

"Sec. 12. The Twelfth District shall be composed of the counties of Hood, Coryell, Hamilton, Comanche, Brown, Coleman, Shackelford, Palo Pinto, Eastland, Erath, Somerville, Jack, Young, and the unorganized counties of Jones, Taylor, Runnels, Callahan, Stephens, Haskell and Throckmorton.

"Sec. 13. The Thirteenth District shall be composed of the counties of Hill, Navarro, Limestone, Bosque, Johnson and Freestone.

"Sec. 14. The Fourteenth District shall be composed of the counties of McLennan, Bell and Falls.

"Sec. 15. The Fifteenth District shall be composed of the counties of Austin, Fayette, Bastrop, Caldwell, Hays and Blanco.

"Sec. 16. The Sixteenth District shall be composed of the counties of Washington, Lee, Travis and Williamson.

"Sec. 17. The Seventeenth District shall be composed of the counties of Burnet, Lampasas, San Saba, Llano, Mason, Menard, Gillespie, and the unorganized counties of Concho, McCulloch and Kimball.

"Sec. 18. The Eighteenth District shall be composed of the counties of Waller, Wharton, Fort Bend, Brazoria, Matagorda and Jackson.

"Sec. 19. The Nineteenth District shall be composed of the counties of Colorado, Lavacca, Gonzales, Guadalupe and Wilson.

"Sec. 20. The Twentieth District shall be composed of the counties of El Paso, Tom Green, Pecos and Crockett.

"Sec. 21. The Twenty-first District shall be composed of the counties of Harris and Montgomery.

"Sec. 22. The Twenty-second District shall be composed of the counties of Comal, Bexar and Atascosa.

"Sec. 23. The Twenty-third District shall be composed of the counties of DeWitt, Victoria, Calhoun, Refugio, Goliad, Bee, Aransas, San Patricio, Karnes, Live Oak and McMullin.

"Sec. 24. The Twenty-fourth District shall be composed of the counties of Kendall, Kerr, Bandera, Medina, Frio, Uvalde, Zavala, Kinney, Maverick, Dimmit, La Salle and Edwards.

"Sec. 25. The Twenty-fifth District shall be composed of the counties of Cameron, Hidalgo, Starr, Zapata, Webb, Encinal, Nueces and Duval.

"Sec. 26. The Twenty-sixth District shall be composed of the county of Galveston.

"Sec. 27. *Be it further ordained,* That for all purposes connected with the first election provided for by this Convention, this ordinance shall take effect and be in force from and after its passage; and should the constitution be ratified by the people, this ordinance shall be and remain in force until otherwise changed by the Legislature of this State; but should the constitution be rejected by the people, this ordinance shall thereafter be of no force or effect."

"Article —, Legislative Apportionment," taken up, pending Mr. Moore's amendment.

On motion, the main question was ordered.

Mr. Moore's amendment lost by the following vote:

YEAS—Abernathy, Arnim, Bruce, Cooke of San Saba, Davis of Brazos, Fleming, Graves, Henry of Limestone, Henry of Smith, Holt, McCormick, Moore, Nugent, Nunn, Ramey, Reagan, Robison of Fayette, Sessions, Spikes, Whitfield—20.

NAYS—Abner, Allison, Ballinger, Barnett, Blassingame, Brown, Burleson, Chambers, Cline, Cook of Gonzales, Davis of Wharton, DeMorse, Dillard, Douglas, Erhard, Ford, Haynes, Johnson of Collin, Kilgore, Killough, Lacy, Lockett, McCabe, McKinney of Denton, Martin of Navarro, Mills, Mitchell, Pauli,

Rentfro, Reynolds, Robertson of Bell, Sansom, Scott, Smith, Stewart, Stockdale, Weaver, West, Whitehead, Wright—40.

The article was then passed by the following vote:

YEAS—Abernathy, Allison, Arnim, Barnett, Blake, Blassingame, Brown, Bruce, Burleson, Chambers, Cline, Cook of Gonzales, Davis of Brazos, DeMorse, Dillard, Douglas, Erhard, Ferris, Fleming, Ford, Graves, Haynes, Henry of Limestone, Holt, Johnson of Collin, Johnson of Franklin, Killough, Lacy, McCormick, McKinney of Denton, Martin of Navarro, Moore, Murphy, Norvell, Nugent, Pauli, Ramey, Reagan, Robertson of Bell, Robison of Fayette, Ross, Sansom, Scott, Sessions, Smith, Spikes, Wade, Weaver, Whitehead, Whitfield, Wright—51.

NAYS—Abner, Davis of Wharton, Henry of Smith, Lockett, McCabe, Martin of Hunt, Mills, Mitchell, Nunn, Rentfro, West—11.

"Article —, Judicial Department," was then taken up and read a third time.

Mr. Davis, of Brazos, offered the following amendment to section 1:

Strike out all after the word "law," in line 11.

Lost.

Mr. Reagan proposed to amend section 1 by inserting the proviso in lines 11 and 12, after the word "census," in line 8.

Adopted.

Also amend section 6 by striking out all of line 66, after the word "jurisdiction," and insert "in civil cases its opinions shall not be published, unless the publication of such opinon be required by law."

Adopted.

Mr. Wright offered the following amendment:

Amend line 275 by inserting between the words "into" and "Commissioner," the word "four," in section 18.

Mr. Reagan proposed to amend section 7, by striking out the words "tyenty-five," in line 83, and inserting "twenty-six."

Adopted.

Also, amend section 16, by striking out of line 226 the words "such estates," and inserting "estates of deceased persons."

Adopted.

Mr. Ballinger propoed to amend section 2, line 24, by striking out the word "more" and inserting "less;" and after the word "dollars," in line 24, insert, "which shall not be increased or diminished during their continuance in office."

Lost by the following vote:

YEAS—Abernathy, Abner, Ballinger, Blake, Brown, Burleson, Cline, Cook of Gonzales, Darnell, Davis of Brazos, Davis of Wharton, Dohoney, Erhard, Ferris, Flanagan, Henry of Smith, Kilgore, Killough, King, McCabe, McCormick, McKinney of Walker, Martin of Hunt, Moore, Murphy, Norvell, Nugent, Nunn, Pauli, Reagan, Rentfro, Reynolds, Ross, Russell of Harrison, Smith, Spikes, Stewart, Stockdale, Weaver, West, Whitfield, Wright—42.

NAYS—Arnim, Barnett, Blassingame, Brady, Bruce, Chambers, Cooke of San Saba, Crawford, DeMorse, Dillard, Douglas, Fleming, German, Graves, Haynes, Henry of Limestone, Holt, Johnson of Collin, Johnson of Franklin, Lacy, Lockett, McKinney of Denton, Martin of Navarro, Mills, Mitchell, Ramey, Robertson of Bell, Ross, Robison of Fayette, Sansom, Scott, Sessions, Whitehead—32.

Mr. McCormick moved to strike out section 14.

Mr. Reagan offered the following amendment:

Amend by adding after the word " law," in line 96, as follows: " *Provided,* that this limitation shall not apply to the Galveston district."

Mr. Scott moved the main question on the passage of the article.

Carried.

Mr. McCormick's amendment to strike out section 14 lost.

Mr. Reagan's amendment lost.

The article was then passed by the following vote:

YEAS—Abernathy, Allison, Arnim, Barnett, Blassingame, Brown, Bruce, Burleson, Chambers, Cook of Gonzales, Cooke of San Saba, Darnell, DeMorse, Dillard, Dohoney, Douglas, Ferris, Fleming, Flournoy, German, Graves, Henry of Limestone, Holt, Johnson of Collin, Johnson of Franklin, Killough, Lacy, McCormick, McKinney of Denton, McKinney of Walker, Martin of Navarro, Martin of Hunt, Moore, Nugent, Ramey, Reagan, Robertson of Bell, Ross, Sansom, Scott, Sessions, Spikes, Wade, Weaver, Whitehead, Whitfield, Wright—47.

NAYS—Abner, Ballinger, Blake, Brady, Cline, Davis of Brazos, Davis of Wharton, Erhard, Flanagan, Ford, Haynes, Henry of Smith, Kilgore, King, Lockett, McCabe, Mills, Mitchell, Murphy, Norvell, Nunn, Pauli, Rentfro, Reynolds, Robison of Fayette, Russell of Harrison, Smith, Stewart, Stockdale, West—30.

Mr. Murphy submitted the following protest:

To the Hon. E. B. Pickett, President of the Convention:

SIR—I respectfully present my disapproval of the action of this Convention, wherein a majority have affixed the salaries for

Judges of the Supreme and District Courts at such low figures as will in my opinion prevent reliable and competent lawyers, in many parts of the State, from becoming candidates, and as a sequence, life, liberty and property will be inadequately protected.   It will furthermore bring censure on this Convention. now endeavoring to frame a good and liberal constitution for this great State.   I therefore enter my solemn protest against such action, and request that this be spread on the journals.

J. B. MURPHY.

The hour having arrived for considering the special order, viz., "Spanish land grants," was taken up.

Mr. Reagan offered the following amendment:

Section 3, by inserting after the date "1835," in line 26, the following words, "by the person or persons so claiming, or those under whom he or they so claim from that date."

Adopted.

Also, amend by adding to the end of section 4, line 40, the following:

"By the words 'duly recorded,' as used in sections 2 and 4 of this article, it is meant that such claim of title or right to land shall have been recorded in the proper office, and that mere error in the certificate of registration, or informality not affecting the fairness and good faith of the holder thereof, with which the record was made, shall not be held to vitiate such record."

Adopted.

Mr. Murphy offered the following amendment:

Amend section 2 by adding, "*provided,* it shall be considered duly recorded, if extant on the records, in the language of the title."

[Mr. Stockdale in the chair.]

Mr. West offered the following as a substitute for Mr. Murphy's amendment:

Strike out of section 2 the following words in line 12, "or not in the actual possession of the grantee thereof, or some person claiming under him."   And in line 15 strike out the words, "under circumstances reasonably calculated to give notice to said junior grantee has never had, and—"

Mr. West's amendment lost.

Mr. Ballinger moved to strike out the word "such" preceding the word "notice," in line 17.

Mr. Dillard moved the previous question.

A call of the Convention was demanded.

Absentees——Messrs. Erhard, Ferris and Morris.

Mr. Ramey submitted the following report:

COMMITTEE ROOM, ⎫
AUSTIN, November 20, 1875. ⎭

To the Hon. E. B. Pickett, President of the Convention:

SIR—Your Committee on Engrossed and Enrolled Ordinances would respectfully report to your honorable body that they have examined and compared "Article —, General Provisions," and find the same correctly engrossed. Respectfully.

WM. NEAL RAMEY, Chairman.

Mr. German moved to suspend the rules and take up the article on General Provisions for consideration, whereupon the yeas and nays were called, and the Convention refused to suspend the rule by the following vote:

YEAS—Abernathy, Arnim, Barnett, Blake, Blassingame, Brown, Bruce, Burleson, Chambers, Cook of Gonzales, Cooke of San Saba, Dillard, Dohoney, Douglas, Flournoy, German, Graves, Haynes, Henry of Limestone, Henry of Smith, Holt, Johnson of Collin, Johnson of Franklin, Killough, Lacy, McKilney of Denton, McKinney of Walker, Martin of Navarro, Martin of Hunt, Mills, Moore, Ramey, Ross, Sansom, Scott, Sessions, Spikes, Stewart, Wade, Weaver, Whitehead, Whitfield, Wright—43.

NAYS—Abner, Arnim, Ballinger, Brady, Cline, Crawford, Davis of Brazos, Davis of Wharton, DeMorse, Flanagan, Ford, Kilgore, King, Lockett, McCabe, McCormick, Mitchell, Murphy, Norvell, Nugent, Nunn, Pauli, Reagan, Rentfro, Reynolds, Robertson of Bell, Robison of Fayette, Smith, Stockdale, West 30.

Mr. Cline moved to have two hundred copies of "Article —, General Provisions," printed.

Carried.

Mr. Reagan moved to suspend call.

Lost.

Second special order, viz: "Article —, Counties," taken up and read second time.

Mr. Douglas offered the following amendment:

After the word "taken," in line 17, insert as follows: "*Provided,* that in counties of fifty miles or more in length, a division line may be run nearer than twelve miles of a county site whenever the same may be desired by a majority of the voters of said county."

On motion of Mr. Murphy, the article was considered section by section.

On motion of Mr. Darnell, the Convention adjourned to 2½ o'clock P. M., pending Mr. Douglas's amendment.

EVENING SESSION—2½ o'clock.

Convention met pursuant to adjournment; roll called; quorum present.

"Article—, Spanish Land Titles," taken up, with pending amendments.

Mr. Murphy's amendment lost.

Mr. Ballinger's amendment lost.

Mr. Reagan moved to amend the amendment by inserting the words "or actual," between the words "such" and "notice," in line 17.

Adopted.

Mr. Stockdale proposed to amend section 3 by inserting in line 26, after the date "1835," the following: "not recorded or archived as provided in section 2."

Adopted.

Mr. Nunn proposed to amend section 2, line 18, after "annexed," the following: "to such grants not archived or recorded of which possession was not taken as aforesaid."

The main question was ordered.

Mr. Nunn's amendment lost.

Mr. West's amendment lost.

Mr. Murphy's amendment lost.

The article was then ordered engrossed by the following vote:

YEAS—Abernathy, Allison, Arnim, Ballinger, Barnett, Blake, Blassingame, Brown, Bruce, Burleson, Chambers, Cook of Gonzales, Cooke of San Saba, Crawford, Darnell, Davis of Brazos, DeMorse, Dillard, Dohoney, Douglas, Ferris, Flournoy, German, Graves, Haynes, Holt, Johnson of Collin, Johnson of Franklin, Kilgore, Killough, Lacy, McCormick, McKinney of Denton, Martin of Navarro, Martin of Hunt, Nugent, Nunn, Ramey, Reagan, Robertson of Bell, Robison of Fayette, Ross, Sansom, Scott, Sessions, Spikes, Wade, Weaver, Whitehead, Whitfield, Wright—52.

NAYS—Abner, Brady, Cline, Davis of Wharton, Erhard, Fleming, Ford, Henry of Smith, King, Lockett, McCabe, Mills, Mitchell, Murphy, Norvell, Pauli, Rentfro, Reynolds, Stewart, Stockdale, West—21.

Mr. Abernathy moved to suspend the rules and place the article on its third and final reading.

Lost by the following vote:

YEAS—Abernathy, Allison, Arnim, Ballinger, Barnett, Blassingame, Brown, Bruce, Burleson, Chambers, Cook of Gonzales, Cooke of San Saba, Darnell, Davis of Brazos, Dillard, Dohoney,

Douglas, Ferris, Fleming, Flournoy, German, Graves, Haynes, Henry of Limestone, Holt, Johnson of Collin, Johnson of Franklin, Killough, Lacy, McCormick, McKinney of Denton, Martin of Navarro, Martin of Hunt, Moore, Nugent, Ramey, Reagan, Robertson of Bell, Robison of Fayette, Ross, Sansom, Scott, Sessions, Spikes, Wade, Weaver, Whitehead, Whitfield, Wright—49.

Nays—Abner, Blake, Brady, Cline, Crawford, Davis of Wharton, DeMorse, Erhard, Flanagan, Ford, Henry of Smith, Kilgore, King, Lockett, McCabe, McKinney of Walker, Mitchell, Mills, Murphy, Norvell, Nunn, Pauli, Rentfro, Reynolds, Stewart, Stockdale, West—27.

Mr. Johnson, of Collin, introduced the following ordinance:

"AN ORDINANCE

"IN RELATION TO RAILROADS.

"*Be it ordained by the people of Texas, in convention assembled,* That in view of the financial misfortunes now existing, no railroad company, chartered or holding grants under this State, which has heretofore organized and commenced work in good faith shall be considered as having lost any of its rights, privileges or grants prior to the close of the next session of the Legislature of this State, by virtue of lapse of time between now and that time; and said Legislature shall have the power, if deemed compatible with the public interests, to grant such relief in time as may be deemed best for the interest of the State; *provided,* that this ordinance shall not be so construed as to relieve railroad companies from compliance with the condition contained in article—of the constitution in relation to railroads."

Mr. German moved to refer the ordinance on "Railroad Corporations."

Mr. German, by leave, withdrew his motion to refer, and moved to lay the ordinance on the table:

Yeas—Arnim, Barnett, Blassingame, DeMorse, German, Haynes, Henry of Smith, McCabe, McKinney of Denton, Norvell, Nugent, Robertson of Bell, Ross, Stewart—14.

Nays—Abernathy, Abner, Allison, Ballinger, Blake, Brady, Brown, Bruce, Burleson, Chambers, Cline, Cook of Gonzales, Cooke of San Saba, Crawford, Darnell, Davis of Brazos, Davis of Wharton, Dillard, Dohoney, Douglas, Erhard, Ferris, Flanagan, Fleming, Flournoy, Ford, Graves, Henry of Limestone, Holt, Johnson of Collin, Johnson of Franklin, Kilgore, Killough, King, Lacy, Lockett, McCormick, McKinney of Walker, Martin of Navarro, Martin of Hunt, Mills, Mitchell, Moore, Murphy, Nunn, Pauli, Reagan, Rentfro, Reynolds, Robison of

Fayette, Sansom, Scott, Sessions, Spikes, Stockdale, Wade, Weaver, West, Whitehead, Whitfield, Wright—61.

Mr. Dillard moved the main question.

A call of the Convention was demanded.

Absentees—Ramey, and Russell of Harrison.

Mr. Flanagan moved to suspend the call.

Carried.

Mr. Dillard's motion for the previous question was then carried by the following vote:

YEAS—Abernathy, Abner, Allison, Ballinger, Barnett, Blake, Brady, Brown, Burleson, Chambers, Cline, Cooke of San Saba, Darnell, Davis of Brazos, Davis of Wharton, Dillard, Dohoney, Douglas, Ferris, Flanagan, Flournoy, Fort, Graves, Henry of Limestone, Henry of Smith, Holt, Johnson of Collin, Johnson of Franklin, Kilgore, Killough, King, Lacy, Lockett, McKinney of Denton, Martin of Navarro, Martin of Hunt, Murphy, Norvell, Nunn, Ramey, Reagan, Rentfro, Reynolds, Robison of Fayette, Sansom, Scott, Sessions, Spikes, Wade, Weaver, West, Whitehead, Whitfield, Wright—52.

NAYS—Arnim, Blassingame, Bruce, Cook of Gonzales, Crawford, DeMorse, Erhard, Fleming, German, Haynes, McCormick, McKinney of Walker, Mills, Moore, Nugent, Pauli, Robertson of Bell, Ross, Stewart—19.

Mr. DeMorse offered the following amendment:

"And further provided, that this ordinance shall be submitted to the people of this State for their approval, and shall have no effect if disapproved."

Adopted by the following vote:

YEAS—Abernathy, Arnim, Ballinger, Barnett, Blake, Blassingame, Bruce, Burleson, Cook of Gonzales, Crawford, DeMorse, Dillard, Dohoney, Douglas, Fleming, Flournoy, German, Graves, Haynes, Henry of Smith, Johnson of Collin, Johnson of Franklin, McCormick, McKinney of Denton, McKinney of Walker, Moore, Norvell, Nugent, Nunn, Pauli, Ramey, Robertson of Bell, Robison of Fayette, Ross, Sansom, Scott, Smith, Stewart, Wade, Weaver, Whitfield—41.

NAYS—Abner, Allison, Brady, Brown, Chambers, Cline, Cooke of Sen Saba, Darnell, Davis of Brazos, Davis of Wharton, Ferris, Flanagan, Ford, Henry of Limestone, Holt, Kilgore, Killough, King, Lacy, Lockett, Martin of Navarro, Martin of Hunt, Mills, Mitchell, Murphy, Reagan, Rentfro, Reynolds, Sessions, Spikes, Stockdale, West, Whitehead, Wright—34.

Mr. Nugent offered the following amendment:

Strike out the proviso, and insert: "*provided,* that this ordinance shall not take effect unless said companies shall, before the first day of January, A. D., 1875, file in the office of the Secretary of State, a complete acceptance of the provisions of the constitution framed by this onvention, which authorize the Legislature from time to time to establish maximum rates for the transportation of freight and passengers."

Lost by the following vote:

YEAS—Abernathy, Arnim, Barnett, Blassingame, Bruce, Robertson of Bell, Wright—7.

NAYS—Abner, Allison, Ballinger, Blake, Brady, Brown, Burleson, Chambers, Cline, Cook of Gonzales, Cooke of San Saba, Crawford, Darnell, Davis of Brazos, DeMorse, Dillard, Dohoney, Erhard, Ferris, Flanagan, Fleming, Flournoy, Ford, German, Graves, Haynes, Henry of Limestone, Henry of Smith, Holt, Johnson of Collin, Johnson of Franklin, Kilgore, Killough, King, Lacy, Lockett, McCormick, McKinney of Walker, Martin of Navarro, Martin of Hunt, Mills, Mitchell, Murphy, Norvell, Nugent, Nunn, Pauli, Ramey, Reagan, Rentfro, Reynolds, Robison of Fayette, Ross, Russell of Harrison, Sansom, Scott, Sessions, Smith, Spikes, Stockdale, Wade, Weaver, West, Whitehead, Whitfield—65.

Mr. Dillard moved to reconsider the vote adopting Mr. DeMorse's amendment.

Mr. McKinney, of Walker, made the point of order that the motion was out of order, as the Convention was voting under the operation of the previous question.

The chair submitted the question as to whether the motion should be entertained to a vote of the Convention, which resulted as follows:

YEAS—Abernathy, Abner, Allison, Ballinger, Barnett, Brady, Brown, Burleson, Chambers, Cline, Cook of Gonzales, Cooke of San Saba, Darnell, Davis of Brazos, Dillard, Ferris, Flanagan, Ford, Henry of Limestone, Holt, Kilgore, Killough, King, Lockett, Martin of Navarro, Martin of Hunt, Mills, Murphy, Ramey, Reagan, Russell of Harrison, Sansom, Scott, Spikes, Stockdale, West, Whitfield, Wright—39.

NAYS—Arnim, Blake, Blassingame, Crawford, DeMorse, Dohoney, Douglas, Fleming, Flournoy, Gaither, German, Graves, Henry of Smith, Johnson of Collin, Johnson of Franklin, Lacy, McCormick, McKinney, of Denton, McKinney of Walker, Mitchell, Moore, Norvell, Nugent, Nunn, Pauli, Rentfro, Robertson of Bell, Robison of Fayette, Ross, Sessions, Smith, Stewart, Wade—33.

So the Convention agreed to entertain the motion.

The question then as to whether the vote should be reconsidered, the same was put and carried by the following vote:

47

YEAS—Abner, Allison, Barnett, Brady, Brown, Burleson, Chambers, Cline, Cooke of Gonzales, Cooke of San Saba, Darnell, Davis of Brazos, Dillard, Erhard, Ferris, Flanagan, Ford, Henry of Limestone, Holt, Kilgore, Killough, King, Lockett, Martin of Navarro, Mills, Murphy, Ramey, Reagan, Rentfro, Russell of Harrison, Sansom, Scott, Sessions, Spikes, Stockdale, Wade, Weaver, West, Whitehead, Whitfield, Wright—41.

NAYS—Abernathy, Arnim, Ballinger, Blassingame, Bruce, Crawford, DeMorse, Dohoney, Douglas, Fleming, Flournoy, German, Graves, Haynes, Henry of Smith, Johnson of Collin, Johnson of Franklin, Lacy, McCormick, McKinney of Denton, McKinney of Walker, Martin of Hunt, Mitchell, Moore, Norvell, Nugent, Nunn, Pauli, Reynolds, Robertson of Bell, Robison of Fayette, Ross, Smith, Stewart—34.

The question then recurring on the adoption of the amendment, the same was put and amendment lost by the following vote:

YEAS—Abernathy, Arnim, Ballinger, Blassingame, Bruce, DeMorse, Dohoney, Douglas, Flemin, Flournoy, German, Graves, Haynes, Henry of Smith, Johnson of Collin, Johnson of Franklin, Lacy, McCormick, McKinney of Denton, McKinney of Walker, Moore, Norvell, Nugent, Nunn, Pauli, Robertson of Bell, Robison of Fayette, Ross, Smith, Stewart, Weaver, Whitehead—32.

NAYS—Abner, Allison, Barnett, Blake, Brady, Brown, Burleson, Chambers, Cline, Cooke of Gonzales, Cooke of San Saba, Darnell, Davis of Brazos, Dillard, Erhard, Ferris, Flanagan, Ford, Henry of Limestone, Holt, Kilgore, Killough, King, Lockett, McCabe, Martin of Navarro, Martin of Hunt, Mills, Mitchell, Murphy, Reagan, Rentfro, Reynolds, Russell of Harrison, Sansom, Scott, Sessions, Spikes, Stockdale, Wade, West, Whitfield, Wright—43.

The question then recurring on the passage of the ordinance, the same was put and the ordinance passed by the following vote:

YEAS—Abner, Allison, Barnett, Brady, Brown, Burleson, Chambers, Cline, Cooke of Gonzales, Cooke of San Saba, Darnell, Davis of Brazos, Dillard, Dohoney, Erhard, Ferris, Flanagan, Ford, Henry of Limestone, Holt, Johnson of Collin, Johnson of Franklin, Kilgore, Killough, King, Lockett, McCabe, Martin of Navarro, Martin of Hunt, Mills, Mitchell, Murphy, Ramey, Reagan, Rentfro, Reynolds, Russell of Harrison, Sansom, Scott, Sessions, Spikes, Stockdale, Wade, Weaver, West, Whitehead, Whitfield, Wright—48.

Nays—Abernathy, Arnim, Ballinger, Blake, Blassingame, Bruce, DeMorse, Douglass, Fleming, German, Haynes, Henry of Smith, Lacy, McCormick, McKinney of Denton, McKinney of Walker, Moore, Norvell, Nugent, Nunn, Pauli, Robertson of Bell, Robison of Fayette, Ross, Smith, Stewart—26.

Mr. Darnell moved to reconsider the vote put, taken, and to lay the motion on the table.

A call of the Convention was demanded.

Absentee, Mr. Crawford.

Mr. Crawford appearing, the call was exhausted, and the Convention proceeded to vote upon Mr. Darnell's motion, which was carried by the following vote:

Yeas—Abner, Allison, Blake, Brady, Brown, Burleson, Chambers, Cline, Cook of Gonzales, Cooke of San Saba, Darnell, Davis of Brazos, Davis of Wharton, Dillard, Dohoney, Erhard, Ferris, Flanagan, Flournoy, Ford, Henry of Limestone, Holt, Johnson of Coliln, Johnson of Franklin, Kilgore, Killough, King, Lockett, McCabe, Martin of Navarro, Martin of Hunt, Mills, Mitchell, Murphy, Ramey, Reagan, Rentfro, Reynolds, Robison of Fayette, Russell of Harrison, Sansom, Scott, Sessions, Spikes, Stockdale, Wade, Weaver, West, Whitehead, Whitfield, Wright—51.

Nays—Abernathy, Arnim, Ballinger, Barnett, Blassingame, Bruce, Crawford, DeMorse, Douglas, Fleming, German, Graves, Haynes, Henry of Smith, Lacy, McCormick, McKinney of Denton, McKinney of Walker, Moore, Norvell, Nugent, Nunn, Pauli, Robertson of Bell, Ross, Smith, Stewart—27.

"Article —, Counties and County Lands," with pending amendment by Mr. Douglas, was taken up.

Mr. Dillard offered the following amendment:

Sec. 2, line 12, strike out "450," and insert "750"; in line 14 strike out "450," and insert "750"; in line 15 strike out "12," and insert "16"; strike out in line 17, after the word "taken," to the word "when," in line 22.

[Mr. Brown in the chair.]

Mr. Graves moved to lay both amendments on the table.

A division on the question was ordered, and Mr. Dillard's amendment was laid on the table by the following vote:

Yeas—Abernathy, Allison, Barnett, Blassingame, Brady, Brown, Bruce, Burleson, Chambers, Cline, Cook of Gonzales, Cooke of San Saba, Davis of Wharton, Dohoney, Douglas, Erhard, Graves, Haynes, Henry of Smith, Holt, Kilgore, Killough, King, Lacy, Lockett, McCabe, Martin of Navarro, Mitchell,

Moore, Pauli, Reagan, Rentfro, Reynolds, Smith, Spikes, Stockdale, West—37.

NAYS—Abner, Arnim, Ballinger, Blake, Crawford, Darnell, Davis of Brazos, DeMorse, Dillard, Ferris, Flanagan, Fleming, Henry of Limestone, McCormick, McKinney of Denton, McKinney of Walker, Martin of Hunt, Murphy, Norvell, Nugent, Nunn, Ramey, Robertson of Bell, Russell of Harrison, Scott, Sessions, Stewart, Wade, Weaver, Whitehead, Wright—31.

The question recurring on laying Mr. Douglas's amendment on the table, the same was put and lost by the following vote:

YEAS—Abner, Arnim, Blake, Cook of Gonzales, Dillard, Flanagan, Fleming, Kilgore, Killough, King, Lacy, McCabe, McCormick, Martin of Navarro, Murphy, Norvell, Nugent, Nunn, Reagan, Robertson of Bell, Robison of Fayette, Russell of Harrison, Sanson, Sessions, Smith, Spikes, Stockdale, Wade, Whitehead, Wright—30.

NAYS—Abernathy, Allison, Barnett, Blassingame, Brady, Brown, Bruce, Burleson, Chambers, Cline, Cooke of San Saba, Darnell, Davis of Brazos, Davis of Wharton, DeMorse, Dohoney, Douglas, Erhard, Ferris, Haynes, Henry of Limestone, Henry of Smith, Holt, Lockett, McKinney of Denton, McKinney of Walker, Martin of Hunt, Mills, Mitchell, Pauli, Ramey, Rentfro, Reynolds, Stewart, West, Whitehead—36.

The question recurring on the adoption of Mr. Douglas' amendment, the same was put and the amendment lost by the following vote:

YEAS—Abernathy, Allison, Blassingame, Brady, Chambers, Cooke of San Saba, Crawford, Dohoney, Douglas, Haynes, Henry of Smith, Holt, McKinney of Denton, Pauli, Ramey, Rentfro, Stewart, West, Whitehead—19.

NAYS—Abner, Arnim, Ballinger, Blake, Bruce, Cook of Gonzales, Davis of Wharton, DeMorse, Dillard, Erhard, Flanagan, Fleming, Graves, Henry of Limestone, Kilgore, Killough, King, Lacy, McCabe, McCormick, McKinney of Walker, Martin of Navarro, Martin of Hunt, Mills, Mitchell, Moore, Murphy, Norvell, Nugent, Nunn, Reagan, Reynolds, Robertson of Bell, Russell of Harrison, Sansom, Scott, Sessions, Spikes, Whitfield, Wright—40.

Mr. Robertson, of Bell, offered the following amendment:

In line 23, after the word "to," insert "or created into."

Mr. Fleming moved to adjourn to 7½ o'clock to-night.

Mr. Rentfro moved to adjourn to 9 o'clock A. M. to-morrow.

Lost by the following vote:

YEAS—Abner, Ballinger, Brady, Cline, Cook of Gonzales,

Cooke of San Saba, Crawford, Darnell, Davis of Wharton, DeMorse, Erhard, Flanagan, Flournoy, Killough, Lockett, McCabe, Martin of Hunt, Mills, Mitchell, Murphy, Pauli, Rentfro, Reynolds, Russell of Harrison, Stockdale—25.

NAYS—Abernathy, Allison, Arnim, Barnett, Blassingame, Brown, Bruce, Burleson, Chambers, Davis of Brazos, Dillard, Dohoney, Douglas, Ferris, Fleming, Graves, Haynes, Henry of Limestone, Henry of Smith, Holt, Locy, McCormick, McKinney of Denton, McKinney of Walker, Moore, Norvell, Nugent, Nunn, Ramey, Reagan, Robertson of Bell, Robison of Fayette, Sansom, Scott, Sessions, Smith, Spikes, Stewart, Wade, West, Whitehead, Whitfield, Wright—43.

Mr. Kilgore offered the following resolution:

Be it resolved, That, at the request of the people of the city of Austin, Miss Nettie Powers Houston have the use of the Hall of the House of Representatives any night next week, to be designated by her, for a public reading.

Adopted.

Mr. Rentfro moved to adjourn to 9½ o'clock A. M. Monday.

The Convention adjourned to 7½ o'clock to-night.

NIGHT SESSION—7½ o'clock.

Convention met pursuant to adjoudnment; roll called; quorum present.

Mr. Barnett moved to suspend the rule and take up "Article —, on General Provisions."

Lost by the following vote:

YEAS—Abernathy, Allison, Barnett, Blake, Bruce, Burleson, Cook of Gonzales, Dohoney, Douglas, Ferris, Fleming, Flournoy, Graves, Haynes, Henry of Limestone, Henry of Smith, Holt, Johnson of Franklin, Killough, McCormick, McKinney of Denton, McKinney of Walker, Martin of Navarro, Norvell, Reagan, Robertson of Bell, Robison of Fayette, Ross, Sansom, Scott, Sessions, Spikes, Stewart, Wade, Whitehead, Whitfield, Wright—37.

NAYS—Arnim, Blassingame, Brady, Brown, Chambers, Cline, Crawford, Darnell, Davis of Brazos, Davis of Wharton, DeMorse, Dillard, Flanagan, Ford, German, Lacy, Lockett, McCabe, McLean, Martin of Hunt, Mills, Mitchell, Moore, Murphy, Nugent, Nunn, Pauli, Rentfro, Reynolds, Smith, Stockdale, West—32.

Mr. Rentfro moved to adjourn to 9 o'clock Monday morning. Lost by the following vote.

YEAS—Brady, Cline, Crawford, Davis of Wharton, DeMorse, Flanagan, Pauli, Rentfro, Reynolds, Sansom, West—11.

NAYS—Abernathy, Allison, Arnim, Ballinger, Barnett, Blake, Blassingame, Brown, Bruce, Chambers, Cook of Gonzales, Darnell, Davis of Brazos, Dillard, Dohoney, Douglas, Ferris, Fleming, Flournoy, German, Graves, Haynes, Henry of Limestone, Henry of Smith, Holt, Johnson of Franklin, Killough, Lacy, Lockett, McCormick, McKinney of Denton, McKinney of Walker, McLean, Martin of Navarro, Moore, Norvell, Nugent, Ramey, Reagan, Robertson of Bell, Robison of Fayette, Ross, Scott, Sessions, Smith, Spikes, Stockdale, Wade, Whitehead, Whitfield, Wright—51.

"Article—, Counties and County Lands," with pending amendment by Mr. Robertson, of Bell, taken up and amendment adopted.

Mr. Arnim offered the following amendment:

Amend section 2 by striking out in line 12 "450," and insert "700," the same change to be made in line 14. In line 15 strike out "12" and insert "18;" and strike out all after "taken" in line 17 to "vote" in line 22.

Mr. Murphy proposed to substitute the amendment by the following:

Strike out "450" wherever it occurs in section 2 and insert "600."

Mr. Arnim's amendment lost by the following vote:

YEAS—Arnim, Blake, Cooke of San Saba, Crawford, Darnell, DeMorse, Dillard, Flanagan, Fleming, Lacy, McCabe, McCormick, Martin of Hunt, Mills, Moore, Murphy, Norvell, Nugent, Robertson of Bell, Robison of Fayette, Ross, Scott, Sessions, Smith, Stewart—25.

NAYS—Abernathy, Allison, Ballinger, Barnett, Blassingame, Brady, Brown, Bruce, Burleson, Chambers, Cline, Cook of Gonzales, Davis of Brazos, Dohoney, Douglas. Ferris, Graves, Haynes, Henry of Limestone, Henry of Smith, Holt, Killough, Lockett, McKinney of Denton, McKinney of Walker, McLean, Martin of Navarro, Nunn, Pauli, Ramey, Reagan, Rentfro, Reynolds, Sansom, Spikes, Stockdale, Wade, West, Whitehead, Wright—40.

Mr. Darnell moved to amend Mr. Murphy's amendment by striking out "six hundred" and inserting "seven hundred."

Mr. Brady moved to lay the amendment on the table.

Lost by the following vote:

YEAS—Abernathy, Allison, Blassingame, Brady, Brown, Burleson, Chambers, Dohoney, Douglas, Graves, Haynes, Holt, Killough, Lockett, McKinney of Denton, Pauli, Reagan, Rentfro, Reynolds, Ross, Sansom, Spikes, Stockdale, Wade, West—24.

NAYS—Arnim, Ballinger, Barnett, Blake, Bruce, Cline, Cook of Gonzales, Cooke of San Saba, Crawford, Darnell, DeMorse, Dillard, Ferris, Flanagan, Fleming, Henry of Smith, Lacy, McCabe, McCormick, McKinney of Walker, McLean, Martin of Navarro, Martin of Hunt, Mills, Moore, Murphy, Norvell, Nugent, Nunn, Robertson of Bell, Robison of Fayette, Smith, Stewart, Whitehead, Whitfield, Wright—37.

Mr. Blassingame moved the main question.

Carried.

Mr. Darnell's amendment adopted as an amendment to Mr. Murphy's amendment, and as an amendment to the article.

The article was then ordered engrossed by the following vote:

YEAS—Abernathy, Arnim, Ballinger, Barnett, Blake, Blassingame, Bruce, Burleson, Chambers, Cook of Gonzales, Cooke of San Saba, Darnell, Dillard, Dohoney, Ferris, Flanagan, Fleming, Graves, Haynes, Henry of Limestone, Henry of Smith, Killough, Lacy, McCormick, McKinney of Walker, McLean, Martin of Navarro, Martin of Hunt, Moore, Norvell, Nugent, Nunn, Robison of Fayette, Ross, Sansom, Scott, Spikes, Stewart, Stockdale, Wade, Whitehead, Whitfield, Wright—42.

NAYS—Abner, Allison, Brady, Brown, Cline, Crawford, Davis of Brazos, Davis of Wharton, DeMorse, Douglas, Holt, Lockett, McCabe, McKinney of Denton, Mills, Murphy, Pauli Ramey, Reagan, Rentfro, Reynolds, Robertson of Bell, Sessions, Smith, West—26.

Mr. Stockdale moved to suspend the rule to put the article on its third reading and final passage.

Carried by the following vote:

YEAS—Mr. President, Abernathy, Arnim, Ballinger, Barnett, Blake, Blassingame, Bruce, Burleson, Chambers, Cook of Gonzales, Cooke of San Saba, Dillard, Dohoney, Flanagan, Fleming, German, Graves, Henry of Limestone, Henry of Smith, Holt, Killough, McCabe, McCormick, McKinney, of Denton, McKinney of Walker, McLean, Martin of Navarro, Martin of Hunt, Moore, Norvell, Nugent, Nunn, Robison of Fayette, Ross, Sansom, Scott, Spikes, Stewart, Stockdale, Wade, Whitehead, Whitfield, Wright—44.

NAYS—Abner, Brady, Cline, Crawford, Darnell, Davis of Brazos, Davis of Wharton, DeMorse, Douglas, Lacy, Lockett, Mills, Murphy, Pauli, Ramey, Reagan, Rentfro, Reynolds, Robertson of Bell, Sessions, Smith, West—22.

The article was then read a third time.

Mr. Rentfro offered the following amendment:

Amend by adding the words: *"Provided,* that in any county

whose county seat has never been located by a vote of the people, and is more than ten miles distant from the centre, the electors of said county may, by a majority of all votes cast at the election, remove said county seat to any point in said county.; *provided further,* that such removal be to a point near the centre than ten miles. Said election to be ordered by the Commissioners' Court at any regular session within a year from and after the adoption of this constitution."

Mr. Dillard moved to lay the amendment on the table.

Lost by the following vote:

YEAS—Abernathy, Allison, Blassingame, Brown, Bruce, Burleson, Chambers, Cooke of San Saba, Dillard, Ferris, Graves, Henry of Limestone, Henry of Smith, Holt, Lacy, McCormick, Murphy, Norvell, Reagan, Ross, Scott, Sessions, Smith, Spikes, Stewart, Stockdale, Wade, West, Whitehead, Whitfield, Wright —31.

NAYS—Abner, Arnim, Ballinger, Barnett, Blake, Brady, Cline, Crawford, Darnell, Davis of Brazos, Davis of Wharton, DeMorse, Dohoney, Douglas, Flanagan, Fleming, Ford, German, Haynes, Johnson of Franklin, Killough, Lockett, McCabe, McKinney of Denton, McKinney of Walker, McLean, Martin of Navarro, Martin of Hunt, Mills, Moore, Nugent, Nunn, Pauli, Ramey, Rentfro, Reynolds, Robertson of Bell, Robison of Fayette—38.

The question then recurring on the adoption of the amendment, the same was put and the amendment lost by the following vote:

YEAS—Abner, Blake, Brady, Burleson, Cline, Davis of Wharton, DeMorse, Douglas, Ferris, Flanagan, Lockett, McKinney of Walker, Mills, Pauli, Ramey, Rentfro, Reynolds, West—19.

NAYS—Abernathy, Allison, Arnim, Barnett, Blassingame, Brown, Bruce, Chambers, Cooke of San Saba, Darnell, Flournoy, German, Graves, Haynes, Henry of Limestone, Henry of Smith, Holt, Killough, Lacy, McCormick, Martin of Navarro, Moore, Murphy, Norvell, Nugent, Nunn, Reagan, Robertson of Bell, Robison of Fayette, Ross, Sansom, Scott, Sessions, Smith, Spikes, Stewart, Stockdale, Wade, Whitehead, Wright—40.

Mr. Brady moved to adjourn to 9 o'clock Monday morning.

Lost.

[Mr. Reagan in the chair.]

Mr. Ramey offered the following amendment:

Add in section 2, line 17, after "taken," "except when a water course may be the boundary line dividing the two counties, in which case said dividing line shall not approach the county seat of the old county so near as to place said county seat more than five miles from the geographical centre of said county."

Lost by the following vote:

YEAS—Abner, Allison, Blake, Brown, Cline, Cooke of San Saba, Douglas, Flanagan, Graves, Johnson of Franklin, Lacy, Mills, Ramey, Rentfro, Stockdale, West, Whitehead, Wright—18.

NAYS—Abernathy, Arnim, Barnett, Blassingame, Brady, Bruce, Burleson, Chambers, Darnell, Davis of Brazos, De-Morse, Dillard, Dohoney, Ferris, Fleming, Flournoy, German, Henry of Limestone, Henry of Smith, Holt, Killough, McCormick, McKinney of Walker, Martin of Navarro, Moore, Murphy, Norvell, Nugent, Nunn, Pauli, Reagan, Reynolds, Robertson of Bell, Robison of Fayette, Ross, Scott, Sessions, Smith, Spikes, Stewart, Wade—41.

Mr. Rentfro moved to adjourn to 9 o'clock Monday morning.

Lost by the following vote:

YEAS—Abner, Brady, Cline, Darnell, DeMorse, Douglas, Mills, Pauli, Rentfro, West—10.

NAYS—Abernathy, Allison, Arnim, Ballinger, Barnett, Blake, Blassingame, Brown, Bruce, Burleson, Chambers, Cooke of San Saba, Davis of Brazos Dillard, Dohoney, Flanagan, Fleming, Flournoy, Ford, German, Graves, Haynes, Henry of Limestone, Henry of Smith, Holt, Killough, Lacy, Lockett, McCabe, McCormick, McKinney of Denton, McKinney of Walker, Martin of Navarro, Martin of Hunt, Moore, Murphy, Norvell, Nugent, Nunn, Ramey, Reagan, Robertson of Bell, Robison of Fayette, Ross, Sansom, Scott, Sessions, Smith, Spikes, Stewart, Stockdale, Wade, Whitehead, Whitfield, Wright—55.

On motion of Mr. Scott, the main question was ordered, which being the final passage of the article, it was passed by the following vote:

YEAS—Abernathy, Allison, Arnim, Ballinger, Barnett, Blake, Blassingame, Bruce, Burleson, Chambers, Cline, Cooke of San Saba, Dillard, Dohoney, Ferris, Flanagan, Fleming, Flournoy, German, Graves, Haynes, Henry of Limestone, Henry of Smith, Johnson of Franklyn, Killough, Lacy, McCormick, McKinney of Walker, Martin of Navarro, Martin of Hunt, Moore, Murphy, Norvell, Nugent, Nunn, Robison of Fayette, Ross, Sansom, Scott, Sessions, Smith, Spikes, Stewart, Stockdale, Wade, Whitehead, Whitfield, Wright—48.

NAYS—Abner, Brady, Brown, Darnell, Douglas, Holt, Lockett, McKinney of Denton, Mills, Pauli, Ramey, Reagan, Rentfro, Robertson of Bell, West—15.

On motion of Mr. Stockdale, "Article —, The Powers of Government," was taken up, read a second time, and ordered engrossed, by the following vote:

YEAS—Abernathy, Allison, Arnim, Ballinger, Barnett, Blassingame, Brown, Bruce, Burleson, Chambers, Cline, Cooke of San Saba, Darnell, Davis of Brazos, Dillard, Dohoney, Douglas, Flanagan, Fleming, Flournoy, Graves, Haynes, Henry of Limestone, Henry of Smith, Holt, Johnson of Franklin, Killough, Lacy, Lockett, McCormick, McKinney of Denton, McKinney of Walker, Martin of Navarro, Martin of Hunt, Murphy, Norvell, Nugent, Nunn, Ramey, Reagan, Robertson of Bell, Robison of Fayette, Ross, Sansom, Scott, Sessions, Smith, Spikes, Stewart, Stockdale, Wade, Whitehead, Whitfield, Wright—55

NAYS—Abner, Brady, German, Mills, Rentfro—5.

On motion of Mr. Flanagan, the rule was suspended, article read third time, and passed by the following vote:

YEAS—Abernathy, Allison, Arnim, Ballinger, Barnett, Blake, Blassingame, Brown, Bruce, Burleson, Chambers, Cline, Cooke of San Saba, Crawford, Darnell, Davis of Brazos, Dillard, Dohoney, Douglas, Ferris, Flanagan, Fleming, Flournoy, Ford, German, Graves, Haynes, Henry of Limestone, Henry of Smith, Holt, Killough, Lacy, Lockett, McCormick, McKinney of Denton, McKinney of Walker, Martin of Navarro, Martin of Hunt, Moore, Murphy, Norvell, Nugent, Nunn, Ramey, Reagan, Robertson of Bell, Robison of Fayette, Ross, Sansom, Scott, Sessions, Smith, Spikes, Stewart, Stockdale, Wade, Whitehead, Whitfield, Wright—59.

NAYS—Abner, Brady, Mills, Rentfro—4.

Mr. Ford called up "Article —, Reserving Lands for Public Buildings," read second time, and ordered engrossed by the following vote:

YEAS—Abernathy, Abner, Allison, Arnim, Ballinger, Barnett, Blassingame, Brown, Bruce, Burleson, Chambers, Cooke of San Saba, Darnell, Davis of Brazos, Dillard, Dohoney, Douglas, Ferris, Flanagan, Fleming, Flournoy, Ford, German, Haynes, Henry of Limestone, Henry of Smith, Johnson of Franklin, Lacy, McCormick, McKinney of Denton, McKinney of Walker, Martin of Navarro, Martin of Hunt, Mills, Moore, Murphy, Norvell, Nugent, Nunn, Ramey, Robertson of Bell, Robison of Fayette, Ross, Sansom, Scott, Sessions, Stewart, Wade, West, Whitehead, Whitfield, Wright—52.

NAYS—Brady, Cline, Crawford, Graves, Holt, Reagan, Rentfro, Spikes—8.

On motion of Mr. Flournoy, the rule was suspended, and the article read the third time.

Mr. Brady offered the following amendment:

Amend by adding, "*provided,* one league of land be set apart for the use of each organized county to erect public buildings."

On motion of Mr. Chambers, laid on the table.

Mr. Cline moved to strike out "three million," and insert "one million."

On motion of Mr. Whitfield, laid on the table.

Mr. Wade offered the following amendment:

Strike out "ten years," and insert "under the direction of the Legislature."

Adopted.

Mr. Flanagan moved to strike out "three million," and insert "five million."

Laid on the table.

Article passed by the following vote:

YEAS—Allison, Arnim, Ballinger, Barnett, Brown, Bruce, Burleson, Chambers, Cooke of San Saba, Darnell, Davis of Brazos, Dillard, Dohoney, Douglas, Ferris, Flanagan, Fleming, Flournoy, Ford, German, Graves, Haynes, Henry of Limestone, Henry of Smith, Johnson of Franklin, Lacy, McCormick, McKinney of Denton, Martin of Navarro, Martin of Hunt, Moore, Murphy, Norvell, Nugent, Nunn, Robertson of Bell, Robison of Fayette, Ross, Sansom, Scott, Sessions, Stewart, Stockdale, Wade, West, Whitehead, Whitfield, Wright—48.

NAYS—Abner, Blassingame, Brady, Cline, Crawford, Holt, Lockett, McKinney of Walker, Pauli, Ramey, Reagan, Rentfro, Reynolds, Spikes—14.

On motion of Mr. Ballinger, the Convention adjourned to 9 o'clock Monday morning.

SIXTY-SIXTH DAY.

HALL OF REPRESENTATIVES,
AUSTIN, TEXAS, November 22, 1875.

Convention met pursuant to adjournment; roll called; quorum present. Prayer by the Rev. Mr. Wright, of the Presbyterian Church, at Austin.

Journal of Saturday read and adopted.

Mr. McCormick submitted the following motion:

[Mr. Brown in the chair.]

HALL OF THE CONVENTION,
AUSTIN, TEXAS, November 22, 1875.

To the Hon. E. B. Pickett, President of the Convention:

The undersigned represents that there are some clerical omissions in the Article on the Judiciary, heretofore passed by this Convention, and asks that the Enrolling Committee be required to make the following corrections in said article, to-wit:

Section 6, line 65, add the word "or" between the words "original appellate,"

Section 8, line 107, add after the word "land" the words "and for the enforcement of liens thereon."

Section 16, line 207, strike out the words "or to enforce liens upon real estate."

Respectfully,   GEO. McCORMICK.

Adopted.

Mr. Cook, of Gonzales, reported as follows:

COMMITTEE ROOM,
AUSTIN, November 22, 1875.

To the Hon. E. B. Pickett, President of the Convention:

Your Committee on Printing and Contingent Expenses are of opinion that as much publicity as possible, consistent with the public interest, should be given to the new constitution which we are about submitting to the people of Texas for their ratification, in order that they may have a full knowledge of the matter to be submitted.

Your Committee believe that a very large proportion of the citizens of the State will not be able to procure pamphlet copies of the constitution, whatever care may be exercised in the distribution of them; but that if, in addition to the distribution so made, the constitution be printed in all the newspapers of the different localities in the State, it may be made accessible to nearly all the voters of the State.

In view of the premies, your committee have instructed me to report the following resolution, and recommend its adoption by the Convention, viz.:

"*Resolved,* That any newspaper in the State of Texas which shall publish the constitution about to be submitted to the people of the State for their ratification, not to occupy more than four weeks in its publication, the last issue not less than two weeks before the time fixed for voting on the same, shall each receive as compensation for such publication the sum of twenty dollars; *provided,* that satisfactory proof of such publication shall be made to the secretary of this Convention, who shall certify the same to the Comptroller of Public Accounts, and he shall draw his warrant on the Treasurer of the State, who shall pay the same out of the fund appropriated to pay the expenses of this Convention."

All which is respectfully submitted.

W. D. S. Cook, Chairman.

The yeas and nays were called on the adoption of the resolution, and the resolution lost by the following vote:

Yeas—Abernathy, Allison, Arnim, Brady, Brown, Burleson, Chambers, Cline, Cook of Gonzales, Davis of Wharton, DeMorse, Dohoney, Flanagan, Henry of Limestone, Henry of Smith, King, Lacy, McCabe, McCormick, Martin of Hunt, Ramey, Reagan, Rentfro, Reynolds, Ross, Sansom, Spikes, Weaver, Wright—29.

Nays—Abner, Ballinger, Barnett, Blake, Blassingame, Cooke of San Saba, Crawford, Darnell, Dillard, Douglas, Erhard, Fleming, German, Haynes, Holt, Killough, Lockett, McKinney of Denton, Mills, Mitchell, Moore, Norvell, Nugent, Pauli, Robertson of Bell, Robison of Fayette, Scott, Sessions, Wade, Whitehead—30.

Mr. Ramey submitted the following report:

COMMITTEE ROOM, }
AUSTIN, TEXAS, November 22, 1875. }

To the Hon. E. B. Pickett, President of the Convention:

Sir—Your Committee on Engrossed and Enrolled Ordinances would respectfully report to your honorable body that they have examined and compared the following articles and ordinances: "Article —, Division of the Powers of Government"; "Article —, Spanish and Mexican Land Titles"; "An Ordinance in relation to Railroads," and "A provision setting apart three millions of acres of the public lands for the erection and repairing of public buildings," and find them all correctly engrossed.

Respectfully,   WM. NEAL RAMEY, Chairman.

Mr. Cook, of Gonzales, reported as follows:

COMMITTEE ROOM, }
AUSTIN, TEXAS, November 22, 1875. }

To the Hon. E. B. Pickett, President of the Convention:

Sir— Your Committee on Printing and Contingent Expenses beg leave to report the following bills and accounts, embracing the entire amount allowed by them for current printing and all other contingent expenses of the Convention up to the present date.   W. H. Cook, Chairman.

1875.	ITEMS.		
Sept. 11	Bill of stationery bought of Thompson & Nagle by Capt. Voight..............	165	63
	Amount postage, stamps, etc., Serg't-at-arms	224	00
Sept. 17	Amount paid Capt. Voight for repairs and arranging hall	126	86
Sept. 18	Bill of J. D. Elliot for various items, printing procured by Secretary, as per resolution	137	50
Sept. 20	Paid Austin Ice Factory for ice.........	4	00
Sept. 23	Paid for stamps and postage............	127	40
Sept. 24	Amount paid J. D. Logan & Co. for printing	206	50
	Allowed for repairs to hall..............	75	00
Oct. 2	Bill for gas to date....................	82	20
	Postage, stamps, etc., to this date........	166	40
	Paid to J. D. Logan & Co. for printing, etc.	95	50
Oct. 4	Paid Thompson & Nagle for stationery...	130	25
Oct. 5	Paid for one gas torch..................	5	10
Oct. 7	Paid I. Steen for glasses and pitchers....	5	25
Oct. 8	Bill of C. F. Millet for four blinds......	80	00
Oct. 9	Bill of J. D. Logan & Co. for printing....	149	50
Oct. 11	Amount paid for postage, stamps, etc.....	187	50
Oct. 16	Amount paid J. D. Logan & Co. for printing	113	50
	Paid I. Steen	15	65
Oct. 19	Paid for postage, wrappers, etc..........	213	10
Oct. 22	Paid for five cords of wood at $5 50.....	27	50
Oct. 23	Paid J. D. Logan & Co. for printing......	211	50
Oct. 25	Allowed *State Gazette* for papers—100 copies during the first eight days of session	40	00
Oct. 26	Paid for postage. stamps, etc..........	146	60
Oct. 30	Bill of J. A. Nagle for stationery........	97	85
Nov. 1	Paid for postage and wrappers..........	132	10
	Paid J. D. Logan & Co. for printing.....	273	50
Nov. 2	Paid Gas Company for gas..............	89	40
Nov. 15	Paid A. S. Roberts for oil and candles....	26	75
	Bill of Capital Ice Company for ice to Nov. 1, 1875	63	28
	Bill of J. D. Logan & Co. for printing....	191	00
Nov. 16	Bill of J. D. Logan & Co. for printing....	119	50
Nov. 17	Bill of G. W. Irwin for water...........	3	00
Nov. 18	Paid for postage, stamps, etc., to Nov. 17th	364	02
	Paid Val. C. Giles for four and a half cords of wood at $5 50....................	23	38
Nov. 20	Paid Wm. Braatz for locks and keys......	54	50
	Total.......................	$4174	72

Mr. DeMorse submitted the following protest:

HALL OF THE CONVENTION, }
AUSTIN, TEXAS, November, 20, 1875. }

To the Hon. E. B. Pickett, President of the Convention:

The undersigned, members of the Constitutional Convention, representing the people of their districts, protest against the action of the Convention in passing ordinance with the force of law, and in the interest of railroad corporations, and refusing to submit to the people for their approval, thereby assuming power not granted to them by the people, and in derogation of the supremacy of the people; and the undersigned respectfully ask that their protest be entered upon the journals.

CHARLES DEMORSE, of Red River County.
E. STERLING C. ROBERTSON, of Bell County.
JOEL W. ROBISON, of the 26th District.
J. F. ARNIM, of the 25th District.
H. G. BRUCE, of Johnson County.
W. BLASSINGAME, of Grayson County.
T. L. NUGENT, of Erath County.
Jos. E. HAYNES, of the 27th District
J. L. GERMAN, of Fannin County.
J. R. FLEMING, of Comanche County.
GEO. McCORMICK, of Colorado County.
A. T. McKINNEY, of Walker County.
S. A. McKENNEY, of Denton County.
G. PAULI, of Lee County.
BENNETT BLAKE, of Nacogdoches County.
ROBERT LACEY, of Leon County.
JOE P. DOUGLAS, of Cherokee County.
L. W. MOORE, of Fayette County.
JNO. L. HENRY, of Smith County.
L. S. ROSS, of McLennan County.
W. P. BALLINGER, of Galveston County.
L. I. NORVLL, of Jasper County.
D. A. NUNN, of Houston County.

Mr. Mills offered the following resolution:

WHEREAS, At the close of the late civil war many citizens of the Southern States, unwilling to live under our national government, betook themselves with their families to Brazil, and there became impoverished, disappointed in their hopes, losing everything, and enduring among strangers cruel hardships; and

WHEREAS, The President of the American Republic, learning the distressful condition of these voluntary exiles, has at various times furnished them free passage to their native land, and has recently dispatched a government steamship to Brazil, to provide for the free return to the United States of these unfortunates; therefore, be it

Resolved, That the thanks of this Convention are due and are hereby tendered to the President of these United States for the generous and considerate conduct thus displayed in behalf of Texans and other Southerners, which has invested his name and personal character with enduring honor; and

Resolved, That our presiding officer be instructed to convey to President Grant this expression of the feelings of this Convention.

Mr. Ballinger offered the following as a substitute for the resolution:

Resolved, That the Constitutional Convention of Texas tender thanks to President Grant for his efforts to assist the return of American citizens in distress, among whom was a number of citizens of Texas, from Brazil to the United States; and that the same be communicated by the President of this Convention to President Grant.

Accepted by Mr. Mills.

Mr. Crawford moved to lay the resolution on the table.

Lost by the following vote:

YEAS—Abernathy, Barnett, Blassingame, Brady, Cook of Gonzales, Crawford, Dohoney, Erhard, German, Henry of Limestone, Holt, Johnson of Franklin, Killough, King, Lacy, McKinney of Denton, Norvell, Pauli, Rentfro, Robison of Fayette, Scott, Stewart, Weaver, West—24.

NAYS—Arnim, Ballinger, Brown, Bruce, Burleson, Cline, Cooke of San Saba, Darnell, Davis of Brazos, DeMorse, Dillard, Douglas, Fleming, Flournoy, Haynes, Henry of Smith, Lockett, McCormick, McKinney of Walker, Martin of Navarro, Mills, Mitchell, Moore, Murphy, Nugent, Nunn, Ramey, Reagan, Robertson of Bell, Ross, Russell of Harrison, Sansom, Smith, Spikes, Stockdale, Whitehead, Whitfield, Wright—38.

On motion of Mr. Fleming, the previous question was ordered and the resolution adopted.

Mr. Murphy called up his motion to reconsider the vote adopting the resolution to adjourn *sine die.*

Mr. Rentfro moved to lay the resolution on the table.

Lost, vote reconsidered, and the consideration of the same postponed to 5 o'clock P. M. Wednesday.

Mr. Ramey offered the following resolution:

Resolved, That Nat. Q. Henderson be, and is hereby allowed the sum of $20 00, for five days service rendered the Convention in the beginning of the session.

Adopted.

On motion of Mr. Murphy, the vote postponing the resolution to adjourn *sine die* was reconsidered, and the resolution was so amended as to read that the Convention should adjourn *sine die* at 5 o'clock, P. M. Wednesday next.

Mr. Cook, of Gonzales, offered the following resolution:

Resolved, That the Secretary of the Convention be required, after the adjournment of the Convention *sine die,* to proceed at once to Galveston, with the manuscript copies of the journal and constitution, and superintend the printing of the same, and to make a complete index to the journal; and to distribute two hundred and twenty copies of the constitution in English, and one copy of the journal, to each member of the convention, and deposit the remainder with the Secretary of State. He shall also make an equal *pro rata* distribution of the copies of the constitution printed in the German, Spanish and Bohemian languages to delegates having constitutents speaking said languages.

Resolved further, That in order to pay the postage and to defray the expenses of the Secretary in carrying out the object of this resolution, and for his services, the sum of $1850 is hereby appropriated out of the fund appropriated to pay the expenses of this Convention to be drawn by the Secretary for that purpose.

Resolved further, That the certificate of the Secretary that the work has been done according to contract, shall be sufficient authority for the Comptroller to audit and the Treasurer to pay the accounts for the printing of the journal and constitution aforesaid, the same to be paid out of the fund appropriated to pay the expenses of this Convention.

Mr. Stockdale proposed to amend the resolution by sending three copies of the journal instead of one.

Adopted.

Mr. Reagan moved to amend by inserting "and the address prepared by the Convention for the people," and that "$1900" be inserted instead of "$1850."

Adopted.

Mr. McKinney, of Walker, reported as follows:

COMMITTEE ROOM, }
AUSTIN, November 22, 1875. }

To the Hon. E. B. Pickett, President of the Convention:

A majority of the members of the Committee on Judicial Apportionment instruct me to report the following ordinance,

48

fixing the terms of the District Courts of this State, for the consideration of the Convention:

"An Ordinance
FIXING THE TERMS OF THE DISTRICT COURTS OF THE STATE OF TEXAS.

"*Be it ordained by the people of the State of Texas in Convention assembled,* That until otherwise provided by law, the terms of the District Courts of the several Judicial Districts shall be as hereinafter prescribed:

"Sec. 1. That the District Courts of the First Judicial District be holden at the times hereinafter specified, to-wit:

"In the county of Chambers, on the first Mondays in March and September, and may continue in session one week.

"In the county of Liberty, on the first Mondays after the first Mondays in March and September, and may continue in session three weeks.

"In the county of San Jacinto, on the fourth Mondays after the first Mondays in March and September, and may continue in session two weeks.

"In the county of Polk, on the sixth Mondays after the first Mondays in March and September, and may continue in session three weeks.

In the county of Tyler, on the ninth Mondays after the first Mondays in March and September, and may continue in session three weeks.

"In the county of Jasper, on the twelfth Mondays after the first Mondays in March and September, and may continue in session two weeks.

"In the county of Newton, on the fourteenth Mondays after the first Mondays in March and September, and may continue in session two weeks.

"In the county of Orange, on the sixteenth Mondays after the first Mondays in March and September, and may continue in session one week.

"In the county of Jefferson, on the seventeenth Mondays after the first Mondays in March and September, and may continue in session two weeks.

"In the county of Hardin, on the nineteenth Mondays after the first Mondays in March and September, and may continue in session one week.

"Sec. 2. That the District Courts of the Second District be holden on the times hereinafter specified, to-wit:

"In the county of Sabine, one the first Mondays in January and July, and may continue in session two weeks.

"In the county of Shelby, on the second Mondays after the first Mondays in January and July, and may continue in session three weeks.

"In the county of Panola, on the fifth Mondays after the first Mondays in January and July, and may continue in session four weeks.

"In the county of Rusk, on the ninth Mondays after the first Mondays in January and July, and may continue in session six weeks.

"In the county of Harrison, on the fifteenth Mondays after the first Mondays in January and July, and may continue in session until the business is disposed of.

"Sec. 3. That the District Courts of the Third Judicial District be holden at the times hereinafter specified, to wit:

"In the county of San Augustine on the first Mondays in September and February, and may continue in session two weeks.

"In the county of Nacogdoches on the second Mondays after the first Mondays in February and September, and may continue in session three weeks.

"In the county of Cherokee, on the fifth Mondays after the first Mondays in February and September, and may continue in session four weeks.

"In the county of Houston on the ninth Mondays after the first Mondays in September, and continue in session five weeks; and on the ninth Mondays after the first Mondays in February, and may continue in session six weeks.

"In the county of Anderson, on the fourteenth Mondays after the first Mondays in September, and the fifteenth Mondays after the first Mondays in February, and may continue in session until the business is disposed of.

"Sec. 4. That the District Courts of the Fourth Judicial District be holden at the times hereinafter specified, to wit:

"In the county of Angelina, on the first Mondays in March and September, and may continue in session two weeks.

"In the county of Trinity, on the second Mondays after the first Mondays in March and September, and may continue in session three weeks.

"In the county of Walker, on the fifth Mondays after the first Mondays in March and September, and may continue in session three weeks.

"In the county of Grimes, on the eighth Mondays after the first Mondays in March and September, and may continue in session four weeks.

"In the county of Madison, on the twelfth Mondays after the

first Mondays in March and September, and may continue in session two weeks.

"In the county of Leon, on the fourteenth Mondays after the first Mondays in March and September, and mbay continue in session until the business is disposed of.

"Sec. 5. That the District Courts of the Fifth Judicial District shall be holden at the times hereinafter specified, to wit:

"In the ounty of Cass, on the first Mondays in February and September, and may continue in session three weeks.

"In the county of Bowie, on the third Mondays after the first Mondays in February and September, and may continue in session two weeks.

"In the county of Morris, on the fifth Mondays after the first Mondays in February and September, and may continue in session one week.

"In the county of Titus, on the sixth Mondays after the first Mondays in February and September, and may continue in session two weeks.

"In the county of Franklin, on the eighth Mondays after the first Mondays in February and September, and may continue in session one week.

"In the county of Camp, on the ninth Mondays after the first Mondays in February and September, and may continue in session two weeks.

"In the county of Marion, on the eleventh Mondays after the first Mondays in February and September, and may continue in session eight weeks, or until the business of the term can be disposed of.

"Sec. 6. That the District Courts of the Sixth Judicial District be holden at the times hereinafter specified, to wit:

"In the county of Grayson, on the first Mondays in January and July, and may continue in session seven weeks.

"In the county of Fannin, on the seventh Mondays after the first Mondays in January and July, and may continue in session four weeks.

"In the county of Lamar, on the eleventh Mondays after the first Mondays in January and July, and may continue in session six weeks.

"In the county of Red River, on the seventeenth Mondays after the first Mondays in January and July, and may continue in session four weeks.

"Sec. 7. That the District Courts of the Seventh Judicial District be holden at the times hereinafter specified, to wit:

" In the county of Smith, on the second Mondays in March and September, and may continue in session six weeks.

" In the county of Henderson, on the sixth Mondays after the second Mondays in March and September, and may continue in session two weeks.

" In the county of Van Zandt, on the eighth Mondays after the second Mondays in March and September, and may continue in session three weeks.

" In the county of Rains, on the eleventh Mondays after the second Mondays in March and September, and may continue in session one week.

" In the county of Wood, on the twelfth Mondays after the second Mondays in March and September, and may continue in session three weeks.

" In the county of Upshur, on the fifteenth Mondays after the second Mondays in March and September, and may continue in session three weeks.

" In the county of Gregg, on the eighteenth Mondays after the second Mondays in March and September, and may continue in session two weeks.

" Sec. 8. The District Court of the Eighth Judicial District be holden at the times hereinafted specified, to wit:

" In the county of Hunt, on the first Mondays in January and July, and may continue in session four weeks.

" In the county of Delta, on the fourth Mondays after the first Mondays in January and July, and may continue in session one week.

" In the county of Hopkins, on the fifth Mondays after the first Mondays in January and July, and may continue in session four weeks.

" In the county of Kaufman, on the ninth Mondays after the first Mondays in January and July, and may continue in session four weeks.

" In the county of Rockwell, on the thirteenth Mondays after the first Mondays in January and July, and may continue in session one week.

" In the county of Collin, on the fourteenth Mondays after the first Mondays in January and July, and may continue in session six weeks.

" Sec. 9. That the District Courts of the Ninth Judicial District be holden at the times hereinafter specified, to wit:

" In the county of Brazos, on the first Mondays in February and September, and may continue in session four weeks.

" In the county of Burleson, on the fourth Mondays after the first Mondays in February and September, and may continue in session four weeks.

"In the county of Milam, on the eighth Mondays after the first Mondays in February and September, and may continue in session six weeks.

"In the county of Robertson, on the fourteenth Mondays after the first Mondays in February and September, and may continue session until the business is disposed of.

"Sec. 10. That the District Courts of the Tenth Judicial District be holden at the times hereinafter specified, to wit:

"In the county of Cooke, on the first Mondays in February and July, and may continue in session three weeks.

"In the county of Denton, on the third Mondays after the first Mondays in February and July, and may continue in session three weeks.

"In the county of Tarrant, on the sixth Mondays after the first Mondays in February and July, and may continue in session four weeks.

"In the county of Parker, on the tenth Mondays after the first Mondays in February and July, and may continue in session three weeks.

"In the county of Wise, on the thirteenth Mondays after the first Mondays in February and July, and may continue in session two weeks.

"In the county of Clay, on the fifteenth Mondays after the first Mondays in February and July, and may continue in session two weeks.

"In the county of Montague, on the seventeenth Mondays after the first Mondays in February and July, and may continue in session until the business is disposed of.

"Sec. 11. That the District Courts of the Eleventh Judicial District be holden at the times hereinafter specified, to wit:

"In the county of Ellis on the second Mondays in May and November, and may continue in session five weeks.

"In the county of Dallas on the fifth Mondays after the second Mondays in May and November, and may continue in session until the business is disposed of.

"Sec. 12. That the District Courts of the Twelfth Judicial District be holden at the times hereinafter specified, to wit:

"In the county of Coryell on the first Mondays in March and September, and may continue in session three weeks.

"In the county of Hamilton on the fourth Mondays in March and September, and may continue in session two weeks.

" In the county of Comanche on the second Mondays in April and October, and may continue in session two weeks.

" In the county of Brown on the fourth Mondays in April and October, and may continue in session two weeks.

" In the county of Coleman on the second Mondays in May and November, and may continue in session one week.

" In the county of Shackelford on the third Mondays in May and November, and may continue in session one week.

" In the county of Young on the fourth Mondays in May and November, and may continue in session one week.

" In the county of Jack on the first Mondays in June and December, and may continue in session one week.

" In the county of Palo Pinto on the first Mondays in June and December, and may continue in session one week.

" In the county of Hood, on the third Mondays in June and December, and may continue in session two weeks.

" In the county of Somerville, on the second Mondays in July and January, and may continue in session one week.

" In the county of Erath, on the third Mondays in July and January, and may continue in session two weeks.

" In the county of Eastland, on the first Mondays in August and February, and may continue in session one week.

" For Judicial purposes, Runnels shall be attached to Coleman; Taylor and Callahan to Eastland; Jones, Haskell, Throckmorton and Stephens to Shackelford.

" Sec. 13. That the District Courts of the Thirteenth Judicial District be holden at the times hereinafter specified, to-wit:

" In the county of Limestone, on the first Mondays in March and September, and may continue in session four weeks.

" In the county of Freestone, on the fourth Mondays after the first Mondays in March and September, and may continue in session four weeks.

" In the county of Navarro, on the eighth Mondays after the first Mondays in March and September, and may continue in session four weeks.

" In the county of Hill, on the twelfth Mondays after the first Mondays in March and September, and may continue in session three weeks.

" In the county of Johnson, on the fifteenth Mondays after the first Mondays in March and September, and may continue in session four weeks.

" In the county of Bosque, on the nineteenth Mondays after the first Mondays in March and September, and may continue in session two weeks.

"Sec. 14. That the District Courts of the Fourteenth Judicial District be holden at the times hereinafter specified, to-wit:

"In the county of Falls, on the first Mondays in March and September, and may continue in session four weeks.

"In the county of Bell, on the first Mondays in April and October, and may continue in session four weeks.

"In the county of McLennan, on the first Mondays in May and November, and may continue in session until the business is disposed of.

"Sec. 15. That the District Courts of the Fifteenth Judicial District be holden at the times hereinafter specified, to-wit:

"In the county of Blanco, on the first Mondays in March and September, and may continue in session one week.

"In the county of Hays, on the first Mondays after the first Mondays in March and September, and may continue in session two weeks.

"In the county of Caldwell, on the third Mondays after the first Mondays in March and September, and may continue in session three weeks.

"In the county of Bastrop, on the sixth Mondays after the first Mondays in March and September, and may continue in session four weeks.

"In the county of Fayette, on the tenth Mondays after the first Mondays in March and Septetmber, and may continue in session six weeks.

"In the county of Austin, on the seventeenth Mondays after the first Mondays in March and September, and may continue in session four weeks.

"Sec. 16. That the District Courts of the Sixteenth Judicial District be holden at the times hereinafter specified, to-wit:

"In the county of Washington, on the first Mondays in January and July, and may continue in session eight weeks.

"In the county of Lee, on the eighth Mondays after the first Mondays in January and July, and may continue in session three weeks.

"In the county of Williamson, on the eleventh Mondays after the first Mondays in January and July, and may continue in session four weeks.

"In the county of Travis, on the fifteenth Mondays after the first Mondays in January and July, and may continue in session until the business is disposed of.

"Sec. 17. That the District Courts in the Seventeenth Judicial District be holden at the times hereinafter specified, to-wit:

" In the county of Burnet, on the first Mondays in March and September, and may continue in session two weeks.

" In the county of Lampasas, on the second Mondays after the first Mondays in March and September, and may continue in session two weeks.

" In the county of San Saba, on the fourth Mondays after the first Mondays in March and September, and may continue in session two weeks.

" In the county of Menard, on the sixth Mondays after the first Mondays in March and September, and may continue in session two weeks.

" In the county of Mason, on the eighth Mondays after the first Mondays in March and September, and may continue in session two weeks.

" In the county of Llano, on the ninth Mondays after the first Mondays in March and September, and may continue in session one week.

" In the county of Gillespie, on the tenth Mondays after the first Mondays in March and September, and may continue until the business is disposed of.

" The counties of Concho and Kimble are attached to Menard county for judicial purposes; and the county of McCulloch is attached for judicial purposes to the county of San Saba.

" Sec. 18. That the District Courts of the Eighteenth Judicial District be holden at the times hereinafter specified to-wit:

" In the county of Waller, on the first Mondays in January and July, and may continue in session three weeks.

" In the county of Fort Bend, on the third Mondays after the first Mondays in January and July, and may continue in session three weeks.

" In the county of Wharton, on the sixth Mondays after the first Mondays in January and July, and may continue in session three weeks.

" In the county of Jackson, on the ninth Mondays after the first Mondays in January and July, and may continue in session two weeks.

" In the county of Matagorda, on the eleventh Mondays after the first Mondays in January and July, and may continue in session two weeks.

" In the county of Brazoria, on the thirteenth Mondays after the first Mondays in January and July, and may continue in session until the business is disposed of.

" Sec. 19. That the District Courts of the Nineteenth Judicial District be holden at the times hereinafter specified, to-wit:

" In the county of Lavaca, on the first Mondays in February and August, and may continue in session four weeks.

" In the county of Colorada, on the fourth Mondays after the first Mondays in February and August, and may continue in session four weeks.

" In the county of Gonzales, on the eighth Mondays after the first Mondays in February and August, and may continue in session five weeks.

" In the county of Guadalupe, on the thirteenth Mondays after the first Mondays in February and August, and may continue in session four weeks.

" In the county of Wilson, on the seventeenth Mondays after the first Mondays in February and August, and may continue in session two weeks.

" Sec. 20. That the District Courts of the Twentieth Judicial District be holden at the times hereinafter specified, to wit:

" In the county of El Paso, on the first Mondays in March and September, and may continue in session three weeks.

" In the county of Presidio, on the fourth Mondays after the first Mondays in March and September, and may continue in session two weeks.

" In the county of Pecos, on the seventh Mondays after the first Mondays in March and September, and may continue in session two weeks.

" In the county of Tom Green, on the tenth Mondays after the first Mondays in March and September, and may continue in session three weeks.

" The county of Crockett is attached to Tom Green county for judicial purposes.

" Sec. 21. That the District Courts of the Twenty-first Judicial District be holden at the times hereinafter specified to-wit:

" In the county of Montgomery on the first Mondays in February and September, and may continue in session four weeks.

" In the county of Harris on the second Mondays in March and October, and may continue in session until the business is disposed of.

" Sec. 22. That the District Courts of the Twenty-second Judicial District be holden at the times hereinafter specified, to-wit:

" In the county of Comal on the first Mondays in April and October, and may continue in session two weeks.

" In the county of Atascosa on the second Mondays after the first Mondays in April and October, and may continue in session two weeks.

"In the county of Bexar on the fourth Mondays after the first Mondays in April and October, and may continue in session until the business is disposed of.

"Sec. 23. That the District Courts of the Twenty-third Judicial District be holden at the time hereinafter specified, to-wit:

"In the county of DeWitt, on the first Mondays in March and September, and may continue in session three weeks.

"In the county of Victoria, on the third Mondays after the first Mondays in March and September, and may continue in session three weeks.

"In the county of Calhoun, on the sixth Mondays after the first Mondays in March and September, and may continue in session two weeks.

"In the county of Refugio, on the eighth Mondays after the first Mondays in March and September, and may continue in session one week.

"In the county of Aransas, on the ninth Mondays after the first Mondays in March, and September, and may continue in session one week.

"In the county of San Patricio, on the tenth Mondays after the first Mondays in March and September, and may continue in session one week.

"In the county of Goliad, on the eleventh Mondays after the first Mondays in March and September, and may continue in session two weeks.

"In the county of Bee, on the thirteenth Mondays after the first Mondays in March and September, and May continue in session one week.

"In the county of Live Oak, on the fourteenth Mondays after the first Mondays in March and September, and may continue in session two weeks.

"In the county of Karnes, on the sixteenth Mondays after the first Mondays in March and September, and may continue session two weeks.

"McMullen county is attached to Live Oak county for judicial purposes.

"Sec. 24. That the District Courts of the Twenty-fourth Judicial District be holden at the times hereinafter specified, to-wit:

"In the county of Kendall, on the first Mondays in March and September, and may continue in session one week.

"In the county of Kerr, on the second Mondays after the first Mondays in March and September, and may continue in session one week.

"In the county of Bandera, on the third Mondays after the

first Mondays in March and September, and may continue in session one week.

"In the county of Medina, on the fourth Mondays after the first Mondays in March and September, and may continue in session two weeks.

"In the county of Frio, on the sixth Mondays after the first Mondays in March and September, and may continue in session one week.

"In the county of Uvalde, on the seventh Monday after the first Mondays in March and September, and may continue in session two weeks.

"In the county of Kinney, on the ninth Mondays after the first Mondays in March and September, and may continue in session one week.

"In the county of Maverick, on the tenth Mondays after the first Mondays in March and September, and may continue in session until the business is disposed of.

"The unorganized counties of Dimmitt and Zavalla are attached for judicial purposes to the county of Maverick.

"Edwards county is attached for judicial purposes to Kerr county, and LeSalle county to Frio county.

"Sec. 25. That the District Courts of the Twenty-fifth Judicial District be holden at the times hereinafter specified, to wit:

"In the county of Cameron, on the third Mondays in February and August, and may continue in session four weeks.

"In the county of Hidalgo, on the fourth Mondays after the third Mondays in February and August, and may continue in session one week.

"In the county of Starr, on the fifth Mondays after the third Mondays in February and August, and may continue in session one week.

"In the county of Zapata, on the sixth Mondays after the third Mondays in February and August, and may continue in session one week.

"In the county of Webb, on the seventh Monday after the third Mondays in February and August, and may continue in session two weeks.

"In the county of Nueces, on the tenth Mondays after the third Mondays in February and August, and may continue in session four weeks.

"Encinal county is attached for judicial purposes to Webb county, and Duval county to the county of Nueces.

"Sec. 26. That the District Courts of the Twenty-sixth Judicial District be holden at the times hereinafter specified, to-wit:

" In the county of Galveston on the first Mondays in February, April, June, October and December, and may continue in session until the business is disposed of.

" Sec. 27. All writs and process, civil and criminal, heretofore issued by or from the District Courts in the several counties of this State, and made returnable to the former terms of said courts, as said terms are now fixed by law, shall be returnable to the next ensuing terms of said District Courts, in each county, as they are prescribed in this ordinance, and all such writs and process that may be issued by or from said courts, at any time within five days next before the holding of the next ensuing terms of said courts, as prescribed herein, are hereby made returnable to said terms, respectively, and all such writs and process, hereinbefore mentioned, are hereby legalized and validated to all intents and purposes, as if the same had been made returnable to the term or terms of said court, as the terms thereof are herein prescribed.

" Sec. 28. That in case where the time has partly elapsed for holding any term of the District Court, as herein prescribed, at the time of the qualification of the District Judges of said District, then said Judge shall proceed to hold said court for the remainder of said term."

On motion of Mr. Dohoney, the consideration of the article was postponed until after action on the article on Judicial Districts.

" Article —, Judicial Apportionment," was taken up.

Mr. McCormick moved the engrossment of the article, and that the reading be dispensed with.

Mr. King moved to consider the article sentence by sentence. Withdrawn.

Mr. McCormick's motion to dispense with the reading adopted.

Mr. Dohoney offered the following amendments:

Amend section 6 by striking out the word " Grayson."

Amend section 10 by striking out " Tarrant," and insert the word " Grayson."

Amend section 11 by adding at the end of the section the word " Tarrant."

Mr. Pickett moved to reconsider the vote just taken.

Mr. Nugent moved the previous question, on engrossment.

Carried by the following vote:

YEAS—Abernathy, Allison, Arnim, Ballinger, Barnett, Blake, Blassingame, Bruce, Burleson, Chambers, Cook of Gonzales, Cooke of San Saba, Crawford, Darnell, Davis of Brazos, Dillard, Douglas, Ferris, Fleming, Haynes, Henry of Limestone, Henry of Smith, Holt, Killough, Lacy, McCormick, McKinney of Denton, McKinney of Walker, Martin of Navarro. Martin of Hunt, Moore, Murphy, Norvell, Nugent, Nunn, Ramey, Robison of Fayette, Ross, Scott, Sessions, Stewart, Wade, Whitehead—43.

NAYS—Abner, Brady, Brown, Cline, Davis of Wharton, Dohoney, Flanagan, German, King, Lockett, McCabe, Mills, Mitchell, Pauli, Rentfro, Reynolds, Robertson of Bell, Russell of Harrison, Sansom, Smith, Spikes, Stockdale, Weaver, West, Wright—25.

Mr. Dohoney's amendment lost, and the article ordered engrossed by the following vote:

YEAS—Abernathy, Allison, Arnim, Ballinger, Barnett, Blake, Blassingame, Brown, Bruce, Burleson, Chambers, Cline, Cook of Gonzales, Cooke of San Saba, Crawford, Darnell, Davis of Brazos, Dillard, Douglas, Ferris, Fleming, Flournoy, Haynes, Henry of Limestone, Henry of Smith, Holt, Johnson of Franklin, Killough, Lacy, McCormick, McKinney of Walker, Martin of Navarro, Martin of Hunt, Moore, Norvell, Nugent, Nunn, Reagan, Rentfro, Ross, Scott, Sessions, Smith, Spikes, Stewart, Wade, Whitehead—47.

NAYS—Abner, Brady, Davis of Wharton, Dohoney, Flanagan, German, King, Lockett, McCabe, Mills, Mitchell, Murphy, Pauli, Ramey, Robertson of Bell, Robison of Fayette, Russell of Harrison, Sansom, Stockdale, Weaver, West, Wright—22.

On motion of Mr. Scott, the rule was suspended, and the article placed upon its third and final reading.

On motion of Mr. Nugent, the reading of the article was dispensed with, and the article passed by the following vote:

YEAS—Abernathy, Arnim, Ballinger, Barnett, Blake, Blassingame, Bruce, Burleson, Chambers, Cline, Cook of Gonzales, Crawford, Davis of Brazos, Dillard, Erhard, Ferris, Fleming, Flournoy, Haynes, Henry of Limestone, Henry of Smith, Holt, Johnson of Franklin, Killough, Lacy, McCormick, McKinney of Walker, Martin of Navarro, Martin of Hunt, Moore, Norvell, Nugent, Nunn, Reagan, Robison of Fayette, Ross, Scott, Sessions, Smith, Spikes, Stewart, Wade, Whitehead, Whitfield—44.

NAYS—Abner, Allison, Brady, Darnell, Davis of Wharton, DeMorse, Dohoney, Douglas, Flanagan, German, King, Lockett, McCabe, Mills, Mitchell, Murphy, Pauli, Rentfro, Reynolds, Robertson of Bell, Russell of Harrison, Sansom, Stockdale, Weaver, West, Wright—26.

"Article —, fixing the times of holding the District Courts," was taken up.

Mr. Nugent moved to dispense with the reading of the article.

Lost, and the article read a second time and ordered engrossed by the following vote:

YEAS—Abernathy, Allison, Arnim, Ballinger, Barnett, Blake, Brown, Burleson, Chambers, Cook of Gonzales, Crawford, Darnell, Davis of Brazos, Davis of Wharton, DeMorse, Dillard, Dohoney, Douglas, Erhard, Ferris, Flanagan, Fleming, Flournoy, German, Haynes, Henry of Limestone, Henry of Smith, Holt, Johnson of Franklin, Killough, King, Lacy, McCabe, McCormick, McKinney of Walker, Martin of Navarro, Martin of Hunt, Mitchell, Moore, Norvell, Nugent, Nunn, Ramey, Reagan, Rentfro, Reynolds, Robison of Fayette, Ross, Scott, Sessions, Smith, Spikes, Stewart, Wade, Whitehead, Whitfield, Wright—57.

NAYS—Abner, McKinney of Denton, Mills, Murphy, Robertson of Bell, Russell of Harrison, Sansom, Stockdale, Weaver, West—10.

On motion of Mr. Whitfield, the rule was suspended and the article taken up and passed by the following vote:

YEAS—Abernathy, Allison, Arnim, Ballinger, Barnett, Blake, Blassingame, Brown, Bruce, Burleson, Chambers, Cline, Crawford, Darnell, Davis of Brazos, DeMorse, Dillard, Dohoney, Douglas, Erhard, Ferris, Flanagan, Fleming, Flournoy, German, Haynes, Henry of Limestone, Henry of Smith, Holt, Johnson of Franklin, Killough, Lacy, McCormick, McKinney of Walker, Martin of Navarro, Martin of Hunt, Moore, Norvell, Nugent, Nunn, Reagan, Rentfro, Robison of Fayette, Ross, Scott, Sessions, Smith, Spikes, Stewart, Wade, Whitehead, Whitfield, Wright—53.

NAYS—Abner, Brady, Cook of Gonzales, Davis of Wharton, Lockett, McCabe, McKinney of Denton, Mills, Mitchell, Murphy, Pauli, Reynolds, Robertson of Bell, Russell of Harrison, Sansom, Stockdale, Weaver, West—18.

"Article—, Spanish and Mexican Land Titles," was then taken up.

Mr. Reagan offered the following amendment:

Amend section 2 by striking out the word "thereto," in line 19, and inserting the words "to such grant not archived or recorded, or occupied as aforesaid."

Adopted.

Also amend section 3 by adding after the word "city," in line 33, the words "or town."

Adopted.

Also amend section 4, line 37, by striking out the word "existed," and insert "issued."

Mr. Ferris proposed to amend by adding after the word "continue," in line 59, the word "as."

The article then passed, by the following vote:

YEAS—Abernathy, Allison, Arnim, Barnett, Blake, Blassingame, Brown, Bruce, Burleson, Chambers, Cook of Gonzales, Cooke of San Saba, Crawford, Darnell, DeMorse, Dillard, Dohoney, Douglas, Ferris, Fleming, Flournoy, German, Haynes, Henry of Limestone, Holt, Johnson of Franklin, Killough, Lacy, McCormick, McKinney of Walker, Martin of Navarro, Martin of Hunt, Moore, Nugent, Nunn, Reagan, Robertson of Bell, Robison of Fayette, Sansom, Scott, Sessions, Smith, Spikes, Stewart, Weaver, Whitehead, Whitfield, Wright—48.

NAYS—Cline, Flanagan, Lockett, Mills, Mitchell, Murphy, Norvell, Pauli, Rentfro, Stockdale, West—11.

Mr. McKinney, of Walker, offered the following:

"ORDINANCE.

"No ordinance passed by this Convention, and not submitted for the ratification of the people, except that postponing the election and that submitting the constitution to a vote of the qualified electors, shall in any sense be deemed operative as affecting the rights of the State, or the rights and obligations of any person, association or corporation within the State, or having rights therein, or obligations thereto, either to confirm, release, relieve or modify the same, unless this constitution shall be ratified by the qualified electors of the State of Texas."

Mr. Mitchell moved to lay the ordinance on the table.

The yeas and nays were demanded, and the motion lost by the following vote:

YEAS—Abner, Brady, Cline, Cooke of San Saba, Darnell, Dohoney, Erhard, Flanagan, Ford, Holt, Lockett, McCabe, Mills, Mitchell, Russell of Harrison, Sansom, Stockdale, West, Whitfield, Wright—20.

NAYS—Allison, Arnim, Barnett, Blassingame, Brown, Bruce, Burleson, Chambers, Cook of Gonzales, Crawford, DeMorse, Dillard, Douglas, Ferris, Fleming, Flournoy, German, Haynes, Henry of Limestone, Henry of Smith, Killough, Lacy, McCormick, McKinney of Denton, McKinney of Walker, Martin of Navarro, Martin of Hunt, Norvell, Nugent, Nunn, Pauli, Robertson of Bell, Robison of Fayette, Ross, Scott, Sessions, Smith, Spikes, Stewart, Weaver, Whitehead—41.

Mr. Nugent moved the main question.

[The President resumed the chair.]

Mr. West made a point of order, that Mr. Darnell was entitled to the floor, and that Mr. Nugent's motion was not in order.

Mr. Stockdale moved to adjourn to 2½ o'clock P. M.

Lost.

The chair ruled that Mr. Nugent having been recognized by Mr. Brown, who was in the chair at the time the motion was made, was entitled to the floor, and the motion was in order.

Mr. Darnell appealed from the decision of the chair.

Appeal sustained by the following vote:

YEAS—Abernathy, Arnim, Ballinger, Barnett, Blassingame, Bruce, Burleson, Chambers, DeMorse, Fleming, German, Haynes, Henry of Smith, Holt, McCormick, McKinney of Denton, McKinney of Walker, Martin of Navarro, Moore, Norvell, Nugent, Robertson of Bell, Robison of Fayette, Scott, Sessions, Smith, Spikes, Stewart—27.

NAYS—Abernathy, Brady, Cline, Cooke of San Saba, Crawford, Darnell, Davis of Brazos, Davis of Wharton, Dillard, Dohoney, Douglas, Erhard, Ferris, Flanagan, Henry of Limestone, Killough, Lacy, Lockett, McCabe, Martin of Hunt, Mitchell, Murphy, Pauli, Rentfro, Reynolds, Ross, Russell of Harrison, Sansom, Stockdale, Weaver, West, Whitehead, Whitfield, Wright—34.

On motion of Mr. Stockdale, the Convention adjourned to 2½ o'clock P. M.

EVENING SESSION—2½ O'CLOCK.

Convention met pursuant to adjournment; roll called; quorum present.

The ordinance submitted by Mr. McKinney, of Walker, again taken up.

Mr. Nugent moved the previous question.

Carried.

The ordinance was then passed by the following vote:

YEAS—Abernathy, Allison, Arnim, Barnett, Blassingame, Brown, Bruce, Burleson, Chambers, Cook of Gonzales, DeMorse, Dillard, Douglas, Fleming, Flournoy, German, Graves, Haynes, Henry of Smith, Johnson of Collin, Johnson of Franklin, Killough, Lacy, McCormick, McKinney of Denton, McKinney of Walker, Martin of Navarro, Martin of Hunt, Moore, Norvell, Nugent, Robertson of Bell, Robison of Fayette, Ross, Scott, Sessions, Smith, Spikes, Stewart, Wade, Weaver, Whitehead—42.

NAYS—Abner, Ballinger, Brady, Cline, Cooke of San Saba, Darnell, Davis of Brazos, Davis of Wharton, Dohoney, Erhard, Ferris, Flanagan, Ford, Henry of Limestone, Holt, King,

49

Lockett, McCabe, Mills, Mitchell, Murphy, Nunn, Pauli, Reagan, Rentfro, Reynolds, Russell of Harrison, Stockdale, West, Whitfield, Wright—31.

Mr. Flournoy moved to reconsider the vote just taken, and to lay the motion on the table.

A call of the Convention was demanded.

On motion of Mr. Moore, Mr. Blake was excused on account of sickness.

On motion of Mr. West, Mr. Sansom was excused.

On motion of Mr. Dillard, Mr. McLean was excused.

The Convention being full, the motion to reconsider and lay on the table was carried by the following vote:

YEAS—Abernathy, Allison, Arnim, Barnett, Blassingame, Bruce, Chambers, Cook of Gonzales, DeMorse, Dillard, Douglas, Fleming, Flournoy, German, Graves, Haynes, Henry of Smith, Johnson of Collin, Johnson of Franklin, Lacy, McCormick, McKinney of Denton, McKinney of Walker, Martin of Navarro, Martin of Hunt, Moore, Norvell, Nugent, Nunn, Ramey, Robertson of Bell, Robison of Fayette, Ross, Scott, Sessions, Smith, Spikes, Stewart, Wade, Weaver, Whitehead—41.

NAYS—Abner, Brady, Brown, Burleson, Cline, Cooke of San Saba, Crawford, Darnell, Davis of Brazos, Davis of Wharton, Dohoney, Erhard, Ferris, Flanagan, Ford, Haynes, Holt, Killough, King, Lockett, McCabe, Mills, Mitchell, Murphy, Pauli, Reagan, Rentfro, Reynolds, Russell of Harrison, Stockdale, West, Whitfield—33.

Mr. Stockdale reported as follows:

To the Hon. E. B. Pickett, President of the Convention:

The Committee on Impeachment instruct me to report the accompanying article and recommend the adoption of the same as a part of the constitution.

F. S. STOCKDALE, Chairman.

" ARTICLE—.

" IMPEACHMENT.

" Section 1. The power of impeachment shall be vested in the House of Representatives.

" Sec. 2. Impeachment of the Governor, Lieutenant Governor, Attorney General, Comptroller, Treasurer, Commissioner of the General Land Office, and the Judges of the Supreme Court, Court of Appeals and District Court, shall be tried by the Senate.

" Sec. 3. When the Senate is sitting as a Court of Impeachment, the senators shall be on oath or affirmation impartially to try the party impeached; and no person shall be convicted without the concurrence of two-thirds of the Senators present.

" Sec. 4. Judgment in cases of impeachment shall extend only to removal from office and disqualification from holding any office of honor, trust or profit under this State. A party convicted on impeachment shall also be subject to indictment, trial and punishment according to law.

" Sec. 5. All officers against whom articles of impeachment may be preferred shall be suspended from the exercise of the duties of their office during the pendency of such impeachment. The Governor may make a provisional appointment to fill the vacancy occasioned by the suspension of an officer until the decision on the impeachment.

" Sec. 6. Any judge of the District Court of this State, who is incompetent to discharge the duties of his office, or who shall be guilty of partiality or oppression, or other official misconduct, or whose habits and conduct are such as to render him unfit to hold such office; or who shall negligently fail to perform his duties as judge, or who shall fail to execute in a reasonable measure the business in his courts, may be removed by the Supreme Court. The Supreme Court shall have original jurisdiction to hear and determine the causes aforesaid, when presented in writing, upon the oaths taken before some judge of a court of record, of not less than seven citizens of this State, at least three of whom shall be practicing lawyers, licensed to practice in the Supreme Court; said presentment to be founded either upon the knowledge of the persons making it, or upon the written oaths as to the facts of credible witnesses. The Supreme Court may issue all needful process, and prescribe all needful rules to give effect to this section. Causes of this kind shall have precedence and be tried as soon as practicable.

" Sec. 7. The Legislature shall provide by law for the trial and removal from office of all officers of this State, the modes for which have not been provided in this constitution."

Mr. Stockdale reported as follows:

To the Hon. E. B. Pickett, President of the Convention:

The Committe on Ordinances have duly considered " The Ordinance to provide for submitting the constitution to a vote of the people," and have instructed me to report the accompanying substitute therefor, and to recommend its adoption by the Convention.

Respectfully submitted,   F. S. STOCKDALE, Chairman.

"An Ordinance

"SUBMITTING THE NEW CONSTITUTION TO A VOTE OF THE PEOPLE,
"AND FOR OTHER PURPOSES.

"Section 1. *Be it ordained by the people of Texas in Convention assembled,* That the new constitution, framed by this Convention, shall be submitted to the electors of this State at an election, which shall be held throughout the State on the third Tuesday in February, A. D. 1876, for their ratification or rejection. Those electors in favor of ratification shall have written or printed on their ballots, "For the constitution." Those electors opposed to ratification shall have written or printed on their ballots, "Against the constitution." If a majority of all the votes cast at said election, and returned to the Secretary of State, shall be in favor of ratification, the Governor shall within five days next succeeding the return day issue his proclamation declaring the fact, and then the new constitution shall, on the third Tuesday in April, A. D. 1876, become, and thereafter be, the organic and fundamental law of the State. If, however, a majority of all the votes so cast and returned be against ratification, then the new constitution thall have and be of no effect whatever.

"Sec. 2. *Be it further ordained,* That at the same time there shall be a general election held throughout the State, for all State, district, county and precinct officers, created and made elective by the new constitution. The electors, as far as practicable, shall be held and conducted as now provided by law, but no registration of voters shall be required, and every elector shall vote in the precinct of his residence; *provided,* that electors residing in unorganized counties may vote in any precinct of the county to which their respective counties are attached for judicial purposes. The qualification of electors shall be as defined in the article regulating suffrage in the new constitution.

"Sec. 3. *Be it further ordained,* That the County Courts now existing shall meet at their respective county seats within twenty days after the adjournment of this Convention, or as soon thereafter as practicable, and re-divide their respective counties into the number of precincts provided for by the new constitution, and make immediate proclamation thereof for the information of the people. Said courts shall establish at least one voting place in each precinct, and, where deemed necessary for public convenience, they shall establish two or more voting places in any precinct.

"Sec. 4. *Be it further ordained,* That the returns of said election shall be made as now provided by law, to the Presiding

Justice of each county, and to the returning officer of each returning county named in the ordinance apportioning the State into Senatorial and Representative Districts, passed by this Convention, as is now required by law, and to the Secretary of State, where by law it is now required. In all cases the returns shall be made, opened, counted, and the result recorded and declared by the proper officers, as is provided by existing laws; and the returns of the election of all judges shall be made by the Presiding Justice of each county to the Secretary of State.

" Sec. 5. If the new constitution shall be ratified by the people, then the County Judges, County Attorneys, and other county officers created by the new constitution, shall, until otherwise provided, receive such fees as were allowed by the constitution and laws of 1866.

" Sec. 6. *Be it further ordained,* That in case the new constitution shall be ratified at said election, the Senators and Representatives then elected shall assemble as the Fifteenth Legislature, at the seat of government, on the third Tuesday in April, A. D. 1876.

" Sec. 7. *Be it further ordained,* That after the first election herein provided for, until otherwise prescribed by law, the regular biennial elections of this State for State, district, county and precinct officers, after the year 1876, shall be held on the ...... Tuesday next after the first Monday in November every second year, commencing with November, 1878. All officers elected at the election herein provided for shall hold their offices as though they had been elected in November, 1876, whether the tenure of their offices by the new constitution be for two, four, or six years.

" Sec. 8. *Be it further ordained,* That all judicial, district, county and precinct officers, elected in accordance with the provisions of this ordinance, shall be installed in office on the third Tuesday in April, A. D. 1876; *provided,* that persons so elected who may be prevented from qualifying by reason of illness or absence shall have twenty additional days in which to do so. The Governor and all State officers not named before in this section shall be installed on the first Tuesday after the assemblage of the Legislature elected, as herein provided. As each newly elected officer may be qualified, his predecessor, if any, shall cease his functions, and deliver to his successor all books, papers, archives and records, and all property, of whatever nature or kind, pertaining to his office, or in his possession or charge.

" Sec. 9. There shall be no session of the Legislature in January, 1876, unless specially called by the Governor, nor except under the provisions of the new constitution and this ordinance, or under the ordinance of this Convention postponing the election of December, 1875.

"Sec. 10. That this ordinance shall take effect and be in full force from and after its passage."

On motion of Mr. Dohoney, two hundred copies were ordered printed.

On motion of Mr. Mills, two hundred copies of the "Article on Impeachment" were ordered printed.

Mr. Wade moved to reconsider the vote ordering the printing of two hundred copies of the ordinance submitting the constitution to the people. Carried.

Mr. Bruce moved to suspend the rules and take up the ordinance.

Carried by the following vote:

YEAS—Abernathy, Allison, Barnett, Blassingame, Brown, Bruce, Burleson, Chambers, Cook of Gonzales, Cooke of San Saba, Davis of Brazos, Dillard, Flanagan, Fleming, German, Graves, Henry of Limestone, Henry of Smith, Holt, Johnson of Collin, Johnson of Franklin, Killough, King, Lacy, Lockett, McCormick, McKinney of Denton, McKinney of Walker, Martin of Navarro, Moore, Norvell, Nugent, Nunn, Reagan, Robertson of Bell, Robison of Fayette, Ross, Scott, Sessions, Spikes, Stewart, Wade, Weaver, Whitehead, Whitfield, Wright—46.

NAYS—Arnim, Ballinger, Brady, Cline, Darnell, DeMorse, Dohoney, Erhard, Martin of Hunt, Mills, Mitchell, Murphy, Pauli, Rentfro, Reynolds, Russell of Harrison, Smith, West—18.

Mr. Ballinger proposed to amend by striking out the election for officers on the same day with the election for the constitution.

Mr. Fleming moved to amend by striking out "March" and inserting "the first Tuesday in February;" and strike out "the first Tuesday in May" and insert "the first Tuesday in April."

On motion of Mr. Scott, Mr. Ballinger's amendment was laid on the table by the following vote:

YEAS—Abernathy, Allison, Arnim, Barnett, Blassingame, Bruce, Burleson, Chambers, Cook of Gonzales, Cooke of San Saba, Crawford, Darnell, Davis of Brazos, DeMorse, Dillard, Dohoney, Douglas, Erhard, Fleming, Flournoy, German, Graves, Haynes, Henry of Limestone, Henry of Smith, Holt, Johnson of Collin, Johnson of Franklin, Killough, Lacy, McKinney of Denton, McKinney of Walker, Martin of Navarro, Martin of Hunt, Moore, Murphy, Norvell, Nugent, Ramey, Reagan, Robertson of Bell, Robison of Fayette, Ross, Scott, Sessions, Spikes, Stewart, Wade, West, Whitehead, Whitfield, Wright—52.

Nays—Arnim, Cline, Flanagan, King, Lockett, McCabe, Mills, Mitchell, Pauli, Rentfro, Reynolds, Russell of Harrison, Smith, Stockdale, Weaver—14.

Mr. Reagan proposed to amend the amendment by striking out "March" and inserting "third Tuesday in February"; and striking out "first Tuesday in May" and inserting "third Tuesday in April." Accepted.

Mr. Rentfro proposed to amend by striking out "second of March" and inserting "first of April."

Lost.

Mr. McCormick moved to amend by striking out the "first Tuesday in February" and inserting the "first Tuesday in April."

Mr. Fleming's amendment adopted.

Mr. Fleming offered the following amendment:

Amend by striking out on page 8 from the words "the ratification" the remainder of the page.

Adopted.

On motion of Mr. Holt, Mr. Reagan was indefinitely excused from to-day.

Mr. Wright proposed to amend by inserting after "State officers" the words "and judicial officers."

Adopted.

[Mr. Stockdale in the chair.]

Mr. DeMorse offered the following amendment:

Amend by inserting in its proper place, and also upon their tickets, the words "in favor of ordinance extending time of railroad charters," or the words "opposed to extension of time of railroad charters."

Laid on the table, and the ordinance then passed by the following vote:

Yeas—Abernathy, Allison, Arnim, Barnett, Blassingame, Brown, Bruce, Burleson, Chambers, Cook of Gonzales, Cooke of San Saba, Crawford, Darnell, Dillard, Dohoney, Ferris, Fleming, Flournoy, German, Graves, Haynes, Henry of Limestone, Henry of Smith, Holt, Johnson of Collin, Johnson of Franklin, Killough, Lacy, McCormick, McKinney of Denton, McKinney of Walker, Martin of Navarro, Martin of Hunt, Moore, Murphy, Norvell, Nugent, Nunn, Ramey, Robertson of Bell, Robison of Fayette, Ross, Scott, Sessions, Smith, Spikes, Stewart, Stockdale, Wade, Weaver, Whitehead, Whitfield, Wright—52.

Nays—Abner, Ballinger, Brady, Cline, Davis of Wharton, DeMorse, Erhard, Flanagan, Lockett, McCabe, Mills, Mitchell, Pauli, Rentfro, Reynolds, Russell of Harrison, West—18.

Mr. Norvell reported as follows:

COMMITTEE ROOM, }
AUSTIN, November 22, 1875. }

To the Hon. E. B. Pickett, President of the Convention:

The undersigned member of the Committee on Impeachment begs leave to report that while he concurs with the majority of the committee in all the provisions of the article reported by them, except those contained in section 6, he believes that the provisions of that section are unnecessary, and might be extremely mischievous in their operations, by subjecting the Judges of the District Courts to undue influences, and to frequent harrassing, expensive and groundless prosecutions. He therefore recommends that the said section be stricken out.

Respectfully submitted,   LIPSCOMB NORVELL.

Mr. Whitfield moved to take up " Article —, University." Lost.

On motion of Mr. Barnett, the Convention adjourned to 7 o'clock P. M.

NIGHT SESSION— 7 o'CLOCK.

Convention met pursuant to adjournment; roll called; quorum present.

Mr. Brown offered the following resolution: ·

Resolved, That on the departure of the Hon. John H. Reagan, a member of this body, to take his seat in the Congress of the United States as a Representative from Texas, we, his associates, express our regrets at the separation, and individually extend to him a tender of our personal esteem, with the hope that his career in another field may redound to the honor and welfare of Texas and our common country.

Unanimously adopted.

"Article —, General Provisions," taken up and read third time.

Mr. Ferris offered the following amendment:

In section 6 strike out all of the section down to the word "and," inclusive, in line 42.

Mr. Ballinger offered the following amendment:

In section 56, line 296, after the word " Texas," insert " and to the surviving widows, continuing unmarried, of such soldiers and signers."

Adopted.

Mr. Moore moved to strike out section 20.

Mr. Graves moved to lay the amendment on the table.

Carried by the following vote:

YEAS—Abner, Allison, Arnim, Barnett, Blake, Blassingame, Bruce, Burleson, Cooke of San Saba, DeMorse, Dillard, Dohoney, Fleming, German, Graves, Haynes, Henry of Limestone, Henry of Smith, Holt, Johnson of Franklin, Kilgore, Killough, Lacy, McCormick, McKinney of Denton, Martin of Navarro, Martin of Hunt, Norvell, Nugent, Robertson of Bell, Robison of Fayette, Ross, Scott, Sessions, Spikes, Wade, Whitehead, Whitfield—39.

NAYS—Ballinger, Brady, Chambers, Darnell, Davis of Wharton, Erhard, Ferris, Flanagan, Lockett, McCabe, McKinney of Walker, Mills, Mitchell, Moore, Pauli, Rentfro, Reynolds, Stockdale, West, Wright—20.

Mr. West offered the following amendment:

Strike out in section 52, line 269, the first proviso, and in line 271 strike out the word "also."

Lost by the following vote:

YEAS—Bruce, Burleson, Cooke of San Saba, Darnell, DeMorse, Flanagan, Fleming, Ford, German, Graves, Haynes, Johnson of Franklin, McCormick, McKinney of Denton, Martin of Hunt, Mills, Norvell, Nugent, Rentfro, Reynolds, Sessions, Spikes, Stewart, Wade, West, Whitehead, Whitfield, Wright—28.

NAYS—Allison, Arnim, Ballinger, Barnett, Blake, Blassingame, Brady, Brown, Chambers, Cline, Crawford, Dillard, Dohoney, Erhard, Ferris, Flournoy, Henry of Limestone, Henry of Smith, Holt, Kilgore, Killough, Lacy, Lockett, McKinney of Walker, Martin of Navarro, Nunn, Pauli, Robertson of Bell, Robison of Fayette, Stockdale—30.

Mr. Murphy offered the following amendment:

Strike out section 35, and insert in section 23, in line 121, between the word "counties" and the word "provided," the following words: "and shall have power to pass general and special laws for the inspection of cattle, stock and hides, and for the regulation of brands."

Adopted.

Mr. Darnell offered the following new section:

"Sec. ——. The Legislature shall make provision by law to have all claims and demands justly and lawfully due by the existing State government, or by any of its predecessors, and which shall be presented within one year from a date specified by law, and not thereafter either adjudicated or audited; *provided,* that such claims and demands have not heretofore been either adjudicated or audited; *and provided also,* that said claims and demands originated prior to the 28th day of January,

1861, or subsequent to the 5th day of August, 1865, and that they are not in contravention of the constitution and laws of the United States; and all claims and demands not so presented shall be and remain forever barred." Lost.

Mr. Wright offered the following amendment:

Amend section 18 by adding after the word "and," at the end of the sentence, the following: "*and provided further,* that no cause of action heretofore barred shall be revived."

Adopted.

Mr. Martin, of Navarro, proposed to amend section 21 in line 103, by inserting after the words "stationery and printing," the words "except proclamations and such printing as may be done at the Deaf and Dumb Asylum."

Strike out the words "and distributing," in line 105, and insert the word "and," after the word "printing."

Adopted.

Mr. Fleming offered the following amendment:

Amend section 2, line 269, by striking out all after the word "provided," down to and including the word "family," in line 270, and insert "that the same may include both the place of residence and the place to exercise the calling of the head of a family, and that the same may be on lots not contiguous."

Lost by the following vote:

YEAS—Barnett, Blassingame, Brady, Bruce, Burleson, Chambers, Cooke of San Saba, Darnell, Davis of Brazos, Davis of Wharton, DeMorse, Flanagan, Fleming, Flournoy, Ford, Graves, Haynes, McCormick, McKinney of Denton, Mills, Murphy, Norvell, Nugent, Nunn, Ross, Spikes, Stewart, Stockdale, Wade, West, Whitehead, Whitfield—32.

NAYS—Abernathy, Allison, Arnim, Ballinger, Brown, Cline, Crawford, Dillard, Dohoney, Ferris, German, Henry of Limestone, Henry of Smith, Holt, Kilgore, Lacy, Lockett, McKinney of Walker, Martin of Navarro, Mitchell, Pauli, Rentfro, Reynolds, Robertson of Bell, Robison of Fayette, Scott—26.

Mr. McCormick offerred the following amendment:

After the word "government," in line 104, section 20, add the words "except the judicial department."

Adopted.

Mr. Barnett offered the following amendment:

Amend section 31, line 154, after "Legislature" strike out "shall" and insert "may."

Mr. Bruce proposed to substitute the amendment:

In section 31 strike out after the word "laws," in line 154, down to and including "State," in line 155. Lost.

Mr. Barnett's amendment adopted.

Mr. Dohoney proposed to amend section 45, line 240, by inserting after the word "Treasurer" the words "and a County Surveyor." Also strike out the word "his" when it occurs in lines 240 and 241, and insert "their." Also strike out the word "is," in line 241, and insert "are." Adopted.

Mr. Ferris proposed to amend section 15, line 83, by striking out all after the word "property."

Adopted.

Mr. McCormick moved to strike out all of section 56, after the word "Texas," in line 296.

Lost by the following vote:

YEAS—Brown, Burleson, Cline, Cooke of San Saba, Darnell, DeMorse, Ferris, Flanagan, Fleming, Ford, Graves, Johnson of Franklin, Kilgore, McCormick, McKinney of Walker, Murphy, Norvell, Ramey, Ross, Sessions, Spikes, Wade, Whitehead, Whitfield—24.

NAYS—Abernathy, Allison, Arnim, Ballinger, Barnett, Blassingame, Brady, Bruce, Chambers, Crawford, Davis of Brazos, Dillard, Dohoney, Flournoy, German, Haynes, Henry of Limestone, Henry of Smith, Holt, Lacy, Lockett, McCabe, McKinney of Denton, Martin of Navarro, Mills, Mitchell, Nugent, Nunn, Pauli, Rentfro, Reynolds, Scott, Stewart, Stockdale, Wright—35.

Mr. Holt offered the following amendment:

In section 45, line 240, after the word "shall" strike out "reside," and insert "have an office."

On motion of Mr. Whitfield, the main question was ordered.

Mr. Holt's amendment adopted.

The article then passed by the following vote:

YEAS—Abernathy, Allison, Ballinger, Barnett, Blassingame, Brown, Bruce, Burleson, Chambers, Cooke of San Saba, Crawford, Darnell, Davis of Brazos, Dillard, Dohoney, Ferris, Fleming, Flournoy, Ford, German, Graves, Haynes, Henry of Limestone, Henry of Smith, Holt, Johnson of Franklin, Kilgore, Lacy, McCormick, McKinney of Denton, McKinney of Walker, Martin of Navarro, Martin of Hunt, Murphy, Norvell, Nugent, Nunn, Ramey, Robertson of Bell, Robison of Fayette, Ross, Scott, Sessions, Spikes, Stewart, Stockdale, Wade, Whitehead, Whitfield, Wright—50.

NAYS—Arnim, Brady, Cline, Davis of Wharton, Flanagan, Lockett, McCabe, Mills, Mitchell, Pauli, Rentfro, Reynolds, Weaver—13.

On motion of Mr. Allison, the Convention adjourned to 9 o'clock A. M. to-morrow.

SIXTY-SEVENTH DAY.

HALL OF REPRESENTATIVES, }
AUSTIN, TEXAS, November 23, 1875. }

Convention met pursuant to adjournment; roll called; quorum present. Prayer by the Rev. Mr. Wright, of the Presbyterian Church, at Austin.

Journal of yesterday read and adopted.

Mr. Wade offered the following resolution:

Resolved by this Convention, that George Flournoy, W. P. Ballinger and W. H. Stewart, members of this body, be and they are hereby appointed a committee to supervise the printing of the constitution, and see that the work is done in accordance with the enrolled copy.

Adopted.

On motion of Mr. Fleming, the Secretary of the Convention was instructed to distribute to each delegate two hundred copies of the constitution, instead of two hundred and twenty as per resolution of yesterday, and to deposit two thousand copies with the Secretary of State.

Mr. Brown offered the following ordinance:

"AN ORDINANCE

"SUPPLEMENTARY TO AN ORDINANCE 'TO PROVIDE FOR SUBMITTING THE CONSTITUTION TO A VOTE OF THE PEOPLE, AND FOR A GENERAL ELECTION UNDER ITS PROVISIONS.'

"Section 1. *Be it ordained by the people of Texas, in Convention assembled,* That all returns of the election to be held on the third Tuesday in February, 1876, under the provisions of the ordinance to which this is supplementary, shall be made to the Presiding Justice of each county by the proper election officers, on or before the Saturday next succeeding the said day of election, on which day the Presiding Justice, or in his absence or refusal to act, the District Clerk, shall open, compare and record the votes for all officers, and on the ratification or rejection of the constitution, as is provided for other elections by law. The Presiding Justice or District Clerk, as the case may be, shall immediately make return of the vote for and against the constitution, for all State officers, all judicial officers, and for District Attorneys in the districts in which they are to be chosen. The returns for Governor and other State officers shall be made separately, and addressed to the Speaker of the House of Representatives, to the care of the Secretary of State. The returns for and against the constitution, for Judges of the Supreme, Appellate, and District Courts, and for District Attorneys, shall be addressed to the Secretary of State. On the third Tuesday in March the Governor, Secretary of State and Attorney General shall open, count, record and declare the result in the returns for and against the constitution, for Supreme, Appellate, and District Judges, and for District Attorneys; whereupon, within five days, the Governor shall make proclamation of the result, as to the ratification or rejection of the constitution, and, if the constitution be ratified, issue certificates of election to the persons who may be chosen to the respective judicial and district officers herein referred to.

Passed November 23, 1875.

E. B. PICKETT,
Pres. of the Convention.

LEIGH CHALMERS,
Sec. of the Convention.

Read first time and passed by the following vote:

YEAS—Abernathy, Abner, Allison, Arnim, Ballinger, Barnett, Blake, Blassingame, Brown, Bruce, Burleson, Chambers, Cook of Gonzales, Cooke of San Saba, Darnell, Davis of Brazos, DeMorse, Dillard, Dohoney, Erhard, Ferris, Flanagan, Fleming, Flournoy, Graves, Haynes, Henry of Limestone, Henry of Smith, Holt, Johnson of Collin, Johnson of Franklin, Kilgore, King, Lacy, McCormick, McKinney of Denton, Martin of Navarro, Martin of Hunt, Moore, Murphy, Norvell, Nugent, Nunn, Rentfro, Robertson of Bell, Robison of Fayette, Ross, Russell of Harrison, Sansom, Scott, Sessions, Spikes, Stewart, Wade, Weaver, Whitehead, Whitfield, Wright—58.

NAYS—Mills—1.

"Article —, University," taken up and read second time.

Mr. Lockett proposed to amend section 5, line 58, by striking out "Austin" and inserting "Brenham."

Adopted.

Mr. Whitfield moved to strike out the preamble down to section 1.

Carried.

Mr. Robertson, of Bell, proposed to amend section 1, after "Austin," by inserting "or Salado."

Mr. Scott offered the following as a substitute for the amendment:

Section 1, line 19, strike out the words "to be located at or near the city of Austin," and insert "to be located by a vote of the people of the State."

Mr. Robertson's (of Bell) amendment lost.

The question on Mr. Scott's amendment was put and adopted by the following vote:

YEAS—Abernathy, Allison, Arnim, Barnett, Blake, Blassingame, Brady, Bruce, Burleson, Chambers, Cooke of San Saba, Crawford, DeMorse, Dillard, Dohoney, Ferris, Fleming, German, Graves, Henry of Limestone, Henry of Smith, Johnson of Collin, Johnson of Franklin, Kilgore, Killough, Lacy, McKinney of Denton, Martin of Navarro, Norvell, Rentfro, Robertson of Bell, Scott, Sessions, Smith, Spikes, Wade, Weaver, Whitehead, Wright—39.

NAYS—Abner, Ballinger, Cline, Cook of Gonzales, Erhard, Flanagan, Haynes, King, Lockett, McCormick, Mills, Mitchell, Moore, Murphy, Nugent, Nunn, Pauli, Robison of Fayette, Russell of Harrison, Sansom, Stewart, Stockdale, West, Whitfield—24.

Mr. Wade proposed to amend as follows:

Section 2, line 25, after "sale," insert "or lease." Section 3, line 40, after "sold," insert "or leased." Also, in line 44, after "sold," insert "lease."

Lost.

Mr. McCormick offered the following amendment:

Section 5, line 56, strike out the words "college or," and insert "a."

Lost.

Mr. Sansom proposed to amend line 19 by inserting in lieu of the amendment just adopted the words "at or near the town of Georgetown, county of Williamson."

Lost.

Mr. Darnell offered the following amendment:

Section 4, line 50, insert "Fort Worth."

Lost.

Mr. Graves offered the following amendment:

Section 5, lines 56 and 57, strike out "to be located at or near the city of Austin," and insert "to be located by a vote of the people."

Adopted by the following vote:

YEAS—Abernathy, Allison, Arnim, Blassingame, Brown, Burleson, Cooke of San Saba, DeMorse, Dillard, Dohoney, Ferris, Fleming, Flournoy, German, Graves, Haynes, Henry of Limestone, Holt, Johnson of Collin, Johnson of Fronklin, Kilgore, Killough, Lacy, McKinney of Denton, Martin of Navarro, Martin of Hunt, Norvell, Nugent, Robertson of Bell, Scott, Sessions, Smith, Spikes, Stewart, Wade, Weaver, Whitehead, Whitfield—38.

NAYS—Abner, Brady, Chambers, Cline, Darnell, Davis of Brazos, Erhard, Flanagan, Henry of Smith, Lockett, McCormick, Mills, Mitchell, Nunn, Pauli, Rentfro, Reynolds, Russell of Harrison, Sansom, West, Wright—21.

Mr. Dohoney offered the following amendment to section 4, line 50:

By inserting after "therewith" the words "and there shall be established a branch of said university at some eligible point in Northern Texas." Lost.

Mr. Moore offered the following amendment:

Amend line 19 by adding after the word "located" the words "by commissioners, to be appointed by the Governor, as may be provided by law."

Mr. Dillard moved the main question on engrossing the article.

Carried.

Mr. Moore's amendment lost by the following vote:

YEAS—Abner, Ballinger, Brady, Burleson, Cline, Cooke of San Saba, Davis of Brazos, Erhard, Flournoy, Henry of Smith, Kilgore, King, Lockett, Mitchell, Moore, Murphy, Nunn, Pauli, Rentfro, Russell of Harrison, Sansom, Stewart, Stockdale, Wade, West, Whitfield—27.

NAYS—Abernathy, Allison, Arnim, Barnett, Blassingame, Bruce, Cook of Gonzales, Crawford, Darnell, DeMorse, Dillard, Ferris, Fleming, German, Graves, Haynes, Henry of Limestone, Holt, Johnson of Collin, Johnson of Franklin, Killough, McCormick, McKinney of Denton, Martin of Navarro, Martin of Hunt, Norvell, Nugent, Robertson of Bell, Scott, Sessions, Smith, Spikes, Weaver, Whitehead, Wright—35.

The article was then ordered engrossed by the following vote:

YEAS—Abernathy, Allison, Ballinger, Burleson, Chambers, Cook of Gonzales, Cooke of San Saba, Darnell, Davis of Brazos, DeMorse, Dillard, Ferris, Flournoy, Graves, Haynes, Henry of Smith, Johnson of Franklin, Kilgore, Killough, King, Lacy, Moore, Norvell, Pauli, Ramey, Smith, Stewart, Stockdale, Weaver, Whitehead, Whitfield, Wright—32.

NAYS—Abner, Arnim, Barnett, Blassingame, Brady, Bruce, Cline, Davis of Wharton, Flanagan, Fleming, German, Henry of Limestone, Holt, Lockett, McCabe, McCormick, McKinney of Denton, Martin of Navarro, Martin of Hunt, Mills, Mitchell, Murphy, Nugent, Pauli, Rentfro, Reynolds, Robertson of Bell, Russell of Harrison, Scott, Spikes, Wade—31.

Mr. Whitfield moved to suspend the rules and put the article on its third reading. Carried.

Article read third time.

Mr. Cline moved to strike out all relative to location, in line 19, and insert "to be located near the capital of the State."

Lost by the following vote:

YEAS—Abernathy, Abner, Ballinger, Barnett, Brady, Burleson, Cline, Cook of Gonzales, Cooke of San Saba, Davis of Brazos, Davis of Wharton, Flanagan, Flournoy, Haynes, Kilgore, King, Lockett, McCabe, McCormick, Martin of Navarro, Mills, Mitchell, Moore, Murphy, Nugent, Nunn, Pauli, Rentfro, Reynolds, Russell of Harrison, Sansom, Sessions, Smith, Stewart, Stockdale, West, Whitfield—37.

NAYS—Allison, Arnim, Blassingame, Bruce, Chambers, Crawford, DeMorse, Dillard, Dohoney, Ferris, Fleming, German, Graves, Henry of Limestone, Henry of Smith, Holt, Johnson of Franklin, Killough, Lacy, McKinney of Denton, Martin of Hunt, Norvell, Robertson of Bell, Scott, Spikes, Wade, Weaver, Whitehead—28.

Mr. McCormick offered the following amendment:

Amend line 56 so as to read "of a branch college or university."

Mr. McCabe moved to table the amendment.

Lost, and amendment lost.

Mr. Brady proposed to amend by striking out the word "Austin," in line 58, section 5, and insert "Brenham."

Lost.

The article was put upon its final passage, and passed by the following vote:

YEAS—Abernathy, Allison, Ballinger, Chambers, Cook of Gonzales, Cooke of San Saba, Crawford, Darnell, Davis of Brazos, DeMorse, Dillard, Ferris, Flournoy, Graves, Haynes, Henry of Smith, Johnson of Franklin, Kilgore, Killough, Lacy, Moore, Murphy, Norvell, Nunn, Robertson of Bell, Robison of Fayette, Sansom, Sessions, Smith, Stewart, Stockdale, Wade, West, Whitehead, Whitfield, Wright—35.

NAYS—Abner, Arnim, Barnett, Blassingame, Brady, Bruce, Burleson, Cline, Davis of Wharton, Dohoney, Flanagan, Fleming, German, Holt, King, Lockett, McCabe, McCormick, McKinney of Denton, Martin of Navarro, Martin of Hunt, Mills, Mitchell, Mooris, Nugent, Pauli, Rentfro, Reynolds, Russell of Harrison, Spikes—30.

Mr. Crawford offered the following ordinance:

Be it ordained by the people of Texas, in Convention assembled, That at the election to be holden on the third Tuesday in February, 1876, and at each biennial election thereafter there shall be elected by the qualified voters of the following named counties, a collector of taxes for each of said countites, who shall hold his office for two years, and shall receive such compensation as may be fixed by law, to-wit: Marion, Cass, Bowie, Red River, Lamar, Fannin, Grayson, Hunt, Hopkins, Montgomery, Washington, Brazos, Tarrant, Limestone, Freestone, Navarro, Smith, Grimes.

That this ordinance continue and be in force until the adjournment of the first Legislature after the next United States or other lawful census of the inhabitants of Texas shall be taken and returned.

On motion of Mr. Dillard, the ordinance was made the special order for 2½ o'clock P. M.

"Article —, Qualified Suffrage," was taken up and read a second time.

Mr. Mills moved to lay the ordinance on the table.

Carried by the following vote:

YEAS—Abner, Arnim, Ballinger, Barnett, Blassingame, Bruce, Chambers, Cline, Crawford, Davis of Wharton, Flanagan, Flournoy, German, Graves, Haynes, Henry of Limestone, Johnson of Collin, Johnson of Franklin, Lockett, McCabe, McKinney of Denton, McKinney of Walker, Martin of Navarro, Martin of Hunt, Mills, Mitchell, Norvell, Nugent, Rentfro, Reynolds, Russell of Harrison, Scott, Sessions, Spikes, Stewart, Weaver, Whitehead—37.

NAYS—Allison, Blake, Burleson, Cook of Gonzales, Cooke of San Saba, Darnell, DeMorse, Dillard, Fleming, Holt, Kilgore, Killough, King, Lacy, McCormick, Moore, Murphy, Robertson of Bell, Robison of Fayette, Sansom, Smith, Stockdale, Whitfield, Wright—24.

Mr. Henry, of Smith, was paired off with Mr. Russell, of Wood, but for which he would vote "nay."

"Article —, Private Corporations," taken up and read second time.

[Mr. Dohoney in the chair.]

Mr. German offered the following amendment as a new section:

"Sec. —. No corporation shall issue stock or bonds, except for money paid, labor done, or property actually received, and all fictitious increase of stock shall be void."

Adopted by the following vote:

YEAS—Arnim, Ballinger, Barnett, Blassingame, Bruce, Cline, Cook of Gonzales, DeMorse, Dillard, Flournoy, German, Graves,

Haynes, Holt, Johnson of Collin, Lacy, McCormick, McKinney of Denton, McKinney of Walker, Martin of Hunt, Moore, Nugent, Robertson of Bell, Robison of Fayette, Sansom, Scott, Stewart, Stockdale, Weaver, Wright—29.

NAYS—Abernathy, Abner, Blake, Cooke of San Saba, Flanagan, Fleming, Henry of Limestone, Henry of Smith, Kilgore, Lockett, Norvell, Russell of Harrison, Sessions, Spikes, West, Whitehead—16.

Mr. Nugent offered the following amendment as section 7:

"Sec. 7. Nothing in this article shall be construed to divest or affect rights guaranteed by any existing grant or statute of this State or of the Republic of Texas."

Mr. Ramey submitted the following reports:

COMMITTEE ROOM,　　　}
AUSTIN, November 23, 1875.　}

To the Hon. E. B. Pickett, President of the Convention:

SIR—Your Committee on Engrossed and Enrolled Ordinances would respectfully report that they have examined and compared "An Ordinance fixing the times of holding the District Courts of the State of Texas, and find the same correctly engrossed.

Respectfully,　　　WM. NEAL RAMEY, Chairman.

COMMITTEE ROOM,　　　}
AUSTIN, November 23, 1875.　}

To the Hon. E. B. Pickett, President of the Convention:

SIR—Your Committee on Engrossed and Enrolled Ordinances beg leave to report that they have examined and compared "An ordinance submitting the new constitution to a vote of the people, and for other purposes," and find the same correctly engrossed.

Respectfully,　　　WM. NEAL RAMEY, Chairman.

On motion of Mr. Flanagan, the Convention adjourned to 2¼ o'clock P. M., pending Mr. Nugent's amendment.

EVENING SESSION—2½ o'CLOCK.

Convention met pursuant to adjournment; roll called; quorum present.

Mr. Ramey reported as follows:

COMMITTEE ROOM, }
AUSTIN, November 23, 1875. }

To the Hon. E. B. Pickett, President of the Convention:

SIR—Your Committee on Engrossed and Enrolled Ordinances would respectfully report to your honorable body that they have carefully examined and compared "An ordinance to divide the State of Texas into Judicial Districts," and "An ordinance to determine the effect of ordinances," and find the same correctly engrossed."

Respectfully,   WM. NEAL RAMEY, Chairman.

Special order, viz., Mr. Crawford's ordinance to elect collectors in certain counties taken up, and on motion of Mr. Murphy, postponed till pending business should be disposed of.

"Private Corporations" taken up, pending Mr. Nugent's amendment.

[Mr. Brown in the chair.]

Mr. Stockdale, by leave, submitted the following reports:

COMMITTEE ROOM, }
AUSTIN, November 23, 1875. }

To the Hon. E. B. Pickett, President of the Convention:

SIR—The Committee on Ordinances have duly considered the memorial of I. H. Hutchins and Alfred Grooms, and also an ordinance on the same subject, that is, to provide a means of ascertaining and paying certain claims against the State. The committee instruct me to report that the same subject has been considered by another committee and acted upon. They, therefore, report back the matters before stated, and recommend that they be laid upon the table. Respectfully submitted,

F. S. STOCKDALE, Chairman.

Adopted.

COMMITTEE ROOM, }
AUSTIN, November 23, 1875. }

To the Hon. E. B. Pickett, President of the Convention:

SIR—The Committee on Ordinances, to which was referred an ordinance to validate the judgments of the County Courts of Lamar and Fannin counties, has duly considered the same, and a majority of the committee instruct me to report: That they regard the question involved as judicial, involving private rights, such as the Convention cannot wisely settle. If the court had jurisdiction, its judgments, if otherwise without error, are valid. If the Legislature, at the date of the act conferring jurisdiction upon these courts, had no power to do so, any act of this

Convention, validating these courts and their judgments, would be retroactive. The committee, therefore, return the ordinance, and recommend that it do not pass.

F. S. STOCKDALE, Chairman.

Adopted.

COMMITTEE ROOM, }
AUSTIN, November 23, 1875. }

To the Hon. E. B. Pickett, President of the Convention:

The Committee on Ordinances, to which was referred the ordinance to declare the land certificates issued under the act of March 10, 1875, void, has duly considered the same, and I am instructed to report: That the question as to the validity of said certificates is judicial, and may be investigated by the courts, either under existing laws, or laws to be passed hereafter. The constitution framed by this Convention, if adopted, will prevent such use of the public domain hereafter.

The ordinance is therefore returned, with the recommendation that it do not pass.   F. S. STOCKDALE, Chairman.

Adopted

Mr. Scott moved the main question.

Carried.

Mr. Nugent's amendment was then adopted by the following vote:

YEAS—Abner, Ballinger, Blake, Brady, Brown, Burleson, Cline, Cooke of San Saba, Davis of Brazos, DeMorse, Dohoney, Ferris, Flanagan, Ford, Henry of Smith, Holt, Kilgore, Lockett, Moore, Murphy, Norvell, Nugent, Nunn, Pauli, Rentfro, Reynolds, Russell of Harrison, Sansom, Smith, Stewart, Stockdale, Weaver, West, Whitehead, Whitfield—35.

NAYS—Abernathy, Allison, Arnim, Barnett, Blassingame, Bruce, Chambers, Crawford, Dillard, Fleming, Flournoy, Graves, Haynes, Henry of Limestone, Johnson of Collin, Killough, Lacy, McCormick, McKinney of Walker, Martin of Navarro, Ramey, Robertson of Bell, Robison of Fayette, Ross, Scott, Sessions, Spikes, Wade, Wright—28.

Mr. Stockdale moved that when the Convention adjourns it adjourns to meet at 7 P. M.

Carried.

The question then recurring on the engrossment of the article, it was ordered engrossed by the following vote:

YEAS—Abner, Allison, Arnim, Barnett, Blassingame, Brown, Bruce, Chambers, Crawford, Dillard, Dohoney, Fleming, Flournoy, Graves, Haynes, Henry of Limestone, Johnson of Collin. Johnson of Franklin, Killough, Lacy, McCormick, McKinney of

Denton, McKinney of Walker, Martin of Navarro, Martin of Hunt, Ramey, Rentfro, Robertson of Bell, Robison of Fayette, Ross, Scott, Sessions, Smith, Wade, Whitehead, Whitfield, Wright—37.

NAYS—Ballinger, Blake, Brady, Burleson, Cline, Davis of Brazos, DeMorse, Ferris, Flanagan, Henry of Smith, Holt, Kilgore, Lockett, Mills, Moore, Murphy, Norvell, Nugent, Nunn, Pauli, Russell of Harrison, Sansom, Stewart, Stockdale, Weaver, West—26.

Mr. Allison moved to suspend the rule, and to place the article on its third reading.

Lost.

Mr. Flannagan offered, by leave, the following resolution:

Resolved, First—That the Constitutional Convention of Texas has heard with deep regret the death of the Hon. Henry Wilson, of Massachusetts, Vice-President of the United States.

Second—That in the death of the Hon. Henry Wilson, this country has lost one of its most illustrious citizens, a profound statesman, a self-sacrificing and zealous patriot, a pure and distinguished public servant.

Third—That the President of this Convention forward copies of this resolution to the President of the United States and to the family of the deceased.

Fourth—That this Convention, as a tribute to the deceased, do now stand adjourned.

Adopted unanimously.

NIGHT SESSION—7 o'CLOCK.

Convention met pursuant to adjournment; roll called; quorum present.

Mr. Ramey reported as follows:

COMMITTEE ROOM, }
AUSTIN, November 23, 1875. }

To the Hon. E. B. Pickett, President of the Convention:

SIR—Your Committee on Engrossed and Enrolled Ordinances beg leave to report to your honorable body that they have examined and compared "Article ——, University," and an ordinance supplementary to an ordinance "to provide for submitting the constitution to a vote of the people, and for a general election under its provisions," and find the same correctly engrossed.

Respectfully,   WM. NEAL RAMEY, Chairman.

Special order, viz: ordinance authorizing the election of Collectors of Taxes, taken up, and postponed for the present.

Municipal Corporations taken up and read second time.

Mr. Crawford offered the following amendment:

Add to section 4, "and all license and occupation tax levied, and all fines, forfeitures, penalties and other dues accruing to cities and towns shall be collectable only in current money."

Adopted.

Mr. McCormick proposed to strike out section 10.

Adopted.

Mr. Robertson, of Bell, moved to strike out section 11.

Mr. Nugent proposed to amend the section by striking out "a majority," and inserting "two-thirds," in line 70.

Mr. Graves moved to close debate on the pending amendments.

Carried.

Mr. Nugent's amendment adopted.

The question recurring on the adoption of Mr. Robertson's (of Bell) amendment, it was lost by the following vote:

YEAS—Abernathy, Arnim, Blassingame, Bruce, Cooke of San Saba, Flournoy, German, Graves, Henry of Limestone, Holt, Johnson of Collin, McKinney of Denton, Martin of Navarro, Murphy, Norvell, Robertson of Bell, Robison of Fayette, Scott, Sessions, Spikes, Whitehead, Wright—22.

NAYS—Allison, Ballinger, Barnett, Brady, Brown, Burleson, Chambers, Cline, Cooley, Crawford, Davis of Brazos, DeMorse, Dohoney, Ferris, Fleming, Ford, Haynes, Henry of Smith, Johnson of Franklin, Kilgore, Lacy, McCabe, McCormick, McKinney of Walker, McLean, Martin of Hunt, Mills, Mitchell, Moore, Nugent, Nunn, Pauli, Rentfro, Ross, Smith, Stewart, Stockdale, West, Whitfield—39.

Mr. Blassingame moved to strike out section 8.

Lost by the following vote:

YEAS—Blassingame, Bruce, Crawford, Dillard, Dohoney, German, Graves, Holt, Johnson of Collin, Lacy, McKinney of Denton, Martin of Hunt, Rentfro, Robertson of Bell, Scott—15.

NAYS—Abernathy, Arnim, Ballinger, Barnett, Brady, Brown, Burleson, Chambers, Cline, Cooke of San Saba, Cooley, Davis of Brazos, DeMorse, Ferris, Fleming, Flournoy, Ford, Haynes, Henry of Smith, Kilgore, McCormick, McKinney of Walker, McLean, Martin of Navarro, Mills, Moore, Murphy, Nugent, Nunn, Pauli, Robison of Fayette, Sessions, Smith, Stewart, Stockdale, West, Whitehead, Whitfield—38.

Mr. Brown proposed to amend section 2, in lines 3 and 4, by striking out the words "the removal of county seats."

Adopted.

Also, add to line 58 the words "and from taxation."

Adopted.

Mr. Ferris offered the following, to come in at the end of Mr. Brown's amendment just adopted:

"*Provided,* nothing herein shall prevent the enforcement of the vendor's liens, the mechanic's or builder's lien or other liens now existing."

Adopted.

Mr. Moore moved to strike out, in line 21, the word "five," and insert "two and one-half."

Mr. Flournoy moved to amend the amendment by inserting "two and one-half" instead of "three."

Lost, and Mr. Moore's amendment adopted.

Mr. Dillard offered the following amendment:

Section 8, add after "Gulf Coast," in line 46, "Red River, Sulphur, Caddo Lake and its tributaries."

Mr. Stockdale proposed to amend the amendment as follows:

Amend by inserting "all other rivers and lakes in the State."

Lost.

Mr. Dillard's amendment lost by the following vote:

YEAS—Blassingame, Brady, Crawford, DeMorse, Dillard, Dohoney, Holt, McLean, Rentfro, Whitfield—10.

NAYS—Abner, Allison, Arnim, Brown, Bruce, Burleson, Chambers, Cline, Cooke of San Saba, Cooley, Davis of Brazos, Fleming, Flournoy, Ford, German, Graves, Haynes, Henry of Limestone, Henry of Smith, Johnson of Collin, Kilgore, Lacy, McCormick, McKinney of Denton, McKinney of Walker, Martin of Navarro, Martin of Hunt, Mills, Moore, Murphy, Norvell, Nugent, Nunn, Pauli, Robertson of Bell, Robison of Fayette, Ross, Scott, Sessions, Smith, Spikes, Stockdale, West, Whitehead—44.

Mr. Robertson, of Bell, proposed to amend section 11 by adding "*provided,* that said tax shall never exceed more than one-fourth of one per cent. in any year."

Lost.

On motion of Mr. Nunn, the main question was ordered, and the article ordered engrossed by the following vote:

YEAS—Abernathy, Allison, Arnim, Ballinger, Barnett, Brown, Burleson, Cline, Crawford, DeMorse, Dillard, Ferris, Flournoy, Ford, Graves, Haynes, Henry of Limestone, Henry of Smith, Johnson of Franklin, McCormick, McKinney of Walker, McLean, Martin of Navarro, Moore, Murphy, Norvell, Nugent, Nunn, Ross, Sessions, Smith, Stewart, Stockdale, West, Whitehead, Whitfield—36.

NAYS—Blassingame, Brady, Bruce, Cooke of San Saba, Cooley, Dohoney, Fleming, German, Holt, Johnson of Collin, Kilgore, Lacy, McKinney of Denton, Martin of Hunt, Mills, Pauli, Rentfro, Robertson of Bell, Robison of Fayette, Scott, Spikes—21.

[Mr. Stockdale in the chair.]

"Article —, Public Lands and Land Office," taken up and read third time.

Mr. Dohoney offered the following amendment:

Amend section 2, in line 23, by striking out "of" and inserting the words "or in."

Adopted.

The article then passed by the following vote:

YEAS—Abernathy, Allison, Arnim, Barnett, Brown, Burleson, Crawford, Davis of Brazos, Dillard, Dohoney, Ferris, Flournoy, Ford, Graves, Haynes, Henry of Limestone, Holt, Kilgore, McKinney of Walker, Martin of Navarro, Moore, Nunn, Scott, Sessions, Smith, Spikes, Stewart, Stockdale, West, Whitehead, Whitfield—31.

NAYS—Blassingame, Brady, Bruce, Chambers, Cline, De Morse, Fleming, German, Henry of Smith, Johnson of Collin, McCormick, McKinney of Denton, McLean, Martin of Hunt, Mills, Mitchell, Norvell, Nugent, Pauli, Rentfro, Robertson of Bell, Robison of Fayette, Ross—23.

Mr. Brown, by leave, offered the following resolution:

Resolved, That there shall be printed for the use of the Convention, in hand bill form, 500 copies of the ordinance submitting the constitution to a vote of the people, and the ordinance supplementary thereto, both duly authenticated by the President and Secretary of the Convention.

Adopted.

On motion of Mr. Davis, of Brazos, the rule was suspended, and "Article —, Municipal Corporations," was taken up and read third time.

Mr. Martin, of Hunt, offered the following amendment:

Amend section 8 by adding "*provided,* such appropriation shall only be made by two-thirds vote of both houses of the Leglature."

Lost.

Mr. Brady moved to adjourn to 9'clock A. M. to-morrow.

Lost.

The article then passed by the following vote:

YEAS—Abernathy, Allison, Arnim, Ballinger, Barnett, Brown, Burleson, Cline, Cooke of San Saba, Crawford, Davis of Brazos, DeMorse, Ferris, Fleming, Flournoy, Graves, Haynes, Henry of

Limestone, Henry of Smith, Johnson of Collin, Johnson of Franklin, Kilgore, Lacy, McCormick, McKinney of Walker, McLean, Martin of Navarro, Moore, Norvell, Nugent, Nunn, Rentfro, Robison of Fayette, Ross, Sessions, Smith, Stewart, West, Whitehead, Whitfield—40.

NAYS—Blassingame, Brady, Bruce, Dohoney, German, Holt, McKinney of Denton, Martin of Hunt, Mills, Pauli, Robertson of Bell, Scott, Spikes—13.

On motion of Mr. Pickett, the rule was suspended and "Article—, Impeachment," was taken up and read second time.

Mr. Norvell moved to strike out section 6.

[The President resumed the chair.]

Mr. Dohoney offered the following amendment:

Strike out the words "seven citizens of the State, three of whom, at least, shall be lawyers," and insert the words "lawyers practicing in the courts held by such Judge."

Adopted.

Mr. Norvell's amendment lost by the following vote:

YEAS—Barnett, Blassingame, Brady, Bruce, Burleson, Cline, Ferris, Graves, Haynes, Johnson of Collin, McKinney of Denton, Martin of Navarro, Mills, Norvell, Nugent, Rentfro, Robertson of Bell, Robison of Fayette, Sessions, Spikes, Stewart, Wade, Whitehead—24.

NAYS—Abernathy, Abner, Allison, Arnim, Ballinger, Chambers, Cooke of San Saba, Davis of Brazos, DeMorse, Dillard, Dohoney, Fleming, Flournoy, Henry of Limestone, Henry of Smith, Holt, Johnson of Franklin, Kilgore, Lacy, McCormick, McKinney of Walker, McLean, Murphy, Nunn, Reagan, Scott, Stockdale, West, Whitfield—29.

The article was then ordered engrossed, by the following vote:

YEAS—Abernathy, Allison, Arnim, Ballinger, Barnett, Blassingame, Burleson, Chambers, Cook of San Saba, Davis of Brazos, DeMorse, Dillard, Dohoney, Ferris, Fleming, Flournoy, Graves, Haynes, Henry of Limestone, Henry of Smith, Holt, Johnson of Collin, Johnson of Franklin, Kilgore, Lacy, McCormick, McKinney of Walker, McLean, Murphy, Nunn, Ramey, Robison of Fayette, Ross, Scott, Sessions, Stockdale, Wade, Whitehead, Whitfield—39.

NAYS—Brady, Cline, McKinney of Denton, Martin of Navarro, Mitchell, Norvell, Nugent, Rentfro, Robertson of Bell, Spikes, Stewart, West—12.

Mr. Dillard moved to suspend the rule, and place the article on its third and final reading.

Carried by the following vote:

YEAS—Abernathy, Allison, Arnim, Ballinger, Barnett, Blassingame, Burleson, Chambers, Cooke of San Saba, Davis of Brazos, Dillard, Dohoney, Fleming, Flournoy, Graves, Haynes, Henry of Limestone, Henry of Smith, Holt, Johnson of Collin, Johnson of Franklin, Kilgore, Lacy, McCormick, McKinney of Walker, McLean, Martin of Navarro, Moore, Murphy, Nunn, Robison of Fayette, Ross, Scott, Sessions, Spikes, Stockdale, Wade, Whitehead, Whitfield—39.

NAYS—Abner, Brady, Bruce, Cline, Mills, Mitchell, Norvell, Nugent, Rentfro, Robertson of Bell, Stewart, West—12.

The question then recurring on the final passage of the article, it was passed by the following vote:

YEAS—Abernathy, Allison, Arnim, Ballinger, Barnett, Blassingame, Burleson, Chambers, Cooke of San Saba, Davis of Brazos, Dillard, Dohoney, Ferris, Fleming, Flournoy, Graves, Hayes, Henry of Limestone, Henry of Smith, Holt, Johnson of Collin, Johnson of Franklin, Kilgore, McCormick, McKinney of Walker, McLean, Moore, Murphy, Nunn, Robison of Fayette, Ross, Scott, Sessions, Stockdale, Wade, Whitehead, Whitfield—37.

NAYS—Abner, Cline, German, Lacy, McKinney of Denton, Martin of Navarro, Mills, Norvell, Nugent, Robertson of Bell, Smith, Stewart, West—13.

Mr. West moved to adjourn to 9 o'clock A. M to-morrow.

Lost by the following vote:

YEAS—Ballinger, Bruce, Cline, Cooke of San Saba, Ferris, Johnson of Collin, Kilgore, McCabe, Martin of Hunt, Murphy, Nugent, Nunn, Rentfro, Stewart, Stockdale, West—16.

NAYS—Abernathy, Abner, Allison, Arnim, Barnett, Blassingame, Brady, Burleson, Chambers, Davis of Brazos, Dillard, Dohoney, Fleming, Flournoy, German, Graves, Haynes, Henry of Limestone, Henry of Smith, Holt, Lacy, McCormick, McKinney of Denton, McKinney of Walker, McLean, Martin of Navarro, Mills, Moore, Norvell, Roberston of Bell, Robison of Fayette, Ross, Scott, Sessions, Spikes, Wade, Whitehead, Whitfield—38.

Mr. Scott moved to suspend the rules and take up the article on private corporations.

Mr. West moved to adjourn to 9 o'clock A. M. to-morrow.

A call of the Convention was demanded.

Absent—Abner, Blake, Brown, Cook of Gonzales, Cooley, Crawford, Darnell, DeMorse, Erhard, Flanagan, Ford, Killough, King, Lockett, McCabe, Martin of Hunt, Pauli, Ramey, Reynolds, Russell of Harrison, Sansom, Smith, Weaver, and Wright.

On motion of Mr. Kilgore, the call was suspended, and the

motion to suspend the rules and take up "Article ——, Private Corporations," carried by the following vote:

YEAS—Abernathy, Allison, Arnim, Ballinger, Barnett, Blassingame, Brady, Bruce, Burleson, Chamebrs, Cooke of San Saba, Davis of Brazos, Dillard, Dohoney, Ferris, Fleming, Flournoy, German, Graves, Haynes, Henry of Limestone, Holt, Johnson of Collin, Johnson of Franklin, Kilgore, Lacy, McCormick, McKinney of Denton, McKinney of Walker, McLean, Martin of Navarro, Martin of Hunt, Moore, Murphy, Norvell, Nugent, Nunn, Rentfro, Robertson of Bell, Robison of Fayette, Ross, Scott, Sessions, Spikes, Stewart, Stockdale, Wade, West, Whitehead, Whitfield—50.

NAYS—Cline, Mills—2.

Mr. Scott moved the main question on the passage of the article.

Carried by the following vote:

YEAS—Abernathy, Allison, Arnim, Ballinger, Barnett, Blassingame, Brady, Bruce, Burleson, Chambers, Cooke of San Saba, Davis of Brazos, Dillard, Ferris, Fleming, Flournoy, German, Graves, Haynes, Henry of Limestone, Holt, Johnson of Collin, Lacy, McKinney of Denton, McKinney of Walker, McLean, Martin of Navarro, Murphy, Norvell, Nugent, Nunn, Rentfro, Robertson of Bell, Robison of Fayette, Ross, Scott, Sessions, Wade, Whitehead, Whitfield—40.

NAYS—Cline, Dohoney, Henry of Smith, Kilgore, Mills, Mitchell, Moore, Stewart, Stockdale, West—10.

The article was then read third time and passed by the following vote:

YEAS—Abernathy, Allison, Arnim, Barnett, Blassingame, Bruce, Burleson, Chambers, Cooke of San Saba, Dillard, Dohoney, Fleming, Flournoy, German, Graves, Haynes, Henry of Limestone, Johnson of Collin, Johnson of Franklin, Lacy, McCormick, McKinney of Denton, McKinney of Walker, McLean, Martin of Navarro, Ramey, Robertson of Bell, Robison of Fayette, Ross, Scott, Sessions, Spikes, Wade, Whitehead, Whitfield—35.

NAYS—Ballinger, Brady, Cline, Davis of Brazos, Ferris, Henry of Smith, Holt, Kilgore, Mills, Mitchell, Moore, Murphy, Norvell, Nugent, Nunn, Rentfro, Stewart, Stockdale, West—19.

Mr. Rentfro moved to adjourn to 9 o'clock A. M. to-morrow.

Lost.

Mr. Norvell offered the following resolution:

Resolved, That the following shall be incorporated in the constitution as a section of the Judicial Department:

"Sec. —. The Judges of the Supreme Court, Court of Appeals, and District Courts, shall be removed by the Governor, on the address of two-thirds of each house of the Legislature, for willful neglect of duty, incompetency, habitual drunkenness, oppression in office, or other reasonable cause, which shall not be sufficient ground for impeachment; *provided, however,* that the cause or causes for which such removal shall be required shall be stated at length in such address, and entered on the journals of each house; *and provided further,* that the cause or causes shall be notified to the judge so intended to be removed, and he shall be admitted to a hearing in his own defense before any vote for such address shall pass; and in all such cases the vote shall be taken by yeas and nays, and entered on the journal of each house respectively."

Mr. Norvell moved to suspend the rules and take up the resolution for consideration.

Carried by the following vote:

YEAS—Allison, Arnim, Ballinger, Barnett, Blassingame, Bruce, Burleson, Chambers, Cooke of San Saba, Dillard, Fleming, Flournoy, German, Graves, Haynes, Henry of Limestone, Henry of Smith, Holt, Johnson of Collin, Johnson of Franklin, Kilgore, Lacy, McKinney of Denton, McKinney of Walker, McLean, Martin of Navarro, Moore, Morris, Murphy, Nugent, Nunn, Ramey, Robertson of Bell, Robison of Fayette, Ross, Scott, Sessions, Spikes, Stockdale, Wade, West, Whitehead, Whitfield—43.

NAYS—Abernathy, Brady, Cline, McCormick, Mills, Mitchell, Rentfro—7.

Resolution read second time.

Mr. Dillard moved the main question.

Carried, and resolution ordered engrossed.

Mr. Stockdale submitted the following protest:

Mr. President—As a delegate, responsible to my own conscience for the proper performance of my duty to the State, I beg, respectfully, to enter upon the journal this my protest against the passage of the "Articles on Railroads and Private Corporations." I protest for this: That the said articles can not lawfully effect their assumed purpose as to existing railroad and other private corporations, while no existing corporations can be affected—they being protected by the Constitution of the United States and their charters, which are contracts between the State and the corporators. The articles are a sure prevention of any further investment in railroads and other like works for public improvement; and of the construction of all wharves and bridges, so necessary to the general public and private convenience.

Respectfully submitted,   F. S. STOCKDALE,
Delegate from Calhoun County,
C. S. WEST,
J. B. MURPHY,
C. B. KILGORE.

On motion of Mr. Dillard, the rule was suspended, and Mr. Norvell's resolution read third time, and passed by the following vote:

YEAS—Allison, Arnim, Ballinger, Barnett, Blassingame, Bruce, Burleson, Chambers, Cooke of San Saba, Davis of Brazos, Dillard, Ferris, Fleming, Flournoy, German, Graves, Haynes, Henry of Limestone, Holt, Johnson of Collin, Johnson of Franklin, Kilgore, Lacy, McKinney of Denton, McKinney of Walker, McLean, Martin of Navarro, Moore, Murphy, Norvell, Nugent, Nunn, Ramey, Robertson of Bell, Robison of Fayette, Scott, Sessions, Spikes, Stewart, Stockdale, Wade, West, Whitehead, Whitfield—44.

NAYS—Abernathy, Brady, Henry of Smith, McCormick, Mills, Mitchell, Rentfro, Ross—8.

On motion of Mr. Chambers, the Convention adjourned to 9 o'clock A. M. to-morrow.

SIXTY-EIGHTH DAY.

HALL OF REPRESENTATIVES, ⎫
AUSTIN, TEXAS, November 24, 1875. ⎰

Convention met pursuant to adjournment; roll called; quorum present. Prayer by the Rev. Mr. Wright, of the Presbyterian Church, at Austin.

Journal of yesterday read and adopted.

Mr. West submitted the following protest:

AUSTIN, November 24, 1875.

To the Hon. E. B. Pickett, President of the Convention:

SIR—The undersigned respectfully ask permission to have entered on the journal their protest against certain parts of the homestead clause, as contained in the article on General Provisions, placing conditions on the use of the homestead. They believe said clause ambiguous, obscure, unfair and unjust, in attempting to make an invidious discrimination between a country and a town homestead. It places, in our opinion, limitations and restrictions on the use of the homestead that have never before been placed on it by any law or constitution. It makes a part of the homestead, under certain circumstances, liable to forced sale for the payment of ordinary debts, and prevents widows, artisans, mechanics and persons of small means from using homestead lots fully and without restriction for their support. The clause subjects, in certain contingencies, the homestead to forfeiture and sale, without the consent of the husband and wife.

Believing the clause unjust and unusual, and calculated to impair the homestead right, we beg to enter our protest against it.

Respectfully submitted,   C. S. WEST,
                                           B. H. DAVIS,
                                           T. L. NUGENT,
                                           B. D. MARTIN,
                                           S. H. RUSSELL,
                                           LIPSCOMB NORVELL,
                                           W. W. WHITEHEAD,
                                           N. H. DARNELL,
                                           R. B. RENTFRO,
                                           G. PAULI,
                                           E. W. BRADY,
                                           HENRY C. KING,
                                           JOHN S. FORD.

Mr. DeMorse submitted the following protest:

AUSTIN, November 24, 1875. ⎱
CONVENTION HALL,   ⎰

To the Hon. E. B. Pickett, President of the Convention:

The undersigned, delegate from Red River county, desires to enter his protest against the passage of the Ordinance on Private Corporations, which has been hurried through by suspension of the rules, without affording delegates such time to scrutinize its provisions as its effect upon important interests demanded. The undersigned had prepared, and desired to offer, an amendment qualifying the arbitrary assumptions of the third section, and affirming the control of the State over private corporations only to the extent that rights were obtained by such corporations from concession by the State; denying that the Legislature can rightfully control the property of private citizens used solely in their own interest and without infringement upon the rights of other citizens, or prevention or interference with the use, by other citizens, of the public highways, whether of land or water.

The undersigned deems the section referred to, nugatory, in so far as it affects private rights, but is unwilling that this Conven tion should assume an attitude inconsistent with vested rights, which have not been conceded as a matter favor by the State.

CHARLES DEMORSE,

Delegate from Red River, Titus, Franklin and Morris.

Mr. Mills introduced the following ordinance:

"*Be it ordained, etc.,* That the Board of Equalization, pro- vided for in article ——, section ——, of the present constitution, shall have power, and is hereby authorized, to modify erroneous and excessive valuations of property rendered for the assessment of taxes since the year 1870; and that the State, county and special taxes for each year be computed on such modified valua- tion, and paid to the Sheriff of the county in which the property is situated, and that the party or parties so paying shall receive duplicate tax receipts, one of which he shall forward to the Comptroller of Public Accounts; and that in case suit has been instituted for the taxes on the original assessment or judgment obtained, the owner shall pay all the costs of suit; and that this ordinance be in force and take effect from and after its passage, and continue in force for six months."

Read the first time.

Mr. Mills moved to suspend the rules and take up the ordi- nance.

Lost.

Mr. Brown offered the following resolutions:

Resolved, That on the enrollment of the constitution it shall be first signed by the President of the Convention, and attested by the Secretary. The roll of members shall then be called alphabetically, and each member may sign the instrument, add- ing the name of the county of his residence; *provided,* that in view of the facts that the Hon. Nicholas H. Darnell is the oldest member of the Convention, and the only member of this body who participated in the formation of the first constitution of Texas as a State of the Union, his name shall be first called, and the Hon. Joel Robison and B. Blake, sign with him.

Resolved, That the ordinances of the Convention shall be authenticated by the signature of the President, attested by the Secretary.

Resolved, That the constitution and ordinances, when thus duly authenticated, shall be deposited in the office of the Secre- tary of State, by the President of the Convention, to be therein preserved among the archives of the State; and that members of the Convention now absent shall have the right to sign the constitution at any time before the promulgation, by the Governor, of its ratification.

Adopted.

Resolved, That instead of twenty thousand there shall be printed forty thousand copies of the constitution and ordinances in English, two thousand of which shall be deposited in the office of the Secretary of State, and thirty-eight thousand distributed equally among the members of the Convention by the Secretary, as heretofore provided.

Adopted.

Resolved, That in closing its labors this Convention recommends to all future Legislatures the propriety, wisdom, and justice of having printed for distribution among the people, through the County Clerks, such number of copies of the general laws of each session, half bound, as will be equal to one-tenth of the number of voters in the State, in order that the people may always have an opportunity of understanding the laws of the State.

Adopted.

Mr. Dillard submitted the following ordinance:

WHEREAS, The Senate and House of Representatives of the Republic of Texas, in Congress assembled, did, on the 26th day of January, A. D. 1839, create and incorporate a college at De-Kalb, in Red River county, to be known as the "DeKalb College;" and

WHEREAS, By said act four leagues of the public lands of Texas were granted to said college, "to be located upon any vacant lands in the Republic of Texas;" and

WHEREAS, James Browning, David . . . ., James N. Smith, Richard Graham, Wilson . . . ., John H. Dyer, Jackson Titus, Hiram H. Allen, Richard Ellis, Isaac Jones, George Wright, John Fowler, Holland Jones, and their successors, were appointed trustees of said College of DeKalb, and were constituted a body politic and corporate in deed and law; and

WHEREAS, The trustees of said college had four leagues of land surveyed, in compliance with the act of 26th of January, 1839; and

WHEREAS, By act of Texas Congress, passed February 3, A. D. 1845, the Commissioner of the General Land Office was required to issue patents upon the field notes of such surveys, in the same manner and form as if certificates had been issued for the same by the Board of Land Commissioners, to the trustees of said institution; and

WHEREAS, From some cause not known, said patents were never issued; and

WHEREAS, By act of the Legislature of Texas, passed the 10th of February, 1852, " requiring the field notes of all surveys made previous to the passage of this act, to be made out and returned in the manner now required by law, to the General Land Office, on of before the 31st day of August, 1853, or to become null and void; and the same surveys shall become vacant land, and be subject to be located and surveyed, as in other cases, by any person holding a genuine land certificate or other legal evidence or claim to land;" and

WHEREAS, By said act of 10th of February, 1852, said College of DeKalb lost the claim to all lands which had been surveyed; therefore

Be it ordained by the people of Texas, in Convention assembled, That the Commissioner of the General Land Office be and is hereby authorized and directed to issue to the trustees of " DeKalb College " certificates for four leagues of land, to be located upon any vacant land in the State.

Read first time and passed by the following vote:

YEAS—Abernathy, Ballinger, Barnett, Blake, Brady, Brown, Burleson, Chambers, Cline, Cook of Gonzales, Crawford, Darnell, DeMorse, Dillard, Henry of Limestone, Johnson of Franklin, Kilgore, Lockett, McKinney of Walker, Martin of Navarro, Mills, Mitchell, Pauli, Rentfro, Russell of Harrison, Sessions, Smith, Stockdale, Weaver, Whitehead, Whitfield, Wright—32.

NAYS—Blassingame, Bruce, Davis of Brazos, Graves, Henry of Smith, Lacy. McCormick, Moore, Norvell, Nugent, Robertson of Bell, Robison of Fayette, Stewart, West—14.

Mr. Brady offered the following resolution:

WHEREAS, Morris Jahn, a citizen of Texas, was convicted of manslaughter, and was sentenced to confinement in the State Penitentiary, which sentence he has fully and faithfully served out, and has been discharged therefrom; and

WHEREAS, The said Morris Jahn is now, and has been since his release from confinement in the penitentiary, laboring under the disqualifications in regard to voting at any election held in this State, and in regard to giving testimony in courts of justice, both of which rights he is prohibited from exercising because of having been convicted of a felony; and

WHEREAS, The said Morris Jahn is now, and has been ever since his release from confinement in the penitentiary, a resident of Grimes county, and has proven himself to be now a good citizen, worthy of being restored to all the rights and privileges

51

which he enjoyed as a citizen and freeman of Texas; therefore be it

Resolved by the people of Texas, in Convention assembled, That the said Morris Jahn, a resident citizen of Grimes county, be, and he is hereby, relieved from all disabilities and disqualifications he may have incurred or suffered by reason of having been once convicted of a felony.

Lost by the following vote:

YEAS—Brady, Brown, Cline, DeMorse, Dillard, Lockett, McKinney of Walker, Mills, Mitchell, Pauli, Rentfro, Reynolds, Russell of Harrison, Smith, Whitehead, Whitfield—16.

NAYS—Mr. President, Abernathy, Arnim, Barnett, Blake, Blassingame, Bruce, Burleson, Chambers, Cooke of San Saba, Crawford, Graves, Henry of Limestone, Henry of Smith, Holt, Johnson of Collin, Kilgore, Killough, Lacy, McCormick, McKinney of Denton, Moore, Norvell, Nugent, Robertson of Bell, Sessions, Stewart, Stockdale, Weaver, Wright—30.

On motion of Mr. Whitfield, the Convention adjourned to 2½ o'clock P. M.

EVENING SESSION—2½ o'CLOCK.

Convention met pursuant to adjournment; roll called; quorum present.

Mr. West submitted the following report:

AUSTIN, November 24, 1875.

To the Hon. E. B. Pickett, President of the Convention:

The undersigned protests against the passage of the Judiciary Article, because he believes that it will not answer the purpose designed. Instead of reducing, he believes it will be found to have increased the expense of the administration of justice; instead of diminishing, it will be found to have increased the number of officers. The system is believed to be cumbersome, complex and when put to the test of experiment, will be found impracticable.

In addition to all this, the salaries have been so much reduced that the best legal talent of the State is virtually excluded from the bench, and thus, in its most vital point, the best interests of the State will suffer from the action of this body.

C. S. WEST.

COMMITTEE ROOM, ⎱
AUSTIN, November 24, 1875. ⎰

To the Hon. E. B. Pickett, President of the Convention:

SIR—Your select committee, to which was referred a resolution concerning depredations upon the people of the Texas frontier by bands of marauders, organized beyond the limit thereof to invade the territory of the United States, and murder and plunder its citizens, have had the same under consideration, and beg leave to report:

That they find that since the time of the annexation of Texas to the United States, and especially since the termination of the war between Mexico and our government, resulting in the acquisition by us of an immense and valuable territory, theretofore belonging to the Republic of Mexico, the people of the latter government, especially those of the northern and frontier States of Mexico, have entertained feelings of bitter hostility toward Americans. They have also coupled with that sentiment a vehement desire to avenge their defeats and retrieve their losses. This feelings has been evinced in various ways.

They have robbed, murdered and maltreated citizens of the United States who were residing or traveling in Mexico, in violation of positive treaty stipulations, the laws of nations, and the laws of humanity; they have passed legislative enactments hostile to the interests of Americans living adjacent to Mexican States, injurious to American commerce, and entailing great damage to and upon the revenues of the United States; they have set on foot expeditions upon Mexican soil, or allowed the same to be done, for the purpose of invading the territory of the United States, and of waging a depredatory war upon her citizens and their property; and they have made themselves the allies of Indians whose mode of warfare respects neither age nor sex. These acts of savage aggression have been perpetrated upon our peaceful citizens for more than twenty years.

In 1859 they became open and unconcealed. During that year Juan Nepomuceno Cortina organized an expedition, mostly in the Mexican State of Tamaulipas, made a descent upon the territory of Texas, and captured the city of Brownsville. He murdered unsuspecting citizens in cold blood, robbed houses, and committed other acts of violence. This outlaw prosecuted an inhuman war upon the flag and the people of the United States for eight months. He did so with the knowledge, tacit consent, and secret co-operation of the Mexican authorities. He drew supplies of men and means from Mexico, and used her territory for the purpose of reorganizing his forces, depositing his stolen property, and as an asylum for himself and followers.

No attempt was then made by the government of Mexico to restrain her citizens. When once upon her soil they were free from arrest and molestation, and received the protection of her laws and her autthorities.

This robber chief was the representative man of that day in Mexico. The masses recognized him as the champion of their sentiments of hatred and revenge. He was their favorite, because his hands were stained with American blood. He rose in the estimation of the authorities. They rewarded crime by promoting him; and he is now a brigadier general in the Mexican army. During the presidency of Mr. Juarez he was sent to the Rio Grande as the commander of the line of the Bravo, and the representative of the supreme government of Mexico. He resumed his position as the leader and protector of the desperadoes, thieves and criminals who were depredating upon the people of Texas. He was retained on the Rio Grande against the protests of General McCooke, of the United States army, and of an indignant people he had outraged. His presence upon our border in any official capacity was an insult to the government and the people of the United States.

He was the first to give coherence and form to the Mexican feeling of hostility to Americans; and his admiring countrymen have faithfully followed his example.

Notwithstanding General Cortina had been recently arrested for disobedience of orders to his government, and for nothing more, yet the border war he inaugurated has been persistently and energetically carried on by his followers. We are informed, and believe it true, that he will soon be upon the Rio Grande to rejoin his plundering partisans, and to finish a historical record which he has written in letters of blood.

The *Zona Libre,* or free belt, was first established by a decree of the Governor of the State of Tamaulipas. It provided that goods, wares, and merchandise could be introduced and sold free of duty, in a belt six miles in width and about three hundred in length. It commenced at the mouth of the Rio Grande and extended to the upper boundary line of the State of Tamaulipas. This decree received the sanction of the supreme government of Mexico, notwithstanding it is in direct violation of the constitution thereof. Its object is expressed on its face. It was a blow aimed at the commerce and the merchants of the United States. It encouraged smuggling, and did much to concentrate upon the Rio Grande a horde of lawless Mexican adventurers. It has shifted business from the American to the Mexican side, and has well nigh ruined American traders in the valley of the Rio Grande. The custom-house records show that goods introduced by the way of Brazos Santiago, and the mouth of the Rio

Grande previous to the late Civil War between the States amounted to more than $10,000,000 per year, and that the amount now scarcely exceeds $3,000,000 annually. The government of the United States requested that of Mexico to abolish a system which discriminated against her commerce and her interests, and produced to many results prejudical to her revenues and the welfare of her people. The answer to this just demand was an extension of the free belt to about double its former length.

The border warfare which has been waged upon the territory of the United States and the people of Texas and their property, has been characterized by savage atrocities. Men have been murdered in cold blood in almost every conceivable way—they have been shot, stabbed, burned alive and strangled; and their bodies have been indecently mutilated; women have been captured, and their persons violated; captive children have been held and sold as slaves. In the latter enormities the Mexicans and Indians have co-operated. In proof whereof, the evidence taken before the United States Frontier Commissioners, in 1873, in the cases of Smith and others, is respectfully referred to. To be brief: On our exposed frontier, especially on the Rio Grande, a reign of terror has existed which prevented citizens from attending to their vocations; the prices of real and personal property have depreciated; population has not increased; hundreds of lives have been sacrificed, and millions of dollars worth of property have been taken into Mexico and into the haunts of their savage allies. It is a question of supremacy. The homes, the property, and the lives of frontiersmen hang upon the issue. On the Rio Grande the decision will consign the country to Mexican bandits or secure it to the American settlers. It is abandonment on the one side, and re-conquest on the other. It is a contest between civilization and savagery.

The outrages on the part of the Mexicans have been committed boldly and defiantly; citizens and soldiers have participated. Officers of the Mexican army have crossed the Rio Grande at the head of their commands, and have committed outrages upon the persons and the property of our people. Mexican officials, civil and military, have been participants in the profits arising from this border war. They have given their sanction to acts of violence and rapine; they have protected the perpetrators, and, as far as they could, they have legalized robbery and murder. To the dishonor of the supreme government of Mexico, the proceeds of the sale of cattle stolen from the people of Texas have found their way into the public treasury. The custom-house authorities of Reynosa and Camargo have seized stolen cattle, knowing they had been feloniously acquired.   They have refused to deliver them to the authorized agents of the American owners, and have condemned and sold them, on the ground that they had been introduced into the country contrary to law.   A municipal tax has been assessed and paid upon property publicly known to have been robbed from Texans.   This has been done in Matamoros and other places.

It has been the practice of the Mexican authorities to throw insuperable obstacles in the way of recovering property stolen from Americans, and carried into Mexico.   Our citizens have been threatened and imprisoned for daring to ask for the restitution of property.

To be concise, we have suffered the evils and the calamities of war from a people with whom we are professedly at peace.

The supreme government of Mexico has been notified of the hostile and piratical aggressions of her authorities and citizens upon the territory, people and property of a neighboring and peaceful power, and no adequate steps have been taken to prevent the fitting out of expeditions upon her soil.   Her territory has been used as a place of deposit for stolen property; the same has been sold publicly in her markets, and the marauders have found refuge upon her territory.   Once across the Rio Grande, and the outlaw is safe from molestation; he is covered by the flag of Mexico, and is the peculiar object of protection by her authorities.   For these and many other hostile acts Mexico stands condemned by the law of nations as the indorser of the aggressions of her citizens.   She has utterly failed to comply with her treaty obligations.   She has been an inactive spectator of the murders and robberies committed by her citizens and soldiers upon citizens of the United States and their property.   Her failure to comply with her duties, under the obligations of international law, and to extend to a neighboring and friendly power the offices of comity and good neighborhood, attach to her a fearful responsibility.   By so doing she has encouraged her citizens in their wanton acts of robbery; and even up to the present time, as we are informed by dispatches from the distracted frontier of the Rio Grande, those depredations are still continuing upon our peaceful people and their property, in the immediate vicinity and in sight of the armed forces of the United States.

Again, our extensive northwestern frontier has for forty years been exposed to constantly recurring inroads of the nomadic tribes that dwell in the regions beyond that line, resulting in the murder of men, women and children, and the stealing and destruction of property of immense value, often leaving whole settlements of hardy frontiersmen (the pioneers of civilization) utterly divested, by wholesale plunder, of all the accumulations of an industrious life, acquired in rescuing from the savage fertile plains, and devoting them to industrious civilization.

THEREFORE, In consideration of the premises, which are abundantly established, by the testimony of the civil and military officers, and various citizens of the United States.

We, the Delegates of the people of Texas, in Constitutional Convention assembled, Do most respectfully but earnestly invoke the interposition of the government of the United States, through its legitimate and constituted authorities, to take such prompt and efficient action as shall secure to her citizens security of person and property, and just compensation for the injuries they have so wrongfully suffered at the hands of the people and officers of the government and Republic of Mexico, claiming to be at peace with our government, so that in the future there shall not be the constantly impending danger of war between the two countries, and our people be left to enjoy their rights of person and property in peace and security, and that they be compensated for the losses and injuries they have sustained, and the State of Texas be reimbursed for the sums of money she has expended in defense of her exposed and suffering frontier, along the entire Mexican and Indian border.

In making these requests, which we prefer to the honorable the Congress of the United States, we feel that we are but asking that which as citizens of that great government, we are justly entitled to; nor can we entertain a doubt that the relief will be granted when the facts shall be made known to the properly constituted authorities.

We, therefore, request that His Excellency the Governor of the State of Texas, transmit a copy of this report and memorial to His Excellency the President of the United States; and that a copy thereof be transmitted by the President of the Convention to our Senators and Representatives in Congress, that the subject may be properly presented to the consideration of the Congress of the United States.

GEORGE FLOURNOY, Chairman.	E. L. DOHONEY,
J. R. FLEMING,	Jo. W. BARNETT,
L. S. ROSS,	JOHN S. MILLS,
JOHN S. FORD,	C. S. WEST,
D. A. NUNN,	HENRY C. KING.
B. D. MARTIN,	

Mr. Graves offered the following:

Resolved, That in consideration of the extra work done by Joseph Jenkins, Engrossing and Enrolling Olerk, after night, in engrossing and enrolling the articles and ordinances of this Convention, he be allowed six days' extra pay as clerk.

Adopted.

Mr. Cook, of Gonzales, offered the following resolution:

Resolved, That in order to carry out the provisions of a resolution adopted this morning, ordering the distribution of 20,000 additional copies of the constitution and ordinances of this Convention, the sum of one thousand dollars, or so much thereof as may be necessary, be appropriated out of the same fund, and to be drawn in the same manner, as the amount appropriated in a former resolution providing for the distribution of said constitution and ordinances.

Adopted.

Ordinance authorizing the election of collectors of taxes in certain counties was taken up, read and lost by the following vote:

YEAS—Blake, Crawford, Darnell, Davis of Brazos, DeMorse, Dillard, Ferris, Fleming, Flournoy, Ford, German, Kilgore, Killough, King, Lockett, Martin of Navarro, Moore, Rentfro, Reynolds, Robison of Fayette, Scott, Wade, West, Wright—24.

NAYS—Abernathy, Allison, Abner Arnim, Barnett, Blassingame, Bruce, Burleson, Chambers, Cline, Cook of Gonzales, Cooke of San Saba, Davis of Wharton, Graves, Haynes, Henry of Smith, Holmes, Holt, Lacy, McCormick, Mills, Murphy, Norvell, Pauli, Robertson of Bell, Russell of Harrison, Stockdale, Weaver, Whitehead—29.

Mr. Stockdale made the following report:

COMMITTEE ROOM,
AUSTIN, November 24, 1875.

To the Hon. E. B. Pickett, President of the Convention:

The committee appointed under Mr. Martin's resolution, to investigate the charges made by the *Statesman* newspaper against certain members of the Convention, beg leave to report: That the chairman, by direction of the committee, called upon the persons named in the *Statesman* as having knowledge on the subject, and upon the editor and the proprietor of that paper, to make a statement of the facts in their knowledge in regard to said charges, to-wit: Mr. Reagan, Mr. Nugent, Mr. Wade, Gen. Whitfield, and Gen. Ross, members of this Convention, and upon

Mr. DuPre and Mr. Cardwell of the *Statesman.* Of these all have made the statements requested, except Gen. Ross and Gen. Whitfield, which statements are herewith submitted. These statements were made upon oath. The members of the committee have been so occupied with the business of a more public nature, and, as they deemed, of much greater public interest, appertaining to their duties as members of this Convention, that they have not had time, if they had had the disposition, to make any further investigation of these charges, and none of the parties interested have given the committee any information of other evidence or requested any further inquiry. The gentlemen accaused (Messrs. Johnson, of Collin, and Russell, of Harrison) have neither of them proposed to make a statement or requested any further investigation; nor has the committee called upon them to make any statement.

Respectfully submitted,   F. S. STOCKDALE, Chairman.

STATEMENT OF JOHN H. REAGAN.

Of my own knowledge, I know nothing of any bargain or agreement between any members of the Convention to support or to oppose any part of the suffrage article of the constitution, or any other measure.

I heard it said, in a general way, several times; but by whom, I do not remember, that there was some agreement between Mr. Johnson, of Collin, and Mr. Russell, of Harrison, that certain members were to unite to secure some action by the Convention; but precisely what this was I did not understand.

On Friday morning, being the day after the vote was taken refusing to impose a poll tax on voters, as a condition to their voting, in passing to the rear of the capitol, I found together some gentlemen, including among them General Whitfield, Mr. Wade, and, I believe, Mr. Nugent, members of the Convention; also Mr. DuPre, who, I understand, is one of the editors of the *Statesman* newspaper. They were conversing about the vote of the day before on the question of imposing a poll tax on voters. General Whitfield said he had heard from General Ross, I believe, that Mr. Johnson and Mr. Russell had entered into an agreement, which it seemed to be understood was to unite their friends to defeat that measure. I understood Mr. Wade to say he heard the agreement made. (This was afterwards explained by Mr. Wade in the Convention to have been some days before that vote was taken.) When the above statements were made, I said if that was true, it ought to be exposed and denounced.

This is all I know, or heard, or said of this matter, except what was said afterwards in open Convention, or in general conversations afterwards, in which the matter was referred to as a sort of joke, and in which what Mr. Johnson said and did was supposed to have been free from any improper or corrupt purpose; but was thought to have exhibited some vanity, growing out of the supposition, on his part, that he was acting as one of the leaders of the Convention.   JOHN H. REAGAN.

STATEMENT OF T. L. NUGENT.

A few days preceding that upon which the vote was taken on what is known as the " poll tax proposition," a conversation took place at my boarding house, between Col. Dupree, editor of the *Statesman,* Hon. H. W. Wade, member of the Convention, myself, and others. During this conversation, Col. Dupree said that a report was current on the streets of Austin to the effect that the Grangers and Republicans of the Convention had formed an alliance for mutual assistance in passing measures through the Convention. I expressed astonishment, as I had heard of no such combination, when Mr. Wade declared that there was some foundation for the report, and that he had heard a conversation between Mr. Johnson, of Collin county, and Mr. Russell, of Harrison, in which the former proposed to furnish Granger votes and the latter Republican votes for the purpose indicated. He further said that this conversation occurred in the hearing of several delegates. Mr. Wade's statement left the impression upon my mind that the alliance between the parties named, if not actually made, was seriously contemplated, and I at once denounced it. Mr. Wade, either during the conversation referred to or subsequently, stated that Mr. Russell, of Harrison, proposed to Mr. Johnson to reduce agreement to writing, but that Mr. Johnson declined to do this. He further stated that Mr. Brady, Republican member, asked him how the arrangement suited him, and that he told Mr. Brady that he (Wade) voted for himself, and no other man. I know nothing myself of any alliance or combination between the Grangers and Republicans, and only propose to state the substance of the conversation which induced me to make statements in reference to it.

T. L. NUGENT.

COMMITTEE ROOM,
CITY OF AUSTIN, Oct. —, 1875. }

THE STATE OF TEXAS, }
  County of Travis. }

H. W. Wade, delegate from Hunt county, after being duly sworn, says that in the latter part of September, 1875, within the Hall of Representatives, after the Convention had adjourned, I heard a conversation between delegates of Constitutional Convention: Mr. Johnson, of Collin county, Texas, said to Mr. Russell, of Harrison county, Texas, that if he (Russell) would furnish the Republican vote in the Convention, he (Johnson) would furnish enough Grange votes to carry any measure through the Convention. Russell acceded to the proposition. I was walking the floor of the hall and not engaged in the conversation. There were several delegates present. I had understood that Johnson was a Granger and Russell a Republican. Mr. Brady (Republican) said to me: "Wade, how do you like the trade?" I stated that "I voted Wade and no one else." On or about the 4th of October, 1875, about a week later, at dinner table where Col. DuPre, assistant editor of *Democratic Statesman,* Mr. Nugent, of Erath county, and I board, Col. DuPre remarked that it was currently rumored on the streets of Austin that the Radicals and the Grangers had formed an alliance to control the action of the Convention. I remarked that it was, perhaps true, rehearsing the conversation hereinbefore stated, except that I did not give the name, Brady. There were many things said that I do not now remember. Nugent denounced the alliance spoken of by Col. DuPre. This was while the question of suffrage was pending. On the morning of the 8th of October 1875, Col. DuPre, editor, Mr. Nugent and myself, in going to the capitol, met Judge Reagan and Gen. Whitfield. I do not remember who introduced the subject of the alliance. Gen. Whitfield said it was so, and that he was going to get up in the Convention and denounce it; that he would have done it on last Monday, but for the interposition of Gen. Ross, who requested him not to do it. Judge Reagan stated that if it was so, it ought to be denounced. Many things were said by all parties, (about poll tax and suffrage.) This is all that pertains to the alliance that I remember.

[Signed,]   H. W. WADE, of Hunt county.

The article of the *Statesman* assumed to be quoted in the resolution ordering the investigation is not properly quoted. The *Statesman* asked, "Does not even Whitfield know that Grangers, all except nine—we think that the number—in the Convention were transferred to the Radicals for a special purpose and known consideration? Was not the district which Gen. Whitfield represents sacrificed"? etc. This clause is only partially quoted and the *Statesman,* in the resolution adopted by the Convention, is made to assert positively "that all the Grangers in the Convention, except nine," were sold out to radicalism. The fact was stated hypothetically, as shown by the above extract from the Statesman of the 9th inst.

About a week previous to this supposed trade or "alliance" was talked about Colonel Cardwell told me that General Whitfield had spoken of it and I referred to the matter at the breakfast table, where Messrs. Nugent and Wade, members of the Constitutional Convention, were present. Mr. Wade said he had heard a conversation on the subject, and an agreement made between a leading Republican—Mr. Russell, I believe—and Mr. Johnson, of Collin. The purport of it was, that the two leaders would consolidate their forces—Republicans and Grangers—and control the action of the Convention. This was four or five days before the suffrage tax question came up, and we thought that with special reference to this measure the alliance was effected. Mr. Wade further stated that another Granger, whose name I do not recollect, asked him if he (Wade) would become a member of the ring, or alliance. Wade answered "no"; that he "always voted Wade, and nobody else." Mr. Nugent heard this conversation, shared in it, and denounced the conduct of parties to the alliance in unmeasured terms.

On the 8th instant—some four, five or six days later than this —with Messrs. Wade and Nugent, I was crossing Capitol square, and encountered Gen. Whitfield, Judge Reagan and some other members of the Convention. The subject of the Radical-Granger alliance was mentioned and Gen. Whitfield said he had intended to denounce it on the floor of the Convention but Gen. Ross had interposed and prevented it; that he would denounce it that morning. I said to him that if such was his purpose I would tell in the *Statesman* what I had heard said about it and I added editorially suppositions and inferences incident to such a state of facts. Judge Reagan said, in the conversation alluded to, that it was Gen. Whitfield's duty to have the facts developed, and I left them and wrote the article which is inaccurately quoted in the resolution ordering this investigation.

I thought the Grangers, or a large majority of them—somebody said all but nine, as well as I recollect—had agreed with the Radicals to defeat the restriction of suffrage, and the consideration agreed to be given by the Radicals was supposed to be their consolidated vote and influence in behalf of a Granger for the Governor's or United States Senator's place. The matter became the talk of the town, and I heard much more, but these are the material facts.

I append the article quoted from the *Statesman:*

"GEN. WHITFIELD, MR. REAGAN, MR. WADE AND GEN. ROSS.

"Gen. Whitfield has said, very properly, that he was not a party to any agreement with the Radicals in the Convention. The General has also as truthfully stated, as shown in all his acts and speeches, that when he came to Austin he left his Grangerism with his regalia at his own home. Everybody has seen and confesses this fact. But this is not the question we would have the distinguished gentleman answer. The *Statesman* never said and never believed that Gen. Whitfield was involved in this trade with Radicalism; but Gen. Whitfield believes, nevertheless, that it was made and subsists, and was operative day before yesterday. Let him and Gen. Ross and Mr. Wade and Mr. Reagan tell what they know and believe and *have said* of the conduct of other Grangers who have never denied the allegations of the *Statesman.* Does not Gen. Whitfield *know* that Grangers, all except nine—we think that the number—in the Convention were transferred to the use of Radicalism for a special purpose and known consideration?"

The proceedings of the Convention show that Judge Reagan said in that body as he had been made a witness on the stand, he would have to testify. He read extracts from the *Statesman,* and then explained that yesterday morning, as he was walking in the rear of the capitol, he passed several gentlemen, among them Mr. Nugent, Mr. Whitfield and others. A representative of one of the papers in this city was present, and a conversation was going on in reference to what had been charged in the *Statesman.* Some one said that Gen. Ross had stated that a bargain had been made between the Grangers and Republicans to carry certain measures. He (Mr. Reagan) then said, if such a bargain had been made, that the dignity of the Convention had been degraded, and in duty to the country it ought to be denounced and exposed. He did not say that the bargain had been made. He denied that any one had the right to transfer the Grangers, and sell them as he pleased. He would now say what he had not said before on this floor, and what but few knew, that he was a Granger himself. He could not deny that an impression had been produced derogatory to the Convention, and that there was some ground for the position assumed by the *Statesman,* as it had been said in the presence of one of the editors of that paper that a coalition had been formed between the Grangers and Republicans.

In the same debate Gen. Whitfield said he had but a few remarks to make. One day, about a week since, he had a conversation with Gen. Ross, and was told that a gentleman had proposed to Mr. Russell, of Harrison, (who is a Republican,) that if he (Russell) would give him thirteen Republican votes to control the suffrage matter, he would give him enough votes to control other matters that might come before the Convention. He (Whitfield) became mad, *good mad,* when he heard it. When he had first heard of this conversation, he had threatened to denounce it on the floor of this Convention, but he was over-persuaded not to do it, being told that Mr. Johnson, of Collin, was only joking, but he must say it was very serious.

Judge Reagan, Gen. Whitfield, Mr. Wade and other gentlemen attest every material fact stated as an ascertained fact by the *Statesman.*

I was also told by some member of the Convention (perhaps it was Mr. Wade, but of this I am not sure) that when the proposition to make the payment of a poll tax a condition precedent to the exercise of the right of suffrage, that Mr. Johnson, of Collin, and the leader of the Radicals, were seen to congratulate each other in the most extravagant manner.

Sworn to and subscribed by   L. J. DuPre.

All I know in regard to the combination referred to in the above statement has been substantially stated in the testimony of Col. L. J. DuPre. I will state that upon the first morning that Gen. Whitfield, and others in the Convention made public comment upon the attacks of the *Statesman,* I met him (Whitfield) outside the bar of the House, when he spoke to me, in the presence of Mr. Lynch, and told me that his remarks upon the floor of the House were not in antagonism really to the *Statesman,* but were made for the purpose of bringing out and exposing Mr. Johnson, of Collin, and he further stated that he had been satisfied for a number of days that Mr. Johnson was a party to the trade referred to, and that he would have brought the matter days before that before the Convention, had it not been that Gen. Ross remonstrated against his doing so. Mr. Lynch also expressed his belief in the combination, and said he was glad the *Statesman* had the courage to comment upon it.

Sworn and subscribed by

JOHN CARDWELL.

On motion of Mr. Russell, of Harrison, the whole subject was laid on the table.

Mr. West offered the following resolution:

Resolved, That the resolution heretofore adopted by this body, to adjourn *sine die* at 5 o'clock P. M. this day, be and the same is hereby rescinded. Adopted.

[Mr. Brown in the chair.]

Mr. Rentfro offered the following resolution:

Resolved, That the thanks of this Convention, and of the members thereof, be tendered to the Hon. E. B. Pickett, President, for the efficient and impartial manner in which he has discharged the duties incumbent upon him as presiding officer of this body, and that in retiring from his said position, he bears with him our best wishes for his future prosperity and happiness.

Unanimously adopted.

Mr. Flournoy offered the following resolutions:

WHEREAS, the officers of this Convention have labored attentively and assiduously in the discharge of their respective duties; and

WHEREAS, they received no mileage and no extra compensation for night service during the session; therefore,

Resolved, that this Convention give them mileage, on return to their respective homes, being only half the mileage allowed to delegates; and that the Secretary be empowered to issue warrants on the Treasurer for such mileage, according to the mileage schedule adoped for the benefit of delegates to this Convention.

Adopted by the following vote:

YEAS—Mr. President, Abernathy, Abner, Arnim, Brady, Burleson, Davis of Wharton, DeMorse, Fleming, Flournoy, Ford, Henry of Smith, Kilgore, King, Lockett, McCabe, Mills, Mitchell, Murphy, Pauli, Reynolds, Russell of Harrison, Spikes, Stockdale, Wade, Weaver, West, Wright—28.

NAYS—Allison, Barnett, Blassingame, Chambers, Cook of Gonzales, Davis of Brazos, Dillard, Dohoney, Graves, Haynes, Holmes, Holt, Johnson of Collin, Lacy, McCormick, McKinney of Denton, Martin of Navarro, Martin of Hunt, Moore, Norvell, Nunn, Rentfro, Robertson of Bell, Robison of Fayette, Scott, Whitehead, Whitfield—27.

Mr. Russell, of Harrison, offered the following resolution:

Resolved, that the thanks of this Convention are tendered Capt. F. Voight, in consideration of services rendered in decorating the hall of the Convention.

Adopted.

Mr. Kilgore offered the following resolution:

Resolved, that the thanks of this Convention are hereby tendered to Temp. Houston and Lafayette Fitzhugh, Pages of the Convention, for the faithful and efficient manner in which they have discharged the duties incumbent on them.

Adopted.

Mr. Cook, of Gonzales, offered the following resolution:

Resolved, that the sum of fourteen dollars and sixty-eight cents ($14 68) be appropriated to pay the balance due W. F. Bengener, for repairs on the capitol, as per bill annexed, and that the Comptroller is hereby authorized to issue his warrant for said amount.

Mr. Brady asked leave to introduce a resolution.

Refused, by the following vote:

YEAS—Abernathy, Brown, Cline, Cook of Gonzales, Davis of Wharton, DeMorse, Lockett, Martin of Navarro, Murphy, Norvell, Nunn, Pauli, Reynolds, Russell of Harrison, Smith, Stockdale, Whitehead—17.

NAYS—Arnim, Barnett, Blake, Blassingame, Bruce, Burleson, Chambers, Cooke of San Saba, Dohoney, Fleming, Graves, Haynes, Henry of Limestone, Henry of Smith, Holmes, Holt, Killough, King, Lacy, McCormick, McKinney of Walker, Nugent, Robison of Fayette, Scott, Sessions, Spikes, Wade, West, Wright—29.

The Secretary then proceeded to read the constitution as an entirety, as adopted by the Convention.

Mr. Murphy moved to adjourn to 7 o'clock.

Lost.

Mr. Flournoy moved to reconsider the vote adopting the resolution giving half mileage to officers.

Carried, and by leave Mr. Flournoy withdrew the resolution.

Mr. Brown made the following report:

COMMITTEE ROOM, }
AUSTIN, November 24, 1875. }

To the Hon. E. B. Pickett, President of the Convention:

The Committee of the Convention on Style and Arrangement, having carefully examined the entire constitution and all the ordinances of the Convention, as enrolled, find them correctly enrolled and prepared for authentication by the signatures of the President, Secretary and members of the Convention.

JOHN HENRY BROWN, Chairman.
WM. P. BALLINGER,
F. S. STOCKDALE,
WM. H. STEWART,
WM. NEAL RAMEY.

Mr. Ramey reported as follows:

COMMITTEE ROOM, }
AUSTIN, November 23, 1875. }

To the Hon. E. B. Pickett, President of the Convention:

SIR—Your Committee on Engrossed and Enrolled Ordinances

would respectfully report to your honorable body that they have examined and compared "Article —, Municipal Corporations," "Article —, Private Corporations," and "Article —, Impeachment Address," and find the same correctly engrossed.

WM. NEAL RAMEY, Chairman.

COMMITTEE ROOM,
AUSTIN, November 24, 1875.

To the Hon. E. B. Pickett, President of the Convention:

SIR—Your Committee on Engrossed and Enrolled Ordinances would respectfully report that they have examined and compared the new constitution, embracing the following articles and accompanying ordinances, to wit:

Preamble.
Article I. Bill of Rights.
Article II. Division of the Powers of Government.
Article III. Legislative Department.
Article IV. Executive Department.
Article V. Judicial Department.
Article VI. Suffrage.
Article VII. Education.
Article VIII. Taxation and Revenue.
Article IX. Counties.
Article X. Railroads.
Article XI. Municipal Corporations.
Article XII. Private Corporations.
Article XIII. Spanish and Mexican Land Titles.
Article XIV. Public Lands and Land Office.
Article XV. Impeachment.
Article XVI. General Provisions.
Article XVII. Mode of Amending Constitution.

1. An ordinance submitting the constitution for ratification and other purposes.

2. An ordinance supplementary to the ordinance submitting the constitution for ratification and other purposes.

3. An ordinance dividing the State of Texas into senatorial and representative districts.

4. An ordinance dividing the State of Texas into judicial districts.

5. An ordinance fixing the times of holding the District Courts in the different counties in the State.

6. An ordinance in relation to railroads.

7. An ordinance defining the effect of ordinances.

And find the same correctly enrolled.

Yours respectfully,   WM. NEAL RAMEY, Chairman.

[The President resumed the chair.]

The constitution having been read through, Mr. Nugent offered the following amendment:

In "Article —, Judicial Districts," strike out section 14 and insert:

"Sec. 14. The judicial districts in this State, and the time of holding the courts therein, are fixed by ordinance, forming part of this constitution, until otherwise provided by law."

Adopted.

The constitution then passed by the following vote:

YEAS—Abernathy, Allison, Arnim, Barnett, Blassingame, Brown, Bruce, Burleson, Chambers, Cook of Gonzales, Cooke of San Saba, Darnell, Davis of Brazos, DeMorse, Dillard, Dohoney, Ferris, Fleming, Flournoy, Ford, German, Graves, Haynes, Henry of Limestone, Henry of Smith, Holmes, Holt, Johnson of Collin, Johnson of Franklin, Kilgore, Killough, King, Lacy, McCormick, McKinney of Denton, McKinney of Walker, Martin of Hunt, Moore, Norvell, Nugent, Nunn, Ramey, Robertson of Bell, Robison of Fayette, Ross, Scott, Sessions, Spikes, Stockdale, Wade, Weaver, Whitehead, Wright—53.

NAYS—Ballinger, Brady, Cline, Cooley, Lockett, Mitchell, Murphy, Rentfro, Reynolds, Smith, West, Whitfield—11.

Mr. Stockdale offered the following resolution:

Resolved, that the Governor be authorized and requested, immediately upon the adjournment of this Convention, to issue his proclamation for the elections contemplated by "An ordinance submitting the new constitution to a vote of the people, and for other purposes," passed by this Convention on the 22d day of November, A. D. 1875, and "An ordinance supplemental thereto," passed on the 23d day of November, 1875; and that said election be holden in the manner prescribed in said ordinance and supplement, and by such officers as are authorized by law to hold general elections under existing laws.

Adopted.

Mr. Stockdale offered the following resolution:

Resolved, that, instead of the number heretofore provided, there shall be published five thousand copies of the constitution in the German language.

Adopted.

Mr. Ballinger submitted the following protest:

To the Hon. E. B. Pickett, President of the Convention:

I make my respectful protest against the provisions of the constitution regulating the salaries and terms of executive and judicial officers, and against the election of judicial officers.

The short terms of office, to be filled by popular elections, will convert the State into a great partisan electioneering camp, in which office-seeking will act on the public morals of the people, and the interests and passions of the people will react on the standard and conduct of officers of evil tendencies, in my judgment, to the character and destines of this great State.

The salaries are not such as ought to be given to our State officers.

If the effect should not be, as I believe it will, to prevent many men of the highest qualifications from holding office who would be the choice of the people, if considerations of patriotism and public duty should be adequate motives to induce them to accept of office, I have still the strong, undoubting conviction that public services will be obtained by the State at hard, stinting, insufficient salaries, which are not honorable or just on the part of this great State.   W. P. BALLINGER,
Delegate from Galveston County.

Mr. Cook, of Gonzales, reported as follows:

COMMITTEE ROOM, ⎫
AUSTIN, November 24, 1875. ⎰

To the Hon. E. B. Pickett, President of the Convention:

Your Committee on Printing and Contingent Expenses ask to make the following supplemental report of the contingent expenses of the Convention.   W. D. S. COOK, Chairman.

Nov. 23—Amount of J. D. Logan & Co.'s bill, printing, etc	200	00
Amount of J. D. Logan & Co.'s bill, printing, etc	207	50
Bill of J. A. Nagle, for stationery	67	75
Nov. 24—Printing 25,000 copies of address	250	00
Printing 500 copies ordinance providing for the election, and four days *Evening News.*	75	00
J. A. Nagle, for stationery	22	00
A. S. Roberts, for candles	8	40
Ice from November 1 to November 13	10	00
Carried forward	$840	65

Brought forward	$840	65
Postage stamps, etc...................	99	71
Austin Gas Company for gas...........	100	20
	$1040	56
Amount of expenses previously reported...	4174	50
Total contingent expenses	$5215	06

Mr. Flournoy moved that the Secretary of State be requested to furnish a certified copy of the constitution to the committee at Galveston, to compare the same with the proof-sheet of the printer.

Adopted.

The delegates present then came forward and signed the enrolled copy of the constitution.

Mr. Ford offered the following resolution:

Resolved, That the thanks of this Convention are hereby tendered to the clergy of Austin, who have generously served as chaplains free of charge.

Adopted.

Mr. Ford offered the following resolution:

Resolved, That the assistant secretaries of the Convention be allowed twenty-five dollars extra pay for services rendered during night sessions.

Adopted.

Mr. West offered the following resolution:

Resolved, That the Secretary of State be requested to employ a sufficient number of clerks to furnish a certified copy of the constitution at the earliest possible moment, and that the sum of one hundred dollars, or so much thereof as may be necessary, be appropriated out of the fund appropriated to pay the expenses of this Convention, to pay for said work, to be drawn upon the certificate of the Secretary of State that the holder of the certificate has performed the work charged for.

Adopted.

Messrs. Reynolds and McCabe submitted the following report:

Whereas, Sundry papers of this State have, early in the session of this honorable body, asserted that the Republicans, and especially the colored members of this Convention, have been controlled in their action by the member from Grimes county, Hon. J. S. Mills; and

Whereas, Such assertions are untrue, unjust and unfair, and reflects much to the discredit of the colored members of this honorable body, etc.

We, therefore, enter this our protest against the same, and ask in justice to ourselves and the public, that this our protest be entered upon the journals of this Convention, etc.

W. REYNOLDS,
L. H. McCABE.

Mr. Stockdale moved to adjourn *sine die.*
The President said:

Gentlemen of the Convention:

I thank you for the expression of confidence and good will contained in the resolution adopted by the Convention. I will say, and need say, but a few words in reply.

Our labors are finished. The work we were sent here to do is now ready to be committed to the people for their approval or disapproval. I will not now review the Organic Act we have made; to you it would be needless, for you made it, and know what it contains. The people will examine it for themselves. But I may be permitted to express the hope and the conviction that the constitution we have framed will be found suited to the condition of this great young State, and not unsuited to its expanding and promising future. If such should be the case we need have no fears that our work will not meet the approval of those who sent us here. Your labors have been earnest and arduous, but they have been harmonious and agreeable to a degree almost without parallel. This should be cause for mutual congratulation.

I will only add, we are about to separate, to return to our respective homes and constituencies, and you must allow me to say to each and all of you that you will carry with you my best wishes for your prosperity and happiness.

I do now declare this Constitutional Convention adjourned *sine die.*

Approved:

E. B. PICKETT,
President of the Convention.

Attest: LEIGH CHALMERS, Secretary.

INDEX.

A

B

2

Check Out More Titles From HardPress Classics Series In this collection we are offering thousands of classic and hard to find books. This series spans a vast array of subjects – so you are bound to find something of interest to enjoy reading and learning about.

Subjects:
Architecture
Art
Biography & Autobiography
Body, Mind &Spirit
Children & Young Adult
Dramas
Education
Fiction
History
Language Arts & Disciplines
Law
Literary Collections
Music
Poetry
Psychology
Science
…and many more.

Visit us at www.hardpress.net